Lecture Notes in Computer Science

Commenced Publication in 1973
Founding and Former Series Editors:
Gerhard Goos, Juris Hartmanis, and Jan van Leeuwen

Mingshu Li   Barry Boehm
Leon J. Osterweil (Eds.)

Unifying
the Software Process
Spectrum

International Software Process Workshop, SPW 2005
Beijing, China, May 25-27, 2005
Revised Selected Papers

 Springer

Volume Editors

Mingshu Li
Chinese Academy of Sciences, Institute of Software
No. 4 South Fourth Street, Zhong Guan Cun, Beijing 100080, China
E-mail: mingshu@iscas.ac.cn

Barry Boehm
University of Southern California, University Park Campus
Los Angeles, CA 90089, USA
E-mail: boehm@cse.usc.edu

Leon J. Osterweil
University of Massachusetts, Department of Computer Science
Amherst, MA 01003, USA
E-mail: ljo@cs.umass.edu

Library of Congress Control Number: 2005937780

CR Subject Classification (1998): D.2, K.6.3, K.6, K.4.2, J.1

ISSN   0302-9743
ISBN-10   3-540-31112-2 Springer Berlin Heidelberg New York
ISBN-13   978-3-540-31112-6 Springer Berlin Heidelberg New York

Springer is a part of Springer Science+Business Media

springer.com

© Springer-Verlag Berlin Heidelberg 2005
Printed in Germany

Typesetting: Camera-ready by author, data conversion by Scientific Publishing Services, Chennai, India
Printed on acid-free paper   SPIN: 11608035   06/3142   5 4 3 2 1 0

Preface

This volume contains papers presented at SPW 2005, the Software Process Workshop held in Beijing, P. R. China, on May 25-27, 2005, and prepared for final publication.

The theme of SPW2005 was "Unifying the Software Process Spectrum." Software process encompasses all the activities that aim at developing or evolving software products. The expanding role of software and information systems in the world has focused increasing attention on the need for assurances that software systems can be developed at acceptable speed and cost, on a predictable schedule, and in such a way that resulting systems are of acceptably high quality and can be evolved surely and rapidly as usage contexts change. This sharpened focus is creating new challenges and opportunities for software process technology. The increasing pace of software system change requires more lightweight and adaptive processes, while the increasing mission criticality of software systems requires more process predictability and control as well as more explicit attention to business or mission values. Emergent application requirements create a need for ambiguity tolerance. Systems of systems and global development create needs for scalability and multi-collaborator, multi-culture concurrent coordination. COTS products provide powerful capabilities, but their vendor-determined evolution places significant constraints on software definition, development, and evolution processes.

The recognition of these needs has spawned a considerable amount of software process research across a broad spectrum. Much of the research has addressed the overall characteristics and needs of software processes, focusing on such issues as process architectures, process behavioral characteristics, and how processes fit with higher-level organizational systems and characteristics. We refer to these investigations as macroprocess research. Simultaneously, there has also been considerable research directed towards the precise, complete, detailed and unambiguous definition of software processes, focusing on such issues as detection of process flaws and facilitation of the human–machine synergies inherent in software processes. We refer to these investigations as microprocess research. A major goal of this workshop was to suggest ways in which to integrate these two complementary lines of research to create a rigorous, orderly discipline of software process engineering. One approach to integration explored at the workshop addressed how high-level process behaviors might be predicted, and modified, through lower-level analyses and optimizations. Another explored how best to integrate objective microprocesses based on explicit knowledge with more subjective collaboration processes based on tacit knowledge.

The workshop achieved its aim of bringing together a critical mass of leading software researchers and practitioners in a forum for assessing current and emerging software process capabilities with respect to the challenges, and for obtaining insights into the software process research directions needed so as to address the challenges and to make progress toward overriding goals. It included initial presentations by leading international software process researchers and users, presentations of contributed papers on process challenge areas and solution approaches, tool demonstrations, and a closing panel on software process research directions.

In response to the call for papers, 111 submissions were received from 10 different countries and regions: Australia, Canada, China, France, Germany, Hong Kong, Japan, New Zealand, UK and USA. Every paper was rigorously reviewed and held to very high quality standards, and finally 30 papers were accepted as regular papers for presentation at the workshop, representing a 27% acceptance rate for regular papers. In addition, 18 were selected as poster papers.

SPW2005 consisted of five regular sessions — "Process Content" (8 papers), "Process Tools and Metrics" (4 papers), "Process Management" (4 papers), "Process Representation and Analysis" (7 paper) — and "Experience Reports" (7 papers), and a poster session (18 papers). Eight software development support tools were demonstrated in the workshop, including: Cost Xpert Project Estimation Tool of Cost Xpert Group, USA; Spiral Pro of Software Process Group, Inc. USA; Mobile Tools for Requirements Discovery of Johannes Kepler University Linz, Austria; Risk Assessment and Tracking System of RATS Software Research Associates Inc., Japan; Concern-Based Business Process Modeling of IBM China Research Laboratory, China; Performance Testing Tool for Wireless Applications of The Hong Kong Polytechnic University, Hong Kong; Integrated Software Process Services Management System and UDCORE (User-driven Domain-specific COmponent-based Requirements Elicitation tool) of the Institute of Software, Chinese Academy of Sciences, China.

The SPW2005 program was highlighted by 11 keynote speeches, delivered by (in alphabetical order by surname): Victor R. Basili (University of Maryland, "Evolving Defect 'Folklore': A Cross-Study Analysis of Software Defect Behavior"), Barry Boehm (University of Southern California, "The Future of Software Processes"), Jacky Estublier (French National Research Center in Grenoble, "Software are Processes Too"), Watts S. Humphrey (Carnegie Mellon University/SEI, "Software: A Paradigm for the Future"), Ross Jeffery (University of New South Wales and NICTA, "Achieving Software Development Performance Improvement Through Process Change"), Mingshu Li (Institute of Software at the Chinese Academy of Sciences, "Expanding the Horizons of Software Development Processes: A 3-D Integrated Methodology"), Leon J. Osterweil (University of Massachusetts Amherst, "Unifying Microprocess and Macroprocess Research"), Arthur Pyster (Science Applications International Corporation, "What Beyond CMMI Is Needed to Help Assure Program and Project Success?"), H. Dieter Rombach (Fraunhofer IESE & University of Kaiserslautern, "Integrated Software Process & Product Lines"), Wilhelm Schäfer (University of Paderborn, "A Rigorous Software Process for the Development of Embedded Systems"), and Brian Warboys (University of Manchester, "Active Models: A Possible Approach to the Integration of Objective and Subjective Process Models").

Among the 235 registered participants, 50 were from North America, Europe, Australia, and Asian countries outside China. The others were from various Chinese cities, such as Beijing, Shanghai, Nanjing, Xi'an, Wuhan, Chengdu, Changchun, Guangzhou, Shenyang, Kunming, Hangzhou, Changsha, Zhengzhou, Zhuzhou, Luoyang and they covered most of the best universities and research organizations in China.

Chaired by Leon J. Osterweil, SPW2005 ended with a closing panel on the discussion of the future directions for software process research: "Where Are We Now? Where Should We Go Next?" The panelists included: Barry Boehm, Mingshu Li,

Ross Jeffery, and Wilhelm Schäfer, representing SPW 2005 participants from North America, Asia, Australia and Europe, respectively. The panel and audience reached a strong consensus that the future software process challenges were real and significant; that attractive new concepts and capabilities were emerging to address the challenges; and that further research, experimental application, and international collaboration would have significant payoffs. A follow-on workshop is being planned in concert with ICSE 2006 in Shanghai.

A conference such as this can only succeed as a team effort. All of this work would not have been possible without the dedication and professional work of many colleagues. We wish to express our gratitude to all contributors for submitting papers. Their work forms the basis for the success of the workshop. We also would like to thank the Program Committee members and reviewers because their work guarantees the high quality of the workshop. Particular thanks also go to the keynote speakers for giving their excellent presentations at the workshop.

We also wish to express our thanks to the organizers for their hard work. The workshop was jointly organized by four units: ISCAS Laboratory for Internet Software Technologies, China; ISCAS State Key Laboratory of Computer Science, China; USC Center for Software Engineering, USA; and UMASS Laboratory for Advanced Software Engineering Research, USA. We greatly appreciate the financial support from The National Natural Science Foundation of China, the largest national grant managing organization in China for fundamental research. We also want to acknowledge the financial support from the Institute of Software, the Chinese Academy of Sciences, a national research unit for fundamental research and development in software. Finally, we acknowledge the editorial support from Springer for the publication of these proceedings.

For more information, please visit our website at http://www.cnsqa.com/~spw2005.

June 2005   Program Co-chairs
Mingshu Li, Institute of Software, Chinese Academy of Sciences, P.R.China
Barry Boehm, University of Southern California, USA
Leon J. Osterweil, University of Massachusetts, USA

Software Process Workshop 2005

Beijing, China
May 25-27, 2005

General Chair

Mianheng Jiang, Chinese Academy of Sciences, China

Program Co-chairs

Mingshu Li, Institute of Software, Chinese Academy of Sciences, China
Barry Boehm, University of Southern California, USA
Leon J. Osterweil, University of Massachusetts, USA

Program Committee Members

Victor R. Basili	University of Maryland, USA
Keith C.C. Chan	Hong Kong Polytechnic University, Hong Kong, China
Sorana Cimpan	University of Savoie at Annecy, France
Bill Curtis	Borland Software Corporation, USA
Jacky Estublier	French National Research Center in Grenoble, France
Anthony Finkelstein	University College London, UK
Paul Grünbacher	Johannes Kepler University Linz, Austria
Valker Gruhn	University of Leipzig, Germany
Jinpeng Huai	Beijing University of Aeronautics and Astronautics, China
Liguo Huang	University of Southern California, USA
Watts S. Humphrey	Carnegie Mellon University, USA
Hajimu Iida	Nara Institute of Science and Technology, Japan
Katsuro Inoue	Osaka University, Japan
Ross Jeffery	University of New South Wales, Australia
Natalia Juristo	Universidad Politécnica de Madrid, Spain
Kouichi Kishida	Software Research Associates, Inc., Japan
Jyrki Kontio	Helsinki University of Technology, Finland
Philippe Kruchten	University of British Columbia, Canada
Barbara Staudt Lerner	Williams College, USA
Jian Lü	Nanjing University, China
Hong Mei	Peking University, China
Flavio Oquendo	University of South Brittany, France
Dewayne E. Perry	University of Texas at Austin, USA

Arthur Pyster	Science Applications International Corporation, USA
David Raffo	Portland State University, USA
H. Dieter Rombach	University of Kaiserslautern, Germany
Kevin Ryan	University of Limerick, Ireland
Walt Scacchi	University of California, Irvine, USA
Wilhelm Schäfer	University of Paderborn, Germany
Stanley M. Sutton Jr.	IBM T. J. Watson Research Center, USA
Colin Tully	Middlesex University, UK
Huaimin Wang	National University of Defense Technology, China
Qing Wang	Institute of Software, Chinese Academy of Sciences, China
Brian Warboys	University of Manchester, UK
Alex Wolf	University of Colorado at Boulder, USA
Ye Yang	University of Southern California, USA

Organizing Committee Chair

Yongji Wang, Institute of Software, Chinese Academy of Sciences, China

External Reviewers

Jesal Bhuta
Wei Chen
Yue Chen
Zhihao Chen
Liping Ding
Shuanzhu Du
Lang Gou
Meng Huang
Juan Li
Nao Li
Kuien Liu
Mohammad S. Raunak
Fengdi Shu
Lei Tang
Lijing Tong
Jizhe Wang
Dan Wu
Zhanchun Wu
Junchao Xiao
Qiusong Yang
Feng Yuan
Chen Zhao
Xinpei Zhao

Listing of Posters

A Case Study of a Multimedia System Using an Integrated Approach of Usability Evaluation
    Sanxing Cao *(Communication University of China)*,
    Natalie L.S Pang *(Monash University)*,
    Dan Li *(Communication University of China)*,
    and Don Schauder *(Monash University)*

Measuring, Analyzing and Diagnosing a Single Software Process
    Bo Gong *(BeiHang University, and Institute of Command and Technology of Equipment)* and Xingui He *(Peking University)*

A Method of Component Selection within Component-based Software Development Process
    Jun Guo, Bin Zhang, Kening Gao, Hongning Zhu, and Ying Liu *(Northeastern University)*

Negotiation-Based Service-Oriented Software Process in Peer-to-Peer Environments
    Yuan He, Kuien Liu, Jian Zhai *(Institute of Software, The Chinese Academy of Sciences, and Graduate School of the Chinese Academy of Sciences)*, and Jiang Guo *(University of Toronto)*

The Elements of Software Process Optimization: Dealing with the Process Dynamics
    Masao Ito *(Nil Software Corp.)*

Toward Quantitative, Rational and Scientific Software Process
    Zenya Koono *(Nara Institute of Science and Technology)* and Hui Chen *(Kokushikan University)*

A Process Meta-Model Supporting Domain Reuse
    Changyun Li *(Zhuzhou Institute of Technology, and Zhejiang University)*, Jin Gou *(Zhejiang University)*, Wu Huifeng *(Zhejiang University)*, and Gansheng Li *(Zhuzhou Institute of Technology)*

Research on the Inheritance of Process Ontology
    Changyun Li *(Zhuzhou Institute of Technology, and Zhejiang University)*, Xingmin Sun *(Hunan University)*, Liao Lijun *(Zhuzhou Institute of Technology)*, and Yunliang Jiang *(Zhejiang University)*

Table of Contents

Keynote Speech

Process Content

Process Tools and Metrics

Process Management

Process Representation and Analysis

Experience Reports

Evolving Defect "Folklore":
A Cross-Study Analysis of Software Defect Behavior

Victor Basili[1] and Forrest Shull[2]

[1] Dept. of Computer Science, University of Maryland,
College Park, MD, 20742, USA
basili@cs.umd.edu
[2] Fraunhofer Center - Maryland, 4321 Hartwick Road,
Suite 500, College Park, MD, 20740, USA
fshull@fc-md.umd.edu

Abstract. Answering "macro-process" research issues – which require understanding how development processes fit or do not fit in different organizational systems and environments – requires families of related studies. While there are many sources of variation between development contexts, it is not clear *a priori* what specific variables influence the effectiveness of a process in a given context. These variables can only be discovered opportunistically, by comparing process effects from different environments and analyzing points of difference.

In this paper, we illustrate this approach and the conclusions that can be drawn by presenting a family of studies on the subject of software defects and their behaviors – a key phenomenon for understanding macro-process issues. Specifically, we identify common "folklore," i.e. widely accepted heuristics concerning how defects behave, and then build up a body of knowledge from empirical studies to refine the heuristics with information concerning the conditions under which they do and do not hold.

1 Introduction

Answering "macro-process" research issues – specifically, being able to make statements about the effectiveness of processes in different contexts, and understanding how processes fit or do not fit in different organizational systems and with different organizational characteristics – requires families of related studies. This is true because of two difficulties inherent in software process research:

- It is clear that there are many sources of variation between one development context and another;
- It's not clear *a priori* what specific variables influence the effectiveness of a process in a given context.

That is, we expect it to be an almost impossible task to predict ahead of time what factors are likely to crucially affect the results of applying a process in one environment or another: for example, the motivation of the practitioners, their experience/skill level with various tasks, the various business goals of the organization. Yet

M. Li, B. Boehm, and L.J. Osterweil (Eds.): SPW 2005, LNCS 3840, pp. 1–9, 2005.

we know that these variables do exist and we are able to reason about their influence if we work bottom-up, that is, starting with the observation of process effectiveness in various environments and identifying the possible causes of discrepancies.

For example, one study provided some indications that the application of a particular software inspection process was influenced by the experience of the developers applying it: novice inspectors seemed to gain some improvement from the new technique while experts seemed to fall back on their own, proven practices [1]. This effect was traced to a particular context variable in this study, the time limit given for the inspection: Since the participants felt pressured to get the inspection completed in time, experts fell back on their own techniques rather than try to deal with the learning curve. In a context where the time limit was open-ended or subjects were more motivated to learn the new process, it is impossible to say whether the same effect would still have been observed. Such unexpected inter-relationships between variables are always a possibility in software process research.

For this reason, we have argued [2] that knowledge at the macro-process level must be built from families of studies, in which related studies are run within similar contexts as well as very different ones. At one level this ensures that conclusions are verified and false conclusions are not drawn due to problems or idiosyncrasies with any one study. For drawing macro-process conclusions, however, it also allows the space of context variables to be explored *opportunistically*; conclusions about influencing factors are drawn bottom-up, by understanding the context similarities and differences that may have caused differences in process effectiveness.

Multiple authors have discussed the idea of software replication, that is, how to design related studies so as to document as precisely as possible the values of likely context variables and be able to compare with those observed in new studies [e.g. 3, 4, 5, 6]. While such a top-down approach is important, given the overwhelming number of potential context variables – including differences in developer experience and motivation, in development tools and approaches, in other processes used, in business goals (e.g. high quality products vs. fastest time to market) – we argue that a bottom-up approach is also necessary, in which results from multiple individual studies can be fitted together after the fact as appropriate. Such a bottom-up approach is necessary for enabling recommendations to be made about process effectiveness in context.

To make such a bottom-up approach work, it is necessary to have an overall framework that allows the relationships among individual studies to be understood so that data can be accumulated and variations in effectiveness determined. Such a framework allows independent researchers to relate the results of their studies more easily to the growing body of knowledge so that macro-process conclusions can be drawn.

In this paper, we illustrate this approach and the conclusions that can be drawn by presenting a family of studies on the subject of software defects and their behaviors – a key phenomenon for understanding macro-process issues. Specifically, we identify some common "folklore," i.e. widely accepted heuristics concerning how defects behave, and then build up a body of knowledge to show whether empirical results can confirm whether such heuristics are accurate and under which conditions.

2 Software Defects

The comparison of lessons learned about software defects between studies has been complicated by the fact that there are multiple taxonomies of defects that have been proposed over time (e.g. [7], [8], [9]). Thus building up a body of knowledge on defects and their behaviors is made even more complicated: Not only do studies in different contexts have many different sources of context variation, which are impossible to identify ahead of time as discussed above, but they may have additionally used different vocabulary to describe similar types of defects.

To make sense of the knowledge learned about defects across multiple contexts and taxonomies, we need to go to a higher level up abstraction, to what we call "folklore." Folklore in this context refers to the informal, subjective lessons learned by developers based on experience. Due to the well-documented fact that human subjective experience is not always the best basis for drawing generalizable lessons, as well as the fact that experiences in one context may not always generalize to others, it is important to use such lore to formulate testable hypotheses that can then be subjected to more formal scrutiny. In this way, folklore is one source of information that should be used to focus new empirical studies in high-payoff areas. The hope is that the basic heuristics encoded in folklore reflect such basic knowledge about software phenomena that they are relatively insensitive to the variations in the precise definition of defect.

To facilitate the comparison across studies, in this paper we will use the IEEE definitions [10] for defects and related phenomena:

- Error: a defect in the human thought process made while trying to understand given information, to solve problems, or to use methods and tools;
- Fault: a concrete manifestation of errors within the software (note that one error may cause several faults and various errors may cause identical faults);
- Failure: a departure of the operational software system behavior from users' expected requirements (a particular failure may be caused by several faults and some faults may never cause a failure).

As examples of folklore about software defect behaviors, we introduce the following heuristics and rationales:

- *The vast majority of defects are interface defects.* This heuristic describes the common belief that implementing individual modules with clearly defined functional requirements is rather straightforward. Instead, the majority of defects is believed to come at the interfaces of such modules, that is, getting them to work together to achieve higher-level functionality.
- *Applying more sophisticated programming languages can eliminate a significant number of defects, but not all.* Another way of saying this is that most implementation defects are believed to come from coding mistakes that could be minimized by better programming languages, which would reduce the likelihood of developers making such mistakes. This is consistent with the belief that most code defects are introduced because of the complexity of solving the problem on the computer, not from problems in analyzing the solution to be produced in the first place.

- *Small modules (say, modules with fewer than fifty LOC) are the least defect prone.* It is assumed that breaking functionality down into the smallest coherent pieces, and implementing each in a separate module, minimizes the number of defects introduced. Said another way, larger modules are assumed to have on average more complexity, which leads them to be more error-prone.
- *If you are not sure what to do – do something and fix it later.* As a general implementation strategy, it is assumed that the effort to modify code is not prohibitive, so it is viable to implement functionality by adding code, testing it, and perfecting the implementation over time.
- *There are patterns in the defect classes found in projects within a particular organization.* This suggests that there are problems common to the organization and application. Thus collecting data for a particular environment will allow the organization to identify opportunities for improvement within that organization.

3 Drawing Conclusions Bottom-Up

In this section, we give a brief overview of a collection of datasets that provide partial evidence addressing the folklore introduced in Section 2. As was emphasized in our discussion of building up bodies of knowledge from families of studies, each study in the family need not be a "strict" replication of one another, with the same overall design and data collection [2].

Also as proposed in [2], we use the Goal – Question – Metric paradigm (GQM) to provide the framework that relates studies within the family to one another. The GQM requires explicit identification of an *object of study* as well as a *focus* for the study (i.e. a model of how the object of study is being characterized or evaluated). Specifying both the object and focus of study helps to make similarities and differences among studies explicit. All of the studies which produced data included in this collection, whatever their specific goals, all have GQMs which at a high level of abstraction have the same form:

> Analyze **software defects** in order to **characterize** them with respect to **various classification schemes** from the point of view of the **knowledge builder** in the **development context in which they were generated**.

As a first pass for demonstration purposes, the datasets in our collection are ones the authors are very familiar with. They include defect data from:

- Endres75: A new release of an operating system, where "defect" was defined as any code fault that caused a failure during system testing. (Faults generated from unit or integration testing were not included.) [11]
- Weiss79: A simulator of various computer architectures, in which all defects were found due to failures reported during the first year of operations after system delivery. [12]
- Basili/Weiss81: The development of an on-board flight control program for a new aircraft. Defects were defined as fixes necessary to the requirements

document, within a 15-month period after the requirements were baselined. (Since the defects were not tracked over the entire lifecycle of the project, this cannot be taken as a complete set of requirements defects.) The problems with the document were found during reviews as well as when it was used as a basis for design. [13]

- Basili/Perricone84: A system designed for satellite planning studies at NASA. Defect data was collected starting with the baselining of the code through the three years of maintenance. [14]
- Mashiko/Basili97: A set of four projects dealing with communication software. [7]
- Weiss/Basili85: A set of three projects dealing with ground support software for satellites. [15]
- Selby/Basili91: A single release of a code library tool. [16]

4 Drawing Conclusions Across Studies

Results from abstracting up across our various data sets show that not all of the folklore was an accurate reflection of software development realities:

The majority of defects are not interface-related. Five of our datasets had collected enough information about the defects to categorize them somehow as interface or non-interface related. The Endres75 dataset defined interface-related issues as any issue that required a change to more than one module in order to fix. Defined this way, the clear majority of defects (85% of the entries in the dataset) were non-interface, i.e. required changes to only one module.

Using a similar definition, the other datasets were in agreement. In the Weiss79 dataset, 94% of defects were non-interface; in Basili/Weiss81 dataset it was 85%. Concerning the Basili/Weiss85 dataset, although an absolute number is not given, the statement is made that "interface errors are not especially troublesome."

However, [14] offered a second definition of an interface defect: a defect is an interface defect if one has to examine more than one module to understand how to fix the defect. Thus even if only one module has to be changed, it can still be an interface defect. Using this definition of interface defect, 39% of the defect could have been classified as interface defects, and these interface defects were the largest single category of defects − 39% of faults involved interface. Using a similar definition of interface defects, [7] report a similar number of interface defects − 40%. Therefore, it can be concluded that across all datasets, although the vast majority of changes made to fix a defect were made to only one module, the need to examine more than one module in order to make a fix was a common problem, even if it did not involve the majority of defects.

Where the datasets showed some disagreement was on the subject of how expensive it was to correct the interface-related defects. Two datasets collected information sufficient to address this issue: In Weiss79, interface design defects were relatively inexpensive. However, in Basili/Weiss81 interface defects took more effort to fix. Since the Basili/Weiss81 defects were collected in the requirements phase, while Weiss79 were defects found in operation, interface defects may simply be more difficult to repair at the requirements level compared to other types.

Defects that could be addressed by better programming languages account for a significant portion of defects, but less than half. Our datasets also contained information about defect categories that can shed some light on what type of misunderstanding on the part of developers caused the defect to enter the system in the first place.

In the Endres75 set, approximately half of the defects (46%) originated due to misunderstanding the problem to be solved or potential solutions. A further 16% were related to textual/clerical mistakes or to not following standards. Thus only 38% of defects could have been avoided had improved programming techniques been used.

In Weiss79, only 31% of the defects were related to the implementation. The remainder were related to requirements, design, or clerical issues.

In Basili/Weiss81, the requirements document contained more defects related to the correctness or completeness of the solution (80%) than with the way it was represented in the given notation (18%). Thus, although in a different lifecycle phase, these results can be taken to agree with the earlier datasets in the sense that the primary cause of defects was misunderstanding of the problem to be solved.

Small modules are no less error-prone than large modules. Two datasets (Endres75 and Basili/Perricone84) traced the defects recorded back to the modules in which they were found, and the size of those modules. In the Endres75 dataset the defect rate (i.e. the number of defects per module divided by the size in LOC of the module) is no different for large modules than for small ones. The Basili/Perricone84 data showed the counter-intuitive result that larger modules, within limits, may even be less fault prone.

"Do something and fix it later" is not always a safe strategy. In Selby/Basili91, it was noted that during design and code review, the total time to correct a fault (identify and fix) of omission was less than the time to correct faults of commission. This result was surprising, given the folklore. Mashiko/Basili97 supports this conclusion when one considers all faults. However, when one limits the faults to those reported by the customer, the results are not consistent, i.e., faults of omission, after delivery of the system, are more expensive to fix than faults of commission when considering customer reported faults. It seems that the context here makes the difference and examining that context offers the opportunity for some insight. During development faults of omission tend to be smaller parts of the system, thus it is better to mark the spot where there is a concern, minimizing the time to identify the fault, and define the correct solution later. However, once a system is delivered, the faults of omission may take on a different flavor, i.e. an omission fault might represent a complex functional capability that the customer assumed was part of the system.

Both the Weiss79 and the Basili/Weiss81 datasets contained information about the time-to-fix needed for defects in an environment where the customers' needs were well understood. For the faults found after delivery in Basili/Weiss81, the effort required to make changes was in most cases relatively small; 68% of defects were repaired in less than one hour. In fixes required to the requirements document described in Weiss79, 84% of defects were fixed in less than a few hours each. However, it should be noted that in both cases a small minority took an exceptionally long time to repair; in Weiss79, for example, 1% of the defects took more than a few days to repair.

It should also be noted that the Basili/Perricone84 study concluded that it's more expensive to repair reused modules than ones developed from scratch. So, in some cases, it may be more cost-effective to try out a solution and then throw away the early proto-type, rather than try to continue to modify the early version of solutions until they work correctly.

Patterns exist in defect classes found in projects within a particular organization. The Basili/Weiss85 dataset was used to identify patterns in the change and defect history of projects developed in NASA's Software Engineering Laboratory. For example, most defects in the development of ground support systems were due to problems in the design and development of single components. This was due in part to the fact that systems were being developed by experienced developers and the single components were coded by novice programmers. It should be noted that the Basili/Perricone85 data showed that for a different application, in the same environment, a majority of the defects were due to requirements and functional specification. The Mashiko/Basili97 data also exhibited a pattern in the defect classes, though this pattern was quite different. Thus, there are patterns that can be detected within a given context, although these patterns will not hold from one environment to another.

5 Summary

Having looked at a collection of datasets and abstracted up a set of conclusions on specific topics, we should also examine what kinds of general lessons learned we have found about cross-study conclusions. We feel that the work described in this paper demonstrates that:

- *There is value in multiple studies for both supporting and not supporting hypotheses.* There are several instances above where the conclusions from multiple datasets all point in the same direction, thus making the overall conclusion much stronger than if it came from any single study in isolation. And, in several important instances, the results from additional studies identify important caveats by examining processes in new environments.
- *Care must be taken to make sure that the objects of the comparison are actually like things that can support the conclusions being drawn.* For example, although all of the datasets described in this paper contain defect data, it was necessary to know in each study the definitions of the various categories of defect taxonomies (e.g. interface vs. non-interface), the definition of defect (especially with respect to injection time, detection time, environment, subjects, phase of data collection), etc.
- *A researcher needs to vary the classification to check the effects along the various values.* For example, in this instance we saw that to investigate the overall impact of interface-related defects, not only is it necessary to investigate the relative number of interface defects in the dataset, but the relative time required to fix those defects.
- There are insights to be gained from the collection and analysis of defects according to different classification schemes, independent of the scheme. Our results show that interesting abstractions can be drawn by comparing defect information opportunistically, based on points of similarity where they occur.

Based upon our experiences to date, we are evolving our methodology for building an effective set of folklore using empirical evidence from multiple studies. The methodology considers information found in papers published about the focus of the study. There is a specific approach to reading and extracting information from the paper. The information is extracted, summarized to create new knowledge that identifies possible context variables and expands the domain of study that is reported in an experiment in any one paper. This approach identifies three levels of abstraction: (1) the hypotheses from a particular study as presented in a paper and the information that can be extracted from that paper by identifying hypotheses, definitions, context variables, etc., (2) a broadened hypothesis from a family of focused related studies, built bottom-up by identifying the relevance of context variables to create integrated knowledge from two or more papers, and (3) vetted guidance or advice based upon empirical evidence abstracted so that it is useful to the software engineering community. Such abstractions are necessary for presenting information relevant for decision support to software developers and managers, for example through the Best Practices Clearinghouse project funded by the US Department of Defense [17] which aims at providing software developers and acquisition managers with robust knowledge based on empirical data.

References

1. Basili, V. R., Green, S., Laitenberger, O., Lanubile, F., Shull, F., Sorumgaard, S.L., Zelkowitz, M.V.: The Empirical Investigation of Perspective-based Reading. Empirical Software Engineering, An International Journal, Volume 1, Number 2, pp 133-164, Kluwer Academic Publishers, October 1996.
2. Basili, V. R., Shull, F., Lanubile, F.: Building Knowledge through Families of Experiments, IEEE Transactions on Software Engineering, Vol. 25, No. 4, pp. 456-473, July 1999.
3. Brooks, A., Daly, J., Miller, J., Roper, M., Wood, M. (1996). Replication of experimental results in software engineering. Technical Report ISERN-96-10, Department of Computer Science, University of Strathclyde, Glasgow.
4. Lott, C. M., Rombach, H. D.: Repeatable software engineering experiments for comparing defect-detection techniques, Journal of Empirical Software Engineering, 1(3), 1996.
5. Wohlin, C., Runeson, P, Host, M., Ohlsson, M., Regnell, B., Wesslen, A.: Experimentation in Software Engineering: An Introduction. Kluwer Academic Publishers: Boston. 2000.
6. Juristo N., Moreno, A. M. (eds.): Lecture Notes on Empirical Software Engineering. World Scientific: New Jersey. 2003.
7. Mashiko, Y., Basili, V.R.: Using the GQM Paradigm to Investigate Influential Factors for Software Process Improvement, The Journal of Systems and Software, Volume 36, Number 1, pp 17-32, January 1997.
8. Chillarege, R., Bhandari, I., Chaar, J., Halliday, M., Moebus, D., Ray, B., Wong, M.: Orthogonal Defect Classification: A Concept for In-process Measurements, IEEE Transactions on Software Engineering, November 1992.
9. Basili, V.R., Weiss, D.M.: A Methodology for Collecting Valid Software Engineering Data, IEEE Transactions on Software Engineering, pp 728-738, November 1984.
10. IEEE. Software Engineering Standards. IEEE Computer Society Press, 1987.
11. [Endres75]

12. Weiss, D.: Evaluating Software Development By Error Analysis: The Data from the Architecture Research Facility, J. Systems and Software, V 1, 1979, 57-70.
13. Basili, V.R., Weiss, D.M.: Evaluation of the A-7 Requirements Document by Analysis of Change Date, Proceedings of the Fifth International Conference on Software Engineering, pp 314-323, March 1981.
14. Basili, V.R., Perricone, B.: Software Errors and Complexity: An Empirical Investigation, Communication of the ACM, vol. 27, no. 1, pp 42-52, January 1984.
15. Weiss, D.M., Basili, V.R.: Evaluating Software Development by Analysis of Changes: The Data from the Software Engineering Laboratory, IEEE Transactions on Software Engineering, pp 157-168. February 1985.
16. Selby, R.W., Basili, V.R.: Analyzing Error Prone System Structure, IEEE Transactions on Software Engineering, pp. 141-152, February 1991.
17. Dangle, K., Hickok, J., Turner, R., Dwinnell, L.: Introducing the Department of Defense Acquisition Best Practices Clearinghouse. CrossTalk, pp. 4-5, May 2005.

The Future of Software Processes

Barry Boehm

University of Southern California,
University Park Campus, Los Angeles, CA 90089
boehm@cse.usc.edu
Copyright USC-CSE, 2005

Abstract. In response to increasing demands being put onto software-intensive systems, software processes will evolve significantly over the next two decades. This paper identifies seven relatively surprise-free trends – increased emphasis on users and end value; increasing software criticality and need for dependability; increasingly rapid change; increasingly complex systems of systems; increasing needs for COTS, reuse, and legacy software integration; and computational plenty – and two "wild card" trends: increasing software autonomy and combinations of biology and computing; and discusses their likely influences on software processes between now and 2025. It also discusses limitations to software process improvement, and areas of significant software process research and education needs.

1 Introduction

Between now and 2025, ever-increasing demands will be put on computer software to provide safe, secure, and reliable information technology; to provide competitive discriminators in the marketplace; to support the coordination of multi-cultural global enterprises; to enable rapid adaptation to change; and to help people cope with complex masses of data and information. These demands will cause major differences in the processes currently used to define, design, develop, deploy, and evolve a diverse variety of software-intensive systems.

This paper elaborates on the nature of these increasing demands on software and their process implications. Section 2 will identify seven relatively surprise-free trends and two less-predictable "wild card" trends, and discuss their likely influence on software processes between now and 2025. Section 3 will attempt to bound expectations about the perfectibility of software processes by discussing basic limitations of software process improvement. Section 4 will describe some high-level software process research and education areas that are likely to have significant payoffs in addressing the software process challenges identified in Section 2, and Section 5 will present the resulting conclusions.

2 Information Technology (IT) Trends and Their Influence on Software Processes

The seven relatively surprise-free trends are:

1. An increased emphasis on users and end value;
2. Increasing software criticality and need for dependability;

M. Li, B. Boehm, and L.J. Osterweil (Eds.): SPW 2005, LNCS 3840, pp. 10–24, 2005.
© Springer-Verlag Berlin Heidelberg 2005

3. Increasingly rapid change;
4. Increasing IT globalization and need for interoperability;
5. Increasingly complex systems of systems;
6. Increasing needs for COTS, reuse, and legacy software integration;
7. Computational plenty.

The two "wild card" trends are:

8. Increasing software autonomy;
9. Combinations of biology and computing.

2.1 User/Value Emphasis Trends and Process Implications

A recent Computerworld panel on "The Future of IT" indicated that usability and total ownership cost-benefits, including user inefficiency and ineffectiveness costs, are becoming IT user organizations' top priorities [2]. A representative quote from panelist W. Brian Arthur was "Computers are working about as fast as we need. The bottleneck is making it all usable." A recurring user-organization desire is to have technology that adapts to people rather than vice versa. This is increasingly reflected in users' product selection activities, with evaluation criteria increasingly emphasizing product usability and value added vs. a previous heavy emphasis on product features and license costs. Such trends ultimately will affect software producers' product and process priorities, marketing strategies, and competitive survival.

Some technology trends strongly affecting usability and cost-effectiveness are increasingly powerful enterprise support packages, data access and mining tools, and Personal Digital Assistant (PDA) capabilities. Such products have tremendous potential for user value, but determining how they will be best configured will involve a lot of product experimentation, shakeout, and emergence of superior combinations of capabilities.

2.1.1 Software Process Implications

In terms of future software process implications, the fact that the capability requirements for these products are emergent rather than prespecifiable has become the primary challenge. Not only do the users exhibit the IKIWISI (I'll know it when I see it) syndrome, but their priorities change with time. These changes often follow a Maslow need hierarchy, in which unsatisfied lower-level needs are top priority, but become lower priorities once the needs are satisfied [35]. Thus, users will initially be motivated by survival in terms of capabilities to process new workloads, followed by security once the workload-processing needs are satisfied, followed by self-actualization in terms of capabilities for analyzing the workload content for self-improvement and market trend insights once the security needs are satisfied.

It is clear that requirements emergence is incompatible with past process practices such as requirements-driven sequential waterfall process models and formal programming calculi; and with process maturity models emphasizing repeatability and optimization [39]. In their place, more adaptive [27] and risk-driven [6] models are needed. More fundamentally, the theory underlying software process models needs to evolve from purely reductionist "modern" world views (universal, general, timeless, written) to a synthesis of these and situational "postmodern" world views (particular, local, timely, oral) as discussed in [45]. A recent theory of value-based software engineering (VBSE) and its associated software processes [9] provide a starting point for addressing these challenges. The associated VBSE book [4] contains further insights and emerging directions for VBSE processes.

For example, the [24] chapter in the VBSE book addresses the need to evolve from software products, methods, tools, and educated students strongly focused on individual programming performance to a focus on more group-oriented interdisciplinary collaboration. Negotiation of priorities for requirements involves not only participation from users and acquirers on each requirement's relative mission or business value, but also participation from software engineers on each requirement's relative cost and time to develop and difficulty of implementation. As we will discuss further under Globalization in Section 2.4, collaborative activities such as Participatory Design [19] will require stronger process support and software engineering skill support not only across application domains but also across different cultures.

Some additional process implications of people- and value- oriented trends are addressed in the ICSE 2000 Software Process Roadmap [21]. They include the need for process modeling languages to allow for incomplete, informal, and partial specification; the need for process-centered environments to be incremental and ambiguity-tolerant; and for software process metrics and empirical studies to be value-driven.

2.2 Software Criticality and Dependability Trends

Software is increasingly becoming the most critical success factor for future products (automobiles, aircraft, radios) and services (financial, communications, defense). It provides both competitive differentiation and rapid adaptability to competitive change. It facilitates rapid tailoring of products and services to different market sectors, and rapid and flexible supply chain management.

Although people's and organizations' dependency on software is becoming increasingly critical, dependability is generally not the top priority for software producers. In the words of the 1999 PITAC Report, "The IT industry spends the bulk of its resources, both financial and human, on rapidly bringing products to market." [41].

Recognition of the problem is increasing. ACM President David Patterson has called for the formation of a top-priority Security/Privacy, Usability, and Reliability (SPUR) initiative [38]. Several of the Computerworld "Future of IT" panelists in [2] indicated increasing customer pressure for higher quality and vendor warranties, but others did not yet see significant changes happening among software product vendors.

This situation will likely continue until a major software-induced catastrophe similar in impact on world consciousness to the 9/11 World Trade Center catastrophe stimulates action toward establishing accountability for software dependability. Given the high and increasing software vulnerabilities of the world's current financial, transportation, communications, energy distribution, medical, and emergency services infrastructures, it is highly likely that such a software-induced catastrophe will occur between now and 2025.

2.2.1   Software Process Implications

Process strategies for highly dependable software systems and many of the techniques for addressing its challenges have been available for quite some time. A landmark 1975 conference on reliable software included papers on formal specification and verification processes; early error elimination; fault tolerance; fault tree and failure modes and effects analysis; testing theory, processes and tools; independent verification and validation; root cause analysis of empirical data; and use of automated aids for defect detection in software specifications and code [8].

These have been used to achieve high dependability on smaller systems and some very large self-contained systems such as the AT&T telephone network [37]. Also, new strategies have been emerging to address the people-oriented and value-oriented challenges discussed in Section 2.1. These include the Personal and Team Software Processes [29, 30] and value/risk-based processes for achieving dependability objectives [22, 28].

The major future challenges for software dependability processes are in scaling up and integrating these approaches in ways that also cope with the challenges presented by other future trends. These include the next four trends to be discussed below: rapid change and agility; globalization; complex systems of systems; and COTS/legacy integration. The remaining trends – computational plenty, autonomy, and bio-computing – will offer further attractive solution avenues, but also further challenges, as we will also discuss below.

2.3   Rapid Change Trends

The increasingly rapid pace of IT change is driven by technology trends such as Gordon Moore's Law (transistor density and performance doubles roughly every 18 months), plus the continuing need for product differentiation and tornado-like processes for new technology introduction [36]. Global connectivity also accelerates the ripple effects of technology, marketplace, and technology changes. Rapid change also increases the priority of development speed vs. cost in capitalizing on market windows. A good example of successful software process adaptation to rapid change was Hewlett Packard's initiative to reduce product line software development times from 48 to 12 months [23].

When added to the trend toward emergent requirements, the pace of change places a high priority on process agility and investments in continuous learning for both people and organizations. Such investments need to be organization-wide. Many organizations have invested in agility and continuous learning for their technical people, but have left their administrative and contract people to propagate the THWADI (That's how we've always done it) syndrome. This usually leads to unpleasant surprises when their agile technical processes run afoul of slow, outdated, and inflexible procurement or approval procedures.

Completely eliminating THWADI is not a good idea either, as it includes an organization's corporate memory and best practices. The big challenge is to determine which legacy processes and principles to keep, modify, or eliminate.

2.3.1 Software Process Implications

A similar challenge is presented by the needs to achieve high levels of agility while simultaneously achieving the high level of discipline needed to develop highly dependable systems. In Balancing Agility and Discipline [10], we provide an overall framework for doing this. As shown in Figure 1, it involves a risk-driven spiral approach to determine whether a primarily agile or primarily plan-driven development approach is best, or if both are needed. If the latter, it involves identifying the partitions of the application most needing agility and encapsulating them in a plan-driven framework. A critical factor is the ability to pass a Life Cycle Architecture (LCA) milestone review before proceeding from concept exploration to development.

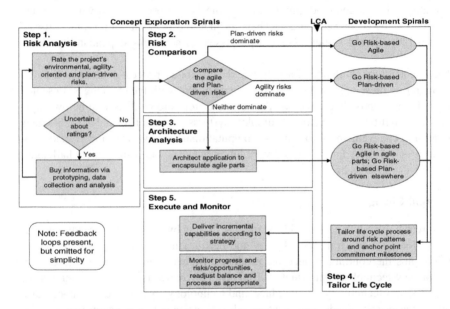

Fig. 1. Risk-Driven Spiral Approach to Balancing Discipline and Agility

For systems already in operation, a rapid pace of change requires a pro-active, risk-driven monitoring and experimentation activity to identify and prepare for major changes. An excellent example is the spiral process used to evolve the Internet (even before the spiral model was defined and published). Using the approach shown in Figure 2, the Internet principals were able to experiment, pilot, evaluate, and redefine the Internet standards to evolve from wire-based communication through packet radio, satellite, and optical communication while providing continuity of service [17]. Another good example of technology monitoring, empirical experimentation, and process improvement was the NASA Goddard/U. of Maryland/CSC Software Engineering Laboratory [5].

Rapid change prompts an additional significant change in software engineering education. This is to help students not only learn concepts, processes, and techniques, but also to learn how to learn. In some of our software engineering courses, we have

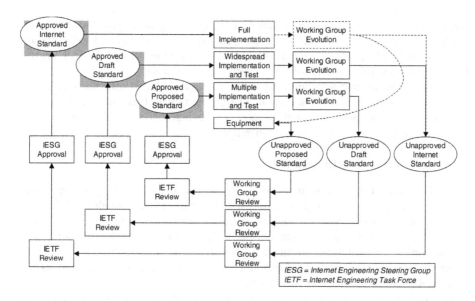

Fig. 2. The Internet Spiral Process [USAF-SAB Information Architectures Study, 1994]

addressed this challenge by adding assignments for students to obtain information from as many sources as possible to evaluate the maturity of an emerging technology and recommend a strategy that an organization could use with respect to adoption of the technology. Other strategies for helping students learn how to learn, such as the use of game technology, appear worth exploring.

2.4 Globalization and Interoperability Trends

The global connectivity provided by the Internet provides major economies of scale and network economies [3] that drive both an organization's product and process strategies. Location-independent distribution and mobility services create both rich new bases for synergetic collaboration and challenges in synchronizing activities. Differential salaries provide opportunities for cost savings through global outsourcing, although lack of careful preparation can easily turn the savings into overruns. The ability to develop across multiple time zones creates the prospect of very rapid development via three-shift operations, although again there are significant challenges in management visibility and control, communication semantics, and building shared values and trust.

On balance, though, the Computerworld "Future of IT" panelists felt that global collaboration would be commonplace in the future. The primary driver would evolve away from cost differentials as they decrease, and evolve toward the complementarity of skills in such areas as culture-matching and localization [2]. Some key culture-matching dimensions are provided in [26]: power distance, individualism/collectivism, masculinity/femininity, uncertainty avoidance, and long-term time orientation. These often explain low software product and process adoption rates across cultures. One example is the low adoption rate (17 out of 380 experimental users) of the more individual/masculine/short-term U.S. culture's Software CMM by organizations in the more collective/feminine/long-term Thai culture [40]. Another example was a much higher Chinese acceptance level of a workstation desktop organized around people, relations, and knowledge as compared to Western desktop organized around tools, folders, and documents [proprietary communication].

As with railroads and telecommunications, a standards-based infrastructure is essential for effective global collaboration. The Computerworld panelists envision that standards-based infrastructure will become increasingly commoditized and move further up the protocol stack toward applications.

2.4.1 Software Process Implications

A lot of work needs to be done to establish robust success patterns for global collaborative processes. Key challenges as discussed above include cross-cultural bridging; establishment of common shared vision and trust; contracting mechanisms and incentives; handovers and change synchronization in multi-timezone development; and culture-sensitive collaboration-oriented groupware. Most software packages are oriented around individual use; just determining how best to support groups will take a good deal of research and experimentation.

One collaboration process that still has significant differences about its future is open-source software development. Security experts tend to be skeptical about the ability to assure the secure performance of a product developed by volunteers with open access to the source code. Feature prioritization in open source is basically done by performers: this is generally viable for infrastructure software, but less so for corporate applications software. Proliferation of versions can be a problem with volunteer developers. But most experts, including the Computerworld futures panel, see the current success of open source development for products like Linux, Apache, and Firefox as sustainable into the future.

2.5 Complex Systems of Systems Trends

Traditionally (and even recently for some forms of agile methods), software development processes were recipes for standalone "stovepipe" applications with high risks of inadequate interoperability with other stovepipe applications. Experience has shown that such collections of stovepipe applications cause unacceptable delays in service, uncoordinated and conflicting plans, ineffective or dangerous decisions, and inability to cope with rapid change.

During the 1990's, standards such as ISO/ISE 12207 [31] began to emerge that situated software project processes within an enterprise framework. Concurrently, enterprise architectures such as the IBM Zachman Framework [48], RM-ODP [42] and the U.S. Federal Enterprise Framework [20], have been developing and evolving, along with a number of commercial Enterprise Resource Planning (ERP) packages.

These frameworks and support packages are making it possible for organizations to reinvent themselves around transformational, network-centric systems of systems. As discussed in [25], these are necessarily software-intensive systems of systems (SISOS), and have tremendous opportunities for success and equally tremendous risks of failure. Examples of successes have been Federal Express, Frito-Lay, and Wal-Mart; examples of failures have been the Confirm travel reservation system, K-Mart, and the U.S. Advanced Automation System for air traffic control.

2.5.1 Software Process Implications

Our work in supporting SISOS development programs has shown that the use of a risk-driven spiral process with early attention to SISOS risks and systems architecting methods [43] can avoid many of the SISOS development pitfalls [7]. A prioritized list of the top ten SISOS risks we have encountered includes several of the trends we have been discussing: (1) acquisition management and staffing; (2) requirements/architecture feasibility; (3) achievable software schedules; (4) supplier integration; (5) adaptation to rapid change; (6) software quality factor achievability; (7) product integration and electronic upgrade; (8) software COTS and reuse feasibility; (9) external interoperability; and (10) technology readiness.

In applying risk management to this set of risks, the outlines of a hybrid plan-driven/agile process for developing SISOS are emerging. In order to keep SISOS developments from becoming destabilized from large amounts of change traffic, it's important to organize development into plan-driven increments in which the suppliers develop to interface specs that are kept stable by deferring changes, so that the systems can plug and play at the end of the increment (nobody has yet figured out how to do daily builds for these kinds of systems). But for the next increment to hit the ground running, an extremely agile team needs to be concurrently doing continuous market, competition, and technology watch, change impact analysis, COTS refresh, and renegotiation of the next increment's prioritized content and the interfaces between the suppliers' next-increment interface specs. This requires new approaches not just to process management, but also to staffing and contracting, which SISOS programs are in the process of wrestling with.

2.6 COTS, Reuse, and Legacy Integration Challenges

A recent ACM Communications editorial stated, "In the end – and at the beginning – it's all about programming." [13]. Future trends are making this decreasingly true. Although infrastructure software developers will continue to spend most of their time programming, most application software developers are spending more and more of their time assessing, tailoring, and integrating COTS products.

Figure 3 illustrates these trends for a longitudinal sample of small e-services applications going from 28% COTS-intensive in 1996-97 to 70% COTS-intensive in 2001-2002, plus an additional industry-wide 54% COTS-based applications (CBAs) in the 2000 Standish Group survey [44, 46]. COTS products are particularly challenging to integrate. They are opaque and hard to debug. They are often incompatible with each other due to the need for competitive differentiation. They are uncontrollably evolving, averaging about to 10 months between new releases, and generally unsupported by their vendors after 3 subsequent releases. These latter statistics are a caution to organizations outsourcing applications with long gestation periods. In one case, we observed an outsourced application with 120 COTS products, 46% of which were delivered in a vendor-unsupported state [46].

Open source software, or an organization's reused or legacy software, is less opaque and less likely to go unsupported. But these can also have problems with interoperability and continuing evolution. In addition, they often place constraints on a

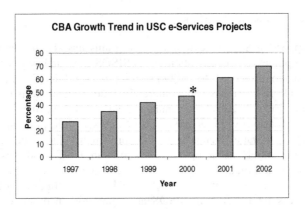

Fig. 3. CBA Growth in USC E-Service Projects — *Standish Group, Extreme Chaos (2000)

new application's incremental development, as the existing software needs to be decomposable to fit the new increments' content and interfaces. Across the maintenance life cycle, synchronized refresh of a large number of continually evolving COTS, open source, reused, and legacy software elements becomes a major additional challenge.

In terms of the trends discussed above, COTS, open source, reused, and legacy software will often have shortfalls in usability, dependability, interoperability, and localizability to different countries and cultures. As discussed above, increasing customer pressures for COTS usability, dependability, and interoperability, along with enterprise architecture initiatives, will reduce these shortfalls to some extent.

2.6.1 Software Process Implications

COTS economics generally makes sequential waterfall processes (in which the prespecified requirements determine the capabilities) incompatible with COTS-based solutions (in which the COTS capabilities largely determine the requirements; it's not a requirement if you can't afford it). Some initial COTS-based applications (CBA) development processes are emerging. Some are based on composable process elements covering the major sources of CBA effort (assessment, tailoring, and glue code integration) [46, 47]. Others are oriented around the major functions involved in CBA's, such as the SEI EPIC process [1].

However, there are still major challenges for the future, such as processes for synchronized multi-COTS refresh across the life-cycle; processes for enterprise-level and systems-of-systems COTS, open source, reuse, and legacy evolution; and processes and techniques to compensate for shortfalls in multi-COTS usability, dependability, and interoperability.

2.7 Computational Plenty Trends

Assuming that Moore's Law holds, another 20 years of doubling computing element performance every 18 months will lead to a performance improvement factor of $2^{20/1.5} = 2^{13.33} = 10,000$ by 2025. Similar factors will apply to the size and power consumption of the computing elements.

This computational plenty will spawn new types of platforms (smart dust, smart paint, smart materials, nanotechnology, micro electrical-mechanical systems: MEMS), and new types of applications (sensor networks, conformable or adaptive materials, human prosthetics). These will present process-related challenges for specifying their configurations and behavior; generating the resulting applications; verifying and validating their capabilities, performance, and dependability; and integrating them into even more complex systems of systems.

2.7.1 Potential Process Benefits

Besides new challenges, though, computational plenty will enable new and more powerful process-related approaches. It will enable new and more powerful self-monitoring software and computing via on-chip co-processors for assertion checking, trend analysis, intrusion detection, or verifying proof-carrying code. It will enable higher levels of abstraction, such as pattern-oriented programming, multi-aspect oriented programming, domain-oriented visual component assembly, and programming by example with expert feedback on missing portions. It will enable simpler brute-force solutions such as exhaustive case evaluation vs. complex logic.

It will also enable more powerful software tools that provide feedback to developers based on domain knowledge, programming knowledge, or management knowledge. It will enable the equivalent of seat belts and air bags for user-programmers. It will support show-and-tell documentation and much more powerful program query and data mining techniques. It will support realistic virtual game-oriented software engineering education and training. On balance, the added benefits of computational plenty should significantly outweigh the added challenges.

2.8 Wild Cards: Autonomy and Bio-computing

"Autonomy" covers technology advancements that use computational plenty to enable computers and software to autonomously evaluate situations and determine best-possible courses of action. Examples include:

- Cooperative intelligent agents that assess situations, analyze trends, and cooperatively negotiate to determine best available courses of action.
- Autonomic software, that uses adaptive control techniques to reconfigure itself to cope with changing situations.
- Machine learning techniques, that construct and test alternative situation models and converge on versions of models that will best guide system behavior
- Extensions of robots at conventional-to-nanotechnology scales empowered with autonomy capabilities such as the above.

Combinations of biology and computing include:

- Biology-based computing, that uses biological or molecular phenomena to solve computational problems beyond the reach of silicon-based technology.
- Computing-based enhancement of human physical or mental capabilities, perhaps embedded in or attached to human bodies or serving as alternate robotic hosts for (portions of) human bodies.

Examples of books describing these capabilities are Kurzweil's The Age of Spiritual Machines [33] and Drexler's books Engines of Creation and Unbounding the Future: The Nanotechnology Revolution [14, 15]. They identify major benefits that can potentially be derived from such capabilities, such as artificial labor, human shortfall compensation (the five senses, healing, life span, and new capabilities for enjoyment or self-actualization), adaptive control of the environment, or redesigning the world to avoid current problems and create new opportunities.

On the other hand, these books and other sources such as Dyson's Darwin Among the Machines: The Evolution of Global Intelligence [18] and Joy's article, "Why the Future Doesn't Need Us" [32], identify major failure modes that can result from attempts to redesign the world, such as loss of human primacy over computers, over-empowerment of humans, and irreversible effects such as plagues or biological dominance of artificial species. From a software process standpoint, processes will be needed to cope with autonomy software failure modes such as undebuggable self-modified software, adaptive control instability, interacting agent commitments with unintended consequences, and commonsense reasoning failures.

As discussed in Dreyfus and Dreyfus' Mind Over Machine [16], the track record of artificial intelligence predictions shows that it is easy to overestimate the rate of AI progress. But a good deal of AI technology is usefully at work today and, as we have seen with the Internet and World Wide Web, it is also easy to underestimate rates of IT progress as well. It is likely that the more ambitious predictions above will not take place by 2025, but it is important to keep both positive and negative potentials in mind in risk-driven experimentation with emerging capabilities in these wild-card areas between now and 2025.

3   Limitations to Software Process Perfectibility

Some of the negative wild-card scenarios above indicate that achieving perfectibility of software engineering and its processes will be difficult. Here are some other limitations that bound such expectations.

Brooks' Four Essentials Plus Two – Brooks' "No Silver Bullet" article and its update in [11] identify four "essential" (vs. "accidental") difficulties making it unlikely that a "silver bullet" solution for software development will be found. These four difficulties and their recent trends are: complexity (growing with larger COTS components, systems of systems, and the needs for competitive differentiation); conformity (growing with the increased needs for dependability and interoperability); changeability (growing with the increasing pace of technology, marketplace, and competitor changes); and invisibility (causing more difficulties due to COTS opacity and increases in complexity). For 21st century software, two further essential difficulties involve the centrality of software (its criticality to products and services, and to stakeholders' power bases) and the need for community-oriented products and processes (compounded by globalization, multiple cultures, and unfamiliar new models of electronic collaboration). Silver bullet solutions look even less likely as we consider these trends and the additional complexity problems with wild-card technologies.

Lampson's Continuing Software Crisis [34] – Lampson points out three reasons why the software crisis will always be with us: (1) Moore's Law enables the feasibility of new applications, requiring new and often complex software; (2) It is easier to handle complexity via software as compared to elsewhere, making it good engineering practice to address system complexities via software; and (3) Physical laws impose few limits on software applications, making it easy to overreach with proposed software solutions.

Conway's Law and Its Converse – Conway's Law [12] and its extension to user organizations states that, "The structure of a computer program reflects the structure of the organizations that build and use it." Its converse states that, "We will learn how to build perfectly functioning software as soon as we learn how to build perfectly functioning organizations." It is not likely that this will happen by 2025, or for some time thereafter.

4 Areas of Significant Research and Education Needs

4.1 Software Process Research Needs

These research needs are roughly prioritized by strengths of needs, based on the results of USC-CSE workshops with its industry and government affiliates.

1. Lean, Hybrid Processes for Balancing Dependability and Agility. The trends in simultaneous need for high dependability in Section 2.2 and high agility in Section 2.3 dominate here. Additional concerns for special cases are the additional need for scalability and incrementality for large, software-intensive systems of systems involving COTS and legacy systems as discussed in Sections 2.5 and 2.6; and the needs to address multi-location and multi-cultural development as discussed in Section 2.4. Using a value-risk-based approach as discussed in Section 2.1 is an attractive approach option. Other specific concerns are metrics for gauging progress during concurrent engineering, and performing concurrent engineering of multiple quality attributes.
2. Integrated Technical and Acquisition Processes. As discussed in Section 2.3, improvements in administrative and contracting processes tend to lag behind improvements in technical processes, causing the technical process to become overconstrained and unstable. Again, balancing dependability and agility is important, and the ability to administer and incentivize collaborative efforts that are performing concurrent plan-driven increments and agile next-increment preparation across multiple supplier chains as discussed in Section 2.5.1 are important.
3. Empirically-Evolved Process Languages, Methods, Metrics Models, and Tools. The need for such capabilities to be incremental and ambiguity tolerant, and to allow for incomplete, informal, and partial specifications are important, as are techniques for bridging gaps between less and more formal specifications and gaps or inconsistencies across life cycle phases or suppliers. The use of empirical evaluation testbeds to accelerate maturity and transition of research results, and to support collection of baseline process data for evaluating improvement priorities is important as well. A further attractive avenue is the development of capabilities to capitalize on computational plenty, as discussed in Section 2.7. The empirical framework could also be extended to monitor and evaluate progress and risk areas in the wild card autonomy and bio-computing areas.

4. <u>Virtual Process Collaboration Support</u>. Shifting the GUI focus from individual performance to distributed team, multi-stakeholder, and multi-cultural collaboration is a significant need, as discussed in Section 2.1.1 and 2.4.1.
5. <u>Game Technology for Process Education and Training</u>. Game engines complemented by virtual reality modeling and simulation have become tremendously powerful, and provide an excellent support base for developing "acquire and develop the way you train; train the way you acquire and develop" capabilities.

4.2 Software Process Education Needs

Some key skills much in demand are combinations of computer science and applications domain skills; COTS assessment, tailoring, and integration skills; stakeholder teambuilding and negotiation skills; combinations of technical and acquisition skills; and education in technologies emerging from the research areas above. Real-client project courses are the strongest mechanism for these kinds of education. The game technology discussed above will become a valuable addition to both education and training.

As discussed in Section 2.3.1, the most important future educational need is the need to learn how to learn.

5 Conclusions

In response to increasing demands being put on software-intensive systems, software processes will evolve significantly over the next two decades. The basic vocabulary will be different, with "goals" and "objectives" replacing such terms as "requirements", and "system evolution" replacing "software maintenance". Value-neutral methods will be largely replaced by value-based methods. The diversity of system stakeholders and values will increase the emphasis on collaborative processes to resolve multidimensional decision issues. Essential practices and skills will increasingly emphasize the integration of software engineering and systems engineering; the ability to integrate software components in place of traditional programming in most software development areas; and the accomplishment of most software development via user programming. The most important skill of all as the pace of change continues to accelerate will be the skill of learning how to learn.

Although perfectibility of software processes is unlikely, there are a number of software process research and education initiatives that would generate a high return on investment in meeting future IT challenges with better software solutions.

References

1. Albert, C., and L. Brownsword. Evolutionary Process for Integrating COTS-Based Systems (EPIC): An Overview. CMU/SEI-20030/TR-009. Pittsburgh, PA: Software Engineering Institute, 2002
2. Anthes, G.: The Future of IT. Computerworld, (March 7, 2005) 27-36
3. Arthur, W. B.: Increasing Returns and the New World of Business. Harvard Business Review (July/August, 1996) 100-109

4. Aurum, A., Biffl, S., Boehm, B., Erdogmus, H., Gruenbacher, P. (eds.): Value-Based Software Engineering. Springer Verlag (2005)
5. Basili, V., Zelkowitz, M., McGarry, F., Page, J., Waligora, S., Pajerski, R.: Special Report: SEL's Process-Improvement Program. Software (November, 1995) 83-87
6. Boehm, B.: A Spiral Model for Software Development and Enhancement. Computer (May, 1988) 61-72
7. Boehm, B., Brown, A.W., Basili, V., Turner, R.: Spiral Acquisition of Software-Intensive Systems of Systems, CrossTalk (May, 2004) 57-63
8. Boehm. B., Hoare, C.A.R. (eds.): Proceedings, 1975 International Conference on Reliable Software, ACM/IEEE (April, 1975)
9. Boehm, B., Jain, A.: An Initial Theory of Value-Based Software Engineering. In: Aurum, A., Biffl, S., Boehm, B., Erdogmus, H., Gruenbacher, P. (eds.): Value-Based Software Engineering, Springer Verlag (2005)
10. Boehm, B., Turner, R.: Balancing Agility and Discipline. Addison Wesley (2004)
11. Brooks, F.: The Mythical Man-Month (2nd ed.). Addison Wesley (1995)
12. Conway, M.: How Do Committees Invent?, Datamation (April, 1968) 28-31
13. Crawford, D.: Editorial Pointers. Comm. ACM (October, 2001) 5
14. Drexler, E.K.: Engines of Creation. Anchor Press (1986)
15. Drexler, K.E., Peterson, C., Pergamit, G.: Unbounding the Future: The Nanotechnology Revolution. William Morrow & Co. (1991)
16. Dreyfus, H., Dreyfus, S.: Mind over Machine. Macmillan (1986)
17. Druffel, L., Loy, N., Rosenberg, R., Sylvester, R., Volz, R.: Information Architectures that Enhance Operational Capability in Peacetime and Warfare. USAF-SAF Study Report (February, 1994)
18. Dyson, G. B.: Darwin Among the Machines: The Evolution of Global Intelligence, Helix Books/Addison Wesley (1997)
19. Ehn, P. (ed.): Work-Oriented Design of Computer Artifacts, Lawrence Earlbaum Assoc. (1990)
20. FCIO (Federal CIO Council).: A Practical Guide to Federal Enterprise Architecture, Version 1.0. (February, 2001)
21. Fuggetta, A.: Software Process: A Roadmap. In: Finkelstein, A. (ed.): The Future of Software Engineering. ACM Press (2000)
22. Gerrard, P., Thompson, N.: Risk-Based E-Business Testing. Artech House (2002)
23. Grady, R.: Successful Software Process Improvement. Prentice Hall (1997)
24. Gruenbacher, P., Koeszegi, S., Biffl, S. Stakeholder Value Proposition Elicitation and Reconciliation. In: Aurum, A., Biffl, S., Boehm, B., Erdogmus, H., Gruenbacher, P. (eds.): Value-Based Software Engineering, Springer Verlag (2005)
25. Harned, D., Lundquist, J.: What Transformation Means for the Defense Industry. The McKinsey Quarterly, (November 3, 2003) 57-63
26. Hofstede, G.: Culture and Organizations. McGraw Hill (1997)
27. Highsmith, J.: Adaptive Software Development. Dorset House (2000)
28. Huang, L.: A Value-Based Process for Achieving Software Dependability. Proceedings, Software Process Workshop 2005 (May, 2005)
29. Humphrey, W.: Introduction to the Personal Software Process. Addison Wesley (1997)
30. Humphrey, W.: Introduction to the Team Software Process. Addison Wesley (2000)
31. ISO (International Standards Organization).: Standard for Information Technology – Software Life Cycle Processes. ISO/IEC 12207 (1995)
32. Joy, B.: Why the Future Doesn't Need Us: Wired (April, 2000)
33. Kurzweil, R., The Age of Spiritual Machines. Penguin Books (1999)
34. Lampson, B.: Computing Meets the Physical World. The Bridge (2003) 4-7
35. Maslow, A.: Motivation and Personality. Harper and Row (1954)
36. Moore, G.: Inside the Tornado. Harper Collins (1995)

37. Musa, J.: Software Reliability Engineering. McGraw Hill (1999)
38. Patterson, D.: 20th Century vs. 21st Century C&C: The SPUR Manifesto. ACM Comm. (March, 2005) 15-16
39. Paulk, M., Weber, C., Curtis, B., Chrissis, M.: The Capability Maturity Model. Addison Wesley (1994)
40. Phongpaibul, M., Boehm, B.: Improving Quality Through Software Process Improvement in Thailand: Initial Analysis. Proceedings, ICSE 2005 Workshop on Software Quality (May, 2005)
41. PITAC (President's Information Technology Advisory Committee).: Report to the President: Information Technology Research: Investing in Our Future (1999)
42. Putman, J.: Architecting with RM-ODP. Prentice Hall (2001)
43. Rechtin, E.: Systems Architecting. Prentice Hall (1991)
44. Standish Group: Extreme Chaos. http://www.standishgroup.com (2001)
45. Toulmin, S.: Cosmopolis. University of Chicago Press (1992)
46. Yang, Y., Bhuta, J., Port, D., and Boehm, B.: Value-Based Processes for COTS-Based Applications. IEEE Software (2005, to appear)
47. Yang, Y., and Boehm, B.: A Contextualized Study of COTS-Based E-Service Projects. Proceedings, ICCBSS 2005 (February, 2005)
48. Zachman, J.: A Framework for Information Systems Architecture. IBM Systems Journal (1987)

Software Are Processes Too

Jacky Estublier

LSR-IMAG, 220 rue de la Chimie BP53,
38041 Grenoble Cedex 9, France
Jacky.Estublier@imag.fr

Abstract. A process defines the way activities are organized, managed, measured, supported and improved to reach a goal. It has been shown, 15 years ago [1] that processes are software too; more precisely that their description can also be software. We hypothesize that a system can be characterized by its *goal* and by answering the questions: *why, what* and *how*.

We show that software process work investigated only a tiny subset of processes, where only the *how* have been addressed. "Meta-process" research tried to address the *why* to change a process model, but was largely unfruitful

This paper first relates processes, software production and humans in the framework of the meta pyramid proposed by the OMG MDA. We show that programs and process models are fully similar, but not at the same level in the meta pyramids. Therefore the claim: software are processes too.

The meta pyramid framework is used to show and contrast new and original potential uses of process technology. It is shown in particular that strategic software management requires a kind of process support where the *what* is not humans, but the software itself. Finally it is shown that autonomic computing will soon require process support where the *why*, the *what* and the *how* will have to be fully formalized and the process models automatically executed.

We believe that this new and demanding context will foster new research on process modeling and support.

1 Introduction

A process is the way activities are organized, managed, measured, supported and improved to reach a goal. For example, in the software process, the activity is software development (design, implementation, test, ...) and the goal is to deliver the planned software product.

A process model is the formal expression of a part of the process, with the goal to understand, communicate, improve, support or automate the process. Process technology supports a process in order to consistently reach the goal within predefined time, budget, and quality constraints.

The process, therefore, encodes a part of the company know-how which otherwise is only in the performer's head. It is acknowledged that this (partial) transfer of know-how allows the company to master its assets, to transfer more easily the know-how to newcomers, to increase repeatability, and to allow process analysis and improvement.

From this perspective, in the software process community, the *goal* is the repeatability of the process with optimal human resource consumption, focusing on

M. Li, B. Boehm, and L.J. Osterweil (Eds.): SPW 2005, LNCS 3840, pp. 25 – 34, 2005.

how the job (designing, developing and maintaining a software) should be done. The job is performed by humans on documents (*what*) on the time scale of a software project (weeks and months) [2] [3] [4].

It is interesting to see that any interactive software system also has a goal to support (and constrain) human activities in order to reach a goal in a repeatable and predictable way, optimizing the human resource. From this perspective, interactive software is a process support system. *How*, is often defined by the functions the system supports and *what* is often the values of some data managed by the software system. Time scale is minutes.

The software process line of work, and most interactive programs, hypothesize that the context is constant (technology, market, goals). But the context permanently evolves, on a larger time scale (years), and successful software (and models) must evolve to adapt to its changing context. This long-term evolution is also a process, often carefully planned (strategic view of the product). The *goal* is to adapt the software product (*what*) to new markets and technologies, changing (*how*) the software product content. The time scale is years. This is *why* software evolves. So far, this kind of process has not been formally described and supported.

Today, in autonomic computing for example, a software must evolve continually at execution, changing its architecture and its features, under the constraints of its environment. This is typically what a process is. The *goal* is to adapt to evolving contextual conditions, *why* is to maintain an optimal software service, *what* is the software system, *how* is architectural and feature changes; in the time frame of seconds. Because of the very short time frame, these changes must be performed fully automatically, and therefore the *why*, *how* and *what* must be formalized.

We discuss these new dimensions of processes, at the light of the MDA framework, and we show what are the differences and synergies.

2 Meta-pyramids

The "meta" prefix is used very often in research, but it is a relative notion. A meta-language is a language that describe languages; meta-data is data that describes data, and a meta-model is a model that models model. The "meta" notion occurs at different levels, in different domains and under different terms.

2.1 The Software Meta-pyramid

The meta notion can be composed. For instance a meta-meta-model is a model that describes meta-models. Clearly each composition step leads to a level that is increasingly difficult to grasp. In practice after a few levels of abstraction, adding more levels is not useful. Figure 1 presents the classical "meta-pyramid".

The language technology provides a good example of meta-tower. The Backus Normal Form (BNF) is a meta-language that is useful for describing languages. One might use the BNF grammar to describe the Java or C++ grammar. The Java grammar describes how to write valid Java programs [5] [6][7].

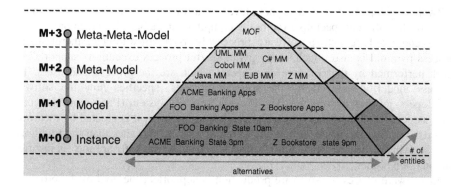

Fig. 1. The MDA Software pyramid [8]

The relationship between two levels is the "conformity" relationship. Conformity can be defined in different ways. It can be the instantiation conformity (an instance conforms to its class); it can be linguistic conformity (a sentence conforms to the language in which it is written), ontological conformity (an instance conforms to the definition of its ontological class) and so on. MDA uses instantiation conformity between M+0 and M+1, linguistic conformity otherwise.

At the lowest level (M+0), instances (or objects) represent abstractions of real world entities (e.g., "tom" is a client of the ACME bank). Each state of the program execution is a model (an abstraction) of a state in the real world. The program is a model of the evolution of the real world.

M+1 is the level where programs reside. Program are models describing the application concepts (e.g., "client" and "account") and the rules that govern all possible states (e.g., "balance>0").

The meta-model level (M+2) describes the concepts that are used to describe models. For instance the concepts of "class" and "association" are used in UML class diagrams, the concepts of "class", "method", "field", and "inheritance" are used in Java programs, etc.

At the meta-meta-model level (M+3), there is the MOF. The MOF is used to describe itself, and to describe arbitrary meta-models including meta-models for UML, Cobol, Java, C, etc. Roughly speaking the MOF is the equivalent of the BNF in the context of UML.

2.2 The Software Process Meta-pyramid

Aside from the MDA pyramid, called here the technology pyramid, we can find the human pyramid, representing the humans working at each level. In this pyramid, the conformity relationship is informal: the persons at one level define the tools and methods to be used at the next lower level [9].

At the model level are software developers; they produce the software. One level higher, the software experts are designing and developing the technologies needed for the developers, including programming languages (compilers), middleware and other piece of enabling technology. These persons are much less numerous than the software developers. At the meta-meta-level are a few specialists that develop (meta) tools for the software specialists (compiler compilers, meta parsers and so on).

As claimed long ago, a software process is itself software [1], therefore, the process pyramid is also a technology pyramid. But process execution "supports" the work performed by the software developers, which are the process' end users. The process model, developed by the software experts, specifies *how* the software developers' job has to be done. The Process Support System (PSS) is the language (and associated support tools) in which models are written; it is created by metaware experts. We find the usual technology pyramid, one level higher than the traditional one, showing clearly that the claim "software processes are software too" is justified, but one step higher.

In software processes, software production is supported, the goal of the processes is support and automation. The software process community has considered the most critical issue to be the modeling and support of activities in a non-deterministic world; non-deterministic because the humans that perform the job (*who*) are non-deterministic. In these software processes, human are producing, consuming and changing "products," which are the final product, the targeted software (*what*). To increase efficiency, predictability, and reduce errors, the process, when supported, prohibits the user from doing anything, and instead lets him perform only some predefined task, in a predefined order; usually the process engine handles the "products" on behalf of the user.

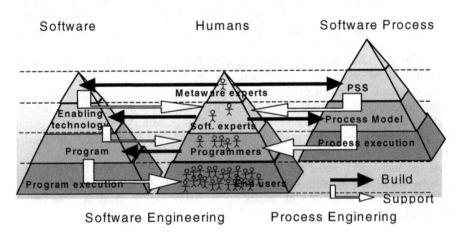

Fig. 2. Software engineering and process engineering

Now consider an interactive program. The program simply manages some data (product) on behalf of its users, it prohibits the user from doing anything with the data and instead proposes only predefined operations (activities) in a predefined order; it handles the issues around concurrent work on the same data. The program is very similar to a process model, and the machine to a process engine. We can say the program *supports* its users in pretty much the same way as a process supports its users. A model (program) expresses *how* humans are supposed to interact with software artifacts (data); it expresses the sequence of actions (*how*) to be performed by these humans of these artifacts (*what*) to reach a goal. In both cases the goal is the repeatability of the process, the consistency of the resulting data and the optimization of human time. This shows that our claim "software are processes too" is fully justified.

The relationships between the human and technology pyramids are *build* and *support*. At a given level, the humans are building the tools at the same level in the technology pyramid. As an exception, at the base level, the end users are not (necessarily) developing any software.

The execution of software succeeds one level down in the technology pyramid, using the instantiation conformity (see fig 1). Therefore, these tools, when executed (1 level down) are *supporting* the work performed by the human at that level. It is the typical relationship between a process and the humans it "manages" or supports.

This consideration is true for any interactive software; this is true for the Process Support System (PSS), that supports the software expert in defining the process model, and it is also true for most of the enabling technology found at the M2 level of the technology pyramid: IDEs and other tools are supporting the software engineers work.

This is why we claim that "software are processes too". This analogy, once established, makes it interesting to revisit process technology and its use.

3 New Uses of Processes

3.1 Program Coordination

Orchestration and choreography are nice names for the coordination of independent programs. Indeed, it means that the *what* are programs and that the goal is to provide control to these program in order to reach a goal. These program can be seen as performing an activity, in which case orchestration and choreography can be seen as a process, with a *goal* to implement a complex application, acting on other programs (the *what*), providing control to these program (the *how*) [18].

In contrast with software processes, the job is not performed by a human, but by programs. Programs are usually deterministic, hence, coordination languages are seen as programming languages, with the same characteristics and constraints. But communication often occur through the internet, which is not fully reliable, introducing another reason for non-determinism. This is why exception handling is an important issue. The point of program coordination, since it is fully automatic, is to get clear an unambiguous semantics; it is a microprocess line of work [10] [12][14].

It is interesting to see that this kind of automated coordination is recognized by the software engineering community as being a process (under name workflow), even if no humans are involved in their execution. Indeed, "process (or workflow) driven" XX is becoming a common expression to indicate that process technology is used to coordinate XX [15].

3.2 Meta Process

In most work on "meta-processes", the meta-process is not the level above the process in the meta pyramid, but a completely different process, which (tries to) support the software experts when updating/changing a process model, in order to solve the discrepancies found during process execution (process instance evolution) [11], to adapt the model to new methods and tools (process evolution), or to improve the model (process improvement).

Indeed the work on "meta-processes" were among the first attempts to formalize the know-how of software experts when deciding to react to contextual changes during process execution. This know-how is the analysis of the changes, and the decision of *what* changes are to be performed in order to maintain some fundamental properties of the process (the *why*). Considering that the process model is also a program, the "traditional" software process, defining *how* to change the model, can be applied [17] [3].

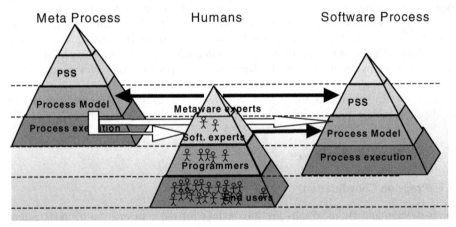

Fig. 3. The Meta-process pyramid

It is interesting to see that virtually all the work performed on meta-processes addressed *why* to change the model, and *what* to change; leaving *how* to change to the "traditional" software process. This is an important difference.

Unfortunately, the least we can say, is that meta-processes have not been successful so far. This is not surprising, since modeling the *why* (modeling motivations, choices in non deterministic space, behavior in non planned context..) is intrinsically more complex than modeling the *how*.

The time scale of such meta-processes is weeks for process instance evolution, but years for process adaptation and software improvement.

3.3 Process for Strategic Software Evolution

The long process by which a software product evolves from its current state to a future desired state is often carefully planned. For example, a development plan may state that product XX, currently on Linux must be available also on Windows XP, must support multi-threading and must provide support for YY and ZZ features in the next 2 years. For a professional product, it is likely that the long list of changes to be performed to reach the goal will be analyzed and the process will be identified (steps, duration, resources …). Companies would like to have support during this long period of time, for example, for each change to be performed (e.g., normal maintenance) to assess if it is consistent with the long term goal or not. This is similar to civil engineering: before performing work is an area, checks are performed to see if there are conflicts with other planned future work (highway, ...).

This is typical software process: it formalizes an evolution to reach a goal (the future desired state of the software), it contains a lot of know-how, and has to be performed in a highly non-deterministic context (technology and market evolve permanently at that time scale).

This long-term process is different from the "usual" one in the sense that it focuses on the structure and technical content of the software (the *what*) while traditional processes focuses the humans and documents (semantically neutral from the process perspective). It defines the changes (*what*) that must be applied to the content and structure of the software, in order for the software evolve as planned. The entities the process acts upon are not humans, but the software itself, not files, but its content and structure.

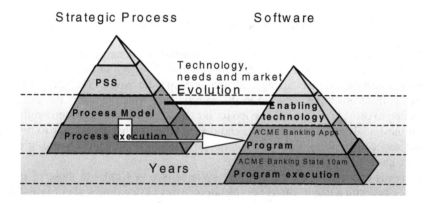

Fig. 4. Strategic software evolution

It means the strategic process should control and coordinate the different production processes (governing *how* the changes are to be performed). In general, it involves the coordination of two or more different processes, possibly handled by different process engines, in different geographical locations. These issues have been addresses by the Workflow Management Coalition (WfMC), but with many restrictions [20][21]. The problem still needs to be addressed in a more general context [19].

3.4 Process for Dynamic Software Evolution

The fact modern software applications are gradually supported by a network of computers, has dramatic consequences. Provided the number of machines potentially involved in such an application (up to thousands), the variability of the network bandwidth and availability, and even the mobility of some "machines" (laptops, PDA, phones), the administration of these complex software application cannot be done manually. It gives birth to so called autonomic computing systems. These systems are commonly defined as exhibiting self-monitoring, self-configuration, self-optimization, self-healing, and/or self-protection [22][23].

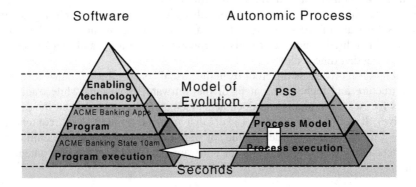

Fig. 5. Dynamic software evolution

This means that autonomic systems are permanently changing their architecture and their features in response to the changing context. The *goal* of these changes is to maintain a service in an evolving and non-deterministic world. The *why* of these changes is that something occurred in the environment which hampers the software application to provide an optimal service (or no service at all). An autonomic software system must analyze the new context, and decide *what* to change in order to restore optimal service (the *why*). Since the autonomic system performs the change, it must therefore know *how* to perform the change.

The needs and ambitions of autonomic systems is very similar to those of meta-processes, but with a major difference: meta-processes have a time scale of years, and therefore are at least partially performed by humans. In autonomic computing, these changes occur in the time frame of a few seconds and are performed on many machine simultaneously: decisions must be made and performed fully automatically. It is very interesting to consider that autonomic computing will require processes that fully formalize the *why*, the *what* and the *how*.

4   Conclusion

Process technology has explored a number of issues and technologies, but with implicit hypothesis : humans are doing the job, the process expresses how to perform the job, in a rather stable world. The difficult issue is the non-deterministic of humans. From the process point of view, the software product (the *what*) is a set of documents whose content is not really of concern. Work on meta-processes tried to address other issues, the product (the process model) being known and changed to adapt to changes that have occurred in the environment. The meta-process work tried to address the *what* and the *why*. Unfortunately, this work was not so successful.

In recent years, process technology has been used for a number of other purposes, in which the *what* became the content and structure of programs (or models), where the major issue is no longer human non-determinism, but the non-determinism of context evolution, either over very long periods of time (market, needs and technology) or very short periods of time for widely distributed and dynamic applications executing in non-predictable environments   (mobility, bandwidth, availability, services and so on). This evolution considers software as both a process and the subject of a process, blurring even more the traditional distinction between processes and software.

We believe that this new and demanding context should resurrect the old work performed on meta-processes and foster a new trend of research activity on process support in general, and on how to formalize the *why* and *what* in processes.

Acknowledgement

We are grateful to Jean-Marie Favre for the discussion and initial ideas leading to that short paper. I hope an extended version will be produce in common soon.

References

[1] L. Osterweil. "Processes are software too". Proceedings of the 9th international conference on Software Engineering. Monterey, California, United States, Pages: 2 – 13. 1987

[2] Conradi, R., Fernstrom, C., Fuggetta, A., Snowdown, B. Towards a Reference Framework for Process Concepts. In Proc. EW SPT'92, 2nd European Workshop on Software Process Technology, Trondheim, Norway (Sept. 1992)

[3] J.C. Derniame (ed). « Software Process : Principles, Methodology and Technology ». LNCS 1500. Springer Verlag 1999.

[4] B. Curtis, M.. I. Kellner, J. Over. "Process Modeling", Communications of the ACM, Volume 35, No. 9, September 1992.

[5] Dsouza, D. "Model-Driven Architecture and Integration: Opportunities and Challenges" Version 1.1, document available at www.kinetiuym.com, February 2001.

[6] OMG Model Driven Architecture A Technical Perspective Architecture Board MDA Drafting Team Draft 21st February 2001

[7] John Poole. "Model-Driven Architecture: Vision, Standards And Emerging Technologies". ECOOP 2002.

[8] J.M. Favre. "CacOphoNy: Metamodel-Driven Architecture Reconstruction". Working Conference on Reverse Engineering (WCRE 2004). November 2004, Delft, The Netherlands

[9] J.M.Favre, S. Ducasse "Using Meta-Model Transformation to Model Software Evolution". ATEM2004, Workshop with WCRE 2004) Delft, The Netherlands, November 8th-12, 2004. And in Electronic Notes in Theoritical Computer Science

[10] C. Godart, F. Charoy, O.Perrin and H. Skaf-Molli: "Cooperative Workflows to Coordinate Asynchronous Cooperative Applications in a Simple Way.". 7th International Conference on Parallel and Distributed Systems (ICPADS'00). Iwate, Japan, July 2000

[11] P.Y. Cunin, R.M. Greenwood, L. Francou, I. Robertson and B. Warboys. "The PIE Methodology - Concept and Application". 8th European Workshop on Software Process Technology (EWSPT). Dortmunt, Germany. June 19, 2001.

[12] G. Valetto, G. Kaiser. Using Process Technology to Control and coordinate Software Adaptation. ICSE, Portland May 2003.

[13] Wise, A., Cass, G.A., Staudt Lerner, B., McCall, E.K., Osterweil, L.J., Sutton Jr., S.M.: Using Little-JIL to Coordinate Agents in Software Engineering. Proceedings of the Automated Software Engineering Conference ASE 2000, Grenoble, France (September 2000) 155-163.

[14] Estublier, J., Sanlaville, S.: Business Processes and Workflow Coordination of Web Services. IEEE International Conference on e-Technology, e-Commerce and e-Service (EEE-05), Hong Kong (March 2005).

[15] Estublier, J., Villalobos, J., Le, A.T., Sanlaville, S., Vega, G.: An Approach and Framework for Extensible Process Support System. 9th European Workshop on Software Process Technology EWSPT 2003, Helsinki, Finland (September 2003).

[16] Leymann, F.: Web Services Flow Language (WSFL 1.0). IBM Software Group (May 2001).

[17] Minh Ngoc Nguyen, Reidar Conradi: "The Software Meta-process: Taxonomy and Assessment", p. 167-175, Proc. 3rd Int'l Conference on Software Process (ICSP'3), IEEE-CS Press, 10-11 Oct. 1994 Washington.

[18] Leymann, F., Roller, D.: Workflow-based applications. IBM System Journal. Vol. 36, No.1 (1997) 102-123.

[19] Jacky Estublier, Pierre-Yves Cunin, Noureddine Belkhatir. « An architecture for process support interoperability". ICSP 5, Pages 137-147. 15-17 June 1998 Chicago, Illinois, USA.

[20] Workflow Management Coalition: Interface 1: Process Definition Interface. WfMC TC-1016 (August 1996)

[21] Workflow Management Coalition "Workflow Standard - Interoperability - Abstract Specification", Document Number WFMC-TC-1012, Version 2.0b, 30 November 1999.

[22] IBM Systems Journal: Special Issue on Autonomic Computing, Vol. 42, No. 1, Jan 2003.

[23] J.O. Kephart and D.M. Chess, The Vision of Autonomic Computing, IEEE Computer, Vol. 36, No. 1, pp. 41-50, Jan 2003.

The Software Process: Global Goals

Watts S. Humphrey

Software Engineering Institute (SEI) of Carnegie Mellon University,
4500 Fifth Avenue, Pittsburgh 15213, USA
watts@sei.cmu.edu

Abstract. The software industry appears to have reached a plateau. While improvements have been made in the last 20 years, progress has been limited in scope and degree. Researchers, tool and method developers, and process specialists are all doing creative and promising work. However, as we continue making impressive technical and process advances, and even though occasional projects produce extraordinary results, broad and effective use of even generally-available best processes and methods has been slow and limited.

Where new processes and methods have been properly introduced, the results have generally been positive. This would be considered success by many definitions but most software work continues to be done with ill-defined processes, poor tools and methods, and ineffective management systems. Modern software work involves many topics and there are many different specialties. Because our field is now so broad and so many different topics are now important, we have developed a wide variety of disciplines which each has its own experts. Unfortunately, these experts all have different views and, because we don't agree among ourselves on what is important, our story is incoherent. To improve our industry so that it can meet the growing demands of society, we, the software process research community, must develop a coherent, consistent, and forceful position.

1   The Issues

Few of the issues in software work are complex, but their significance is not obvious to even highly-qualified and perceptive managers and executives. It is not that the issues we raise are unimportant, but that most executives face a constant stream of many important issues and are deluged with specialized solutions to the many parts of their software operations. Without a clear and compelling way to present the software process story, each of our individual technical successes has too narrow a scope to be a priority for those who lead and control today's software development work. If our process, method, and tool advances do not address goals that are already near the top of their priority lists, busy executives will feel that, while possibly important, incorporating these advances in their work is not anything they must address right now.

It is as if we were building the Tower of Babel. We work on this enormous edifice but we can't even communicate among ourselves. It is not surprising that we have trouble communicating with our users. The problem is goals. What important goals do we face and what do we recommend as goal priorities? Should we really recommend that our potential users apply every one of our advances at once, or is there

M. Li, B. Boehm, and L.J. Osterweil (Eds.): SPW 2005, LNCS 3840, pp. 35–42, 2005.
© Springer-Verlag Berlin Heidelberg 2005

some order and framework we could agree upon? To get our work on the priority list of busy people, we must address the goals that are important to them. And we must do it in a way that makes sense, is not technically controversial, and that fits coherently with what other experts tell them.

2 What We Need

So we need goals, but our current goals are overly focused. We must not just consider the goals of one or two people; everyone must be involved. We all work on this enormous elephant of a problem but we each work on only a small part: if one person concentrates only on the trunk, or the tusks, or the toenails then no one can describe the entire beast. And, what is worse, those of us who work on tusks or trunks don't recognize the legs or toenails as important, and we are even likely to belittle what is actually very good and necessary work. We are not only foregoing the likely synergies among our efforts, but we are not even aware that such synergies could exist. Few of us have the time to even consider them.

We need to understand our own goals and also to see where our goals fit into an overall framework that characterizes both the local and the systemic problems of the entire field of software process and technology. Further, since our process concepts must address the entire universe of software issues, we must consider all of the communities involved: the consumers who use the software products and services; the suppliers who produce software systems, products, and services; and the generators who produce the processes, tools, methods, environments, technologies, and skills that the consumers, suppliers, and generators need to do their work. As members of the generator group, we must understand the goals of our own work but also understand how these goals address the needs of the three classes of constituents. With such a coherent framework, we could tell a compelling story, and we could support each other while doing so. Because the problems will not get better by themselves and because the need for solutions is growing daily, a logical and coherent goal framework for the entire software field would have an enormous impact. Developing such a framework for the software process research community would be a useful start and might motivate an effort to produce a coherent set of goals for all of software technology.

3 A Goals Framework

To produce a coherent and meaningful set of goals, we must consider both how process work fits into the entire software field and how process research relates to the broader spectrum of process activities. The ultimate focus of all software-related goals must be on the software users. If these users don't sooner or later benefit from our work, our products will not be used or our activities well-supported. This means that the first goals to define are for those groups that supply products and services directly to software users.

Developers and service providers are interested in processes only if these processes appear likely to help them produce more attractive products, provide more effective services, or improve their business performance. Therefore, our goals must ultimately concern ways to help product developers and servicers produce better products for lower costs and on shorter schedules. This, in turn, requires that we provide process-related products and services that will help both developers and servicers produce these better products.

From this point, the next step in the goals discussion must consider the groups that provide process-related products and services to software developers and servicers. The goals for these groups are much like those of the product developers and servicers. They will be interested in process research work only if it can help them to produce more attractive process-related products and services or to improve their own business performance.

The next logical step would appear to be to define the goals for process research. However, goals like those for product developers are not appropriate for research groups. Research groups are not in the business of identifying market opportunities, defining and developing products, or providing user services. Our business is developing knowledge and understanding, so it is more appropriate for the process research community to think in terms of questions than goals. What are the critical questions that the process developers and service providers face in their work, and what might the process research community do to help address these questions? Presumably, by having answers to the right set of questions, the people who provide process products and services would be better able to do their jobs.

4 Critical Questions

While there are many ways to group the critical process questions, this paper divides them into four categories.

Designing processes
Using processes
Analyzing processes
Supporting processes

There are many questions that one could ask in each area, but based on recent work at the SEI, the following appear to be some of the more fundamental ones.

5 Designing Processes

Here, one of the most basic questions is the following.

- To what extent is it possible to design software development processes that are both sufficiently precise to provide useful guidance and sufficiently general to be widely applicable?

Work to date with the Personal Software Process (PSP)^{SM} shows that, at least for individual developers, a single simple process can be used by most software developers to guide the development of small programs [Humphrey]. This work has also shown that, with a precise and well-defined process and sufficient motivation, devel-

---

^{SM} Personal Software Process and PSP are service marks of Carnegie Mellon University.

opers will actually change their behavior and produce higher-quality and work on more predictable schedules than they did before.

This same PSP work also shows that such a process can constrain the programming style of some users. While relatively simple process modifications can make these processes suitable for almost any programming style, few software developers have the skill and motivation to make such changes themselves, particularly if their initial process experiences felt constraining.

While the results to date appear helpful, substantial additional work is required to produce a broader answer to the question of process precision vs. generality. This work should include steps like the following.

- Identify the particular facets or sub-processes of software work that could profitably use precise but generic processes.
- Define how these sub processes should relate.

Establish a generalized architectural framework for these processes, with appropriate standards for nomenclature, measures, data formats, and interfaces.

6 Using Processes

Regarding process use, one fundamental open question is the following.

- What combination of process features, tool support, user training, and user experience is required to enable broad and effective use of a process?

Experience to date shows that a substantial preparatory effort is required before software developers will use a defined process on their own. Even after they are using it, however, the consistent and effective use of that process is still widely variable. While many teams of developers have successfully used the Team Software Process (TSP)[SM], many of the processes that they used were ones that they had personally defined under the guidance of an experienced TSP coach [Davis]. Then, with proper coaching and management support, these teams have generally obtained impressive results.

Continued effective use of these team-defined processes appears to require substantial management support and ongoing professional team coaching. The problems that cause these needs concern process tool support and automation; developer experience, education, and training; the quality of the coaching provided; and the consistency and nature of management support.

One question where an answer could help clarify the process usage issues is as follows.

- If developers had been required to use defined and measured processes when they first learned to write programs during their formal education, would they be more likely to use processes consistently and effectively later in their careers?

While some universities have started to introduce process concepts and methods in initial programming courses, not enough developers have been trained in this way to provide a reliable answer to this question. Another important usage question concerns the developers' working environment.

[SM] Team Software Process and TSP are service marks of Carnegie Mellon University.

- If developers worked in an environment where consistent and regular use of defined and measured processes was normal, would new members of these groups learn and use these processes more readily?

Limited experience indicates that the answer is probably yes, but experience also shows that there will be exceptions. A few developers will refuse to follow generally accepted practices regardless of their benefits or of management and peer pressure. Typically, such developers change jobs under these conditions. A third and related usage question concerns creativity.

- Would the broad and effective use of defined processes enhance developer creativity?

While there is insufficient evidence to date to answer this question, early experience in the medical profession provides an interesting and possibly pertinent analogy. Before the late 1800s, the practice of medicine was severely limited by what was then called sepsis. We now know that sepsis was caused by bacterial infection. Since patients almost always died of sepsis after extensive or complicated surgery, there was little demand for such procedures, and the practice of surgery was severely limited. Even though surgeons had many creative ideas, and many surgical tools and methods had been invented, it was not until Lister introduced antiseptic techniques around 1870 that advanced surgical methods began to be widely used and that the startling advances we have since seen in surgical technology could be developed.

Unfortunately, with current software practice, the severity of cost, schedule, quality, safety, or security problems often results in the premature demise of our projects. While there is no way to prove the point, it seems likely that the current rudimentary state of software practice is limiting the nature of software applications in much the way that sepsis limited the practice of surgery. On the positive side, there is growing evidence that all of these problems could be solved or substantially reduced by the proper use of suitably defined and measured software processes and practices.

7 Analyzing Processes

One of the more interesting and possibly most fundamental set of process questions concerns our ability to study processes independently of the people and projects that enact them. One such question is the following.

- What can we learn about the usefulness and performance of processes by studying the processes themselves?

One way to think about this question is to consider the degree to which process performance can be characterized independently of the people or projects that enact that process. The SEI has PSP data on many thousands of process enactments by several thousand software developers. Because the PSP, as taught in the SEI's standard course, consists of six upwardly-compatible processes, developer performance can be examined across the range of processes [Hayes]. Even though the performance variation among individuals is generally larger than the performance variation across process levels, statistical studies have shown that the variation between process levels is significant. On average, the SEI has found that process differences can cause significant changes in the performance of individuals and even of large groups of developers.

However, the really important issue is not learning about a process by studying the results of using that process, it is learning about the process from studying the process itself. For example, if we could devise a framework and measurement system for characterizing the performance of process elements, what could we say about the performance of various combinations of these elements? Based on what we can deduce from the PSP data, we are a long way from answering this broader question. While it is not clear that we ever could draw useful conclusions about a process without studying data on its enactment, it seems likely that, if we were to ever do so, we must use scientific principles to develop verifiable theories.

8 The Scientific Method

To follow the scientific method, we must follow these steps.
- Produce theories about our processes.
- Make hypotheses about our theories.
- Postulate experiments to test these hypotheses.
- Conduct and measure these experiments.
- Use the experimental data to either verify the hypotheses or to modify the theories and hypotheses and repeat the experimental cycle.

Hopefully, after conducting enough scientifically-based experiments on enough enactments of a sufficiently varied family of processes, this approach would yield a family of experimentally-verified theories which could guide useful process analysis. If we could ever get to this point, a few of the more interesting questions we might address would be the following.
- To minimize cost and schedule, what would be the optimum balance of development, defect prevention, quality assessment, and defect repair activities?
- To maximize planning accuracy at each stage of a process, what is the proper mix of planning and development activities for any given process or process family?

Another series of questions might address process performance limits. An example is the following.
- Are there limits to the quality levels that skilled developers can achieve with a process or process family and, if so, how do these limits vary with the tools and methods used?

Finally, there is the more fundamental question which is at the root of many software research activities.
- Are there limits to software process automation and, if there are, what are they and how can we characterize them?

While great strides have been made in automating many aspects of the software development process, there is some essence of this process that appears unlikely to ever be automated. It concerns those aspects of the work involving learning, communicating, motivating, committing, and adapting. Could we somehow characterize the limits of software process automation and define ways to measure our progress against these limits?

Such a demonstrably sound theoretical foundation for our work would be of tremendous value. To help advance scientifically sound studies of the software process, the SEI is willing to consider requests for using its large volume of PSP and TSP data for qualified research studies.

9 Supporting Processes

The many important categories of process support include training, coaching, management, and tools. Of these, the one area that would be of most immediate value is tool support. The two principal areas of tool support are support for enacting existing processes and support for developing or enhancing processes.

10 Tool Support for Enacting Processes

Regarding tool support for supporting process enactment, the single biggest complaint developers have about using almost any process is inadequate tool support. To facilitate scientifically-sound process studies, the highest priority focus should be automated data gathering. For this, the tool should
- use the data that are potentially available from the development environment
- provide maximum assistance to the developers in performing whatever data-gathering tasks they must perform
- analyze the current and historical data and draw useful inferences regarding project and product status
- generate individual and team reports on project and product status

To capitalize on the potential for automated data gathering, analysis, and reporting, we will likely need to integrate process support tools into development environments.

11 Tool Support for Developing and Enhancing Processes

As we have learned from the PSP and TSP work, many of the process needs of development teams are unique to that team, project, and time. Therefore, tool support could greatly facilitate process development and evolution. As teams gain experience, their process needs change. So, if they are to continue using the process, that process should also change. Similarly, as teams use processes, they find areas where the process is inconvenient, incomplete, or even incorrect, and must be updated. While the frequency and magnitude of these changes is generally low during a project, each new project invariably requires new or modified processes.

The PSP and TSP facilitate this process evolution process by using a Process Improvement Proposal (PIP) form that developers are encouraged to submit whenever they see process problems or have process improvement ideas. The PIP provides a way to both capture many improvement ideas from developers and to give all process users a sense of ownership and control over the processes they use. Some important questions about process development and enhancement support are the following.

- How do you modify a process that is currently being used?
- How do multiple developers work effectively together with a common team process while individually using tailored personal processes?
- How can process data be gathered and managed so that these data can be used to analyze dynamic and varied processes?

12 Next Steps

Hopefully, the SPW 2005 discussions and proceedings will provide a useful first step in assembling a coherent set of critical questions for software process research. While this in itself would be an enormous contribution, an even greater achievement would be to use this work as the springboard for developing a coherent and comprehensive goals framework for the entire field of software research and engineering. I hope that the issues I have raised with this paper will provide a starting point for the goals discussion that is needed to launch the next wave of technological advancement in the software industry.

References

1. N. Davis and J. Mullaney, "Team Software Process (TSP) in Practice," SEI Technical Report CMU/SEI-2003-TR-014.
2. Will Hayes and James W. Over, "The Personal Software Process: An Empirical Study of the Impact of PSP on Individual Engineers," SEI Technical Report CMU/SEI-97-TR-001.
3. Watts S. Humphrey, PSP: A Personal Improvement Process for Software Engineers, Reading, MA: Addison Wesley, 2005.

Achieving Software Development Performance Improvement Through Process Change

Ross Jeffery

Empirical Software Engineering Program, National ICT Australia & School of Computer
Science and Engineering, The University of New South Wales,
Locked Bag 9013, Alexandria, NSW, 1435, Australia
ross.jeffery@nicta.com.au

Abstract. This paper summarizes the results of process improvement activities
in two small software organizations. One of these made use of macro process
modelling. These results, along with the reported results of CMMi adoption, are
interpreted in the light of organizational theory, a process improvement research
framework, and process innovation theory. It is concluded that the evidence
supports process innovation or variations on innovation as a means of achieving
large scale improvements in productivity or quality. It also argues (1) for the
use of the process research framework to identify research limitations, and (2)
that consideration of process alone is unlikely to provide sufficient evidence for
generalization.

1 Introduction

In a presentation made at the pre-ICSE 2006 *Workshop on International Cooperation
in Software Engineering* in Shanghai [1], the argument was made that evolutionary
process improvement in the Allette Systems corporation context studied has had only
limited success in significantly changing their performance in software development.
The process modelling and experience management technologies developed for Allette Systems have been beneficial to the organization and shown a positive return on
investment. But these technologies have not provided an order of magnitude improvement or significant multiplier for software development efficiency or effectiveness in this organisation. Thus it was not that improvement had not occurred, but that
it was a relatively small improvement, and we believed that to achieve truly significant continuing improvement, revolutionary change was needed if significant inroads
into productivity and quality were to be achieved. In this paper we explore the context in which software process improvement occurs and the topic of process innovation. We compare this with the research in process modelling, process improvement
and experience management that has been carried out in the software engineering
research community in recent years.

In sections two, three and four the paper introduces concepts from the literature
which provides the means by which interpretation of the industrial case studies presented later is provided. In section two of the paper we provide background to the
context in which process improvement will occur. In section three we present a

M. Li, B. Boehm, and L.J. Osterweil (Eds.): SPW 2005, LNCS 3840, pp. 43–53, 2005.
© Springer-Verlag Berlin Heidelberg 2005

means of interpreting the research type applied to process improvement. In section four we investigate the proposition that process innovation rather than process improvement is a necessary condition to significant performance changes. Here we use the work of Davenport to make this argument. The paper then compares these frameworks and arguments with process modelling and process improvement activities carried out in two SME's.

2 The Process Improvement Context

Software process improvement does not occur in a vacuum. One easy way of visualising this is the model provided in the Scott Morton MIT90's framework [2]. This is shown in Figure 1. This model shows that improvements to process occur within an organization and within an organizational culture.

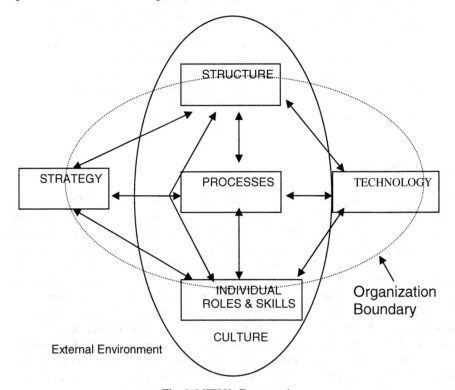

Fig. 1. MIT90's Framework

In addition technology, strategy, individual roles and skills and the organizational structure will all interact with the processes and any process improvement activities. We return to examples of this in the case studies and research frameworks presented later in the paper.

3   A Process Improvement Research Framework

In the paper by Sambamurthy and Kirsch [3] a software development process research framework is presented which provides a useful background for our considerations in software process improvement. This framework classifies software process literature into four categories:

Factors-oriented which associates contextual factors with process outcomes.
This category includes research that treats process as a black box and investigates the relationships between input, context and output variables. The results of this research might enable improvement in outcomes as a consequence of change or control of inputs and context.

Process as explanation.
This type of research takes on step further than the factors-oriented work. It involves the use of process logic to explain why outcomes result from factors. Thus it is a logic-based rather than empirically-based explanation of the outcomes.

Process as a category of concepts.
In this category of process research the researchers explicitly investigate processes and then test associations between the process variables and outcomes.

Process as a sequence of events.
This category of research recognizes that processes are a sequence of events and investigates that sequence and the relationships between the documented sequences and outcomes that can be associated with the sequences.

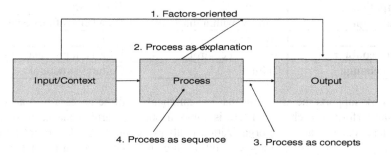

Fig. 2. Process Research Framework

From this investigation the authors conclude that systems development processes are "the *tasks* undertaken to construct a …system, and the management of this effort, by a group of *stakeholders* with *agendas*, who engage in *transactions* over time within an institutional *context* by applying *structure* to their work with a set of tools and methodologies, and who judge *outcomes* of their efforts and act accordingly." The concepts in italics are considered the core concepts to guide process research in a way that will make it more likely to address the inherent complexities of process enactment within organizations. It can also be noted that there is an echo of the MIT90's framework in this definition. The concepts can be diagrammed as in Figure 2. In this figure the fours categories of research are shown. Category 1 seeks relationships between inputs/context and outcomes; category 2 seeks to explain these relationships from process; category 3 explores the process factor relationships and category 4 seeks a deeper understanding of process sequence and its impact.

All of these are valid research categorizations but the question remains as to which research strategy will provide significant output improvement opportunities in an industrial context?

4 Davenport's Model

In his book Davenport [4] argues that continuous process improvement might achieve 5% to 10% improvement in performance levels but that increases in the order of 50% to 100% are needed to be competitive. Admittedly he is discussing business process rather than software process, but if your business is software then they are a part of the same puzzle. Craig and Yetton [5] identify six themes of Davenport's work as illustrated in Table 1 which is taken from their paper

Table 1. Process improvement versus process innovation

	Process Improvement	Process Innovation
Level of change	Incremental	Radical
Starting point	Existing processes	Clean slate
Frequency of change	One-time/continuous	One-time
Time required	Short	Long
Participation	Bottom up	Top down
Typical scope	Narrow, within functions	Broad cross functional
Risk	Moderate	High
Primary enabler	Statistical control	Information technology
Type of change	Cultural	Cultural/structural

This work supports the argument that radical change will be necessary to achieve significant performance change. There is some dispute concerning the need to start from a clean slate because the organization is always going to be dependant on the capabilities of the people and these capabilities are anchored in the current technologies, processes and environment. It has also been recognised that innovation will be a higher risk strategy, and that failure to achieve a 100% improvement in one year will likely be worse than success at achieving a compound 10% improvement each year for seven years say. However there has been some support for this strategy in industry. For example a company in Canberra has adopted one of the agile methodologies and report significant improvements in productivity and quality through what was a radical change in development process

Craig and Yetton highlight six themes of Davenport's work. These are:

1. Process innovation is different to process improvement.
2. Process innovation must be undertaken explicitly.
3. Process innovation is technology dependent.
4. Process innovation is large scale change with people and organization as key enablers.

5. Process innovation should be guided by a vision linked to strategy.
6. Process innovation can be undertaken in all types of industries and processes.

But then they proceed to illustrate by example some of the weaknesses of Davenport's argument and instead provide evidence for what is termed a "dynamic improvement" model which is shown as column three in Table 2

Table 2. Dynamic Improvement

	Dynamic Process Improvement	Process Innovation
Level of change	Incremental	Radical
Starting point	Existing Processes	Clean slate
Frequency of change	Continuous	One-time
Time required	Long	Long
Participation	Top down /bottom up	Top down
Typical scope	Broad cross functional	Broad cross functional
Risk	Moderate	High
Primary enabler	Technology	Technology
Type of change	Individual roles and skills / technology/ management processes	Cultural/structural

The essential difference in the Craig and Yetton argument is that the evidence suggests that (1) it may not be possible to pursue a strategically directed change in process, (2) that the risk of this large-scale change is too high, and (3) that a more complex expression of organizational dynamics is needed to understand the evidence concerning process improvement. "Implementing process redesign is itself the real activity, out of which strategic options will emerge. It is not a planned, top down process that begins with strategy formation and structural design, followed by implementation." [5]

5 The Allette Case

The work carried out with Allette Systems is documented in a number of publications but most fully in the recent Information and Software Technology paper [6]. In this work we have been developing intra-net instantiated macro process models and technologies for the generation of these models. In addition we have initiated a software process experience base and a process model-integrated time recording system.

In the software engineering domain, several Electronic Process Guides (EPGs) of proprietary processes like RUP [7] and Mentor [8] have been available for some time, and tools such as Spearmint [9], ARIS [10] and Adonis [11] have been developed to generate EPGs. Some studies showing the application of knowledge management in software engineering are the experience factory work of Basili et al. within NASA Goddard's SEL [12] and the Daimler-Chrysler research center project [13]. Research has also been done on tools to support experience storage and retrieval [14], [15], [16], [17], [18].

Most publications on the experience gained in organisations that have used software engineering repositories present qualitative descriptions of the setup of, and lessons learned. For example, Conradi and Dingsoyr [19] provided notes on the experience repositories in four organisations. Lindvall et al. [20] outlined three case studies and described some high level lessons learned and Brossler [21] describes experience in one company. More recently, Schneider and Hunnius [22] identified user guidance, usability, process conformance, feedback mechanism and maintainability as quality aspects that determined the chances for success of an experience repository based on their work at Daimler-Chrysler. But it must be concluded however that this work does not appear to have provided software development performance improvement of the order that would be desired to achieve a competitive advantage for the companies pursuing these technologies. This supports the experience in Allette Systems. The technology used in Allette is shown in Figure 3.

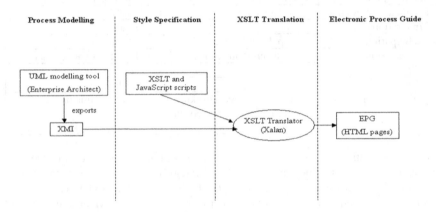

Fig. 3. EPG Generation

UML activity diagrams are used to graphically specify the processes. These are then exported into XML Metadata Interchange (XMI) format. An XSLT translator is then used to transform the exported XMI using EXtensible Stylesheet Language (XSL) and JavaScript scripts that define the layout and functionality of produced EPGs. The UML modelling tool used is Enterprise Architect [23] and the XSLT translator used is Xalan [24]. Figure 4 shows an example page of the EPG/ER. Each page of the EPG/ER consists of two frames. The diagrammatic overview on the left-hand side displays the UML diagram of the process that supports browsing and hyper-navigation of the process. The description section on the right-hand side displays the description of the currently displayed entity and any textual attributes such as entry and exit criteria and responsibilities.

In evaluating this technology we found that the EPG/ER is extensively used in the organisation and remains in regular use. Furthermore, users appear to have learned to create more sophisticated forms of experiences such as lessons learned for reuse. The results validate the effectiveness of the tool as an SPI tool by bringing about not only benefits such as improved documentation and release of experts from guidance of novices, but also a bolstered confidence in the organisation to plan and execute software projects. These results serve as supporting evidence that user guidance is an

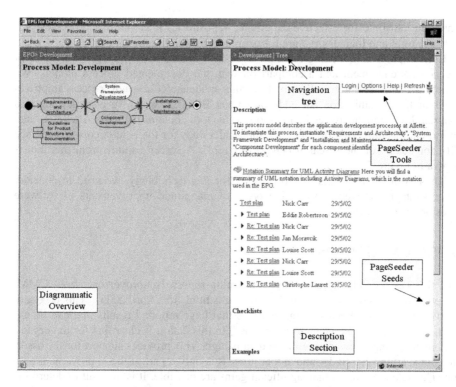

Fig. 4. Layout Example of the EPG/ER

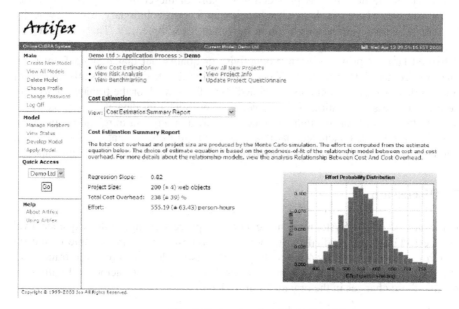

Fig. 5. Estimation Screen

important attribute for effective experience repositories [22] and that processes provide a natural and logical structure for people to consider their work [25].

Current process modelling research with this organization concerns an analysis of the process enactment and a comparison with the documented process model. We expect that this research will provide further evidence concerning process improvement in this organization. In addition to the EPG/ER work we also developed a tailored development cost estimation tool. This tool contains the basic Allette productivity relationships, cost drivers and empirical values for the Allette cost drivers (see [26] for details of the research behind this tool). A screen capture from this tool is shown in Figure 5.

Thus even if the results are so positive for this technology, we need to consider other strategies if we are to enable order of magnitude improvements in software development performance.

6 The CMMi Results

The SEI has recently released data concerning reported improvements from CMMi adoption (http://www.sei.cmu.edu/cmmi/results.html 15th April 2005). This is "quantitative information from 18 organizations that have reported results that can be expressed as performance changes over time." In this data it is clear that for the organizations reporting, the variance in the data is high. This provides support for the assertions in sections 2, 3 and 4 above that process is only a part of the improvement puzzle. The data also shows that significant gains are possible. It is difficult to determine the nature of the change from the information provided by the SEI however. It is likely, given the descriptions provided that many of the changes reported have occurred in cases where the change has been dynamic or revolutionary. This is typically the case when a level one organization moves to level three, say. There is clear evidence in one Australian organization that moving from level three to level five has not delivered large improvements in productivity or quality but that moving from level one to three had delivered these. It is disappointing that the reported statistics do not provide details such as contained in the MIT90's framework or the framework used to describe process innovation or improvement. Without this data it is impossible to identify the reasons for the high variance in the data or any causal relationships. So at this stage it must be concluded that this evidence is still insufficient to provide insight into the complexities of process improvement and its relationship with performance.

7 Discussion

In the case of Allette Systems we made a one-off process change at the sequence level via the EPG/ER and studied its impact on outcomes. This is an example of the research framework category 4 research type. We also undertook a research framework category 1 research project in identifying the effort estimation factors and values. In making these changes in the organization we have:

1.   Introduced new technology,
2.   Made use of existing skills in the organization,

3. Modified the software process and made it explicit,
4. Slightly modified the structure of the organization by changing some roles for individuals.

We have not affected the business strategy however. Thus these interventions are an example of a dynamic improvement process according to the Craig and Yetton model. One element that we believe is important but seems not to have been addressed in this type of literature is the issue of organization size. We hypothesize that one of the major determinants of appropriate improvement strategy will be organizational unit size. If the organization is small, we believe that dynamic process improvement and possibly process innovation can achieve large scale positive outcomes. However if the organizational unit is large then we hypothesize that continuous process improvement will most often be the appropriate model. There is evidence that large scale change in large organizations can be achieved, such as in moving from CMM level one to level three. There is also evidence that this is a costly and time consuming activity [see 27]. It is suggested that the success of this initiative is dependent on the clear and precise definition of the change required and the management of that change. The issue becomes one of managing the organizational change.

The set of models presented can also be used to explain behavior we have seen in other organizations in Australia. For example, one medium sized software organization that has adopted agile processes reported in a private communication (April 13th 2005) that their process change can be classified as part innovation and part dynamic improvement. The level of change was seen as radical but implementation was incremental. The initial starting point was existing processes but more recently they have moved to a clean slate application. Thus the change can be seen as a one-time change but it continues to evolve. Risk was seen as moderate because it was managed via incremental adoption and the type of change was more cultural than skill based. These are highlighted in Table 3. Significant organizational benefits are claimed. An earlier study in the organization had rejected CMM-based continuous improvement. The overriding conclusion is that the process improvement implemented was part dynamic improvement and part innovation.

The industrial implications of these models and cases are, (1) Competitive advantage through process improvement is more likely to be achieved via dynamic process

Table 3. SME Process Improvement Example

Dynamic Process Improvement		Process Innovation
Incremental	←-----------	Radical
Existing Processes	-------------→	Clean slate
Continuous	←-----------	One-time
Long		Long
Top down /bottom up		Top down
Broad cross functional		Broad cross functional
Moderate Risk		High Risk
Technology		Technology
Individual roles and skills / technology/ management processes		Cultural/structural

improvement or process innovation, (2) large organizations are likely to use continuous process improvement unless they approach innovation through incremental strategies or large-scale change management, (3) small organizations are well placed because of their size to implement process innovation or dynamic process improvement, (4) organizations need to recognise that software process improvement needs to be considered in the context of individual roles and skills, organizational strategy and size, available technology and organizational structure. The research implications are that, (1) the process improvement framework can position the research method and highlight the likely outcomes and limitations of the research, (2) consideration of process alone is unlikely to provide sufficient evidence for generalization.

References

1. R. Jeffery, Presentation at Pre-ICSE 2006 Workshop on Research Directions in Software Process, 14 and 15 October, 2004, Shanghai, China.
2. M.R. Scott Morton, The Corporation of the Nineties, Oxford University Press, Oxford, 1991.
3. V.Sambamurthy & L.J.Kirsch, An Integrative Framework of the Infortmation Systems Development Process, Decision Sciences, 31,2, Spring ,2000, pp. 391-411.
4. T.H.Davenport, Process Innovation: Reengineering Work Through IT, Harvard Business School Press, Boston, 1993.
5. J.Craig & P.Yetton, Business Process Redesign: A Critique of Process Innovation by Thomas Davenport as a Case Study in the Literature, Australian Journal of Management, Australian Graduate School of Management, 17,2, December, 1992
6. F.Kurniawati & R.Jeffery, The Use and Effects of an EPG/ER in a Small Software Organization, accepted for publication in Journal of Information & Software Technology.
7. P. Kruchten, "Rational Unified Process – An Introduction", Addison-Wesley, 2000
8. Object-Oriented, Managing Successful Software Projects with Process MeNtOR, Object Oriented Pty Ltd, 1998
9. U. Becker-Kornstaedt, D. Hammann, R.Kempkens, P. Roesch, M. Verlage, and J. Zettel, Support for the Process Engineer: The Spearmint Approach to Software Process Definition and Process Guidance., Proceedings of the 11th Conference on Advanced Information Systems Engineering CaiSE'99, 1999, pp. 119-133
10. ARIS. 2000: www.ids-scheer.de.
11. Adonis. 2001: www.boc.at.
12. V. Basili, G. Caldiera and H.D. Rombach, "The Experience Factory", Encyclopedia of Software Engineering vol. 1, J.Marciniak, Ed. John Wiley Sons, 1994, pp. 469-476.
13. K. Schneider, "LIDs: A Light-Weight Approach to Experience Elicitation and Reuse", Product Focused Software Process Improvement: Second International Conference vol. LNCS 1840, 2000, pp. 407-424.
14. K. Althoff, A. Birk, S.Hartkopf, W.Muller, M.Nick, D.Surmann and C. Tautz, "Systematic Population, Utilization and Maintenance of a Repository for Comprehensive Reuse", Proceedings of the 11th International Conference on Software Engineering and Knowledge Engineering, 1999, pp.25-50.
15. F. Houdek and H. Kempter, "Quality Patterns – An approach to packaging software engineering experience", Proceedings of the 1997 Symposium on Software Reusability vol. 22, 1997, pp. 81-88

16. S.Henninger, J. Schlabach, "A Tool for Managing Software Development Knowledge", Proceedings of Product Focused Software Process Improvement: Third International Conference vol. LNCS 2188, 2001, F. Bomarius, Komi-Sirvio, S, Ed. Springer, pp. 182-195.

17. B. Lewis, "On-Demand KM: A Two-Tier Architecture", IT Professional vol. 4, 2002, pp. 27-33

18. Y. Ye and G. Fischer, "Supporting Reuse by Delivering Task-Relevant and Personalized Information", Proceedings of 2002 International Conference on Software Engineering, 2002, pp.513-523

19. R. Conradi and T. Dingsoyr, "Software Experiences Bases: a Consolidated Evaluation and Status Report," Proceedings from the 2nd International Cofnerence on product focused Software Process Improvement (PROFES 2000), vol. LNCS 1840, 2000, pp. 391-406

20. M. Lindvall, M. Frey, P. Costa and R. Tesoriero, "Lessons learned about Structuring and Describing Experience for Three Experience Bases, " Proceedings of the third International Workshop. Advances in Learning Software Organisations (LSO 2001, 2001), pp. 106-119

21. P. Brossler, "Knowledge Management at a Software Engineering Company – An Experience Report," Proceedings of the Workshop on Learning Software Organisations, 1999, pp. 77-86

22. K. Schneider, J. von Hunnius, "Effective Experience Repositories for Software Engineering", Proceedings of the 25th International Conference on Software Engineering, 2003, pp. 534-539

23. Enterprise Architect 2003: http://www.sparxsystems.com.au/

24. Xalan-Java. 2003: http://xml.apache.org/xalan-j/index.html

25. H. Holz, A. Konnecker and F. Maurer, "Task-Specific Knowledge Management in a Process-centered SEE," Proceedings of the 3rd International Workshop on Advances in Learning Software Organisations, 2001, pp. 163-177

26. M.Ruhe, R.Jeffery & I.Wieczorek, Cost Estimation for Web Applications, Proceedings of 25th International Conference on Software Engineering, IEEE Computer Society, Los Alamitos, California, 2003, pp. 285 – 294

27. The Report of the Software Quality Accreditation Working Party, Software Quality Accreditation in the Australian Context, Australian Government, Department of Communications, Information Technology and the Arts, February, 2005, 39pp.

Expanding the Horizons of Software Development Processes: A 3-D Integrated Methodology*

Mingshu Li

State Key Lab of Computer Science and Lab for Internet Software Technologies,
Institute of Software at Chinese Academy of Sciences,
No. 4 South Fourth Street, Zhong Guan Cun, Beijing 10 00 80, China
mingshu@iscas.ac.cn

Abstract. This paper investigates how to define and improve software development processes. Based on examining the software development during last two decades, it proposes a breakthrough point of an updated view of requirements, called *Great Requirements*, and presents a 3-D *integrated software engineering* methodology for improving software development activities. It expands the horizons of possible future software development processes.

1 Introduction

Software, as the core of any modern product or service, is becoming increasingly important. However, most software projects are unsuccessful. The Standish Group (www.standishgroup.com) found in its survey (2004 3rd Quarter Research Report) [1], as shown in Figure 1, only 29% of the projects finished on time, on budget, with required features and functions; and 18% were canceled before delivery or delivered but never used. Moreover, the remaining projects, 53%, which all finished late, over budget and/or with less than the required features and functions. The problems associated with software development are critical issues. Improving software development processes is a key challenge for software community.

Fig. 1. Most Software Projects are not Successful

SE (Software Engineering), from 1968, introduced tremendous techniques for software development to combat the "software crisis". It is defined as "the establishment and use of sound engineering principles in order to obtain economically software that is reliable and works efficiently on real machines"[2], or "the application of a systematic, disciplined, quantifiable approach to the development, operation and maintenance of software; that is, the application of engineering to software"[3].

---

* Supported by the National Natural Science Foundation of China (Grant Numbers: 60273026, 60473060) and the Hi-Tech Research and Development Program (863 Program) of China (Grant Numbers: 2004AA112080, 2005AA113140).

M. Li, B. Boehm, and L.J. Osterweil (Eds.): SPW 2005, LNCS 3840, pp. 54–67, 2005.

There are hundreds of definitions for SE and all of them stress on the term of *"engineering"*. Philippe Kruchten argued in [4]: "Is software development really a form of engineering? Or is it just some kind of elaborate craftsmanship? Are we just fooling ourselves thinking that we are doing engineering? If so, it is certainly not from lack of trying hard over the last 20 years. But maybe we tackled the problem from the wrong end: we tried to impose techniques from other engineering disciplines onto software development models without understanding the real nature of software". He explored SE's five key differentiating characteristics from other engineering fields: it has limited usable underlying theory, it is very "soft" by nature, it has high technological churn, it has no manufacturing cost, and it has few international borders.

The "software crisis" presented several decades ago never seemed to materialize. As an engineering discipline, SE still has a long way to go before it matures and is able to produce quality software products through quality software development processes.

2 Related Work

A *software development methodology* can be defined as [5]: (1) an integrated set of software engineering methods, policies, procedures, rules, standards, techniques, tools, languages, and other methodologies for analyzing, design, implementing, and testing software and (2) a set of rules for selecting the correct methodology, process, or tools for use. The SE-based software development methodologies generally used in the past and on today include *Structured Analysis and Design* [6], *Object-Oriented* Methods [7], *Agile* Methods [8], *CASE* Tools [9], *CBSE* (Component-Based Software Engineering) [10], *AOSD* (Aspect-Oriented Software Development) [11], and so on.

SE is a layered technology, from a quality focus, an organizational commitment to quality, to process, methods, and tools [12]. SE process is the glue that holds the technology layers together and enables rational and timely development of computer software; SE methods provide the technical how-to's for building software; and SE tools provides automated or semi-automated support for the process and the methods. There are eight fundamental SE notions that form the basis for an effective discipline of SE [13]: (1) abstraction; (2) analysis and design methods and notations; (3) user interface prototyping; (4) software architecture; (5) software process; (6) reuse; (7) measurement; (8) tools and integrated environments.

The software development process is sometimes called the software life cycle, because it describes the life of a software product from its conception to its implementation, delivery, use, and maintenance [13]. The *Waterfall Model* is the oldest software development process model. It suggests a systematic, sequential approach to software development that begins at the system level and progresses through five distinct and linear stages: requirements, design, implementation, testing and maintenance. There are some drawbacks of the Waterfall Model, e.g., it imposes a project management structure on system development; it is inflexible in handling requirement changes; it presents a manufacturing view of software development and tells us nothing about the typical back-and-forth activities that lead to creating a final software product.

The push for software process improvement came as a response to the failures of software projects [14]. The success of total quality management (TQM) has inspired the software process movement. The origins of software process maturity can be traced back to the principles of product quality management that have existed for nearly 70 years. The effective use of software technology is limited by several factors [15]: an ill-defined process, inconsistent implementation, and poor process management. Software technology cannot be fully effective until these problems have been adequately addressed.

A *software process* can be defined as the coherent set of policies, organizational structures, technologies, procedures, and artifacts that are needed to conceive, develop, deploy, and maintain a software product [16]. More specifically, the software process sets out the technical and management framework for applying methods, tools, and people to the software task, while the process definition identifies roles and specifies tasks [17]. Viewing software development as a process has significantly helped identify the different dimensions of software development and the problems that need to be addressed in order to establish effective practices. The focus of SE process research during the past two decades mostly concentrated on *Process Modeling* [18], *Process Programming* [19], *PSEEs* [20], and Software Process Management, Improvement, and Assessment like *ISO 9000* [21] and *SEI-CMM/CMMI* [22].

CMMI ® (Capability Maturity Model® Integration) was released by the Software Engineering Institute (SEI) at Carnegie Mellon University in January 2002 [23]. It is designed to help organizations improve their product and service development, acquisition, and maintenance processes. The SEI continues to advocate the adoption of CMMI models as the best process improvement models available for product and service development and maintenance. These models build on and extend the best practices of the Capability Maturity Model for Software (SW-CMM®), the Systems Engineering Capability Model (SECM), and the Integrated Product Development Capability Maturity Model (IPD-CMM). There are 25 Process Areas (PA) in Continuous Representation of CMMI and they are divided into 4 categories: (1) Process Management; (2) Project Management; (3) Engineering; (4) Support.

CMMI provides a systematic perspective on organizational process improvement. However, it stresses too much only about the managerial aspects of software development. It does not give an implementation details and is a little bit difficult for small size software organizations to adopt it without a full guidance of methods and tools. Also it does not suit highly flexible, dynamic, market-driven, innovative software organizations very well. And it is at over cost in the beginning period and hardly affordable for some software organizations.

Addressing software development problems and issues is not just a matter of introducing some effective tool and environment. It is insufficient to select a reasonable lifecycle strategy either. It must be paid attention to the complex interrelation of a number of organizational, cultural, technological, and economic factors [16].

SE economics tries to measure software quality and process characteristics [24]. *COCOMO II* (COnstructive COst MOdel) [25], is a fully documented and widely accepted model, which targets the estimation of software projects. *CORBA* (Cost Estimation, Benchmarking, and Risk Assessment) and *Web-CORBA* [26], combines expert knowledge with data on a small number of projects to develop cost estimation models, which can also be used for risk analysis and benchmarking purpose.

Most SE economics methods lack software project management and technology details, which makes them risky in cost/duration estimation and control.

In a short summary of the related work, people usually only paid attention to some key technologies independently, such as software development programming and tools, project management, software process improvement, schedule and cost estimation, and so on. Some elements necessary to develop software successfully were often discussed too abstractly and obviously, or even ignorantly.

3 The Horizons of Software Development Processes

In 1990, Robert Balzer presented eight unresolved process support problems in his paper entitled "What We Do and Don't Know about Software Process" [27]: (1) Abstraction/instantiation relationships between generic and specific processes and between specific processes and their enactments; (2) Involve people in automated processes; (3) Measure process; (4) Measure process progress; (5) Use process status as basis for prediction; (6) Improving process; (7) Change process in midstream; (8) Manage inconsistency & incompleteness.

A lot of efforts had been made during past years, e.g., eight systems were demonstrated at ISPW9 [28]: *Hakoniwa,* from Osaka University (Japan); *LEU,* from Lion Gesellschaft fur Systementwicklung mbH (Germany); *MVP-S,* from University of Kaiserslautern (Germany); *Oikos,* from Pisa University (Italy); *Oz,* from Columbia University (USA); *Synervision,* from HP (USA); *Regatta,* from Fujitsu (Japan); *SPADE,* from Politecnico di Milano (Italy). Some of them have newer versions more recently. Based on *Oz, OzWeb* extends to a hypermedia collaboration environment in which people may collaborate by accessing and manipulating hypermedia documents [29].

However, most problems mentioned above still remain to date. As a matter of fact, few (if any) of the proposed approaches have been transferred into industrial practice [16]. There are several problems related to defining process from industrial experience[30]: (1) Attempting to define a "one-size-fits-all" process or process framework for different kinds of systems where knowledge content and knowledge availability is quite different; (2) Failing to differentiate between knowledge discovery and knowledge application in process definition; (3) Attempting to define a single level of abstraction for all process types; (4) Depositing our process knowledge in book form or leaving it in brain form rather than developing automated systems that assist the knowledge acquisition and application process; (5) Not properly allowing for the nature of the learning activity in setting up processes, particularly the nature of cognition and problem understanding.

We have to think about what should be a starting point in further improving software development processes? Requirements may be a good choice. Getting requirements right might be the single most important and difficult part of a software project [31]. *Requirements engineering (RE)* denotes both the process of specifying requirements by studying stakeholder needs and the process of systematically analyzing and refining those specifications. Despite heterogeneous terminology throughout the literature, RE must include four separate but related activities: elicitation, modeling, validation, and verification. In practice, they will most likely vary in timing and intensity for different projects.

Numerous tools are available to support RE [32], e.g., *Ciliber-RM*, Borland; *CARE* (Computer-Aided RE), Sophist Technologies; *DOORS*, Telelogic; *IRqA* (Integral Requisite Analyzer), TCP Sistemas & Ingenieria; *Reqtify*, TNI-Valiosys; *Requisite Pro*, IBM Rational; *RM Trak*, RM Trak; *RTM Workshop*, Integrated Chipware; *Truereq*, Truereq; *Vital Link*, Compliance Automation. The worst thing that can happen in RE is that the set of requirements, however expressed, doesn't accurately represent the users' needs and consequently leads the team down the wrong development path. The risk is greatest at several points [33]: (1) Overlooking a crucial requirement; (2) Inadequate customer representation; (3) Modeling only functional requirements; (4) Not inspecting requirements; (5) Attempting to perfect requirements before beginning construction; (6) Representing requirements in the form of designs.

To address the system development challenges of the 21st century, people must rethink RE's role in software development and integrate the processes of RE with system implementation [34]. The artificial separation of these activities leads to a situation where customers do not realize how much time and effort is required to deliver their requirements, and where suppliers can not deliver the best value to customers using their specialist knowledge and existing software.

We should revisit software characteristics to better understand the nature of software. Some presentations of my conclusions are learnt from Osterweil's paper title to give an updated view of the classic understanding [19].

3.1 Requirements Are Software Too

The traditional software requirements document is not a complete specification of the software to be implemented. During software development processes, requirements always change. Requirements are about wants and needs, but people usually don't know what they want until they know it exists. Requirements and other software artifacts may change throughout the whole development phase and even after that. No one can understand them completely before starting system development or even operational use. Stakeholders have to continue to gain new insights into the requirements. Requirements are not only engineered within the traditional requirements analysis stage, but also throughout the whole life cycle; and requirements are not only functional/non functional specifications, but also need to guarantee achieving quality goals, being on time and within budget, etc.

3.2 Software Is a Process Too

Although the industry is moving toward component-based assembly (like a car and a house), most software continues to be custom built. It is due to the lack of a strong underlying theory to rigorously define the software components and especially their interfaces, like in the classic industry. A process is a set of practices performed to achieve a given purpose; it may include tools, methods, materials, and/or humans.

The task of software development needs effective cooperation from all of the tools, methods, materials, and/or humans, through the software process.

3.3 Software Is Not Software Only

Software, like other design work, is developed or engineered. It is not mechanized or manufactured in the classical sense and not able to be totally preplanned in a standardized and detailed process model. Although software consists of program codes plus documents, it has to be produced in an integration way not only from software technologies/tools, but also from process managements, and human efforts. All the codes and documents may be seen, but not able to be inspected by machines. Humans play the most important role. Software in development and/or in use has to consider all the stakeholders, how to involve the right people, no matter how busy they are or how difficult they understand the software, at the right time, and at the right place...particularly the users! It is impossible to improve quality and productivity through importing some equipment like that in traditional manufacturing industry. Software is always potentially complicated, even for a system whose software is comparatively less important. We must develop software by integrating the technical, cognitive, social, organizational processes and others necessary to satisfy the requirements.

Recently, the focus on individual productivity has gradually evolved to a focus on development/tools integration, process integration and collaboration among humans. A number of emerging approaches were introduced for their potential to set new directions of software development processes. Some of the approaches are still in an academic stage, others are at the level of small market shares. They broaden the horizons of possible future developments.

From last 90s, software development processes have evolved to integration or unification trends: e.g., *WinWin Spiral Process Model* (Humans and Process Framework) [35]; *OPT* (Organization and Process Together) Approach [36]; *ACME* Integrating Process and Collaboration [37]; Integrating the reference models for software processes (human activities) and for CASE environments (machinery activities) [38]; *Open Process Architecture Toaster Model* [39]; Both products and processes may benefit from analysis in terms of families and family relationships [40]; Multi-View Process Modeling Project (*MVP-Project*) [41]; *Pynode* framework which integrates different aspects, e.g. product, process, role, etc, in a unified manner [42]; Reuseworks integrating concepts, processes, models and tools [43]; *RUP* (Rational Unified Process)[44]; *COSE* (Component-Oriented Software Engineering) [45]; Agile Software Quality Assurance [46]; *PRAISE* (Process and Agent-based Integrated Software development Environment) [47]; Assumptions on all three objects of people, processes and products [48].

Many of the practical challenges in SE are not limited to technological issues. Managements, communications, personnel relationships, and other factors often have a substantial impact on a software project's success. Next section will discuss a three-dimensional integrated methodology.

4   A 3-D Integrated Methodology

Figure 2 shows the famous *Technology-Process-Human* triad for a software project success. In this triad, all three items are almost at the same importance. Without process, it is impossible to leverage all the resources. Without technology, it will be difficult to deal with this ever-changing world. Lastly, humans always play a very important role in coordinating process and technology.

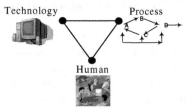

Fig. 2. *Technology-Process-Human* Triad

The *Technology-Process-Human* triad may also be considered the "glue" that unifies the other aspects of software development processes. It is easy to imagine that a software supplier improves its quality and productivity through improving its technology. Also, it should try to improve its software development process and human involvements all the way. However, the software supplier seldom improves them together. Usually these elements are not integrated and have to be remedied by human efforts. Software development processes should be improved integrating from three perspectives, *Technology, Process,* and *Human*.

Recently, the focus on individual productivity has gradually evolved to a focus on team efforts or integrated tools. This expanded view incorporates the benefits gained from integrations among technologies, processes and humans. Based on the *Technology-Process-Human* triad conception and successful SE methodologies in the past, we present a 3-D integrated methodology for software development processes.

TRISO-Model (TRidimensional Integrated SOftware development Model) is a 3-D integrated model, described in three dimensions: *SE Technology, SE Process* and *SE Human,* as shown in Figure 3. It is written as:

$$TRISO\text{-}Model = (SE\ Technology,\ SE\ Process,\ SE\ Human)$$

where *SE Technology* perspective focuses on software product; *SE Process* perspective on software management; *SE Human* perspective on software cost.

The horizontal axis, described in terms of software managements, represents SE Process and shows disciplines that logically group the process activities. The vertical axis represents SE Technology and shows the life cycle aspects of software product development. The third axis is SE Human and shows a cost estimation before or at different phases.

TRISO-DEVELOPER (TRidimensional Integrated SOftware DEVELOPment EnviRonment) is a 3-D integrated SE environment.

TRISO-Model and *TRISO-DEVELOPER* represent the 3-D integrated methodology for software development processes. It is a kind of solid concept and approach, with multiple perspectives.

As shown in Figure 4, a *TRISO-DEVELOPER* Integrated Framework consists of six integrations: (1) Development Integration; (2) Process Integration; (3) Service Integration; (4) Data Integration; (5) Management Integration; and (6) Use Integration. The former three are internal integrations, and the later three are external integrations.

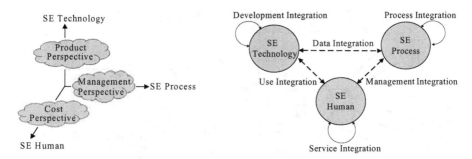

Fig. 3. A 3-D Integrated Software
Development Model *TRISO-Model*

Fig. 4. *TRISO-DEVELOPER*: Integrated Framework

Usually the task of software development is unable to be achieved simply by only one or even a few tools, and it needs effective integration from all the perspectives through the software development process. *TRISO-DEVELOPER* Integrated Framework suggests integrated relationships and a hierarchically ordered decomposition. For internal integrations, three systems/platforms may be developed for integrating development technologies as a SE Technology-based system/platform, integrating process improvements as a SE Process-based system/platform, and integrating human services as a SE Human-based system/platform respectively. For external integrations, the SE Technology-based system/platform may be integrated with the SE Process-based system/platform through data integration; the SE Process-based system/platform may be integrated with the SE Human-based system/platform through a management integration; and the SE Human-based system/platform may be integrated with the SE Technology-based system/platform through a use integration. All the three systems/platforms and six integrations, no matter internal or external, should progress toward lower-level modules, starting with the high-level abstraction, to meet component integration's synthetic nature. By addressing high-priority requirements at high-level abstract before considering low-priority ones, we can significantly reduce project costs and duration.

5   Practical Experiences

Based on our 3-D integrated methodology, ISCAS makes a lot of efforts in improving software development processes, as shown in Figure 5: (1) Research: requirements elicitation, process modeling, measurement model, knowledge management, collaborative work and so on; (2) Platforms: development of an integrated framework with three platforms, PQM (Quality Management), PPE (Product Engineering) and PSS (Service Support); (3) Tools: integration of each platform with a series of tools providing a collaborative working environment for senior managers, project managers, developers, SQAs, customers, suppliers and so on. PQM includes four tools: PM (Project Management), PAL (Process Asset Library), MA (Measurement and Analysis) and SQA (Software Quality Assurance). PPE also includes four tools: UDCORE (User-driven Domain-specific Component-based Requirements Elicitation), TFrame (Test Framework),

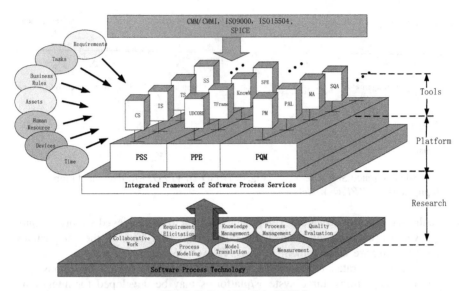

Fig. 5. Related Work in ISCAS

KnowM (Knowledge Management) and SPE (Software Product Evaluation). PSS currently provides customer service (CS), general information service (IS), training service (TS) and supplier service (SS).

TRISO-DEVELOPER presents a 3-D integrated solution based on the mainstream SE achievements: (1) SE Technology, i.e., "Requirements" Dimension, based on Waterfall development. Those features are considered in developing, e.g., development methodologies, domain analysis, creative activities, culture, functional requirements and nonfunctional requirements such as look and feel, ease of use, operational environment, performance, maintainability, security, legality, efficiency, flexibility, repeatability, evolvability, and visibility. (2) SE Process, i.e., Process Dimension, based on CMMI management. Those features are dealt with in managing, e.g., software process and quality assurance, as well as improvability, usability, sustainability, and robustness. (3) SE Human, i.e., Economy Dimension, based on COCOMO II Service Support (in progress). We need to pay more attention to human/cost (the use of the time, money, etc), risk, predictability and so on.

The software characteristics revisited in Section 3 have expanded the role of traditional requirements in software developments. Requirements now should be taken as a solid abstract in real world or problem world, rather than only a specification of software in computer or solving world. So, we give a new name to them, *Great Requirements*.

Different stakeholders, like domain experts, system analysts, software engineers, software testers, SQA, SEPG, project managers, senior managers, managers, users, customers, and so on, are highly collaborative, interactive during software development. We distinguish them into three kinds of stakeholders: SE technology stakeholders, SE process stakeholders and SE human stakeholders, and we leave the most important

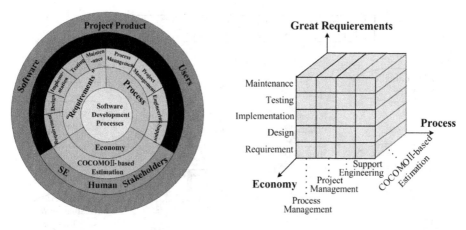

Fig. 6. *TRISO-DEVELOPER*: Integrated Implementation and 3D Stakeholders

Fig. 7. *TRISO-DEVELOPER*: A 3-D Solid View

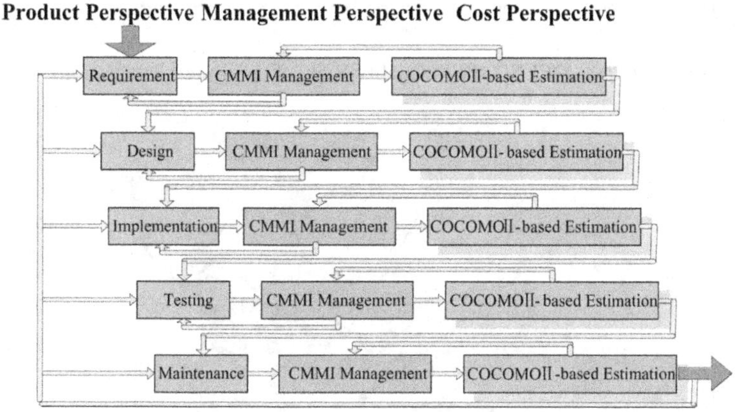

Fig. 8. *TRISO-DEVELOPER*: Integrated Life Cycle

stakeholders, users/customers, as independent ones. The integrated implementation and 3D stakeholders are shown in Figure 6. The core part is software development processes. The foundation for improving software development processes is the 3-D model layer and then followed by the implementation layer, currently based on waterfall, CMMI and COCOMO II. Of course, different people may have other choices. The third layer is stakeholders. All the three layers provide a fully support for software project/product users.

Figure 7 shows a 3-D solid view of *TRISO-DEVELOPER*. The horizontal axis *Process* shows CMMI-based four categories, process management, project management, engineering, and support. The vertical axis *Great Requirements* (in contrast with traditional term of "requirements") shows a Waterfall-based 5 staged life cycle aspects of software product development. The third axis *Economy* shows a COCOMO II-based cost estimation.

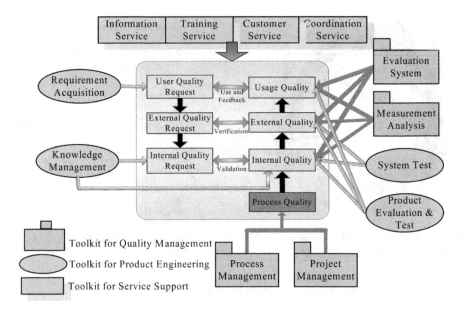

Fig. 9. *TRISO-DEVELOPER*: Quality View of the System Integrations

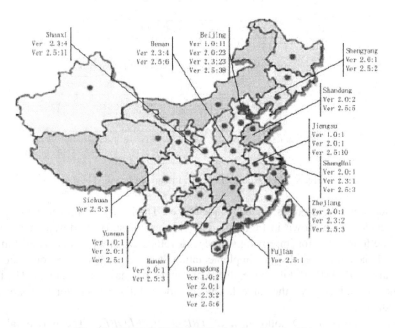

Fig. 10. *TRISO-DEVELOPER*: Applications in China

Figure 8 shows the integrated life cycle of TRISO-DEVELOPER. It's not a sequential process, but an integrated solid iteration among products, managements and cost perspectives. The iteration can be treated as a miniature waterfall life cycle. It also shows that TRISO-DEVELOPER, similar to agile methods, deals with unstable and volatile requirements by using a number of techniques, i.e., (1) simple planning, (2) short iteration, (3) earlier release, and (4) frequent customer feedback.

Figure 9 shows *TRISO-DEVELOPER* quality view of the system integrations of our three current platforms and toolkits: *Quality Management*, *Product Engineering* and *Service Support*.

As shown in Figure 10, our *TRISO-DEVELOPER*-based system has been used in many areas in China, including 8 of the total 11 national software industry bases Beijing, Shanghai, Guangzhou, Xi'an, Chengdu, Jiangshu, Zhuhai and Changsha; all of the National Hi-Tech Planning Program (863) software incubators Beijing, Shanghai, Guangdong, Xian, Sichuan, Shenyang, Henan and Kunming; and more than 130 software organizations. Applications of our products have generated tremendous economic and social benefits. According the statistical data from 10 representative software organizations, the total net-savings has exceeded 40 million dollars due to the use of our systems.

6 Conclusions and Future Work

Requirements exist in situation beyond the defined scope in traditional software developments, i.e. requirements analysis and system design. They run through the whole life cycle of software developments. Also they have to be involved in achieving quality goals, being on time and within budget, etc. In contrast to traditional methodologies, this paper presented a new conception, *Great Requirements*. It needs a multiple dimensional integrated methodology.

We believe software development processes may be fully improved only in some integrated way. A new direction of SE methodologies may be needed to think about more in the future: *Integrated Software Engineering*. It expanded the horizons of possible future software development processes.

Tony Hoare presented in his Turing Award lecture [49], "There are two ways of constructing a software design: One way is to make it so simple that there are obviously no deficiencies, and the other way is to make it so complicated that there are no obvious deficiencies". The idea presented in this paper may result in more complicated and more interactive in developing software projects, and leave new challenges to software development processes.

Acknowledgements

The presentation was supported partly by the National Natural Science Foundation of China (Grant Numbers: 60273026, 60473060) and the Hi-Tech Research and Development Program (863 Program) of China (Grant Number: 2004AA112080). Also, I appreciate all the help offered by my colleagues (particularly to Qing Wang, Yongji Wang, Chen Zhao, Zhanchu Wu, Hui Jiang, Hui Lei, Ye Chen and Fengdi Shu) and students (specially to Jizhe Wang, Xinpei Zhao, Da Yang, Juan Li, Feng Yuan, Xia Liu, Qiusong Yang and Lang Gou) in the Lab for Internet Software Technologies, Institute of Software at Chinese Academy of Sciences.

References

1. The Standish Group, 2004 Third Quarter Research Report, www.standishgroup.com (2004)
2. P.Naur and B.Randall (eds.): Software Engineering: A Report on a Conference Sponsored by the NATO Science Committee. NATO, Brussels, Belgium (1969)
3. IEEE Standard 610.12:1990, Glossary of Software Engineering Terminology, IEEE Standards Association (1990)
4. P.Kruchten: Putting the "Engineering" into "Software Engineering". In: Proc. of the 2004 Australian Software Engineering Conference (ASWEC'04) (2004)
5. R.H.Thayer and M.Dorfman (eds.): System and Software Requirements Engineering. IEEE Computer Society Press Tutorial (1990)
6. E.Yourdon and L.Constantine: Structured Design. Prentice-Hall (1979)
7. I.Jacodson, G.Booch and J.Rumbaugh: The Unified Software Development Process. Addison-Wesley (1999)
8. K.Beck and C.Andres: Extreme Programming Explained: Embrace Change. 2nd edition, Addison-Wesley (2005)
9. T.Bergin et al.: Computer-Aided Software Engineering: Issues and Trends for the 1990s and Beyond. Idea Group (1993)
10. A.W.Brown and K.C.Wallnau: The Current State of CBSE. IEEE Software (Sept./Oct. 1998) 37-46
11. http://www.aosd.net
12. R.S.Pressman: Software Engineering: A Practitioner's Approach. 5th edition, McGraw-Hill (2001)
13. S.L.Pfleeger: Software Engineering: Theory and Practice. 2nd edition, Prentice-Hall (2001)
14. S.Zahran. Software Process Improvement: Practical Guidelines for Business Success. Addison-Wesley (1998)
15. W.S.Humphrey: Managing the Software Process. Addison-Wesley (1989)
16. A.Fuggetta: Software Process: A Roadmap. In: Proc. of 22nd Int. Conf. on Software Engineering - Future of Software Engineering (2000) 25-34
17. W.S.Humphrey. A Discipline for Software Engineering. Addison-Wesley (1995)
18. A.Finkelstein, J.Kramer and B.Nuseibeh (eds.): Software Process Modeling and Technology. Research Studies (1994)
19. L.J.Osterweil: Software Processes are Software too. In: Proc. of 9th Int. Conf. on Software Engineering (ICSE 9) (1987) 2-13
20. P.K.Garg and M.Jazayeri: Process-Centered Software Engineering Environments. IEEE Computer Society (1996)
21. International Standard: ISO 9001 Quality Management System – Requirements (2000)
22. http://www.sei.cmu.edu/
23. M.B.Chrissis et al.: CMMI: Guidelines for Process Integration and Product Improvement. Addison-Wesley (2003)
24. B.W.Boehm: Software Engineering Economics. Prentice-Hall (1981)
25. B.W.Boehm et al.: Software Cost Estimation with COCOMO II. Prentice-Hall (2000)
26. M.Ruhe, R.Jeffery and I.Wieczorek: Cost Estimation for Web Applications. In: Proc. of 25th Int. Conf. on Software Engineering (ICSE 25) (2003) 270-279
27. Robert Balzer: What We Do and Don't Know about Software Process. In: Proc. of the 6th Int. Software Process Workshop (ISPW 6) (28-31, October, 1990) 61-64
28. M.H.Penedo: ISPW 9 Process Demonstrations – Summary. In: Proc. of the 9th Int. Software Process Workshop (ISPW 9) (5-7, October, 1994) 19-32
29. G.E.Kaiser et al.: An Architecture for WWW-based Hypercode Environments. In: Proc. of 19th Int. Conf. on Software Engineering (ICSE 19) (1997)

30. P.G.Armour: The Laws of Software Process: A New Model for the Production and Management of Software. CRC Press (2004)
31. H.F.Hofmann and F.Lehner: Requirements Engineering as a Success Factor in Software Projects. IEEE Software (July/August 2001) 58-66
32. R.Wieringa and C.Ebert: RE'03: Practical Requirements Engineering Solutions. IEEE Software (March/April 2004) 16-18
33. B.Lawrence, K.Wiegers and C.Ebert: The Top Risks of Requirements Engineering. IEEE Software (November/December 2001) 62-63
34. Ian Sommerville: Integrated Requirements Engineering: A Tutorial. IEEE Software (January/February 2005) 16-23
35. B.Boehm and P.Bose: Humans and Process Frameworks: Some Critical Process Elements. In: Proc. of the 9th Int. Software Process Workshop (ISPW 9) (5-7, October, 1994) 82-84
36. C.B.Seaman and V.R.Basili: OPT: Organization and Process Together. In: Proc. of the 9th Int. Software Process Workshop (ISPW 9) (5-7, October, 1994) 57-59
37. J.E.Arnold: Toward Collaborative Software Process. In: Proc. of the 9th Int. Software Process Workshop (ISPW 9) (5-7, October, 1994) 107-109
38. T.Ajisaka: Meta-Integration for Process Integrated CASE Environments. In: Proc. of the 9th Int. Software Process Workshop (ISPW 9) (5-7, October, 1994) 62-66
39. B.Boehm and S.Wolf: An Open Architecture for Software Process Asset Reuse. In: Proc. of the 10th Int. Software Process Workshop (ISPW 10) (17-19, June, 1996) 2-4
40. S.M.Sutton, Jr. and L.J.Osterweil: Product Families and Process Families. In: Proc. of the 10th Int. Software Process Workshop (ISPW 10) (17-19, June, 1996) 109-111
41. M.Verlage: Towards Software Process Modules. In: Proc. of the 10th Int. Software Process Workshop (ISPW 10) (17-19, June, 1996) 112-114
42. D.Avrilionis et al.: A Unified Framework for Software Process Enactment and Improvement. In: Proc. of the 4th Int. Conf. On Software Process, 2-6 December (1996) 102-111
43. C.D.Klingler and R.Creps: Integrating and Applying Processes and Methods for Product Line Management. In: Proc. of the 4th Int. Conf. On Software Process, 2-6 December (1996) 102-111
44. P.Kruchten: The Rational Unified Process—An Introduction. Addison-Wesley (2000)
45. A.H.Dogru and M.M.Tanik: A Process Model for Component-Oriented Software Engineering. IEEE Software (March/April 2003) 34-41
46. M.Huo et al.: Software Quality and Agile Methods. In: Proc. of the 28th Annual International Computer Software and Applications Conference (COMPSAC'04) (2004)
47. C.-H.Chang et al.: An Integrated Software Development Environment with XML Internal Representation. In: Proc. of the 28th Annual International Computer Software and Applications Conference (COMPSAC'04) (2004)
48. J.Carver, J.VanVoorhis and V.Basili: Understanding the Impact of Assumptions on Experimental Validity. In: Proc. of the 2004 International Symposium on Empirical Software Engineering (ISESE'04) (2004)
49. C.A.R Hoare: The Emperor's Old Clothes. In: C.B. Jones (ed.), Essays in Computing Science, Prentice-Hall (1989)

Unifying Microprocess and Macroprocess Research

Leon J. Osterweil

Laboratory for Advanced Software Engineering Research,
Department of Computer Science,
University of Massachusetts,
Amherst, MA 01003, USA
ljo@cs.umass.edu

Abstract. This paper proposes the unification of two complementary approaches to software process research. The two approaches can be characterized as macroprocess research, focused on phenomenological observations of external behaviors of processes, and microprocess research, focused on the study of the internal details and workings of processes. The paper suggests that it is time to bring these approaches together with the goal of using microprocess methods to provide definitive explanations of observed macroprocess behaviors. The paper suggests that this unification could lead to improved understandings leading to improvements in software development practice. The paper observes that such positive outcomes have resulted when the macro- and micro- approaches have been synthesized in domains such as Economics, Physics, and the Life Sciences.

1 Introduction

The recent years have been gratifying for the community of people who focus attention on the importance of process. Process has long been recognized by manufacturing industries as the key to achieving control over such core issues as costs and quality levels. In such industries there is considerable agreement that "quality products result from quality processes", for example. Recognition of the possibility that these same ideas hold for software development has been more recent. One key event in advancing the importance of process was the 1984 Software Process Workshop [1], held at Runnymede, England, although many will point out that there had already been a focus on process (e.g., in large companies such as IBM), prior to this event.

The past two decades have seen a steady growth in interest in the application of process to the solution of many problems and issues in software development. Process has been identified as being a vehicle for controlling development costs and achieving product quality (in strong analogy to the situation in industries that manufacture tangibles). Process has also been identified as a vehicle for supporting more effective training, for superior project coordination, for improved management visibility (leading to more effective management), and for studying how to achieve the most effective deployment of resources.

With this diversity of applications of software process, it is no wonder that there is also a diversity of approaches to the development of process technology. This paper

M. Li, B. Boehm, and L.J. Osterweil (Eds.): SPW 2005, LNCS 3840, pp. 68–74, 2005.

explores the possibility that two complementary types of software process technology research might be integrated so as to support each other and provide substantial benefits to the development community.

We propose the term *macroprocess research* to describe investigations that have emphasized the study of overall behaviors of process, and the term *microprocess research* to describe investigations that have emphasized the study of the internal workings of processes. There seems to be a natural complementarity between these two approaches, with the former investigating gross external effects, and the latter investigating the root causes of these observed effects. In this way, this dichotomy strongly mirrors similar dichotomies in such other disciplines as economics, physics, and the biological sciences. As in those other disciplines, it seems promising to consider the integration of these approaches.

This paper proposes that software process research increasingly focus on the systematic investigation of how external process behaviors are definitively explained (and potentially improved) by examination (and modification) of the internal structure and details of the processes themselves.

2 Macroprocess Research

We propose that macroprocess research be characterized as investigations whose focus is on the study of the external behaviors of processes. Such behaviors include the speed of execution of processes, the characteristics of the software products they produce, the way in which resource infusion affects product nature and process speed, and the effect of changes in production timetables upon products, and the processes themselves. Much of this research emphasizes the determination of appropriate measures of such characteristics as product quality, worker productivity, and process efficiency. It is not surprising, and indeed appropriate, that much of this research is empirical in nature.

Some of the most notable directions in this research are represented by such projects as the Software Engineering Institute's Capability Maturity Models (e.g., CMM and CMMI) [2, 3], the Experience Factory project [4, 5], and the many attempts to define measures of software quality and process characteristics [6]. It is undeniable that these efforts have had a noticeable positive effect on the way in which software is developed, and upon industrial understanding of many of the principal issues that need to be understood if software development is to be practiced as an order, disciplined, predictable activity. These is, for example, now a general understanding that, despite the obvious difficulties, effective measures must be defined and applied to software products in order to determine their size, cost, and quality. There is general agreement that processes themselves must be studied in order to determine how to change them in order to achieve desired improvements.

As the macroprocess work progresses, however, it becomes increasingly apparent that there will be considerable value in complementing a strictly external, phenomenological view of software process by investigations of process internals in order to develop explanations of the causes of observed phenomena. Later in this paper, we support this view with some analogies. For now, however, we simply suggest that the desire to understand *why* something works is more than just natural human curiosity. Knowing the cause of a phenomenon provides an avenue for approaching its control. We may observe that there seems to be a linear relationship between cost decrease and infusion of additional resources. But does that linear relationship extrapolate indefinitely? Or can the relationship be expected to hold only over a restricted range of circumstances? If so, then how can that range of circumstances be characterized? Certainly additional empirical studies can provide additional insight, but a firm grip on the causes of a phenomenon can provide predictive power that should be expected to reduce the need for empirical studies, or eliminate them entirely.

The macroprocess research community has demonstrated a clear recognition of the need to determine the causes of the external behaviors that have been observed and codified. Often the search for causal relations has been based upon empirical studies and statistical investigations. Other approaches have been based upon process models. At this point, the macroprocess approach begins to take on the character of microprocess research.

3 Microprocess Research

We propose that microprocess research be characterized as investigations that focus on investigation of the precise specification of the details of software processes, for the purpose of inferring how those details effect the external behaviors of the processes. Much of this research has focused on the identification of languages and semantic features that are effective in supporting precise process definition. Other research has focused on the use of such linguistic features to describe and define specific processes (e.g., system evolution [7]). These process descriptions and definitions are then sometimes used as the basis for supporting process automation, or semi-automation, and for supporting reasoning about and analysis of these processes. An important goal of some of this work is to create a discipline of process engineering, in which process definitions can be crafted to deliver desired process behaviors, and product characteristics.

Some examples of work in this area include the Process Instance Evolution (PIE) Project [8], as well as process language efforts such as Adele [9, 10], Spade/Slang [11], Marvel/Oz [12, 13], and Little-JIL [14, 15]. It is worth noting that there are parallel efforts at identifying languages effective in supporting definitions of process in other domains. For example workflow research aims to support definition of business processes, and enterprise framework modeling aims to support definition of internet-based processes for supporting innovative business models that use emerging network technologies [16]. A common theme in all of this research is the determination of how to characterize processes effectively, so that they can be carried out more satisfactorily, and so that their properties (both positive and negative) can be predicted accurately.

As such microprocess research can be seen both as providing something that macroprocess research needs, and needing something that macroprocess research provides. A key goal of microprocess research is to provide detailed, accurate, low-level definitions of processes, and reasoning capabilities that are able to predict and explain the high level phenomena discovered by macroprocess investigations. On the other hand, the phenomena that have been identified, and shown to be of greatest interest, by macroprocess research seem to be of central importance to microprocess research, in indicating the phenomena whose explanation seems to be of greatest interest and importance. Given that there are an infinite number and variety of process properties that might be studied, and a wide spectrum on analysis approaches that might be applied to process definitions, microprocess research needs a focus on the phenomena of greatest interest. Macroprocess research can provide just such a focus.

Here too, we note that microprocess research is just beginning to identify, and evaluate, process properties about which reasoning seems possible and useful. In this respect, microprocess research is beginning to address issues that might more accurately be characterized as macroprocess subject matter.

Thus, it seems that the two approaches, macroprocess and microprocess, are starting to reach tangency with each other, and have much to offer each other. The suggestion that an integration of these research directions therefore seems both logical and timely.

4 Some Analogies

The use of complementary approaches such as those suggested here is certainly not unique, and is indeed long predated by, similarly complementary approaches in such other disciplinary areas as Economics, Physics, and the Life Sciences. The success of such complementarity should be instructive and encouraging.

Economists have long distinguished among themselves using the complementary approaches of macroeconomics and microeconomics. The analogy to software process is particularly striking. Macroeconomics studies large-scale phenomena, and the gross behaviors of economies in response to large-scale forces. Such relations as how economic growth responds to interest rates, and fiscal policy are within the purview of macroeconomics. Microeconomics, on the other hand, emphasizes the creation of models of smaller scale behaviors and phenomena, seeking to use them to explain and predict the phenomena of macroeconomics. Thus, for example, microeconomists may employ systems of linear inequalities, and analytic approaches such as game theory, using complex mathematics, in order to explain the behaviors and properties of markets that have been observed by macroeconomists. This dichotomy seems to provide a strong and close parallel to our suggestions about the complementarity between microprocess and macroprocess research. To go further with this analogy, it seems important to note that microeconomics can support a diversity of reasoning about its models, but the reasoning that is most important and most relevant is that which is directed towards explanation of behaviors whose importance has been established by macroeconomists.

Physics provides other analogies that seem interesting and relevant. Early physicists, such as Boyle, determined that air was "springy". When enclosed in an airtight container, pressure on the enclosed air was resisted, and when the pressure was released, the air sprang back. Compressing the air seemed to heat it up. Careful investigations of this, and other, external behavioral phenomena eventually resulted in the formulation of Boyle's Law, which related air pressure, volume, and temperature. Boyle's Law provided useful guidance for centuries before an explanation of this behavior was provided by statistical mechanics. Eventually it was explained that air consists of myriad molecules bouncing unceasingly off of each other and the sides of containers. Mathematics was used to demonstrate how this internal structure and behavior explained Boyle's Law. Conversely Boyle's Law's external verification of the predictions of statistical mechanics helped confirm the hypothesis that air is composed of molecules with elastic properties, leading to innumerable other scientific advances. Other examples from Physics are not hard to find. We note, for example, that various behaviors of electricity were observed, and even described by formulas, before physics determined the root causes of these behaviors. Light was bent and focused long before its wavelike nature was understood. But that understanding led to better engineering of light.

Indeed, Physics provides a long list of illustrations that the observation of phenomena generally precedes their explanation, but that the explanations generally lead to improved management and engineering of the phenomena. The Life Sciences provide more examples of this.

Physicians, and primitive healers before them, have had growing success in treating human ailments simply by observing external phenomenology. Even the earliest healers understood that bleeding and high fevers were dangerous and problematic. They focused attention on controlling them long before there was an understanding of the role of blood (and hence the danger posed by its loss), or the specific impact of increased body temperature upon the functioning of the body's organs and systems. The importance of cleanliness, both in public health, and in treatment therapies, was observed long before there was a recognition of the existence, and dangers posed by, microorganisms. Once the nature of microorganisms was understood, and the details of the processes by which they caused disease understood, superior therapies (e.g., antiseptics and antibiotics) could be deployed to greater effect.

Currently we are seeing that basic understandings of DNA, molecular biology, and cell biology are leading to clearer understandings of viruses, and are leading to the more effective treatment of maladies ranging from the common cold to cancer. It is noteworthy that these advances are being derived from micro-level understandings of their causative factors, while phenomenological observation of these diseases has been relatively ineffective in advancing their treatment.

Thus, there seem to be numerous examples of the complementarity of macro- and micro- level research in other disciplines, and considerable reason to expect that parallels with software process research are valid. This seems to us to add more credence to the suggestion that this complementarity should be studied and pursued.

5   Future Directions

As macroprocess research and microprocess research continue to widen their scopes, their intersections can be expected to continue to increase. What seems needed now is some consensus about one or more projects that have the potential to cause each to gain a better understanding of the other, and to find in the other the sort of complementarity that will lead to added value for both. While there would seem to be many such projects, one will be suggested here, more in the spirit of being specific than in an attempt to be prescriptive or exhaustive.

A principal problem in software project management is the need to determine what mix of skills and other resources are needed at different phases of a software project in order to maximize productivity. Numerous empirical studies have suggested various behaviors that seem useful and applicable. Thus, for example, there have been numerous examinations of software design. These studies have suggested, for example, that experienced designers tend to be more productive and effective than novices, especially on larger, more unprecedented, projects. But highly experienced designers may be overkill for some less ambitious projects. Similarly, adding more designers seems to be effective in larger projects. But it is all too possible to put too many designers to work on a project. Empirical studies have come up with statistics and numerical measures that suggest how to quantify these qualitative observations. Still, however, the quantifications are generally interpolations and extrapolations from relatively small sets of observations. And the possibility that some of these observed behaviors may be affected by yet-undetermined factors still exists.

It would seem reasonable to propose that microprocess approaches might help here. Microprocess research [17] has resulted in the development of definitions of processes that seem to help novices produce better designs more rapidly. These processes seem to rely importantly upon the ability to apply design constraints over specified scopes, and upon the ability to accurately describe, and thus more effectively support, the elusive notion of "rework". This seems to be a good example of how microprocess research, focused on developing appropriate process definition language constructs, and using them to develop more precise and accurate process definitions, can develop understandings of the nature of a key software process like design. We suggest that understandings such as these, drawn from microprocess research be used to create definitions of specific design processes, indicating precisely how various designers, of various skill levels, and other resources, could be used to develop designs. We suggest it might then be possible to then apply analyzers and reasoning approaches to explore how different numbers and mixes of resources and design expertise levels might affect the progress of a design. Many different design processes have been defined, and more could be defined. But macroprocess research would, in this case, be used to suggest specific characteristics and desiderata in a design process that would make it particularly worth studying, and would then focus the process definition and analysis.

Other such integrative projects would seem to be relatively easy to identify. Joint pursuit of them would seem to offer important benefits for both macroprocess and microprocess research, and for the overall discipline of software engineering.

Acknowledgments

This material is based upon work supported by the US National Science Foundation under Award Nos. CCR-0427071, CCR-0204321 and CCR-0205575. The views and conclusions contained herein are those of the author and should not be interpreted as necessarily representing the official policies or endorsements, either expressed or implied, of The National Science Foundation, or the U.S. Government.

References

1. *Software Process Workshop*, in *Software Process Workshop*. 1984. Runnymede, England.
2. Paulk, M.C., et al., *Capability Maturity Model Version 1.1*. IEEE Software, 1993: p. 18-27.
3. *Capability Maturity Model® Integration*. http://www.sei.cmu.edu/cmmi/
4. Basili, V.R. *Software Development: A Paradigm for the Future*, in *COMPSAC'89*. 1989. Orlando, FL.
5. Basili, V.R., *The Experience Factory and its Relationship to Other Quality Approaches*, in *Advances in Computers*. 1995, Academic Press, Inc.
6. Boehm, B.W., *Software Engineering Economics*. 1981, Englewood Cliffs, NJ: Prentice-Hall.
7. Valetto, G. and G. Kaiser. *Using Process Technology to Control and Coordinate Software Adaptation*, in *Twenty-fifth International Conference on Software Engineering*. 2003. Portland, OR.
8. Cunin, P.Y., et al. *The PIE Methodology - Concept and Application*, in *EWSPT-8*. 2001. Witten, Germany: Springer-Verlag.
9. Estublier, J. *A Configuration Manager: The Adele Data Base of Programs*, in *Workshop on Software Engineering Environments for Programming-in-the-Large*. 1985. Harwichport, MA.
10. Estublier, J., et al. *An Approach and Framework for Extensible Process Support System*, in *9th European Workshop on Software Process Technology (EWSPT 2003)*. 2003. Helsinki, Finland.
11. Bandinelli, S., A. Fuggetta, and S. Grigolli. *Process Modeling in-the-large with SLANG*, in *Second International Conference on the Software Process*. 1993. Berlin, Germany: IEEE Computer Society Press.
12. Kaiser, G.E., P.H. Feiler, and S.S. Popovich, *Intelligent Assistance for Software Development and Maintenance*. IEEE Software, 1988. **5**(3): p. 40-49.
13. Ben-Shaul, I.Z. and G. Kaiser. *A Paradigm for Decentralized Process Modeling and its Realization in the Oz Environment*, in *16th International Conference on Software Engineering*. 1994.
14. Wise, A., *Little-JIL 1.0 Language Report*. 1998, Department of Computer Science, University of Massachusetts: Amherst: Amherst, MA.
15. Wise, A., et al. *Using Little-JIL to Coordinate Agents in Software Engineering*, in *Automated Software Engineering Conference*. 2000. Grenoble, France.
16. Estublier, J. and S. Sanlaville. *Business Processes and Workflow Coordination of Web Services*, in *IEEE International Conference on e-Technology, e-Commerce and e-Service*. 2005. Hong Kong.
17. Cass, A.G., S.M. Sutton, and L.J. Osterweil. *Formalizing Rework in Software Processes*, in *Ninth European Workshop on Software Process Technology*. 2003. Helsinki, Finland: Springer-Verlag.

What Beyond CMMI Is Needed to Help Assure Program and Project Success?

Arthur Pyster

Science Applications International Corporation,
1710 SAIC Drive,
McLean, VA 22102 USA
pystera@saic.com

Abstract. The U.S. Department of Defense and other parts of the U.S. government use the Capability Maturity Model Integrated (CMMI) for process improvement to reduce the risk of poor performance by its major contractors. Acquisition officials have reported that many of its major programs suffer from cost, schedule, and technical performance problems even though those programs are being implemented by companies which rate high with respect to the CMMI. This paper explores possible reasons why companies with high CMMI ratings can still have significant performance problems and suggests possible remedies.

1 Introduction

At last November's CMMI Conference, which was sponsored by the U.S. National Defense Industrial Association (NDIA), I participated in an industry panel that discussed what beyond CMMI is needed to help assure program and project success. The panel was motivated by reports from government acquisition executives that companies with high CMMI maturity ratings were still having problems meeting their commitments on major government programs. Throughout the conference and subsequent to it, this issue was raised again and again. The paradox can be stated:

> If high maturity ratings are a strong predictor of good performance, then programs run by organizations with high maturity ratings should consistently perform well. Yet many problems persist.

At the NDIA Capability Maturity Model Integrated (CMMI) conference, Mr. Mark Schaeffer, the Director of Systems Engineering for the U.S. Department of Defense (DoD), presented information showing that the actual correlation between high maturity ratings and high performance is not as strong as the Department of Defense leadership expects [1]. He said that "DoD expects that if you have achieved high maturity, the next program will perform at that maturity." This mismatch between expectations and performance was raising anxiety within DoD about whether the CMMI is actually an effective risk reduction tool. Throughout the rest of the conference and in the intervening months, the dialog about the effectiveness of the CMMI for risk reduction in large acquisitions has continued within the CMMI community, especially within the NDIA and the Department of Defense. This paper elaborates on that issue and proposes some steps that could be taken to address it.

M. Li, B. Boehm, and L.J. Osterweil (Eds.): SPW 2005, LNCS 3840, pp. 75–82, 2005.

2 What Is the CMMI?

The CMMI is a relatively complete and widely used framework for improving the processes of organizations that build complex engineering products. It has been published in several variants, all of which are available on Carnegie Mellon University's Software Engineering Institute (SEI) website [2].   Developed over several years under the auspices of DoD, the NDIA, and SEI, the current version of the CMM, version 1.1, was released in 2001. Results from using the model in more than 30 different countries are also reported on the SEI website.

The CMMI is largely a derivative of three earlier CMM-related standards – the CMM for Software version 2 draft, the Electronic Industries Alliance interim standard 731 on the Systems Engineering Capability Model, and the integrated Product Development Capability Maturity Model version 0.98. The CMMI is now being updated to simplify aspects of the model, to incorporate improvements based on user experience, and to better support organizations that do engineering services and acquire systems rather than build them. Other enhancements will surely follow over time.

The next several paragraphs present a brief description of the CMMI. In order to keep the explanation simple, **I have taken a number of liberties with how the model really works**. For example, I have blurred the distinction between the two major model variations – *staged* and *continuous*. Nevertheless, this explanation provides the essence of the model and how it is used.

In brief, the CMMI can be applied either at an individual program level or at a higher level within a company or government agency. Companies and agencies that are new to the CMMI often begin applying it to isolated programs and gradually expand its use. The CMMI itself divides the primary processes used to develop engineering products into 25 project management, technical, process management, and supporting areas such as requirements management, integrated teaming, and configuration management.   Each process area has associated goals which the adopting organization is expected to meet and best practices which it is expected to implement. The adopting organization is rated from level 0 to 5 on how capable each process area is, with five being the best score. The levels are established using fairly well-defined criteria that require a rigorous appraisal consisting of interviews with staff who perform the processes and an examination of artifacts that demonstrate processes execution. The appraisal team is well-structured and is typically led by an experienced person who has been authorized by the SEI. As of December 2004, the SEI had authorized over 350 people to lead CMMI appraisals [3].

A capability level of 0 for a process area means that one or more of the goals is not met, often by a failure to perform one or more of the prescribed best practices. For example, one of the goals of the project management process area is to establish estimates, specifically, that "estimates of project planning parameters are established and maintained." Several specific best practices are identified that are normally performed to establish estimates. Process performance by a level 0 organization is typically erratic, with wide fluctuations in cost, schedule, and technical performance. Such performance should not be surprising for an organization that doesn't consistently do good estimation. On the other hand, a capability level of 5 means that an organization has institutionalized its processes, uses a common implementation of best practice across the entire organization, has well-defined ways to collect data about process performance, and consistently uses that data to refine the process in order to improve performance. Strong consistent performance is expected from organizations that have achieved high levels (and therein lies the dilemma for the DoD).

Finally, recognizing that it is natural to improve several related process areas concurrently, the CMMI defines *maturity levels* around the simultaneous achievement of capability levels in selected process areas. For example, realizing capability level 2 in requirements management, project management, project monitoring and control, supplier agreement management, measurement and analysis, process and product quality assurance, and configuration management means that a project or large organization also has a maturity level of 2. Hence, maturity levels also go from 0 to 5.

Most major companies that build large complex systems for the U.S. government each invest millions of dollars annually in CMMI-based process improvement (and earlier in the CMM for Software) and have achieved maturity levels of 3, 4, or 5 for significant parts of their companies. SAIC, for example, has a robust CMMI-based process improvement program in which nearly all the company participates. Broad segments of the company are at maturity levels 3, 4, and 5, and have achieved substantial gains in such measures as the cost per line of developed code. At conferences and in publications, speakers from across many industry segments widely extol the benefits of using the CMMI. The SEI publishes results on its website reporting major gains in productivity, cost, and schedule, customer satisfaction, and quality for organizations with high maturity levels. The results are impressive with many testimonials cited.

3 Limitations of CMMI Maturity Levels

Given that the major industrial suppliers for the U.S. government generally have achieved high maturity levels, and there is a wealth of published data reporting impressive performance by organizations with high maturity levels, one could certainly expect government organizations to have few troubled programs. Yet, as reported by DoD officials, by the U.S. Office of Management and Budget, which is part of the Executive Office of the President and by the General Accounting Office, which is part of the U.S. Congress, the U.S. government has many troubled programs. How is this possible? The answer lies in four flaws in how the CMMI is understood and used.

Flaw 1.   A large organization can receive a high maturity level rating even if portions of that organization do not systematically use high maturity processes.

Flaw 2:   After contract award, government program offices often do not appraise the actual team working on the contract, which according to Flaw 1, may not be using a mature process even if it is part of an organization that has a high maturity level.

Flaw 3:   Many (most?) government source selection and program management organizations themselves do not have mature acquisition processes. This can lead to such problems as unstable requirements from the government.   Moreover, these same organizations may not fully understand and appreciate the importance of mature processes. They may be unwilling to fund the contractor's execution of mature processes, which can lead to shortchanging such activities as quality assurance and systems test.

Flaw 4:   Excellent process is not enough.   Strong program performance is based on a combination of excellent process, people, technology, and program environment.   Shortcomings in any one of these four areas will drive down overall program performance and can even lead to outright program failure.

3.1   Flaw 1 – Misunderstanding the Significance of the Maturity Level

A single appraisal will typically involve interviews with dozens of people and the review of hundreds of documents. An appraisal for a higher maturity level will normally examine only a handful of programs within an organization, even if that organization has many times that number of programs. For large organizations, which may have many individual programs, it is only practical to appraise a sample of programs. Scaling up to large organizations can be addressed incrementally by appraising each of the component organizations and aggregating the results appropriately.   Yet, even with this approach, only a small percentage of the total program population will be examined.

Under this appraisal approach, the validity of the resulting rating depends heavily on whether the chosen sample is representative of the larger population. If the sample programs are weighted towards the best performers in the organization, the organization will receive an artificially high maturity level. Similarly, if the sample programs are weighted towards poor performers, an artificially low maturity level will emerge.   Selecting a good representative sample is absolutely necessary, but for businesses with a very diverse business base, this can be difficult.

When a company is focused internally on improving its processes solely to better its performance, then that company is strongly motivated to pick the most representative sample that it can.   Even then, if the company's programs are quite diverse in size, complexity, and other important characteristics, this will be hard to do. When a company's maturity level is a factor in winning business, choosing the most representative sample becomes even harder.

In a government request for proposal, it is common for the government to ask the offerer to explain its implementation of CMM for Software or CMMI. This request is normally in the context of the government seeking to reduce risk by hiring a contractor that has high performing processes. A company typically responds by explaining its process improvement program in the proposal and by citing the maturity level of the organization bidding for the work. The company may even include in the proposal a copy of the certificate from the appraiser who rated the bidding organization. Yet, as was discussed earlier, the program bidding the work may, in fact, not use the high maturity process that was appraised.

This problem can be partially addressed in three ways:

- Government acquisition offices involved in source selection need to better understand the limitations of a maturity level, so they do not draw inappropriate conclusions from it. They should likewise require that if an offerer references an organizational level in its proposal, the performing team must use the high maturity process that is referenced.

- The Software Engineering Institute needs to improve guidance on how to select representative samples, and on how to aggregate results from subordinate organizations when appraising a large organization. This will improve the accuracy of the ratings within the limitations of the overall appraisal method.

- Government acquisition offices involved in source selection need to recognize that this problem will lessen over time. The CMMI is relatively new. It takes time to fully permeate companies, even those making serious and thoughtful investments in process improvement. Over the next several years, strong mature processes will become commonplace in nearly every corner of major government contractors.

Some have suggested that this problem can be addressed by providing the acquisition organization performing source selection with more detailed information about an offerer's processes and process improvement program; e.g., by delivering as part of a proposal the underlying data on which an appraisal team drew its conclusions or by delivering the individual capability levels of each of the 25 process areas rather than the summary maturity level rating that an organization has achieved. Unfortunately, this additional information will not solve the problem. As discussed above, the difficulty is not that the acquisition organization has too little information about an offerer's processes. The difficulty is that the performing team may not use those mature processes. Moreover, the detailed information prepared for internal process improvement will likely be voluminous and written in a style and terminology that is well-suited for internal use, but ill-suited for external audiences. Recasting that information into language suitable for those involved in source selection would require extensive effort on the part of the contractor with nominal gain for the government. Moreover, without extensive additional training of acquisition officials, they will have significant difficulty understanding the new information they receive.

3.2   Flaw 2 – Missing Appraisal

When a proposal for a government contract is submitted by an offerer, the *full* team that will actually do the work probably doesn't exist yet. Only parts of the team will have been assembled before the contract is awarded. It is simply too expensive to assemble full program teams in advance of contract award. Hence, even if an organization that has a high maturity level wants to assemble a team that will use the mature appraised process, it will need time to do so. A proposal can describe the planned process, but a fully trained and operational team to execute that process won't yet exist. Of course, a high maturity organization should be able to stand up a team and train them in the process more quickly and more successfully than a low maturity organization.

Even if a program team uses the high maturity process taken from its surrounding organization, the team must tailor that process to the unique characteristics of the specific program. This tailoring is normal and customary when using any organizational process. The best way for the government to ensure that the program has a suitably tailored high performing process is to perform an appraisal sometime after contract award and periodically thereafter (for long running programs).

Because appraisals require interviews with dozens of people and the review of hundreds of artifacts, an appraisal will last several weeks (including preparation) and typically cost tens of thousands of dollars (or more) to conduct. Government program offices (which become responsible for an acquisition after source selection) sometimes are not willing to pay for such an appraisal. However, given the importance of good process to program performance, such an appraisal is actually a prudent investment. The contract between government acquirer and company should require the correction of process deficiencies that are found during that appraisal. By conducting an appraisal early in the lifecycle of a contract, problems can be quickly found and corrected. By repeating an appraisal periodically (perhaps with a focus on potential problem areas rather than on all process areas), continued improvements in process should be achieved.

3.3   Flaw 3 – Immature Source Selection and Program Management Organizations

Not only must the contractor have mature processes, so must the acquirer, to include both the office that performs source selection and the program office that manages the acquisition after contractor selection. The government cannot simply shift responsibility for the performance of the acquisition onto the contractor. It must share that responsibility. The government acquisition office must be strong at earned value management, technical performance measurement, requirements management, systems architecture, transition planning, source selection, project scheduling, and a myriad of other processes when acquiring large complex systems. Unfortunately, over the past decade, there has been a general erosion in government acquisition capability. Many of the most talented acquisition managers and engineers have left the government. Even though there are still many highly talented government acquisition managers and engineers remaining, their numbers are down.

Despite this erosion in workforce skill, there has been a steady increase in the quantity and complexity of government acquisitions. Moreover, few acquisition organizations have embraced CMMI-based process improvement or similar approaches, such as the Federal Aviation Administration's (FAA) iCMM, which the FAA uses to improve its own acquisition community [4]. Acquisition organizations have often expected mature processes from their contractors, but have not always demanded it from themselves. This mismatch between acquirer and supplier has broad negative consequences. Four resulting problems are:

1.   Unstable and imprecise requirements from the government that lead to significant rework on the part of the contractor and a strained relationship between acquirer and contractor.

2. Poorly planned adoption of the new system by the government; i.e., the adoption of a complex system often requires significant preparation at the sites into which the new system will be housed, extensive end-user training, and detailed planning for migrating end-users from legacy systems onto the new system. The government is often directly responsible for many of these activities.

3. A misunderstanding by the government of how to effectively use advanced acquisition techniques; e.g., insisting on "big bang" adoption of a complex system rather than spiral or incremental deployment simply because the new system is so important to the agency's mission.

4. A failure by the government to appreciate just how important certain processes such as quality assurance and systems test really are to success. This can lead a contractor to back away from its robust process because the government will not pay for these activities and believes they needlessly add to the delivery schedule.

Solving the problem of immature acquisition organizations for both source selection and program management will require a dramatic increase in commitment to educating the acquisition workforce, providing them the necessary tools to become more mature, and finding suitable rewards to retain the best talent. This is a systemic problem within the government that will take years to address.

3.4 Flaw 4 – Expecting Too Much from Mature Processes

Four factors drive program performance: process, people, technology, and environment. Relying too heavily on excellent process as *the* key performance driver will lead to disappointment and failure. A balanced approach that recognizes the need for strength in all four factors is required. Three examples illustrates this point well.

In the last decade, the U.S. Federal Aviation Administration (FAA) decided to augment the Global Positioning System (GPS) so that it would be reliable and accurate enough to use for aircraft navigation. Moreover, it decided that the augmented GPS would eventually become the *sole means of navigation,* replacing traditional ground-based approaches. The primary rationale for this decision was that a satellite-based GPS system would be much cheaper to operate, maintain, and expand than the elaborate ground-based system then in use. The proposed system was unprecedented. A large-scale GPS-based system with the performance characteristics needed to support safe flight had never been built. There were tremendous technical challenges. A contractor was hired to deliver the augmented GPS-based system. That system took years longer than originally planned, much of that due to the requirement that augmented GPS become the sole means of navigation. The technology required to meet that requirement simply did not exist. That requirement was eventually dropped as impractical. No process can make up for the fact that there is no generally accepted way to accurately predict cost, schedule, and technical performance of unprecedented systems.

As a second example, the FAA hired a contractor to develop another system to build a system for controller/pilot datalink communications (CPDLC). CPDLC allows pilots and controllers to transmit digital data messages directly between computers on the ground and computers on board the aircraft rather than relying on voice communications. Success of the program depended on two factors. First, aircraft needed to upgrade their equipment to send and receive the digital messages, and second the FAA needed to expand the operation to cover much of the U.S. national airspace. Initially, CPDLC was piloted only in the Miami, Florida area. Even though CPDLC worked largely as expected in trial use in Miami, last year the program was postponed until the end of this decade because of inadequate funding. The FAA has faced continuing budget reductions and most U.S. airlines have been struggling financially since the terrorist attacks on September 11, 2001. No process can make up for an environment in which the acquiring agency and the airlines lack the funds to deploy the system.

Finally, it is impossible to overstate the importance of having people working on a program who deeply understand their customer and their customer's domain. Government requests for proposals routinely ask the offerer to demonstrate its understanding of the acquiring organization's mission, problems, operational constraints, and existing systems. A prime contractor assembles its team, in part, to ensure a strong customer understanding by the team as a whole. Nevertheless, some program teams fall short. Even if an organization as a whole has strong domain understanding, the program team itself might not reflect that strong understanding. A contractor may have difficulty staffing all of its programs with the requisite talent. Government requests for proposals try to mitigate this problem by requiring an offerer to state by name and qualification certain key personnel for a contract. However, on large programs that last for years, deep domain knowledge by many people is needed. Source selection organizations generally have no way of gauging the overall strength of the proposed team and cannot account for personnel changes over time. No process can make up for a contractor team that lacks an understanding of its customer.

4 Final Thoughts

The process improvement community owes a large measure of debt to the innovative, thoughtful, and dedicated public servants who have embraced the CMMI and have encouraged its use. That same process improvement community must now work closely with government policy makers to correct misunderstandings in what the CMMI does and to improve how the government and industry together apply the CMMI. Failure to take such action could lead the U.S. government to reduce its commitment to the CMMI and to process improvement with a consequent deterioration in acquisition performance.

References

1. Schaeffer, Mark: DoD Systems Engineering and CMMI. CMMI Technology Conference and User Group. (17 November 2004), http://www.dtic.mil/ndia/2004cmmi/CMMIGS/SchaefferCMMI17Nov04v3.pdf.
2. Software Engineering Institute: http://www.sei.cmu.edu/cmmi.
3. National Defense Industrial Association: Systems Engineering Division Meeting (8 February 2004), http://www.ndia.org.
4. Federal Aviation Administration: http://www.faa.gov/aio.

Integrated Software Process and Product Lines

Dieter Rombach

Fraunhofer IESE & University of Kaiserslautern,
Kaiserslautern, Germany
dieter.rombach@iese.fraunhofer.de
Copyright Fraunhofer IESE, 2005

Abstract. Increasing demands imposed on software-intensive systems will require more rigorous engineering and management of software artifacts and processes. Software product line engineering allows for the effective reuse of software artifacts based on the pro-active organization of similar artifacts according to similarities and variances. Software processes – although also variable across projects – are still not managed in a similar systematic way. This paper motivates the need for Software Process Lines similar to Product Lines. As a result of such organization, processes within an organization could be organized according to similarities and differences, allowing for better tailoring to specific project needs (corresponds to application engineering in product lines). The vision of SPPL (integrated product and process line) engineering is presented, where suitable artifacts and processes can be chosen based on a set of product & process requirements and project constraints. The paper concludes with some resulting challenges for research, practice, and teaching.

Keywords: Reuse of artifacts & processes, commonalities and variabilities, software product lines, software process lines (SPL), integrated software process & product lines (SPPL), experience factory.

1 Introduction

Increasing demands imposed on software-intensive systems will require more rigorous engineering and management of software artifacts and processes. For example, software embedded in automobiles exceeds 10 million lines of code already today and has to satisfy extreme safety requirements. Such developments can only be mastered with highly modular architectures enabling the reuse of verified and validated components and the checking of safety requirements at the system integration level. The processes used will highly depend on the degree of safety or reliability to be achieved and on other project characteristics. Choosing trustable components and performing needed module adaptations and additionally required verification & validation, and checking adherence to safety or reliability requirements at the system integration level with the appropriate processes are the key engineering decisions.

Software product line engineering allows for the effective reuse of software artifacts based on the pro-active organization of similar artifacts for a given domain according to similarities and variances. Software processes – although also variable across projects – are still not managed in a similar systematic way. It must not only be the objective to establish software process lines in order to choose the appropriate and proven processes,

M. Li, B. Boehm, and L.J. Osterweil (Eds.): SPW 2005, LNCS 3840, pp. 83–90, 2005.
© Springer-Verlag Berlin Heidelberg 2005

but to establish integrated software process & product lines (SPPL) in order to systematically choose both artifacts and processes needed for a given project.

This paper motivates the need for Software Process Lines similar to Product Lines. As a result of such organization, processes within an organization could be organized according to similarities and differences allowing for better tailoring to specific project needs (corresponds to application engineering in product lines). The vision of SPPL (integrated product and process line) engineering is presented, where suitable artifacts and processes can be chosen based on a set of product and process requirements and project constraints. The paper concludes with some resulting challenges for research, practice, and teaching.

2 Motivation for Proactive Reuse

Engineering requires reuse of proven artifacts. In software engineering, the major challenge to reuse stems from the fact that such artifacts typically have to be changed and tailored to the needs of unique projects. One approach to support such adaptation in a systematic way is to differentiate between commonalities and variations across all systems to be developed within a given domain, and to pre-define limits for variations that can be supported.

2.1 Mature Software Engineering

Mature software engineering requires, among other things, a focus on all engineering and management processes, the application of techniques, methods and tools suitable for practical engineering, and effective reuse.

2.2 Reuse Challenges

Assumptions for successful reuse include the following [1]:

- All experience can be reused: Traditionally, the emphasis has been on reusing concrete objects of 'source code'. This limitation reflects the traditional view that software equals code. It ignores the importance of reusing all kinds of software-related experiences including artifacts at all levels of abstraction ranging from requirements to test cases, processes, and other knowledge, such as reliability, cost or resource models.
- Reuse typically requires some modification: Under the assumption that software developments are typically different in some way, modification of reuse candidates from previous projects must be anticipated. The degree of modification depends on how many, and to what degree, existing characteristics of a reuse candidate differ from the ones needed in the target system.
- Reuse must be integrated into (tailored to) the target projects: Reuse is intended to make software development more effective. In order to achieve this objective, we need to tailor reuse practices to the respective development processes.

The question is how we can minimize the tailoring actually needed and how we can systematically guide the actual tailoring.

2.3 Commonality and Variation

Software systems within any domain can be characterized by their

-   Commonalities: These are functionalities that are contained in all (or at least a large number of) systems within that domain.
-   Variabilities: These are functionalities that are unique to one (or some number of) system(s) within some domain.

These commonalities and variabilities are then implemented via an architecture of components with

-   Fixed commonalities: Such components can be reused across all (or at least a large number of) systems of a domain without change.
-   Controlled variabilities: Such components can be reused with limited and controlled change. Examples include parameterized components or components with optional or modifiable functionalities (e.g., via conditional compilation at the code level, via decision models at the UML modeling level). Modifiable functionalities may be defined in a binary way (include or not include!) or in a continuous way (e.g., ranges of parameters such as reliability [0.9 … 0.99]).
-   Adhoc variabilities: Such components may be unique to one system and will have to be developed from scratch. However, in order to prevent architecture erosion, the interfaces for the inclusion of such components should be well defined, and they should not address nonfunctional requirements (e.g., reliability, performance or safety), as such requirements are known to carry the risk of architecture discontinuities.

A good architecture should

-   maximize the percentage of components with fixed commonalities and controlled variation, and
-   be stable across the entire family of systems within a domain.

3 Product and Process Lines

'Software product line (SPL) engineering' represents the most promising approach to proactive reuse based on pre-designed commonalities and controlled variabilities across a family of systems. This chapter briefly summarizes the state-of-the-art and – practice in SPL engineering, motivates why processes would also benefit from similar treatment as artifacts, and suggests the expansion of SPL engineering to ' Software Process Line engineering'. Based on the hypothesis in chapter 2.2 – that effective reuse must comprise all experiences (artifacts and processes) – the vision of 'integrated software process & product line engineering' (SPPL) is created.

3.1 Software Product Lines

Software Product Line (SPL) engineering has been proposed by the Software Engineering Institute (SEI) at Carnegie Mellon University. However, the underlying ideas of differentiating between the development of experiences reusable across projects and the project-specific development of a software system by means of reusing available experiences have been formulated as early as the 1980s under the label 'experience factory' [2].

The main characteristics of SPL engineering include:

- Two (2) separate development processes: One distinguishes between the domain engineering process, by which artifacts for reuse are being created, and the application engineering process, by which project-specific systems are being developed.
- An artifact repository: Reusable artifacts at all abstraction levels – from requirements to test cases – are made available.
- A systematic reuse process: For each predefined choice of variabilities, the choice of components is pre-defined (e.g., via 'product maps').
- A systematic artifact management process: For each exception (e.g., an unintended change to a component of a supposedly controlled variability) it will be decided whether this exception will be factored into the component or not.

The objectives of using SPL engineering are – as in the case of all reuse approaches - increased quality, reduced cost and time, and reduced risk. Especially a reduction of cost can be achieved only if the requirements engineering process within the domain engineering process is based on sound 'scoping'. Scoping attempts to maximize the common functionalities and controlled variabilities so that they can be addressed with one stable architecture and domain engineering effort can be amortized over the number of possible applications.

Several real-world implementations of SPL engineering exist and show remarkable results. Especially time to market reductions by orders of magnitudes and reduced quality risks are reported. One example includes the company Market Maker which produces stock trading software for professionals and non-professionals, and which recently reported about such experiences from five years of product line engineering [ICSE 2005]. Fraunhofer IESE assists companies in establishing SPL engineering based on PuLSE – an SPL approach supporting effective scoping, providing tools for variability specification and management at all abstraction levels, and providing means for incremental build-up of product lines. Example implementations exist at Bosch (automotive supply company), Ricoh (printer business) and Market Maker (stock trading).

The artifacts created with an SPL development organization can be organized according to an 'is_a' relationship. Each component created from a domain artifact (without or with controlled change) is in an 'is_a' relationship with the reused domain artifact. This direct relationship (instead of the multiple derivation sequences in non-SPL settings, where application N+1 is derived from application N) avoids all the configuration management problems we know from release- or variant-based developments.

3.2 Problems with Software Processes

Today we can distinguish mainly two kinds of software processes – the prescriptive company processes and the processes actually executed in projects. The former are typically phase-based, serve to control projects company-wide wrt. cost and time, and allow synchronization with other processes, such as system engineering processes (combining development of mechanical, electronic and software components in embedded system domains) or non-engineering processes, such as acquisition or distribution. However, such processes provide little guidance for software developers. The latter processes are the processes by which software systems have been developed. Mostly they are implicit and have an unclear relationship with the company-wide prescriptive processes.

Some of the problems resulting from this current situation include:

- Lack of guidance for software developers from a process that is too generic.
- Problems with measurement due to the lack of process adherence to the process for which metrics have been defined.
- Problems with feedback due to the fact that the lessons learned during projects cannot be related to the company-wide process.

What is missing is a clear relationship between a generic company process and the actual instantiations (either for a specific business unit or for a concrete project). It is unclear what the commonalities and controlled variabilities are across all process instances. The commonalities should be captured in the company-wide process; the controlled variabilities should be specified and guidelines for tailoring should exist. The discriminators for the 'is_a' relationship between processes would be

- Product & process requirements: Examples could include degree of reliability or certain sets of functionalities and effort distributions or time.
- Project characteristics: Examples could include the experience of developers.

3.3 Software Process Lines

Software process lines would be based on the same principles described in chapter 3.1. That means we would, by means of a domain engineering process, create a generic (set of) process(es) that capture the commonalities and controlled variabilities across a domain. The variabilities – and thereby the discriminators for process instances - in the case of processes are product and process goals as well as project characteristics. The knowledge about these variabilities – as well as their instantiation into concrete processes - comes from empirical studies on the impact of processes on goals under given project characteristics (often referred to as context).

For example, we might have a generic inspection process associated with a certain development milestone. Variabilities of the developments could be different degrees of reliability (highly reliable, normally reliable) of the software under development, and the experience of the inspectors (high, medium). In this case we might create – and by means of empirical studies validate – the following hypotheses:

- Perspective-based reading is best suited for software with high reliability requirements and medium experience.
- Ad-hoc reading is best suited for software with normal reliability requirements and highly experienced inspectors.
- Checklist-based reading is most suitable for all other combinations.

Here we would have three 'is_a' relationships between ad-hoc/checklist-based/perspective-based inspections and a generic inspection process.

The main characteristics of software process line engineering would be similar to the ones listed in chapter 3.1:

- Two (2) sepaoprate development processes: One distinguishes between the domain engineering process, by which processes for reuse are being created, and the application engineering process, by which project-specific processes are being developed.
- A process repository: Reusable processes at all abstraction levels are made available.
- A systematic reuse process: For each predefined choice of variabilities, the choice of process components is pre-defined (e.g., via empirically justified 'project maps').
- A systematic process management process: For each exception (e.g. an unexpected behavior of the process occurs) it will be decided whether this exception will be factored into the generic process or not.

The objectives of using software process line engineering are – as in the case of all reuse approaches - increased predictability, reduced cost and time, and reduced risk. The way to build such process hierarchies is either bottom-up or top-down. Top-down establishment reflects the typical standardization process. Bottom-up approaches look at commonalities and variabilities across a number of projects, perform a commonality analysis [3], and model the process in terms of commonalities and controlled variances.

Several real-world implementations of software process lines have been started. Examples include the process architecture (created bottom-up) at NASA Goddard Space Flight Center's SEL, and the newly proposed and top-down developed V-Model XT for public development sub-contracts in Germany [http://www.v-model-xt.de].

3.4   Integrated Software Process and Product Lines

There exists a strong correlation between process and products in the sense that the product goals are achieved as a function of executing some process under certain project characteristics. It would be desirable to establish a focus on reusing experience like software artifacts and processes. Such an organization would be called a 'Software Process & Product Line (SPPL)". Here artifacts and processes are captured and organized according to discriminators combining product and process requirements, and project characteristics.

It might be obvious that such an organization could also be viewed as a 'comprehensive Experience Factory' implementation. The interesting vision would be that one wants to start a project by characterizing it and submitting a query (e.g., in the form of a set of GQMs [4]) to the repository. Then a combined set of artifacts and processes would be provided to plan and run a project with.

4   Future Work

Process lines and even integrated process and product lines can be built today. How-ever, efforts in research, practice, and education & training are needed in order to support the establishment of SPPLs.

4.1   Research

The most important research tasks needed include:

- The design of process modeling languages with features for variability specifi-cation: Example languages with features for variability specification MVP-L.
- More effective methods for creating empirically grounded 'process → prod-uct' models. Here the research thread on 'evidence-based software engineer-ing' or 'value based software engineering' as well as portals for evidence on process effectiveness and efficiency such as 'CeBASE' or 'VSEK', or even books like [5].
- Theoretical & engineering foundations for process lines (especially organiz-ing) and integrated SPPLs. Discrepancies will be handled separately.

4.2   Practice

The most important practice changes include:

- Acceptance of the importance of processes and the need to manage them.
- Empirical model building based on studies imposed upon projects.
- Wide-spread adoption of SPL.
- Expansion of the SPL idea to the SPPL vision.

4.2   Education and Training

In the case of embedded systems:

- Higher focus on process, more specifically on the appropriate use of process
- Training of new methods in laboratory settings
- Role-based education & training. Especially in the product line context, we have to separate developers (top-down problem solvers) from domain engi-neers (bottom-up abstractors).

5   Conclusions

Delivery of increasingly complex software systems in more and more customer varia-tions requires effective (pro-active) reuse in the form of product lines. In these prod-uct lines, all kinds of experience (mostly artifacts and processes) need to be stored and managed. We call such product lines 'software process and product lines'. This paper suggests an expansion of the well-defined and proven principles of software product line engineering to processes, and an integration of both based on the ideas of the 'Experience Factory'.

References

1. Basili, V.R., and H. D. Rombach. Support for Comprehensive Reuse. IEE British Computer Society, Software Engineering Journal (May, 1991.
2. Basili, V.R., G. Caldiera and H. D. Rombach. The Experience Factory. Encyclopedia of Software Engineering I, Wiley (1994) 469-476.
3. Ocampo, A., F. Bella and J. Münch. Software Process Commonality Analysis. Accepted for publication in Software Process Improvement and Practice (October, 2005).
4. Basili, V.R., G. Caldiera and H.D. Rombach. Goal Question Metric Paradigm. Encyclopedia of Software Engineering I, Wiley (1994) 528-532.
5. Endres, A. and H.D. Rombach. A Handbook of Software and Systems Engineering - Empirical Observations, Laws and Theories. Pearson Education Ltd, Addison Wesley (2003).

A Rigorous Software Process for the Development of Embedded Systems

Wilhelm Schäfer

Software Engineering Group, University of Paderborn,
Warburger Str. 100, D-33098 Paderborn, Germany
wilhelm@uni-paderborn.de

Abstract. The paper reports about a rigorous software process for embedded system development. The process is based on specifying the software by a well-chosen and well-defined subset of UML diagrams. The process together with a formally defined semantic of the various diagram types supports requirements tracking, consistency checking and formal verification across the various parts of a UML-based specification. An existing software development environment illustrates the concepts of the paper.

1 Introduction

Software has become an intrinsic part of so-called embedded systems. Software is usually employed to implement the control of these systems and to extend and improve their functionality. In many cases these systems are used in a safety-critical environment and implement themselves safety-critical applications. Consequently, the development of their software has to undergo a rigorous process which guarantees a high-quality software product when it is shipped the first time.

A first example for such an embedded safety-critical system is the Paderborn-based Railcab project (http://www-nbp.upb.de/en), which aims at combining a passive track system with intelligent shuttles that operate individually and make independent and decentralized operational decisions. The project is funded by a number of German research organizations. A test track has been built in the scale of 1:2.5 such that the ideas of the project are not only tested "on paper" but in real operation.

The vision of the railcab project is to provide the comfort of individual traffic concerning scheduling and on-demand availability of transportation as well as individually equipped cars on the one hand and the cost and resource effectiveness of public transport on the other hand. The modular railway system combines sophisticated undercarriages with the advantages of new actuation techniques as employed in the Transrapid (http://www.transrapid.de/en) to increase passenger comfort while still enabling high speed transportation and (re) using the existing railway tracks.

As a second example consider a state-of-the-art production system in a factory. Such a system is composed of more or less autonomous production agents like manufacturing cells, shuttles carrying goods, or gates in a track-based transportation system. Although the system is not really safety-critical, a bad design and implementation may result in weeks of downtime for reconfiguration or repair. This time frame is, of course, unacceptable, if a company wants to stay in business and thus the careful design of such a system.

M. Li, B. Boehm, and L.J. Osterweil (Eds.): SPW 2005, LNCS 3840, pp. 91–99, 2005.

The next section describes the proposed rigorous process in more detail whereas section 3 gives an example of the application of this process using the above mentioned production system. The whole approach is based on using UML 2.0 as an international standard for system specification. Section 4 finishes with some concluding remarks.

2   The Software Process

Requirements Elicitation Phase: The whole process starts with the gathering of requirements supported by the notion of UML-component and sequence diagrams as well as statecharts. Component diagrams are used to describe the coarse-grained system architecture based on the constituent hardware components of the system to be constructed. The physical behavior of these components is described by statecharts. The communication with other system components is then modeled using sequence diagrams. Sequence diagrams describe typical scenarios of system execution as well as examples for non-intended behavior. The definition of the consistency between the various scenarios and the component behavior is a topic of current research in our group [1].

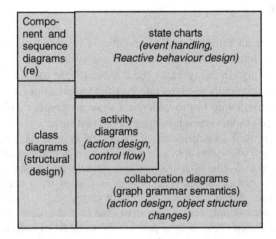

Fig. 1.   Main process phases and diagram types

Design Phase: In the next step, one derives the initial (UML) class diagram of the software system. Here, each component (type) as identified in the component diagram generates a class in the class diagram which can, of course be later on refined into more than one. Communication between components as expressed by the scenario definitions is reflected by an association between the corresponding classes. Ports are refined into operation signature definitions of classes which are identified either as signals or methods. Signals correspond to events which connect the software control with hardware-related events whereas methods are mainly used to specify the communication between the various software objects. The detailed partly automatic synthesis of a class diagram and further behavioral specifications, as explained later on, from the output of the requirements phase is currently the topic of a new research project. As a first step in this direction see [2].

Reactive Behavior Modeling Phase: In this phase the reaction of each class to the invocation of its signals is specified by (hybrid) real-time statecharts [3, 4]. Each signal as defined in the class interface must appear in the statechart definition. Each class which corresponds to an active system component, i.e. a component which requires some control functionality, has exactly one statechart associated. Hybrid statecharts support the definition of underlying continous controller functionality, i.e. a state in a statechart may express that a predefined continous controller becomes active on entering this state. Real-time annotations to transitions and states support the definition of time constraints on the execution of state transitions and associated actions as well as on the execution of entry- do-and exit actions.

Action Modeling Phase: Statecharts specify in which states a certain object as the instance of the corresponding class reacts to a particular signal. In response to a signal an object might change its state and execute some additional activities. For a flexible production agent, for instance, these activities might again include complex computations. These complex computations might employ or modify complex object-oriented data structures in order to reflect the surrounding world as e.g. the execution of manufacturing plans for certain products. For the specification of such complex computations we use UML-like collaboration diagrams. Consequently, we use collaboration diagrams to specify complex control flows of methods employed as actions within statecharts.

Frequently, one will need more than a single collaboration diagram to model a number of object structure modifications. Therefore, we combine statecharts (and activity diagrams) with collaboration diagrams to a powerful visual specification language. Basically, we employ collaboration diagrams as the specification of activities instead of just pseudo-code statements as offered in many other statechart-based approaches and tools, e.g. [5,6].

Code Generation Phase: Once all aspects of the system are specified, a complete, executable (Java-) implementation is generated from the class and behavior diagrams. This implementation is further used for the following simulation phase. Our approach also supports the generation of other more domain specific languages like PLC or subsets of C.

Simulation Phase: The implementation is not only the full program of the desired control software but is also used for simulation purposes, i.e. the software which is supposed to run later on in the real system is simulated upfront using (in the long run) sophisticated graphic facilities. This is in contrast to many approaches where simulation is based on the interpretation of a model of the software which runs of course the risk that the finally implemented software is inconsistent with the model (and the simulation results).

Although, the above sketched process is by no means surprising, it has important differences compared with e.g. the Rational Unified Process (RUP) and other "classical" software processes. In our approach, the different diagrams are logically and mutually dependent on each other and carry a formal static and dynamic semantics. The main dependencies are that component diagrams specify the minimal number of classes of the control software and their corresponding associations. In addition, each (active) class is associated with one main statechart. This statechart has to define the response to all signals of the corresponding class. In addition to state changes, this response might include actions. Each of these actions is specified using one behavior diagram (which in turn may apply additional diagrams for sub-activities). Thus, within the resulting overall specification each aspect of the system is specified by exactly one diagram and it is absolutely clear how these different diagrams are related to each other and how they form the whole specification. In addition, a specification is complete only if all aspects identified in the component and sequence diagrams are covered by class diagrams and statecharts and if in turn all auxiliary aspects introduced in these diagrams are covered by additional behavior diagrams (until transitive closure is reached).

In addition, model-based verification is possible and done for the output of the reactive behavior modeling and action modeling phase resp.. Verification is based on the definition of a formal semantics for our statechart and collaboration diagram models. Real-time hybrid statecharts are mapped to timed automata and the semantics of a collaboration diagram is given by a graph transformation system. These mappings enable the formal check of system properties, especially safety properties by using available tools such as UPAAL and GROOVE [7, 8]

Note that the mentioned completeness of specification diagrams is enforced for the final system specification only. One might use additional UML behavior diagrams in order to analyze certain scenarios during early informal requirements gathering. Such diagrams need not to be complete and there may be multiple diagrams that overlap in several aspects. One may study such scenarios at any time during the specification process and one should keep such diagrams for documentation purposes.

3 The FUJABA Environment

The application of the above described process and its support by a software development environment is demonstrated using a simplified example of a production line. This example stems from the case-study of the ISILEIT project which is funded by the German National Science Foundation (DFG) [9].On this production line bottle

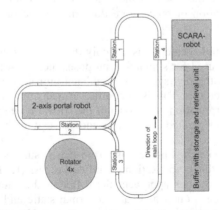

Fig. 2. Schematic overview of the Sample Factory

openers are produced which consist of several (hardware) components. The system works in such a way that an external job allocation system, which is beyond the scope of this paper, assigns a task to a shuttle, which means that the shuttle becomes responsible for initiating the production of certain components by traveling to the right stations in a certain order (see Fig. 2). A simplified production process (not the software process) could look like the following. In a first step a shuttle moves to station 1 where somebody (a machine or a human) equips the shuttle with the appropriate raw material. After finishing the loading process, the shuttle moves to station 2 where the portal robot takes the material from the shuttle and hands it over to the rotator which performs the required manufacturing step. After that, the portal robot takes the finished product from the rotator and puts it on the waiting shuttle. The shuttle now takes the good to station 4 where the good is stored. Shuttles rotate on the main loop as long as no job is assigned to them. Shuttles run on a track-based system which is easily extensible to provide further stations and consequently a more complex production process.

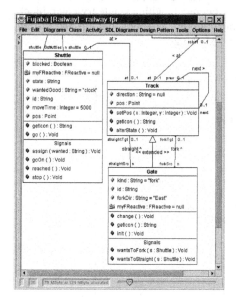

Fig. 3a. Fujaba showing the example class diagram

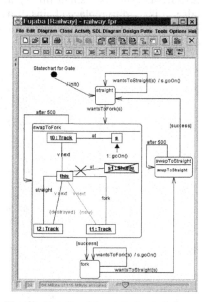

Fig. 3b. Details of the statechart of class Gate

The software development environment which is being used to illustrate our approach, is called FUJABA (From UML to Java and Back Again) [10]. It has been developed over the last seven years in our group and is available as public domain software at www.fujaba.de. It especially supports to check many consistency constraints between the various UML diagrams as mentioned above. Figure 3a shows an excerpt of the example class diagram as developed with FUJABA and the definition of classes shuttle, track and gate with their interfaces and associations which have been synthesized from the component and scenario diagrams of the requirements phase.

Figure 3b shows some details of the statechart of class Gate. A gate is either in state straight or in state fork. When a shuttle arrives at a gate, it signals its desired direction via a wantsToStraight or wantsToFork event, respectively. Depending on its current state, the gate may have to swap its current direction first, cf. activity swapToFork. Finally, the gate sends a goOn event to the shuttle, signaling that it may proceed.

The body of the activity swapToFork shows a collaboration diagram modeling the swap operation. This collaboration diagram shows a cut-out of the object structure surrounding the current gate (the this object). The crossed-out shuttle object s1 defines that the gate must not operate during a shuttle crossing. If this condition holds, the next link from this to track t2 is destroyed and a new next link from this to t1 is created, as indicated by the the {destroyed} and {new} constraints, respectively.

Note that this notation is syntactically different from the definition of UML-collaboration diagrams but it has been shown that this notation is just a condensed notation and can be easily mapped to the UML syntax [11].

Figure 4 shows the Java code generated from activity the swapToFork. Note, that JavaSDM.ensure is a small library method, throwing an exception if its argument is false. It is used to replace chains of nested if-statements with a single try-catch block. Note the use of association encapsulating methods for neighbor look-up and testing, e.g. in lines 8 and 9, and for modifications, cf. 23 and 24.

```
1:  public void doAction0SwapToFork () {
2:      Object sdmTmpObject = null;
3:      Track t0 = null; Track t1 = null; Track t2 = null;
4:      boolean sdmSuccess = false;
5:      try {
6:          sdmSuccess = false;
7:          // check link 'at' between this and s1
8:          JavaSDM.ensure (this.getAt () == null);
9:          t2 = this.getStraightTgt();            // bind t2 : Track
10:         JavaSDM.ensure (t2 != null);
11:         // check link 'next' between this and t2
12:         JavaSDM.ensure (this.getNext() == t2);
13:         t1 = this.getForkTgt ();               // bind t1 : Track
14:         JavaSDM.ensure (t1 != null);
15:         // check isomorphic binding
16:         JavaSDM.ensure (t2 != t1);
17:         t0 = this.getPrev();                   // bind t0 : Track
18:         JavaSDM.ensure (t0 != null);
19:         // check isomorphic binding
20:         JavaSDM.ensure (t2 != t0 && t1 != t0);
21:         // check link 'at' between s and t0
22:         JavaSDM.ensure (s.getAt() == t0);
23:         this.setNext (null);                   // delete link
24:         this.setNext (t1);                     // create link
25:         s.goOn();                              // 1:
26:         sdmSuccess = true;
27:     } catch (JavaSDMException sdmInternalException) {
28:         sdmSuccess = false;
29:     } // try catch
30: }
```

Fig. 4. Java code of the swapToFork activity

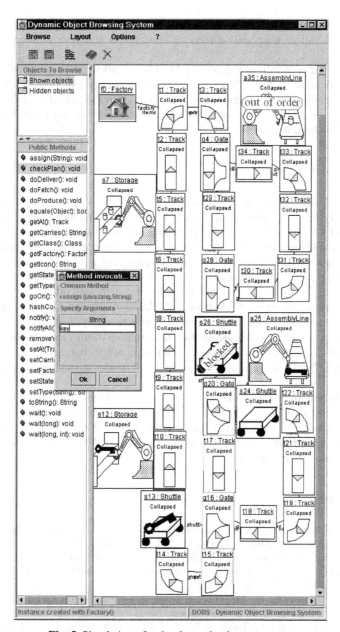

Fig. 5. Simulation of a simple production system

Fujaba focusses on modeling graph-like object structures. It does not yet include a graphical user-interface builder. (Integration with GUI builders is under development.) However, Fujaba provides a generic standard user interface, called Mr. Dobs, that shows a graphical view of graph-like objects structures and allows to call methods on objects, interactively. Fig. 5 displays a small track system with three shuttles running. Note, shuttle s26 is currently blocked, since it wants to pass gate g20 straight but gate g20 had to wait until shuttle s24 had left it and is now about to swap its direction.

The standard graphical user-interface Mr. Dobs works fine as an initial aid for testing a specification. It also allows to adapt the appearance of objects and to define more specifically which objects should be visible and which should be hidden. In some cases, one may use this standard user interface as starting point for the development of the final user interface.

4   Conclusions

This paper illustrated that using (a subset of) UML as a specification language for embedded systems is a feasible approach. It also shows, however, that "just" providing a profile for schedulability, performance and time specifications as the OMG does, is not sufficient to fulfill the need of a verifiable consistent software design. It also needs a rigorously defined software development process and a corresponding formally defined set of specification documents which describe the various system properties and functions in detail and are consistent with each other.

The software development environment FUJABA illustrating and supporting our approach is currently extended in various directions by a developer community around the world. It is already being used in a number of university projects at different places, especially in teaching object-oriented concepts but also in some real-world applications. Check the web pages for more details under the address as given above.

Acknowledgements. The work described here is joint work with a number of colleagues and current and former students. Concerning the process definition, in particular Albert Zündorf, Ulrich Nickel and Robert Wagner were instrumental in developing the approach. I am also indebted to Robert Wagner for discussing former versions of this paper with me.

References

1. Giese, H., Kindler, E., Klein, F. and Wagner, R.: Reconciling Scenario-Centered Controller Design with State-Based System Models, Proceedings of the 4th Workshop on Scenarios and State Machines: Models, Algorithms, and Tools (in Conjunction with the International Conference on Software Engineering), St. Louis, MO, USA/ (Yves Bontemps et al., ed.). IEEE, (2005) 1-5, accepted.
2. Giese, H., Burmester, S.: Analysis and Synthesis for Parameterized Timed Sequence Diagrams. Proceedings of the 3rd International Workshop on Scenarios and State Machines: Models, Algorithms and Tools (SCESM, ICSE 2003 Workshop W5S). Edinburgh, Scotland (2004)
3. Giese, H., Tichy, M., Burmester, S., Schäfer, W., Flake, S.: Towards the Compositional Verification of Real-Time UML Designs, Proceedings of the European Software Engineering Conference (ESEC) Helsinki, Finland, ACM Press, (2003) 38-47
4. Giese, H., Burmester, S., Schäfer, W., Oberschelp, O.; Modular Design and Verification of Component-Based Mechatronic Systems with Online-Reconfiguration, Proceedings of 12th ACM SIGSOFT Foundations of Software Engineering 2004 (FSE 2004), Newport Beach, USA, ACM Press, (2004)

5. Henzinger, T.A.: Masaccio: A Formal Model for Embedded Components, Proceedings of the First IFIP International Conference on Theoretical Computer Science (TCS), Springer Verlag, Lecture Notes in Computer Science, Vol. 1872, Berlin (2000) 549-563
6. Harel, D. and Gery, E.: Executable Object Modeling with Statecharts, Proceedings of the 18th International Conference on Software Engineering, Berlin, Germany (1996) 245-257
7. Jensen, H. E., Larsen, K.G., Skou, A.: Scaling up Uppaal Automatic Verification of Real-Time Systems using Compositionality and Abstraction, Proceedings of the 6th International Symposium on Formal Techniques in Real-Time and Fault-Tolerant Systems (FTRTF 2000), Pune, India, Springer Verlag, Lecture Notes in Computer Science, Vol. 1926, Berlin (2000)
8. Rensink, A.: Towards Model Checking Graph Grammars, in Leuschel, M. and Gruner, S., and Presti, S. L.: Technical Report DSSE—TR—2003—2. University of Southampton, (2003) 150-160
9. Schäfer, W., Wagner, R., Gausemeier, J., Eckes, R.: An Engineer's Workstation to support Integrated Development of Flexible Production Control Systems. In: Ehrig, H., Damm, W., Desel, J., Große-Rhode, M., Reif, W., Schnieder, E., Westkämper, E.: Integration of Software Specification Techniques for Applications in Engineering, Lecture Notes in Computer Science, Vol. 3147, Springer Verlag, Berlin, (2004), 48-68
10. Köhler, H. J., Nickel, U., Niere, J., Zündorf A.: Integrating UML Diagrams for Production Control Systems, Proceedings of the 22nd International Conference on Software Engineering (ICSE), Limerick, Ireland, ACM Press, (2000) 241-251
11. Nickel, U., Schäfer, W., Zündorf, A.: Integrative Specification of Distrubuted Production Control Systems for Flexible Automated Manufacturing, in DFG-Workshop: Modelle, Werkzeuge und Infrastrukturen zur Unterstützung von Entwicklungsprozessen (M. Nagl and B. Westfechtel, eds.), , Wiley-VCH Verlag GmbH and Co. KGaA, (2000) 179-195.

Active Models: A Possible Approach to the Integration of Objective and Subjective Process Models

Brian Warboys

School of Computer Science, University of Manchester,
Oxford Road, Manchester, United Kingdom, M13 9PL
brian@cs.man.ac.uk

Abstract. This paper suggests that the workshop problem of managing the integration of processes based on both explicit and tacit knowledge needs to be addressed by questioning the classical software engineering paradigm. It illustrates a possible approach through a short description of the recently prototyped ArchWare system.

1 Introduction

In the announcement for the workshop, the challenges that were outlined for process technology identified the important conflict facing us.

"The increasing pace of software system change requires more lightweight and adaptive processes, while the increasing mission-criticality of software systems requires more process predictability and control, as well as more explicit attention to business or mission values."

Further it identified the problem with the modern trend towards component-driven engineering as

"COTS products provide powerful capabilities, but their vendor-determined evolution places significant constraints on software definition, development, and evolution processes."

The call went on to identify the integration of objective and subjective based process technology , somehow addressing the problem of dealing with the inevitable real world mixture of explicit and tacit knowledge, as perhaps holding the key to the solution to this issue.

This paper not only supports this conjecture but argues that such an exploration also offers the opportunity to exploit the endemic nature of 'emergent' behaviour in human endeavour as an asset to be nurtured rather than a trait to be suppressed. It argues that software engineering has suffered, from its inception, from the curse of twentieth century reductionism. This logico-mechanistic approach to software engineering flows from the recognition of a problem through phases of problem analysis, system specification, implementation, installation and maintenance. The conventional 'Waterfall' process [1] still continues to dominate software development practices.

M. Li, B. Boehm, and L.J. Osterweil (Eds.): SPW 2005, LNCS 3840, pp. 100–107, 2005.

2   On Classical Software Engineering

Software Engineering emerged during the sixties as a necessity to manage the very large software engineering projects that had arisen, in some sense, without planning. The environment for this initiative was one on which very little or no prior research had been conducted into the nature of the software development process. The proceedings of the two landmark conferences of the late sixties [2, 3] make clear that both the conference discussions and recommendations were derived from informal observations of the nature of the problem. Basically large software developments were happening everywhere, they were never really completed, were full of errors and did not meet their requirements. Not a lot has really changed in the last forty years!

The context had really been set from the beginning of modern computing in the proceeding twenty years and had essentially followed the classical model of numerical computation that had characterized the early computing machines.

This is still the case, and modern development processes still in general follow a requirements, specification, implementation series of steps. This is usually considered adequate for systems that restrict themselves to operating in a priori environments. The situation is made worse by the fact that much of our research focus has historically been on methodologies which semi-automate these different classical software engineering phases. It is surprising, given the failure of the software industry to really solve the problems with large software systems, that no real alternative approach has emerged or even been thoroughly researched.

3   The Need for a More Flexible Approach

Modern business systems, and in fact social systems as well, are characterized by the need to change their processes ever more frequently. This rapid change environment is further enforced by the fact that humans are a highly adaptive species. Although all social systems increasingly prescribe the processes to which they wish their members to subscribe, in practice humans are extremely well equipped to make such processes 'work' by small adaptation. The world functions by people 'nearly' following the many processes prescribed, informed by explicit knowledge, to make organizations (and social systems) operate efficiently, by taking into account their tacit knowledge.

Further, the desire of these social systems, in general, is to get the citizen (or employee) more deeply involved in all the aspects of the running of these systems. This is an immensely complex task and there is no doubt that a large part of the solution will come from the application of computer systems. However, for the computer to fulfill this role, it needs to operate in closer harmony with natural social behaviour. This implies that the software can be adapted at a rate consistent with the social rate of change. We term such a system as one supporting the notion of co-evolution.

Taking a holistic view of the system we see the social and computer system acting in harmony with one another. The interface between the parts being the shared behaviour of the two. Thus the social system interacts with the computer system, and vice versa, through the interfaces provided by this shared behaviour. Clearly the processes that provide this shared behaviour need to be determined by both systems and are crucial to real co-evolution. This is a characteristic which is typical of all such autopoietic systems in that they can only understand the sensations and messages, in whatever form they are received, that they have evolved to understand.

If we now examine, in more depth, the technical implications for such co-evolutionary systems then we discover that the traditional 'Waterfall' type approach to software development is clearly unsuitable. Traditional practice, exaggerated by quality control pressures, encourages the view that the functionality of the system should be defined through a top-down requirements, specification and implementation approach. In practice we need the specification and implementation to evolve at a rate that reflects the needs of the real world; that is somewhere where the requirements change as a result of tacit knowledge, which include the reactions to the software system . Further such evolution needs, potentially, to be determined by all of the members of a social system.

The process models, that are a key part of this co-evolutionary system, need to be constructed so that change is possible at any level, and at any granularity, of the system. This includes the management system that controls such change. Once we accept that we cannot predict the overall behaviour of such complex systems then we need also to accept that we cannot predict the appropriate complex management system either.

4   A Proposed Structure for Co-evolving Systems

Typically we can break the process components of our co-evolutionary system into two sets. Those that are concerned with the production or operational aspects of running the social system and those that are concerned with the management of these operational processes. We shall term this latter set, the set of meta-processes which manage the operational processes. One key aspect of this management is, of course, the change process that allows for continuous system evolution. We can denote these two sets of processes as a produce set (P) and an evolve set (E). Essentially P is responsible for the operational system and E, the meta-process set, is responsible for the fitness for purpose of this set P. Each member of these sets P and E, P_i and E_i, are then individually responsible, respectively, for both some fragment of the operation of a social system and also the fitness for purpose of that operation. If we wish to change an operational process P_i then we can appeal to the responsible E_i, to manage this change.

So what properties are required to ensure that the sets of P_i and E_i pairs can meet these obligations? Well we begin, as process modelling engineers, by describing our computer systems as enacting models of behaviours in complex systems (rather like simulations). However the nature of our co-evolutionary system is such that humans are a very important component of this system. The inclusive nature of both development (evolution) and the context for development extends this to a view that such models are part of the complex system itself. Basically the models are the system. In particular we note the importance of the meta-processes as a part of the system as a whole. This view-point means that one general rule about a co-evolutionary system is that it is adaptive. The engineer is part of this adaptive behaviour rather than, as in traditional approaches, external to it; indeed the end-user is a valid engineer of such a system.

We term such systems, "active models" [12], since the model of the system remains consistent with the real world system that it supports, and we shall refer to the processes comprising such a system as behaviour. In order to produce such an active system, we have previously noted [13] that it should possess at least the following properties:

- Dynamic:
    - The topology of the components and their interactions are determined dynamically
    - New components and interactions may be created during execution
- Updatable:
    - The components may be replaced dynamically
    - Whereas dynamic evolution is additive, update evolution may be regarded as subtractive and then additive (atomically)
- Decomposable:
    - The running system may be (partially) stopped and split into its constituent components and interactions
- Reflective:
    - the specification of the components and interactions may be evolved during their execution

These capabilities allow the system to be developed in an extremely flexible way. However, a highly undesirable characteristic of such a system is that it also allows the simple development of nonsense systems. In order to bring order to this chaotic environment we need to introduce the notion of meta-behaviours, that is behaviours that manage and constrain the possible behaviours that might be evolved. An important property of these meta-behaviours is that they must, of course, still exist within this active co-evolving process system. This means that the vital meta-behaviours are also behaviours and, as such, subject to the same requirements for co-evolution.

In active architectures, in order to ensure continuing compliance to the needs of the supported social system, the specification of the architectural model needs to change in lock-step with the model execution. Thus changes during execution will change the specification and changes to the specification will affect the execution. At any time in the execution of the model the specification is kept dynamically up-to-date.

So, fundamentally the specification is in the computational model. However, without some special efforts, all changes are still of an a priori nature and thus must be pre-programmed into the process definitions. For co-evolution we require a single computational model that can also accept change stimulus from outside and hence deal with emergent change.

Consideration of the properties that such a system requires, leads naturally to the definition of a style of specification development that is naturally supportive of an evolutionary software paradigm. Clearly evolution can be thought of as a form of refinement, however the need to deal with emergent behaviour means that this refinement is not smooth and is thus akin to the notion of retrenchment [14]. In retrenchment we are seeking to deal with such ragged refinement.

To summarize the nature of the development process is one of starting with an abstract definition of some system and then gradually adding and changing detail to support the emergent properties of the active system. In this process we start by outlining the architectural properties that fix the immutable features of our active system. This is classically the role of an architecture definition language and indeed it is appropriate to term our active system process modelling notation, an architecture definition language. The required properties of architecture definition and those of process model specification appear, to me at least, to be the same. We are in both cases defining a set of behaviours and their possible interconnections.

5   An Example Implementation

Our latest approach to implementing a process modelling notation is termed the ArchWare Architecture Definition Language (ADL). Our goal was to provide a unified, software architecture-based framework for the development and maintenance of active process systems. Support for this framework requires the following:

- an architecture description language (ADL) supporting architecture specifications which capture both the structure and the behaviour of components and interactions so that observations and changes may be made within a single framework.
- specification of constraints mechanisms for feedback and change, thus supporting the notion of emergent bahaviour.
- support for integrating commercial off-the-shelf (COTS) components into active systems to address the problem of relaxing the constraints imposed by vender-determined rather than user-determined evolution.
- a structuring methodology designed for change which maintains the integrity of this potentially chaotic environment.

ArchWare ADL [4] is the architecture description language used by the framework and exploited here as a process modelling language. It is a strongly-typed executable architecture description language based on higher-order polyadic π-calculus [5] and was developed as part of the ArchWare project [6]. The language and its support for constraints [7], feedback [8], change [9] and integration of COTS components [10] have been described elsewhere. [13] also enumerated that the following kinds of change are supported by the ADL:

- replacement
- static and dynamic generation of new components
- dynamic evolution (decomposition, reification, reflection, recomposition)

Components are modelled by behaviours (analogous to processes in π-calculus) in the ArchWare ADL. They communicate via connections (channels in π-calculus) using send and receive actions. Behaviours can be composed together to form a system and the compose operator creates a single handle to these executing behaviours. Abstractions abstract over behaviours in the same way as functions abstract over expressions. Mutability is explicitly modelled by locations and replacement of statically defined components is supported by simply assigning a new component to a location containing the old one. In this paper we are concerned with a more general form of adaptation, where part of a system has to be (partially) disassembled, changed and put back together to create an evolved system while the unaffected part still executes. This is in the nature of co-evolving systems. This change requires support for

- decomposition,
- reification,
- reflection
- recomposition.

Decomposition [11] takes (part of) an executing system, breaks it up into its constituent components and returns them in a partially suspended state. The ADL supports a decompose operator which takes a composite component and returns a sequence of its constituent components (behaviours).

Reification allows introspection of a component so that its specification can be used as the basis for any change. The specification of a component is always available including during execution and after decomposition via the ArchWare ADL hyper-code system [19]. The specification of a component can be edited using the hyper-code system to produce an evolved specification. Using hyperlinks to denote existing values allows for the preservation of shared data through this evolution.

Reflection allows new or evolved components to be bound back into an executing system. The evolved specification is brought into the execution domain by dynamic compilation. A callable compiler is provided as a built-in function in the ADL to implement reflection.

Recomposition, using the compose operator of ADL, takes the evolved set of components and composes them together to form a new system.

If we now look at the most abstract specification of such a system then it consists of a null produce process P_{NULL} and some evolve process E_0. Recall that any produce process is some purposeful operational process, and any evolve process is responsible for ensuring that this operational process is fit for purpose. The evolve process E_0 must be capable of handing emergent behaviour. In its most abstract state this emergent behaviour takes the form of direct user input of ADL text through an editor supporting the ADL hyper-code system. This system can then just evolve into the active system we require. Significantly, this entire process of evolution, that has been created, can remain as part of the final system and thus we may evolve the system at any level. The hyper-code environment gives us the capability of doing this at any level of code granularity, in the sense that any primitive ADL construct may be manipulated.

6 Conclusions

So how does this active approach help to address the issue of explicit and tacit knowledge derived process integration identified in the call for this workshop? The main contribution lies in outlining an approach aimed at simply removing the distinction; to argue that a process model should be seen as an abstract definition of a co-evolvable system. This process model sets the boundaries on the style of the various behaviours, based on either explicit or tacit knowledge, that populate this system. These behaviours should then be seen as the set of the refinements of this abstract definition, produced by a process of continuous evolution of the initial specification. Explicit knowledge behaviours usually being added by the process engineer and tacit knowledge usually driving the end-user evolutions of these, but not necessarily.

What this paper suggests is that we need to not only address the contexts for so called macroprocess and microprocess definitions in order to integrate them, but also address the underlying software engineering paradigm that currently constrains system designers to seek to suppress emergent behaviour. It argues that emergent behaviour is an inevitable property of future, and indeed current, systems and that therefore emergent behaviour is a characteristic to be exploited rather than suppressed. The short example demonstrates a possible and, to date, promising approach to such a system. [10] also suggests that this active system approach can also be used to reduce many of the constraints placed on process systems by COTS products. It argues that by embedding COTS products into an active system, the end-user can achieve greater control over remaining compliant to the changing requirements of the target social system.

Acknowledgements

Some of the work presented in this paper has been supported by the EC grant IST-2001-32360 (the ArchWare project). My thanks to fellow partners of the project for useful discussions relevant to the work described. Special thanks go to Ron Morrison and his research team at the University of St Andrews and to my team at the IPG in Manchester for the many years of highly productive collaboration in this field.

References

[1] Royce, W.W. "Managing the development of large software systems:concepts and techniques." Procs IEEE WESTCON, Los Angeles, CA (1970)

[2] Naur, P. and Randell, B."Software Engineering" Report of NATO conference, Garmisch, Germany (1968)

[3] Buxton, J.N. and Randell, B. "Software Engineering Techniques" Report of NATO conference, Rome, Italy (1969)

[4] Balasubramaniam, D, Morrison, R, Kirby, GNC, Mickan, K, Norcross, S. ArchWare ADL - A User Reference Manual. 2004. ArchWare Project Report.

[5] Milner, R. Communicating and Mobile Systems: The Pi- Calculus. 1999: Cambridge University Press.

[6] Oquendo, F, Warboys, BC, Morrison, R, Dindeleux, R, Gallo, F, Occhipinti, C. ArchWare: Architecting Evolvable Software. In: Proc. First European Workshop on Software Architecture (EWSA'04). 2004. St Andrews, UK. Springer-Verlag. pp 257-271.

[7] Cimpan, S, Oquendo, F, Balasubramaniam, D, Kirby, GNC, Morrison, R. ArchWare ADL:Definition of Textual Concrete Syntax. 2002. ArchWare Project Report.

[8] Balasubramaniam, D, Morrison, R, Mickan, K, Kirby, GNC, Warboys, BC, Robertson, I, Snowdon, R, Greenwood, RM, Seet, W. Support for Feedback and Change in Self adaptive Systems. In: Proc. ACM SIGSOFT Workshop on Self-managed Systems (WOSS04). 2004. Newport Beach, CA, USA. ACM.

[9] Morrison, R, Kirby, GNC, Balasubramaniam, D, Mickan, K, Oquendo, F, Cimpan, S, Warboys, BC, Greenwood, RM. Support for Evolving Active Architectures in the ArchWare ADL. In: Proc.4th Working IEEE/IFIP Conference on Software Architecture (WICSA 2004).

[10] Warboys, BW, Snowdon, R, Greenwood, RM, Seet, W, Robertson, I, Morrison, R, Balasubramaniam, D, Kirby, GNC, Mickan, K. An Active Architecture Approach to COTS Integration. To be published in: IEEE Software Special Issue on Incorporating COTS into the Development Process 2005

[11] Warboys, BC, Balasubramaniam, D, Greenwood, RM, Kirby, GNC, Mayes, K, Morrison, R, Munro, DS. Collaboration and Composition: Issues for a Second Generation Process Language. In: Proc. 7th European Software Engineering Conference (ESEC'99). 1999. Toulouse, France. Springer-Verlag. pp 75-91.

[12] Greenwood, R.M., Robertson, I., Snowdon, R.A., and Warboys, B.C. Active Models in Business. In: Procs 5th Annual Conference on Business Information Technology (BIT'95). Manchester. 1995.

[13] Balasubramaniam, D, Morrison, R, Mickan, K, Kirby, GNC, Warboys, BC, Robertson, I, Snowdon, R, Greenwood, RM, Seet, W. A Software Architecture for Structuring Autonomic Systems. To be published in: Procs ICSE 2005 Workshop on the design and evolution of Autonomic Application Software (DEAS 2005)

[14] Banach R., Poppleton M. (1998); Retrenchment: An Engineering Variation on Refinement. in: Proc. B-98, Bert (ed.), LNCS 1393, 129-147, Springer Verlag

A Value-Based Process for Achieving
Software Dependability

Liguo Huang

Computer Science Department, University of Southern California,
Los Angeles, CA 90089-0781, USA
liguohua@usc.edu

Abstract. Since different systems have different success-critical stakeholders, and these stakeholders depend on the system in different ways, using traditional one-size-fits-all dependability metrics to drive the system and software development process is likely to lead to delivered systems that are unsatisfactory to some stakeholders. This paper proposes a Value-Based Software Dependability Achievement (VBSDA) process generated from the WinWin Spiral Model's risk-driven approach coupled with a set of value-based dependability analysis frameworks, methods, and models for reasoning about software and system dependability. It helps project success-critical stakeholders define, negotiate and develop mission-specific combinations of dependability attributes. The NASA/USC Inspector SCRover (ISCR) project is used as a case study to elaborate the process.

1 Introduction

The key objectives of the NASA High Dependability Computing Program (HDCP) are to develop NASA mission-relevant definitions of system and software dependability metrics, to use the metrics to drive development processes, and to evaluate the contributions of existing and new computing technologies to the improvement of an information-intensive system's dependability. Such evaluations require one or more evaluation criteria or metrics that enable quantitative comparisons of candidate technology solutions to be performed. Ideally, one would like to have a single dependability metric by which the development process could be driven, and by which the contributions of each technology could be ranked. However, in practice, such a one-size-fits-all metric is unachievable. Different systems have different success-critical stakeholders, and these stakeholders depend on the system in different ways [1].

This paper proposes a Value-Based Software Dependability Achievement (VBSDA) process generated from the WinWin Spiral Model's risk-driven approach coupled with a set of value-based dependability analysis frameworks, methods, and models for reasoning about software and system dependability. It helps project success-critical stakeholders define, negotiate and develop mission-specific combinations of dependability attributes. The NASA/USC Inspector SCRover (ISCR) project [2] is used as a case study to elaborate the process.

M. Li, B. Boehm, and L.J. Osterweil (Eds.): SPW 2005, LNCS 3840, pp. 108–121, 2005.
© Springer-Verlag Berlin Heidelberg 2005

1.1 Case Study: NASA/USC Inspector SCRover (ISCR) Project

The ISCR system was developed to serve as a distributable HDCP testbed for evaluating current and emerging dependability-enhancing technologies. It involved obtaining requirements from the USC Department of Public Safety (DPS) for an autonomous robot that could investigate the possible presence of hazardous materials in an environment unfit or dangerous for human intervention. Such an environment could be caused due to an earthquake or a failed chemical/biological experiment in a chemistry/biological laboratory. It would have several risks, such as loss of human health or life due to failure to identify a dangerous target with chemical leak or radiation, and the damage of robot itself.

Here are the top-level requirements that were determined for the ISCR system. The robot shall be able to autonomously maneuver around in the area designated by the robot operator and identify the potentially hazardous targets. The robot shall simultaneously return pictures taken by the camera mounted on the robot and the available sensor information to the designated host computer. Additionally, the robot shall maintain enough power so that it can return back to the initial designated location.

The development of the SCRover was planned in 3 increments. The case study is based on the increment 3 of the project which covers most of the important mission scenarios.

2 Related Work

The International Federation for Information Processing Working Group WG 10.4 on Dependability Computing and Fault Tolerance (IFIP/WG 10.4) defines dependability as "the trustworthiness of a computing system which allows reliance to be justifiably placed on the service it delivers" [13]. IFIP/WG 10.4 also mentions that, in different circumstances, the focus will be on different properties of services such as continuity, performance, real-time response, etc. Therefore, dependability is not a single aspect of a computing system but a combination of various aspects of stakeholders' interests such as availability, reliability, safety, confidentiality, integrity, maintainability and so on.

Because different stakeholders depend on different system capabilities in different situations, dependability is necessarily a multi-attribute construct with situation-dependent attribute values. At the Economics-Driven Software Engineering Research (EDSER) workshops (www.edser.org) and elsewhere [14, 15], researchers have developed general frameworks for making software engineering decisions that enhance the value of delivered software systems. Some contributions that explicitly address dependability aspects include

- Carnegie Mellon University's work on value-based security investment analysis [16], warranty models for software [17], and value-based software fault detection [18]
- The University of Virginia's application of real-options theory to the value of modularity [19] and application of utility-theory and stochastic control approaches to reliable delivery of computational services [20]

- University of Maryland's work on modeling dependability for a diverse set of stakeholders [21]

3   Value-Based Software Dependability Achievement Process

Scenario-based stakeholder/value dependency analysis and risk-driven concurrent engineering are two critical factors emphasized in our VBSDA process. In order to avoid using one-size-fits-all metrics to measure the achievement of software dependability, we use a scenario-based approach to identify stakeholders' value propositions with respect to dependability (D-) attributes and to help stakeholders define the detailed D-attribute requirements in different scenarios. This approach also helps to identify and resolve their value conflicts on D-attributes and to perform tradeoff analyses in order to engineer the stakeholder WinWin-balanced D-attribute requirements. Further the scenario-based approach enables us to use real earned value to monitor and control the progress toward achieving the D-attribute requirements. Finally, the VBSDA process generated from the WinWin Spiral Model provides a workable framework for dealing with risk-driven concurrency.

This section discusses the major steps in the VBSDA process and identifies other sources of methods and tools for elaborating each step. The most complete source is the "Guidelines for Model-Based (System) Architecting and Software Engineering (MBASE)" [3] at http://cse.usc.edu/research/MBASE. Shorter summaries are [4] and [12]. The top-level process steps are listed as following:

1. Identify top-level mission objectives and stages
   – including dependability objectives
2. Develop results chain and identify success-critical stakeholders and their top-level value propositions
3. Stakeholders negotiate mutually satisfactory (Win-Win) dependability (and other) goals and relevant mission scenarios
4. Concurrently engineer top-level D-attribute and other requirements and solution tradeoff spaces
5. Identify top-level risks, execute risk-mitigation spirals
6. Develop initial Feasibility Rationale; hold Life Cycle Objective Review
   – Pass: go to 7.   Fail: go to 5.
7. Concurrently engineer detailed D-attribute and other requirements and solutions; resolve risks
8. Develop detailed Feasibility Rationale; hold Life Cycle Architecture Review
   – Pass: go to 9.   Fail: go to 7.
9. Construct, test, and deploy system
   – Use the mission scenarios and D-attribute requirement levels as progress metrics and test cases
   – Monitor progress and change requests; perform corrective actions

3.1   Identify Top-Level Mission Objectives and Stages

The top-level objectives and stages for the Inspector SCRover were summarized in Section 1.1.

3.2 Develop Results Chain and Identify Success-Critical Stakeholders

The Results Chain technique, developed by the DMR Consulting Group [5] is a way to identify missing initiatives and success-critical stakeholders in a system development project. It involves initially defining the project's Initiatives (rectangles), Contributions (arrows), Outcomes (circles, ovals), and Assumptions (hexagons) for its nominal-case operation. It then involves identifying risks and vulnerabilities that may go wrong with the initial Results Chain, and establishing additional Initiatives, Contributions, and Outcomes to avoid or resolve them.

Fig. 1 shows the dependability-elaborated Results Chain for developing the Initial Operational Capabilities (IOC) of the ISCR increment 3 operational scenarios. We have omitted the Assumptions for simplicity, but added the identification of success-critical stakeholders in parallelograms. Note that the text in italic shows the original simple initial Results Chain for the project developing the Initial Operational Capability (IOC) of the ISCR increment 3 information processing (IP) and operational capabilities without the dependability considerations. The full Results Chain identifies additional success-critical Initiatives, such as prevention and avoidance of ISCR risks and vulnerabilities (R&Vs), training operator and maintainers. Besides the Acquirers and Developers identified in the simple initial Results Chain, the additional dependability initiatives identify success-critical stakeholder class (Dependability Experts), and also the employment of additional dependability-enhancing tools and techniques such as verification and validation (V&V). Other success-critical stakeholders are also identified whose inputs are needed for the risk and vulnerability analysis: ISCR System Dependents (i.e. USC Lab Faculty, Students and Staff), Operators and Maintainers.

3.3 Stakeholders Negotiate Dependability Goals and Relevant Mission Scenarios

Table 1 identifies a matrix of the primary ISCR success-critical stakeholders as rows and their prioritized goals with respect to the ISCR system development, operation, and evolution as columns. The specific columns represent the primary categories of system requirements to be negotiated by the stakeholders.

Project goals and requirements include desired constraints on the system and project such as choices of programming language, infrastructure packages, and computing platforms; development and operational standards; and constraints on budgets, schedules, and other scarce resources as listed in Table 2. Capability goals include the functions the SCRover should perform. Interface goals include message formatting and content, and interaction protocols with other interoperating systems. Level of Service goals include the dependability attributes, except for cost and schedule (covered under Project goals) and interoperability (covered under Interface goals). Evolution goals include downstream goals that the initial system architecture should support, such as deferred capabilities or scalability to accommodate workload growth.

Instead of using one number to define the ISCR system availability goal, we distinguished three classes of mission scenarios. As shown in Table 3, the ISCR system

112   L. Huang

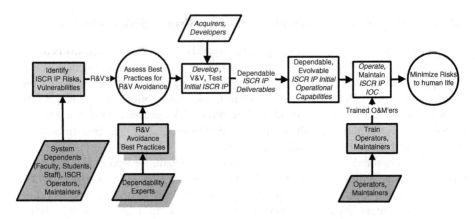

Fig. 1. Dependability-Elaborated Results Chain for ISCR Increment 3

Table 1. Inspector SCRover (ISCR) Stakeholder/Goal Matrix (Priorities: High, Medium, Low)

Goals / Stakeholders	Project	Capability	Interface	Level of Service	Evolution
ISCR System Dependents (USC lab faculty, students, staff, etc.)			►Table 3 ──────────────────────────────►		
ISCR Operators	Table 2				
ISCR Acquirers (USC DPS)					
ISCR Developers, Maintainers (USC CSE)	▼				

Table 2. Inspector SCRover (ISCR) Stakeholder/Goal Matrix (Priorities: High, Medium, Low)

Goals / Stakeholders	Project Goals	Priority
ISCR System Dependents (USC lab faculty, students, staff, etc.), Operators	Develop an autonomous mobile robot that shall help the USC DPS perform its goals of investigating hazardous agents in the USC labs.	H
	Post-Mission data analysis	M
ISCR Acquirers (USC DPS)	Acquire the Core Initial Operational Capabilities (IOC) within budget and schedule	H
ISCR Developers, Maintainers (USC CSE)	Develop IOC within $200K and 9 months	H
	Use MDS (Mission Data System) Framework	H

Table 3. Inspector SCRover (ISCR) Stakeholder/Goal Matrix II: ISCR System Dependents/Operators Goals and Priorities (High, Medium, Low)

Stakeholders / Goals	ISCR System Dependents/Operators
Project	...
Capability	...
Interface	...
Level of Service	H: Availability >= 0.9998 for ISCR mission critical scenarios H: Availability >= 0.993 for ISCR on-line operational scenarios M: Availability >= 0.807 for ISCR post-mission data analysis scenarios H: Accuracy of Target Sensing >= 99% ...
Evolution	...

dependents' and operators' goals for system availability are 0.9998 for mission-critical scenarios, 0.993 for on-line operational scenarios, and 0.807 for post-mission data analysis scenarios. Such numbers are traditionally difficult to determine. We will show how the Information Dependability Attribute Value Estimator (iDAVE) [6] helps determine them.

iDAVE Analysis of ISCR Availability Goals. Multiple stakeholder negotiation of ISCR system goals involves a mix of collaborative win-win option exploration with prototyping and analysis of candidate options. Here, the iDAVE model can be used to help the stakeholders determine how much availability is enough for the three primary classes of ISCR scenarios. Table 4 shows the key availability-related parameters for the software related to the three classes of ISCR scenarios; the size in thousands of source lines of code (KSLOC), the cost per line of code and total cost independent of investments in software reliability, and the dollar mission value of risk if the class of the scenarios fails. For example, there is 15 KSLOC of software for mission-critical scenarios: *Target Sensing* and *Target Rendezvous*. Its cost per instruction of a Nominal COCOMO II Required Reliability level is $6.24/LOC (at graduate-student labor rates), leading to a nominal cost of $93.6K. A failure in the mission-critical software is likely to cause complete contamination and replacement of the robot and the lab, with an impact equal to the $2.5M of an entire lab. A failure and loss of availability of the on-line operational ISCR scenario (i.e., display continuous video images and sensor data to operator) would require repair and rerun of the mission, possibly losing $200K of lab equipments. A failure of post-mission data analysis would require debugging, fixing, and regression testing the software, typically costing about $14K.

Table 5 summarizes an iDAVE analysis of the return on investment involved in increasing the reliability level from Nominal to High; High to Very High; and Very High to Extra High. As determined from the calibrated parameters in the COCOMO II [22], and COQUALMO [23] models on which iDAVE is based [6], increasing the reliability level of the ISCR On-Line Operational software from Nominal to High involves an additional $45K(0.10) = $4.5K investment. It results in an increase in MTBF from 300 to 10,000 hours, which at an experienced-based Mean Time To Repair (MTTR) of 72 hours results in an increase in availability from .807 to .993. Using a linear relation between fraction of downtime and fraction of lost value as in [24], this 0.186 increase applied to the $200K risk impact of the On-Line Operational scenario results in an added benefit of $200K (0.186) = $37.2K, and a resulting ROI = (37.2-4)/4 = 7.29. However, an additional $45K (0.16) = $7.19K investment to take the software from High to Very High only gains in a ($200K)(.9998-.993)=$1.38K benefit, for a negative ROI of -0.81.

Table 4. Size, Cost, and Risk Impact of Three Classes of SCRover Scenarios

Classes of Scenarios	Size (KSLOC)	Nominal		Risk Impact ($K)
		$/LOC	$K	
Mission-Critical	15	6.24	93.6	2500
Online-Operational	8	5.62	45	200
Post-Mission Data Analysis	6	4.48	26.9	14

Table 5. iDAVE Analysis of ISCR Availability Goals for Three Classes of Scenarios

COCOMO RELY Level	Nom	High	Very High	Extra High
MTBF(hrs)	300	10,000	300,000	1,000,000
Availability (MTTR=72hrs)	.807	.993	.9998	.99993
Incremental Availability		.186	.0069	.00001
Incremental Cost		0.10	0.15	0.24
Mission-Critical				
Incr. Cost @ $93.6K		$9.36K	$14.55K	$16.84K
Incr. Benefit @ $2.5M		$466K	$17.27K	$.42K
ROI = (B-C)/C		+48.8	+0.15	-0.98
Online-Operational				
Incr. Cost @ $45K		$4.5K	$7.19K	
Incr. Benefit @ $200K		$37.28K	$1.38M	
ROI = (B-C)/C		+7.29	-0.81	
Post-Mission Data Analysis				
Incr. Cost @ $26.9K		$2.69K	$4.3K	
Incr. Benefit @ $14K		$2.61K	$100	
ROI = (B-C)/C		-0.03	-.0.98	

This and the ROI results for the other two classes of ISCR scenarios calculated in Table 5 are summarized in Fig. 2. The incremental cost of achieving the higher availability levels still keeps the total cost below $200K. From a pure calculated ROI standpoint, one could achieve some potential savings by interpolating to find the availability-requirement levels at which the ROI goes from positive to negative, but it is best to be conservative in a safety-related situation. Or one can identify desired and acceptable availability levels to create a tradeoff space for balancing availability with other dependability attributes.

3.4 Concurrently Engineer Top-Level D-Attribute and Other Requirements and Solution Tradeoff Spaces; Identify Top-Level Risks and Execute Risk-Mitigation Spirals

Step 4 and 5 are often coupled with each other during the software development process. In this section, we propose a scenario-based approach to identify stakeholders' value propositions on dependability attributes and help stakeholders define the detailed D-attribute requirements in different scenarios. The approach also helps identify and resolve value conflicts on dependability attributes and to perform tradeoff analysis on dependability attributes in order to engineer stakeholder WinWin-balanced dependability attribute requirements. Fig. 3 shows the process elements for stakeholders to engineer top-level dependability attribute requirements, identify dependability risks and select the most cost-effective dependability technology combination to mitigate risks for different scenarios. The entry criteria of the D-attribute requirement engineering and risk mitigation process are shown in the box in the top-left corner of Fig. 3.

E1. Identify dependability (D) attributes
This is the entry of the process where the top-level dependability attributes for the whole project are established. The results obtained from Step 1 and 3 in the VBSDA process are usually used as the inputs of this step.

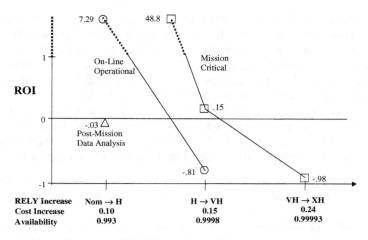

Fig. 2. Summary of iDAVE Analysis of ISCR Availability Goals

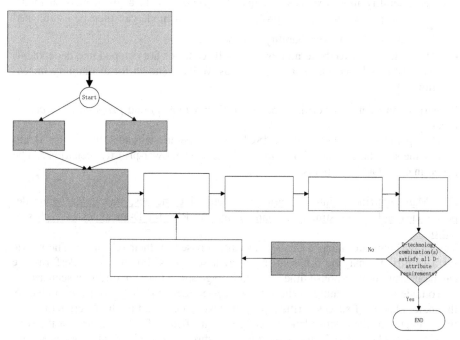

Fig. 3. A Scenario-Based Approach to Engineer Dependability Requirements and Risk Mitigation Plans

The top-level dependability attributes for the ISCR project are availability, accuracy, performance, usability, cost and schedule.

E2. Establish system operational profile scenarios and prioritize scenarios

The scenarios can be defined as mission sequences, environmental inputs or D-objective threats and their frequencies. A scenario is used to describe a proposed use

case of the system and/or an interaction of one of the stakeholders with the system
[7]. Scenarios provide a vehicle for converting vague dependability attrib-
utes/requirements into concrete use cases of a system and make dependability attrib-
ute/requirements measurable and testable. The top-level scenarios of a software system can be established from its use case description (e.g., MBASE Operational Concept [3] use case description). A complex scenario can be decomposed into several
component scenarios if it's necessary for testing purposes. On the other hand, several
component scenarios can be composed into a high-level scenario for analysis or testing purposes. We provide a framework with three factors to be associated with each
scenario S_i, which will be directly leveraged in our scenario-based approach:

- **Value (v).** The value loss (can be measured either in dollars or in utility) if a
  scenario execution fails. It indicates the impact of a scenario on the total mission
  value.
- **Probability of occurrence (p).** The probability that a scenario occurs in a specific mission mode. When several scenarios have the comparable value impact on
  the entire mission, a scenario that is more frequently executed affects the system
  dependability more extensively, than if it were less. In a given mission mode,
  $\sum p_i = 1$. The operational profile of a mission mode can then be established
  based on the scenario probability distribution.
- **Dependability attribute metrics (m).** All scenarios are mapped into dependability attributes based on their relevance, as we have shown for availability in section 3.3.

Scenarios can then be prioritized based on their *value (v)* and *probability of occurrence (p)*.

The operational scenarios of the ISCR initial operational capability (IOC) identified by the stakeholders are shown in the Table 6. The lower-priority scenarios can be
added in post-IOC increments.

E3. Map D-attributes into scenarios and determine metrics, stakeholder/value dependencies and value estimating relationships (VER's) for D-attributes of each scenario

The D-attributes are mapped into each scenario based on their relevance. The metric
for a D-attribute may be different in different scenarios. For instance, Performance
can be measured in response time (s) or in storage space (MB) in different scenarios.

To understand the nature of the software system dependability, we have to identify
the major classes of success-critical project stakeholders, and to characterize the relative strengths of their dependencies on various attributes of each scenario of the software system [1]. Table 7 shows the top-level direct stakeholder/value dependencies
on the D-attributes in the *Target Sensing* scenario. Acquirers, developers, and maintainers are not directly concerned with availability and accuracy, but become concerned with them when their operational stakeholders are.

If needed, the value estimating relationships (VER's) of each D-attribute can be
also established based on the impact of the D-attribute on a particular scenario. Note
that the VER's for a D-attribute may also be different in different scenarios since the
same D-attribute's impact on different scenarios may be different.

Table 6. ISCR Increment 3 Operational Profile Scenarios

Scenarios	Component Scenarios	Priority
Target sensing		H
Target rendezvous	Trajectory planning	H
	Localization	
	Obstacle avoidance	
Display environment state information to operator	Return target state info state variable to operator	H
	Return terrain state variable to operator	
Display sensor and actuator health state information to operator	Return camera state variable to operator	H
	Return range finder health state variable to operator	
	Return wheel motor health state variable to operator	
	Return battery state of charge to operator	
Display continuous camera video images to operator		M
Post-mission data analysis		L
Goal conflict identification and resolution		L

Table 7. Target Sensing Scenario: Top-level Stakeholder/Value Dependencies on D-attributes (** Critical, * Significant, () Insignificant or indirect)

Stakeholders / D-attributes	System Dependents	Operators	Acquirers	Developers	Maintainers
Availability	*	**			*
Accuracy		**			
Cost			**	*	
Schedule			**	**	
Evovability					**

E4. For each scenario, stakeholders define their acceptable and desired values for concerned D-attributes
The results of the iDAVE ROI analysis for three ISCR scenario classes discussed in section 3.3 can be used as guidance for stakeholders to define their expected and desired levels for D-attributes based on the priority of a particular scenario and their value dependencies on the scenario-related D-attributes.

E5. For each scenario, identify the risks of not achieving the acceptable values of D-attributes
E6. For each scenario, identify the D-technologies to mitigate the risks
E7. D-technologies evaluation
Scenario-based Fault Tree Analysis (FTA) [8], Failure Modes and Effects Analysis [8] and Dependability Cases [9] are three useful techniques to trace scenario failures to the potential risks causing them.

Risks are quantitatively linked to the D-attributes of each scenario. For each pair of risk and D-attribute in each scenario, stakeholders provide an estimate (expert judgement) of the potential impact of the risk in the scenario. We define the "impact" as the proportion of the scenario value that would be lost were that risk occur. The probability of occurrence of each risk is also estimated. D-technologies are quantitatively linked to risks. For each pair of risk and D-technology in each scenario, we provide an estimate (expert judgement) of the mitigation of the risk in the scenario. We define the "mitigation" as the proportion by which the risk would be reduced were that D-technology to be applied. At the same time, the cost/effort of applying a particular D-technology should also be recorded. Tools such as the JPL Defect Detection and Prevention (DDP) model [25] can be used for such analysis.

In addition, the parameters used in the iDAVE analyses may be based on incompletely-validated assumptions such as the scalability of a model-checking tool. This is also identified as a risk, and a risk-mitigation plan to validate the scalability of the model-checking tool is developed and executed. The next step is to look for conflicting combinations of D-attributes.

E8. Identify conflicting D-attributes and perform tradeoff analysis
E9. Stakeholders negotiate WinWin balanced D-attribute requirements and redefine the acceptable and desired values for conflicting D-attributes
If the existing technologies can't satisfy the acceptable values of all the D-attributes, or if the estimated cost/schedule to satisfy all the D-attribute requirements is too high, then the tradeoff function between the conflicting D-attributes will need to be constructed and the tradeoff analysis will be performed in conjunction with additional stakeholder negotiation. Multi-attribute preference analyses [10] and stakeholder win-win negotiation support tools [26] are useful techniques to help stakeholders perform such negotiations based on the stakeholders' value propositions. Note that the conflicting D-attribute tradeoff analysis can be performed concurrently with the D-technology evaluation.

3.5 Develop Initial Feasibility Rationale; Hold Life Cycle Objective Review

The initial Feasibility Rationale Description (FRD) [3] furnishes the rationale for the product being able to satisfy the stakeholders' system requirements and specifications. The initial FRD in LCO stage includes an initial business case analysis (i.e., cost, benefits and ROI analysis) based on the Results Chain.

Then a Life Cycle Objective (LCO) Review is to be held with the participation of all the project key stakeholders, and independent experts (these were NASA Jet Propulsion Laboratory (JPL) planetary mission software experts for ISCR). This indicates a milestone of the LCO phase in the WinWin Spiral Model. The exit criteria of LCO Review are to provide at least one feasible architecture to satisfy the requirements, and to provide proofs of requirement satisfaction including the dependability requirements.

The initial risk analysis should identify all the major risks and propose an initial risk mitigation plan. Risks without mitigation in LCO stage have to be resolved in Life Cycle Architecture (LCA) stage.

The result of LCO ARB was to Pass and go to Step 7. However, a risk was identified that the tool evaluation needs for the HDCP tool researchers had been incompletely defined for ISCR.

3.6 Concurrently Engineer Detailed D-Attribute and Other Requirements and Solutions; Resolve Risks

Thus, the major new activity in Step 7 involved surveying HDCP interventionists for additional evaluation needs. The primary emerging need identified was for a three-dimensional graphic uses interface (3D GUI).

Originally, developers planned to use Player/Stage as the robot simulator platform. Because of the 3D GUI requirement, we had to reevaluate the existing technologies or identify new technologies to cover this D-risk. In this case, since Stage doesn't support a 3D GUI, the developers had to find a replacement. After the evaluation, stakeholders finally chose Gazebo because it supports the new stereo camera model and a 3D GUI which also enabled most devices to be directly controlled/inspected through the simulator GUI. Since Stage and Gazebo are both Player-compatible, client programs written using one simulator can usually be run on the other with little or no modification. The key difference between these two simulators is that whereas Stage is designed to simulate a very large robot population with low fidelity, Gazebo is designed to simulated a small population with high fidelity [27]. Thus Gazebo fits with most of DPS missions which can be accomplished by a few robots. Furthermore, Gazebo is more valuable to stakeholders since it improved the usability and evolvability of the system.

3.7 Develop Detailed Feasibility Rationale; Hold Life Cycle Architecture Review

The Life Cycle Architecture (LCA) Review was held with the participation of all the project key stakeholders and the JPL experts. The exit criteria of LCA Review is to commit one architecture to satisfy all the requirements of the system. Thus the LCA FRD has to provide detailed proofs of all requirement satisfaction including the dependability requirements.

The LCA FRD risk analysis should propose a detailed risk mitigation plan to resolve all known risks.

The result of the LCA ARB was again to Pass, and proceed to Step 9.

3.8 Construct, Test, and Deploy System

ISCR Increment 3 is currently under development. It is using the dependability scenarios to simulate the ISCR performance and evaluate whether the dependability attribute levels will be achieved. The framework of the value-realization feedback process [11] is shown in Fig. 4.

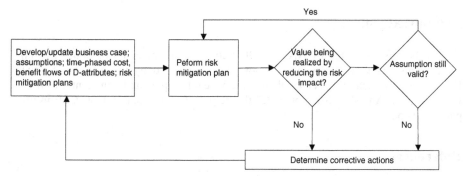

Fig. 4. A Value-Realization Feedback Process to Monitor and Control the Achievement of D-attribute Requirements

A matrix with the capability to track the value-based expected versus actual outcomes (i.e., dependability cost, reduced value loss, ROI) is a useful technique to support the monitoring and control of the actual progress of the dependability achievement. A case study on how to perform the value-based monitoring and control using such a matrix is discussed in [11].

4 Conclusions and Lessons Learned

In practice, value-dependencies on D-attributes vary significantly by stakeholders and scenarios. The universal one-size-fits-all metrics for software dependability (SWD) achievement are unachievable in most project situations. We need to balance stakeholders' value propositions on D-attributes. Thus, a critical first step in understanding the nature of information system dependability is to identify the major classes of success-critical information system stakeholders, and to characterize the relative strengths of their dependencies on various attributes of a given software system. Furthermore, stakeholder value dependencies are often in conflict and require negotiated situations. There is an increasing need for value-based approaches to SWD analysis and its achievement monitoring and control.

The iDAVE model provides a technique for reasoning about the ROI of software dependability. It helps project decision-makers determine how much dependability investment is enough based on their project's business case. It also provides a way to define different dependability levels for different software classes or scenarios based on stakeholders' value propositions, which can avoid the one-size-fits-all dependability metrics for a project. Based on the stakeholder/value dependency analysis frameworks, and value-based methods and models for reasoning about software and system dependability, we have developed and are experimentally applying a value-based process for using these artifacts integrated with the scenario-based approach to cost-effectively achieve desired dependability attribute levels for a given project, and for improving the cost-effectiveness of an organization's capability to develop dependable software and systems. It helps project success-critical stakeholders define, negotiate and develop mission-specific combinations of dependability attributes. To date, the value-based process and scenario-based approach have enabled us to successfully perform value-based feedback control of the actual progress of the ISCR project's dependability achievement.

Acknowledgements

This work was supported by NASA-HDCP contract to University of Southern California. This material is also based upon work supported by the National Science Foundation. The author specially thanks the valuable inputs and comments from Dr. Barry Boehm. And she also appreciates the help of Zhihao Chen in USC CSE in preparing this paper.

References

1. Boehm B., Huang L., Jain A., and Madachy R.: The Nature of Information System Dependability: A Stakeholder/Value Approach (Draft 6). USC-CSE (2004)
2. USC-CSE Inspector SCRover Project Team: Inspector SCRover Project, http://cse.usc.edu/iscr/pages/ProjectDescription/home.htm (2004)
3. Guidelines for Model-Based (System) Architecting and Software Engineering (MBASE), http://cse.usc.edu/research/MBASE. USC-CSE (2003)
4. Boehm B. and Hansen W.: Understanding the Spiral Model as a Tool for Evolutionary Acquisition. CrossTalk May (2001) 4-11

5. Thorp J. and DMR: The Information Paradox. McGraw Hill (1998)
6. Boehm B., Huang L., Jain A. and Madachy R.: The ROI of Software Dependability: The iDAVE Model. IEEE Software, Vol. 21, No. 3, May/June (2004) 54-61
7. Clements P., Kazman R., and Klein M.: Evaluating Software Architecture: Methods and Case Studies. Addison Wesley (2002)
8. Leveson N. G.: Safeware, System Safety and Computers. Addison Wesley (1995)
9. Weinstock C. B., Goodenough J. B.: Dependability Cases. Technical Note, CMU/SEI-2004-TN-016 May (2004)
10. Keeney R. L., Raiffa H.: Decisions With Multiple Objectives. Cambridge University Press (1993)
11. Boehm B. and Huang L.: Value-Based Software Engineering: A Case Study. IEEE Computer, Vol. 36, No. 3, March (2003) 33-41
12. Boehm B. and Port D.: Balancing Discipline and Flexibility With the Spiral Model and MBASE. CrossTalk, Vol. 14, No. 12, December (2001) 23-28
13. Laprie J.C. (ed.): Dependability: Basic Concepts and Terminology. Springer-Verlag, Vienna (1992)
14. Reifer D.: Making the Software Business Case. Addison-Wesley (2002)
15. Nejmeh B. and Thomas I.: Business-Driven Product Planning Using Feature Vectors and Increments. IEEE Software, Nov./Dec (2002) 34–42
16. Butler S.: Security Attribute Evaluation Method: A Cost-Benefit Approach. Proc. of 24th Int'l Conf. Software Eng. (ICSE 02), IEEE CS Press (2002) 232–240
17. Li P., Shaw M., Stolarick K., and Wallnau K.: The Potential for Synergy between Certification and Insurance. Special edition of ACM SIGSOFT from the 1st International Workshop on Software Reuse Economics (in conjunction with the 7th International Conference on Software Reuse) (2002) http://www.sei.cmu.edu/staff/kcw/icsr02.pdf
18. Raz O. and Shaw M.: Software Risk Management and Insurance. Proceedings of 3rd International Workshop on Economics-Driven Software Engineering Research. IEEE CS Press (2001) http://www.cs.virginia.edu/~sullivan/edser3/raz.pdf.
19. Sullivan K. et al.: Software Design as an Investment Activity: A Real Options Perspective. Real Options and Business Strategy: Applications to Decision Making. Trigeorgis L. (ed.), Risk Books (1999)
20. Cai Y. and Sullivan K.: Stochastic Optimal Switching. Proceedings of 4th Workshop on Economics-Driven Software Eng. Research, IEEE CS Press (2002) 71-72
21. D. Huynh, M. Zelkowitz, V. Basili, and I. Rus: Modeling Dependability for a Diverse Set of Stakeholders. The International Conference on Dependable Systems and Networks (2003) (DSN-2003) http://hdcp.org/Publications/dsn-fast-abstract-031603.pdf
22. Boehm B. et al.: Software Cost Estimation with COCOMO II. Prentice Hall (2000)
23. Steece B., Chulani S., and Boehm B.: Determining Software Quality Using COQUALMO. Case Studies in Reliability and Maintenance. Blischke W. and Murthy D. (eds.), John Wiley & Sons (2002)
24. DeMillo R.: Why Software Falls Down. Mutation Testing for the New Century. Wong W.E. (ed.), Kluwer Academic (2001)
25. Feather M. S., Cornford S. L., Dunphy J.: A Risk-Centric Model for Value Maximization. Proceedings of 4th Workshop on Economics-Driven Software Engineering Research, IEEE CS Press (2002)
26. WinWin Spiral Model & Groupware Support System. http://sunset.usc.edu/research/WINWIN/index.html
27. Koenig N. and Howard A.: Gazebo: 3D Multiple Robot Simulator With Dynamics. http://playerstage.sourceforge.net/gazebo/gazebo.html

A Development Process for Building OSS-Based Applications

Meng Huang[1,2], Liguang Yang[1,2], and Ye Yang[3]

[1] Lab for Internet Software Technologies, Institute of Software,
The Chinese Academy of Sciences, P.O.Box 8718, Beijing, 100080, China
[2] Graduate School of the Chinese Academy of Sciences,
Beijing 100039, China
{hm, yanglg}@itechs.iscas.ac.cn
Http://www.cnsqa.com
[3] Center for Software Engineering, University of Southern California,
Los Angeles CA 90089-0791,USA
yangy@sunset.usc.edu

Abstract. It has become great prominence that business organizations are considering open source software (OSS) when looking for software system solutions. However, building applications based on open source software remains an essential issue for many software developers since the new development process differs from traditional in-house development. In this paper, we present a development process based on our experience on using open source software in application development. The new process emphasizes the early assessment to improve the architecture stability and project manageability by assessing available OSS. A set of measurable assessment criteria is established in assessing OSS candidates and making optimal decisions in the development process. A case study is discussed to show the application of this process.

1 Introduction

It is becoming more popular that business organizations apply open source software (OSS) for their IT needs [1,2,3,4,5]. Some important motivation include cost reduction, technology reuse, organizational and environmental considerations. In many cases, users' needs cannot be fulfilled exactly by the existent OSS. Building applications basing on existent OSS is essential tasks for the developers in such scenarios. Though the approach of building OSS-Based Applications (OBAs) has been widely adopted, there is a lack of well-established development process that accommodates the many distinguished OSS features which can lead a seemingly simple development to disaster, if not handled properly. OBAs' developers often feel confused about what to do next when blindly following certain traditional process models, and results in schedule delay and cost overrun due to tremendous rework over time. Building software applications from OSS requires modifying, improving and integrating existent OSS instead of reinventing wheels. Traditional in-house development cannot work well in such scenarios.

M. Li, B. Boehm, and L.J. Osterweil (Eds.): SPW 2005, LNCS 3840, pp. 122–135, 2005.
© Springer-Verlag Berlin Heidelberg 2005

What is open source software is still defined unclearly [1]. In this paper, we adopt a loose concept of OSS that includes publicly available source code and community-source software that can be freely distributed and modified. We define OBAs as "applications including one or more OSS". Goals of building OBAs are :(1) building or improving an OSS' functionality, performance or qualify to fulfill customers' needs; (2) Integrating multiple OSS to deliver a more complex integrated system solution; (3) including (1) and (2).

In most case, building OBAs is similar to developing COTS-Based Applications (CBA). The essential tasks consist of selecting suitable OSS or COTS product, adjusting them as needed, and integrating them with custom components, OSS, or COTS. However, this is a significant difference between OBAs and CBA development. In developing CBA, developers cannot modify COTS components for their special needs because they rarely have access to the source code of COTS products, therefore are hardly able to modify COTS [6,7]. In building OBAs, developers not only need to integrate existent OSS, but also need to modify existent OSS because their quality are irregular or their functionality cannot fully satisfy desired system functionality. Therefore, developers cannot use the process of developing CBA to build OBAs directly.

Our paper offers a development process of building OBAs that is analogous to the process of developing CBA [7]. The new process emphasizes the early assessment to improve the architecture stability and project manageability by assessing available OSS. A set of measurable assessment criteria is established in assessing OSS candidates and making optimal decisions in the development process.

2 Related Work

COTS-based development is based on the acquisition and integration of commercial off-the-shelf products over in-house development [8]. Acquiring COTS products includes identifying alternative candidate COTS products; assessing candidates; and designing architecture based on selected COTS. Integrating COTS products includes tailoring COTS components and developing glue code.

Assessing candidate COTS components is key factors of system development lifecycle (SDL) [8,9,10]. Some recent research focuses on assessment method [10,11,12]. These methods establish assessment criteria according to requirements specification. Some methods in them assume the requirements specifications pre-existed before doing COTS assessment [11,12], while others propose that establishing assessment criteria and eliciting requirement should be performed concurrently [10]. Tradeoff between desired requirements and available COTS packages is usually the key to success within COTS-Based development [8,13]. Multiple criteria are needed to establish in assessment process [14,11,15]. Which are used to collect data from various COTS candidates for doing such tradeoff analysis [8,15]. Some recent researchers focused on designing CBA development process that includes evaluation and integration [7,16,17,18,19]. They believe an iterative process for developing CBA should meet volatility of COTS products and concurrent evolution of requirements, architecture, and COTS choices. Those process frameworks put acquisition and integration of COTS in the background of SDL and support flexible and concurrent development process.

The following actions are carried out in developing CBA by developers:

· Assessing candidate COTS according to criteria
· Negotiating with customer about requirements and available COTS and making decisions
· Designing architecture on available COTS
· Integrating COTS products
· Merging the process of developing CBA into SDL

Those actions are performed similarly when building OBAs. OBAs approach may accelerate development and cut costs, but the consequences of selecting the wrong component can erase these benefits [3]. There are some researches about how to assess OSS [1,3,5, 20] although they only focus on deploying OBAs in business organizations. Some reported the importance of tradeoff among requirements, available OSS and other project factors such as cost and schedule [3,5]. Further, although developers can design architecture for OBAs, OBAs' architecture relies upon available OSS largely. Integrating OSS into OBAs also like integrating COTS components into CBA except OBAs' developers should improve selected OSS in functionality or quality. Merging the process of building OBAs into SDL is a challenge for OBAs' developers also [21].

Those analogous actions imply that OBAs' developers could use a similar process for developing CBA. Nevertheless, there are some differences between OSS and COTS that require appropriate adjustments to accommodate the special OBA development needs. These adjustments include the following three aspects:

1. Designing high-level architecture should be implemented before assessment.

Developers cannot afford to freeze high-level architecture design in early stage of CBA development because interfaces among selected COTS cannot be fixed and system architecture should be designed concurrently while assessing candidate COTS products. However, in building OBAs, it is possible and reasonable to have high-level architecture selected early in the development since interfaces between OSS can be adjusted, customized, and even modified to meet particular system needs.

2. Particular attributes of OSS should be considered carefully during assessment.

In developing a CBA, developers evaluate candidate COTS packages by a set of established evaluation criteria. Evaluation criteria often include attributes of system functionality and performance, organization constraints, and priorities [22]. These are equally important criteria for assessing different OSS if they are appropriately adjusted. Additionally, in building an OBA, developers have to read and change source code for their needs. Reading and changing source code require considering some other attributes. In section 3, we explain which particular attributes should be considered.

3. The process of integrating OSS is similar to that of integrating COTS, but with greater complicity.

In developing CBA, the integration actions include tailing COTS components and developing glue code to make them work together. In this case, COTS is integrated as black-box reuse. Since COTS is often not free, it always comes with sufficient documentation and vendor support. However, since integrating OSS frequently involves changing OSS source code without any "vendor" support, developer must read through and understand the source code, determine which part should be modified and how to modify, consider the resultant issues possibly cause by code modification. In section 3, we define related actions during integrating OSS.

3   A Development Process for Building OBAs

Firstly, a development process for building OBAs is presented in 3.1, which is an analogous process of developing CBA. Because the special OBAs development needs should be considered, we discuss the important issues about high-level architecture design, special attributes of OSS and OSS integration of the process for meeting those special needs in 3.2.

3.1   Descriptions of the Development Process for Building OBAs

The process for building OBAs is shown in Figure 1.

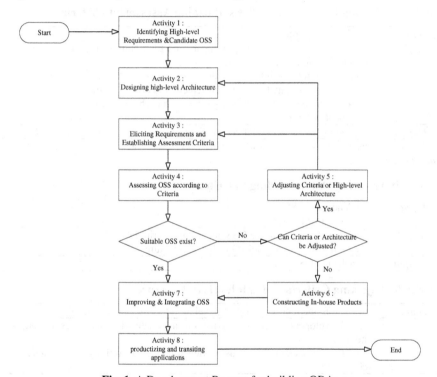

Fig. 1. A Development Process for building OBAs

Activity 1: Identifying High-level requirements & Candidate OSS

Input	· Conceptions of desired system and project restraints*
Step	1.1 Identify high-level requirements 1.2 Identify Candidate OSS according to OSS project profiles and high-level requirements**
Output	· High-level requirements and project restraints which describe boundary of the project · An inventory of candidate OSS that may be used possibly in the applications

Project restraints include cost, schedule and software & hardware environments.

**The project profiles [1,20,25] include project' age, application domain, programming language, size, developers' state, number of users, modularity level, documentation level, popularity, status, and vitality. By OSS project profiles and high-level requirements, a group of OSS, which may be used in the application, is sorted out initially.

Activity 2: Designing High-Level Architecture

Input	· High-level requirements, project restraints and inventory of candidate OSS
Step	2.1 Dividing the desired system into a set of modules. Each module is an OSS and reflects one or more high-level requirements. 2.2 Sorting candidate OSS for every module in high-level architecture
Output	· High-level architecture

Activity 3: Eliciting Requirements & Establishing Assessment Criteria

Input	· High-level architecture
Step	3.1 Eliciting low-level requirements and distributing them into modules' attributes of high-level architecture 3.2 Define total weights of the desired system as distributable benchmark 3.3 Assign weights for each requirement and project restraints*** 3.4 Accumulating requirements weights in each module's attributes as assessment criteria
Output	· a set of OSS assessment criteria for modules in high-level architecture

***Developers must negotiate with users about how much weights are assigned to a requirement.

Activity 4: Assessing OSS according to Criteria

Input	· Candidate OSS · Assessment criteria
Step	4.1 Assessing candidate OSS according to criteria 4.2 Choosing the suitable OSS for architecture
Output	· Selected OSS

Activity 5: Adjusting Criteria or High-level Architecture

Input	· If assessment criteria or high-level architecture can be adjusted
Step	5.1 Developers return to Activity 3 to negotiate with customers and adjust criteria 5.2 If criteria cannot be adjusted, developers go to Activity 2 to reconsider architecture
Output	· Adjusted assessment criteria and high-level architecture

Activity 6: Constructing In-house Products.

Input	· Requirements cannot be met by selected OSS
Step	6.1 Building in-house products for those requirements
Output	· In-house products****

****Those in-house products may be OSS or not according to the OSS' license of other part in the applications and organizations' policy.

Activity 7: Improving & Integrating OSS.

Input	· Selected OSS · In-house Product

Step	7.1 Defining Necessary Interfaces of OSS.
	7.2 Analyzing OSS' architecture, source code, and location of modification.
	7.3 Improving Code and Unit Testing.
	7.4 Integrating OSS and Integration Testing.
Output	· OBAs system

Activity 8: productizing and transiting applications.

Input	· OBAs system
Step	8.1 Doing βtest, documenting user manual
	8.2 Collecting users' feedback and fixing reported bugs.
	8.3 Transiting products to operation.
Output	· OBAs product

3.2 Important Issues in the Process

Because the special OBAs development needs should be considered, we discuss the important issues about high-level architecture design, special attributes of OSS and OSS integration of the process for meeting those special needs.

3.2.1 Designing High-Level Architecture Before Assessment

In activity 2 of the process, the OBAs were divided into modules by high-level architecture. Modularity improves maintainability of OBAs and development efficiency by adding alternative OSS.

Although OBAs' low-level architecture relies on selected OSS largely, Developers still design high-level architecture early since interfaces between OSS can be adjusted, customized, and even modified to meet particular system needs by changing source code.

Basing on requirements and currently candidate OSS, developers start to design high-level architecture. Developers will divide the desired system into a set of modules. Each module is according to a set of requirements. The degree of success of this activity is decided by developers' knowledge and experience on candidate OSS.

3.2.2 Attributes of OSS

In activity 3 of the process, attributes of OSS are used to build assessment criteria. Attributes of COTS components are suitable for OSS also if they are adjusted slightly. Furthermore, reading and changing source code in building OBAs require considering more other attributes. The stability of OSS' architecture should be considered because modularity and repairing architecture of OSS are important issues while OSS evolving. OSS' architecture instability will prevent developers to reuse OSS [2,23]. Another attribute that should be considered is the development tools of OSS. OSS' low cost has contributed to the widespread adoption of sophisticated tools [21]. Developers should accept the development tools of selected OSS if they want to change source code. Otherwise, transferring the selected OSS to their familiar development circumstance would consume many development resources. The third attribute is understandability and revisability of source code; the quality of source code is an important problem in reusing OSS [1,5,24]. Chaos in source code cuts the productivity of reading and changing source code. Beside all these attributes coming from reading and changing source code, attribute of OSS' legality should be considered too. A risk in reusing OSS is third parties' patents or other intellectual-property rights [25].

Based on COTS' attributes and OSS' particular attributes, our process uses the following set of attributes to assess OSS (Table 1).

It is very important to assign weight appropriately for every attribute based on stakeholders' agreement to facilitate the quantitative evaluation analysis later on. Detailed scales, either qualitative or quantitative, should also be defined for each criteria in order to measure candidate OSS' score with respect to that criteria.

Table 1. Attributes of OSS

Attributes of OSS	Description
Correctness of Functionality	If the functionality of OSS consists with its statement?
Flexibility of Interface	The easy degree that the OSS' interfaces can be used in different environment.
Availability/Robustness	The degree that the OSS operate correctly when using.
Installation/Upgrade Ease	The easy degree that install/upgrate the OSS within a hardware or software environment.
Security	The degree that the OSS prevents unauthorized access and harm
Portability	The easy degree that the OSS can be transferred from one environment to another.
Product Performance	OSS' performance in execution, data capacity, response time, and so on.
Functionality	The degree that the OSS fulfills function needs.
Understandability of Interface	Document quality, simplicity, and testability of development interfaces.
Ease of Use in Interface	The easy degree that developers use the OSS' interface.
Maturity	The length of time that the OSS is available and team of OSS exist.
Version Compatibility of Interface	Compatibility of interface between earlier and later versions.
Inter-Component Compatibility	The easy degree that OSS exchange data with other OSS
Training	The degree that OSS' vendor/developers provide training in using the OSS
Cost of Procurement and Maintenance	The cost of procurement and periodic maintenance
Developers' Support	Response time for problem, capacity in dealing with problem
Architecture Stability	Evolution speed of the OSS' architecture
Usability of Development Tools	The easy degree that in-house developers use the OSS' development tools
Understandability and Revisability of Source Code	Quality of source code and their documents
Legality of Source Code	The legality of OSS' source code

3.2.3 Improving and Integrating OSS

In activity 7 of the process, selected OSS and in-house products are improved and integrated to OBAs. If selected and in-house products can be integrated to fulfill customers' needs without improvement in interfaces or quality, developers integrate them and test the integrated system against defined test cases. Else, developers improve the selected OSS in interfaces or quality with custom coding.

This activity consists of the following steps, which accommodates the differences of OSS integration from COTS integration, as illustrated in Figure 2.

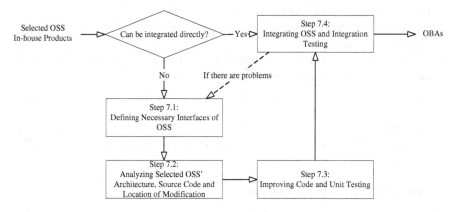

Fig. 2. Actions of Improving & Integrating OSS

Step 7.1: Defining Necessary Interfaces of OSS.

If it is needed to integrate multiple OSS with custom coding, necessary interfaces between multiple OSS should be defined according to high-level architecture.

Step 7.2: Analyzing OSS' Architecture, source code and location of modification.

Developers analyze architecture and source code of selected OSS that needs to be improved, then locate where code will be improved for implementing new interface or enhancing quality of selected OSS.

Step 7.3: Improving Code and Unit Testing.

After locating where code will be improved, developers perform code modification as needed. Then, the units testing are carried out to verify the correct modification.

Step 7.4: Integrating OSS and Integration Testing.

All OSS are integrated and OBAs are tested. If there are problems during integration, developers should enter Step 7.1 to improve the system.

4 Case Study

The case was a project of building an email system using open source software. The process introduced in Section 3 was used to build the system, which kept the project under control and end up with an extremely satisfying OBA. The most important part of the email system, Mail Transfer Agent (MTA), is used as an example to show how to assess the candidate OSS.

4.1 Identifying High-Level Requirements and Candidate OSS

After eliciting requirement from customer, the high-level requirements were identified. High-level requirements include:

1. Mail Transfer Agent (MTA) which supporting SMTP (Simple Mail Transfer Protocol) to receive and relay email.
2. To allow users to receive and send email from their remote computers, the email system supports the standard email protocols -- Interactive Message Access Protocol (IMAP4) and Post Office Protocol (POP3).
3. To allow users to receive and send email by web browser, the email system supports webmail.
4. To improving the security of the email system, the email system provides SMTP authentication and defend spam and virus by content filter.

The project restraints include platform (LINUX), cost (less than 20PM), schedule (less than 3 month), etc.

We searched current email systems and efficient authentication technologies; secure technologies; configuration technologies, etc. Then we identified a set of candidate OSS (Table 2).

4.2 Designing High-Level Architecture

High-level architecture design of the email system is illustrated in Figure 3. The high-level architecture design based on common experience of email system.

The results of sorting candidate OSS for architecture are shown in Table 2.

Table 2. Candidate OSS

Modules in High-level Architecture	Candidate OSS
MTA	Sendmail
	Postfix
	Qmail
User Authentication	Syrus SASL
	Courier
POP3/IMAP	Syrus IMAPD
	Free pop3
	Gavamail Server
	Mercur POP3 and IMAP Server
Webmail	TWIG webmail
	SQwebmail
	IMP webmail
	Open webmail
Email Database	Unified Mail Queue*****

*****This is not an OSS, but a standard for mail database. We chose the standard for keeping compatibility among modules.*

At the time, there was not an OSS offering content filter. We decided to build a content filter by in-house development.

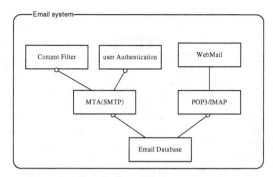

Fig. 3. High-Level Architecture of the Email System

4.3 Eliciting Requirements and Establishing Assessment Criteria

After designing high-level architecture, we elicited requirements and established assessment criteria of the email system. We first elicited low-level requirements and distributed them into modules' attributes. For an example, some functionality requirements distributed into MTA functionality attributes are shown in table 3. Then, we defined 4,000 as total weights for distributable benchmark and assigned weights to requirements basing on discussions between team members and customers. Lastly, each attributes' weights of module in high-level architecture were calculated as assessment criteria. The table 4 was an example for the assessment criteria of MTA; the last column presents corresponding weights assigned.

Table 3. An Example for Weights of Some Functionality Requirements That Were Distributed into MTA Functionality Attribute

No.	Requirements	Weights
1	Email Queue Manager	15
2	Smtpd Parameters Control	15
3	Address Verification	10
4	Maillist Support	10
5	Clients Connect Control	10
6	Relay Rules	10
7	Proxy Support	10
8	Queue Configuration	15
9	Mailbox Limit	10
10	Icp Control	10
11	Email Head Control	10
12	UCE (unsolicited commercial email) Control	15
13	Address Classes	10
14	Access Policy Delegation	10
15	Address Rewriting	10
16	Multi Domain Support	10
17	Virtual Domain Support	10
18	Log Support	10

Table 4. Assessment Criteria of MTA

No.	Attributes	Weights
1	Correctness of Functionality	150
2	Flexibility of Interface	80
3	Availability/Robustness	100
4	Installation/Upgrade Ease	60
5	Security	120
6	Portability	80
7	Product Performance	60
8	Functionality	200
9	Understandability of Interface	80
10	Ease of Use in Interface	60
11	Maturity	80
12	Version Compatibility of Interface	100
13	Inter-component Compatibility	80
14	Training	100
15	Cost of Procurement and Maintenance	80
16	Developers' Support	60
17	Architecture Stability	150
18	Usability of Development Tools	80
19	Legality of Source Code	60
20	Understandability and Revisability of Source Code	100
Total weights		**1880**

Table 5. Result of Assessing Candidate MTA

No.	OSS attributes	Scores of Candidates		
		Sendmail	Postfix	Qmail
1	Correctness of Functionality	150	150	120
2	Flexibility of Interface	60	80	80
3	Availability/Robustness	90	90	80
4	Installation/Upgrade Ease	30	50	60
5	Security	100	110	80
6	Portability	60	80	70
7	Product Performance	50	60	40
8	Functionality	180	180	160
9	Understandability of Interface	60	80	70
10	Ease of Use in Interface	40	60	50
11	Maturity	80	70	60
12	Version Compatibility of Interface	90	80	80
13	Inter-component Compatibility	70	80	80
14	Training	90	90	60
15	Cost of Procurement and Maintenance	80	80	80
16	Developers' Support	60	60	50
17	Architecture Stability	150	150	120
18	Usability of Development Tools	70	70	60
19	Legality of Source Code	60	60	60
20	Understandability and Revisability of Source Code	90	90	80
	Total	**1650**	**1720**	**1540**

4.4 Assessing Candidate OSS

We assessed the candidate OSS according to the set of assessment criteria. For an example, assessment results of MTA are shown in table 5. According to assessment result, we chose Postfix as MTA of the email system.

As the same process, we chose Cyrus IMAPD as the POP3/IMAP, Cyrus SASL as SMTP user authentication, and Sqwebmail as webmail.

4.5 Improving, Integrating OSS and Productizing

The selected OSS cannot fully meet customers' needs in content filter; therefore, after designing and implementing content filter by in-house development, we defined necessary interfaces between content filter and Postfix. At the same time, Postfix is needed to improve in Chinese language support and users configuration modules. We analyzed the architecture and source of Postfix. After analyzing, we realized those new interfaces between content filter and Postfix by coding functions such as GetHeadOfMail, GetContentOfMail, FilterMailByKeywords, FilterMailByDB, etc while improved the code in Chinese language support and users configuration modules. Then, we combined those new functions and improved code into Postfix. After unit testing and integration testing, we delivered the email system to users.

4.6 Lessons Learned

1. Building OBAs from existent OSS can cut cost, accelerate schedule, and improve quality of products. If we developed the email system from the first line code, it would use more than 200 PM based on experiential estimation. However, by using existent OSS, we cost only 15 PM to finish our product. We got an email system with high performance and security. Now it ran steadily in 2 companies.
2. OBAs' developers must select OSS carefully during building OBAs on existent OSS. Many researches in deploying OSS indicate qualities of existent OSS are irregular and functionality of them contrast clearly with each other. Our experiences in the case validate those findings.
3. During building OBAs, there are many tradeoffs among available OSS, requirements, designing, and other projects factors such as cost and schedule. Those tradeoffs aggravate the complexity of selecting OSS.
4. During building the OBAs, we adapt a strategy that we only considered stable versions of OSS in identifying candidate OSS. The benefits of the strategy are we need not consider those new versions that are validated deficiently during identifying candidate OSS. The disadvantages are we cannot fully utilize the OSS' features in new versions. We believe the strategy will induce a bit of extra works in future maintenance and upgrade of our email system.

5 Conclusions

With many excellent OSS coming forth, it is more popular that deploy OSS in business organizations. Many developers build OBAs on existent OSS instead of build them from beginning. The process of in-house development cannot work well in such scenarios.

In most case, the process that builds OBAs on existent OSS is largely similar with the process of developing CBA. Selecting correct OSS, adjusting them as needed, and integrating them are essential actions during system development lifecycle. OBAs' developers can use an analogous process with developing CBA to build OBAs. However, there is a significant difference between OSS and COTS in right and motivation of modifying source code. Therefore, developers cannot use the process of developing CBA to build OBAs directly.

Our paper offers a development process of building OBAs. The process is analogous to the process of developing CBA in emphasizing the early assessment of OSS. For difference exists between OSS and COTS, we adjusted the process of developing CBA to accommodate OBAs development in early high-level architecture design, attributes of OSS, and OSS integration. A case study is discussed to show the application of this process.

OSS community is a rapidly evolving world that complicates the OBAs development reality. As for future work, we plan to enhance the process by introducing accommodating mechanisms and strategies to address the OSS refreshment during both development phase and maintenance phase. Future experimental studies will also be performed on more projects to validate the applicability of our process and further refine it accordingly.

Acknowledgement. Work reported in this paper is supported by the National Natural Science Foundation of China under grant Nos. 60273026, 60473060 and the Hi-Tech Research and Development Program (863 Program) of China under grant Nos. 2004AA112080, 2005AA113140.

References

1. Wang, H., Wang, C.: Open Source Software Adoption: A Status Report. IEEE Software, Vol. 18, No. 2 (2004) 90-95
2. Fitzgerald, B.: A Critical Look at Open Source. IEEE Computer IEEE Software, Vol. 37, No. 7 (2004) 92-94
3. Norris, J., Kamp, P.: Mission-Critical Development with Open Source Software: Lessons Learned. IEEE Software, Vol. 21, No. 1 (2004) 42-49
4. Dedrick, J., West, J.: An Exploratory Study into Open Source Platform Adoption. Proceedings of the 37th Annual Hawaii International Conference on System Sciences. 2004
5. Madanmohan, TR., De', R.:Open Source Reuse in Commercial Firms. IEEE Software, Vol. 21, No. 6 (2004) 62 -69
6. Barros, M., Werner, C., Travassos, G.: Scenario Oriented Project Management Knowledge Reuse within a Risk Analysis Process. International Conference on Software Engineering and Knowledge Engineering (SEKE'01). (2001)
7. Yang, Y., Port, D., Boehm, B., Buhta, J., Abts, C.: Composable Process Elements for COTS-Based Applications, 5th International Workshop on Economics-Driven Software Engineering Research (EDSER-5). (2003).
8. Alves, C., Finkelstein, A.: Challenges in COTS decision-making: a goal-driven requirements engineering perspective. Proceedings of the 14th international conference on Software engineering and knowledge engineering. (2002) 789-794

9. Dean, J. Vidger, M.: COTS Software Evaluation Techniques. Proceedings of The NATO Information Systems Technology. Symposium on Commercial Off-the-shelf Products in Defence Applications. (2000).

10. Ncube, C. Maiden, N.: PORE: Procurement-Oriented Requirements Engineering Method for the Component-Based Systems Engineering Development Paradigm. International Workshop on Component-Based Software Engineering. (1999).

11. Kontio, J.: A COTS Selection Method and Experiences of Its Use. Proceedings of the 20th Annual Software Engineering Workshop. (1995).

12. Kunda, D., Brooks, L.: Applying Social-Technical Approach for COTS Selection. Proceedings of the 4th UKAIS Conference. (1999).

13. Carney, D.: COTS Evaluation in the Real World. SEI Interactive, Carnegie Mellon University,December (1998).

14. Alves, C., Castro, J.: CRE: A Systematic Method for COTS Components Selection. XV Brazilian Symposium on Software Engineering (SBES). (2001).

15. Sivzattian, S., Nuseibeh, B.: Linking the Selection of requirements to Market Value: A Portfolio-Based Approach. 7th International Workshop on Requirements Engineering: Foundation for Software Quality. (2001).

16. Basili, V., Boehm, B.: COTS Based System Top 10 List. IEEE Computer, Vol. 34, No. 5 (2001) 91-93.

17. Benguria, G., Garcia, A., Sellier, D., Tay, S.: European COTS Working Group: Analysis of the Common Problems and Current Practices of the European COTS Users. COTS-Based Software Systems (Proceedings, ICCBSS 2002), Springer Verlag, Dean, J., Gravel, A. (eds.). (2002)44-53.

18. Albert, C., Brownsword, L.: Evolutionary Process for Integrating COTS-Based Systems (EPIC): An Overview. CMU-SEI-2002-TR-009, (2002).

19. Morisio, M., Seaman, C., Parra, A., Basili, V., Kraft, S., Condon, S.: Investigating and Improving a COTS-Based Software Development Process. Proceedings of the 22nd International Conference on Software Engineering (ICSE 22). (2000) 32-41.

20. Capiluppi, A., Lago, P., Morisio, M.: Characteristics of Open Source Projects. Proceedings of the 7th European Conference on Software Maintenance and Reengineering(CSMR 2003). (2003)317-328

21. Spinellis, D., Szyperski, C.: How Is Open Source Affecting Software Development?. IEEE Software (Vol. 21, No. 1): (2004)28-33.

22. Boehm. B., Abts, C., Brown, A.W., Chulani, S., Clark,B., Horowitz, E., Madachy, R., Reifer, D., Steece,B.: Software Cost Estimation with COCOMO II. Prentice Hall. (2000).

23. Tran, J., Godfrey, M., Lee, E., Holt, R.: Architectural Repair of Open Source Software. Proceedings of the 2000 International Workshop on Program Comprehension (IWPC'00). (2000)

24. Godfrey, M., Tu, Q.: Evolution in open source software: A case study. Proceedings of the International Conference on Software Maintenance (ICSM'00). (2000) 131-142

25. Ruffin, M., Ebert, C.: Using Open Source Software in Product Development: A Primer. IEEE Software, Vol. 21, No. 1(2004)82-86

A Study on the Distribution and Cost Prediction of Requirements Changes in the Software Life-Cycle

Chengying Mao, Yansheng Lu, and Xi Wang

College of Computer Science and Technology,
Huazhong University of Science and Technology, 430074 Wuhan P.R. China
maochy@yeah.net

Abstract. Software development is a dynamic process. Requirements change (RC) is inevitable and brings great challenges to the software development. How to precisely predict requirements change is especially important in the field of requirements engineering. In this paper, an assessment framework for the factors of RCs' distribution is constructed firstly. Apart from the rough prediction method based on the statistic process control of RCs, an artificial neural network method for predicting RCs' distribution is presented. In this case, the weight of each factor is calculated by a fuzzy logic method, called experts ranking. Furthermore, we propose a model to pre-evaluate the cost caused by RCs. With some practical projects data, a validation experiment has been drawn, whose result shows that our method and model are practical and efficient to predict the distribution and cost of RCs.

1 Introduction

With the rapid increase of size and complexity of software systems, the difficulty resulting from requirements change becomes outstanding and greatly bothers software developers. They profoundly understand the claim made by Fred Broochs [1], "The hardest single part of building a software system is deciding precisely what to build". The status of requirements analysis and definition in the whole software development life-cycle is increasingly significant, which directly influences the success of the development. As a result of that, the *Requirements Engineering* (RE), a newly occurring subject which mainly focusing on the study of software requirements appears. In the recent years, RE becomes one of the hottest issues in the fields of software engineering all over the world.

Generally speaking, RE is an engineering of implementing the requirements analysis. Requirements analysis refers to revising the unformulated requirements statements into the detailed requirements definition, even formulizing it into requirements specification. It is noted that requirements analysis is not always for good. Software development is a dynamic process. This often causes software requirements to change while development is still in progress. Though there are plenty of effective and applicable techniques, tools and methods used for capturing and managing requirements [2,3], software requirements inevitably change throughout system development and maintenance process. These changes are driven by several factors, including system complexity, techniques, market demands and government regulation

M. Li, B. Boehm, and L.J. Osterweil (Eds.): SPW 2005, LNCS 3840, pp. 136–150, 2005.

[4]. Requirements change makes it so hard to estimate the schedule and cost of a project that the product quality is uncontrollable, which brings great challenges to the project [5,6,7]. As a consequence, we need to identify a better approach to manage the impacts of continuously changing requirements. We believe that the sufficient measurement and precise prediction are the most important steps towards better and effective managing requirements change.

In this paper we analyze the main factors resulting in the requirements change firstly. Secondly, we discuss their quantitative evaluation in experts ranking approach, and apply the *Artificial Neural Network* (ANN) to predict the distribution of requirements change in the software life-cycle. According to the distribution, we evaluate the cost of software development produced by the requirements change.

The rest of the paper is organized as follows: In the next section, it is a brief overview of the recent software requirements change researches, and a simple introduction of the ANN is displayed. In Section 3, the methods of predicting the requirements changes occurring throughout the entire software development process are discussed. Based on the content of Section 3, the method of evaluating requirements change cost is introduced in Section 4. In Section 5, we use a case study to validate the correctness and feasibility of our methods. Section 6 presents the conclusion and future work in this area.

2 Background

2.1 Software Requirements Change

Requirements analysis is particularly a complex task. It requires developers have the knowledge of management and psychology as well as proficient skills. Software projects often start at the time when the requirement is not obvious and complete enough [7,8]. Even though the intention is for software requirements specifications to be captured and formed correctly in the initial stage of development, there are still some other inevitable factors that will lead to the requirements change throughout the entire process of development and maintenance. We name this change as the *Requirements Change* (RC), and *Requirements Volatility* (RV) is the rate of RC. The formal definitions of them can be presented as follows:

Definition 1. Requirements Change *is the number of changes (addition, deletion, and modification) in a given period of development life-cycle, and* Requirements Volatility *is the ratio of changes to the total number of requirements.*

According to the occurrence of changing the requirements, RCs can be classified into two categories [9]: (1) Pre-SRS RC, which refers to the requirement modification before the complete software requirements document is fixed (at the early stage of software development), (2) Post-SRS RC, which occurs during the later phases of software development (i.e. design, coding, testing and maintenance). We argue that the former type of RC is constructive while the second is possibly destructive because it is claimed that it will affect the productivity of the software development process, scope creep and the quality of final product. For instance, the rate of the progress is hard to control, so the cost of the project is hard to budget. In this paper, we focus on the study of post-SRS RC. The RC in the following parts all refers to the second one.

Recently there are quite a few investigations concerning the requirements change and its influence. T. Hall et al. [10] made a survey by having an informal discussion with developers, project managers and senior managers from twelve software companies. They found that most of the RCs were caused by the organization instead of the techniques, and the maturity of a company had a close relation with the pattern of requirements. Via E-mail from the 430 software corporations in Australia, Didar Zowghi et al. [9] discovered that the requirements change had a great impact on the expiration of the project process as well as the finance overspending. They also pointed out two key factors influencing the RC: One is the communication between software users and developers, the other is the method of requirements analysis and modeling. N Nurmuliani et al. [6] had another point, they analyzed the requirements changes in the life-cycle of a system called GDS and concluded three important factors of RC: (1) Customers' needs (market demands); (2) Developers' understanding of the software product domain; (3) The change of the organization policy. N. F. Schneidewind et al. [11] made a detailed discussion about the risk of the software reliability and maintainability from the RC.

At present, studies concerning the analysis of RCs distribution and prediction are rare. Q. Wang employs the *Statistic Process Control* (SPC) to make a statistic for the historical projects information [12]. It can discover the statistical distribution of RCs in some specific software development organizations and enable the guidance of the RC prediction of a new project (the method will be introduced in Section 4), but it is lack of self-adaptability. In summary, the analysis of RCs in software project development mainly focuses on the software productivity, software releases, or on its impact on an isolated phase [11,13,14,15]. We apply the model ANN to predict the RCs distribution in each stage of software development life-cycle. Based on that, we propose a cost assessment model for the RCs.

2.2 Artificial Neural Network

ANN is a newly mathematical model grounded on the biological neural systems of modern science. It has many favorable properties, such as intelligent, self-adaptive, learning ability and so on. Due to these good characteristics, it has gradually been applied in the field of software engineering and achieved better effect [16,17,18,19]. For example, Charles Anderson et al. [18] applied ANN to direct the optimization of test suite. Reun Kumat et al. [19] also employed the ANN to evaluate the quality of software.

Back-propagation (BP) [20] is the most popular training algorithm for multilayer neural networks. Except input and output layers, BP network has one or more hidden layers. The network training is gained by a two-stage learning algorithm, i.e., forward pass and backward pass. The forward pass propagates the input vector $X=(x_1, x_2, ..., x_n)$ through the nodes of hidden layers until it reaches the output layer $Y=(y_1, y_2, ..., y_m)$ (see Figure 1). In the second stage of network training, the output error propagates backward to update network weights. BP network is a highly non-linear mapping system from input-end to output-end, i.e., $f: R^n \rightarrow R^m$, $f(X)=Y$. The Kolmogrov's theorem tells us that any continuous function can be accurately approximated by a three-layer BP network [20]. Here, we adopt the three-layer BP network to predict the distribution of RCs in each stage of software life-cycle.

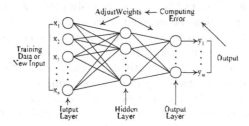

Fig. 1. Basic configuration of the BP network

3 Prediction of Requirements Changes

3.1 Factors of Requirements Change

The inducements of RC are various, which involve a number of factors such as technology, management, work environment and psychology science. The analysis of the factors causing requirements change is the effective measures to avoid changes, especially good for the prediction of the frequency and distribution of RCs. So called frequency of RCs is the ratio of the number of RCs to the total number of requirements. There are plenty of studies involved in the RCs' causation. One style employs the statistical analysis from the *Change Request* (CR) [21] of systems in practice [6]. The other gains the main factors by the conversation or poll from the developers or project managers [10]. Our major task is to reflect the factors that lead the frequency of RC to change, but the change reasons of RCs' distribution have something with causation of RCs. Grounded on the conclusions of references [4,6,8,9,10,14,22], we attribute the factors relating to the change of RCs' frequency and distribution to four major factors: (1) Project character, (2) software developers' condition, (3) users' condition and (4) project management. Each factor is composed of a set of items, and each item is presented in the quantitative form of the *difficulty coefficient*. In other words, it shows the possibilities of project failure risk caused by that item. Its value can be evaluated by the developers, administrators and experts in software engineering.

3.1.1 Factor of Project Character

The major feature of a software project under investigation is its ultimate size. It is often characterized by the number of code lines, the size of the source files and so on. We employ the predicted number of sub-systems (also called modules) to measure the project. The prediction result is highly reliable because the alteration of the number of main functional modules is rare after the completion of the requirements analysis. In general, we consider that the difficulty coefficient increases with the number of modules. The subsequent feature is the number of manpower. Generally speaking, it is fit for about three persons to participate in one sub-system, but the granularity can be adjusted according to the practical situation. If the number of participants per module is more or less than the average, the difficulty coefficient will increase. Suppose the total number of the persons involved in a project is P, and the number of predicted sub-systems is M, we can use the formula $|P/M - 3|$ to calculate the difficulty. The amount of the available budget (especially in the phase of requirements analysis) is also one of the factors affecting project. The more sufficient cost is provided, the lower the difficulty coefficient is. Furthermore, the techniques applied in the project and techniques risk also do influence the RC, as well as the technology accumulation in the past. If the system has preferable reuse resources (e.g. source codes, project documents, development experience, etc.), it will decrease the risk of RC.

Some projects are forced to end up curtly due to the pressure from the limitation of schedule budget, so it is very necessary to make assessment of the sufficiency of requirements analysis activity. Here we use the style of developers' self-evaluation. The sufficiency of requirements analysis increases while the risk of RC decreases. The details of project character are as follows, weight of significance is referred to the RC risk of each sub-item.

Table 1. The guideline of assessing project character

No.	Sub-items	Difficulty coefficient	Weight
1	The number of sub-systems (or modules)	0.2(≤10), 0.4(10~20), 0.6 (20~30), 0.8(30~40), 1.0 (>40)	0.2
2	Total number of developers	0.2, 0.4, 0.6, 0.8, 1.0	0.1
3	Project budget	0, 0.5, 1.0	0.05
4	Complexity of techniques and its risk	0, 0.5, 1.0	0.15
5	Reusable resource	0, 0.5, 1.0	0.2
6	Sufficiency of requirements analysis	0.2, 0.4, 0.6, 0.8, 1.0	0.3

3.1.2 Factor of Developers

Similar to the classification in Section 3.1.1, the factor of developers can also be divided into six sub-items: (1) Developers' experience, that is to say, development-years they experienced and their ages, we can notice that the age between twenty and thirty-five is the best period to employ software development. On the other hand, it reflects that developers with more experience take the lower RC risk. (2) The condition of mastering development approaches and tools. If developers are familiar with the approaches and tools, it will help them to consider project's requirements more comprehensively. (3) The familiarity with the business knowledge. (4) The experience training for project development, such as requirements analysis strategies and methods of writing requirements documents. (5) Degree of communication between developers and users. It can be evaluated from the aspects of the times of interviews and the capability of interactions. We conclude that bad communication leads to great challenge to RC. (6) Internal communication and cooperation in development team.

Table 2. The guideline of assessing factor of developers

No.	Sub-items	Difficulty coeff.	Weight
1	Developers' experiences	0.2, 0.4, 0.6, 0.8, 1.0	0.15
2	Familiarity with development approaches and tools	0, 0.5, 1.0	0.1
3	Familiarity with the business knowledge	0.2, 0.4, 0.6, 0.8, 1.0	0.2
4	The training for development	0, 0.5, 1.0	0.1
5	Degree of communication	0.2, 0.4, 0.6, 0.8, 1.0	0.3
6	Internal communication and cooperation	0.2, 0.4, 0.6, 0.8, 1.0	0.15

3.1.3 Factor of Users

The influences to RC distribution caused by the users can be precisely categorized as following: (1) The span of their occupations and working experiences. Their sufficient understanding of the business is advantageous to the software development. (2) The definitude of users' requirements goal. The more explicit goal means the more sufficient in early requirements analysis. (3) Internal negotiation and consistency of the requirements. When sufficient internal negotiation and the consistency of requirements are achieved, we define the difficulty coefficient as 0. Otherwise the coefficient is 0.5 or 1.0. (4) The enthusiasm of the participation. If the users are against the project, the difficulty coefficient will be defined as 1.0. (5) The extent of the users' mastery of computer knowledge. The difficulty coefficient will rise when the users know little about the relative computer skills. (6) The users' satisfaction at the initial requirements specification documents. There will be few changes in the later stages if the initial documents are fit for the users' taste.

Table 3. The guideline of assessing factor of users

No.	Sub-items	Difficulty coeff.	Weight
1	Working experience	0.2, 0.4, 0.6, 0.8, 1.0	0.1
2	Definitude of users' requirements goal	0.2, 0.4, 0.6, 0.8, 1.0	0.25
3	Internal negotiation and consistency	0, 0.5, 1.0	0.2
4	Enthusiasm of the participation	0, 0.5, 1.0	0.1
5	Mastery of computer knowledge	0, 0.5, 1.0	0.05
6	Satisfaction at the initial specification	0.2, 0.4, 0.6, 0.8, 1.0	0.3

3.1.4 Factor of Project Management

Similarly, the factor of project management has five measurement indexes shown as follows.

Table 4. The guideline of assessing factor of project management

No.	Sub-items	Difficulty coeff.	Weight
1	Sufficiency of requirements inspection	0.2, 0.4, 0.6, 0.8, 1.0	0.4
2	Configuration of requirements tools	0.2, 0.4, 0.6, 0.8, 1.0	0.2
3	Formalization of requirements documents	0.2, 0.4, 0.6, 0.8, 1.0	0.2
4	Configuration management for RC	0, 0.5, 1.0	0.1
5	Rationality of organization and management	0.2, 0.4, 0.6, 0.8, 1.0	0.1

The above table provides a quantitative framework for evaluating the factors which will influence the frequency and distribution of RCs. The factors and their sub-items can be adjusted on the basis of the actual situation of software development organizations. This framework is a combination of existing research results and our accumulated experience during information systems development. More detailed evaluation framework can be constructed by the correlation analysis which is presented in Reference [11]. Furthermore, the correlation analysis technique can also be applied to merge some closely related sub-items.

3.2 Method of Predicting RC

RCs are affected by various factors. But as for specific software development organization, the RCs' frequency and distribution still follow some rules in the sense of statistics. Based on the employment of the statistical analysis and ANN learning on the related historical data of RCs, we can easily predict the distribution of RCs. For constructing a prediction model of RCs, we give the following assumptions:

➢ Assume the recorded data are from the software development processes in which exists some relativity. For example, they are all derived from the information system under development. In general, the projects developed by a software organization are almost under a similar background.

➢ Assume the granularity of all requirement items is comparative. Software companies usually have referential standards for their developers so that the granularity can't be of great difference.

➢ Assume all projects under analysis are not groping, because this type of projects is too indeterminate to make a rational prediction.

From the assumptions mentioned above, it is easy for us to conclude that the data used for analysis can't be collected from different development organizations. In other words, a company's historical data can't be used to predict another's RCs. Here we will address two approaches for the prediction.

3.2.1 Prediction of RCs' Distribution Based on SPC

Wang's study demonstrated that [12]: (1) For a software organization, the frequency of RCs is a relatively steady value when its capability of software process is mature. (2) The distribution of RCs has a relatively stable statistical rule. Based on their research, we can adopt a method for predicting RCs as below: Firstly, we calculate the average value μ_p of the RCs' frequency of previous projects, and set the number of original requirement items as N_{or}, so the probable number of RCs is $N_{rc} = \mu_p \cdot N_{or}$. Secondly, we get the distributed proportions of RCs in each stage of development processes, that is, the design, coding, testing and maintenance. As a consequence, we can get the number of probable RCs in each stage.

This approach is easy to operate. But the capability of software organizations is constantly upgrading, and the early distribution can't well reflect current condition, i.e., this approach belongs to static prediction. The improvement is to use the most of the latest data to execute statistical analysis. We'll introduce a dynamic and self-adaptive approach to the prediction in the next sub-section.

3.2.2 RC Prediction Based on ANN

As illustrated in Section 3.1, four factors play crucial roles in the distribution of RCs. Hence, it is necessary to present a quantitative evaluation for these factors. In this paper, we apply the method of experts ranking to quantify them. Assume the risk values resulting from the *Project Character* (PC), *Developers' Condition* (DC), *Users' Condition* (UC) and *Project Management* (PM) are V_{pc}, V_{dc}, V_{uc}, V_{pm} respectively. The process of quantitative evaluation is as following: Take the PC for example, suppose PC has n sub-items, and the weight of each sub-item is w_i *($1 \leq i \leq n$)*. We choose m experienced ones from the project developers or administrators as "judge experts". An evaluation matrix R corresponding to this factor can be produced by ranking each sub-item when the assessment framework in Section 3.1 is referenced.

$$R = \begin{bmatrix} r_{11} & r_{12} & \cdots & r_{1m} \\ r_{21} & r_{22} & \cdots & r_{2m} \\ \vdots & \vdots & \ddots & \vdots \\ r_{n1} & r_{n2} & \cdots & r_{nm} \end{bmatrix} (r_{ij} \in [0,1], 1 \le i \le n, 1 \le j \le m)$$

Then associating with weight of each sub-item, the quantitative result of the factor PC can be drawn as follows:

$$V_{pc} = \frac{1}{m} \sum_{i=1}^{n} (w_i \sum_{j=1}^{m} r_{ij}) \tag{1}$$

Obviously, the value of V_{pc} is between 0 and 1. For instance, the probable RCs risk caused by the factor PC in a project is described as below:

$$R = \begin{bmatrix} 0.4 & 0.4 & 0.6 & 0.4 & 0.4 \\ 0.6 & 0.2 & 0.4 & 0.4 & 0.2 \\ 0 & 0 & 0 & 0.5 & 0 \\ 0.5 & 0.5 & 1.0 & 0.5 & 0.5 \\ 0.5 & 0.5 & 0.5 & 0 & 0.5 \\ 0.4 & 0.2 & 0.4 & 0.4 & 0.2 \end{bmatrix}$$

Well then, V_{pc}=(0.2*2.2+0.1*1.8+0.15*3+0.2*2+0.3*1.6)/5=0.395. The value of V_{dc}, V_{uc} and V_{pm} can also be calculated by the formula (1). Generally speaking, larger values represent greater occurrence possibility of RCs. The evaluation activity should be synchronous with project development, that is, it is required to make a detailed assessment after the completion of requirements specification documents. When a project is accomplished, we can adjust part of sub-items so as to prepare the prediction for the next project.

We put the above assessment values and N_{or} together as the input of ANN, i.e., $X=(V_{pc}, V_{dc}, V_{uc}, V_{pm}, N_{or})$. The output of ANN is composed of the RCs distribution values in the four stages (i.e., design, coding, testing and maintenance). It is denoted as following: $Y=(N_d, N_c, N_t, N_m)$. We choose the Sigmoid function as the mapping from input layer nodes to hidden layer nodes, such as $f(x) = 1/(1+e^{-x})$. And a linear function is used to relate the hidden layer with output layer.

The prediction of RCs' distribution can be carried out in two steps: Step1, learning phase. Collect the correlative data of previous projects as the input and output vectors respectively, then to train the network. Step 2, prediction phase. When the error of the network reaches a convergent point, we put the data of current project (i.e., V_{pc}, V_{dc}, V_{uc}, V_{pm} and N_{or}) into the network to calculate the number of the possible RCs in each stage after requirements analysis. The whole process of RCs prediction is shown in Figure 2.

As shown in the formula (1), the decision of sub-items' weight is very important. The value in Table 1~4 is only for reference. The difference of the sub-items' weightiness in a factor is merely qualitative, so the assignment on instinct is generally inaccurate. But we can adopt the method of *Analytical Hierarchy Process* (AHP), which has been used for deciding the weight of software quality characteristics in [23], to weight sub-items. This method contains consistency check, so the judgement error is in an acceptable level.

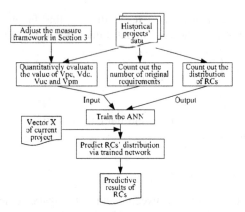

Fig. 2. ANN prediction framework for the RCs distribution

The significant advantage of the prediction approach based on ANN is the ability of dynamic self-adaptive learning. This approach not only makes good use of the statistical rules of RCs' distribution in the historical projects, but also reflects the maturity enhancement of the software organization. Figure 2 shows that it depends on the developers' self-assessment of four factors during the software development. As a consequence, the implementation of this approach can accelerate the quantitative and normative representation for project management, which is in accordance with the demand of the level 4 in CMM [24].

4   Pre-evaluation of the Cost for RC

Although to ascertain the RCs' distribution in each stage of software life-cycle is very important, the management of the cost caused by RCs is also unable to be neglected. Existing research on RC cost only concentrates on one specific stage, or the reliability and maintenance risk. Under such condition, we propose a prediction model for the additional cost caused by RCs.

4.1   Taxonomy of Requirements Changes

There are a few ways used to classify the RCs [6], such as by the RC's reason, or by the change origin etc. Here we mainly concentrate on the RC's change types. The taxonomy to classify the change requests is in terms of:

  ◆ *Requirement addition*: adding a requirement to make up for the omission or meet the customers' requirements;

  ◆ *Requirement deletion*: deleting or removing existing requirements from the business strategy or the requirements redundancy;

  ◆ *Requirement modification*: modifying requirements owing to technical restrict or design improvement. This case doesn't include the rewording of requirements text which is not essential modification.

It is insufficient for us to predict the RC cost only by the RCs' distribution in each stage. It also needs to know the number of each RC type. ANN's prediction ability depends on the training on historical data, so it is important to get RC number of the three types mentioned above in each stage. It can be dealt with under the following two conditions: (1) If the software organization puts good RCs management in practice, the number can be gained from the data analysis framework mentioned in [6]. (2) As for those organizations without requirements management, the number of three RC types can only be worked out by comparing the requirements specifications, detail design documents, testing documents and maintenance documents. Of course, the second case is not as accurate as the first.

For a stage following requirements analysis, such as design, coding and testing etc., we should construct another ANN to predict the number of each RC type. The input is the same as the network in Section 3.2, while the output is modified to the proportion of three RC types, i.e., $Y = (t_a, t_d, t_m)$, where t_a, t_d and t_m represent the rate of the requirement addition, deletion and modification respectively, and $t_a+t_d+t_m=1$. The prediction process is also divided into two steps as above. The number of each type can be calculated via referring the proportion and the total RC number in this stage.

4.2 Model of RC Cost Pre-evaluation

There are many models of software cost estimation at present. Among them the models of *COCOMOII* [25] and *GOM/CGOM* [26,27] are widely accepted. But it is a pity that they all ignore the cost caused by RCs. According to the classification of RCs, we apply ANN to predict the number of each RC type in each stage respectively, then pre-evaluate the RC cost in the whole software life-cycle. The total RC cost (C) consists of the additional cost caused by RCs in the phases of Design (C_d), Coding (C_c), Testing (C_t) and Maintenance (C_m), i.e., $C=C_d+C_c+C_t+C_m$. We discuss each one as follows:

(1) The calculation of C_d: During the phase of detailed design, the requirements specification documents are analyzed and classified to establish a detailed implementation plan. The endeavor of requirement addition, deletion and modification is nearly equivalent, so it is not necessary to distinguish them. In this case, we denote the extra cost for a RC as α, so the RC cost in the design stage is

$$C_d = \alpha \cdot N_d \tag{2}$$

(2) C_c: Unlike the design stage, the cost of realizing requirement addition, deletion and modification is different in the phase of coding. Generally, the additional cost of a requirement modification is the biggest, denoted as β_m. And the cost of addition (β_a) takes the second place, the least is the deletion cost (β_d), i.e., $\alpha<\beta_d<\beta_a<\beta_m$. So the RC cost in the coding stage can be calculated by the following formula.

$$C_c = \beta_a \cdot t_a \cdot N_c + \beta_d \cdot t_d \cdot N_c + \beta_m \cdot t_m \cdot N_c = (\beta_a \cdot t_a + \beta_d \cdot t_d + \beta_m \cdot t_m)N_c \tag{3}$$

(3) C_t: It is similar to the coding stage. The additional costs for each requirement addition, deletion and modification are noted as γ_a, γ_d and γ_m ($\gamma_d <\gamma_a <\gamma_m$) respectively. And there is such a relation: $\beta_a<\gamma_a, \beta_d<\gamma_d, \beta_m<\gamma_m$. Hence,

$$C_t = (\gamma_a \cdot t_a' + \gamma_d \cdot t_d' + \gamma_m \cdot t_m')N_t \tag{4}$$

(4) C_m: The maintenance is more complex than the above three stages. In general, only a part of project maintainers are developers, or even they are all not developers.

When RCs happen, the foremost thing is to understand the correlative parts with changes. We adopt an approach proposed in [28] to quantify the degree of changes comprehension. It proceeds in two aspects: *Software Understanding Increment* (SU) and *Programmer Unfamiliarity* (UNFM). SU is determined by maintainers' self-assessment on the facets of documents and source code. Each facet is divided into five ranks (the value ranges from 0.1 to 0.5). The higher value represents the worse understanding, and vice versa. The last value of SU is the average of their evaluations on both facets. The value of UNFM is expressed quantitatively in Table 5.

Table 5. Rating scale for programmer unfamiliarity (UNFM)

UNFM increment	Level of unfamiliarity
0.0	Completely familiar
0.2	Mostly familiar
0.4	Somewhat familiar
0.6	Considerably familiar
0.8	Mostly unfamiliar
1.0	Completely unfamiliar

The difference between C_m and C_t is merely the increment produced by the SU and UNFM, because the modifications in these two stages are all made for a completed system.

$$C_m = (\gamma_a \cdot t_a " + \gamma_d \cdot t_d " + \gamma_m \cdot t_m ")(1 + SU \cdot UNFM)N_m \qquad (5)$$

The factors we considered may be insufficient, so the above is only a rough pre-evaluate model of RC cost at present.

5   Case Study

In order to validate the methods of predicting RCs' distribution and cost, a case study was employed with the projects' data of our laboratory in the recent two years. The survey of the six selected projects is shown in the Table 6.

The risk weights of factors that will possibly influence the RCs' distribution in each project are determined by the self-assessments of developers and administrators. Among them, the risk values of the first four projects are evaluated following the completion of the project, while the latter two are given in development process. The RCs' distribution of a project is calculated by the statistic analysis of CR data, which will be described in Table 7.

While validating the prediction method of RCs' distribution, the data of the former five projects were picked up to train the BP network. While the network was stable, we used it to predict the RCs' distribution of the sixth project. The experiment was drawn in the environment of Matlab 7.0 and adopted the 5×35×4 BP Network, whose configurative parameters were as follows: $epochs=2\times10^4$, $goal=0.005$, $min\_grad=1.0\times10^{-10}$, $mu\_max=1.0\times10^8$. Because the initial value of network's weight is assigned randomly by the Matlab neural network toolbox, it can't ensure the error convergence

Table 6. Descriptions of the projects for case study

Projects	Description	Development tools
jxhd	A network charging system in Hongdu Air-port	VC, PB, SQL Server
hustmis	An educational administration and students work management system in HUST	PB, JSP, EAServer, SQL Server
lamis	An instrument & assets management system in HUST	PB, .NET, SQL Server
gzsf	A decision support system (DSS) in Guang-zhou bureau of water conservancy	.NET, PB, Oracle, Arcinfo
fcms	A realty management system	Delphi, .NET, SQL Server
whsw	A DSS of a bureau of water resource	similar to (4)

Table 7. RCs' factors and their distribution of projects

Projects	V_{pc}	V_{dc}	V_{uc}	V_{pm}	N_{or}	N_d	N_c	N_t	N_m
jxhd	0.402	0.470	0.255	0.550	45	2	3	2	1
hustmis	0.775	0.652	0.780	0.412	372	34	22	28	21
lamis	0.560	0.640	0.725	0.605	295	20	13	29	24
gzsf	0.285	0.305	0.232	0.260	264	6	5	4	2
fcms	0.325	0.402	0.265	0.300	67	3	2	1	1
whsw	0.395	0.255	0.385	0.300	281	12	9	8	4

of each training. We have to make sure that the error of adopted network is conver-gent. Consequently, the predictive result is: $N_d'=11$, $N_c'=7$, $N_t'=9$, $N_m'=5$. In contrast with Table 7, it is obvious that the RCs' distribution predicted by the ANN is much more precise.

In a similar way, we can apply ANN to predict the number of the three change types in the project *whsw*. Combined with the RC cost prediction model mentioned in Section 4, the project cost increment resulted from the RCs can be worked out. The pre-evaluation's parameters are as following: $\alpha=0.5$, $(\beta_a, \beta_d, \beta_m)=(1.5, 0.5, 2.0)$, $(\gamma_a, \gamma_d, \gamma_m)=(1.8, 1.0, 3.0)$, $SU=0.4$, $UNFM=0.8$.

The results of the pre-evaluation are shown in the row 4 of Table 8. Row 3 indi-cates the extra cost compared with the plan during the practical development. Here, we measure the cost by the scale of person-day (p-d for short). From the comparison we can conclude that the results of the pre-evaluation are reasonable. Because RC is only on reason for cost increase, the RC cost is generally less than the practical cost increment. However, RC plays the most important role in the cost increase, so the two cost increments (predictive and practical) are quite close to each other.

Table 8. Cost increment comparison between the predictive and the practical

RCs & relevant cost	N_d (add.,del.,mod.)			N_c (a., d., m.)			N_t (a., d., m.)			N_m (a., d., m.)		
Num. of predictive RCs	8	2	1	2	1	4	2	1	6	1	0	4
Num. of practical RCs	7	3	2	4	1	4	0	1	7	0	0	4
Predictive RC cost (p-d)	5			11.5			22.6			18.2		
Practical RC cost (p-d)	6			14			24			25		

6 Conclusions and Future Work

In the entire process of software development and maintenance, requirements may evolve constantly. Requirements changes have a significant impact on software project uncertainty, in particular the scopes of schedule overrun and cost overrun. This indicates that requirements change still remains a challenging problem in the field of software engineering. This paper concentrates on the study of prediction of RC distribution and its cost pre-evaluation. Based on the analysis of RC factors in the existing literatures and the investigations on information systems developments of our laboratory, an assessment framework for the factors of RCs' distribution is made. It employs a fuzzy logic method, named experts ranking, to ensure the quantitative results convincible. Subsequently, an ANN method used to predict the RCs' distribution is presented. Following the predictive distribution, a model for evaluating the RC cost is proposed. In addition, we apply some historical data from practical projects to validate them. The results show that ANN is feasible to predict the RCs' distribution, and the RC cost pre-evaluation model is also precise.

This paper only offers some insights based on the exploratory research into the aspect of the RC prediction and its cost evaluation, the proposed framework and model need to be further specified. A critical review of our methods highlights some directions for future research: (1) Apart from ANN, some traditional prediction methods can be also adopted to assist the RCs' prediction. The method of curve fitting has been used to carry out the above experiment, and the result shows that the precision of curve fitting is nearly equivalent to that of ANN when the data set is small. The reason of this phenomenon is that the small data set is not sufficient for training the network. However, the ANN is superior to the curve fitting when training set is adequate. (2) The sensitivity analysis can be employed on the data in Table 7 to get the primary factors that cause the change of RCs' distribution. This is of great benefit to improve the process management of software organizations. (3) The input and output patterns of the neural network need to be further explored. Then a more precise network model can be acquired.

Acknowledgements

This work was supported in part by the Defense Pre-Research Project of the "Tenth Five-Year-Plan" of China under Grant No.41315.9.2, and the Defense Pre-Research Project of the Navy Equipment Ministry under Grant No.10104010201. We'd like to thank all project developers and managers from our laboratory for their support of this research.

References

1. Brooks, F.: The Mythical Man-month: Essays on Software Engineering (2nd edition). Addison-Wesley Publisher, Boston MA (1995) 179–203
2. Zhang, J. Z., Xu, J. F.: Advances in Requirements Engineering. Journal of Computer Research and Development, Vol. 35, No. 1. Science Press, Beijing (1998) 1–5 (in Chinese)

3. Lu, M., Li, M. S.: Review of Methods and Tools of Software Requirements Engineering. Journal of Computer Research and Development, Vol. 36, No. 11. Science Press, Beijing (1999) 1289–1300 (in Chinese)

4. Barry, E. J., Mukhopadhyay, T., Slaughter, S. A.: Software Project Duration and Effort: An Empirical Study. Information Technology and Management, Vol. 3, No. 1–2. Inderscience Publishers, Switzerland (2002) 113–136

5. The Standish Group: CHAOS: A Recipe for Success. (1999) (www.standishgroup.com/sample_research/PDFpages/chaos1999.pdf)

6. Nurmuliani, N., Zowghi, D., Powell, S.: Analysis of Requirements Volatility during Software Development Life Cycle. In: Proc. of the 2004 Australian Software Engineering Conference (ASWEC'04). IEEE Press, New York (2004) 28–37

7. Krasner, H.: Requirements Dynamics in Large Software Projects. In: Proc. of the 11th World Computer Congress (IFIP'89). Elsevier Science Publishers B.V., Amsterdam (1989) 211–216

8. Christel, M., Kang, K.: Issues in Requirements Elicitation. TR.CMU/SEI-92-TR-12, Carnegie Mellon University, Pittsburgh (1992)

9. Zowghi, D., Nurmuliani, N.: A Study of the Impact of Requirements Volatility on Software Project Performance. In: Proc. of the 9th Asia-Pacific Software Engineering Conference (APSEC'02). IEEE Press, New York (2002) 3–11

10. Hall, T., Beecham, S., Rainer, A.: Requirements Problems in Twelve Software Companies: An Empirical Analysis. IEE Proc. of Software Engineering, Vol. 149, No. 5. IEEE Press, New York (2002) 153–160

11. Schneidewind, N. F.: Investigation of the Risk to Software Reliability and Maintainability of Requirements Changes. In: Proc. of IEEE International Conference on Software Maintenance. IEEE Press, New York (2001) 127–136

12. Wang, Q., Li, M. S.: Measurement of Software Requirement Based on SPC. Chinese Journal of Computers, Vol. 26, No. 10. Science Press, Beijing (2003) 1312–1317 (in Chinese)

13. Lane, M., Cavaye, A.: Management of Requirements Volatility Enhances Software Development Productivity. In: Proc. of the 3rd Australian Conference on Requirements Engineering (ACRE'98). Deakin University Press, Geelong (1998)

14. Stark, G., Oman, P., Skillicorn, A., et al.: An Examination of the Effects of Requirements Changes on Software Maintenance Releases. Journal of Software Maintenance: Research and Practice. Vol. 11, No.5. John Wiley & Sons, Inc., Hoboken, NJ (1999) 293–309

15. Malaiya, Y. K., Denton, J.: Requirements Volatility and Defect Density. In: Proc. of the 10th International Symposium on Software Reliability Engineering. IEEE Press, New York (1999) 285–294

16. Idri, A., Mbarki, S., Abran, A.: Validating and Understanding Software Cost Estimation Models based on Neural Networks. In: Proc. of 2004 International Conference on Information and Communication Technologies: From Theory to Applications. IEEE Press, New York (2004) 433–434

17. Yang, G. X., Gao, D. Q., Song, G. X.: An Overall Evaluating Method for Software Qualities Based on Neural Networks. Journal of East China University of Science and Technology, Vol. 30, No.3. East China University Press, Press (2004) 292–295 (in Chinese)

18. Anderson, C., Mayrhauser, A., Tom, C.: Assessing Neural Networks as Guides for Testing Activities. In: Proc. of the 3rd International Software Metrics Symposium. IEEE Press, New York (1996) 155–165

19. Kumar, R., Rai, S., Trahan, J. L.: Neural Network Techniques for Software Quality Evaluation. In: Proc. of Annual Reliability and Maintainability Symposium. IEEE Press, New York (1998) 155–161

20. Hagan, M. T., Demuth, H. B., Beale, M.: Neural Network Design. PWS Publishing Company, Boston MA (1996)

21. Crnkovic, I., Funk, P., Larsson, M.: Processing Requirements by Software Configuration Management. In: Proc. of 25th EUROMICRO Conference, Vol. 2. IEEE Press, New York (1999) 260–265
22. Javed, T., Maqsood, M., Durrani, Q. S.: A Study to Investigate the Impact of Requirements Instability on Software Defects. ACM SIGSOFT Software Engineering Notes, Vol. 29, No. 3. ACM Press, New York (2004) 1–7
23. Xiao, H. M.: A Quantitative method on Software Quality Evaluation. Journal of Northwest Normal University (Natural Science), Vol. 36, No. 4. Northwest Normal University Press, Lanzhou (2000) 31–35 (in Chinese)
24. Software Engineering Institute: The Capability Maturity Model: Guidelines for Improving the Software Process. Addison-Wesley Publisher, Boston MA (1995)
25. Boehm, B., Abts, C., Brown, A. W., et al.: Software Cost Estimation with COCOMOII. Prentice Hall (2000)
26. Pham, H., Zhang, X. M.: A Software Cost Model with Warranty and Risk Costs. IEEE Transactions on Computers, Vol. 48, No. 1. IEEE Press, New York (1999) 71–75
27. Liu, H. W., Yang, X. Z., Qu, F., et al.: A Study on Software Cost Model Based on CGOM. Chinese Journal of Computers, Vol. 26, No.3. Science Press, Beijing (2003) 1333–1336 (in Chinese)
28. Boehm, B., Brown, A. W., Madachy, R., et al.: A Software Product Line Life Cycle Cost Estimation Model. In: Proc. of the 2004 International Symposium on Empirical Software Engineering (ISESE'04). IEEE Press, New York (2004) 156–164

Requirements Engineering Processes Improvement: A Systematic View

Anliang Ning, Hong Hou, Qingyi Hua, Bin Yu, and Kegang Hao

Institute of Software Engineering, Northwest University,
Taibai Road 229#, Xi'an, China (710069)
yiran_ning@163.com, hhong66@sina.com
{huaqy, yubin, hkg}@nwu.edu.cn
http://www.nwu.edu.cn

Abstract. Requirement is the foundation for both software development and project management activities, so an effective requirements process which has a potential influence on the quality of the final software product must be committed by all stakeholders. However current process improvement maturity models pay little attention to requirements engineering process and they are "black-box test" for organizations' competence. It is the precondition for our research to understand the fundamental issues and to identify the characteristic that requirement process possessed. We suggest a systematic view for requirement process improvement that includes measurement-based improvement for activities, methods, peoples as "white-box test", emphasizing the people factor, such as communication and collaboration, etc. Our future work will involve structuring the platform or tools which integrate methods, technologies, checklists, templates, lessons-learned, and providing basic supporting for requirements process improvement and distributed requirements development and management.

1 Introduction

As our societies rely ever more on the transfer and processing of information for day-to-day life, reliance on the quality of software systems is becoming of paramount. To achieve high quality in software, one has to start from high quality requirements [25]. A comment from Sanjiv who was one of CHAOS University participants, "If you don't nail the requirements, you fail the project. If you nail the requirements, you'll deliver." [28]. Understanding the value of good requirements and managing them well can be the single biggest factor in lowering the cost and improving the success rate of software projects. Therefore requirements are regarded as the foundation for both software development and project management activities, all stakeholders must be committed to an effective requirements process. It is well-known that software processes have an important influence on the quality of the final software product, and it has motivated companies to be more and more concerned about software process improvement when they are promoting the improvement of the final products. There are many evidences that process improvement has led to real improvements in both software product quality and organizations' profitability. Software Process Improvement (SPI) already offers the means to improve processes abilities or mature in the later

M. Li, B. Boehm, and L.J. Osterweil (Eds.): SPW 2005, LNCS 3840, pp. 151 – 163, 2005.
© Springer-Verlag Berlin Heidelberg 2005

stages of the software development process. In recent years, the SEI's Capability Maturity Model (CMM/CMMI) for Software and the ISO 9000 quality standard(s) have been enthusiastically embraced throughout the industry [2]. However, the experience of our industrial was neither the CMM nor ISO 9000 address requirements processes adequately; current process improvement and maturity models pay little attention to requirements engineering.

Therefore, to understand the fundamental issues and to identify the characteristic that requirement process possessed was discussed in section 2. To explore the effective approaches (measurement-based white-box test) to improve requirements processes, especially to emphasize the improvement of relationship among the technologies, activities, people from a systematic view in section 3, it is a novel, creative idea for requirements processes and its improvement. On the other hand, by providing the sufficient technology supporting to people factors (i.e. communication and collaboration) improvement, as the more decisive role in requirement development and management is discussed in section 4 in the paper.

2   Requirements Engineering Processes

Brooks, in his classic paper on the essence and accidents of software engineering, stated that "the hardest single part of building a software system is deciding precisely what to build... Therefore, the most important function that the software builder performs for the client is the iterative extraction and refinement of the product requirements" [3].

More and more, the organizations consulted consider the principal problem areas in software development to be the requirements specification and the management of customer requirements. Improving the processes of discovering, documenting and managing customer requirements is critical for future business success. Because of the persistence of these problems, requirements engineering attracts much interest and investment. About requirement engineering process, we all also want to find the most effective way to help industrial practitioners and to identify how they could make best use of existing good practices [1]. In order to do this it is important for us to understand requirements processes, because these requirements processes provide the context within which new practices must be used, and practitioners need to be able to assess their current processes in terms of the requirements problems which they experience and then select practices appropriate to the improvements which they wish to make. From two different perspectives, the context of requirements engineering process and the reason why requirement process is complex are discussed in section 2.1 and 2.2.

2.1   Context of Requirement Engineering Process

Improving the quality of requirements is crucial. But it is a difficult objective to achieve. To understand the reason one should first define what requirements engineering is really about. Broadly speaking, software systems requirements engineering (RE) is a process of discovering the purpose, by identifying stakeholders and their needs, and documenting these in a form that is amenable to analysis, communication, and subsequent implementation[4]. So requirement engineering process is a multi-disciplinary, human-centered process, such as computer science, psycho-social sciences, economics, and engineering converge in RE, contributing to the multi-disciplinary approach that has characterized this discipline for a quarter of a century now [25].

Now the software development world is experiencing an irreversible trend towards the globalization of business [5]. This creates the need to achieve a thorough understanding of collaborative activities such as requirements engineering and design of software in distributed development environments. Collaborative approach to software requirements management is necessary in modern systems development, so as to improve communication between project stakeholders and thereby bring about improvements in productivity and quality.

If we want to improvement requirement process, we should firstly understand it. Up to now, that we know some knowledge on requirements process involve:

- Requirements lie at the heart of every well-run software project, supporting the other technical and management activities. Changes that you make in your requirements development and management approaches will affect other processes, and vice versa [21].
- It is not a discrete front-end activity of the software life cycle, but rather a process initiated at the beginning of a project and continuing to be refined throughout the lifecycle [10].
- Clear requirements as the third most important factor for successful project development which was identified by a Standish Group report; incomplete and changing requirements as the second and third most important factors leading to unsuccessful projects; and incomplete requirements as the number-one factor for canceled projects [23].
- Requirements errors are the most expensive errors to fix because they become magnified as they go uncorrected. These errors become increasingly more difficult to correct as you move further along the software development lifecycle and actually have a snowball effect. Boehm estimated that the late correction of requirements errors could cost up to 200 times as much as correction during such requirements engineering [6].

2.2 Why Requirements Engineering Processes So Complex

Software requirements have been repeatedly recognized during the past 30 years to be a real problem. In early empirical study, Bell and Thayer observed that inadequate, inconsistent, incomplete, or ambiguous requirements are numerous and have a critical impact on the quality of the resulting software [7]. Noting this for different kinds of projects, they concluded that "the requirements for a system do not arise naturally; instead, they need to be engineered and have continuing review and revision". Requirements engineering must address the contextual goals why the software is needed, the functionalities the software has to accomplish to achieve those goals, and the constraints restricting how the software accomplishing those functions is to be designed and implemented. Such goals, functions and constraints have to be mapped to precise specifications of software behavior; their evolution over time and across software families has to be coped with as well [8]. Thus the actual is ([19], [39]):

- The scope is fairly broad as it ranges from a world of human organizations or physical laws to a technical artifact that must be integrated in it; from high-level objectives to operational prescriptions; and from informal to formal. The target system is not just a piece of software, but also comprises the environment that will surround it; the latter is made of humans, devices, and/or other software. The whole system has to be considered under many facets, e.g., socio-economic, physical, technical, operational, evolutionary, and so forth.

- There are multiple concerns to be addressed beside functional ones - e.g., safety, security, usability, flexibility, performance, robustness, interoperability, cost, maintainability, and so on. These non-functional concerns are often conflicting

- Requirement specifications may suffer a great variety of deficiencies [9]. Some of them are errors that may have disastrous effects on the subsequent development steps and on the quality of the resulting software product - e.g., inadequacies with respect to the real needs, incompleteness, contradictions, and ambiguities; some others are flaws that may yield undesired consequences (such as waste of time or generation of new errors) - e.g., noises, forward references, over-specifications, or wishful thinking.

- There are multiple parties involved in the requirements engineering process, each having different background, skills, knowledge, concerns, perceptions, and expression means - namely, customers, commissioners, users, domain experts, requirement engineers, software developers, or system maintainers. Most often those parties have conflicting viewpoints.

- Requirements engineering covers multiple intertwined activities.

  - *Domain analysis:* the existing system in which the software should be built is studied. The relevant stakeholders are identified and interviewed. Problems and deficiencies in the existing system are identified; opportunities are investigated; general objectives on the target system are identified there from.

  - *Elicitation:* alternative models for the target system are explored to meet such objectives; requirements and assumptions on components of such models are identified, possibly with the help of hypothetical interaction scenarios. Alternative models generally define different boundaries between the software-to-be and its environment.

  - *Negotiation and agreement:* the alternative requirements/ assumptions are evaluated; risks are analyzed; "best" tradeoffs that receive agreement from all parties are selected.

  - *Specification:* the requirements and assumptions are formulated in a precise way.

  - *Specification analysis:* the specifications are checked for deficiencies (such as inadequacy, incompleteness or inconsistency) and for feasibility (in terms of resources required, development costs, and so forth).

  - *Documentation:* the various decisions made during the process are documented together with their underlying rationale and assumptions.

  - *Evolution:* the requirements are modified to accommodate corrections, environmental changes, or new objectives.

- There are many appropriate methods and techniques used for requirements engineering, which will have defined standards for requirements documents, requirements descriptions, etc. The organization may use automated tools to support process activities. It will have management policies and procedures in place to ensure that the process is followed and may use process measurements to collect information about the process to help assess the value of process changes.

3 The Systematic View: Measurement-Based Process Improvement for Activities, Techniques, Human

The software process is a production system regulated by a management system. Managerial commitment is paramount in bringing about effective changes in working practices; tools and methods may assist but a clear management lead, supported through sustained reinforcement, is essential if the necessary changes in behavior and culture are to be realized in practice and become a permanent feature ([1], [31]). Software development depends critically on human creativity and talent. [6] has reported, for instance, that people factors have an influence on productivity six times greater than the use of software tools. [3] argues that methodology alone (i.e. process models) will not "inspire the drudge". If the quality of software requirement development want to be improved, then a coherent model of the software requirement process is required that does full justice to both the technical and the social dimensions of the process. A complementary emphasis on people and process is required. Without a broad approach that embraces process, people and technology, the danger is that any attempt to "improve the process" will founder.

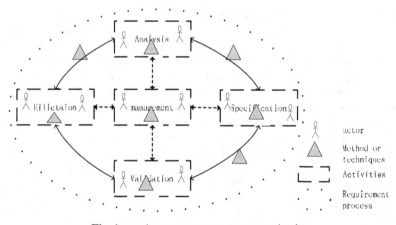

Fig. 1. requirement process - a systematic view

In essence, socio-technical theory conceptualizes organizations as open systems (i.e. as intelligent entities that interact with and adapt to changing environments) composed of technical and social "subsystems". The technical subsystem of an organization refers to tasks, processes and technologies; the social subsystem denotes the people who work for the company, their "psychological need" for fulfilling and satisfying work, and the way that they are organized (e.g. as autonomous groups or in line management structures).

Technical improvements can have social costs (e.g. process automation which restricts individual autonomy, CASE tools which rigidify roles) such that overall performance is worsened rather than improved. It is vital that both technical and social dimensions of the workplace are redesigned together, with the aim of improving performance through increased efficiency. The key to improving performance is to optimize the joint design of the technical subsystem (deliberations) and the social subsystem.

Most RE research is conceptual and concentrates on methods or techniques, primarily supporting a single activity. Moreover, the rare field studies we actually have do not establish a link between RE practices and performance. So in remaining section, based on thorough understanding of requirement and its inherent complexity, we emphatically discussed the process (set of activities) improvement in section 3.1 and 3.2, and social/humanities factors' improvement in section 4.

3.1 Black-Box Test: The Weakness of Existing Standards and Models for Process Improvement

In order to improve an organization's requirements engineering process ability, existing process must be assessed. Developing an accurate process model is a complex business and most assessment techniques tend to require specialist process assessment input. This is achieved by identifying the requirements practices used by assessing them against a checklist of the good practices described in the [10]. The requirements process is much less homogeneous and well understood than the software development process as a whole. There are two complementary classes of standard which are relevant to requirements engineering process improvement:

SPI methods are aimed at evaluating organizations' software processes and providing guidance on what can be improved and how. Although the ISO 9000 family of quality standard(s) has not strictly an improvement standard, but has much in common with those parts of improvement models which deal with the attainment of basic levels of process maturity [11]. There is no section specific to requirements engineering and little is said about the activities involved in eliciting, analyzing and validating the requirements. These standards offer little direct help to an organization committed to serious quality improvements in their requirements process. The SEI's CMM for software version defines standards to be attained by different process areas for the different phases of the development life-cycle. The experience of the industrial organizations show the benefits are harder to gain when applied to the requirements process. In contrast to the CMM, SPICE has a continuous architecture where there is a less rigid correspondence between practices, processes and maturity levels. This is intended to encourage a more flexible approach where improvement effort may be focused on the most needy process areas ([40],[41]).

Life-cycle process standards which are concerned with providing reference models of the software development process. They deal with process models, the activities which comprise a process and their products, and these models or standards apply across the development life-cycle so requirements processes are not the focus. Existing life-cycle standards are a valuable source of basic good practices but the our aims is to provide more focused coverage of how they can be integrated in a requirements process, what their benefits and costs will be and what problems may be encountered.

The major characteristic of all the above standards and models is that they are oriented towards assessing organizations' competence against a set of process criteria using forms, checklists and templates. That is to say, it is black-box test for organizations' competence. Inevitably, process assessment is difficult and is based on a snapshot view of the organization. Organizations are increasingly keen on performing internal assessments, both as a preparation for official accreditation visits but also simply to help identify their process weaknesses. This reflects growing recognition of the potential for cost savings from process improvement and parallels the enthusiasm for business process reengineering (BPR) and total quality management (TQM) in other business areas ([17],[40]).

3.2 White-Box Test: Measurement-Based Process Improvement

Software measurement by itself cannot solve the problems in requirement process improvement, but it can clarify and focus your understanding of them. Moreover, when done properly, sequential measurements of quality attributes of products and processes can provide an effective foundation for initiating and managing process improvement activities. Effective measurement processes help software groups succeed by enabling them to understand their capabilities, so that they can develop achievable plans for producing and delivering products and services. Measurements also enable people to detect trends and to anticipate problems, thus providing better control of costs, reducing risks, improving quality, and ensuring that business objectives are achieved. Business goals and strategies, together with factual data about attribute of product quality and process performance, are the key drivers that lead to actions that improve a software process. In short, measurement methods help to identify important events and trends and effectively separate signals from noise are in valuable in guiding software organizations to informed decisions ([12],[20],[21],[24]).

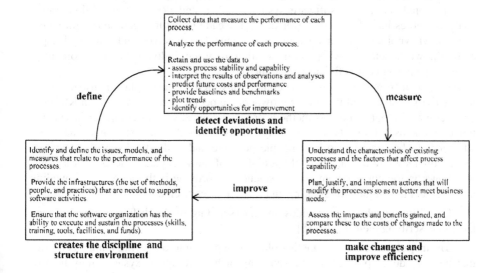

Fig. 2. measurement-based process improvement framework

Figure 2 illustrates our generic requirements process improvement model which defines activities aimed at identifying and resolving requirements defects while coping with those which inevitably emerge at later stages and then measure, improve them. The model:

- encourage a more flexible, continuous approach where improvement effort may be focused on the most needy processes/activities areas.
- can be adopted in a way which allows an organization to plan and evaluate improvements to its requirements process.
- reflect the requirements processes' iterative nature

It must be pointed out that process ability/maturity level is only one of the factors which affect the quality of the final requirements document. Other important factors are the ability and experience of the people involved in the process, the novelty, difficulty and size of the problem and the time and resources available, etc.

4   Humanities Factors and Its Improvement

We cannot ignore the fact that people issues rather than technology underlie the majority of systems development problems [13]. Software development is carried on by people, and indeed many commentators have taken pains to stress that high performance depends decisively on these "people factors". Human, social and organizational (HSO) factors play a decisive role in software development in terms of determining functional and non-functional characteristics of software products. The fundamental rules for collecting requirements are shifting in importance from the data to be processed by the system and the operations which process that data, to human–computer interaction and social and organizational factors. Traditional requirements analysis focus lacks human issues and does not address adequately the impact of social and organizational matters in software systems design and development. Ethnography analysis studies have been used over the last decade to fill this gap and to provide a different viewpoint of how a software system must be conceived and examined, especially in work settings where collaboration between individuals in a computer-supported environment is the primary issue ([14],[23]).

As we seen from the Figure 1 the context in which RE takes place is usually a human activity system, and the problem owners are people. Engagement in an RE process presupposes that some new methods or technologies, such as computer-based system could be useful, but these will change the activities that they supports. Therefore, RE needs to be sensitive to how people perceive and understand the world around them, how they interact, and how the sociology of the workplace affects their actions. RE draws on the cognitive and social sciences to provide both theoretical grounding and practical techniques for eliciting and modeling requirements:

- **Cognitive psychology** provides an understanding of the difficulties people may have in describing their needs [15].

- **Anthropology** provides a methodological approach to observing human activities that helps to develop a richer understanding of how computer systems may help or hinder those activities [16].

- **Sociology** provides an understanding of the political and cultural changes caused by computerization. Introduction of a new computer system changes the nature of the work carried out within an organization, may affect the structure and communication paths within that organization, and may even change the original needs that it was built to satisfy [17].

- **Linguistics** is important because RE is largely about communication. Linguistic analyses have changed the way in which the English language is used in specifications, for instance to avoid ambiguity and to improve understandability. Tools from linguistics can also be used in requirements elicitation, for instance to analyze communication patterns within an organization [18].

Finally, there is an important **philosophical** element in RE. RE is concerned with interpreting and understanding stakeholder terminology, concepts, viewpoints and goals. Hence, RE must concern itself with an understanding of beliefs of stakeholders (epistemology), the question of what is observable in the world (phenomenology), and the question of what can be agreed on as objectively true (ontology). Such issues become important whenever one wishes to talk about validating requirements, especially where stakeholders may have divergent goals and incompatible belief systems. They also become important when selecting a modeling technique, because the choice of technique affects the set of phenomena that can be modeled, and may even restrict what a requirements engineer is capable of observing [4].

So effective communication and collaboration should be recognized and enhanced, that is the good way to improve productivity and quality by fading humanities/social negative influence.

4.1 Communication and Collaboration in Requirement Process

The requirements engineering phase of software development projects is characterized by the intensity and importance of communication activities. And it is widely recognized that communication problems are a major factor in the delay and failure of software projects [35]. During requirements engineering phase, the various stakeholders must be able to communicate their requirements to the analysts, and the analysts need to be able to communicate the specifications they generate back to the stakeholders for validation, etc. Sound requirements processes emphasize a collaborative approach to product development that involves multiple stakeholders in a partnership throughout the project. Identifying the real requirements requires an interactive requirements process, supported by effective mechanisms, methods, techniques, and tools [33]. By extension, therefore, the requirements on particular software are typically a complex combination of requirements from different people at different levels of an organization and from the environment in which the software will operate [31].

Informal communication is very important for coordination of work and for learning the culture of an organization. It is also crucial for the perpetuation of the social relations that underlie collaboration and generally, in any situation that communication is required to resolve ambiguity. Through informal communication, the reaction to a requirement-related issue is propagated much quicker locally than across sites. At the same time, informal communication within one site has a positive impact on the local negotiation process. There is significantly greater ability to tap into immediate knowledge in co-located development. In both organizations, requirements-related communication between remote sites is mostly done through "formal" channels, i.e. the bi-weekly meetings, when the communication is focused on urgent issues and leaves little room for small talk. Outside these meetings, the communication between stakeholders is primarily channeled through the non-interactive email, or phone calls, when improper knowledge management techniques make the communication ineffective. Reliance on asynchronous channels contributes to issues identified at one site, small or big -- which may crop up on a daily basis -- go unrecognized at the other site, and thus unresolved for a long time [35]. Geographically distributed requirements teams is a complex phenomenon that covers several dimensions ([30], [36], [37]):

Inadequate communication. Distance introduces barriers to informal and face-to-face communication, and the stakeholders' communication is dependent on the quality of using synchronous or asynchronous electronic communication tools.

Knowledge management. The sheer quantity of information and knowledge about requirements from multiple sources at remote customer sites was not appropriately shared with the developers.

Cultural diversity. Differences in stakeholders' language and national culture affect global collaboration. Equally important was the impact of differences in organizational and functional culture. Not only did remote sites develop their own organizational culture, but also the distance widened the gap between the different functional departments of the organization (marketing, business management, development and engineering). This had a significant impact on achieving a common understanding and negotiation of requirements.

Time difference. The large distribution of stakeholders introduced large time-zone differences and allowed little overlap available for synchronous collaboration.

4.2 Congruent Tools/Platforms for Humanity Factors' Improvement

While it is known that global projects bring additional challenges to project management, there was an unanimous dissatisfaction with the Project Manager's skills in identifying a clear direction for the RE process and roles to support it. The concept of "not working together" emerged when the impact of distance was discussed with the stakeholders, and resulted in the attitude of "there is no knowledge of what the others are doing, or should do". The lack of well-defined roles and expectations led to misinterpretation of actions, due to stereotyping about cultures and working styles. It often generated negative attitudes, exacerbated by existing conflicts due to political struggles, and hence changed the atmosphere of the requirements negotiations ([36], [38]).

The requirements conflicts and tradeoffs are critical aspects that occur throughout the software development and software engineers need to better understand the technological impacts on the performance of groups resolving requirements issues in distributed development structures. Because of the complexity of software development projects, and also because stakeholders are likely to be geographically distributed, the use of an automated tool to support such collaboration is essential. Recent advances in technology, in conjunction with major changes observed in fundamental concepts of requirements analysis, have altered the way software is produced nowadays. The explosion in telecommunications and the continuous growth of the Internet as a means to communicate, exchange information and trade, caused significant revisions in certain phases of software life cycle models. For example, the need for continuous change in content and functionality in web applications urged the establishment of tentative configuration management mechanisms and forced a quicker development of software products. Multimedia Web-based meeting tools such as NetMeeting are becoming ubiquitous for communication on the Internet. By providing audio and video channels and real time sharing of applications, they emerge as potentially useful tools for such communication ([30], [36], [37]).

5 Future Work and Conclusion

Based on the above understanding on requirement process improvement principle, the next step is to construct a platform or tool, named WbCRE, for requirement development and management, which integrate the practical metrics for white-box test process improvement, and many methods, technologies guider, templates, checklists, lessons-learned, and others basic elements, such as objective data for practical measurement analysis which collected automatically from requirement processes, remote communication and collaboration techniques supporting tools, etc. Although, there are several requirement management tools exercised in industries, such as Analyst Pro, Caliber-RM, DOORS, IRqA, Rational RequisitePro, but none of them adopting quantity technology or methods to help the improvement of requirement process([26],[29],[32]).

It is a systematic engineering problem for us to improve the productivity and quality of requirement engineering product, SRS, but existing models and standards are oriented towards assessing organizations' competence. Organizations are increasingly keen on identifying their process weaknesses and maximizing the ROI (return of invest). Only to improve requirement process can not ideally solve the problem faced. We have announced that to achieve reliable and durable gains in software quality, both the social and the technical dimensions of the software process must be given equal weight within a unified conceptual framework. More generally, it provides a theoretical framework in which a broad debate about the design of process support systems can be conducted which addresses both technical and social concerns.

References

1. J. Carver and V. Basili : Identifying Implicit Process Variables To Support Future Empirical Work, Proceedings of the 17th Brazilian Symposium on Software Engineering (SBES 2003).
2. Humphrey, W., Snyder, T. and Willis, R. : Software Process Improvement at Hughes Aircraft, IEEE Software, 8 (4) (1991) 11-23.
3. F.P. Brooks: "No Silver Bullet : Essence and Accidents of Software Engineering". IEEE Computer, Vol. 20 No. 4 (April 1987) 10-19.
4. B. Nuseibeh and S. Easterbrook : Requirements Engineering: A Roadmap , Proceedings of International Conference on Software Engineering (ICSE-2000), 4-11 June 2000, Limerick, Ireland, ACM Press(2000).
5. Herbsleb JD and Moitra D : Global software development. IEEE Software, (March/June 2001) 16–20.
6. B.W. Boehm : Software Engineering Economics. Prentice-Hall(1981).

7. T.E. Bell and T.A. Thayer : "Software Requirements: Are They Really a Problem?", Proc. ICSE-2: 2nd Intrnational Conference on Software Enginering, San Francisco, (1976) 61-68.

8. P. Zave : "Classification of Research Efforts in Requirements Engineering", ACM Computing Surveys, Vol. 29 No. 4 (1997) 315-321.

9. B. Meyer : "On Formalism in Specifications", IEEE Software, Vol. 2 No. 1, (January 1985) 6-26.

10. Sommervile, I. and Sawyer, P. : Requirements Engineering A Good Practice Guide, Wiley(1997).

11. Paulk, M. : A Comparison of ISO 9001 and the Capability Maturity Model for Software, CMU/SEI-94-TR-12, Software Engineering Institute, USA(1994).

12. William A. Florac, Robert E. Park and Anita D. Carleton : Practical Software Measurement: Measuring for Process Management and Improvement, CMU/SEI-97-HB-003,(1997).

13. Guinan, P.J., Cooprider, J.G. and Faraj, S. : 'Enabling Software Development Team Performance During Requirements Definition: A Behavioral Versus technical Approach', Information Systems Research, 9(2) (1994) 101-125.

14. Andreou, A. : "Promoting Software Quality Through a Human, Social, and Organizational Requirements Elicitation Process," Requirements Engineering, 8(2) (July 2003) 85-101.

15. Posner, M. I. (Ed.) : Foundations of Cognitive Science. MIT Press(1993).

16. Goguen, J. and Jirotka, M. (Ed.) : Requirements Engineering: Social and Technical Issues. London: Academic Press(1994).

17. Lehman, M. M. : Programs, Life Cycles, and Laws of Software Evolution. Proceedings of the IEEE, 68(9) (1980) 1060-1076.

18. Burg, J. F. M. : Linguistic Instruments in Requirements Engineering. Amsterdam: IOS Press(1980).

19. R Jeffery, S Lauesen, D Zowghi and D Damian : Conducting Empirical Research in Requirements Engineering, 6th Workshop on Requirements Engineering, Eds. Aybuke Aurum; Ross Jeffery,The University of New South Wales, Sydney (2001) 49 – 50

20. Mingshu Li : User-Driven Domain-Specific Software Requirements Analysis, 13th International Conferences on System Engineering (ICSE'99), Nevada,USA.(1999).

21. Karl E. Wiegers : Software Requirements, second edition, Microsoft Press(2003).

22. Wang Qing and Li Ming-shu : Measurement of Software Requirement Based on SPC, Chinese Journal of Computers, Vol.26, No.10(2003).

23. Ralph R. Young : Effective Requirements Practices, Addison-Wesley(2001).

24. Ren Fake, Zhou Bosheng and Wu chaoying : Study on Software Measurement Process, Journal of Beijing University of Aeronautics and Astronautics, Vol.29, No.10 (2003)

25. Björn Regnell, Erik Kamsties and Vincenzo Gervasi : Summary of the 10th Anniversary Workshop on Requirements Engineering: Foundation for Software Quality (REFSQ'2004), www.resg.org.uk

26. http://www.volere.co.uk

27. Guide to the Software Engineering Body of Knowledge SWEBOK® 2004 Version, 2.1–2.16, IEEE Computer Society, http://computer.org,

28. http://www.standishgroup.com

29. http://www.incose.org

30. Damian, D., et al. : "An Empirical Study of Facilitation of Computer-Mediated Distributed Requirements Negotiations," Fifth International Symposium on Requirements Engineering, Los Alamitos, California: IEEE Computer Society Press (2001) 128-135.

31. S. Robertson and J. Robertson : Mastering the Requirements Process: Addison-Wesley (1999).

32. Anliang Ning and Hong Hou : Software Economics Concept in Modern Software Development, National Software and Applications Conference (NASAC2004), Beijing University of Aeronautics and Astronautics, (2004).
33. Michael Lang and Jim Duggan : A Tool to Support Collaborative Software Requirements Management, Requirements Engineering (2001) 161–172
34. Katrina Hands, D. Ramanee Peiris and Peter Gregor : Development of a computer-based interviewing tool to enhance the requirements gathering process, Requirements Engineering (2004) 204–216
35. Jane Coughlan and Robert D. Macredie : Effective Communication in Requirements Elicitation: A Comparison of Methodologies, Requirements Engineering (2002) 47–60
36. Damian, D., and D. Zowghi : Requirements Engineering Challenges in Multi-Site Software Development Organizations, Requirements Engineering,8(3) (August 2003) 149-160.
37. Damian, D., et al. : An Exploratory Study of Facilitation in Distributed Requirements Engineering, Requirements Engineering, 8(1) (February 2003) 23-41.
38. Dale, R. : Using a Requirements Management Tool in Technical Requirements Negotiations, Fourteenth Annual International Symposium on Systems Engineering, Seattle, Washington: International Council on Systems Engineering(2004).
39. Axel van Lamsweerde : Requirements Engineering in the Year 00: A Research Perspective, 22nd International Conference on Software Engineering, (2000)June 04 - 11, Limerick, Ireland.
40. Sawyer, Pete, Ian Sommerville and Stephen Viller : Requirements process improvement through the phased introduction of good practice, Software Process - Improvement and Practice, 3(1) (1997) 19-34.
41. www.isospice.com

S-RaP: A Concurrent, Evolutionary Software Prototyping Process

Xiping Song, Arnold Rudorfer, Beatrice Hwong, Gilberto Matos,
and Christopher Nelson

Siemens Corporate Research Inc. 755 College Road East,
Princeton, NJ 08540, USA
{xiping.song, arnold.rudorfer, beatrice.hwong,
gilberto.matos, christopher.nelson}@siemens.com

Abstract. This paper defines a highly concurrent, software rapid prototyping process that supports a sizable development team to develop a high-quality, evolutionary software prototype. The process is particularly aimed at developing user-interface intensive, workflow-centered software. The Software Engineering Department and User Interface Design Center at Siemens Corporate Research (SCR) have successfully practiced this process in prototyping a healthcare information system over the last year. We have evolved this agile, iterative software development process that tightly integrates the UI designers and the software developers with the prototype users (e.g., marketing staff), leading to efficient development of business application prototypes with mature user interfaces. We present the details of our process and the conditions that make it effective. Our experience with this process indicates that prototypes can be rapidly developed in a highly concurrent fashion given a stable prototyping software architecture and access to readily available domain knowledge.

1 Introduction

Rapid software prototyping is an effective way to facilitate communication among the customers, the requirement engineers and the marketing staff by providing them with an executable, intuitive representation of a target system. Prototyping is an effective approach to evaluate and refine software requirements [4][5][6][7]. Prototyping is also used to aid the communications between the company's marketing team and potential customers, promoting the advanced features of the product and gathering customer feedback. It helps to gain early customer buy-in for novel product ideas.

A software prototyping project can be "throwaway" or evolutionary. The throwaway prototyping normally has a short duration and the software code will not be reused for the corresponding product. The evolutionary prototyping has a potential to mature a prototype into the final product and thus it needs to be of high quality and with a software architecture that is compatible with the product software technologies. In this paper we define a rapid software prototyping process that is aimed at developing the evolutionary software prototype and can be applied during the early phases (e.g., Requirements, Analysis and Design of RUP [10]) of the software

M. Li, B. Boehm, and L.J. Osterweil (Eds.): SPW 2005, LNCS 3840, pp. 164–176, 2005.
© Springer-Verlag Berlin Heidelberg 2005

product development. We describe the process with sufficient detail so that other organizations can apply this process as well. This process will be referred to as **S-RaP** (**S**iemens **Ra**pid **P**rototyping) throughout this paper.

A number of rapid prototyping approaches (e.g., agile modeling and software development methods (e.g., Extreme Programming [9]) [5][8], RAD [4])) have been described in the past. Agile methods usually emphasize involving the product users in the prototyping, and encourage a rapid users-to-developers feedback cycle. Project management and tracking are often not emphasized by those methods. Some agile methods rely completely on using experienced developers.

S-RaP is similar to Extreme Programming (XP) method [9] in that it uses a storyboard (XP uses a similar idea called Story Card) and extensively involves product users during the development. Our contribution is that S-RaP is a unique and effective approach that provides specific details for *concurrent* and iterative prototyping of certain kinds of software applications within certain project constraints. Those applications and project constraints are

- **High software quality within short development life cycle** (a few weeks or months)**:** Some of the quality attributes could be reliability, customizability, usability, and code maintainability. In the projects where S-RaP was originated, the company's marketing team planned to use the prototype to communicate with customers at pre-scheduled dates. Thus prototypes need to demonstrate an overall high quality. Because the prototype is required to be highly customizable and high fidelity, "throwaway" prototyping that is built upon hardwired code and scripted scenarios is not acceptable.

- **Support the visibility of project progress:** The effort for which this process originated is to deliver a prototype for a major trade show. This is different from many other prototyping efforts that are only for technology evaluation or for a few potential customers. Thus, project management must be able to evaluate the project progress and manage the risk effectively.

- **Workflow driven:** The targeted prototype is viewed as a piece of software supporting a set of workflows. *A workflow within the scope of this paper refers to a sequence of users' UI interactions to achieve a certain business function.* For example, checking in the patient with the use of a healthcare information system would be a workflow. *Use-case* refers to a specific instantiation of the workflow. For example, checking in a particular patient (e.g., John Smith) would be a use-case.

- **The architecture of the prototype is largely known in advance:** Particularly, S-RaP is aimed at software applications built upon n-tiered web application architecture. With a known architecture at the start of prototyping, the prototyping process can be more focused on the implementation of specific user requirements.

- **Use of inexperienced developers:** The project where this process originated was a series of short-term contracts between SCR and a Siemens company. Due to fluctuations in development resource needs, SCR had to engage quickly new developers. Even if the developers had advanced development skills, they were unfamiliar with the application areas (e.g., medical financial calculation, hospital bed management). Thus the process needs to facilitate their application knowledge ramp-up through early exposure to relevant concepts.

- **Ill-defined requirements:** The initial requirements from the users are unclear and the developers also need time to acquire domain knowledge. However, the *business application has been in practice for a long time* (e.g., the healthcare financial applications).

- **Emphasis on UI interaction:** A mature and intuitive UI is a key acceptance criterion for most software systems. Evaluating alternative UI designs for the software prototype is a key activity.

From the above characteristics, we can see that S-RaP does not have some characteristics and constraints required by other agile methods. For example, some agile methods require using experienced developers while S-RaP is designed to use inexperienced developers. S-RaP is also aimed at supporting the development of the software with specific architectures (i.e., n-tiered, MVC based architectures).

Initially, in our early use of S-RaP, we laid out this process as a project plan that included the definitions of the concurrent activities and key reviewing activities. In this paper we will define the process in detail, following the process engineering approach as suggested in [2]. First we define the requirements in Section 2 for the process and then in Section 3, define the process. Finally, in Section 4, we will discuss our experiences with S-RaP, specifically how we used and managed this process to carry out a successful project.

2 Process Requirements

Because of the prototype characteristics targeted by S-RaP as described in Section 1, S-RaP must provide the following support (note that in this paper the *user* is often referred to the people who will use the prototype to define and validate the product requirements, such as marketing staff or requirements engineers):

- **Support high concurrence in a sizable project team:** It must support a sizable development team (e.g., 20-30 developers) working on the prototype in parallel to facilitate a quick delivery. *This is one of the unique requirements of our process* since many of the software prototyping activities tend to be at small scale and performed with a small team (5-6 developers). The parallelism could be achieved in a number of ways; the activities of same kind (e.g., UI design) are performed concurrently on the different portions of a prototype, or the activities of the different kinds (e.g., UI design and UI implementation) are performed on the same portion of the prototype.

- **Enable user involvement:** because of the vague initial requirements, the process must involve the users in making all the requirements decisions and approve major UI designs.

- **Allow iteration:** Since the requirements are not well defined, the users and UI designers must see the prototyped behaviors to be able to adjust the existing requirements and UI design. Thus, the process must be iterative enough to allow continuous changes to the user interface and system behaviors.

- **Promote cooperation between UI designers and developers:** In order to avoid miscommunication between UI designers and software developers, the process should foster quick feedback on feasibility and usability between these two teams.

- **Sufficient documentation:** Due to the short development life cycle, it is not possible to develop extensive documents since that would create too much over-head for the project. The document should be just sufficient to ensure that the prototype is delivered with the correct UI look-and-feel and behaviors.

3 Process Definition

Figure 2 uses a basic flow chart to define the S-RaP process. The process starts from the top-left corner and finishes at the bottom-right corner. From the project planning and tracking point of view, it consists of three phases. Thus, the project management can evaluate the project progress based upon the numbers of workflows that are being mainly developed in each phase. However, from the development point of view, the activities are performed concurrently through those three phases. For example, the UI Design Phase and the Prototype Implementation Phase are largely carried out in parallel.

The solid-line objects in the diagram are the steps as we defined in our plan of the project where the S-RaP process was originated. The major outputs of the process are the prototype and the storyboard that contains the prototype requirements. *The prototype requirements can be used as the initial requirements document of the corresponding product.* Each workflow will be implemented by using this process. Thus, at one point of the project, there can be a number of instantiations of the S-RaP process that concurrently develops a number of workflows.

3.1 UI Design Phase

The user interface design begins with the initial understanding of the workflow and prior experience in developing similar functions. The UI designer will carry out this activity with extensive involvement of the users and limited participation of the software engineers who will be implementing the user interface. This activity requires a varied number of meetings with the users depending on the different complexities of the targeted workflows. This activity will deliver a document called a *storyboard* that defines each workflow (e.g., check-in of a patient for a healthcare information system). The storyboard is a Microsoft PowerPoint document. The first page is a text description of the function that the workflow achieves. The next page is a diagram (e.g., a flowchart-alike diagram) of the workflow. Following the diagram, each page of the storyboard defines one screen shot of the workflow. The interactions and behaviors embedded in the screen shot are described in the notes area of the document (see Figure 1). A storyboard is an evolving artifact, initially based upon the ideas from the users. However, it will be further refined during the user reviews (either at UI design or UI implementation level) or during the requirements meetings with the users. Since this activity attempts to describe dynamic system behaviors with static screen shots and English, the workflow description in the storyboard is likely incomplete, at least at the beginning of the documentation. However, the storyboard will be further refined and completed along with the maturing prototype throughout the S-RaP process. The finished storyboard contains both the prototype requirements and the UI design.

The UI design can start with an existing preliminary style guide to ensure design consistency. The use of such a style guide can make the UI design and communication with users more effective and efficient. For example, a modification to the UI design can be consistently applied to other similar UI designs via the style guide. The consistent naming of the UI presentations will make the communication easier. However, it is also understood that prototyping will enhance the style guide, so the style guide becomes a deliverable of the prototyping as well.

A long and complex workflow can be divided into two or more sub-workflows to enable multiple UI designers to work concurrently on the same workflow.

Activity Review with Users ensures that all the major users are satisfied with the user interface and the system behaviors. The main user contact must approve the UI design as sufficiently complete so it can be final-reviewed by all the major users. All the major stakeholders will attend this review and decide if the storyboard will be approved. This activity is largely a requirement activity that is focused on the UI look-and-feel and correct interaction sequences. Due to the limited meeting duration, the meeting can be focused on only the important requirement issues. The review meeting will not verify all the behaviors of the workflow with the users.

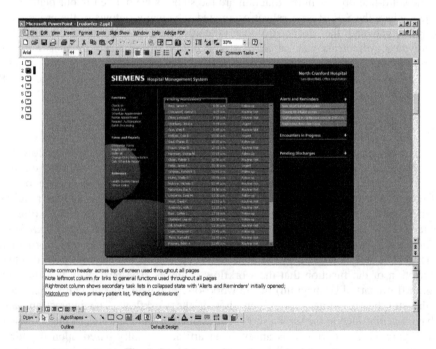

Fig. 1. Sample page from the storyboard

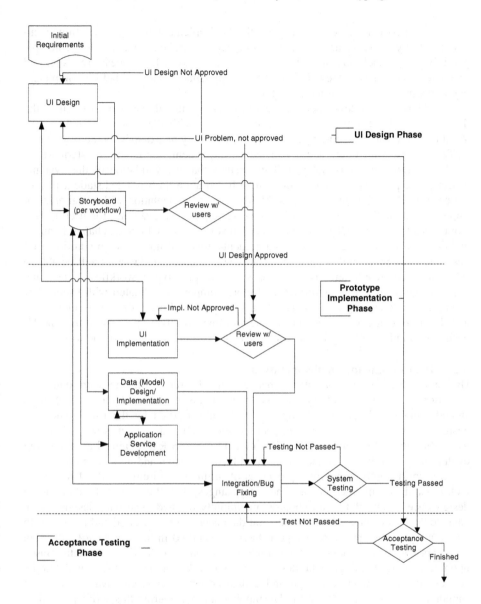

Fig. 2. A diagram illustrating the S-RaP prototyping process

3.2 Prototype Implementation Phase

3.2.1 UI Implementation

The UI Implementation activity starts as soon as a portion of a workflow's storyboard has been developed and its basic layout is relatively stable (e.g., about 30-40% finished). It is not necessary to wait until the storyboard is completed. Implementers can first start implementing the most stabilized UI designs. This enables a high parallelism between the UI Design and the UI Implementation. The UI Implementation activity delivers an executable, interactive user interface of the prototype, possibly using mock-up data. This ensures that the workflow appears realistic, and thus users can easily review the workflow's dynamic behaviors before completely validating more detailed prototype requirements.

For inexperienced developers, this activity can be started even earlier to allow the developers to have extra time to become familiar with the prototype architecture. What they develop during this period of time will likely be extensively modified later.

The Review with Users activity of the UI implementation cannot be started until the UI Design Review is finished. This ensures that the validation of the dynamic aspect of the prototype requirements can be based upon the validated static aspect of the prototype requirements. It is possible that the implementation will reveal areas of improvement in the UI design (e.g., missing required interactions for users). This would lead to an extra UI design iteration. However, if the UI design change is minor and does not require changing the requirements, this will not cause an additional UI design review. Since at this point the prototype is interactive, the users will be able to see some complete interactive use-cases of the prototyped workflow. Thus, the requirements can be further refined and more completely validated with users. For example, for "checking-in patients into a hospital" workflow, since it is interactive and the users can actually execute it, the working prototype can ensure that the UI design is complete at least for one use-case (for a particular patient) of the workflow.

3.2.2 Data Design and Implementation

Unlike a "throwaway" prototype that completely relies on mock-up data, the evolutionary software prototype needs to use realistic data and the data changes should remain realistic after being accessed and modified by the users. The data design can consist of two parts. One is the data model and another is the actual data value set that will be stored in the data model. Since S-RaP is aimed at supporting evolutionary prototyping, it needs to support the data design and implementation.

To support highly concurrent processes of refining requirements of UI look-and-feel, dynamic UI interactions and the data changes, S-RaP can start the data model design once a few of the storyboards are initially defined. The data designers can analyze the UI designs to understand what data needs to be accessed and modified. In addition, by analyzing the prototype behaviors specified in the storyboards, the data designers can better understand the relationships among the different data. Based upon this understanding, data designers can develop a data model that can be converted into a database design and a data access layer (e.g., Java classes) that supports the direct access from the UI implementation. During this activity, the data designers will discuss the data requirements with users as well to gain an overall understanding of the requirements across multiple workflows.

The data design is the second task of this activity. This task is to ensure that the data values are realistic as well as sufficient for exploring a variety of interesting use-cases that would use the varied data values. It will identify a basic data set (e.g., the patient demographics data) and the rules that govern which data should be allowed to appear in certain workflows. Such rules depend heavily on the application domain knowledge. Thus, the development of those rules requires the communication with the users.

3.2.3 Application Service Development

This activity develops the application services that support the prototype behaviors. The application services support the business logic that can be shared among a number of workflows. For example, it supports the calculation of a reimbursement for a patient. Starting this activity early gives the developers extra time to gain the domain knowledge required for implementing the services. This activity is started immediately after a few storyboards are initiated. The developers for this activity must discuss with the users the requirements for the behaviors of the services they will implement. With an in-depth understanding of the application service requirements, the service application developers can provide useful inputs to the data model designers for how the data should be structured to effectively support the data accesses from the application services.

3.2.4 Integration and Bug Fixing

This is the final activity for each workflow to be developed. During this activity, the developers will integrate the UI implementation code and application service code. The developers may need to implement the UI/data interface code to facilitate the data support for each UI (e.g., forms in the Struts architecture [3]). The developers will unit-test the developed workflow against the corresponding storyboard. This is often teamwork between the developers who are involved in the previous activities such as Application Service Development and UI Implementation development. Sometimes, if the data model needs to be changed, it will require the participation of the data designers.

3.2.5 System Testing

The system testing is to test the functional behaviors of a workflow after it has been fully integrated with all the required business logic and persistent support. It differs from the "unit testing" in: 1) it is carried out by testers who do not implement the particular workflow being tested, and 2) it will formally report the defects which will then be tracked by project management and the test lead. The storyboard is used as the testing script for verifying the prototype behaviors. At this stage, the testers verify the prototypes against the storyboard for every detail.

3.3 Acceptance Testing

The prototype users will carry out the acceptance testing. The users are the people who will demonstrate the prototype to their customers for the proposed new product features. Like the system testers, the users use the storyboard as the requirements to verify the prototype behaviors and the user interface compliance. Since the users have previously approved the storyboard, there should be little disagreement between the testers and the implementation team as to whether the prototype UI and behaviors are implemented correctly. Acceptance testing can be viewed as a final step to validate the actual requirements, since the users will perform the testing, based both on the storyboard and their understanding of the application domain.

4 Experience

In using this process, we developed a healthcare information system. The prototype has the attributes as we described in Section 1. Specifically, a Siemens marketing

team planned to use this prototype to communicate with Siemens customers on proposed features. The initial requirements of the prototype were based upon their existing understanding of the customer needs and their knowledge on the prior similar
products. Prior to our prototyping effort, a large portion of existing understanding of
customers' needs was neither well documented nor organized in a way to support
product development. Thus, our prototyping activity had two goals: 1) To develop the
prototype that is a marketing and requirement solicitation tool for the marketing team,
2) To formulate the product requirements elicited from the Siemens customers in an
organized and tangible manner.

The prototype consists of 6 workflows and each workflow was specified with a
storyboard that has on average about 25 screen-shots. The prototype is required to be
customizable; the data displayed in the prototype UI can be customized for different
customer audiences. The business rules can be added or modified to enforce the prototype data compliance. The schedule for the delivery was very tight and firm (we
needed to deliver the prototype in four months) while the prototype was required to be
extremely reliable and with high look-and-feel quality. Our development team had on
average 20 staff members throughout the project duration.

By using S-RaP, we finished the project even a little earlier than the scheduled delivery dates even though at the start, the project was considered as highly risky for
delivering on time. The project size in terms of the number of requirements, projected
lines of implementation code, and number of team members all exceeded those of our
prior projects. *Our success in applying the S-RaP process concurrency indicates that
concurrent and iterative prototyping is highly effective for the development of a large
software prototype within a short development life cycle.* In the following sections we
discuss our observations in detail.

4.1 Progress Visibility

The following diagram provides a combined snapshot view as the project manager
evaluated the project progress. Note that this is not a view directly shown by the project-planning tool (i.e., Gantt Chart), but rather a project progress envisioning by the
project manager based upon the executing project plan. The span of each box indicates roughly where the major activities for each workflow fall. For example, the
diagram shows that Workflow 1 was finished while Workflow 6 was being developed
in parallel in both UI Design and the Prototype Implementation phase. After a workflow development had completely been moved from one phase to another, the project
manager will know most of the work in the past phase had been finished. The span of
a specific workflow across multiple phases (for example, Workflow 5 is in UI Design
and Prototype Implementation) indicates that the activities of both phases are still
taking place. The implementation phase will be under way for the data and service
aspects, or for the parts of the UI whose UI design has been matured and approved.

The S-RaP process provided the project manager with four checkpoints to evaluate
if a workflow has passed certain development phase: 1) "UI Design Review with
Users", 2) "UI Implementation Review with Users", 3) Problem list from System
Testing, and 4) Problem list from the Acceptance Testing. 1) and 2) are two very
specific activities that will either approve or reject the reviewed artifacts Thus, they

provided clear information for the project manager about the progress. Since the problem lists describe specific defects of the prototype found at certain dates for each workflow, they were very informative for evaluating the project progress.

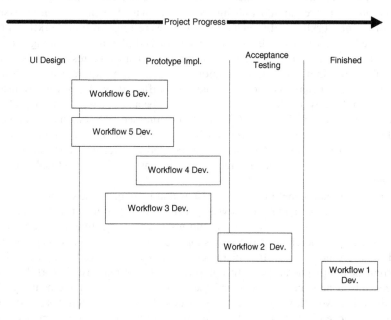

Fig. 3. Project progress envisioning

4.2 Concurrent Prototype Development

We successfully applied the S-RaP concurrency as we planned. Our experience however indicates that the *concurrent activities should be highly interactive* among the different teams (e.g., UI design and UI implementers). Those interactions can trigger the iterations of the activities in a more timely fashion. For example, the requirements of different system aspects (e.g., UI look-and-feel, and the dynamic interactions) were developed concurrently. However, once an initial working prototype was created, the detailed UI interactions and data behavior provided by the prototype affected the UI design again. Reviewing the UI prototype provided an opportunity for users to iteratively refine their UI requirements with the developers. To reduce the time spent on those team interactions, a representative member of one team can participate in the requirement meetings of other teams.

One major issue for the concurrent development is that the concurrent activities can cause substantial rework that outweighs the time gains from the activity execution concurrency. We addressed this issue by allowing the dependent activities to be carried out only on the stable requirements. Thus, the activities can speed up the iterative refinement of requirements rather than cause a complete rework of the requirements. For example, a storyboard draft in our project had over about 40 screen-shots that define UI and interactions. We started the UI implementation on the first 10 screen-shots that were relatively well defined. Thus, while the UI designers worked on the other slides, the developers implemented the first part of the workflow and provided the UI designers with feedback more quickly than if this had been done in a linear order.

Our experience also shows that concurrent development *requires a centralized coordination*, so the requirement changes can be managed to ensure their consistency across different workflows. In our project, there were three to four workflows being implemented concurrently. The project lead tracked the issues coming from the different teams and coordinated some unified approach to address those issues that can be about the implementation techniques or prototype requirements such as the consistent system behaviors. For example, two different workflows allow users to enter the data. However, when to save the data can be an issue (e.g., immediately after the data is entered, or after the "OK" button is pressed). Sometimes, whether we should keep the behaviors consistent depended on different application purposes. The identification of these sorts of issues sometimes led to a team meeting or a meeting with users to resolve the unclear requirements that can have a global impact on multiple workflows.

Another important benefit of this process is that it supports incremental delivery to users. One major issue in our project was that if we delivered the prototype exactly on the scheduled delivery date, the users would not have enough time to acceptance-test the prototype. The incremental delivery supported by S-RaP process very effectively solved this problem since the incremental delivery involved the users in the concurrent development process. In our project, the system-tested workflows were packaged into a number of groups and then delivered to users incrementally. Thus, while the other workflows were still being developed and system-tested, the users were able to acceptance-test the delivered workflows. The early acceptance testing also provided the development team sufficient time to fix the bugs, which would be impossible if the process were completely sequential and the delivery were not made incrementally.

4.3 Start System-Testing Early

One important factor that contributes to the successful use of S-RaP in this project is to start the system testing early. As soon as the integration for a workflow was stable, the system testers started the system testing for this workflow. Sometimes, for a long workflow, the system testing can be started on a finished portion of the workflow. The system testing helped identify quite a few problems that were not identified during the UI Implementation Review. Partially, it was due to the fact that the UI Implementation Review is more oriented towards the requirements validation, not the system verification. Thus, portions of the workflow implementation that were not related to the requirement issues were often not reviewed. The system testing was aimed at testing all the details of the prototype. Thus, it revealed the previously overlooked problems. Thus, it is extremely important to understand that the approved prototype implementation cannot in any way to replace the system testing.

About 10% of the development staff performed the system testing. The project leads played a significant role in the system testing. This helped them to have an accurate estimate about the project progress and to identify issues (e.g., developers' misunderstanding of the requirements) early. Since the project lead had a broad view of the workflows being concurrently developed, the identification of issues helped him to estimate the impacts on the other workflow developments (e.g., efforts required for making the changes).

UI designers who previously worked on the storyboards also tested most of the prototypes with an emphasis on the UI look-and- feel. This helped to identify the detailed UI issues that were often overlooked by the system testers.

5 Conclusions and Future Work

Highly concurrent, evolutionary software prototyping for certain application types that have stable application practice can be very feasible and effective. Even if the user interaction definition is initially unclear, if the application practice is well understood by the users, then the data model design and application services can be developed in parallel with the UI design to a large extent. Hence, the requirements for the different system aspects can be defined concurrently to speed up the prototype development.

The S-RaP prototyping process helps mature the prototype requirements that will then be used as the inputs to the product requirements. The UI design, implementation, system/acceptance testing of the prototype correspond to the different stages of the requirements activities, namely, requirement elicitation, analysis, specification, and validation. UI and the implementation reviews facilitate the above activities. The prototype system testing and acceptance testing can reveal potential requirement issues (e.g., behavior consistency) across different workflows. As with any method that involves customers throughout the software development, S-RaP requires the project management and development leads to manage the customer involvement efficiently and sufficiently. For example, the manager needs to direct the customers to describe only the domain knowledge that is relevant to the desired prototype behaviors. Otherwise, customers and software developers can both waste their time discussing irrelevant issues.

A well-designed software process can be essential to the success of a software prototyping and development project. However, process alone will not guarantee the project success. Its success additionally requires a good understanding of the process (and its rationales) by all key project staff at the project start and by the entire team soon after. The project leads and developers need to understand when they should defer a design decision making to the next prototyping iteration and when they should design and implement the system to the level of perfection. Documenting and representing such knowledge and criteria can be challenging since they are often not very tangible and measurable. We believe that capturing such knowledge however will be very useful for understanding rapid software prototyping and specifically, for using S-RaP more effectively. This should potentially be a future research topic for us.

References

1. Gamma E., et al.: Design Patterns, Addison-Wesley (1977)
2. Song, X., Osterweil, L: Engineering Software Design Processes to Guide Process Execution, IEEE Transactions on Software Engineering, Vol. 24, No.9 (1998) 759-774

3. Cavaness, C.: *Programming Jakarta Struts*. O'Reilly & Associates (2002)
4. Millington, D., Stapleton J.: *Developing A RAD Standard*. IEEE Software. Vol. 12, No. 5, (1995) 54-55
5. Martin, C. R.: Agile Software Development, Principles, Patterns and Practice, Prentice Hall (2002)
6. Hwong B., Laurance, D., Rudorfer A., Song, X.: User-Centered Design and Agile Software Development Processes, CHI, April 25-29, Vienna, Austria, (2004)
7. Gunaratne, J., Hwong, B., Nelson C., Rudorfer A.: Using Evolutionary Prototype to Formalize Product Requirements, workshop with International Conference on Software Engineering (2004)
8. Boehm, B, Turner R.: Balancing Agility and Discipline, Addison-Wesley (2002-2003)
9. Beck K.: Extreme Programming Explained, Addison-Wesley (2000)
10. Kruchten P.: The Rational Unified Processes, Addison Wesley (1999)

Aspect-Oriented Software Development and Software Process

Stanley M. Sutton Jr.

IBM T. J. Watson Research Center,
Hawthorne, NY, 10532 USA
suttons@us.ibm.com

Abstract. Aspect orientation is an increasingly promising approach to software development. It affords benefits deriving from advanced separation of concerns, including concern modeling, encapsulation, extraction, and composition. These may enable the development and evolution of software on a higher semantic level, with unprecedented control and flexibility. Aspect orientation may hold similar benefits for software process. Aspect orientation has implications for process on three levels: aspect-oriented products, aspect-oriented processes, and aspect-oriented process languages. It also facilitates insight into how the software-process spectrum may be unified. Macroprocess and microprocess concerns do not overlap, but some relationship between them is necessary. The relating of macroprocess concerns and microprocess concerns is the concern of a *mesoprocess* level, the principal home for process engineering, the purpose of which is to realize the ends of the macro level in terms of the means provided by the micro level. Aspect orientation should also benefit to a rigorous, orderly, and effective discipline of process engineering.

1 Introduction

Software process is generally about the development of software artifacts, using software tools, and working in software formalisms. Thus software process must necessarily accommodate itself to views and realizations of those artifacts, tools, and formalisms (although it may also seek to influence those views and realizations). Often these reflect programming or data-modeling paradigms, such as procedural or object orientation. *Aspect orientation* is a relatively new paradigm that has emerged from a programming model to stake a legitimate claim to being a software-development paradigm: *aspect-oriented software engineering* (AOSD). AOSD is still an emerging field with many open research issues. However, it has received considerable attention from research and commercial communities and it has produced interesting and significant results, especially in the area of programming but also in other areas of the life cycle. Thus, the implications of AOSD for software process (and process engineering in general) should be considered. Additionally, aspect orientation provides a useful perspective from which to consider the unification of the software-process spectrum and contributions to the formation of a discipline of process engineering. Section 2 of this paper discusses some of the key ideas in

M. Li, B. Boehm, and L.J. Osterweil (Eds.): SPW 2005, LNCS 3840, pp. 177–191, 2005.
© Springer-Verlag Berlin Heidelberg 2005

AOSD. Section 3 then considers implications of aspect orientation for software process on three levels. Section 4 addresses unification of the software process spectrum, using the aspect-oriented perspective to propose a third, integrating level of the spectrum and to consider how aspect orientation may contribute to process engineering. Finally, Section 5 presents conclusions.

2   Aspect-Oriented Software Development

"Aspect oriented" has been given two different meanings in software development. The original and narrower meaning relates to a method of programming that involves special treatment of "aspects", where an aspect was originally defined as (program) property that cannot be cleanly encapsulated in a "generalized procedure" [28]. A later but comparable definition is a program property that forces crosscutting in the implementation [15]. However, aspect-oriented programming in this narrower sense is one of a number of efforts that address the more general topic of "advanced separation of concerns." Examples of these approaches include subject-oriented programming [18], composition filters [1], adaptive programming [30], and multidimensional separation of concerns [45]. The term "aspect-oriented" has also been adopted to refer to this broader field. Unless otherwise stated, that is the sense in which I use the term (and the acronym AOSD). Some important ideas from AOSD are as follows:

- **Advanced separation of concerns:** Practically all approaches to AOSD are founded on the idea that conventional mechanisms for separating concerns are inadequate. The problem is that concerns are separated by means of system decomposition, and this allows only a single, dominant decomposition to be imposed, supporting only a single, dominant structuring of concerns. However, many systems can be decomposed in multiple ways, and no single decomposition can effectively separate all of the concerns that a realistic system must address. This leads to *scattering*, in which some concerns necessarily crosscut the dominant decomposition, and *tangling*, in which some modules necessarily combine multiple concerns. Additionally, for a long-lived system, the concerns of relevance will change over time. Consequently, the initial decomposition is likely to become less and less appropriate to current concerns and more and more problematic to maintain, extend, integrate, and so on. Thus, more "advanced" means of separating concerns are needed.

- **Aspect-oriented programming:** As noted, aspect orientation in the narrow sense is a particular perspective on advanced separation of concerns that addresses the problem of crosscutting concerns. Aspect-oriented *programming* [28] distinguishes these crosscutting concerns as *aspects*. It explicitly recognizes the crosscutting relationships, which are referred to as *pointcut* specifications in many AOP systems. It provides the means to localize the code for an aspect in a single module and provides a mechanism for composing (or weaving) the aspect code into the (dominant) base code of a program according to these crosscutting relationships. This addresses the scattering of aspectual concerns by localizing them in aspect modules, and it addresses tangling in the base program by enabling the omission of aspectual concerns. AOP mechanisms are typically defined in relation to an existing programming language (such as Java [28, 22], C++ [41], C [9] and several others [3]), and so the AOP mechanisms supplement the separation-of-concerns mechanisms already available in those languages.

- **Subject orientation:** Subject orientation [18] is the idea that different participants in a system (whether human or automated) may have different views of various entities in the system. Conversely, any given entity in a program may have to play multiple roles corresponding to multiple users or stakeholders[1]. Subject orientation gives another argument against the suitability of a single, dominant decomposition for software systems, for in general no one decomposition can coherently represent the perspective of all subjects. (The elements of concern to a subject may be scattered over multiple implementation classes, and the implementation classes in a system may tangle the concerns of multiple subjects.)

- **Multidimensional Separation of Concerns:** MDSOC [45] is (in part) a generalization of subject-orientation that holds that elements in a software system should be considered to belong to multiple independent concerns simultaneously. In other words, a system should be decomposable in multiple ways at the same time, for example, by features, behaviors, structures, and qualities [44]. MDSOC provides a basis not only for conceiving, viewing, and organizing software according to multiple dimensions of concern but also for extracting and composing software elements according to multiple dimensions of concern (e.g., as in Hyper/J [22], and the Concern Manipulation Environment (CME) [21,13]). This subverts the tyranny of the dominant decomposition [20] in a way that goes beyond that of strict aspect orientation by obviating the need for any dominant decomposition (or base program) and enabling elements from various decompositions to be used with equal priority.[2]

- **Explicit modeling of concerns:** Another idea that emerges from MDSOC, as first embodied by Hyper/J [22] and generalized in later work [44,31,48], is that concerns should be modeled explicitly, as first class entities in and of themselves, independently of particular software artifacts that may implement them. This can be seen as an application of the principle of separation of concerns to the treatment of concerns in the software life cycle. The importance of concern-modeling as a first-class activity is that it enables stakeholder concerns, and the relationships among them, to be captured explicitly at a high level of semantics. These concerns can be captured independently of the various artifacts and activities through which they will be realized, but the concerns can still be related to those artifacts and activities. This enables a concern model to serve as a high-level, "semantic hyper-index" into the software process and its products [44]. A concern model can be used to organize, analyze, interrelate, navigate, and query life-cycle elements,

---

[1] This is of course very similar to the idea of *Viewpoints* [32], although the subject-oriented authors were initially concerned with more fine-grained elements (such as classes) within a program, whereas the Viewpoints authors were initially concerned with more coarse-grained elements (such as artifacts) within a software development process.

[2] The aspect-base view of (for example) AspectJ [27] is often called asymmetric AOP, while the concern-concern view of (for example) Hyper/J [22] is often called symmetric AOP.

allowing stakeholders to conduct their activities and to access the system under development directly in terms of their interests.

- **Applicability across the life cycle (and beyond):** Although the original ideas relating to aspect orientation were articulated in terms of implementations [18,28,22], much work has since extended these ideas across the life cycle. MDSOC applies across the life cycle [45], and work has been done (for instance) on aspect-oriented requirements engineering [4,7,24,47], aspect-oriented design and architecture [8,5], and aspect-oriented analysis and testing [35,50,38]. Additionally, many ideas in aspect orientation should be applicable outside of the software domain. For example, mechanisms for concern extraction and composition should be applicable to any sort of structured information artifact or work product. Also, concerns can be modeled for any sort of entity that is capable of holding interest in some matters or in reflecting some matters of interest (such as organizations, processes, and artifacts, whether relating to software, engineering in other domains, business, government, manufacturing, and so on).

A number of elements of aspect orientation have process implications. In my opinion, the most important are the explicit modeling of concerns to represent stakeholder interests at a high conceptual level, the ability to conceive, organize, and view software according to concerns, and the ability to extract and compose software elements based on concerns.

It is worthwhile to consider the process implications of aspect orientation for two reasons. First, aspect orientation is a growing movement and, although it is still relatively new, it has produced some significant results. The International Conference on Aspect-Oriented Software Development has been held annually since 2002, and workshops on topics relating to aspect-oriented software development have been held at major software-engineering conferences since well before then. There are research groups in aspect orientation at a growing number of universities. Finally, the promotion and/or use of AOSD has received significant attention from several commercial organizations, including IBM [37,22,21,12,11], BEA [6], PARC (Xerox) [34], JBoss [26], among others (often through open-source projects). Also its applicability to "real-world" projects has been the subject of significant research programs ([16], [10]).

The second reason to consider the process implications of aspect orientation is that aspect orientation holds many prospective benefits for software engineering, including increased understandability, improved maintainability, easier evolution, greater reuse, and more. These qualities would also be of considerable benefit in process engineering. Implications of aspect orientation for software process are discussed in the following section.

3   Implications for Software Process

Aspect orientation has implications for software process on three levels: relating to products, relating to processes or process-programs, and relating to process languages.

3.1   Implications Relating to Products

Aspect orientation has implications for the nature and kinds of software artifacts. Since elements relating to specific concerns can be more fully separated, individual units may become physically smaller and more numerous and semantically simpler and more focused. At the same time, because these elements are smaller, simpler, and more focused, the ability to reuse and share them may increase. Increased sharing and reuse may reduce the total size of the artifact base for a given set of products (or product variants). However, ease of composition for reusable elements may tend to increase the number of products (or product variants) that are be developed. Artifacts representing composition or weaving directives will be necessary, but these will play a role analogous to traditional configuration and build files. Concern models may come to represent an important new category of artifact.

Aspect orientation also has implications for the nature of the activities in which we work with software products. Generically, AOSD will include activities like the identification (or mining) and modeling of concerns, the association of software artifacts to concerns, the organization of artifacts according to concerns, the extraction of new units from existing units to achieve greater specificity of concerns, the composition of new units from existing units to achieve greater breadth of concerns, and the specification of extraction and composition directives.

The specific roles played by aspect-oriented activities in software development depend on the kind of process. For example, in legacy migration, the principal aspect-oriented activities may be to browse, query, and navigate the existing artifact base, identify the concerns represented there, map units and their parts to identified concerns, logically encapsulate and/or physically extract elements according to concerns identified, and recompose extracted elements to obtain the prior system or to introduce new variations. In new development, the activities may be to identify concerns to be addressed by the new system, develop artifacts to address specific concerns, specify composition directives, and compose the new system according to the directives. When a new product is to be based on reuse from existing components, it will be important to browse and query a base of components based on the concerns they address. When the activity is debugging, it may be addressed by composing in code for measuring, monitoring, analyzing, logging, and reporting, applying composition and extraction to address problems, and then removing the diagnostic code from distributed products.

We can also envision some more general consequences for aspect-oriented software products. The ability to include or exclude concern-specific elements from a system should tend to facilitate the development of product families (including the conversion of "single-variant" products into families). The ability to extract concern-specific elements from existing systems (legacy or not) and then to recombine these in comparable or entirely new products should promote reuse. Conversely, the ability to extract and (re)compose concern-specific elements of a system increases the ability to configure, adapt, tailor, and evolve the system. This may help to extend system lifetimes. Better separation of artifacts according to concerns affords the opportunity for better separation of processes since activities on different concerns may proceed in parallel. This may make aspect orientation especially appropriate for open-source projects and may better enable commercial (or other proprietary) developers to provide value-added elements into open-source projects [19].

It is important to note that the adoption of aspect-orientation need not be all-or-nothing [13]. The changes to existing development practices can be minimal. Composition can be used in implementation (coding) without necessarily requiring changes to other parts of the life cycle. Concern modeling can be performed at any stage of development, potentially relating to any sort of artifact, without necessarily affecting those artifacts or requiring the use of composition. Concern mining can operate on an existing artifact base (now typically a code base) without affecting that base. Composition can be used to temporarily inject measuring, monitoring, and logging code into systems for purposes of testing or validation [29].

As noted in Section 2, there are aspect-oriented tools for several common programming languages, and there have been research prototype systems that apply aspect orientation to UML. There are several systems [21,36,17,25] that support some form of querying or modeling of concerns in code or other artifacts. These typically work in the Eclipse [14] open-source software development environment, a modern environment where AOSD tools can be used with "conventional" Java technology and other software tools.

3.2 Implications Relating to Processes and Process Programs

If we view processes and process programs as a kind of software product, then it is natural to imagine that the technologies and methods of aspect orientation may be applied to processes and process programs just as they are to ordinary software. For instance, process languages may be extended to incorporate aspect-oriented elements (similar to the introduction of aspects, pointcuts, and advice into Java by AspectJ [27]), or tools may be developed to enable the aspect-oriented treatment of existing process languages (similar to the ability to treat unmodified Java in an aspect-oriented manner using Hyper/J [22]). Concern modeling can be applied to processes and process programs, reflecting both organizational and implementation issues (such as macroprocess and microprocess concerns). Process elements could then be defined to address specific concerns, and process programs could then be composed to address the set of concerns applicable to a process.

There has already been some work in the aspect-oriented community that addresses process. The aspect-oriented treatment of business rules has been demonstrated [46,2], and there have been efforts on the aspect-oriented modeling of business processes [33,51].

Additionally, process may be an especially suitable domain for aspect-orientation. For instance, many process languages comprise relatively rich collections of language constructs compared to conventional programming languages. This situation has arisen as process-language designers have raised and broadened the scope of process languages in order to address the variety of processes concerns more directly. Thus many process languages already speak directly to a diversity of "microprocess" concerns including activities, activity control, rules, events, transactions, product and process consistency, exception handling, resources, artifacts, and more.

If aspect-orientation can be applied to process, then benefits like those for product development should be obtained for process development. It should be possible to develop specific aspects of a process more or less independently or in parallel. These can be developed by experts in the particular process-aspect domains, whether in the core functional areas (e.g., requirements specification, architecture, etc.) or in "crosscutting" concerns (e.g., security, accounting, resource management, etc.). The aspects addressing particular concerns (functional or nonfunctional) may be more readily reusable in other processes. By varying selected aspects (e.g., the way product requirements are gathered or resource allocation is performed) it may be relatively straightforward to develop process families or to tailor process instances to the particular concerns of particular projects.

The applicability of aspect orientation to processes does not depend on the use of programs to define processes. Aspect-oriented concepts and tools have been applied at most (if not all) stages of the software life cycle, many of which do not involve code at all, such as domain modeling, requirements specification, architecture, and design. Also, concerns are a generic concept, concerns can be modeled independently of any artifact type, and concerns can be modeled to reflect the interests of any sort of stakeholder in any sort of stake. Thus concerns can be modeled for enterprises, processes, agents, models or programs, artifacts or work products, and so on. Regardless of whether processes are conceived as software, processes reflect and address concerns just as software does, and so processes are subject to modeling and manipulation in terms of concerns just as much as software is.

3.3 Implications Relating to Process Languages

In considering the implications of aspect orientation for process languages, we can view the languages in the usual role of languages or in the less usual role of products.

Process Languages as Aspect-Oriented Languages. With respect to process languages, one issue raised by aspect orientation is whether process languages should be aspect-oriented. Some motion in this direction is needed if we want to treat processes and process programs as aspect-oriented artifacts. One path is to add new, aspect-oriented modules and constructs to an existing process language, as AspectJ adds elements representing advice, aspects, and pointcuts to Java. The other is instead to add these notions via distinguished annotations into an unchanged language, as AspectWerkz [6] does for Java. Another path is not to change the language (or programs) at all, but to change (or extend) the technology with which one works with the language, keeping aspect-oriented information separately from programs. This approach is used in Hyper/J [22] for Java, in which ordinary Java elements (classes, members, etc.) can be composed or extracted, and for which concern models and composition relationships are maintained in artifacts separate from the code.

Process Languages as Aspect-Oriented Products. Process languages are a form of software, and, as with other forms of software, we can consider what it might mean to apply aspect orientation to them. In my view, the chief benefit is the prospect of defining families of process languages based on alternative compositions of language constructs and semantics. In the absence of a generally accepted term for such languages, I will refer to them as "composed languages."

The idea of composed languages is somewhat anticipated in the process domain by the idea of "factored" languages such as JIL [42]. JIL contained a variety of high-level constructs that would specifically reflect the variety of concerns evidenced by software processes. However, as software processes reflect a large variety of concerns, software-process languages that attempt to address these concerns can become complex. The idea behind JIL was to enable process programmers to work with subsets of the language, comprising specific subsets of factors, that could be tailored to address the specific concerns of specific processes. Variants of JIL could be defined that might or might not include transactions, triggers, rules, procedures, and so on, depending on the concerns of the processes for which the languages were to be used. These language variants would be smaller and simpler than the full language and thus might be more readily understandable and adoptable. Additionally, because the various factors of the language would correspond to relatively independent concerns, they might be programmed relatively independently, by process programmers with particular expertise in the particular concerns. Little-JIL [49] is a successor to JIL (although not strictly a subset of it) that focuses on the "coordination" concern. It provides an elaboration of the coordination factor of JIL, and it avoids the complexity of concerns that are not intrinsic to coordination.

JIL represents a particular family of languages comprising the various subsets of factors it contains. Members of this language family are obtained, in effect, by extraction from the full language. The idea of composed languages generalizes the factored approach, potentially allowing an open set of factors, or language aspects, including alternative constructs and semantics, and potentially allowing an open set of factor compositions, hence resulting in an open set of composed process languages.

There are a number of reasons that favor consideration of a family of process languages compared to a single process language. No single process language has been widely adopted in practice. This is probably at least in part because the sets of concerns pertinent to processes varies from organization to organization, project to project, and process to process—just as they do for conventional applications—and no single language will be ideal for all sets of concerns. Finally, the ability to tailor the process language to the process may simplify development and maintenance, reduce costs, and improve time to delivery.

There are also a number of reasons that favor the consideration of a family of process languages compared to the use of multiple, independently defined languages. There may be considerable overlap of semantic concerns in the different languages (say, different languages with triggers, different languages with user roles, etc.). These could be regularized and simplified if the same language aspect for a particular concern (say, user roles) could be shared among multiple languages. The impedance mismatch between processes written in different languages might also be reduced if those languages are members of the same family. Additionally, it may be easier to evolve languages as the semantic concerns relevant to the languages evolve.

A major issue in the use of multiple process languages is the burden of understanding the languages and using them effectively. For families of composed languages, this problem may be reduced by the similarity of language aspects across languages. It may also be reduced by the possibility that language factors may be used more or less independently, by developers who are specialists in those factors.

4 Unifying the Software-Process Spectrum

For this workshop the software process spectrum has been defined with respect to two endpoints: microprocess and macroprocess. The challenge is to address how we may unify the spectrum between these endpoints and thereby enable the creation of a rigorous, orderly discipline of software-process engineering. Aspect orientation affords two perspectives on this issue. One is a conceptual perspective on the relationship of the microprocess and macroprocess levels, from which emerges a third level. The other is a practical perspective on an approach to process engineering.

4.1 Microprocess, Macroprocess, and Mesoprocess

To address this issue from an aspect-oriented perspective, we can consider the concerns that characterize each level of process. The topic statement for the workshop listed several concerns for the microprocess level:

Microprocess concerns:
- Description of processes that is precise, complete, detailed, unambiguous
- Detection of process flaws
- Facilitation of human-machine synergies

More generally, we can consider that microprocess concerns typically involve the representation of processes and things that can be done with process representations. These concerns may also suggest an orientation based on software concepts and technologies, since software engineering may be the domain in which these sorts of concerns are most effectively addressed in general. The topic statement for the workshop also listed several concerns for the macroprocess level:

Macroprocess concerns:
- Process architectures
- Process behavioral characteristics
- Process fit with organizational systems and characteristics

More generally, we can consider that macroprocess concerns usually involve the outward manifestations of a process in execution, especially with respect to the organizational context in which it executes. These concerns may not suggest any particular interest in software concepts and technology, as they emphasize the external aspect and effect of processes without consideration of how processes are realized.

These two sets of concerns do not overlap. Evidently, though, they can be interrelated: processes that execute and are observed on the macro level can have a basis in definition and interpretation on the micro level, and the specific requirements relating to concerns on the macro level should be supported by specific process representations that address concerns of the micro level.

What is missing from the opposition of microprocess versus macroprocess is an explicit connection between the two. I believe that there is another significant level of process research, development, and application, namely, the *mesoprocess* level, the purpose of which is to realize process goals as defined on the macro level in terms of formalisms and mechanisms as defined on the micro level. Thus, the mesoprocess level has the following sorts of concerns:

Mesoprocess concerns:
- Process development processes and platforms
- Selection and application of process languages
- Process execution platforms
- Specific processes

More generally, these concerns are involved in establishing the relationship between the macro and micro levels, realizing the organizational process objectives in terms of organizational process means.[3]

Concerns on the macro level motivate the selection of process development processes and platforms, the selection and use of process languages, the choice of process execution platforms, and the choice and execution of specific processes. On the meso level, choices are made, and process-development processes are carried out, to achieve the desired fit of product-development processes with organizational systems and behaviors, and to obtain desired process behaviors, in an architecture that is suitable for the architecture of the organization and its resources. Selections of processes, languages, and technologies on the meso level will be based on their ability to support desired levels of precision, completeness, detail, and clarity, to enable the detection of process flaws, and to facilitate human/machine interactions.

In other words, the mesoprocess level is the level of *meta-processes*, such as process-development processes, which is missing in the dichotomy of macroprocess versus microprocess. The meso level is thus the principal level on which process engineering, as an applied art, occurs.

4.2 Process Engineering

Aspect orientation provides some significantly new approaches to software development. These include

- The promotion of concerns to first-class entities in the software life cycle, thus raising the level of abstraction at which we work with software
- The overthrowing of the tyranny of the dominant decomposition by enriching the means and increasing the flexibility for separating and combining concerns
- A shift of the basic activities of software development toward the identification, encapsulation, extraction, and composition of concerns, thereby facilitating the change and exchange of software

Of course, aspect orientation is not without challenges. These include issues of consistency and correctness (as of composed or extracted elements, or composition and extraction specifications), expressiveness (as of aspects, pointcuts, and composition relationships), generality (as in the tradeoff of power versus ease of use), dynamism (as in the composition of new concerns into running applications), and complexity (as in the detailed modeling of concerns for large applications, or in

---

[3] It may seem that the mesoprocess concerns are based on ideas of "process programming", but that is only one possible approach to addressing concerns on this level. For instance, all processes must be developed and implemented somehow, whether by software engineering or other techniques, and all processes must be defined somehow, whether by programming language, modeling language, or natural language.

managing the composition relationships for large product families). These issues are the subject of research in the aspect-oriented community.

The potential benefits of aspect-oriented approaches are such that they could be of significant value in the domain of process engineering. Thus, at the mesoprocess level, a discipline of process engineering might very well be based on aspect-oriented principles and practices. Similarly, many of the issues that confront the realization of aspect-oriented product development (consistency, correctness, expressiveness, generality, dynamism, complexity) have also been (and remain) issues in software process research and development. So the concerns of aspect-oriented research and software process research have a natural alignment.

Some examples of potential applications of aspect orientation in process engineering are as follows:

- Concern modeling across the process levels: Conventional software development relies on the representation of concerns and their interrelationships in the various artifacts that are developed across the life cycle. Aspect orientation (in part) advocates the reification of concerns in separate models that are independent of life-cycle artifacts. A concern model can thus serve as a domain model where the domain is the application under development. As such, it can serve as a kind of index to the artifacts in the product under development, represent relationships among them, and facilitate traceability and analysis at the semantic level of concerns. This may have special relevance in process engineering, for capturing concerns on the macroprocess level, abstracting concerns from the microprocess level, and (through process-engineering processes on the mesoprocess level) supporting connection, analysis, and traceability between the two.

- Process families: Process families have been a particular concern of software process research (for example, [23]). Organization-wide process families are a part of the Capability Maturity Model [39] at level 3 (defined processes), at which reuse of defined processes in an organization is established. Additionally, process families may be especially relevant for product families [40] and domain-specific software development. Aspect orientation lends itself to product families: concern modeling can play a role analogous to feature modeling, capturing similarities and variations of concerns across family members, and compositional techniques can be used to compose family members from libraries of concern-specific family assets. Also, concern-identification, encapsulation, and extraction capabilities (along with recomposition) are useful in retroactively converting an isolated product into a product line [43]. In process engineering, with defined processes seen in the role of the product, aspect-oriented techniques can be used to define process lines or to evolve process lines from individual defined processes.

- Process integration: Process integration is an important aspect of business integration in commercial and engineering domains. The motivation to integrate processes depends on some complementarity of their concerns. The ability to integrate processes depends on the compatibility of their concerns. It also depends on the ability to achieve the necessary interoperation of activities in the processes. Concern modeling of organizations and processes has the potential to support the analysis of the compatibility of processes at a high semantic level and to facilitate the identification of process elements that are especially important for interoperation. The ability to extract and compose process elements would provide a mechanism whereby incompatible elements of processes could be removed and replaced by compatible elements. Extraction and composition also may provide a means to enhance the interoperability of processes from different organizations, for example, by incorporating processes of one organization as subroutines in the processes of another, or by adding elements for communication and coordination.

Aspect orientation can also play many other roles, such as helping to evolve processes in response to the evolution of organizational systems and characteristics, the tailoring of process languages so as to be more appropriate for organizational process-definition processes, and more. Thus, aspect orientation seems to address a set of concerns that contribute in important ways to the resolution wide variety problems in process engineering. On that basis it seems that aspect orientation can be a substantial part of a rigorous, orderly, and effective discipline of process engineering.

5 Conclusions

Aspect-oriented software development is a relatively new and increasingly promising approach to software development. It offers a number of potential benefits for software engineering, mainly deriving from advanced approaches to separation of concerns, including (multidimensional) concern modeling, encapsulation, extraction, and composition. These may enable the development and evolution of software on a higher (concern-oriented) semantic level with unprecedented control and flexibility.

Aspect orientation may hold the same benefits for software processes and process engineering in general. Aspect orientation has implications for process on three levels: "conventional" processes for aspect-oriented products, aspect-oriented processes and process programs or models (viewing process as products), and aspect-oriented process languages (viewing process languages as products).

Aspect orientation also facilitates insight into how the software process spectrum may be unified. Evidently the concerns of the macroprocess level and the concerns of the microprocess level do not overlap, but both are essential, and some relationship between them is necessary for the success of software process. The relating of macroprocess concerns and microprocess concerns is the concern of a middle level, the mesoprocess level, which is the principal home of meta-processes for process engineering, the purpose of which is to realize the ends of the macro level in terms of the means provided on the micro level. Aspect orientation should also offer benefits to a rigorous, orderly, and effective discipline of process engineering.

Acknowledgements

My perspectives on the issues addressed in this paper have been influenced by many people. In the area of AOSD, I want especially to thank Peri Tarr, Isabelle Rouvellou, Harold Ossher, and William Harrison. In the area of software process I would particularly like to thank Dennis Heimbigner and Lee Osterweil. Of course, any problems in this work are entirely due to me.

References

1. Akşit, M., Wakita, K., Bosch, J., Bergmans, L., and Yonezawa, A. Abstracting object-interactions using composition-filters. In *Object-Based Distributed Processing*, R. Guerraoui, O. Nierstrasz, and M. Riveill, Eds. LNCS 791. Springer-Verlag, Berlin (1993) 152–184.
2. AOP for Business Rules. Website (2003) http://ssel.vub.ac.be/br/index.php
3. AOSD.net. Website (2005) http://www.aosd.net
4. Baniassad, E. and Clarke, S. 2004. Finding aspects in requirements with Theme/Doc. In Early Aspects 2004: Aspect-Oriented Requirements Engineering and Architecture Design Workshop (AOSD) http://trese.cs.utwente.nl/workshops/early-aspects-2004/Papers/Baniassad-Clarke.pdf
5. Bass, L., Klein, M., and Northrop, L. 2004. Identifying aspects using architectural reasoning. In Early Aspects 2004: Aspect-Oriented Requirements Engineering and Architecture Design Workshop (AOSD) (Lancaster, UK). http://trese.cs.utwente.nl/workshops/early-aspects-2004/Papers/BassEtAl.pdf
6. BEA Systems. aspectwerkz-workshopkit Project home (Website). https://aspectwerkz-workshopkit.projects.dev2dev.bea.com/
7. Brito, I, and Moreira, A. 2004. Integrating the NFR framework in a RE model. In Early Aspects 2004: Aspect-Oriented Requirements Engineering and Architecture Design Workshop (AOSD) (Lancaster, UK). http://trese.cs.utwente.nl/workshops/early-aspects-2004/Papers/BritoMoreira.pdf
8. Clarke, S., Harrison, W., Ossher, H., and Tarr, P. Subject-oriented design: Towards improved alignment of requirements, design and code. In *14th Conf. Object-oriented Programming, Systems, Languages, and Applications (OOPSLA)* ACM (1999) 325–339.
9. Coady, Y., Kiczales, G., Feeley, M. and Smolyn, G. "Using AspectC to Improve the Modularity of Path-Specific Customization in Operating System Code", Proceedings of the 8th European Software Engineering Conference held jointly with 9th ACM SIGSOFT International Symposium on Foundations of Software Engineering (2001) 88-98.
10. Defense Advanced Research Projects Agency (DARPA). Program Composition for Embedded Systems (Website) (1999) http://www.darpa.mil/baa/baa00-23.htm.
11. Eclipse AspectJ Development Tools Technology Subproject (Website). (2005) http://www.eclipse.org/aspectj/
12. Eclipse AspectJ Technology Project (Website). (2005) http://www.eclipse.org/aspectj/
13. Eclipse Concern Manipulation Environment Technology Project (Website) (2005) http://www.eclipse.org/cme/
14. Eclipse.org. (Website) http://www.eclipse.org
15. Elrad, T., Filman, R. E., and Bader, A. 2001. Aspect-oriented programming. *Comm. ACM 44*, 10 (Oct.), 29–32.
16. Fraunhofer Institute Computer Architecture and Software Technology FIRST. TOPPrax – Applying Aspect-Oriented Programming in Commercial Software Development (Website) (2005) http://www.first.fraunhofer.de/en/topprax
17. Griswold, W. Aspect Browser for Eclipse (Website). http://www-cse.ucsd.edu/users/wgg/Software/AB/
18. Harrison, W. and Ossher, H. 1993. Subject-oriented programming—a critique of pure objects. In *8th Conf. Object-oriented Programming, Systems, Languages, and Applications (OOPSLA)*, (Washington, D. C.). ACM, 411–428.

19. Harrison, W., Ossher, H., Sutton Jr., S., and Tarr, P. Concern Modeling in the Concern Manipulation Environment. IBM Systems Journal, Special Issue on Open Source Software (2005, to appear)

20. Harrison, W., Ossher, H., and Tarr, P. 2000. Software engineering tools and environments: A roadmap. In *Conf. Future of Software Engineering* (Limerick). ACM, 261–277.

21. IBM. Concern Manipulation Environment (CME): a flexible, extensible, interoperable environment for AOSD. http://www.research.ibm.com/cme/

22. IBM. Hyperspaces. http://www.research.ibm.com/hyperspace/

23. ISPW. 10th International Software Process Workshop: June 17-19, 1996, Dijon, France : Proceedings, IEEE (1998) 119

24. Jacobson, I. and Ng, P-W. Aspect-Oriented Software Development with Use Cases. Addison-Wesley Object Technology Series (2004) 464

25. Janzen, D. and De Volder, K. Navigating Code without Getting Lost. 2nd International Conference on Aspect-Oriented Software Development. ACM (2003) 178—187

26. JBoss. JBoss Aspect Oriented Programming (Website) (2005) http://www.jboss.org/products/aop

27. Kiczales, G., Hilsdale, E., Hugunin, J., Kersten, M., Palm, J., and Griswold, W. G. 2001. Getting started with AspectJ. *Comm. ACM 44*, 10 (Oct.), 59–65

28. Kiczales, G., Lamping, J., Mendhekar, A., Maeda, C., Lopes, C., Loingtier, J.-M., and Irwin, J. 1997. Aspect-oriented programming. In *ECOOP'97 Object-Oriented Programming, 11th European Conference,* M. Akşit and S. Matsuoka, Eds. LNCS 1241. Springer-Verlag, Berlin, 220–242.

29. Kimelman, D., Kruskal, V., Ossher, H., Roth, T., and Tarr, P. HyperProbe(TM) - An Aspect-Oriented Instrumentation Tool for Troubleshooting Large-Scale Production Systems. Demonstration Abstract, 1st Int'l Conf. Aspect-Oriented Software Development (AOSD) (2002) http://trese.cs.utwente.nl/aosd2002/index.php?content=hyperprobe

30. Lieberherr, K.   Adaptive Object-Oriented Software: The Demeter Method with Propagation Patterns. PWS Publishing Company (1996).

31. Lohmann, D., and J. Ebert., J. 2003. A generalization of the hyperspace approach using meta-models. In Early Aspects 2003: Aspect-Oriented Requirements Engineering and Architecture Design Workshop (AOSD) (Boston, USA). http://www.cs.bilkent.edu.tr/AOSD-EarlyAspects/Papers/LohEbe.pdf

32. Nuseibeh, B., Kramer, J., and Finkelstein, A. 1993. Expressing the relationships between multiple views in requirements specification. In *15th Int'l Conf. Software Engineering (ICSE)* (Baltimore, Maryland). IEEE, 187–196.

33. Odgers, B. and Thompson, S.: Aspect-Oriented Process Engineering (ASOPE). In: Moreira, M. D. and Demeyer, S. (eds.): Object-Oriented Technology, ECOOP'99 Workshop Reader, ECOOP'99 Workshops, Panels, and Posters, Lisbon, Portugal, June 14-18, 1999, Proceedings. Lecture Notes in Computer Science 1743 Springer-Verlag, Berlin Heidelberg New York (1999) 295.

34. PARC. AspectJ (2004) http://www.parc.com/research/csl/projects/aspectj/default.html

35. Rajan, H. and Sullivan, K. Generalizing AOP for Aspect-Oriented Testing. Proceedings of the Fourth International Conference on Aspect-Oriented Software Development (AOSD) (2005) 14-18

36. Robillard, M. and Murphy, G. Concern Graphs: Finding and Describing Concerns Using Structural Pro-gram Dependencies. In Proceedings of the 24th Int'l Conf. of on Soft. Eng., (2002) 406—416

37. Sabbah, D. 2004. Aspects—From Promise to Reality. In 3rd International Conference on Aspect-Oriented Software Development (AOSD) (Lancaster, UK). ACM, 1-2.

38. Sereni, D. and de Moor, O.   Static Analysis of Aspects.   Proceedings of the 2nd International Conference on Aspect-Oriented Software Development. ACM (2003) 30-39
39. Software Engineering Institute (SEI).   The Capability Maturity Model: Guidelines for Improving the Software Process. Addison-Wesley Professional (1995) 464
40. Software Engineering Institute (SEI).   A Framework for Software Product Line Practice Version 4.2 (2004) http://www.sei.cmu.edu/plp/framework.html#outline
41. Spinczyk, O., Gal, A. S, and Schröder-Preikschat, W.   Aspect*C++: An Aspect*-Oriented Extension to C++. Proceedings of the Fortieth International Conference on Tools Pacific: Objects for internet, mobile and embedded applications - Volume 10 (2002) 53-60 (see also http://www.aspectc.org/)
42. Sutton Jr., S. and Osterweil, L.   The Design of a Next-Generation Process Language. In: Jazayeri, M. and Schauer, H. (eds.) Proceedings of the 6th European Conference held jointly with the 5th ACM SIGSOFT International Symposium on Foundations of Software Engineering. LNCS 1301. Springer-Verlag, New York, Inc. (1997) 142—158
43. Sutton Jr., S. M. and Rouvellou, I.   Advanced separation of concerns for component evolution. In Workshop on Engineering Complex Object-Oriented Systems for Evolution (Tampa, Florida) (2001) http://www.dsg.cs.tcd.ie/ecoose/oopsla2001/papers.shtml
44. Sutton Jr., S. and Rouvellou, I.   Modeling of software concerns in Cosmos. In Kiczales, G. (ed.) 1st Int'l Conf. Aspect-Oriented Software Development (AOSD) ACM (2002) 127–133
45. Tarr, P., Ossher, H., Harrison, W., and Sutton Jr., S.   N degrees of separation: Multi-dimensional separation of concerns. In 21st Int'l Conf. Software Engineering (ICSE), (Los Angeles). IEEE (1999) 107 – 119.
46. Tarr, P., Ossher, H., and Sutton Jr., S.   Hyper/J: Multi-Dimensional Separation of Concerns for Java (Tutorial) (2001)
http://www.netobjectdays.org/pdf/01/slides/tutorial/sutton.pdf
47. Tekinerdogan, B. ASAAM: aspectual software architecture analysis method. In Early Aspects 2003: Aspect-Oriented Requirements Engineering and Architecture Design Workshop (AOSD) (2003).   http://www.cs.bilkent.edu.tr/AOSD-EarlyAspects/Papers/-Tekinerdogan.pdf
48. Wagelaar, D. A concept-based approach for early aspect modelling. In Early Aspects 2003: Aspect-Oriented Requirements Engineering and Architecture Design Workshop (AOSD) (2003) http://www.cs.bilkent.edu.tr/AOSD-EarlyAspects/Papers/Wagelaar.pdf
49. Wise, A., Cass, A., Lerner, B., McCall, E., Osterweil, L., and Sutton Jr., S.   Using Little-JIL to Coordinate Agents in Software Engineering. 15th IEEE International Conference on Automated Software Engineering (ASE 2000) Proceedings. IEEE (2000) pp. 155—164
50. Zhao, J. Data-Flow-Based Unit Testing of Aspect-Oriented Programs. Proceedings of the 27th Annual IEEE International Computer Software and Applications Conference (COMPSAC'2003) (2003)
51. Zhu, Jun. Personnel communication. IBM Research (2005) zhujun@cn.ibm.com

A Gradually Proceeded
Software Architecture Design Process*

Licong Tian, Li Zhang, Bosheng Zhou, and Guanqun Qian

Software Engineering Institute, Beijing University of Aeronautics and Astronautics,
No. 37 Xueyuan Rd., Haidian District, Beijing, 100083, P.R. China
tianlicong@163.com, lily@buaa.edu.cn, bszhou@cyberspi.com.cn
qianguanqun@process.buaa.edu.cn

Abstract. When design software architecture for large systems, designers often face with the problem how to move from requirements to a coarse-grained abstract architecture, then gradually refine it into more concrete ones, and last to detail design and implementation. Steps involved to implement such a process remain vague. Designers usually implement this process intuitively and opportunistically. We propose a Gradually Proceeded Software Architecture Design Process called GADesign. GADesign divides software architecture design into several phases and provides a sequence of well-defined steps to make this process more transparent and easier to be implemented.

1 Introduction

During the past ten years, architecture-based development has received a lot of attention in academia and industry as evidenced by numerous of architecture related techniques. Such as, architecture description languages (ADLs) [1,2,3,4], architecture styles/patterns [5,6], architecture evaluation methods [7,8], architecture documenting guidance [9,10], architecture design tools [11,12], etc. However, to make full use of these techniques, they must be incorporated into a design process.

As is well known, software architecture design for large systems is complex. Even experienced software architects can't make the complete definition of software architecture all at once, but need to do in a gradual manner: first begin with a coarse-grained abstract architecture which may be partial and incomplete; then gradually refine it into more concrete ones; and last to detail design and implementation. However, the steps involved in such a process remain vague. Designers implement this process mainly depending on intuition and experience. There's a need for a series of well-defined steps to provide systematic guidance for it.

Several software architecture design methods do exist. Bass et al. propose Attribute Driven Design (ADD) [13]. ADD focuses mainly on high-level architecture. The output of ADD is an "initial software architecture design known as the candidate architecture"[14]. Jacobson, Booch and Rumbaugh propose in their Unified Software Development Process [15] an iterative, use case driven method for architecture design. As Kazman et al. argue, this method focuses primarily on functional requirements of

---

* This work is supported by Beijing Government' Sponsor Plan for New Star in Science and Technology (No. H013610270112).

M. Li, B. Boehm, and L.J. Osterweil (Eds.): SPW 2005, LNCS 3840, pp. 192–205, 2005.

the system, while the guidance on quality attribute requirements is insufficient [14]. Meihong et al. propose ABC, an Architecture Based Component Oriented Approach to Software Development [16]. The main contribution of ABC is the mapping of a relatively detailed architecture into implementation, and the realizing of component automatic assembly and deployment.

In this paper, we incorporate some existing techniques and propose a Gradually Proceeded Software Architecture Design Process called GADesign. The main purpose of GADesign is to provide a systematic, step-by-step guidance to software architecture design, so as to make this process clearer and easier to be implemented.

This paper is organized as following: Section 2 presents some concept definitions to establish the vocabulary of the paper. Section 3 gives an overview of the basic ideas of GADesign. Implementation details of GADesign are presented in section 4. Section 5 concludes this paper with future work.

2 Concept Definitions

These concepts are mainly introduced or adapted from references [9,17,18,19].

Software Architecture. Any well-defined form of a system's fundamental organization embodied in its components, their relationships to each other and the environment, and the principles governing its design and evolution [9].

Software Architecture Requirement. Software architecture requirements are those requirements that "shape" the architecture. If these requirements can be met, then the architecture can be satisfactorily designed [17].

Software Architecture Tactic. A software architecture tactic is a technique or principle used to address one or more architecture design issues. Some of them may be captured in patterns of various sorts, others may be general design principles (e.g. information hiding), or measures the designer himself thinks of [18].

UML[19] Related Concepts. UML (Unified Modeling Language) is an industry standard for object-oriented modeling. In this paper, we use several UML related concepts without further explanation, such as use case, use case analysis, sequence diagram, etc. Readers can turn to UML reference books for more information.

3 Basic Ideas of GADesign

The basic ideas underpinning GADesign include:

-- Divide the whole process into several phases. Different phase focuses on different sets of problems and describes the architecture with different level of details. Doing this way, design information can be added incrementally, so it's helpful to reduce the complexity and risk of software architecture design.

-- Clearly define implementation steps for each phase, so as to make the design process more transparent and easier to be understood and implemented.

-- Clearly define finish criteria for each phase, so as to implement architecture evaluation phase by phase, instead of a one-time evaluation after all design work is completed. So, it's helpful to discover potential problems and risks earlier.

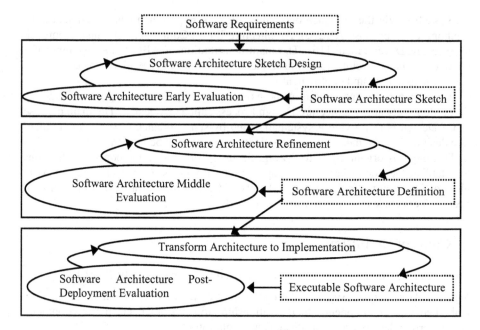

Fig. 1. Outline of GADesign

Fig. 1 gives the process outline of GADesign.

The input to GADesign is a list of software requirements: functional requirements are represented as use cases for their wide acceptance in current software development; quality attribute requirements can be documented in any textual format.

GADesign divides software architecture design into three phases: Software Architecture Sketch Design (for short, SAS Design), Software Architecture Refinement and Transform Architecture to Implementation.

Software Architecture Sketch Design
The main purpose of SAS Design is to provide system stakeholders with an initial sketch of the system's architecture (before diving into its strict definition) to enable an early understanding of the high level structure of the system and roughly reason about its potential ability to meet system's requirements.

At this phase, designers concentrate their efforts on identifying what architecture tactics can be used to meet architecture requirements, and then integrating these tactics to construct a consistent, cohesive structure. Since the main purpose of SAS Design is to make sure whether design decisions are feasible to meet system's requirements, so only core components of the system and their main connections need to be shown. Strict definitions for interfaces and behaviors of single component are information that suggested to be deferred to the next phase. These information are imperative for system implementation and assembly, but not so important if we just want to reason about system's potential ability to satisfy some properties.

So in SAS Design, design results are described with coarse-grained concepts. Semantic information of component may include:

-- a name, to identify the component in the model;

-- a functional description, to describe the role of the component in the system;

-- optional properties, to show auxiliary information, such as thorough outputs, max connections, etc;

-- optional pattern information tags, to show its relationship with pattern roles, if this component is created by instantiating certain pattern template;

-- operations and attributes, they are only treated as placeholders to show components' responsibility, not strict signatures of their methods and variables.

Connections between components are also described in a coarse-grained manner. For example, we may use a common "data flow" connection to show data production and requirement relationship between two components without specifying whether the data is transferred by procedure call, shared variable or message passing. We may connect component A and B with procedure call to imply that component A has the potential to invoke component B's operations, but need not to show exactly through which interface and operation this call is invoked. An example metamodel for SAS modeling is shown in Fig.2.

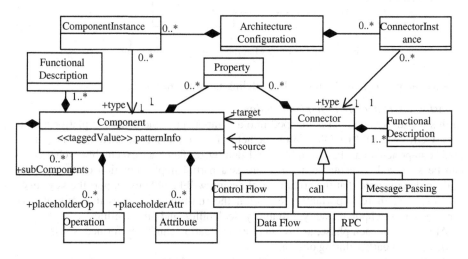

Fig. 2. An Example Metamodel for SAS Modeling

Software Architecture Refinement
The main purpose of software architecture refinement phase is to refine SAS model into a more detailed architecture specification, so as to provide rigorous constraints on software development. In this paper, we call this specification as Software Architecture Definition (for short, SAD). Interface and behavior details of each component and their interaction protocols are identified and defined with precise signatures. More detail implementation mechanisms are identified and determined, such as processes/threads to cope with concurrent activities, inter-process communications, resource managing and/or arbitrating strategies, persistence mechanisms, etc. In order to minimize the effects of specific technique on architecture design, SAD is defined in a platform-independent manner.

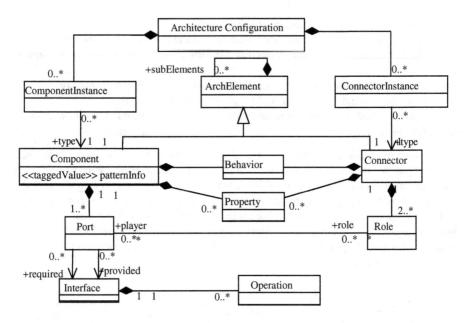

Fig. 3. An Example Metamodel for SAD Modeling

An example metamodel for SAD modeling is shown in Fig. 3.

Transform Architecture to Implementation
In this phase, SAD model is mapped into a component implementation platform (e.g. EJB, CORBA, COM/DCOM). With the help of some tools, code sketch can be generated; components can be assembled and deployed. Thus, an executable architecture can be achieved. Executable architecture is a partial implementation of the system, built to demonstrate that the architectural design will be able to support the key functionality and, more importantly, to exhibit the run-time properties in terms of performance, throughput, capacity, reliability, scalability, and other "-ilities".

At the end of each phase, an architecture evaluation can be performed, so risks can be discovered earlier during design.

Another thing worth mentioning is that phases in GADesign are elastic. Depending on the characteristics of your project, you can compress two phases into one, or divide one phase into two or more smaller ones. And the principle is, when adjust the phases, you must also define/redefine the finish criteria for each phase.

4   Implementation Details of GADesign

4.1   Software Architecture Sketch Design

This design phase can be carried out in five steps. The definitions of these steps are enlightened by several different sources of technique achievements, such as Bass's Attribute Driven Design [13], Bachmann's architectural tactic [18], Buschmann's patterns for applying patterns"[22], use case analysis techniques from UML[19], etc.

Step 1: Identify Software Architecture Requirements
A system may have many requirements, not all of these requirements have relations with software architecture. The first step in software architecture design is to identify those requirements that have influence on architecture design. This can be done by:

-- *Choose architecturally significant use cases*: Architecturally significant use cases are use cases that expose high-risk capabilities that must be mitigated, those have much difficulty to be implemented, or those that represent most important functionality to users of the system.

-- *Choose architecturally significant quality attributes*: Architecturally significant quality attributes are quality attributes that have global influence on the system, or those may be distributed across several components. Quality attributes that only influence some local methods of a single component are not architecturally significant.

Step 2: Identify Candidate Architecture Tactics
After architecture requirements are identified, next to do is to identify candidate architecture tactics that can be used to meet these requirements.

First, consider if there's a reference model exist in this domain, a reference model can help to construct the initial functional decomposition of the architecture.

Then, for every quality attribute requirement, look for technique tactics that help to meet its satisfaction. Architecture or design pattern libraries/catalogues can be taken as the first step to start to search, they provide lots of reusable design solutions for common design problems. Famous general-purpose libraries include POSA[6], GoF[20], Shaw's style list[5], etc. Domain-specific pattern libraries are also exist, such as Douglass's real time pattern catalogue [21]. To effectively use these pattern libraries, designers need to be acquainted with the basic ideas of design patterns.

For requirements that are not addressed by available architectural patterns, architect can make a decision based on conversional design methods and his own experiences and knowledge.

Identified tactics can be recorded in the form shown in Table 1.

Table 1. Candidate Architecture Tactics

Req ID	Tactic ID	Tactic Name	Tactic Description	Tactic Status	Strengthen / Weaken
R_001	S_001_1	POSA.MVC+ POSA.CommandProcessor	decoupling user interface and business process	suggested	R_002 (0.8) R_003 (-0.5)

Establish cross-reference relationships between requirements and tactics. Assign a unique ID, a name, a brief description and a status (may be *suggested, accepted* or *rejected)* for each tactic. Items of Strengthen/Weaken represent the influence of each tactic to other requirements.

Step 3: Trade-off Analysis and Tactic Selection
A large number of tactics may be identified, and these tactics are never standalone. Before applying these tactics, a trade-off analysis must be carried out. For the time being, we can't provide a systematical method for trade-off analysis of architecture tactics. We suppose that architects make this choice by experience.

Step 4: Create Software Architecture Sketch

The task of this step is to apply the selected tactics to construct the software architecture. Since each tactic will impose special constraints to architecture in terms of structure decomposition, functional distribution or how control and data flow through elements, so each tactic implies the existence of some components and connections, or in other words, each tactic relates to a design fragment. For example, The *Localize Changes* tactic for some kind of modifiability requirement suggests a three-tier client-server model be used to allocate the client, database and business rules to separate tiers and, hence, three components represent the three tiers can be identified, and potential interactions between theses tiers are identified as connections between these components. The *Use an Intermediary* tactic suggests that the communication between the tiers be mediated by some abstract interface, so a data access layer may be created as the design decision relate to this design tactic. SAS model is constructed by composing these design fragments. To make this composition process more controllable and easier to be implemented, we introduce the principles of "One Pattern At a Time" and "Design Integration Precedes Implementation" proposed by Buschmann as "patterns for applying patterns"[22].

The idea underpinning "One Pattern At a Time" is to integrate these tactics one by one, with descending order of importance. Doing this way, we can follow their implementation guidelines more easily, since aspects of other, not yet applied tactics, do not need to be considered.

The idea underpinning "Design Integration Precedes Implementation" is that designer should concentrate his focus on how to integrate separated design fragments into a coherent structure to make them work together harmoniously. Before the integration is finished, don't unfolding each fragment's details. Too many details may divert designer's attention from critical decisions. You may create a design that has several perfect design segments but on the whole cannot work properly. For architecture design, this means, designers should pay more attention on how components related to each other, not their interfaces details.

First, apply a large-scale pattern to implement the initial decomposition of the system. Then, composite other tactic's design fragment one by one and take an order according to the requirement's priority. When compositing a fragment, first check whether the existing structure can directly support this fragment, if it can, then

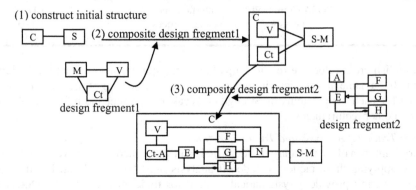

Fig. 4. Design Segment Integration

continue to the next fragment; otherwise, adapt the structure to satisfy the property of this fragment. This process is shown in Fig.4.

Step 5: Behavior Description

Without taking into account how elements behave when connected to each other, there can be no assurance that the system will work as intended. Knowledge of system's behavior can be achieved by analyzing architecturally significant use cases. By use case analysis, we can validate whether components can interact as intended to meet system's function. For example, if a component wants to send message to a destination, however there's no proper component to receive this message, then it implies that new component should be added to the system to meet this requirement. When doing use case analysis, if we can assure that the control or data flows between components are reasonable, then message definitions need not be strictly specified, textual phrases are usable. Since these operations are not the final signature definitions of component's methods, mark these responsibilities with <<placeholderOp>> to mind designers that these operations should be refined further in subsequent design.

With the iterations between structure construction and behavior description, we can finally get a SAS model. SAS model contains the core components of the system and their main connections that reflect main architecture decisions that constrain the system's design and implementation. Because interface and behavior details of each component have not been specified, we can just reason about whether or not the system has the potential ability to meet certain properties, but can't get enough information for implementation.

4.2 Software Architecture Early Evaluation

Before announcing the finish of software architecture sketch design, an evaluation should be performed to this initial architecture model. The main purpose of software architecture early evaluation is to reason about the system's ability to satisfy functional and quality requirements.

Satisfaction of functional requirements can be examined based on use case analysis, quality requirements can be evaluated using SAAM[7] based on quality scenarios. In this paper, we just give the checkout list for architecture evaluation and don't provide details for evaluation process. This is not the focus of this paper. Readers can turn to [7] for more information about how architecture evaluation can be performed.

Checklist for software architecture early evaluation:

-- The key components and their connections have been identified, and every component has a name and a functional description to show its role in the system.

-- The architecture covers all architecture requirements, that is, there's no important requirements remain unconsidered.

-- For each architecturally significant use case, there's at least one interaction diagram to show the realization of this use case.

-- For each architecturally significant quality attribute requirements, architect can illuminate in SAS model how it is satisfied.

4.3 Software Architecture Refinement

SAS model focuses mainly on coarse-grained design, the focus of the architecture refinement phase is shifting to specific technology details, such as precise definition of component communication protocol and the interfaces of each component. The main purpose of software architecture refinement is to define each architecture element strictly to provide real constrains on software development. At the end of this phase, we can get a more detailed model, called SAD (Software architecture definition). For the purpose of design reusability, SAD model is described in a component technology independent manner, no commitment to any component platform. Doing this way, it allows us to potentially substitute one specific implementation mechanism for another without adversely affecting the design.

Software architecture refinement consists of three forms of refinement: component refinement, connector refinement and interface refinement. Component refinement is mainly about the decomposition of high-level abstract components into concrete smaller ones, this activity makes components more understandable and easier to be implemented. Connector refinement is the refinement of the connections between components, which makes interaction relationships between components more clear. Interface refinement is to define the interfaces of components with strict operation signatures. Activities associated with these three kinds of refinements are interleaved.

Following these steps to do software architecture refinement.

Step1: Create a primitive SAD model

A primitive SAD model can be constructed from SAS model according to some mapping rules, as follows:

Rule M1. If a component in SAS is simple and already represent a single logical abstraction, it can be directly mapped, 1:1, to a component in SAD.

Rule M2. An abstract component in SAS can be mapped to several concrete components in SAD.

SAS may not characterize the full behavior of its components, and therefore may use a single component type to represent a group of components that have common behavior but significantly different at the implementation level, as shown in Fig 5.

Rule M3. Divide a component in SAS into several smaller components in SAD, these smaller components together implement the behavior of the original component, as shown in Fig6.

For rule M2 and M3, although the original component is substitute by new components, a virtual packaging component (e.g. Processors in Fig.5 and Dispatch in Fig.6) can be defined to group the derived components.

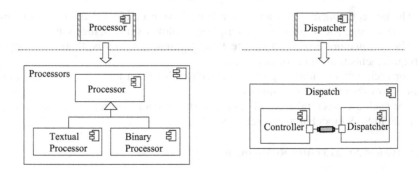

Fig. 5. Mapping Rule M2   **Fig. 6.** Mapping Rule M3

Rule M4. If there's a connection between two components in SAS, then create a port for each corresponding component in SAD, and replace the abstract connection in SAS with a more concrete one, for example, replace data flow connection with shared variables, procedure call or message passing.

This rule doesn't work if an outer component directly connects to the subcomponent of another component. In this situation, Rule M5 should be used.

Rule M5. If a component (or its subcomponent) connects to another component's internal subcomponent, create a port for each outer component and create binding connection between port and subcomponent, as shown in Fig.7.

Rule M6. <<placeholderOp>> operations of SAS components are mapped to provided services of ports of corresponding SAD components.

When doing this mapping, try to give strict definition of each service's signature.

After mapping, connections between components are substituted by connections between ports of components. Components in SAD are defined in an encapsulated manner and can only connect and interact with each other through ports. This primitive model will be adjusted when more details exposed with further refinement. New components, connectors, ports may be identified; Interface types are defined to constrain ports' behavior; Large components may be further decomposed into smaller ones, especially in a situation when the behavior of a certain component is still too complex to be understood.

Step 2: Describe Component Interactions

When the outline of SAD model is obtained, next need to do is to describe the interactions between components, so as to get a profound understanding about how components collaborates with each other, and so be able to define components' interfaces precisely. Components' interactions are described through use case analysis using UML sequence diagrams. Compared with SAS Design, use case analysis in SAD design is more rigorous, with more detail information exposed:

-- Components can only interact with each other through ports.

-- Interactions can only occur between components at the same level, an outer component can't interact directly with another component's internal subcomponents. Use separate interaction diagram to describe a component's internal behavior.

-- Messages passed between components' ports must be defined strictly; types of parameters must be defined.

Interaction diagram in SAS design is shown in Fig.8.

During use case analysis, if one component need to send message to another component, but there's no proper port to receive this message, then refine the structure diagram to add a new port for that component. If there's difficulty to strictly define a component's interface, it may imply that the function of this component is too complex to be understood, then internal structure of this component need to be analyzed and decomposed. By decomposing a component's internal structure, we can get profound understanding of a component's behavior, so it may be helpful to quickly stabilize the interfaces between components.

Step 3: Define Interfaces and Assign Interfaces to Components

After every use case has been analyzed, messages passed through each port will come to be clear. That is, services that a component provides or requires through each

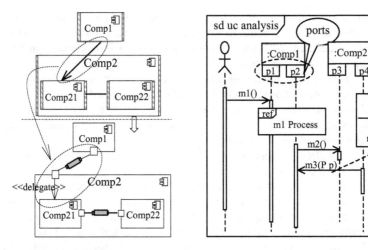

Fig. 7. Mapping Rule M5   **Fig. 8.** Behavior Refinement

port are clear. Divide these services into coherent groups and publish them as interfaces. Then, as part of specifying the overall architecture of an application solution, interfaces are allocated to components and become components' provided and required interfaces. See Fig.9.

To make interface definition more rigorous, pre, post conditions and invariants of interface behavior may be specified. UML protocol state machines can be used to constraint the order that interface operations must obey.

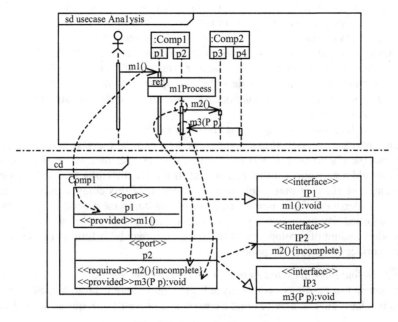

Fig. 9. Interface Refinement

With continuous iterations of these three kinds of activities, SAD model will become more detailed and rigorous. When every component and connector's interface and behavior is clearly defined, SAD design can be thought of being finished.

4.4 Software Architecture Middle Evaluation

Software architecture middle evaluation can be performed to ensure the consistency between SAS and SAD, as well as the completeness of SAD.

When we say SAD is consistent with SAS, we mean SAD obeys the design principles presented in SAS. That is, information defined in SAS must be preserved or transformed in SAD, but can't be lost. For the time being, we assume consistency checking is performed by human review. This needs the architects to present the main design principles of SAS and mapping information between constructs of SAS and SAD. Reviewers evaluate the consistency by brainstorming. More systematic and rigorous consistency checking methods will be discussed in future works.

Completeness of SAD means that all information included in SAD must obey the syntactic and semantic rules of the modeling language, and there must not exist inconsistent information between different parts of the model. Some example completeness checking rules are as follows:

Rule C1. Every component must have at least one port, and components can only interact with each other through ports.

Rule C2. A component must connect to at least one other component (to avoid dangling components).

Rule C3. Every connector must connect to at least two ports.

Rule C4. No dependency relationship should exist between a provided interface and a required interface on the same component (otherwise, it will mean the required services are provided by itself).

Rule C5. Types of parameters included in interface operations must be defined (otherwise, clients of this interface don't know how to prepare parameters).

Rule C6. Every component must participate at least one interaction.

Rule C7. Messages passed between ports must be operation or signal definitions of these ports.

Rule C8. If there's message passing between two ports, then these two ports must be connected by a connector.

Rule C9. Abstract components can't be instantiated.

Rule C10. Outer component can't interact directly with another component's internal subcomponents.

These are some common completeness rules. Other description language specific completeness and consistency rules may exist according to notation used in architecture definition.

4.5 Transform Architecture into Implementation

The task of this design phase is to transform SAD models to platform specific models, bridging the gap between higher-level specification and lower-level implementation. EJB (Enterprise Java Beans), CCM (CORBA Component Model) and COM/DCOM (Distributed Component Object Model) are examples of architectures that used to define and implement platform specific models.

Transformation from SAD to component model can be partially automatized by tools. For example, ABCTool from Beijing University can transform platform independent models to EJB and CORBA, and then automatically implement components composition and deployment [16].

4.6 Software Architecture Post-deployment Evaluation

Software Architecture post-deployment evaluation occurs after the architecture has been implemented and deployed. At this time, architecture run-time properties, such as performance, synchronization, concurrency, can be observed and evaluated by execute the architecture prototype.

5 Conclusions and Future Works

GADesign has been used as development process standard in the project of Hardware-in-Loop Simulation System for Warship taken on by SERI(System Engineering Research Institute) of China. There're four development groups from different organizations participated in this project. With the guidance of GADesign, the following advantages achieved:

-- The schedule of the process was easier to be controlled because the design followed some well-defined steps.

-- Communication between groups was easier because they knew each other's progress.

-- Different groups could be able to exchange design strategies and ideas at early time of the design process, which made it possible to implement similar strategies for similar functions in different subsystems.

Now, GADesign is still in its initial stage and several steps still lack of systematic assistance. Future work includes: 1) Research on evaluation techniques to make evaluation for each phase more systematic; 2) Research on tools to provide automatic transformation between models.

Acknowledgements

We would like to gratefully acknowledge the following persons for contributing ideas and comments to improve this paper: Fan Shengyin, Gao Hui, Gao Juntao,Xu Hongxia, Duan Fang, Zhu Guoping, Zhang Xinjia, Tang ji, Ding Yuzheng, as well as the reviewers of SPW2005 for this paper.

References

1. Garlan, D., Allen, R., Ockerbloom, J.: Exploiting Style in Architectural Design Environments. ACM SIGSOFT Software Engineering Notes, Vol. 19, (1994) 175-188
2. Luckham, D.C.: Rapide: a Language and Toolset for Simulation of Distributed Systems by Partial Ordering of Events. DIMACS Partial Order Methods Workshop IV, Princeton University (1996)

3. Shaw, M., DeLine, R., Klein, D.V.: Abstractions for Software Architecture and Tools to Support Them. IEEE Transactions on Software Engineering, Vol. 21, (1995) 314-335
4. Allen, R.: A Formal Approach to Software Architecture. Technical Report, CMU-CS-97-144, Carnegie Mellon University (1997)
5. Shaw, M., Clements, P.: A Field Guide to Boxology: Preliminary Classification of Architectural Styles for Software Systems. In Proceedings of 21st International Computer Software and Applications Conference (1997) 6-13
6. Buschmann, F., Meunier, R., Rohnert, H.,Sommerlad, P., Stal, M.: Pattern-Oriented Software Architecture: a System of Patterns. Addison-Wesley (1996)
7. Kazman, R., Abowd, G., Bass, L., Clements, P.: Scenario-Based Analysis of Software Architecture. IEEE Software, Vol. 13, (1996) 47-55
8. Kazman, R., Klein, M., Clements, P.: ATAM: Method for Architecture Evaluation (CMU/SEI-2000-TR-004, ADA382629). Pittsburgh, PA: Software Engineering Institute, Carnegie Mellon University (2000). http://www.sei.cmu.edu/publications/documents /00.reports/00tr004.html
9. IEEE Standard 1471: IEEE Recommended Practice for Architectural Description of Software-Intensive Systems. IEEE Computer Society (2000)
10. Clements, P., Bachmann, F., Bass, L.: Documenting Software Architectures: Views and Beyond. MA: Addison Wesley (2002)
11. Kazman, R.: Tool Support for Architecture Analysis and Design. Proceedings of the Second Int. Workshop on Software Architectures, ACM Press (1996) 94-97
12. Grundy, J. and Hosking, J.: Softarch: Tool Support for Integrated Software Architecture Development. International Journal Of Software Engineering and Knowledge Engineering (2003)
13. Bass, L., Clements, P., Kazman, R.: Software Architecture in Practice. Addison-Wesley (2003)
14. Kazman, R., Kruchten, P., Nord, R.L., Tomayko, J.E.: Integrating Software-Architecture-Centric Methods into the Rational Unified Process. TECHNICAL REPORT,CMU/SEI-2004-TR-011, Software Engineering Institute, Carnegie Mellon University (2004), http://www.sei.cmu.edu/publications/documents/04.reports/04tr011.html
15. Jacobson, I., Booch, G., Rumbaugh, J.: The Unified Software Development Process. MA: Addison-Wesley (1999)
16. Meihong, Chenfeng, Feng Yaodong: ABC: Architecture Based, Component Oriented Software Development Method. Journal of Software, Vol. 14. Beijing (2003)721-732
17. Bachmann, F., Bass, L., Chastek, G.: The Architecture Based Design Method. Technical Report CMU/SEI-2000-TR-001, Software Engineering Institute, Carnegie Mellon University (2000), http://www.sei.cmu.edu/publications/documents/00.reports/00tr001.html
18. Bachmann D, Bass L and Klein M. Moving from Quality Attribute Requirements to Architectural Decisions. Proceedings of Second International Software Requirements to Architectures Workshop Located at ICSE'03 (2003)122-130
19. Object Management Group. UML 2.0 Superstructure Specification: Final Adopted Specification. http://www.omg.org/docs/ptc/03-08-02.pdf (August 2003)
20. Gamma, E., Helm, R., Johnson, R., Vlissides, J.: Design Patterns-Elements of Reusable Object-Oriented Software. MA:Addison-Wesley (1995)
21. Douglass, B.P.: Doing Hard Time: Developing Real-Time Systems with UML, Objects, Frameworks, and Patterns. Addison-Wesley (1999)
22. Buschmann, F.: Building Software with Patterns. http://www.daimi.au.dk/~apaipi/dpf/ EuroPLoP.pdf (1998)

Process Patterns for COTS-Based Development

Ye Yang

Center for Software Engineering, University of Southern California,
Los Angeles, California 90089, USA
yey@cse.usc.edu

Abstract. Software development is increasingly moving away from processes to compose pure-custom software from lines of code, toward processes for assessment, tailoring and integration of COTS or other reusable components with each other and with custom code. Beyond that, there are large variations within COTS based applications (CBA) processes that make a one-size-fits-all COTS process model unworkable. In previous work, we developed a general CBA process framework that provides guidance covering the wide range of possible CBA processes. Here, we provide more particular process patterns that we have identified in analyzing the first 9 projects to use the general CBA process framework, along with refinements of the general framework. These include three levels of process patterns: lifecycle patterns, activity patterns, and workflow patterns.

1 Introduction

Trends toward COTS-based applications (CBA) development include the increase in percentage of USC e-services projects from 28% in 1996-1997 to 70% in 2001-2002 [11], and from the Standish Group's 2000 CHAOS survey showing that 54% of the application projects were COTS-based [9]. The underlying reason is that economic imperatives are inexorably changing the nature of software development processes. They are increasingly moving away from processes to compose pure-custom software from lines of code (although these processes still apply for developing the COTS products themselves), and toward processes for assessment, tailoring and integration of COTS or other reusable components. The primary economic drivers of this change are:

- The increasing criticality of software capabilities to a product's competitive success;
- The ability of COTS or other reusable components to significantly reduce a product's cost and development time;
- An increasing number of COTS products available to provide needed user functions.

Empirical studies further show that the activities conducted while developing COTS-based applications (CBA) differ greatly from those conducted while traditional custom development [11, 14]. The new challenges confronted by both COTS researchers and practitioners go beyond the need to acquire new expertise, manage greater project uncertainty and volatility, and demand an entirely new development paradigm.

M. Li, B. Boehm, and L.J. Osterweil (Eds.): SPW 2005, LNCS 3840, pp. 206–221, 2005.

Traditional sequential requirements-design-code-test (waterfall) processes do not work for CBA's [1], simply because the COTS whole life process is not a sequential one [15]. The volatility of COTS products [2] introduces a great deal of recursion and concurrency into CBA processes. Meanwhile, within COTS-based development, there is a large variation in development processes and approaches (e.g. pure selection, pure adaptation, integration [3]) for which a single generic process model is unable to provide adequate development guidance. Our previous CBD classification in [11] identified three types of COTS-based applications: assessment-intensive, tailoring-intensive, and glue code-intensive. Though the classification is based on the intensity of certain COTS related activities, many other activities as well as the entire development process will also be significantly affected by the CBD type. Such process diversity has to be carefully taken into consideration when modeling CBA development processes.

Some recent CBA process models have partially addressed these issues by adding CBA extensions to a sequential process framework [4] or a suitably flexible and concurrent process [5], including our previous work on the composable CBA process decision framework [12]. However, these models only provide partial context profiles identified for developers to select and form an effective and efficient CBA process, which makes CBA developers often find that it is difficult to determine the relevance of these models to their project situation. Therefore, it becomes more important to provide CBA developers with further guidance to select from a series of effective process solution patterns with respect to particular project circumstance.

Many disciplines have identified patterns by analyzing historical project data and experiences [17, 18]. We believe that this approach is also valid for COTS-based development (CBD) processes. An analysis and characterization of CBA process patterns may serve to:

- Identify and avoid high risk development patternsï
- Aid in COTS effort planning, monitoring, and controlï
- Help explore COTS development options and rationalize COTS decision makingï
- Provide evidence to further validate the composable CBA decision frameworkï
- Help illuminate the COTS risks and risk management within COTS development activitiesï

In this paper, we present a series of COTS process patterns identified under the context of the COTS process decision framework established in [12]. Each COTS process pattern captures some common characteristics of the project, process, product, and personnel perspectives under certain circumstances. Following selected process patterns, CBA developers can instantiate process instances from the CBA process decision framework.

The following section will briefly examine related work on process pattern approach and such current COTS process models. Section 3 will discuss the CBA process decision framework and its three composable elements together to accommodate lifecycle implications of CBD. Section 4 will categorize an initial list of proposed process patterns based on empirical results from applying the CBA process decision framework. Lastly, describe follow-on plans of empirical studies for identifying and validating CBA process patterns.

2 Related Work

2.1 Process Pattern Approach

The concept of process pattern has been proposed to address the effective reuse of knowledge and experience during software development. The pattern concept is not new in many other disciplines [17, 18], however, the current focus in software engineering has been on product patterns rather than process patterns. Jim Coplien [25] did the early work on software process patterns by introducing a family of patterns that can be used to shape a new organization and its development processes. Ambler [16] defined a process pattern as a description of a proven, successful approach and/or series of actions for developing software, then a number of researchers have further extended the approach to Requirement Engineering [19], tool support for living software process pattern definition [20], and ProMisE framework for process models customization [21]. Huang [22] introduced the Hierarchical Process Patterns approach to provide a stepwise means to model software process based on patterns. These extensions categorized process patterns at different levels, such as activity and process level [20] and pattern-model-instance level [22], however, none of these work can be applicable to fully address CBD life cycle issues.

2.2 COTS Process Models

Morisio presented a modified waterfall process [4] in performing concurrent COTS package evaluation, selection, and requirements analysis. But committing to requirements on this basis before performing design and glueware integration analysis is likely to run into the kind of architectural mismatch problems causing factor-of-4 schedule overruns and factor-of-5 budget overruns as discussed in [10].

Though the avoidance of premature-commitment problems was addressed by the Spiral-based EPIC model [4], the model is too underdetermined to provide enough planning content to enable projects to monitor progress toward completion. It is good in identifying the important COTS considerations to address – but its lack of intermediate milestones leaves it open to at least three major problem sources. One problem source is the lack of guidance of what steps to take next, or for how long to perform them. Another is the lack of status information for communicating and controlling progress toward completion. A third problem is the likelihood of nonconvergence, as in the "study-wait-study" syndrome.

In analyzing over 20 USC e-services projects and 17 industry COCOTS calibration projects, we found that the CBA effort mostly happens among assessment, tailoring, and glue code activities [11] as shown in Figures 1 (a) and (b). Our definitions of the three primary sources of effort are:

- COTS Assessment is the activity whereby COTS products are evaluated and selected as viable components for a user application.
- COTS Tailoring is the activity whereby COTS software products are configured for use in a specific context.

- COTS Glue Code (also called glueware) development and integration is the activity whereby code is designed, developed, and used to ensure that COTS products satisfactorily interoperate in support of the user application.

We furthered this research by describing a recursive and re-entrant CBA process decision framework within these three activities [12] based on the risk driven spiral model [8] abstracted from the CBA projects. The CBA process decision framework consists of dominant decisions and activities within CBA development to enable developers to "compose" a COTS development process specifically instantiated for their project. Section 3 will describe the CBA process decision framework and its composable process elements.

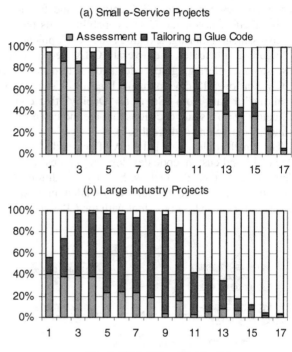

(a) Small e-Service Projects

(b) Large Industry Projects

Fig. 1. CBA Effort Distribution

2.3 Motivation of Defining COTS Process Patterns

It is also clear from Figures 1 that there is no one-size-fits-all effort distribution or development process for CBA's. Some projects, particularly in the small e-services area, were almost exclusively Assessment, in which there was little tailoring or glue code required once the COTS products were selected. Some were almost exclusively Tailoring; these were primarily applications supported by large, single COTS Enterprise Resource Planning or Web Portal packages. Some were almost exclusively glue code development and integration, in which the selected best-of-breed COTS packages were not designed to interoperate with each other. And there were some projects with a nontrivial amount of effort in all three areas.

The motivation behind this study is to exploit the pattern concept and define an initial series of process patterns within the context of CBA process decision framework in order to enhance its accommodation for COTS process diversity. Each process pattern describes certain recurring CBD circumstances and a valid series of navigation steps in the CBA process decision framework as a solution to be performed under these circumstances. Hence, variations in the COTS processes become different combinations of instantiations from particular process patterns.

3 CBA Process Decision Framework

The CBA process decision framework is a recursive and reentrant decision framework consisting of dominant decisions and activities within CBA development. It accommodates concurrent CBA activities and frequent go-backs based on new and evolving client needs and COTS capabilities. Its three composable process elements are assessment, tailoring, and glue code development.

Figure 2 illustrates the overall CBA decision framework that composes the assessment, tailoring, glue code, and custom code development process elements within an overall development lifecycle. The CBA process is undertaken by "walking" a path from "Start" to "Deploy" that connects (via arrows) activities as indicated by boxes and decisions that are indicated by ovals (again, subject to COTS-related backtraching and feedback).

The small circles with letters A, T, G, and C indicates the assessment, tailoring, glue code, and custom code development process elements respectively. Each process element is further defined with entry conditions, a set of sub-activities to be performed, and exit conditions as detailed in [12]. In addition, this scheme was developed from and is consistent with the CBA activity distributions of Figure 1.

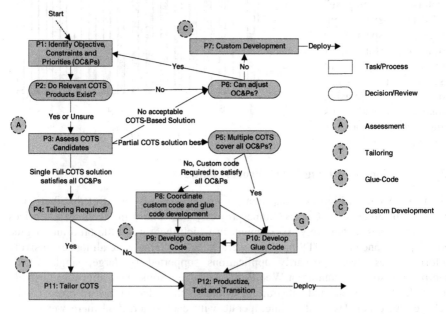

Fig. 2. The CBA Process Decision Framework

The less obvious aspects of each process area are summarized as follows.

P1: Identify stakeholders' desired objectives, constraints, and priorities (OC&P's). This is the entrance to the process framework. As the project goes on, risk considerations, stakeholders' priority changes, new COTS releases and other dynamic considerations may alter the OC&P's. In particular, if no suitable COTS packages are identified (P6), the stakeholders may change the OC&P's and the process is started over with these new considerations.

P2: Relevant COTS products exist? In most cases, stakeholders are aware of some available COTS packages that can provide part of all their needed functionalities. Then a COTS assessment activity will help them to determine the best option. However, the project will follow a custom development approach if the stakeholders realize that there is no relevant COTS available.

P4: Tailoring Required? When a certain COTS product can satisfy all the OC&P's, there is no need to develop application code or glue code. The selected COTS may need to be tailored in order to work for the specific system context.

P5: Multiple COTS cover all OC&P's? If a combination of COTS products can satisfy all the OC&P's, they are integrated via glue-code. Otherwise, COTS packages are combined to cover as much of the OC&P's as feasible and then custom code is developed to cover what remains.

P6: Can Adjust OC&P's? When no acceptable COTS products can be identified, the OC&P's are re-examined for areas that may allow more options. Are there constraints and priorities that may be relaxed? How firm are the objectives and if adjusted slightly will it enable consideration of more products? Are there analogous areas in which to look for more products and alternatives?

P8: Coordinate Application Code development and Glue Code effort. Custom developed components must eventually be integrated with the chosen COTS products. The interfaces will need to be developed so they are compatible with the COTS products and the particular glue code connectors used. This means that some glue code effort will need to be coordinated with the custom development. This coordination needs to continue through the concurrent development of custom code and glue code (P9, P10).

P12: Productize, test, and transition. This is the last area of CBA process framework. It involves some traditional engineering activities of productizing, testing, and transitioning the application to the client.

The recursive and reentrant nature of this general CBA process framework enables it to reflect such project realities as asynchronous go-backs to reflect new developments and the ability to conduct combinations of the process elements in parallel. However, particular CBA projects would like to have more specific information about the relative likelihood of various process patterns, at least within a particular CBA domain. Below, we provide some initial results on such process patterns in the domain of small e-service CBAs, based on the results of the first 9 projects in this domain that have used the general CBA process framework. These results also enabled us to refine the original CBA process framework presented in [12] into the version presented above.

4   CBA Process Patterns

In this section, we will present the identification of CBA process patterns at three levels. Throughout this section, we will be referring to the ID's of process areas within the CBA process decision framework as presented in Section 3.

We adopt a three-tier hierarchical structure [22] to organize the CBA process patterns:

- Lifecycle Pattern: which is a valid walk from "Start" to "Deploy" in the CBA process decision framework;
- Activity Pattern: which organizes a series of activities to be frequently performed together, either in a sequential order or concurrently. An activity sequence pattern reflects certain project characteristics and risk considerations.
- Workflow Pattern: which decomposes a particular CBA process element into a workflow attributed with entry conditions, major tasks, and exit conditions.

4.1 Lifecycle Patterns (LP)

The CBA process decision framework provides a general yet sufficiently specific mechanism to identify all the process conditions that allow CBA processes to be specialized according to their project context factors such as number of COTS packages, percentage of COTS delivered system functionalities, COTS tailoring complexity, new COTS or project developments, or opportunities to execute instances of process elements in parallel.

There are three life cycle patterns identified based on the CBA process decision framework, with respect to the COTS assessment results (i.e. P3 in Figure 2). These include:

- LP-1: <u>No available COTS</u>. If COTS assessment results conclude that there are no available COTS packages providing desired system capabilities, and none of the OC&P's could be adjusted to accept more COTS candidates (i.e. P6), then the development process will follow a custom development approach (i.e. P7).
- LP-2: <u>Single-Full COTS</u>. This condition implies that a single COTS product such as a web portal generator or an Enterprise Resource Planning (ERP) package is finally selected to meet all desired OC&P's, the CBA process will then simply depend on whether tailoring the COTS product is necessary (i.e. P3→ P11→ P12) or not (i.e. P3→ P12). Note that in this situation, no COTS glue code or custom code development is needed.

- LP-3: <u>Partial COTS</u>. This condition means that the selected COTS solution could consist of either only one single COTS package or multiple COTS packages. However, the available COTS products can only partially deliver the desired OC&P's. In this case, the emphasis of the CBA process will be on the glue code development (i.e. P10) and custom code development (i.e. P9), and the coordination of these two (i.e. p8).

Figure 3 depicts the process areas from the CBA process decision framework visited in each of the three Lifecycle patterns, where boxes represent the activities and circles represent decision points.

Again, these patterns are subject to asynchronous go backs, such as the process of COTS glue code generation and tailoring within the Partial COTS (LP-3) process element P10 identifying additional COTS capabilities that make a go-back to a Single Full-COTS (LP-2) process more attractive.

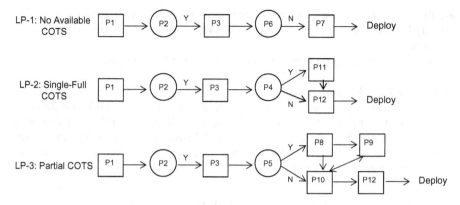

Fig. 3. The Three CBA Lifecycle Patterns

4.2 Activity Patterns (AP)

Table 1 summarizes the results with respect to these activity areas from applying the process CBA decision framework within various e-services projects. We observed that not all projects follow similar activity sequences. For example: Assessment and tailoring were the dominant activity for project 2 in the elaboration spiral, while for project 3 during the elaboration phase the team implemented in parallel tailoring and glue-code activities, and on finding the COTS unsuitable for their need this team revisited he assessment activity during the elaboration phase.

Table 1. CBA Activity Sequence Examples

No.	Activity Sequences			
	Inception	Elaboration	Constructio	Transition
1	A	AC	ATG	C
2	A	AT	A	A
3	A	(TG)A	G	G
4	A	A(TG)	A(TG)	G
5	AT	AT	T	T
6	A	T	TG	G
7	AT	T	T	T
8	AT	(AA) TG	(TGC)	G
9	A	AT	TG	G

The analysis shows each of these CBA projects has a distinct pattern of sequences in which various activities were implemented. Such differences in the activity sequences resulted from a specific set of project characteristics and associated risks reported by the projects. Analyzing the CBA project sequence data showed that there are usually certain patterns that commonly exist in almost all of the CBA projects, and also there are some patterns that reflect the most significant project risks if not being properly handled leading to significant loss in terms of confusion, rework, and delay in schedule.

The observed activity patterns fall into the following two categories.

4.2.1 Anticipated Patterns

Every anticipated pattern maps to a path within the decision framework to address the identified COTS related risks, to avoid such risks where possible, and finally to control or transfer the remaining risks. Table 2 Lists the five identified anticipated activity patterns, with the avoided risk shown in column 4 and probability of occurrence in the 9 observed projects shown in the last column.

Table 2. Anticipated COTS Activity Patterns

No.	Name	Description	Avoided Risks	Prob.
AP-1	Assessment first	After identifying OC&P's and collecting an initial set of COTS candidates, COTS assessment is usually performed.	Selecting faulty COTS candidate; Faulty vendor claim	100%
AP-2	Assessment to tailoring (A=>T).	While assessment is on going or once assessment is done, it becomes clearer what can be customized in a COTS product before being utilized.	COTS is developed for general purpose, not for any particular system	100%
AP-3	Tailoring to glue code (T =>G).	When integrating COTS packages, often tailoring can help prepare unrelated COTS packages to "fit" together with glue-code.	Integrated system did not perform as expected.	33%
AP-4	Assessment to tailoring and glue code (A=>(TG) or A =>T=>G).	This is particularly true with multiple COTS components that require a thorough assessment with tailoring and glue code development to test COTS usability and interoperability.	Insufficient early assessment without prototyping by tailoring and glue coding	67%
AP-5	After Inception, A, T, TG as a repeatable pair (A=>A or T=>T or (TG)=>(TG)).	Due to frequent requirement changes or new COTS insights, re-assessing or retailoring a COTS package is common in addition to possibly a certain amount of rework on glue code to accommodate the changes.	Changes make initial COTS no longer satisfying	67%

4.2.2 Unanticipated Patterns

An unanticipated pattern is a pattern that is not expected to typically occur (and as a result, not often planned for) in a project. Yet it is valid within the CBA framework, has project rationale, and is observed within the case-study projects. Table 3 lists the two identified unanticipated activity patterns.

Table 3. Unanticipated COTS Activity Patterns

No	Name	Description	Indicated Risk	Prob.
AP-6	Tailoring to assessment (T⇒A)	When tailoring COTS, need to re-assess selected COTS due to project changes (e.g. Reqt's, COTS, and priority changes)	1) Requirement changes make initial COTS no longer satisfying; 2) COTS version upgrade during development demands re-evaluation; 3) Tailored package didn't perform as expected.	33%
AP-7	Glue code to assessment (G⇒A)	Integration difficulty causes re-assessing COTS.	1), 2) above and 3) Integrated system did not perform as expected. 4) Lack of interoperability standards to facilitate the integration	20%

4.3 Workflow Patterns (WP)

Our original composable process elements in the CBA process decision framework in [12] (assessment, tailoring, glue code integration) were overly simple. Our experience with the initial 9 project applications of the framework has led to more realistic workflow patterns for these process elements. Each of the three process elements consists of entry conditions, major tasks, and exit conditions, which well fits into the workflow pattern as discussed next.

4.3.1 Assessment Workflow

COTS assessment aims at helping to make buy-or-build choices, evaluating the fitness of COTS candidate package(s), and selecting the most satisfactory COTS or COTS combination based on evaluation results. Figure 4 illustrates the assessment workflow pattern.

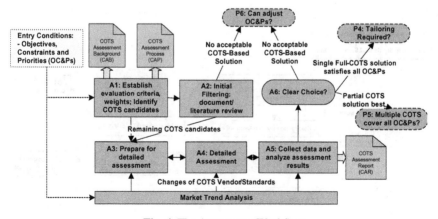

Fig. 4. The Assessment Workflow

Entry Conditions. The entry condition for assessment assumes stakeholder-negotiated OC&P's for the system are present and relevant COTS products are available.

Major Tasks

A1: Establish evaluation requirements.

A2: Initial Filtering.

A3: Prepare for detailed assessment.

A4: Detailed assessment.

A5: Collect evaluation data and analyze evaluation results.

A6: Clear COTS choice?

Along with the steps of A3, A4, and A5, market trend analysis is a very useful and critical technique to gather broader and up-to-date information for comparison and analysis. For example, market-watch activity can be used to get the latest information regarding COTS products or standards, and to collect COTS information from its current users to gain first hand COTS experience.

Exit Conditions

The following three exit directions from step A6 have been identified:

- Single full COTS solution best: it means a single COTS product covering all desired OC&P's;
- Partial COTS solution best: it means that either a single COTS product or a combination of COTS products is selected, however, the COTS products only cover part of the OC&P's, and custom development and/or glue code development is needed to meet all desired OC&P's;
- No acceptable COTS: it means that pure custom development is the optimal solution, unless the stakeholders are willing to adjust unsatisfied OC&P's.

4.3.2 Tailoring Workflow

In most cases, COTS packages need to be adapted in order to work in a specific system context. If these adaptations are directly supported within the COTS packages

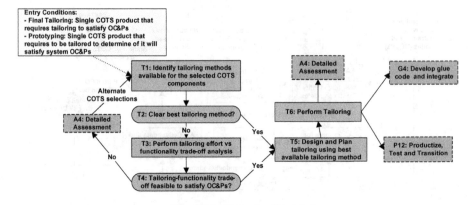

Fig. 5. The Tailoring Workflow

themselves, then this is considered tailoring activity. The tailoring workflow is illustrated in Figure 5.

Entry Conditions. While several COTS products may be tailored simultaneously, the tailoring workflow focuses on tailoring an individual COTS product. This product may be under consideration by the assessment workflow; be adapted for use as a glue code component; or be a fully assessed and ready to use product simply needing some specialization.

Major Tasks
    T1: Identify Tailoring Methods available.
    T2: Clear Best Choice?
    T3: Perform tailoring effort vs. functionality trade-off.
    T4: Tailoring-functionality trade-off feasible?
    T5: Design and Plan tailoring.

T6: Perform Tailoring.

Exit Conditions
COTS package is parameterized, customized, configured, or some scripts are written to tune the COTS ready for detailed assessment, glue code development, or final productization.

4.3.3 Glue Code Workflow
The intent of a glue code activity is to integrate COTS products as basic application components. In some fortunate cases, the combination of COTS components and application components being integrated or assessed will easily plug-and-play together. If not, some glue code needs to be defined and developed to integrate the components, and some evaluation may be necessary to converge on the best combination of COTS, glue code, and application code for the solution. A number of architectural approaches for using glue code or connectors to integrate COTS products have been developed, but less has been done to work out the process for glue

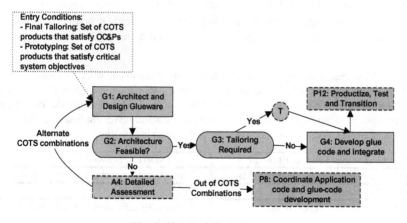

Fig. 6. The Glue Code Workflow

code development and its interactions with other CBA activities. Figure 6 illustrates the activities and decisions during a glue code workflow.

Entry Conditions. The primary entry conditions are a combination of COTS products that require glueware and/or custom code for successful operation.

Major Tasks
   G1: Architect and Design Glueware.
   G2: Architecture Feasible?
   G3: Tailoring Required?
   G4: Develop Glue Code and Integrate.

Exit Conditions
Glue code among selected COTS packages and/or custom components is developed and ready for detailed productization, testing, and transition. If no COTS combinations can be feasibly integrated via glue code, either the OC&P's need to be adjusted or a custom solution pursued (P6).

4.3.4 Workflow Guidance – An Example
Hierarchical definitions of CBA process patterns can help a project team identify and apply an appropriate pattern at any given stage of the project according to the context profile comparison, risk mitigation considerations, and need of workflow guidance.

Example of Workflow Guidance
For example, we have developed a set of three lightweight process guidelines for developing assessment-intensive CBA projects based on the Assessment Workflow Pattern. The three guidelines are COTS Assessment Background (CAB), COTS Assessment Plan (CAP), and COTS Assessment Report (CAR). The CAB document provides the minimum-essential set of objectives, constraints, priorities, and situation background needed to perform the COTS assessment. The CAP document is organized to cover the minimum essential "why/whereas, what/when, who/where, how, and how much" aspects of the COTS assessment activity being planned. The CAR document presents the major results, conclusions, and recommendations of the COTS assessment. The CAB, CAP, and CAR remain lightweight are updated whenever new risks, opportunities, or changes emerge. Figure 4 marks the places that these guidelines can be applied to generate corresponding project artifacts.

Table 4. The overall mapping of artifacts defined by Assessment workflow guidelines and ISO/IEC 14598-4 [7]. We found some specific guidance important to include in the CAB, CAP, and CAR guidelines that were not found in ISO/IEC 14598-4. These include the Result Chain Analysis, System OP&C's (objectives, priorities, and constraints) identification, and process plan for concurrent COTS assessment, tailoring and glue code activities.

CBA Assessment Process Element	ISO/IEC 14598-4
COTS Assessment Background (CAB)	Evaluation Requirement Specification
COTS Assessment Plan (CAP)	Evaluation Plan
COTS Assessment Report (CAR)	Evaluation Specification + Evaluation Records and Results

4.3.5 Summary of the Application of the Three Levels of CBA Process Patterns

In the Fall 2004 semester, an experiment was performed on the 14 USC e-services CBA projects, which were split into two groups. The first group A consists of 8 projects that applied the CBA process patterns in their project planning and management; the second group B includes 6 projects that did not apply.

Table 5. To measure and compare the team performance, data on defects within team deliverables were collected and analyzed. The team performance measurement is derived from the overall number of defects within the LCO and LCA package [8]. The experiment has proven that the application of the CBA process patterns helps to improve development team performance significantly. The quantitative data shows the comparison of Group A and B on team performance.

Group A		Group B	
Team No.	Defect	Team No.	Defect
1	41	2	57.8
6	31	3	76
7	48	4	118
8	37	10	85
14	33	11	72
18	49	12	86.7
21	50		
24	30		
Average	39.8	Average	82.6

A paired t-test was performed on the two group's team performance data. The two-tailed P value equals 0.0029. By conventional criteria, this difference is considered to be very statistically significant.

Other Results

A survey performed on these projects to collect the usage data from the CBA developers. The results of the survey show that different COTS impact profiles exist between projects from the group A and projects from group B.

Figure 7 compares the different aspects of COTS impacts in terms of the magnitude of the impact on the two groups. In average, the group A projects exhibit less schedule delay, less difficult integration issues, and slightly less

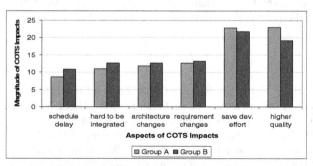

Fig. 7. Comparison of COTS Impacts

changes in requirements and architecture design, they also reported the use of COTS helps to save development effort and produce higher quality system. Note that the number of responses from group A is 44, and that from group B is 26.

Table 6. Among the responses from group A, the developers also cited various advantages gained by applying the framework. This is summarized in the Table 6, where the last column shows the percentage of responses for each listed advantage.

Framework can help with:	Percentage
COTS assessment	81.8%
Risk identification and mitigai	68.2%
Life cycle planning	63.6%

5   Conclusions

In the past, we have tried to incorporate a generic CBS processes but with limited success. This was evidenced by observing numerous teams succumbing to effort allocation pitfalls. For example performing too much COTS assessment and neglecting to allocate enough time for training, tailoring and integration resulting in project delays, inability to implement desired functional capabilities, and so forth.

Process patterns provide an effective means for analyzing complex and often subtle CBA processes. The identifications of the hierarchical CBA process patterns are useful for strategic and tactical development planning as they provide an overview of the viable lifecycle options, potential risks and appropriate mitigation actions, and development workflows.

CBA process patterns are invaluable for validating and refining the CBA decision framework that has already proven to be of substantial value to developers inexperienced in COTS based system development. Additionally, CBA activity patterns provide an empirical means of identifying and avoiding COTS risks. CBA workflow patterns identify the common activity configurations of assessment, tailoring, and glue code development which are significantly different from traditional software engineering activities.

In future work we hope to develop tools that help identify and apply the CBA process patterns and evaluate their utility through empirical experiments.

References

1. Benguria, G., Garcia, A., Sellier, D., Tay, S.: European COTS Working Group: Analysis of the Common Problems and Current Practices of the European COTS Users. In: Dean, J., Gravel, A. (eds.): Proceedings of 1st ICCBSS, Springer Verlag (2002) 44-53
2. Basili, V., Boehm, B.: COTS Based System Top 10 List. IEEE Computer (2001) 91-93
3. Carney, D.: Assembling large systems from COTS components: Opportunities, cautions, and complexities. In SEI Monographs on the Use of Commercial Software in Government Systems. Software Engineering Institute, Carnegie Mellon University (1997)

4. Morisio, M., Seaman, C., Parra, A., Basili, V., Kraft, S., Condon, S.: Investigating and Improving a COTS-Based Software Development Process. Proceedings of 22nd ICSE (2000) 32-41
5. Albert, C., Brownsword, L.: Evolutionary Process for Integrating COTS-Based Systems (EPIC): An Overview. CMU-SEI-2002-TR-009 (2002)
6. Abts, C.: Extending the COCOMO II Software Cost Model to Estimate Effort and Schedule for Software Systems Using Commercial-Off-The-Shelf (COTS) Software Components: the COCOTS Model. Ph.D. Dissertation, University of Southern California (2001)
7. ISO/IEC 14598-4: Software engineering -- Product evaluation -- Part 4: Process for acquirers (1999)
8. Boehm, B., Egyed, A., Kwan, J., Port, D., Shah, A., Madachy, R.: Using the WinWin Spiral Model: A Case Study. IEEE Computer (1998)
9. CHAOS 2001, http://www.standishgroup.com
10. Garlan, D., Allen, R., Ockerbloom, J.: Architectural Mismatch, or, Why it's hard to build systems out of existing parts. Proceedings of 17th ICSE (1995)
11. Boehm, B., Port, D., Yang, Y., Bhuta, J.: Not All CBS Are Created Equally: COTS-Intensive Project Types. Proceedings of 2nd ICCBSS (2003) 36-50
12. Boehm, B., Port, D., Yang, Y., Bhuta, J.,: Composable Process Elements for Developing COTS-Based Applications. Proceedings of ISESE 2003 (2003)
13. Port, D., Yang, Y.: Empirical Analysis of COTS Activity Effort Sequences. Proceedings of 3rd ICCBSS (2004)
14. Brownsword, L., Oberndorf, T., Sledge, C.A.: Developing New Processes for COTS-Based Systems. IEEE Software (2000)
15. Looney, M., Erdogmus, H., Allan, G., Allison, S., Dean, J.C., Sledge, C.A., Oberndorf, P.: COTS Process Issues in Military Applications. Proceedings of ICSE 2000 Workshop on Continuing Collaborations for Successful COTS Development (2000)
16. Ambler, S.: Process Patterns: Building Large-Scale Systems Using Object Technology, Cambridge University Press, New York (1998)
17. Alexander, C.: A Pattern Language, New York, Oxford University Press (1977)
18. Buschmann, F., Meunier, R., Rohnert, H., Sommerlad, P., Stal, M.: Pattern-Oriented Software Architecture – A system of Patterns. Wiley and Sons Ltd (1996)
19. Gaska, M.T., Gause, D.C.: An approach for Cross-Discipline Requirement Engineering Process Patterns. Proceedings of 3rd ICRE (1998) 182-189
20. Gnatz, M., Marschall, F., Popp, G., Rausch, A., Schwerin, W.: Towards a tool support for a Living Software Development Process. Proceedings of 35th Annual Hawaii International Conference on System Sciences (2002) 1529–1537
21. Baldassarre, M.T., Caivano, D., Visaggio, C.A., Visaggio, G.: ProMisE: a framework for process models customization to the operative context. Proceedings of 2002 ISESE (2002) 103-110
22. Heyuan, H., Shensheng, Z.: Hierarchical process patterns: construct software processes in a stepwise way IEEE International Conference on Systems, Man and Cybernetics (2003) 353-1358

Software Testing Process Automation Based on UTP – A Case Study

Wei Chen[1,2], Qun Ying[1,2], Yunzhi Xue[1,2], and Chen Zhao[1]

[1] Laboratory for Internet Software Technologies, Institute of Software,
The Chinese Academy of Sciences, Beijing 100080, China
[2] Graduate School of the Chinese Academy of Sciences, Beijing 100039, China
{chenwei, yingqun, yunzhi, zhaochen}@itechs.iscas.ac.cn

Abstract. Automation of software testing process plays an important role in improving software quality, shortening period of development and reducing development cost. However, most existing testing automation methods tend to rely on various kinds of limited formal models, and make a contrived separation between software testing and other phases in software life cycle. This separation limits wide spread application of these methods. On the other hand, UML, as a unified modeling language that has been widely employed to describe and model software and software process, can provide good basis for testing automation to close the separation. In this paper we introduce an approach that transforms design models represented by UML to testing models represented by UTP (UML Testing Profile), and further more transforms the testing models to TTCN-3 (Test and Test Control Notation) test cases that can be executed on a TTCN-3 execution engine, according to TTCN-3 mapping interface defined in UTP. This approach integrates testing phase with other phases tightly together, and leads to automation or semi-automation of software testing process. Finally, the paper demonstrates the effectiveness of the proposed approach by deriving TTCN-3 test cases for a typical C/S software system.

1 Introduction

In typical software testing process, development and execution of test cases cover most time and money cost. So, automation of software testing process plays a very important role in improving software quality, shortening period of development and reducing development cost. In the past years researchers have proposed many techniques to derive test data or cases automatically. Generally such techniques are based on formal specification that describes the structure and/or behavior of software systems and do generate test cases using algorithms derived from that specification [1]. However these methods are lack of practice in a real-world development process due to several reasons [2]. The first one is of complexity of formal specification and completeness of generating algorithms. Second one is selection criteria of test cases: how to select an efficient set of test cases from commonly infinite space to fit a given testing requirement is quite difficult. The last reason, maybe the most important one,

M. Li, B. Boehm, and L.J. Osterweil (Eds.): SPW 2005, LNCS 3840, pp. 222–234, 2005.

is from formal methods themselves. Most formal methods require good mathematical background and comprehensive understanding of target system for users, so that building a complete formal specification to generate test cases are generally too expensive to practice.

Historically, the appearance of software "testing" activity was later than software development and implementation; this had cause to a trend that separates development of testing and development of implementation away. While developing test cases, experienced tester may refer to design model, and may also introduce some errors for misunderstanding of design models. An ideal development model should be like this: all activities should be implemented in a unified process, these activities should incorporate each other and affect each other, and further more all concepts and methods employed by this process should be consistency [2]. Nowadays it seems that UML is the best one of supporting tools to construct the ideal development model [3], especially after official release of UML Testing Profile (UTP), which can assist testers to build exactly description of (static) structure and (dynamic) behavior of software systems, is released in 2004.

Though UTP can be used to construct testing model for a software system, this kind of construction starting from scratch would be expensive. So it is naturally to try to transform UML model to UTP model with motivation to reduce cost of developing testing model. [5] outlined principles and advices of such transformation, and listed elements in UTP that can be transformed from UML, including test component, test configuration, test control, default, data pool, data partition and timer. [6] discussed an example that applies such transformation to protocol testing. However, these works only expressed principles and description, lack of detailed transformation algorithms. And [7, 8] proposed a transformation method based on MOF four-tier model framework which can be used only to generate structural elements of testing model.

In this paper we propose a transformation approach that transforms UML design models to UTP testing models using three detailed algorithms, and further more transforms the testing models to TTCN-3 testing cases that can be executed on a TTCN-3 execution engine, according to TTCN-3 mapping interface defined in UTP[4,9]. This approach integrates testing phase with other phases tightly together, and leads to automation or semi-automation of software testing process. In order to demonstrate the feasibility and effectiveness of the proposed transformation approach, we try to derive TTCN-3 test cases for a typical C/S software system describe in section 3.

The paper is organized as following. The section 2 gives an introduction of UTP and TTCN-3. The section 3 describes the design model of a C/S communicating software, which is the target system being tested. The section 4 introduces three detailed algorithms that transform design model to testing model, and application to testing of the target system. The following section is execution of testing model by transforming it from UTP model to TTCN-3 model. Section 6 gives concluding remarks and future research directions.

2 Background

The UTP defines a visual language for designing, specifying, analyzing, implementing and documenting test systems. All necessary conceptually elements for description of testing specification and testing model of black-box testing are contained. Generally these elements can be categorized into test architecture, test behavior, test data and timer. Each category describes one specific aspect of testing model, as below:

- Test Architecture: description of test components, interfaces, connections among test components and connections between test components and SUT.
- Test Behavior: description of behavior of test cases, trace of test execution and evaluation of test results.
- Test Data: data used by test cases or test execution.
- Timer: description of time constraint or control of test behavior.

Though UTP can describe test system by itself, it can be integrated with UML together so that design of system and design of testing system can be merged. Section 3 proposes a transformation approach to generate UTP testing model from UML design model.

To generate executable test cases from UTP testing model, these models could be translated to programs written in Java or TTCN-3, as defined in official specification of UTP. This paper refers to the latter.

TTCN-3, the Testing and Test Control Notation, is the test specification and implementation language defined by the European Telecommunications Standards Institute (ETSI) for the precise definition of test procedures for black-box testing of reactive systems. It is a modular language and has a similar look and feel to a typical modern programming language. In addition to the typical programming features, it contains many important features necessary to specify test behavior and campaigns for functional, conformance, interoperability, load and scalability tests like test verdicts, matching mechanism to compare the expected responses with the actual ones, timer handling, distributed test components, synchronous and asynchronous communication and tracing[4].

TTCN-3 allows the description of complicated, distributed, parallel test behavior in terms of sequence, alternatives, loops, parallel stimuli (altsteps and interleaves) and responses. The parallel stimuli are exchanged at the interfaces of SUT, which are defined as a collection of ports being either message-based for asynchronous communication or signature-based for synchronous communication. The test system can use any number of test components, interfaces of which are described as ports likewise to the interface of SUT, to perform test procedure in parallel[4].

3 Design Model

A typical C/S system, which employs socket-based communication to serve business process, is selected as our experimental target system. Figure 1 shows the static structure of the system. Package CSCom contains five classes, ClientApp, Client, ServerApp, Server and Database. Notably, one Server object can serve many Client objects simultaneously.

In addition, figure 2 characterizes a runtime scenario of the system, and describes connections and communications between objects. A *ClientApp* instance, *cApp*, sends connection request to a *Client* instance, *client*, and *client* forwards the request to a specific *server*, an instance of *Server*. Then, *client* receives a message indicating that the connection is established, which will be forwarded to *cApp*. As soon as the connection is set up, *cApp* issues a service request to *server* through *client*, which is processed by *sApp*. The result of the service is sent back in reversed direction. Finally, *cApp* sends a disconnection request to *server* via *client*, and the entire communication is terminated.

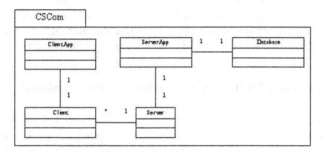

Fig. 1. Class diagram of the system

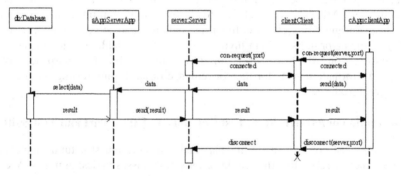

Fig. 2. Sequence diagram of the system

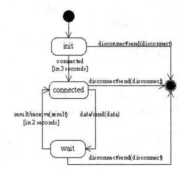

Fig. 3. Statechart diagram of a Client object

Figure 3 shows the state transfers of a *Client* object during system execution. After it is created, *Client* sends a connection request to the *server* and waits for the connected message in init state. A connected message in 3 seconds from the moment the *Client* object enters state init will trigger a state transfer, and the object comes into state connected. Then, a message of data will trigger an action *send(data)* and a state transfer to state wait, where a message of result will trigger an action of *receive(result)* and a state transfer back to state connected. Note that, a message of disconnect at any state to the object will trigger an action of *send(disconnect)* and terminate the life cycle of the object. As we can see, the statechart diagram, together with the sequence diagram, depicts the dynamic features of the system.

4 Transformation from Design Model to Testing Model

After design model is constructed, necessary information needed for modeling test system is ready. UTP, as a complement of testing issues of UML, adopts many concepts and elements from UML, and thus many of its elements can be transformed from UML design model. Three transformation algorithms for automatically transforming from UML design model to UTP testing model are proposed in this section. By applying these algorithms, most elements of UTP testing model can be generated from UML design model, e.g. SUT, test component, utility part, test suite, arbiter, test configuration, test case, timer and defaults, and so on. Notably, to assure usability of the algorithms, human involvement is an inevitable way to append some testing information which is absent in design model. For this purpose, several heuristic transformation rules for the convenience of specifying testing requirements by users are introduced.

4.1 Generation of Arbiter, SUT, Test Component, Utility Part and Test Suite

Arbiter, SUT, test component, utility part and test suite are structural elements of UTP. They merely relate to structural information of classes in design model. We can do generation of these five kinds of elements in a single algorithm.

An arbiter is a special test component, which is a requisite in each testing model. An arbiter object is used as a monitor that determines whether a test output is same as expected. According to our algorithm, an arbiter object named Test-Coordinator is automatically assigned to a testing model.

Generation of SUT is straightforward. Users simply specify classes to be tested in design model. A rule, named sut, is in form of

$$sut(class1, \cdots, classn).$$

in which each parameter refers to a class to be tested, and these classes finally form the SUT in testing model. We have to import these classes into the test package in order to access them.

In testing model, utility part elements represent external classes, which provide some specific services. To generate this kind of element, we introduce a utility rule in form of

$$utility \ (class1, \cdots classn).$$

in which each parameter refers to a class in design model. This rule indicates those classes of utility part. One design model needs at most one utility rule. Similarly, we have to import these classes into test package in order to make these external service classes accessible in testing model.

Apart from classes specified in sut rule and utility rule, each other class is regarded as a single test component in testing model. However, in case of an intricate system, simple one-to-one mapping will leads to large numbers of test components in testing model and aggravate implementation complexity of test system. To avoid this situation, group rule is introduced in form of

$$group\ (id,\ class1,\ \cdots,\ classn),$$

in which the first parameter represents id of such a rule, and each rest parameter represents a class in design model respectively. *Group* rule indicates that some classes of design model are combined into an individual test component element named after the rule. One design model may have more than one *group* rule.

Test suite organizes all test cases together in a UTP testing model. In our transformation method, we just generate default skeleton for a test suite class, which contains a verdict variable, and each of whose methods denotes one test case corresponding to a sequence diagram of design model. Users can refine and complete this automatically generated test suite.

Here we give generation algorithms for arbiter, SUT, test component, utility part and test suite in detail.

ALGORITHM 1:

S1. Initialize set S, which contains all classes in design model; Initialize set $GROUP$, which contains all *group* rules; Initialize mapping set MAP as empty;
S2. Add an *Arbiter* object named *Test-Coordinator* to testing model;
S3. For each parameter p_i in *sut* rule, let $S=S-\{p_i\}$, $MAP.Add(p_i, SUT)$;
S4. If no *utility* rule exists, GOTO S5; otherwise, for each parameter $p_i(i>0)$ in *utility* rule, let $S=S-\{p_i\}$, add an identical class p_i to testing model, $MAP.add(p_i, p_i)$;
S5. $g = GROUP.pop\_First()$, if $g == NULL$, GOTO S7;
S6. Add a test component class named as the first parameter p_1 of g to testing model; for each rest parameter of g, i.e. $p_i(i>1)$, $S=S-\{p_i\}$, $MAP.add(p_i, p_1)$; GOTO S5;
S7. For each class c left in S, add a corresponding test component class in testing model;
S8. Add a test suite class to testing model, which contains a private data member of *verdict*; for each sequence diagram in design model, add a test case method;
S9. Import all classes in design model that relate to utility part or SUT element into test package.

To apply algorithm 1, firstly users should specify rules to be imported. Notably, sut rule is absolutely necessarily for any testing model, and utility rule and group rule are optional. Besides using textual form, users can use role assignment diagram to import these three kinds of rules. For example, for figure 1, we import rules *sut (Server)*, *utility (Database)* and *group (TCClient, ClientApp, Client)*, as shown in figure 4.

After specifying rules, we can get part of UTP structural elements from design model by applying algorithm 1 to target system, i.e. package diagram of the testing system shown in figure 5 and skeleton of the test suite class shown in figure 6. For simplicity, we import all classes in design model into test package, rather than import those classes in design model that correspond to utility part and SUT elements. In addition, algorithm 1 also generates a set *MAP* mapping each class in design model to class in testing model, which will be utilized in next two algorithms.

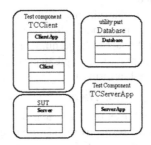

Fig. 4. Role assignment diagram

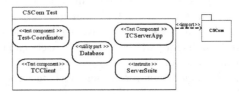

Fig. 5. Package diagram of test system

Fig. 6. Class diagram of Test Suite

4.2 Generation of Test Configuration

Test configuration diagram shows connective relationship between objects in testing model. Since there may be some objects in testing model which belong to same class, we need to import a rule that can describe such a scenario that there are more than one object belong to one test component or one utility part. The rule is in form of

$$instance(par, num).$$

in which *par* refers to a class in testing model, *num* is number of objects. Note that an *instance* rule cannot be imported arbitrarily, and it should be validated according to class diagrams in design model. For example, if there are two instances of *ServerApp*, and only one *Database* instance, then *instance(ServerApp, 2)* is wrong because it disobey the one-to-one relation of *ServerApp* and *Database* in design model.

An arbiter instance is used to evaluate testing result, so it needs to connect with some test component objects and utility part objects. Firstly, all utility part objects need to connect with arbiter objects, and all test component object or SUT object which interacts with utility part objects need to connect with arbiter objects. These two kinds of connections show that all interaction with utility part objects should be executed via an arbiter object. In addition to interactions involved with utility part objects, an arbiter object usually monitors some other events. We introduce monitor rule in form of

$$monitor\ (E_1, \cdots\cdots, E_n).$$

in which every parameter refers to an event $E(Tcom1, Tcom2, operation)$[1] which should be monitored by arbiter object. If an event E is to be monitored, it should notify arbiter object after its execution is finished. If $Tcom1$ is not SUT, it is $Tcom1$ object which informs arbiter object of E, otherwise it is $Tcom2$ which informs arbiter object.

Here we give generation algorithm for test configuration in detail.

ALGORITHM 2:

S1. Create a *SUT* object in test configuration diagram; for each class C in testing system, if there is an *instance* rule *instance(C, k)*, then create k objects of class C in test configuration diagram; otherwise create only one object of class C;

S2. Initialize set of connection relations *CONNECT* as empty;

S3. Set up set of events *EVENT* according to sequence diagram of the system;

S4. For each element $E=(com1, com2, operation)$ in *EVENT*, search *(com1, Tcom1)* and *(com2, Tcom2)* in *MAP*; if $Tcom1 == Tcom2$, delete E from *EVENT*, otherwise, replace E with *(Tcom1, Tcom2, Operation)*;

S5. $E=$ *EVENT.first()*;

S6. If $Tcom1$ or $Tcom2$ is a utility part object, *CONNECT.add(Tcom1, Test-Coordinator)*, *CONNECT.add(E.Tcom2, Test-Coordinator)*; GOTO S10;

S7. *CONNECT.add(Tcom1, Tcom2)*;

S8. If E does not appear in *monitor* rule. GOTO S10;

S9. If $Tcom1$ is not SUT, *CONNECT.add(Tcom1, Test-Coordinator)*; otherwise *CONNECT.add(Tcom2, Test-Coordinator)*;

S10. $E=EVENT.next(E)$, if $E!=NULL$. GOTO S6;

S11. For each element *(Tcom1, Tcom2)* in *CONNECT*, connect every $Tcom1$ object with every $Tcom2$ object in test configuration.

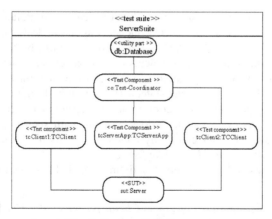

Fig. 7. Test configuration

---

[1] Here a $Tcom1$ object sends an event of *operation* to a $Tcom2$ object.

Rules to be imported should be specified at first. For target system the rules are *instance(TCClient, 2)* and *monitor((Client, Server, con-request), (Server, Client, connected), (Client, Server, data), (Server, Client, result))*. Now we can apply algorithm 2 to target system, and get test configuration diagram of testing model. Figure 7 shows all objects of testing model and connections between these objects. Afterwards, it is easy to ascertain interfaces of these objects. For every pair of objects connected, two relevant interfaces need to be added on the two objects respectively.

4.3   Generation of Test Case and Defaults

Test cases describe execution behaviors of testing model, and they are denoted by UTP in a form like sequence diagram. It is obvious that test cases should be derived from sequence diagrams in design model. Additionally, in order to validate events triggered during execution of a test case, statechart diagram in design model should be referred in the process of translation. For each event in sequence diagram, if there is a corresponding statechart diagram of recipient of the event, a state transfer will be triggered in statechart diagram. A test case will validate corresponding guard condition when an event is received if there is a guard condition in state transfer of the object. Notably, validation of time conditions is different from other guard conditions. For time conditions, it should start a timer before state transfer, and validate value of the timer when state transfer happens. If an object needs to start a timer, it should inform an arbiter object to do.

All execution failures are processed by validating operations which are denoted as defaults diagrams. Generally, for only state transfers of some certain objects are cared in a design model, state rule is imported in form of

$$state(Tcom1, \cdots\cdots, Tcomn).$$

In addition, for a test case we can validate some kinds of data if its value can be evaluated without running the test case. If there is such data in an event and recipient of the event is not SUT, then we can add a defaults object at the point of receiving to validate the data.

Here we give generation algorithm for test case and defaults in detail. The algorithm should be executed for each sequence diagram in design model.

We introduce a state rule, *state(TCClient)*, for system to be tested. One test case diagram along with some defaults objects can be generated from design model by employing algorithm 3. Note that the test case listed in figure 8 is not generated directly from sequence diagram and statechart diagram in design model. Users add an instance rule when generating test configuration diagram, and create a new *TCClient* instance *tcClient2*. Now algorithm 3 does not deal with such object added by user using instance rule. But user can easily add some events for *tcClient2* according to events involved with *tcClient1*, just like figure 8.

There are some differences between figure 8 and the sequence diagram in the design model.

- According to group rule, *Client* and *ClientApp* class are merged into a new class *TCClient*, and there are two *TCClient* objects according to instance rule.
- Add an Arbiter object *Test-Coordinator(co)*, which transmits events between *Database* object and *Server* object.

ALGORITHM 3:

S1. Initialize *CONNECT* and *TIMER* sets as empty; add an empty *defaults* object *Coord_Default* at creating point of *arbiter* object;

S2. Set up an event queue *EVENT_QUEUE* according to order of events in a sequence diagram chosen in design model;

S3. For each element *E=(com1, com2, operation)* in *EVENT*, search *(com1, Tcom1)* and *(com2, Tcom2)* in *MAP*; if *Tcom1== Tcom2*, delete *E* from *EVENT*, otherwise, replace *E* with *(Tcom1, Tcom2, operation)*;

S4. Let *E=EVENT_QUEUE.First()=(Tcom1, Tcom2, operation)*; add a *Tcom1* object in test case diagram; let *new_flag=0*;

S5. If *Tcom2* has not appeared in the test case diagram, then create a *Tcom2* object, let *new_flag=1*;

S6. If *Tcom1* or *Tcom2* is a utility part object, then add events of *(Tcom1, Test-Coordinatort, operation)* and *(Test-Coordinator, Tcom2, operation)* in the test case diagram, GOTO S9;

S7. Add *E* in the test case diagram; if *E* is not in *monitor* rule, then GOTO S9;

S8. If *Tcom1!=SUT*, then add *(Tcom1, Test-Coordinator, operation)* in the test case diagram; otherwise add *(Tcom2, Test-Coordinator, operation)* in it;

S9. If *Tcom2* is not in state rule, GOTO S15;

S10. If *new_flag==1*, GOTO S12;

S11. Delete all pairs of *(Tcom2, t)* from the set of *TIMER*, and add a *stop(t)* action for *Test-Coordinator*;

S12. If current state of *Tcom2* object is s_1, do the state transfer *(s_1, s_2, operation)*; if there is not a guard condition in this transfer, GOTO S14;

S13. If the guard condition is not time guard, then add a defaults object at receiving point of *Tcom2*;

S14. If there is any data in *operation* of which the value is known, then add a Defaults object at the accepting point of the *Tcom2* object;

S15. If there is a state transfer *(s_2, s_i)*, in which there is a time guard condition, then *Tcom2* informs *Test-Coordinator* to do the action of *start(t)*, *TIMER.add(Tcom2, t)*, and add actions in *Test-Coordinator* to process *t.timeout*;

S16. Let *new_flag=0, E=EVENT_QUEUE.NEXT(E)*, if *E!=NULL*, GOTO S5.

- Add timer *T1, T2, T3* and *T4* in co to validate timer guard conditions. In figure 8 events that related with timer are denoted in blue;
- Add a Defaults object *Coord_Default* to deal with all timeout events.

The figure 9 shows a Defaults object Coord_*Default*, which is appended to *co* in figure 8 to deal with timeout events. If co receives a timeout event of *T1, T2, T3* or *T4*, it performs operation *setverdict(fail)*, which sets testing result as fail, and terminates execution of the test case. If co receives some message unexpected, it performs operation *setverdict(inconc)*, and continues to execute the test case.

It should be aware that testing model generated from design model using above algorithms is not final one, and generally some refinement and validation could be done by users. For a complex system, efforts of refinement and validation could be much more than we have done above. Though, for this kind of automated transformation from design model to testing model can provide a good start point, it is still very helpful for constructing testing model, as we showed above.

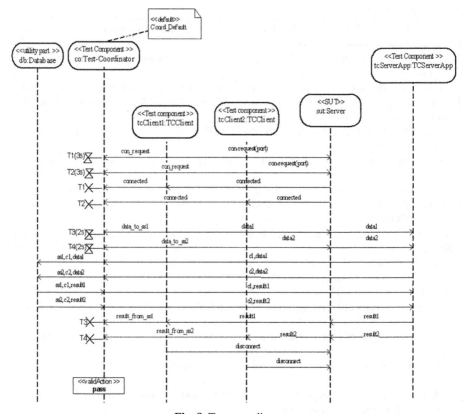

Fig. 8. Test case diagram

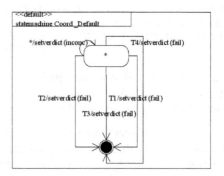

Fig. 9. Coord_Default state diagram

5 Execution of Testing Model

Now UTP is just a means used for denotation, but it can not be executed directly. In order to execute test cases in testing model, UTP introduces two methods. One is to translate testing model into test cases in java, and the other is to translate testing model into test cases in TTCN-3. Although both of these two methods can be used to execute test cases in testing model, it is simple and natural to use TTCN-3 solution rather than java solution for UTP references many concepts and models from TTCN-3[4]. Also, TTCN-3 solution does not require implement languages of target system. For our system to be tested, we employ the TTCN-3 mapping defined in UTP standard to generate executable test cases from UTP testing model. We execute such test cases using the TTCN-3 execution engine implemented by us in C++, so that testing tasks can be quickly implemented with high quality.

6   Conclusion

Most existing testing automation methods rely on various kinds of formal models, and make a contrived separation between software testing and other phases in software life cycle. This limits the wide spread application of these automation methods. In this paper we propose an automated approach that transforms existing UML design model to UTP testing model so as to assist construction of a testing model. And further more, we also transform UTP testing model to TTCN-3 model to execute it on TTCN-3 execution engine, according to TTCN-3 mapping interface defined in UTP. The two-step transformation leads to automation or semi-automation of software testing process, including development, execution and verify phases. Application of these transformations to a typical C/S style communication system demonstrates efficiency of this approach. By that, we have shortened period of development, reduced cost of development, and improved quality of software that illustrated in section 3.

Future research will concern on flexibility and completeness of this approach. According to the algorithms above, for a single sequence diagram, only one test case is generated so that only part of state transfers can be covered in statechart diagram. And, may be more important, considering there is more and more concurrency in modern software systems, extending these transformation methods to concurrency testing will become one of the most important research areas in the near future.

Acknowledgements

This work/paper was partially supported by the National Natural Science Foundation of China under grant Nos. 60473060, 60273026 as well as the Hi-Tech and Development Program (863 Program) under grant Nos.2004AA1Z2100, 2005AA113140.

References

1. B. Beizer, Software Testing Techniques. International Thomson Computer Press (1990)
2. Bertolino, "Software Testing Research and Practice", Invited presentation at 10th International Workshop on Abstract State Machines ASM 2003, Taormina, Italy, LNCS 2589 (2003) 1-21
3. L. C. Briand and Y. Labiche, "A UML-Based Approach to System Testing", Software and Systems Modeling, vol. 1 (1) (2002) 10-42

4. OMG, UML 2.0 Testing Profile Specification (04-04-02)
5. Z. R. Dai, Model-Driven Testing with UML 2.0. Second European Workshop on Model Driven Architecture (MDA) with an emphasis on Methodologies and Transformations, Canterbury, England, September (2004)
6. Z. R. Dai, J. Grabowski, H. Neukirchen, From Design to Test with UML – Applied to a Roaming Algorithm for Bluetooth Devices. TestCom 2004, LNCS 2978 (2004) 33-49
7. Schieferdecker, G. Din, A Meta-model for TTCN-3.FORTE 2004 Workshops, LNCS 3236 (2004) 366-379
8. Duddy, A. Gerber, M. Lawley, K. Raymond, J. Steel, Model Transformation: A declarative, reusable patterns approach. (In: 7th IEEE International Enterprise Distributed Object Computing Conference) (2003) 174-185
9. Schieferdecker, Z. R. Dai, J. Grabowski,The UML2.0 Testing Profile and its Relation to TTCN-3. TestCom 2003, LNCS 2644 (2003) 79-94
10. OMG, UML 2.0 Superstructure Specification (ptc/03-08-02)
11. ETSI ES 201 873 – 1, v2.2.1: "The Testing and Test Control Notation TTCN-3: Core Language " (2002)

Evaluation of the Capability of Personal Software Process Based on Data Envelopment Analysis

Liping Ding[1,3], Qiusong Yang[1,3], Liang Sun[1,3],
Jie Tong[1,3], and Yongji Wang[1,2]

[1] Laboratory for Internet Software Technologies, Institute of Software,
The Chinese Academy of Sciences, Beijing 100080, China
{dingliping, qiusong_yang, sunliang, tongjie, ywang}
@itechs.iscas.ac.cn
[2] Key Laboratory for Computer Science,
The Chinese Academy of Sciences, Beijing 100080, China
[3] Graduate School, The Chinese Academy of Sciences, Beijing 100039, China

Abstract. Personal Software Process (PSP) is a defined and measured software process designed to be used by an individual software engineer. For PSP users, it's important to evaluate the impact of the PSP upon their own personal capabilities of software development. However, the evaluation of capability of PSP is a Variable Return to Scale (VRS) and multivariate input and output problem, which makes traditional evaluation methods useless. In this paper, an evaluation framework for the capability of PSP based on Data Envelopment Analysis (DEA) is proposed. This framework has the advantage of dealing with VRS issues with multivariate input and output. In addition, the input or output variables of the framework can have different measurement units. Therefore, a quantitative and comprehensive result can be returned by this relative efficiency evaluation method and it can support the continuous improvement of PSP.

1 Introduction

Due to the research of software process and its improvement, the focus of software quality has moved from the software test to the whole software development process. The wide adoption of the Software Engineering Institute's Capability Maturity Model (SEI CMM) has improved software quality, and it is also established that the implementations of CMM can improve the performance of organizations continuously. In order to answer the question about how to effectively implement CMM in small organizations, Watts S. Humphrey introduced some fundamental principles of CMM into the practices of small organizations and individuals, and proved that those principles of process management can also be applied to the individual work of software engineers. His research formed the basis of the Personal Software Process (PSP).

The PSP provides an alternative, complementary approach which empirically guides software process improvement and is "scaled down" to the level of an individual developer. In the PSP, individuals gather measures related to the software

M. Li, B. Boehm, and L.J. Osterweil (Eds.): SPW 2005, LNCS 3840, pp. 235–248, 2005.

engineers' work products and the process by which they are developed, and use these measures to drive changes to their development behavior. The PSP regards defect reduction and the accuracy of process improvement estimation as the two primary goals of personal process improvement.

Return to scale refers to increasing or decreasing, constant or variable efficiency based on size. [1] points out that small and large software projects likely exhibit *Variable Return to Scale* (VRS, i.e. the relationship between the input and the output is non-linear), whereas medium software projects probably exhibit *Constant Return to Scale* (CRS, i.e. the relationship between the input and the output is linear). Since the size of programs developed by the PSP method ranges from 50 LOC (Line Of Code) to 5000 LOC [2], it is reasonable to assume that the PSP projects have VRS, which is also illustrated in Section 5. On the other hand, there may be many metrics that can be used for the evaluation of PSP capability. For example, if we are interested in the development schedule, we can set the accuracy of schedule estimation as a metric. Meanwhile, we may set the defect density as a metric to pay particular attention to the product quality. So the evaluation of PSP capability is a multivariate input/output problem that must take all the needed metrics into account.

For the PSP users, it is important to evaluate the impact of the PSP upon their own personal capabilities of software development. Because of the VRS and multivariate input/output properties of the PSP, it is not appropriate to use those linear models, as well as those non-linear models, such as COCOMO(Constructive Cost Model) . Hence, we need a new framework for the evaluation of PSP capability.

Data Envelopment Analysis (DEA) developed by A. Charnes and W. W. Cooper in 1978 is a non-parametric mathematical programming approach to frontier estimation. It can be used to evaluate the relative efficiency of a number of decision making units or DMUs, which may have multivariate input and output. Generally speaking, DMU can denote any entity which economically transforms some inputs into outputs. In addition, some DEA models have VRS, which address the variable return to scale issues. Therefore, DEA is a very appropriate tool to evaluate the PSP capability.

In this paper, a DEA-based evaluation framework for the capability of the PSP is presented, and it is illustrated by a case study. This framework utilizes the CCR and BCC models of DEA to analyze the project plan summary data accumulated during the implementations of PSP, and then computes the relative efficiencies and efficiency frontier as the basis of the evaluation result. Compared with the existing methods, this framework has the following advantages:

1) It can deal with multivariate input/output issues even the inputs and outputs have very different measurement units.
2) The VRS model of DEA can handle the VRS property of PSP perfectly, and it does not assume any functional relationship between the inputs and outputs.
3) It provides an efficiency evaluation method which returns a quantitative and comprehensive result.
4) The result of DEA can support the continuous improvement of the PSP.

The rest of this paper is organized as follows. Section 2 discusses two fundamental properties of the evaluation of PSP capability; Section 3 presents a short introduction to DEA, then two typical DEA models named CCR (a kind of CRS models) and BCC (a kind of VRS models) are discussed; Section 4 focuses on the DEA-based evaluation framework for PSP capability; Section 5 presents a case study according to the framework in Section 4. Section 6 concludes the paper.

2 Evaluation of PSP Capability

It is stated in [1] that small and large software projects likely exhibit VRS while medium ones exhibit CRS. This conclusion can be intuitively derived from the following statements: software development can be divided into two parts, application development (user functionality development) and technical infrastructure (TI) development (software configuration, deployment and supporting environment). For a small size project, the return to scale will increase along with the increase of scale since the technical infrastructure holds a relative huge proportion in the whole project. For a large project, the TI has a smaller proportion, the return to scale will decrease when the project size increases because the complexity increases exponentially with the increasing of project scale. The PSP is suitable for the projects ranging from 50 to 5000 LOC, while cyclical methodology is recommended for larger projects [2]. Thus the projects, in which the PSP is applied, likely exhibit VRS since their size is supposed to be small.

All metrics in Table 1 are derived from the Project Plan Summary of PSP [3][4][5]. Among these metrics, only "total schedule" is input. The rest are outputs used for the calculations of the quantity or quality of the product.

Trend diagrams are frequently used to illustrate the positive influence of the adoption of the PSP in [1], [6], and [2]. One example of trend diagram used for depicting defects density is shown in Fig. 1. Many other types of trend diagram, such as Process Yield, Phase Yield, A/FR, Accuracy of Size Estimation etc., are used in the final report of the PSP training. The adoption of the PSP can surely make great positive changes to personal capability, but no accurate quantitative and comprehensive conclusions can be drawn from these diagrams. For example, although programmer A has a better defect density trend diagram than programmer B, programmer B has a better A/FR trend diagram. It's difficult to answer the question that which one has a higher PSP capability. This dilemma is mainly due to the fact that the evaluation must take all the needed metrics into account. That is to say, the evaluation of the PSP capability is a multivariate input/output issue.

The most widely applied productivity model in software engineering is the following univariate CRS model (P = productivity, x = input, y = output) [1]:

$$P=\frac{y}{x}$$

Another sort of productivity model is the cost estimation models, e.g. COCOMO model, which generally have the following form (P = productivity, u = effort, v = function point (FP) or source line of code (SLOC), $b > 1$) [1]:

$$u =\frac{1}{p}v^b$$

These models are widely used, but not suitable for the evaluation of PSP capability. The first one does not take VRS into account and the latter can not deal with the multivariate input/output issues. The evaluation framework proposed later in this paper can handle both the VRS and multivariate input/output issues.

Table 1. PSP recommended metrics

Metric	Formula
Total Schedule	The sum of planned or actual time for all phases of a project
Scale	Source Line of Code
Review Rate	60 * (New and Changed Code in LOC)/Review Minutes
Time Ratios	Design Time/ Coding Time
	Design Review Time /Design Time
	Code Review Time/ Coding Time
Defect Ratios	Remove Defects in Code Review/Defects when Compiling
	Removed Defects in Design Review/Defects when Unit Test
Process Yield	Removed Defects before Compiling and Unit Test/Total Defects
Phase Yield	Defects at Entry/ Defects at Ending
A/FR	(Design Review Time + Code Review Time)/(Compiling time+ Unit Test Time)
LOC/Hour	Total New and Changed Code in LOC / Total Schedule in Hour
CPI	Planned Time/Actual Time
Reuse Rate	Reused LOC/Total LOC
Increased Reuse Rate	The New Increased Reuse Code LOC /New and Changed Code in LOC
Test Defects/KLOC	1000*(Defects Removed in Test)/Actual New and Changed LOC
Defect density	1000*(Total Defects removed)/Actual New and Changed LOC

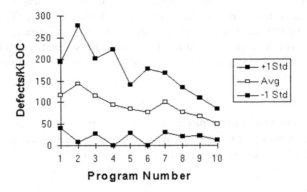

Fig. 1. An example of defects density trend diagram

3 Data Envelopment Analysis

The usual model for the measurement of producers' efficiencies, $efficiency = \dfrac{output}{inupt}$, is inadequate due to the existence of multivariate inputs and multivariate outputs with different measurement units. One way to solve the problem is to assume that there is a common set of weights applied to each input and output. But this leads to the problem of how to determine the set of weights for the model in advance.

However, DEA uses a non-parametric mathematical programming approach to evaluate the relative efficiency of the producers. A producer is usually referred to as a decision making unit (DMU) in DEA. A typical statistical approach is characterized as a central trend approach and it evaluates producers' relative efficiencies through comparing with an average producer's efficiency. In contrast, DEA is an extremum method and compares each producer's efficiency with only the "best" producers'. So DEA can only be used for the evaluation of relative efficiency, not absolute efficiency. In order to make DEA to be automated or semi-automated, many commercial or free software tools for DEA [8] are available now.

At present, DEA has been extensively applied in performance evaluation and benchmarking of city bank branches, schools, hospitals, productivity plants, etc [9]. A recent paper illustrated how to evaluate the efficiency of ERP projects using DEA [1]. However, the applications in the field of software engineering are rare.

In this section we will discuss two classical DEA models: the CCR model by Charnes, Cooper and Rhodes [10] and the BCC model by Banker, Charnes and Cooper [11]. The CCR model's assumption is CRS and the BCC model's assumption is VRS.

Before any further discussions, the following notations are given:

n the number of DMUs to be evaluated

DMU_j the j th DMU

m the number of inputs to each DMU

s the number of outputs to each DMU

x_{ij} amount of the i th input consumed by DMU_j

y_{kj} amount of the k th output produced by DMU_j

eff abbreviation for efficiency

v_i the weight assigned to the i th input

μ_k the weight assigned to the k th output

3.1 CCR Model

The CCR model is probably the most widely applied and best known DEA model. It is the DEA model used in frontier analysis when a constant return to scale relationship is assumed between inputs and outputs.

According to

$$eff \quad DMU_{j_0} = \frac{\sum\limits_{k=1}^{s} \mu_k y_{kj_0}}{\sum\limits_{i=1}^{m} v_i x_{ij_0}}$$

the ratio approach of CCR model can be written as:

$$\text{Maximize} \quad \theta = \frac{u_1 y_{1 j_0} + u_2 y_{2 j_0} + \cdots + u_s y_{s j_0}}{v_1 x_{1 j_0} + v_2 x_{2 j_0} + \cdots + v_m x_{m j_0}}$$

$$\text{subject to} \quad \frac{u_1 y_{1j} + \cdots + u_s y_{sj}}{v_1 x_{1j} + \cdots + v_m x_{mj}} \leq 1 \quad (j = 1, 2, \cdots, n) \tag{1}$$

$$v_1, v_2, \cdots, v_m \geq \varepsilon, \quad u_1, u_2, \cdots, u_s \geq \varepsilon$$

where ε is a positive small constant. The solution to this model provides the weight that maximizes the efficiency of the DMU_{j_0}, and constrains that the efficiency of other DMUs is less than 1. The problem in this form has infinite number of optimal solutions. In fact, if (u^*, v^*) is an optimal solution, then $(\beta u^*, \beta v^*)$ is also optimal for every positive number β.

Then the corresponding dual problem is:

$$\min_{\theta, \lambda, s_i^+, s_k^-} \quad \theta - \varepsilon \left(\sum_{i=1}^{m} s_i^+ + \sum_{k=1}^{s} s_k^- \right)$$

$$\text{s.t.} \quad \theta x_{i j_0} - \sum_{j=1}^{n} x_{ij} \lambda_j - s_i^+ = 0 \qquad i = 1, \ldots, m \tag{2}$$

$$\sum_{j=1}^{n} y_{kj} \lambda_j - y_{k j_0} - s_k^- = 0 \qquad k = 1, \ldots, s$$

$$\lambda_j \geq 0 \qquad j = 1, \ldots, n$$

$$s_i^+ \geq 0 \qquad i = 1, \ldots, m$$

$$s_k^- \geq 0 \qquad k = 1, \ldots, p$$

where θ denotes the efficiency score of the DMU_{j_0}. This score is between 0 and 1. A unit with score of 1 is *relative efficient*, otherwise *relative inefficient*. s_i^+ $(\theta x_{i j_0} - \sum_{j=1}^{n} x_{ij} \lambda_j)$ and s_k^- $(\sum_{j=1}^{n} y_{kj} \lambda_j - y_{k j_0})$ are the relaxation and remaining *variables* for input and output. Relaxation represents the over use of input and remaining represents the insufficient output. It represents the available improvements that can make an inefficient unit become efficient. λ_j is called *dual weight* for the given DMU_j. The linear combination of the original DMUs with the coefficients of λ_j is the projection of the DMU_{j_0} on the efficiency frontier through the origin. The projection is also called the virtual DMU for the given DMU.

From the dual weights of (2), a *peer group* of the DMU_{j_0} is defined as:

$$RS_{j_0} = \{ j : \lambda_j \neq 0, \ j = 1, \cdots, n \}$$

It should be noted that each DMU in the peer group is relative efficient. It provides examples of good operating practice for the relatively inefficient unit to emulate. λ_j of the DMU in the peer group is also called *peer weight*.

We refer to (2) as the dual *input oriented* model since an inefficient DMU is made efficient by reducing the proportions of its inputs but keeping the output proportions constant. From this model, we get the efficiency score of the DMU_{j_0}. All the efficiency scores of the DMUs in question can be get by the similar calculation. Thus, the efficiency frontier (envelope), including all the relatively efficient units and the best performance representation, can be determined.

3.2 BCC Model

The BCC model is used in frontier analysis when a variable return to scale relationship is assumed. The input oriented model is written as:

$$\min_{\theta,\lambda,s_i^+,s_k^-} \quad \theta - \varepsilon\left(\sum_{i=1}^{m} s_i^+ + \sum_{k=1}^{s} s_k^-\right)$$

$$\text{s.t.} \quad \theta x_{ij_0} - \sum_{j=1}^{n} x_{ij}\lambda_j - s_i^+ = 0 \qquad i = 1,\ldots,m$$

$$\sum_{j=1}^{n} y_{kj}\lambda_j - y_{kj_0} - s_k^- = 0 \qquad k = 1,\ldots,s \qquad (3)$$

$$\sum_{j=1}^{n} \lambda_j = 1$$

$$\lambda_j \geq 0 \qquad j = 1,\ldots,n$$

$$s_i^+ \geq 0 \qquad i = 1,\ldots,m$$

$$s_k^- \geq 0 \qquad k = 1,\ldots,p$$

Noting the strong similarity with the CCR model, the difference between the two models is the constraint $\sum_{j=1}^{n} \lambda_j = 1$. This constraint implies that the virtual DMU is the convex combinations of all the original DMUs and ensures that the virtual DMU is of similar scale to the unit being measured.

3.3 The Calculation of Scale Efficiency

The efficiency score obtained from the BCC model is also called *pure technical efficiency* because the impact of scale size is ignored. The DMUs are only compared with the units of similar scale size. However, the efficiency scores obtained from CRS model can be decomposed into two components, one due to the technical inefficiency and one due to the scale inefficiency. The scale efficiency may be calculated through dividing efficiency score (from CCR model) by pure technical efficiency (from BCC model). The efficiency score of the CCR model is also called technical efficiency in the context without conflicts.

One shortcoming of the above approach is that it's difficult to determine whether a DMU is operating in an area of *increasing or decreasing return to scale* (IRS or DRS). IRS (DRS) indicates that an increase in one unit's inputs will yield a greater (or less) proportionate increase of its outputs. The type of return to scale can be determined by conducting a more *non increasing return to scale* (NIRS) DEA model upon the same data. This can be done by altering the DEA model in (3) by substituting the constraint $\sum_{j=1}^{n} \lambda_j = 1$ with $\sum_{j=1}^{n} \lambda_j \leq 1$:

$$\min_{\theta, \lambda, s_i^+, s_k^-} \quad \theta - \varepsilon \left(\sum_{i=1}^{m} s_i^+ + \sum_{k=1}^{s} s_k^- \right)$$

$$\text{s.t.} \quad \theta x_{ij_0} - \sum_{j=1}^{n} x_{ij} \lambda_j - s_i^+ = 0 \qquad i = 1,\dots,m$$

$$\sum_{j=1}^{n} y_{kj} \lambda_j - y_{kj_0} - s_k^- = 0 \qquad k = 1,\dots,s$$

$$\sum_{j=1}^{n} \lambda_j \leq 1$$

$$\lambda_j \geq 0 \qquad j = 1,\dots,n$$

$$s_i^+ \geq 0 \qquad i = 1,\dots,m$$

$$s_k^- \geq 0 \qquad k = 1,\dots,p$$

$$(4)$$

If there is difference between the results calculated by the two models, (3) and (4), then the DMU has IRS, otherwise it has DRS.

4 The DEA-Based PSP Capability Evaluation Framework

In this section, we will briefly discuss how to perform each step in our DEA framework for PSP capability. The task of evaluating the relative efficiency can be divided into four steps [12]: deciding the purpose of the evaluation; selecting DMU; establishing the input/output variables system; choosing DEA models.

4.1 Deciding the Purpose of the Evaluation

The purpose of DEA evaluation is to explain the relative efficiency of the PSP implementation by comparing the performances and capabilities of PSP at different phases. Obviously, the key issue here is to transform basic concepts of DEA, such as "relative efficiency", "efficiency frontier" and "the mapping of DMUs in the frontier", into corresponding attributes about the PSP.

4.2 Selecting DMUs

Selecting DMUs is to determine reference sets. Because DEA evaluates the relative efficiency among the similar DMUs, the basic requirement of the DMU selection is that the DMUs must be *homogenous*. The homogenous DMUs mean that they are DMU sets satisfying the following three conditions: 1) they have the same purposes; 2) they are in the same environment; 3) they have the same input/output indices. Book [2] gives the exercises of various PSP phases for PSP training. We will consider ten excises from 1A to 10A as DMUs.

4.3 Establishing the Input/Output of DMUs

After selecting DMU, we will establish the input/output of DMUs [13]. Firstly, we must take into account the evaluation purpose. That is to say, the selection of input and output must be consistent with the evaluation purpose. For example, if the evaluation purpose is "the organization efficiency of a sort of DMUs", then we can specify the inputs and outputs as follows. The inputs are flow capital input, fixed capital input, manpower effort, and the outputs are return, actual / plan progress, actual /plan cost. We haven't selected the quality and security variables because they don't accord with the evaluation purpose.

Secondly, we must consider the relationship of the input and output variables. Because the DMUs' input and output variables are not isolated, the variables which have been regarded as input or output can influence the cognizance of other variables. For example, we should discard a variable if the information of it has been covered by other several variables or has strong relationship with some other input/output variables.

Thirdly, we can get all the input and output values for all the DMUs. Note that they are all positive values.

Fourthly, according to the efficiency ratio principle, we prefer the smaller input values and bigger output values.

Fifthly, different input or output variables can have different measurement units, such as the number of individuals, the area, the cost, etc.

We have chosen the following metrics (shown in Table 2) according to the above discussions.

4.4 Choosing DEA Models

There are various forms of DEA models. Which kind of DEA models should we choose when we evaluate efficiencies based on DEA? We should choose the models according to both the actual background and the evaluation purpose. In addition, in

Table 2. Input/output variables to the PSP evaluation

Metric	Formula	Type	Meaning
Schedule	Development time(minute)	Input	Activity Input (or Investment)
Scale	Source line of code	Output	Product Scale
Reciprocal of Defect Density	10000/(Total Defects/(Scale in KLOC))	Output	Product Quality
Scale Estimation Accuracy	10/(|Planned Scale-Actual Scale|/Actual Scale)	Output	Ability of Scale Estimation
Time Estimation Accuracy	10/(|Planned Schedule-Actual Schedule|/Actual Schedule)	Output	Ability of Schedule Estimation
Process Yield	Number of Defects Removed Before Compiling and Unit Test/Total Defects	Output	Process Performance

order to get the different evaluation information, we should choose different forms of DEA models as possible as we can. And then the results of the analysis should be compared and integrated. Therefore, the result will be more complete and accurate. In the case study of Section 5, we will use CCR and BCC models given above to evaluate the capability of PSP.

5   Case Study

According to the approach introduced in Section 4, we use the metrics listed in Table 2 as the output and input of the DMU. The DEA models discussed in Section 3 is used to evaluate the capability of PSP.

Table 3 is derived from the project plan summary data in [14]. The result of DEA algorithm is presented in Table 4,5,6,7.

In Table 3, because PSP0 is used in the first and second exercises, there are not enough data to calculate the accuracy of size estimation. So they are arbitrarily set to 30 and 35 respectively. Table 4 shows what the peer group of each exercise is. One given exercise can emulate some good development practices from its peers. The peer weight indicates the importance of the peer to the given exercise. In Table 5, for a relative inefficient DMU, $s_1^+ > 0$ shows that the DMU has an over use of the input. It indicates that the exercise should be developed using less hours. If $s_k^- > 0$, then the exercise can make more progress in the kth metric as the relative efficient DMU. As for Table 6, for the covexity constraint added by BCC model, there may be more peers for each DUM than CCR model. Table 8 shows that DRS (IRS) exists when the development efficiency drops (rises) along with the increase of software scale.

We can draw the following conclusions from the above results:

1) In Table 4, the efficiency frontier is composed of DMU 7, DMU 5, DMU 4 and DMU 1. DMU 10's technical efficiency is also 1.000 in Table 6, which implies that DMU 10 is positioned on the efficiency frontier in BCC model. That is, DMU 10, DMU 7, DMU 5, DMU 4 and DMU 1 are fully efficient. This conclusion can also be intuitively derived from the original data directly. Exercise 7 is designed to calculate the correlation between two data sets and the programs developed in exercise 1 can be reused without any modifications. So exercise 7 has a moderate scale but with a relatively shorter schedule. As for exercise 5 and exercise 4, each of them has either high accuracy of schedule estimation or low defect density. Exercise 10 and exercise 1 have a comprehensive higher performance. From the above discussion, we can learn that DEA algorithm can take into account all the metrics and address the multivariate output issues properly.

2) To those inefficient DMUs, whose technical efficiency is less than 1.000, $s_k^- > 0$ shows that the DMU can make further improvement on the kth metric, the absolute value of s_k^- indicates that what the margin of the improvement is. So based on the analysis result of DEA, we can select those metrics with relatively larger s_k^- and analyze the factors which can improve the metric. Thus we can learn what we should do to make further improvement on the PSP. That is to say, the result of DEA can help the continuous improvement of PSP.

Table 3. Measures derived from Project Plan Summaries listed in [14]

Exercise	Scale (LOC)	Reciprocal of Defect Density	Size Estimation Accuracy	Schedule Estimation Accuracy	Process Yield	Schedule
1	94	78	NA(35)	48	58	114
2	233	75	NA(30)	55	71	214
3	263	109	23	15	50	310
4	236	157	63	28	87	188
5	178	93	32	455	89	182
6	568	75	45	53	67	315
7	678	43	72	66	95	198
8	458	63	49	18	87	393
9	824	74	25	60	80	342
10	1202	61	85	23	85	498

3) The DMU's return to scale property, which indicates whether a DMU has IRS or DRS, can be obtained by comparing the result of NIRS and BCC model. The result is listed in table 8.

In Table 8, all the DMUs except the third one has DRS, so the PSP exercises have decreasing return to scale. The reason is that there are few technical infrastructure development tasks in the PSP exercises, the complexity of programs, which increases exponentially when scale increases, lead to the decrease return to scale.

Table 4. Efficiency scores and referencing relations obtained from CCR model

DMU	Efficiency Score	Peer 1	Peer Weight 1	Peer 2	Peer Weight 2
1	1.000	1	1.000		
2	0.664	7	0.225	1	0.856
3	0.497	4	0.650	7	0.162
4	1.000	4	1.000		
5	1.000	5	1.000		
6	0.630	4	0.274	7	0.742
7	1.000	7	1.000		
8	0.452	7	0.605	1	0.509
9	0.757	4	0.153	7	1.162
10	0.705	7	1.773		

4) In general, technical infrastructure is the indivisible part of the real world application development. It's reasonable that the PSP projects, whose scale ranges from 50 to 5000 LOC, should have increasing return to scale. That is, the PSP projects have variable return to scale. Just as noted in Section 3, CCR and BCC are CRS and VRS model respectively. The notable difference between the results of CCR and BCC lies in that the 10th exercise is positioned on the efficiency frontier in BCC. When doing the 10th exercise, the student has had a comprehensive understanding about the PSP and adopts PSP3, the maturest version of PSP, to implement PSP. So the comprehensive performance of the 10th exercise is relatively higher. The BCC model can get the relative efficiency without the influence of return to scale and put

the 10th exercise on the efficiency frontier. As a conclusion, it should be better to evaluate the capability of PSP using BCC model than CCR model.

Table 5. Relaxation and remaining variables of the CCR model

DMU	s_1^+	s_1^-	s_2^-	s_3^-	s_4^-	s_5^-
1	0.000	0.000	0.000	0.000	0.000	0.000
2	0.000	0.000	1.408	16.147	0.918	0.000
3	0.000	0.000	0.000	29.589	13.869	21.907
4	0.000	0.000	0.000	0.000	0.000	0.000
5	0.000	0.000	0.000	0.000	0.000	0.000
6	0.000	0.000	0.000	25.730	3.671	27.387
7	0.000	0.000	0.000	0.000	0.000	0.000
8	0.000	0.000	2.728	12.376	46.366	0.000
9	0.000	0.000	0.000	68.312	20.982	43.712
10	0.000	0.000	15.233	42.646	94.009	83.422

Table 6. The technical efficiencies and peer relations of the BCC model

DMU	Technical Efficiency	Peer	Peer Weight	Peer	Peer Weight	Peer	Peer Weight	Peer	Peer Weight
1	1.000	1	1.000						
2	0.670	7	0.211	5	0.141	4	0.029	1	0.620
3	0.527	7	0.175	4	0.470	1	0.355		
4	1.000	4	1.000						
5	1.000	5	1.000						
6	0.642	10	0.024	7	0.699	4	0.277		
7	1.000	7	1.000						
8	0.457	7	0.586	5	0.208	4	0.030	1	0.176
9	0.989	10	0.476	7	0.297	5	0.054	4	0.173
10	1.000	10	1.000						

Table 7. Relaxation and remaining variables of the BCC model

DMU	s_1^+	s_1^-	s_2^-	s_3^-	s_4^-	s_5^-
10	0.000	0.000	0.000	0.000	0.000	0.000
9	0.000	0.000	0.000	49.469	0.000	8.529
8	0.000	0.000	0.000	7.911	124.4	0.000
7	0.000	0.000	0.000	0.000	0.000	0.000
6	0.000	0.000	0.000	24.815	1.457	25.547
5	0.000	0.000	0.000	0.000	0.000	0.000
4	0.000	0.000	0.000	0.000	0.000	0.000
3	0.000	0.000	0.000	31.639	26.752	28.109
2	0.000	0.000	0.000	13.177	53.611	0.000
1	0.000	0.000	0.000	0.000	0.000	0.000

Table 8. Return to scale of DMUs

DMU	BCC Technical Efficiency	NIRS Technical Efficiency	Return to Scale
1	1.000	1.000	DRS
2	0.670	0.670	DRS
3	0.527	0.497	IRS
4	1.000	1.000	DRS
5	1.000	1.000	DRS
6	0.642	0.642	DRS
7	1.000	1.000	DRS
8	0.457	0.457	DRS
9	0.989	0.989	DRS
10	1.000	1.000	DRS

5) The same characteristics of DMUs that make DEA a powerful tool can also create some problems. When choosing to use DEA in the evaluation of PSP, we should keep these limitations in mind. First, DEA is an extreme point method, so noise (even symmetrical noise with zero mean), such as measurement errors, can cause significant problems. Secondly, DEA is good at estimating "relative" efficiency of a DMU but it converges very slowly to "absolute" efficiency. In other words, it can indicate how well we are doing compared to our peers but not compared to a "theoretical maximum." Thirdly, Since DEA is a nonparametric technique, statistical hypothesis tests are difficult and are the focus of ongoing research. At last, a standard formulation of DEA creates a separate linear program for each DMU, problems can be computationally intensive[15].

6   Conclusion

This paper focuses on two notable characteristics of the evaluation of the PSP: multivariate input/output and VRS. To overcome the difficulties caused by these characteristics, we proposed a DEA-based evaluation framework for the PSP capability in Section 4, and Section 5 presents a case study which illustrates the principle of our framework well. The evaluation framework can deal with VRS issues with multivariate input and output. Another advantage of the framework is the input/output variables can have different measurement units. So we can get accurate quantitative and comprehensive results to evaluate the PSP capability by the proposed framework and make the decision of how to improve the PSP.

Acknowledgements

This paper was partially supported by the National Natural Science Foundation of China (Grant Numbers: 60373053, 60473060), 863 Program (Grant Numbers: 2004AA112080, 2005AA113140), the research collaboration between the Chinese Academy of Sciences and the Royal Society of the United Kingdom (Grant Numbers: 20030389, 20032006), the Plan of Hundreds Scientists in the Chinese Academy of Sciences, the key program of the National High-Tech Research and Development

Program of China (Grant Number: 2004AA1Z2100), and the State Education Ministry's Scientific Research Foundation for the Returned Overseas Chinese Scholars.

References

1. E. Stensrud, I. Myrtveit: Identifying High Performance ERP Projects. IEEE Transaction on Software Engineering, 29(5) (2003) 387-416
2. W. S. Humphrey: A Discipline for Software Engineering. New York: Addison-Wesley (1995)
3. W. S. Humphrey: The Personal Software Process. Technical Report, CMU/SEI-2000-TR-022, (Nov 2000)
4. W. Hayes, J. W. Over: The Personal Software Process: An Empirical Study of the Impact of PSP on Individual Engineers. Technical Report, CMU/SEI-97-TR-001 (1997)
5. W. S. Humphrey: Using a defined and measured personal software process. IEEE Software, 13(3) (1996) 77-88
6. A. M. Disney, P. M. Johnson: Investigating Data Quality Problems in the PSP. Software Engineering Notes, 23(6) (1998) 143-152
7. W. S. Humphrey: Introduction to the Personal Software Process. New York: Addison-Wesley (1997)
8. R. S. Bar: DEA Software Tools and Technology: A State-of-the-Art Survey. Boston: Kluwer Academic Publishers (2004) 539-566
9. Quanling wei: Use DEA to Evaluate the Relative Efficiency—A New Filed of Operational Research. Beijing: China Renmin University Press (1987)
10. A. Charnes. W. Cooper and E. Rhodes: Measuring the efficiency of decision making units. European Journal of Operation Research, 2 (1978) 429-444
11. R. D. Banker, A. Charnes and W Cooper: Some models for estimating technical and scale inefficiencies in data envelopment analysis. Management Science, 30 (1984) 1078-1092
12. A. Charnes, W. W. Cooper, Q. L. Wei, Z. M. Huang and C. Ratio: Data Envelopment Analysis and Multi-objective Programming, The University of Texas at Austin, Center for Cybernetic Studies Report CCS559 (1986)
13. Liang li, CUI Jinchuan: Selection of Input-output Items and Data Disposal in DEA. Journal of Systems Engineering, 18(6) (2003) 487-490
14. V. Putz: The Personal Software Process: an Independent Study.
http:// www.nyx.net/~vputz/psp_index/book1.html
15. A Data Envelopment Analysis (DEA) Home Page: Limitations of DEA.
http://www.emp.pdx.edu/dea/homedea.html#Limitations

Project Management System
Based on Work-Breakdown-Structure Process Model

Akira Harada[1], Satoshi Awane[1], Yuji Inoya[1], Osamu Ohno[1],
Makoto Matsushita[2], Shinji Kusumoto[2], and Katsuro Inoue[2]

[1] Engineering Support Management Division, Solution Systems, Hitachi Ltd.,
890 Kashimada Kawasaki, Kanagawa 213-8567, Japan
{aharada, awane, yinoya, ohno}@itg.hitachi.co.jp
[2] Department of Computer Science,
Graduate School of Information Science and Technology,
Osaka University, 1-3, Machikaneyama, Toyonaka, Osaka 560-8531, Japan
{matusita, kusumoto, inoue}@ist.osaka-u.ac.jp

Abstract. We have developed a "WBS(Work Breakdown Structure) process model" for a business application software development project. We have also developed a project management system called "PRO-NAVI" which works on the "WBS process model." This WBS process model" provides (1) mutual mapping between the "software development processes", "activities", "products", "know-how," "rules", and "standards", and provides (2) comprehensive control. The role of "project management" in a business application software development project is recognized to be of more importance. These projects generally involve huge efforts, and cost heavy payloads to their "project management." Thus, an efficient project management system is needed. We have developed "PRO-NAVI". We have applied and evaluated "PRO-NAVI" with a number of projects and confirmed that it is effective for efficient project fulfillment.

1 Introduction

Digitization and networking of the society is accelerated, such as seen in diffusion of the Internet and the World Wide Web, and in business application software development, requirements for larger scale, higher function, shorter delivery schedule, and lower cost are urged. Accordingly, role of project management is becoming more important to carry out business application software development projects as planned: [1],[2],[3],[4].

Generally in a project management, repetition of so called Plan-Do-Check-Action process, make plan, execute it, check progress situation, and take action if necessary is said to be fundamental. A project is a set of multiple works and their consequential products, and a project management is a facilitation to make these works done with efficiency and to manage works and products. Therefore, a system to support a project management is required.

M. Li, B. Boehm, and L.J. Osterweil (Eds.): SPW 2005, LNCS 3840 pp. 249–261, 2005.
© Springer-Verlag Berlin Heidelberg 2005

This paper is a proposal of a management method of works and products and a project management support method based on WBS(Work Breakdown Structure) process model: [5],[6],[7],[8]

We also show our actual development of "PRO-NAVI", which is a WBS-based project management system.

As project management systems, MS-Project [9], ProcessDirector [10], and KnowledgePLAN [11] are well known products. As Product document management systems, DocumentBroker [12] and documentum [13] are well known products. We thought a new point of view is required, to relate and use with efficiency, of project process information, work information, product information, know-how information, which both of above have. PRO-NAVI" provides [a] clear definition of software development process, work, and products of the project at the project planning phase, [b] grasp of project progress status, [c] standardization of software project development process and navigation, [d] sharing of project knowledge such as project products and "know-how." These improve efficiency of project promotion. PRO-NAVI" is used by more than 1,000 projects by now and will be used more.

In this paper, we will show modeling of a business application software project by WBS in chapter 2, realization of "PRO-NAVI" in chapter 3, we will also show an application example, evaluation and consideration in chapter 4, and we will show a summary and address future issues in chapter 5.

2   WBS

WBS is a hierarchy chart to describe project goals in detail.

2.1   WBS Process Model

Department of Defense handbook "Work Breakdown Structure" defines WBS as below: [5]

(1) A product-oriented family tree composed of hardware, software, services, data, and facilities. The family tree results from systems engineering efforts during the acquisition of a defense material item.

(2) A WBS displays and defines the product, or products, to be developed and/or produced. It relates the elements of work to be accomplished to each other and to the end product.

(3) A WBS can be expressed down to any level of interest. However the top three levels are as far as any program or contract need go unless the items identified are high cost or high risk. Then, and only then, is it important to take the work breakdown structure to a lower level of definition.

"PMBOK" defines WBS as, "A deliverable-oriented grouping of project elements that organizes and defines the total work scope of the project. Each descending level represents an increasingly detailed definition of the project work,: [6]"

In this paper, we will explain according to the definition of [6]. We will also call each element of WBS as "work".

2.2   Project Planning Based on WBS

(1) "Standard PRO-NAVI WBS"

We propose a five layer WBS process model for a software development project and name it "Standard PRO-NAVI WBS".

[a] first layer: project [b]second layer: sub-project [c]third layer: phase [d]fourth layer: work step [e]fifth layer: product.

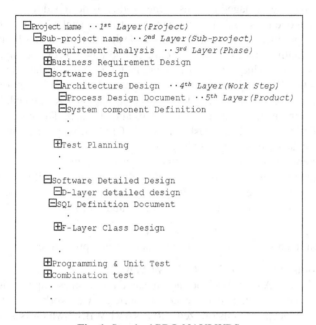

Fig. 1. Standard PRO-NAVI WBS

Figure 1 shows an example of Standard PRO-NAVI WBS".

First layer is the project itself.

We divide the whole software to be developed by a project to several loosely related sub systems and name each project to develop one of these sub systems as sub-project. We define this sub-project as the second layer. For example, for a project to develop a management administration system for an enterprise, first layer will be "management administration system", second layer will be sub systems of the management administration system such as "employee management system," "account management system," "merchandise management system," and so on.

"Standard PRO-NAVI WBS" defines names of works in 3rd, 4th, and 5th layer as shown in Figure 1.

Third layer, that is, phase, is equivalent to waterfall model development phase: [14],[15] , and it divides the project lifecycle into 7 phases, namely, requirement analysis, business requirement design, software design, software detailed design, programming and unit test, combination test, and integrated or system test. These phases proceed with time by the above order.

The fourth layer, or work step, divides the work of each phase into multiple concrete works. Software design for example, will be divided into following 7 work steps: architecture design, test planning, business process design, database layer class design, function layer class design, presentation layer event design, and physical database design.

Fifth layer, or product, includes process design document, system component definition, business flow diagram, display transition diagrams and so on.

Product entities are managed by files. One product is designed to be constituted by one or more than one files so that more than one project members can share the works concerning one product. For example, process design document can be made of two following files, online process design document and batch process design document. We call this file as product file, and this product file will not show up to standard PRO-NAVI WBS. We simply call product file as product when it is not necessary to make distinction. A chronological order do exist among phases as listed, however, no peculiar relation in time exists among work steps and products. These work steps, work items correspond to activities and tasks of SLCP-JCF98, which is a common frame for software centric development and trades: [16]

A project member may need to refer to prerequisite products to do a work.

A project member may also be able to do works efficiently with common project know-how and knowledge of standards, procedures, and worksheets.So, we add two kinds of common information items to each of "Standard PRO-NAVI WBS"[17]:

1)   prerequisite works prior to the current work,
2)   common knowledge required, such as rules and procedures.

(2) Optimization of "Standard PRO-NAVI WBS"

A "Standard PRO-NAVI WBS" defines a standard business application software development process, and may cause excess or deficiency of works for actual projects. So, we made a concept of "customized PRO-NAVI WBS," which is a derivative of "Standard PRO-NAVI WBS", giving more details and layers, adding necessary works, deleting unnecessary works, renaming works, so as to optimize "Standard PRO-NAVI WBS" for a peculiar project. However, we have given restrictions on deletion or change of specific works in the "Standard PRO-NAVI WBS" in order to enforce a certain "common structure" to the "customized PRO-NAVI WBSs" for various projects. By this, we can easily promote standardization of project management method because the "customized PRO-NAVI WBSs" for various projects have same product names, work names, and similar basic structures. When there is no need to make distinctions between "Standard PRO-NAVI WBS" and "customized PRO-NAVI WBS", we simply call them as "PRO-NAVI WBS." We have prepared multiple, not one, Standard PRO-NAVI WBSs", so that the "customized PRO-NAVI WBSs" can be made with ease.

When deriving a "customized PRO-NAVI WBS," we also optimize prerequisite works and common information accordingly. The common information will be added common reference information of the project.

(3) A project Planning Based on "PRO-NAVI WBS"

A project plan can be clearly defined by deciding project start date, project finish date, project members, work start dates, work finish dates, work member assignments.

So, we add two kinds of information items to each work of "PRO-NAVI WBS":

1) assigned members, due dates, and progress status of the work (started, not started, completed, reviewed and approved),
2) product files that constitutes an product, assigned member, updated time, version number and progress status.

By this, we can have following effects:

1) A project plan and its progress status are clear to its members, and project plan and progress information can be easily accessed, because the "PRO-NAVI WBS"structure is identical to the project's development process.

2) Project's common knowledge such as products, rules, procedures and worksheets can be easily found and referred because they are not only uniformly managed but also related to respective works, thus higher quality, higher efficiency and standardization of works can be done.

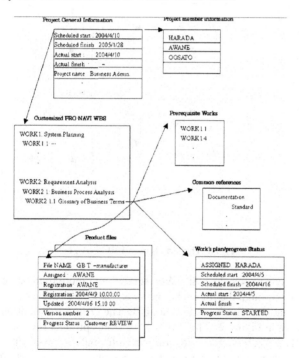

Fig. 2. An example of attached information to PRO-NAVI WBS

Figure 2 shows an example of information added to the "PRO-NAVI WBS". In this example, "customized PRO-NAVI WBS" and project member information are added to project general information of a business administration project. Additionally, plan of work itself and prerequisite works, common references, and product files information are also added. Figure 2 shows one member HARADA is scheduled to finish a glossary of business terms by 2004/4/16, and manufacturer's part of the glossary of business terms is assigned to AWANE and was updated on 2004/4/16.

3 "PRO-NAVI"

We have developed a project management system "PRO-NAVI", based on "PRO-NAVI WBS process model." In this chapter, we explain the schematics, functions and implementation of "PRO-NAVI".

3.1 Structure and Functions of "PRO-NAVI"

(1) Structure of "PRO-NAVI"

Figure 3 shows the structure of "PRO-NAVI".

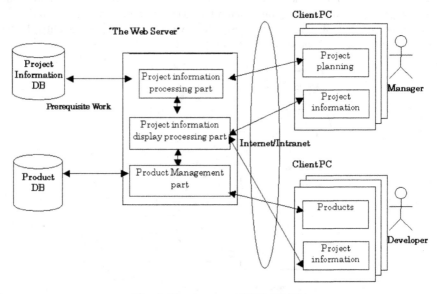

Fig. 3. The structure of PRO-NAVI

"PRO-NAVI" is composed of "the Web server" and more than one client PCs, and they communicate through the Internet or intranet. The "Web server" is connected with the Project information DB and the Product DB. The Project information DB stores the information shown in Figure 2. The Product DB stores product files, which are entities of products. "The Web server" has project information processing part, project information display processing part and product management part. A project plan which is made on a manager's client PC will be sent to "the Web server", and then processed by the project information processing part, and then stored in the Project information DB. A project information which is stored in the Project information DB, will be processed by the project information display processing part, and then sent to the manager's client PC or to a developer's client PC, and then displayed.

(2) Project Information Display Function

Two kinds of project information display functions for each project member's client PC are provided and are called private view and project view.

(a) Private View

The private view is a screen to display the works, a list of product files, and the progress status of the project member who operates his or her client PC. Actual screen example is shown in Figure 4. This example shows multiple projects or sub projects one member participates in, works assigned, a list of product files made and registered. The "project path (in Japanese)"represents first and second layers of the "PRO-NAVI WBS", and "work path (in Japanese)" represents the third layer or below.

The first item of Figure 4 shows he or she is assigned to a "business integration project (in Japanese)", is assigned a project work "definition of non-functional requirements (system requirements) (in Japanese) ", and the due date is "2004/12/10", and the progress status is "started (in Japanese)".If one member belongs to multiple projects, all the works assigned and a list of product files of those projects will be displayed.

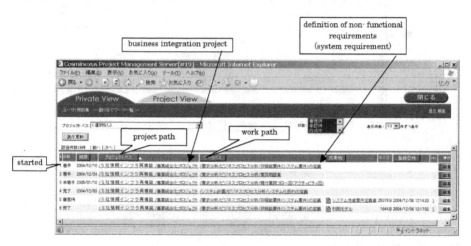

Fig. 4. An example of private view

(b) Project View

The project view is a screen to display "PRO-NAVI WBS," product information of each WORK, and reference information of each WORK. A screen example is shown in Figure 5. If one selects a work on "PRO-NAVI WBS display frame" on the left of the screen, related WORK and a list of product files, assigned members, due dates, and progress status will be displayed as "Product information display frame" on the upper right of the screen. If one selects a product file in addition, he or she can view a file registered as a product.

A "reference information display frame " on the lower right of the screen displays products and common information of the organization to be referenced. If one selects one item, he or she can read a relevant document. For example, in Figure 5, one has selected   "definition of non-functional requirements (system requirements) (in Japanese) " of "PRO-NAVI WBS display frame", and the "Product information display frame" displays assigned member as HARADA (in Japanese), due date (in Japanese) as 2004/12/10, and status (in Japanese) as "started" are displayed. In addition, "definition of non-functional requirements (system requirements) (in Japanese) " is composed of three product files and displayed with assigned member names and status, namely, "system requirement definition document", "use model", "percentage of band-width share – weekly day and time wise."

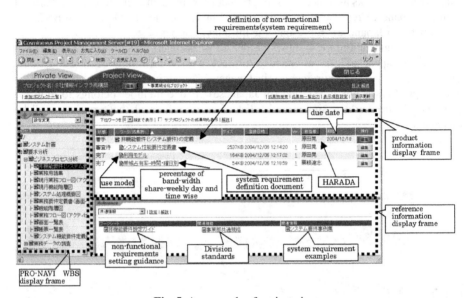

Fig. 5. An example of project view

Also, the "reference information display frame " displays common information to refer when defining non-functional requirements (system requirements), namely, "non-functional requirements setting guidance (in Japanese)", "Division standard", and "system requirement examples".

(3) Other Functions
(a) Managers' Functions

1) Project managers are able to make project plans based on "PRO-NAVI WBS," by putting in necessary information through his or her client PC with ease, because prototypes of WBS, prerequisite WORKs, and common information are provided by "Standard PRO-NAVI WBS." These project plans will be transmitted through the network and then stored in the "Project information DB."

2) Project managers refer to "Product information display frame" of the project view and then evaluate progress status by project planning, and status of works and product files.

3) Project managers may directly read product files and confirm progress status or percentage of completion independent from project member's report, if necessary.

4) Project managers choose one product file from a list which is displayed in the "Product information display frame", and check the contents, review, or approve, and then reflect the result to the "status".

(b) Developers' Functions
1) A developer refers to his or her client PC's private view or project view and confirms assigned works; this is called "To Do management".
2) A developer refers to his or her project view and recognizes participating project's plan and progress status.
3) A developer selects product files and downloads them to the client PC from a list displayed in his or her private view or project view, and then do assigned works, update product files.
4) If prerequisite work products or a common reference of the organization is found to be required while making an assigned product, a developer selects a necessary material from "Reference information display frame", and then downloads it to the client PC and refers to it.
5) An updated most recent product will be sent to the server and then stored in Product DB. At this time, version number of the product file will be also updated by 1, hence version management of product files are also performed by version numbers.
6) On completion of the assigned product, a developer changes status of the product and the product files to "COMPLETED."

By 1), start priorities and due dates of the products are shown, and by 4), directions and examples of contents and formats of the products are shown, and thus these are "Navigator" of works. We name this as "NAVIGATION FUNCTION".

4 Evaluation

We will state the application record and effects of "PRO-NAVI."

4.1 Actual Application Record of "PRO-NAVI"

Figure 6 shows the cumulative number of the projects using "PRO-NAVI." We started the operation of "PRO-NAVI" on March, 2000. By March, 2004, approximately 1200 projects are using "PRO-NAVI." The number of product files registered counts approximately 310,000 by March, 2004. We think "PRO-NAVI" has become the standard project management system of in-house use.

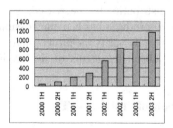

Fig. 6. The cumulative number of the projects using PRO-NAVI

We have added new "standard PRO-NAVI WBSs," as the number of "PRO-NAVI" users grows. We had just two standard WBSs at the beginning. Now we can choose from 13 types of "standard PRO-NAVI WBSs" for each project and then optimize it.

Added "standard PRO-NAVI WBSs" are developed with name-changes, check-process-additions and unnecessary-work-deletions corresponding to our customer's business fields and their organizations, as shown in Figure 7.

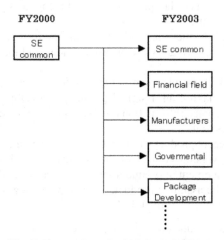

Fig. 7. Types of standard PRO-NAVI WBSs

For example, for the financial field WBS, we have added detailed improvements concerning systems operation. We have added detailed works such as emergency operation manuals and tests. A project manager selects an appropriate "standard PRO-NAVI WBS", related with customer's business field and customer's role in the company, optimizes it, and then starts a project.

We have favorable evaluations from "PRO-NAVI" users, as shown below.

(1) Getting across job of the project standard document and project development plan to its project members has become easier.
(2) Development errors due to "version-mistakes" have disappeared, because most recent products can be shared in a secured manner.
(3) Search job for necessary products has become much easier.
(4) Distribution job of products has become easier.
(5) Hard copy document distribution has decreased.
(6) Version management of products has become possible.
(7) A project manager can easily verify the project status report, because the project manager can directly check the status of the product and its contents with "PRO-NAVI".

4.2 An Application Example of "PRO-NAVI"

A railroad company ticket system construction project: 800 Kilo source lines of code to be developed, by 200 project members in 10 separate development locations. This large scale project applied "PRO-NAVI" to achieve high efficiency development and management level and to share project progress status, product files and project common documents.

(1) Optimized "standard PRO-NAVI WBS" for the project

Figure 8 shows the optimization process of "standard PRO-NAVI WBS" to the project above.

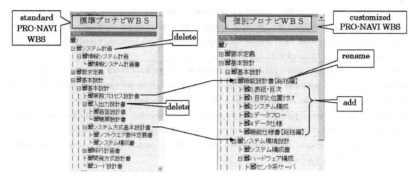

Fig. 8. An example of customization of PRO-NAVI WBS

Optimization points are as follows:

(a) Unnecessary works or products are deleted. Here, (system planning) and (I/O design document) are deleted.

(b) Standard names of works are renamed to that of peculiar ones in the project. In Figure 8, the name of (business process design document) is renamed to (function design document –comprehensive part-).

(c) Divided works are added as 6th layer, so that a project member can be assigned to a divided product. In Figure 8, (function design document –comprehensive part-) is divided to (0. top cover/outline) and (1. Purpose and positioning).

(2) Comprehensive Management of Products and Common Documents

The "PRO-NAVI" managed 391 product files as outcomes of design process, and 173 common documents.

(3) Accurate Grasp of the Project Progress Status

The "PRO-NAVI" 's product information display frame provides products progress status, and a manager may directly access to each product. Thus, a project manager can directly feel and confirm progress status of products and their quality. The project is to have prescheduled progress meetings, and project members are to report their progresses. The project manager compared project member's report with "PRO-NAVI confirmation result", and warned the project member, whose confirmation result was much different, and realized early detection of progress problems and suitable countermeasures.

(4) Application Result of "PRO-NAVI"

Effects of using "PRO-NAVI" are given in Table 1.

On the other hand, product progress status gathering function is pointed out to be an issue.

For example, to grasp project progress status, one needs to select a work in "PRONAVI WBS display frame" of the project view, and then check its progress work

Table 1. Effects of using PRO-NAVI

Effects of using "PRO-NAVI"
Project planning has become easier because "standard PRO-NAVI WBS" lists standard works neatly and "customized PRO-NAVI WBS" can be made without fault.
Project management efficiency for product management and progress management, which were troublesome chores due to the huge number of project members, has been improved 20% .
Project products can be checked with ease.
Specification checks have become easier and rudimentary errors have faded out, and reutilization of other project member's products has become easier and project efficiency has been improved, because the most recent version of the products can be easily accessed by other project members.
Navigation of development jobs has become possible by referring to project's shared common documents such as procedures and writing examples. And it has supported efficient development.
Instantaneous distribution of the most recent information to project members among 10 remote development sites has been realized.

by work in "product information display frame". This operation method has advantage in grasping percentage of completion of products, however, it costs effort to grasp project progress status, and requires a new function to sum up product progress.

4.3   Analysis and Considerations

From application results of "PRO-NAVI" until now, we have confirmed three effects as follows: (1) Clarification and notification of project plan throughout the project. (2) Correct grasp of project progress status. (3) Higher quality, higher efficiency, standardization of the project due to easy access to products and common documents. It is also recognized, with "PRO-NAVI", one can grasp progress status with ease, however to grasp comprehensive project progress status, one needs to select work by work from project view displays, and this costs effort. For this issue, an automatic collection apparatus of project progress status based on products is effective, and we should make research.

5   Conclusions

In this paper, we have proposed a WBS process model to relate project process, project works, project products, and project's common knowledge such as know-how, rules, and standards and a project management system "PRO-NAVI". As is shown in chapter 4, "PRO-NAVI" provides (1) Clarification of software development process, work, and products of the project at the planning phase, (2) a grasp of project progress status, (3) standardization of software project development process and navigation, (4) sharing of project knowledge such as project products and "know-how." We have confirmed the "PRO-NAVI" is an effective system to support a project management.

On the other hand, project progress status gathering is pointed out to be a bothersome and burdensome job and requires much effort. Our next step will be the research and development of an automatic collection and evaluation function of project progress status based on products which are registered in "PRO-NAVI".

References

1. H. Kerzner, Project Management, John Wiley&Sons, Inc. New York (2001)
2. R. Rada, J. Craparo, " Standardizing software projects," Communications of the ACM, vol.43, no.12 (Dec. 2000) 21-25
3. Watts S. Humphrey, Managing the Software Process, Addison-Wesley, Winthrop (1989)
4. Shunichi Fukuyama, Hideo Takagi, Ryoji Tanaka, Michihiro Watanabe, Isao Nakabayashi: Procedures for Implementing Checklists that Provide Guidance for Continuous Improvements in Software Processes, IPSJ Journal, vol.42, no.3 (March 2001) 529-541
5. Department of Defense handbook Work Breakdown Structure(MIL-HDBK-881), Department of Defense, USA (1998)
6. A Guide to the Project Management Body of Knowledge 2000edition, Project Management Institute, Newtown Square (2000) Glossary
7. Gregory T. Haugan, Effective Work Breakdown Structures, Management Concepts, Vienna (2002)
8. Practice Standard for Work Breakdown Structures, Project Management Institute, Newtown Square (2001)
9. Eric Uyttewaal, Dynamic scheduling with Microsoft Project2002, J. Ross Publishing and International Institute for Learning, Boca Raton (2003)
10. KABUSHIKIKIKAISHA NEC, KORABOREISHON-GATA PUROJEKUTOKANRI SISUTEM ProcessDirector (in JAPANESE), http://www.sw.nec.co.jp/cced/processdirector
11. KABUSHIKIKIKAISHA KOUZOUKEIKAKUKENKYUUJYO, SOFUTOUEA MITSUMORI TUURU KnowledgePLAN (in JAPANESE), http://www4.kke.co.jp/sec/service/o1.html
12. KABUSHIKIKIKAISHA HITACHI SEISAKUSHO, BUNSHOKANRIKIBAN DocumentBroker Version2 (in JAPANESE), http://www.hitachi.co.jp/Prod/comp/soft1/docbro/index.html
13. NIPPON DOKYUMENTAMU KABUSHIKIKIKAISHA. documentum (in JAPANESE), http://www.documentum.co.jp
14. C. Jones, Applied Software Measurement, The MeGraw-Hill Companies, New York (1996)
15. H. Kerzner, Applied Project Management, John Wiley&Sons, Inc., New York (2000)
16. KYOUTUUFUREIMU98–SLCP-JCF98-(1998 NENBAN), SLCP-JCF98IINKAI, KABUSHIKIKIKAISHA TSUUSANSIRYOUTYOUSAKAI, TOKYO (1998) (in Japanese)
17. Y. Oka, T. Tanida, S. Konno, C. Hirai, "Operation assistance method and system and recording medium for storing operation assistance method," U.S. Patent no.6799183, (Sep.2004)

Spiral Pro: A Project Plan Generation Framework and Support Tool*

Jizhe Wang[1,2] and Steven Meyers[3,4]

[1] Laboratory for Internet Software Technologies,
Institute of Software, the Chinese Academy of Sciences, Beijing 100080, China
wangjizhe@itechs.iscas.ac.cn
[2] Graduate School of the Chinese Academy of Sciences,
Beijing 100039, China
[3] Center for Software Engineering, University of Southern California,
Los Angeles, California 90089, USA
stevem@cse.usc.edu
[4] Software Process Group,
1968 W. Adams Blvd., Suite 211, Los Angeles, California 90018, USA

Abstract. Project planning is a delicate and on-going activity that requires a great deal of experience and knowledge. Several models and methods are developed which explore the various aspects of planning a project. In this paper, we propose a framework named Spiral Pro that integrates Spiral Model, MBASE and COCOMO II to help project managers do their project planning in a systematic way. In an empirical study, a project plan template, developed following the framework, was provided for thirteen e-service projects and a survey was used at the end to assess the study. Based on the survey, some characteristics are summarized, which help point out the effectiveness of using of Spiral Pro framework. Motivated by the findings in the study, a tool has been developed to help both experienced and inexperienced project managers make better use of the framework for project planning.

1   Introduction

In software development, a rational project plan with proper flexibility is one of the most fundamental success factors. A good plan makes it possible to execute the project efficiently and effectively by calling for the right activities at the right times. Software project planning is also highlighted as one of the key process areas of level 2 in the SEI Capability Maturity Model [1]. However, with a seemingly infinite set of possible combinations of activities, many of which are people-, time-, and environment-dependent, a project plan can be very difficult to get right, and in many ways project planning is regarded as an art rather than a scientific activity.

There is a consensus that the quality of project plan lies highly on the manager's experience. However, at least three problems come with this situation.

---

* Supported by the National Natural Science Foundation of China under grant No. 60273026, 60473060 and The Hi-Tech Research and Development Program (863 Program) of China under grant No. 2004AA112080, 2005AA113140.

M. Li, B. Boehm, and L.J. Osterweil (Eds.): SPW 2005, LNCS 3840, pp. 262–276, 2005.

- Because of the diversity of software projects, there are no clear criteria to define one's level of experience. The characteristics and context of software projects are usually very complex and greatly diverse. Application domain, customers' expectations, engineering culture, capability maturity level, project size and available resource are some examples of the factors that could make projects totally different from each other. Thus it becomes very difficult to judge if one is experienced enough under certain context.
- Secondly, as a result of the above problem, there are often inexperienced project managers who end up doing the project planning. Without sufficient knowledge and past experience, it is highly likely that their plans will lead to project failures.
- The third problem is the high risk of relying too heavily on personal experience. Too much reliance on experience may allow for the same errors or inefficiencies to be repeated over and over, thus stifling improvement. And without a framework for monitoring quantitatively the likelihoods of the project's success, it's hard to make any improvement based on real execution data.

Software process technology is regarded as a solution to these problems and has attracted considerable research focus to date. A typical approach is to define a standard development process, develop some general guidelines, and enable the process to be tailorable for particular projects. The waterfall model [2] and Rational Unified Process [3] are two of the most recognized ones. Such approaches provide a common base for continuous improvement with the feedback from usage. But unfortunately there are still some problems remaining. Firstly, a standard process can only cover certain types of projects and there are always emerging project types that cannot be fit into the existing processes. The latest CHAOS Report [4] shows that only 46% of application projects are developed from scratch, while the rest are either purchased applications or integrated existing components. However, several research results show that the process of COTS based development is quite different from the traditional waterfall processes [5,6,7].

A critical success factor is that software process is just one aspect of a project plan and it's always interacting with other models such as product model, success models and property models [8]. In order to resolve the potential model clashes, the models including process model must be treated as a whole from a higher level, which is the contribution of MBASE (Model-Based Architecting and Software Engineering) [9]. To make it useful, more specific information should be provided to give the project managers more detailed help.

In this study, we propose a plan generation framework named Spiral Pro, which consists of a conceptual architecture and a suggested planning process. In order to deal with different aspects that are essential in software project planning, we integrated the key elements in MBASE and Spiral Model. In this framework, software process is treated inside of this context with interaction with other factors. Spiral Model is used as a basic process generator for evolutionary improvement. COCOMO II (Constructive Cost Model II) [10] and its empirical data are used to estimate and assign the effort and other resource. Based on the framework and the analysis of the data from the study, a tool is developed with the capability of guiding the project managers to follow the process and generating project plan automatically.

2 Related Work

2.1 Spiral Model

Software life-cycle process models provide guidance for staging a software development and its evolution, and to establish the transition criteria for progressing from one phase to another. However, if a life-cycle process is not a applicable for some emerging development approaches and its effectiveness will be significantly reduced. As summarized in [11,12], process models are still in a continuous evolution process. As one of the most accepted and used software process frameworks, spiral model provides a rational balance between flexibility and discipline.

There are six invariants of the Spiral Model including:

- Concurrent determination of key artifacts.
- Each cycle does objectives, constraints, alternatives, risks, review, and commitment to proceed.
- Level of effort driven by risk considerations.
- Degree of detail driven by risk considerations.
- Use of anchor point milestones: LCO, LCA, IOC [9,13].
- Emphasis on system and life cycle activities and artifacts.

In the work described in this paper, these six essentials are used to define the disciplines that are used in the Spiral Pro framework or to define specific tasks.

2.2 MBASE

MBASE provides a model integration framework and a process framework. In the integration framework, the relationship and interaction between every two elements are described. Based on the integration framework, the process framework provides a specific process and guidance on how to use the relationships defined in the integration framework.

Although MBASE is said to be a recent extension of Spiral Model, its stand-alone ability to help projects to escape from model clashes has made it an independent method beyond Spiral Model. In software projects, success models, process models, product models, and property models are used to guide the progress. Unfortunately model clashes occur when incompatible models are combined, thus causing projects to suffer. One example is using waterfall process model in a COTS-driven project [8]. However, few project managers are aware of the problem at this level of abstraction.

In our work on Spiral Pro, we benefit from MBASE in two aspects. First, the description model architecture provides a method to categorize the elements of a project plan at proper conceptual level. Second, the interactions and dependencies between each model imply a feasible process to generate a set of compatible models.

2.3 COCOMO II

Software development is not only a technical activity but also a social economic process. A project is regarded as successful only when it is finished on schedule and within the budget. Thus in terms of project planning, one of the keys to success is an accurate estimate of the expected effort to complete the project.

COCOMO (Constructive Cost Model) is a software cost estimation model based on a set of empirically derived equations, which was first published by Dr. Barry Boehm in 1981[14]. In order to meet the demands of new approaches of software development, a new revised model was developed which is called COCOMO II [10].

The primary use of COCOMO II is to estimate the effort, cost, and schedule of software projects based on the size and other cost drivers, which capture the characteristics of the project and environment. In Spiral Pro Framework, this estimation is both a key element of property model and the basis for following project plan generation.

COCOMO II also provides phase and activity distribution values of effort and schedule, which are generated from empirical data of real software projects. In Spiral Pro Framework, these values are used to allocate effort and other resource to phases and activities.

3   The Spiral Pro Approach

3.1   Fundamental Questions for Project Planning

"Planning is deciding in advance what to do, how to do it, when to do it, and who is to do it."[15] As more specifically indicated in CMM, the purpose of software project planning is to establish reasonable plans for performing the software engineering and for managing the software project [16]. In the software project planning and control framework [14], five major steps are described including the producing of producing of WBS, PERT charts (activity networks), Personnel Plan, Project Work Authorization and Summary Task Planning Sheet. The MBASE Life Cycle Plan Guidelines [18] extend these considerations by providing sections for Purpose (why), Assumptions (whereas), Milestones and Products (what and when), Responsibilities (who and where), Approaches (how) and Resources (how much).

Additionally, since the estimation could not be 100% accurate and the context of the project always tends to be volatile, continuous revising based on the feedback data from the project execution is necessary to reduce risks. Thus we added a further question for project planning:

- How to revise the plan on a regular basis?

3.2   The Spiral Pro Framework

In order to resolve the problems mentioned above, we developed the Spiral Pro Framework, which integrates the essential elements and mechanisms from the Spiral Model and MBASE. COCOMO II is also used to estimate specific resources needed for each project activity.

Conceptual Architecture
Figure 1 illustrates the conceptual architecture of the Spiral Pro framework. It's built up with two elements, which are the concept models and the project plan. COCOMO

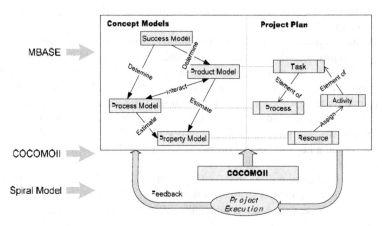

Fig. 1. Spiral Pro Framework: Conceptual Architecture

II is used to revise the cycles based on the feedback from project execution. The use of MBASE, COCOMOII and Spiral Model are also illustrated on the left of the figure 1 (feedback cycles exist but are not included for simplicity).

Concept Models

The concept models in Spiral Pro Framework are simplified and revised from the MBASE Integration Framework. Since the success model is the dominant model, the users' choice on a success model will determine the available optional product and process models. The model clash between a process model and a product model should also be avoided but there are no necessary constraints on the sequence of their selection since no one of them is more important than any other. Process and product models are used to estimate effort, schedule, and other resources needed in the project so that resource allocation can be done in the following process.

Project Plan

In the Spiral Pro Framework, a project plan is defined as a set of tasks with resource allocated, and the order of their execution. Thus, there are four major elements including task, process, activity and resource. The major benefit of using such a structure is that the information from the concept models can be transformed into a project plan in a straightforward way. The elements and their relationship with the concept models are informally defined as follows:

- Task: a set of activities with one or more specific objectives to produce a product, which could be a physical artifact or a logical decision.
- Activity: a set of actions with actors assigned, resources allocated and entry and exit criteria defined.
- Process: a sequential or parallel set of Tasks with entry/exit criteria well defined.
- Resource: effort and cost needed to perform an activity.

COCOMO II and its empirical data

COCOMO II are used to capture and estimate the data in Property Models. COCOMO II also provides the effort and schedule distribution data among the phase and activity categories. The empirical data can be used to calculate the effort and schedule that should be distributed across the project phases and activities.

Continuous revisions of the project plan

According to the essentials of Spiral Model, the level of effort and degree of details all should be driven by risk considerations. Usually such kind of risk assessment should be held in each spiral. In terms of project planning, a thorough and accurate plan for the whole project lifecycle is preferred; actually the plan for future spirals or phases can always be improved based on the data from past phases and current context. Thus in Spiral Pro Framework we suggest and provide guidance on revising the plan in between two spirals.

Planning Process

In [9], an overall process framework is provided for the MBASE approach. Based on this framework, we developed a general process for project planning. As described in figure 2, the planning process can be decomposed into three phases with each composed of some specific activities. During the process, additional fundamental data is provided to help the project managers to follow the whole activity flow. The activity flow and data flow are all illustrated in figure 2.

Phase 1: Model Set Selection

In this phase, a project manager or several critical stakeholders work out a set of models including the success models, product models, process models that are compatible with each other. Since the success model is the dominant one, success

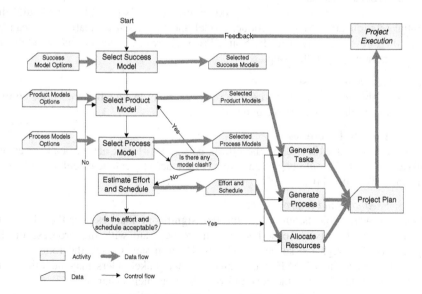

Fig. 2. Spiral Pro Framework: Planning Process

models will drive the choices on other models. And as a support framework, what the framework will be able to do automatically are also described here.

Step 1.1 Select Success Model
There are many success models in software development, such as stakeholder win-win [17], IKIWISI (I know it when I see it), lowest cost, and shortest duration. Once the stakeholders choose one set of success models, the framework will give guidance or tool support on finding the potential conflicts between success models.

Step 1.2 Select Process Model/Product Model
The selection of a success model will determine the available options for process and product models. Thus the users will be provided with lists of process models and product models. An additional manual or automated check on the model clashes is provided at the end of this step [19].

Step 1.3 Estimate Effort and Cost
Effort and Schedule can be estimated based on product and process model chosen along with other context information from the users. Sometimes the users will re-consider the previous three kinds of models when they have a better understanding on the cost and schedule factors. So Step 1.1, 1.2 and 1.3 may be executed for several cycles till the stakeholders get common agreement on them.

Phase 2: Plan Generation
Once a set of compatible models is selected, the project plan can be generated based on the relationships between concept models and project plan that are described in Figure 1. Ideally this process could be automated with the support of some specific knowledge. However, since there might be multiple options, it may be more effective to query the users for a decision.

Step 2.1 Generate Tasks
Since the objective of the Tasks is to produce products, it's possible to pre-build the potential relationships between product model and tasks. These relationships can be part of the knowledge saved in the Spiral Pro Framework. Thus product models are used to generate tasks in this step.

Step 2.2 Generate Process
In this step, the process model is used to build the relationships between tasks so that the processes in the project plan can be defined.

Step 2.3 Allocate Resources
According to COCOMO II data, the efforts between different activity categories are relative. Effort that should be assigned to a certain activity can be calculated based on the ratios provided in [10].

Phase 3: Feedback and Improvement
Because software projects tend to go through significant changes over their lifecycle the estimation of software cost becomes more accurate with the progress of the project [14]. Although the success model is the dominant model, the four kinds of models mentioned in MBASE could interact since stakeholders may negotiate and find the new tradeoffs when the cost, effort or other elements change.

As mentioned above, during the process of project execution, especially in between two spirals, feedback and additional context information will be obtained. Depending on the result of risk assessment, it might be necessary to re-assess the environment and other factors at risk. Based on the assessment and feedback information, the planning process of Spiral Pro should probably be performed again so that the project planning accuracy can be improved.

3.3 Summary

With the Spiral Pro Framework, the eight fundamental questions for project planning, which are mentioned in section 3.1, can now be answered. The set of tasks to be performed in a project is determined by the product models that are chosen based on the success models selected by stakeholders. The sequence of the activities (the process) is defined by the process models that are required to satisfy the success models. However, the selection of these models might be iterative in order to avoid model clashes. COCOMO II and its empirical data are used to record assumptions about some of the fundamental questions (why, who, where, whereas, how), and to allocate the effort to activities (what, when, how much). Between spirals, feedback data from the previous execution of the plan and new risk assessment results are used to improve the plan for following spirals.

4 Implementing Spiral Pro: Empirical Study and a Support Tool

When the initial version of the Spiral Pro Framework was accomplished, we carried out an empirical study on 13 e-services projects in CSCI 577a, a graduate software engineering course taught at the University of Southern California. At the end of the semester, we made a survey on these projects using a questionnaire and analyzed the results.

The main objective of the study is to find opportunities for improvement and to test if the template-centered method is a good way of using the framework. Although we are not using a quantitative method, it still provided abundant firsthand valueable information. From the analysis of the results, we found some characteristics that might reduce the effectiveness of the framework when it is used solely or only with some simple support such as templates, especially when used by inexperienced project managers. Motivated by these findings, a support tool is developed to help them use the framework in an effective and efficient way.

4.1 The Empirical Study

Description of the Study and Its Environment
These projects are all real projects with fixed deadline, limited or no budget, and real clients from such customers as ISD (Information Services Division) or Libraries of USC. The teams are comprised of graduate students who typically have minimal experience in software development. There were totally 18 projects in the class. We chose these 13 projects because they are indicated as COTS (Commercial-Off-The-Shelf) Based Application (CBA) development projects in the pre-assessment.

In this study, we developed a project plan template for CBA projects (using MS Project) based on the Spiral Pro Framework and gave it to the teams. There are several reasons we gave the teams the template rather than just providing the framework description. First, most of the team members lacked prior knowledge of the concepts used in the framework. Even though the COTS concept was taught during the course there would not be enough time for the students to learn and use the framework by themselves. Hence a well-defined template is much easier to use. Second, the Spiral Pro framework was also in the evolution from an initial version to a complete one, and there was not sufficient time for referencing it to MBASE.

The template was not developed from scratch. Instead, it was developed following the Spiral Pro process with the help of MBASE Guideline [18] and CBA Process [5], which consists of a set of process patterns drawn out from the analysis of previous COTS Based Application development projects.

The Results from the Survey

In the 13 projects, 7 teams made use of the template while 6 said they did not use it in the whole process though they might have used it as a reference. For the 6 projects that did not use it, we asked the team members to give their explanation on why they chose to not use it. For the first 7 projects, we asked them to write down their comments for improvement of the template. The results are listed in table 1 and 2.

Table 1. Reasons of not using the template

Project ID	The Reason of Not Using the Template
2	Unaware of its existence; Project type not match
6	Improper schedule; Project type not match
7	Unaware of its existence
10	Project type not match
11	Project type not match
12	Project type not match

Table 2. Feedback from the use of the template

Project ID	Comments for Improvement
1	Over detailed; inaccurate estimation; Lack of certain task
3	Lack of some tasks; lack of further information on tasks
4	Lack of further information on tasks;
14	Lack of detailed information; Lack of certain tasks; To be extended for 577b*
18	To be extended for 577b*
21	Lack of help and detailed example
24	Lack of flexibility for projects with different size

* 577b is a following course of 577a, in which the projects will continue.

Analysis of the Survey Results

The results from the survey are illustrated in figure 3 and figure 4. Although we summarized the answers from the two groups separately, actually together they display aspects that should be noticed when using the template.

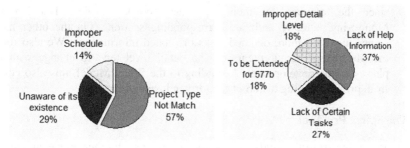

Fig. 3. Reasons of not using the template   **Fig. 4.** Comments for Improvement

There are seven issues mentioned by the teams. However 'unaware of its existence' and 'to be extended for 577b' are excluded from further analysis since they are not relevant to the framework directly. The other five are analyzed in more detail:

- **Project type not match**
  In the six projects where the template was not used, five teams indicated that their projects were not typical CBA projects. This is the entire or partial reason of why they did not make use of the template. For example, in project 6, where a bar-code reading system was developed for Maternal-Child Virology Research Laboratory, no functionality was be provided by the COTS alternatives for avoiding hidden detrimental functionality. Thus custom development has to be involved.

- **Lack of help information**
  In the seven projects that the template was used, four of them mentioned that they needed more detailed help information on the tasks in the plan and how to tailor it. This is quite reasonable since the inexperienced students were not involved in the process of generating the project plan following Spiral Pro Framework. Hence, it's hard for them to have comprehensive understanding.

- **Improper pre-set schedule**
  In one of the projects, improper schedule is listed as an issue that prevented them from using the template. It's quite interesting since we didn't put any constraints on the adjusting of the schedule. However, since no relevant help information was provided, the team was not able to take advantage of such flexibility.

- **Lack of certain optional tasks**
  Three of the seven projects encountered the problem of not being able to find particular tasks in the template. Creation of test plans (in project 14) and periodical meeting with clients (in project 3) were mentioned as absent. There are two reasons. First, the tasks are all based on the documents of the CBA projects that were performed in the CSCI577 course in the past 3-4 years. Hence the knowledge base is relatively limited.

- **Improper detail level**
  Another interesting phenomenon is the teams' opinion on the detail level of the template. Some of them said the template was over detailed, which made it hard to use. For example, 'Identify the number of issues and defects in the current week' and 'Weekly risk assessment and control' could be omitted

since the template for their super-task 'Weekly Project Tracking and Monitoring' already includes corresponding sections. On the other hand, some suggested more detailed tasks or related information. We also found that the teams' requirements on the detail level tend to change with the phases of the development. According to the Spiral Model, this also comes from projects having different risk-driven levels of detail.

4.2 The Spiral Pro Tool

The issues coming from the study are interwoven with each other. For example, the lack of training or help information may prevent the teams from understanding how to modify the template effectively. In project 11, the COTS products were predetermined by the clients thus COTS assessment was not necessary. Finally they didn't use it for 'project type not match'. In such situations, the team would be able to make use of the template simply by omitting the COTS assessment task if they had got enough help information on tailoring the template. Although they look quite perplexing, there are some characteristics in common. Furthermore, most of them can be solved or improved with a tool which could:

- **Provide a systematic and flexible guide on the process**
  In the cases of unsuitable project type, improper schedule, insufficient optional tasks and improper detail level, the root reason is that no systematic guide was provided to make use of the template in a flexible way. Further more, due to the nature of templates, although some options and tailor mechanism are provided, the flexibility is still very limited. Also, the model set selection was not incorporated thus the users didn't have the opportunity to change the underlying models. If a tool could guide them follow the whole Spiral Pro process, even inexperienced project managers will be able to get a better plan more easily.
- **Provide knowledge support on optional models and tasks**
  Another typical comment from the projects was regarding the lack of certain optional tasks and related information. One reason is that the template-centered method is not powerful enough to support an effective knowledge service mechanism for project planning. Another reason is the template is made from a relatively limited set of experience. A tool with well-designed knowledge support mechanism will be very helpful to make much more effective use of the framework.

As described above, the objectives of the tool are to help the users in flexing the Spiral Pro Framework to suit their needs and provide a corresponding mechanism for sharing the experiences of past projects. Inspired by the advantages that may be achieved, we have begun developing the Spiral Pro tool.

Basic Capabilities
The tool will not only benefit the inexperienced project managers by providing a user-friendly interface that is easy to understand and follow, but also help experienced project managers find relative information from the experience database and in automating some of the planning work.

In order to achieve the objectives indicated above, we defined the following basic capabilities for the tool:

- The tool should provide friendly user interface that can help the users follow the Spiral Pro Planning Process, especially in the phase of model selection.
- The tool should be able to help the users to avoid model clashes among the models mentioned in MBASE.
- The tool should provide an interface to interact with a Knowledge Base, either internal or external. And additional help information for detailed tasks is preferred for assisting the users.
- With the support of the knowledge base, the tool should be able to automate the project plan generating process to some extent.

Architecture

Based on the Spiral Pro Framework, a tool is being developed by the Software Process Group, Inc., with the cooperation of the USC Center for Software Engineering. The conceptual architecture of the tool is illustrated in figure 5.

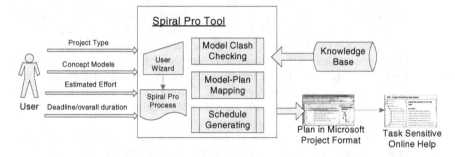

Fig. 5. Spiral Pro Tool

- A user wizard is used to guide the users in following the Spiral Pro Process, which is especially helpful when integrated with the model clash checking mechanism.
- Model clash checking capability is supported by using the pre-defined consistency relationship between each other of the models, which are stored in the knowledge base and will be provided as options for users.
- The knowledge base is used to provide options for different models as well as their relationship including dependency and conflict. Project plan elements and their relationship with the concept models are also stored there. For example, if the 'IKIWISI' (I'll Know It When I See It) is selected as a success model, the 'prototypes' will become one of the recommended product models. In automatic plan generating, prototyping related tasks such as the determination of objectives, development and feedback obtaining would be added in the project plan.
- Task sensitive online help is provided for users to find more information on the tasks in their plans, including explanation, guidelines, document

templates, and worked examples of good usage. The help information can be accessed via Internet by through the hyperlinks in the task information.

- Following the Spiral Pro Process, part of the work of the plan generating is automated, which is implemented in the Model-Plan mapping and Schedule Generating module with the information from the Knowledge Base.

Tool Use Example

In project 24, the team is working on a CSE website to "make sections that students use more user-friendly, such as the courses section, define an XML and develop an attractive front-end". Though they have some rough idea of the capabilities as "the ability to search by course, by semester", the requirements are quite unclear and unstable. When using the tool to generate its project plan, the user is guided by the tool to follow these steps:

1) In the list of success models, we select IKIWISI as one of the success models. Since the website will be used by quite a wide range of stakeholders, 'stakeholders win-win' is also chosen.

2) Product models and process models are displayed but both are categorized into two groups, one consistent with the success models and one inconsistent. For example, 'Prototype' is in the consistent list of product models, and 'Waterfall model' is in the inconsistent list of process models. This checking mechanism is based on the use of a knowledge base.

3) Once a consistent set of models is determined, a list of tasks will be generated automatically, including generic tasks as risk management, and specific ones as 'win-win negotiation', 'prototype development'. User can tailor this list according to their special needs. Estimated effort and deadline (or overall duration) are also prompted to input here.

4) When the task list is set, the tool will automatically generate a complete project plan (in MS Project format) with effort and schedule assigned.

5) In the project plan, there is a column in front of the column of Task Name, in which a hyperlink is provided for each task. By clicking the hyperlinks, the users will be directed to an online help system where corresponding help information and required artifacts for this task are provided.

5   Conclusions and Future Work

Software project planning is regarded as an art because of the great diversity of the projects and complexity of the context. In order to reduce the risks coming with this highly experience dependent way of project planning, some models and methods have been invented and are being introduced to improve the quality and efficiency of project planning. However, they usually focus on some specific aspect of software development, so from a project manager's viewpoint they are hard to follow.

In this paper, our general focus is on developing an integrated software project-planning framework based on Spiral Model, MBASE and COCOMO II. In the framework, we developed a conceptual architecture to present the elements and relationships, and a planning process following which the users can create and modify a project plan in a systematic yet straightforward way.

Concurrently with the Spiral Pro Framework, we carried out an empirical study. This study is not quantitative, yet it provided valueable information for the improvement of Spiral Pro. By summarizing and analyzing the data from a survey at the end of these projects, some characteristics of the framework and this template-centered usage are found. Based on these findings, some new features were added for enhancement. Also the emerging requirements motivated us to develop the Spiral Pro tool to help users make better use of the framework.

Both the framework and the tool are still in the process of improvement. In the current framework, the relationship among models are simplified, however, other interactions and constraints should also be included for more comprehensive discussion especially on more flexible methodologis such as extreme programming [20]. In order to facilitate the reuse of software process assets within the organization, process element [7] will also be incorporated into the framework. We will also try to introduce some solutions using expertise or Delphi method to improve the effort calculation for certain kinds of projects.

References

1. Paulk, M. C., et al. Capability Maturity Model for Software. In: Thayer, R.H., Christensen, M. J. (eds.): Software Engineering, vol.2: The Supporting Processes. John Wiley & Sons, Hoboken, New Jersey, USA (2002) 375-386
2. Royce, W.W.: Managing the Development of Large Software Systems: Concepts and Techniques. In: Proceedings of the 9th ICSE. IEEE Computer Society Press, Los Alamitos, CA, USA (1970) 328-338
3. Jacobson, I., et al.: The Unified Software Development Process. Addison-Wesley Longman, Massachusetts, USA (1999)
4. Standish CHAOS Report 2001, http://www.standishgroup.com
5. Boehm, B., Abts, C.: COTS Integration: Plug and Pray? Computer, Vol.37, No.1 (1999) 135-138
6. Brownsword, L., Oberndorf, T., Sledge, C.: Developing New Processes for COTS-Based Systems. IEEE Software, Vol.17, No.4 (2000) 48-55
7. Boehm, B., Port, D., Yang, Y., Bhuta, J.: Composable Process Elements for Developing COTS-Based Applications. In: Proceedings of ISESE 2003. IEEE Presss, Los Alamitos, CA, USA (2003) 8-17
8. Boehm, B., Port, D., Alsaid, M.: Avoiding the Software Model Clash Spider Web. IEEE Software. Vol.17, No.6 (2000) 120-122.
9. Boehm, B., Port, D.: Balancing Discipline and Flexibility with the Spiral Model and MBASE. Crosstalk. Vol.11, No.12 (2001) 23-28
10. Boehm, B., et al.: Software Cost Estimation with COCOMO II. Prentice Hall, Upper Saddle River, New Jersey, USA (2000)
11. Boehm, B.: A Spiral Model of Software Development and Enhancement. IEEE Computer. Vol.21, No.5 (1988) 61-72
12. Fugetta, A.: Software Process: A Roadmap. In: Finkelstein, A. (eds.): Proceedings of the Conference on The Future of Software Engineering, ACM Press, New York (2000) 25-34
13. Boehm, B.: Anchoring the Software Process. IEEE Software, Vol.13, No.4 (1996) 73-82
14. Boehm, B.: Software Engineering Economics. Prentice Hall, Upper Saddle River, New Jersey, USA (1981)

15. Koontz, H. and O'Donnell, C.: Principles of Management: An Analysis of Managerial Functions (5th ed.). McGraw-Hill, New York, USA (1972)
16. Paulk, M.C., et al.: Key Practices of the Capability Maturity Model. Technical Report, CMU/SEI-93-TR-025. Software Engineering Institute, Carnegie Mellon University (1993)
17. Boehm, B.: Theory-W Software Project Management Principles and Examples. IEEE Transactions on Software Engineering. Vol.15, No.7 (1989) 902-916
18. MBASE Guidelines and MBASE Electronic Process Guide. Center for Software Engineering, University of Southern California, USA. http://sunset.usc.edu/research/MBASE.
19. Al-Said, M.: Identifying, Analyzing, and Avoiding Software Model Clashes. Ph. D. Dissertation. University of Southern California, USA (2003)
20. Beck,K., Andres, C.: Extreme Programming Explained: Embrace Change (2nd ed.). Addison-Wesley, Massachusetts, USA (2004)

A Process Improvement Framework and a Supporting Software Oriented to Chinese Small Organizations

Bo Gong[1,3], Xingui He[2], and Weihong Liu[3]

[1] School of Computer Science and Technology,
BeiHang University, Beijing 100830, China
gongbo@vip.sina.com
[2] School of Electronics Engineering and Computer Science,
Peking University, Beijing 100871, China
hexingui@ns.cetin.net.cn
[3] Institute of Command and Technology of Equipment, Beijing 101416, China

Abstract. Applying the widely accepted process improvement models, such as CMM and ISO 9001, to small software organizations is a challenge for Chinese software industry. Resistance comes from organization structure, software process improvement model, and the market. Small organizations have many characteristics suitable for process improvement, such as rapid communication. How to maximize advantages and minimize shortcomings is a long-term practical task that Chinese software organizations and academe must face. This paper analyzes difficulties that block small organizations, and provides suggestions to resolve these difficulties. And then this paper puts forwards a framework oriented to Chinese small organizations, consisting of three phases. To assist in implementing upper framework, supporting software Project Man was developed, which provides a convenient integrated environment for project management and process improvement. Experiments and practices have proved that the framework and supporting software can largely reduce the difficulties of process improvement in small organizations.

1 Introduction

It has been recognized that software industry is valuable to Chinese economy and that it continues to grow and should contribute more to the economy in the future. However, due to the nature of software products and the growth of the Internet, country markets are faced with increasing global competition. Comparing with India, the number of our overseas contracts is too small. How to earn this kind of contracts and ensure that software products are of higher quality than other countries, the key is to improve software processes.

CMM and ISO 9001 are the most important software process improvement efforts. In recent years, many companies in China tried to apply CMM, but experiences have shown that many small software organizations have been frustrated. In China, 70 percent software companies have 20 or less employees [1]. CMM largely reflects software process practices of large software organizations, and many practices are inappropriate to small projects.

M. Li, B. Boehm, and L.J. Osterweil (Eds.): SPW 2005, LNCS 3840, pp. 277–286, 2005.
© Springer-Verlag Berlin Heidelberg 2005

On the other hand, both ISO 9001 and CMM fail to benefit from the "smallness" which usually means flexibility, fast reaction time, and enhanced communication. As a result, small software organizations or small projects have not progressed very high on software process maturity scale. To satisfy needs of such organizations, different studies addressing "smallness" issues have been launched.

Based on our research on the topic, we summarize related problems surrounding the use of the CMM in Chinese organizations and projects, and define a basic framework for process improvement in such environments. The framework is based SW-CMM and IDEAL, covers all key process areas of CMM Level 2 and 3, and consists of three phases: Process Definition, Process Control, and Process Stability. In every phase, detailed instructions about how to do are provided.

To assist in performing the framework, we have developed a computerized process improvement environment Project Man. The software is developed in Lotus Notes R5, utilizing its workflow mechanism and knowledge management. The improvement framework and its supporting software have been applied in many military organizations and some civil companies, including Beijing International Switch System Corp. and ZhongXin Network Technology Corp.

The remainder of this paper is organized as follows. Section 2 discusses the difficulties of process improvement in small organizations, and introduces other notable research work. Section 3 defines a process improvement framework for small organizations. Section 4 introduces the architecture and characteristics of Project Man, and compares with other well-known systems. A summary of this work and conclusions are thereof in Section 5.

2   Difficulties and Related Work

In the section, we simply summarize the difficulities that small organizations encounter, and related work in the area.

2.1   Difficulties of Process Improvement in Small Organizations

Difficulties can be classified into three related kinds: organization structure, software process improvement model, and the market that small organizations operate in [4].

(1) Organization structure
Organization structure is the most important determinant of any process initiative, prominent difficulties include:
- Lacking of quality conscious personnel. It is very common that the majority of employees lack an understanding of underlying principles, related concepts and techniques in order to participate in process improvement.
- Limited number of personnel. In small organizations, it is often not possible to form a dedicated process improvement group.
- Limited funds. Many small organizations have no money to prepare process improvement, such as assessment and training, and can't reserve resources for a long-term process improvement project.

- States of current processes. Small organizations, in general, rank Level 1; experiences show that it takes 4 to 6 years for a Level 1 company to reach Level 3 maturity. Small organizations can't endure so long.
- Problems of non-software process. Small organizations often lack required maturity of organizational processes not directly related to software development.
- Hacker culture. Small software organizations are generally extremely dependent on a couple of very talented programmers.
- Lacking quantitative data. Lacking quantitative data poses a problem for software process initiatives since the state of the organization before the initiative is unknown, and it is even very difficult to quantify early results of the initiative.
- Lacking suitable approaches to promote communication of ideas and organizational knowledge. The personality of Chinese goes against communication.

(2) Process Improvement Models
Widely applied software process improvement models (such as CMM) have many inherent problems for small organizations:
- Lacking guidance. CMM provides many key process areas, but don't state how to do. Small organizations lack expertise, often need detailed instructions on how to apply such models within their own company [2, 3].
- Failing to benefit from smallness. Existing models fail to benefit from "smallness", which means flexibility, fast reaction time, and enhanced communication.
- Assumption of expertise in diverse fields. Existing models implicitly assume the organization can form different teams working in parallel on different issues. Small organizations with limited personnel fail to adapt the models to their own reality.

(3) Market
Generally, small organizations are in close contact with customers, and are more vulnerable to market economy. The difficulties related to the market include:
- Changeability assumption. In small organizations, the ability of managing requirements and changes is very week, and closing to customers will bring more requirement changes.
- Low RIO. Small software organizations operate in a small market with limited number of customers, the RIO typically is below expectations.
- Treating CMM or ISO 9001 as a measure for contracts. Managers don't attach importance to process improvement, just go in for certificates of CMM or ISO 9001.

2.2 Related Work

Small organizations are the majority of software industry. How to improve the process capability of small organizations has been studied in past several years.

SPIRE (Software Process Improvement in Region of European) project was sponsored by the European Commission under contract ESPRIT/ESSI 23873 and managed by the Center for Software Engineering (CSE). SPIRE aimed at helping small organizations improve their abilities to develop and/or maintain software. Hunter [6] outlined the progress of SPIRE.

Demirrors [4] and [7] introduced a composite model based on CMM, ISO 9001 and ISO 9000-3. Kautz [5] stated how to apply and adjust IDEAL model in small organizations, and provided tailoring guidance. Richard [8] discussed the characteristics that should include in SPI models, and put forward a SPI model. Johnson [9] defined LOGOS Tailored CMM, stating how to tailor CMM and addressing the problems in small organizations.

3 An Improvement Framework Oriented to Small Organizations

Based on the research on process improvement in Chinese small organizations, we summarize a process improvement framework oriented to small organizations [2, 4, 7]. The framework is based on SW-CMM and IDEAL, includes all the key process areas of CMM Level 2 and 3, and consists of three phases. The activities to be carried out in these phases are briefly described below.

(1) Process Definition phase

The phase corresponds to Initiating and Diagnosing phases of IDEAL model. In this phase, senior management first understands the needs of software process improvement (SPI), commits to a SPI program, and defines the context for SPI. At the same time, initial improvement infrastructure is established, the roles and responsibilities for the infrastructure are initially defined, and initial resources are assigned. Key activities to be performed include: obtaining commitment of senior management; assessing current states of organizations and processes, and establishing organization and process baseline; preparing initial improvement infrastructure, providing needed resources and personnel.

(2) Process Control phase

The phase is tailored from Acting and Establishing phases of IDEAL model. In the phase, improvements are developed and deployed across the organization.

Key activities to be performed include: refining a SPI strategic action plan that will provide the guidance and direction to SPI program; developing or refining the software development processes; integrating the process improvements with new or existing project development plans; monitoring and supporting the organization in the process of using the new or modified processes.

In the phase, we tailor three main key process areas: project monitoring and tracking, configuration management, and product engineering.

(3) Process Stability phase

The phase is similar to Leveraging phase of IDEAL model. Product engineering is widely applied throughout the organization. Formal review and testing, quality assurance, and requirement management should be established. Another key task to be performed is to establish measurement program. In our framework and subsequent software, GQM (Goal-Question-Metric) measurement method is applied.

Key activities include: establishing requirement management process, formal testing and review process, quality assurance process, product engineering process, and complete measurement program to monitor software processes; reviewing and analyzing lessons learned from prior phases; developing plan to provide continuous guidance to SPI program.

4   The Supporting Software Based on GQM

During the process of deploying CMM or ISO9001, supporting tools are indispensably. In 2004, a survey on lessons of process improvement in Chinese small organizations is conducted, 30 percent informants deem that failure rests with insufficient and unsuitable tools. And, the most required tools in organizations are configuration management, project management, product engineering, and change management.

To cooperate with upper process improvement framework, we develop an integrated computerized software engineering environment Project Man. Lotus Notes R5 is the development tool. The system consists of two major parts: Organization-Level Management Platform and Project-Level Management Platform, corresponding to characteristics and the model of organization management and project management.

Project Man provides upper four types of tools, covers all key process areas of CMM Level 2 and 3, and supports quantitative management requirements described in CMM Level 4. Figure 1 is the architecture of Project Man.

By virtue of the system, fussy paperwork and management activities will be largely simplified. The system provides a strong mechanism to collect and analyze various quality data, and finally all related data will be stored in history database to guide future projects.

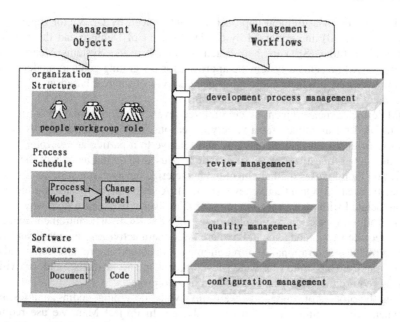

Fig. 1. The architecture of Project Man. The system establishes four main workflows: development process management, review management, configuration management, and quality management.

4.1 System Characteristics

The system has four characteristics.

(1) Quality assurance program based on GQM. The system establishes a quality assurance system based on review and GQM to achieve quantitative management.

For any ongoing project, firstly project goals are defined according to business goals, and customers' expectations. In order to fulfill every business goal, project questions are defined, and each project question is a task. Tasks can be split or incorporated. Projects goals and all tasks compose a to-do network. Every task has some distinguished quantitative properties, which is called metrics.

(2) Integrating an efficient process improvement framework. The system fulfills the basic ideas and requirements of the improvement framework described in Section 3; tailors and realizes all key process areas of CMM Level 2 and 3, and quantitative process managements of CMM Level 4.

(3) Efficient tools and environment support for implementing CMM Level 2 and 3. The system simplifies fussy process management activities and paperwork, improves communication and work efficiency, and finally efficiently addresses the "smallness" problems of small organizations.

(4) A collaborated software development and management environment. The system constructs a safe and reliable collaborated software development and management environment using many advanced technologies, such as Web technology, workflow technology, email technology, and multimedia database.

4.2 Application of GQM

GQM is a proven measurement approach first introduced by Dr. Victor Basili (University of Maryland) and endorsed by the Department of Defense and the Software Engineering Institute (SEI) in their Practical Software and Systems Measurement workshop. GQM presents a systematic approach for integrating goals to models of the software processes, products and quality perspectives of interest based upon the specific needs of the project and the organization.

GQM defines a measurement model on three levels. (1) Conceptual level (goal): A goal is defined for an object, for a variety of reasons, with respect to various models of quality, from various points of view, and relative to a particular environment. (2) Operational level (question): A set of questions is used to define models of the object of study and then focuses on that object to characterize the assessment or achievement of a specific goal. (3) Quantitative level (metric): A set of metrics, based on the models, is associated with every question in order to answer it in a measurable way.

In the following section, we explain how GQM is used for requirement management. In requirement management, there are three main activities: reviewing and validating correctness and rationality of requirements; decomposing requirements and deploying requirements into software development plan, artifacts, and activities; reviewing requirement changes, and combining into projects.

During the process of bringing forward, reviewing, designing, coding, and testing a requirement, the requirement's status will change. In Project Man, we use requirement status library to manage the status of any requirement: Defined, Approved, Designed, Implemented, and Completed.

Table 1 lists goals and corresponding questions of requirement management. Table 2 is the first goal's questions and corresponding metrics. Limiting to the space, other goal's metrics are omitted.

Table 1. goals and corresponding questions of requirement management

	goals	questions
1	Tracking the status and quality of any requirement	How many requirements are in every status?
		What is the result of requirement review?
		Are iffy requirements have been modified?
2	Controlling requirement changes	How many requirement changes are put forward?
		When are requirement changes put forward?
		What types of requirement changes are?
		What effect do requirement changes pose?
3	Tacking the speed of processing requirements	How fast are requirement processed?
		Has the speed of processing requirement been improved?
		Does the proceeding speed of requirements meet expectation?
		How fast are requirement changes processed?
		Has the speed of processing requirement changes been improved?
		Does the proceeding speed of requirement changes meet expectation?

Table 2. the questions and corresponding metrics of goal 1

questions	metrics
How many requirements are in every status?	Number of requirements in "Defined" status
	Number of requirements in "Approved" status
	Number of requirements in "Designed" status
	Number of requirements in "Implemented" status
	Number of requirements in "Completed" status
What is the result of requirement review?	Number of requirements that are reviewed
	Number of requirements that are considered impractical by reviewers
	Number of requirements that are considered improper by reviewers
	Number of requirements that conflict with other requirements
	Number of requirements that canot be testted
Are iffy requirements have been modified?	Number of iffy requirements
	Number of requirements that have been modified and accepted

4.3 Other Related Systems

There are some other well-known software products that can be used by small organizations to manage and improve projects and processes.

(1) Project Assistant

Project Assistant is developed by DingXin Corp., a joint-stock company of TsingHua University and IBM Corp. It is a software process management system based on Lotus Domino/Notes, supporting requirement management, project planning, project monitoring and tracking, quality management, and configuration management. There are many differences between Project Assistant and Project Man:

- Project Man covers 13 KPAs of CMM Level 2 and 3, and provides quantitative management of CMM Level 4. Whereas, Project Assistant covers CMM Level 2, mainly designed for project management.
- Project Man uses GQM to collect and analyze process data, such as schedules, cost, resources, and risks. These process data will be stored in organization or project baseline, guiding future projects. Project Assistant collects few data; process data and experiences cannot be inherited.
- In Project Man, process management, review management, quality management, and configuration management are interrelated. While in Project Assistant, different modules are isolated, data sharing and transfer is a little difficult.

In summary, Project Man is a compound platform, providing more functions, clear workflows, and simple operations.

(2)Software Quality Assurance Platform based on CMM (SQAP)

SQAP is developed by Institute of Software of CAS (Chinese Academy of Sciences), integrating three tools: process asset management, project management, and software measurement. The platform is a C/S system, meets CMM Level 3 specifications. There are following differences between SQAP and Project Man:

- Project Man implements all KPAs of CMM Level 2 and 3, whereas SQAP only covers partial KPAs of CMM Level 3, including organization process definition, and organization process focus.
- Project Man is a compound system, integrating project management and organization management, and modules are closely coupled. While SQAP consists of three isolated tools, the interrelations between them are loose.
- Project Man collects daily-reports, while SQAP collects week-reports. The granularity of process data is different, Project Man provides finer granularity, and can more quickly find abnormal situations and take correct actions.
- Project Man collects diversiform process data, such as workload, cost, review results, configuration items, sub-contracts, realizing quantitative management of CMM Level 4. SQAP are mainly concerned about workload and cost.

As a whole, two systems all support project management and quality measurement. SQAP provides better graphical representations.

(3) JadeBird Configuration Management system (JBCM)

JBCM is a component-based software configuration tool developed by Beijing Beida Jadebird Software Engineering Co., which uses new software configuration management model, and meets related configuration specifications of ISO9000-3 and CMM. There are following differences between JBCM and Project Man:

- JBCM is a dedicated tool for configuration management, while Project Man is a compound platform, covering all phases of software development.
- JBCM implements software configuration management of CMM Level 2; while Project Man implements all KPAs of CMM Level 2 and 3.
- JBCM isn't directly related with a specific project, cannot collect quality data related to configuration items; while in Project Man, as one of core modules, every configuration item is related with specific tasks, and configuration status of every task is displayed real time.

As a whole, JBCM is a powerful and isolated configuration management tool. Project Man is a comprehensive solution for software development management, can better promote all-sided improvement of software processes.

4.4   Feedback from Users

The process improvement framework and related software have been deployed in more than 20 military and civil organizations. Beijing International Switch System Corp. is our first customer. It is a subsidiary company of Siemens Corp., whose development section has about 100 engineers, responsible for localizing switch software.

Before implementing software process improvement, the manager of the section often complained that projects seldom completed before deadline, and the status of every project, workload and related process data are hard to collect. He was busy with solving unforeseen situations, often acted as a fire fighter. He expects to rely on our service and software to standardize software development and project management, improve the efficiency of project development, and finally keep harvests and lessons of past projects.

The project began from Jan. of 2004, lasted three months, and terminated in Apr. of 2004. The process is divided into three phases: (1) Introducing the idea of process improvement, training related personnel, establishing required workgroups; (2) Implementing process improvement framework described in Section 3, standardizing software process, establishing workflows and related specifications, identifying roles and responsibilities; (3) Deploying Project Man, and training every stakeholder.

In Oct 2004, we dispensed a questionnaire to all employees, expecting them to evaluate the process improvement framework, workflows, documents, specifications, and the performance, usability, and functions of Project Man.

We received 88 valid questionnaires, 90 percent of informants deem that the process improvement project largely improves the efficiency and visibility of projects; risks can be forecasted; communication is more convenient; and workload can be quantitatively measured.

5   Conclusions

Through our research, we find following points are very important: (1) According to organization's characteristics, business goals and resources, selecting and tailoring suitable process improvement model. (2) Implementing process improvement as a project, obtaining commitment of senior management. (3) Using suitable tools to assist in process improvement, simplify paperwork and specifications, enhance communication, and automate routines.

The future goals of our research include: (1) Using a formal schema to represent process improvement framework and validate it. (2) Perfecting Project Man to support mobile users, integrate with OAs and other related commercial tools, and so on.

References

1. Xingui He: Capability Maturity Model for Software. TsingHua Press, BeiJing, China (2001)
2. Bo Gong: The Theory and Practices of CMMI. WaterPower Press, BeiJing, China (2003)
3. Bo Gong and Weihong Liu: Software Process Management. WaterPower Press, BeiJing, China (2003)
4. Onur Demirrors and Elif Demirors: Software Process Improvement in a Small Organization: Difficulties and Suggestions. Proceedings 6th European Workshop on Software Process Technology, Paris (1998) 1-26
5. Karlheinz Kautz, Herik Westergaad Hansen, and Kim Thaysen: Applying and Adjusting a Software Process Improvement Model in Practice: The Use of the IDEAL Model in a Small Software Enterprise. Proceedings of ICSE, London (2000) 626-663
6. R.B.Hunter and H.W.Jung: Some Experiences and Results from the SPICE Trails. SPICE 2000, Dublin (2000) 102-234
7. Elif Demirors, Onur Demirors, Oguz Dikenelli, and Billur Keskin: Process Improvement Towards ISO 9001 Certification in a Small Software Organization. Proceedings of ICSE, London (2000) 471-474
8. ITA Richard: SPI Models: What Characteristics are Required for Small Software Development Companies? Software Quality Journal, Vol 10 (2002) 101-114
9. Donna L. Johnson and Judith G. Brodman: Tailoring the CMM for Small Businesses, Small Organizations, and Small Projects. Proceedings of ICSE, New York (2003) 239-257

Incremental Workflow Mining Based on Document Versioning Information

Ekkart Kindler, Vladimir Rubin, and Wilhelm Schäfer

Software Engineering Group, University of Paderborn,
Warburger Str. 100, D-33098 Paderborn, Germany
{kindler, vroubine, wilhelm}@uni-paderborn.de

Abstract. Current enterprises spend much effort to obtain precise models of their system engineering processes in order to improve the process capability of the organization. The manual design of workflow models is complicated, time-consuming and error-prone; capabilities of human beings in detecting discrepancies between the actual process and the process model are rather limited. Therefore, automatic techniques for deriving these models are becoming more and more important.

In this paper, we present an idea that exploits the user interaction with a version management system for the incremental automatic derivation, refinement and analysis of process models. Though this idea is not fully worked out yet, we sketch the architecture of the solution and the algorithms for the main steps of incremental automatic derivation of process models.

1 Introduction

This paper deals with automatically increasing the process maturity of organizations by means of discovering the process from information about versions of documents and assignments of these documents to different users. This information can be derived from data stored in document or version management systems.

The Capability Maturity Model^{SM} (CMM) [1] and the Capability Maturity Model® Integration (CMMI^{SM}) [2] specifications of SEI define several levels of maturity as a foundation for process improvement. The CMM refers to software development processes only; the CMMI is more general and applies to system engineering, which can consist of software and hardware as well, i.e. mechatronic system. In this paper, we present our idea by the help of examples from Software Engineering only, which means that we restrict ourselves to the CMM. But, the ideas should apply to CMMI in general.

Achieving the next level of the maturity framework results in increasing the process capability of the organization. The first level of the CMM model (initial) is characterized by ad-hoc and occasionally chaotic processes; the second (repeatable) implies the existence of the process discipline to repeat earlier successes; the third level (defined) means that the processes are documented, standardized and integrated to the organizational structure; the fourth (managed) level

M. Li, B. Boehm, and L.J. Osterweil (Eds.): SPW 2005, LNCS 3840, pp. 287–301, 2005.

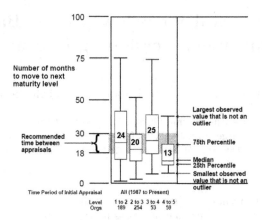

Fig. 1. Time to increase the CMM level

is achieved when the software process and products are quantitatively under-stood and controlled; the fifth (optimizing) level enables a continuous process improvement from innovative ideas and technologies.

The CMM was introduced for incrementally improving the maturity from the first (initial) level to the higher levels. The statistics published in the "Process Maturity Profile of the Software Community" of August 2004, where about 1543 organizations of different size and from different areas were analysed [3], shows that transitions between levels in the CMM are time-consuming. This statistics is based on the information from such appraisals as: CMM-Based Appraisals for In-ternal Process Improvement (CBA IPIs), Software Process Assessments (SPAs) and Standard CMMI Appraisal Method for Process Improvement (SCAMPI). The most interesting statistics in our context is "Organizational Trends", where the time, needed by the organization to improve the process capability is shown. The average time needed to reach the repeatable level is 24 months and from repeatable to the defined level is another 20 months (see Fig. 1). So, automatic process discovery can speed up increasing the CMM level. We call it "incremental workflow mining" and it is discussed in this paper.

"Workflow mining" is ongoing research in the area of Business Process Man-agement [4]. Existing results can be used for generating the System Engineer-ing Processes and for supporting them by a Workflow Management System. Therefore, a brief look into the concepts of Business Process Modeling helps us identifying the information needed for discovering software processes. Busi-ness Process Models cover such aspects as Informational, Organizational, and Behavioural [5, 6, 7] as shown in Fig. 2. When considering different aspects for workflow mining, Wil van der Aalst calls this "Workflow Mining from different perspectives" [8]. To make things even worse, in many enterprises the infor-mation is distributed over different subsystems, such as Document Management and Resource Management systems, which is called "Mining from heterogeneous sources".

Fig. 2. Aspects of BPM of the Enterprise

Usually the information distributed on the different systems is integrated by using ERP or CRM systems. In software development processes, documents are usually maintained by a Version Management System. The logs of the Version Management Systems contain information about the control flow, the documents and the resources of the underlying processes. In this paper, we present an approach for incrementally and automatically generating software process models from these logs. We believe that similar logs can be obtained from ERP or CRM systems, so that our approach carries over to these systems either.

Altogether our approach helps to incrementally obtain a better model of the development process by exploring the real work on this process. Later, this model can be used to enforce the specific style of work in the organization and supply missing information about the actual process. The generated model can be also compared to the predefined process model and the discrepancy report between the prescriptive and the discovered process model can be used to improve the process capability. Automatic generation of the process can also trigger Business Process Reengineering of the Organization, which is necessary for configuration and maintenance of "Process-Aware Information Systems".

The remainder of this paper is organized as follows. First, we discuss the related work and show the state of the art in this field. In Sect. 3, we present the architecture of the process discovering infrastructure and background ideas in the area. Section 5 concludes the paper; and Sect. 4 shows important problems in the related research domains to be treated in future.

2   Related Work

The seminal research in the area of process mining started in the mid 90ties with new approaches to the grammar inference problem proposed by Cook and Wolf in their first articles, which was improved later [9]. This research considers events to be tokens and event streams to be strings of the grammar and, thus, solves the grammar inference problem from event logs. Their research deals with the software engineering process only and proposes three approaches to discovering the process: the RNet, the KTail and the Markov approach. The RNet approach uses neural networks. The KTail is a pure algorithmic approach, building finite state machines, depending on the future behaviour. The Markov approach uses a combination of the statistical and the algorithmic method for constructing the event graph from probability tables. In their work, Mannila and Rusakov [10] present also the Markovian approach, but in a different domain.

The first application of "process mining" to workflow models from workflow logs was presented by Agrawal in 1998 [11]. This approach models business processes as annotated activity graphs and presents an algorithm for finding a "conformal" process graph, assuming absence of cycles in the log. This algorithm is restricted to sequential patterns.

The inductive approach to workflow mining was presented by Herbst and Karagiannis [12]. Their approach uses machine learning techniques for acquisition and adaptation of workflow models. The work of the same authors on integration of machine learning and workflow management [13] is a foundation of the work on "incremental workflow mining", presenting three phases of the workflow acquisition and adaptation cycle: inductive learning, workflow analysis, and adaptation.

Another foundational approach to our work was presented by van der Aalst et al. [14, 4, 15]. Within this approach, workflow logs and classes of sound Workflow Nets are defined. Formal causality relations between events in logs are defined and the "rediscovery problem" is introduced. The α-mining algorithm for discovering workflow models is described in the work.

The work of Schimm [16] presents a mining tool for discovering hierarchically structured workflow processes. The area of workflow mining can also be productively integrated with the research in the area of workflow-based process monitoring and controlling as presented in the work of zur Muehlen and Rosemann [17].

Like Aalst, we use Workflow Nets for modeling workflows and we combine and extend ideas of Herbst et al. and of Aalst et al. for a new "incremental workflow mining" algorithm. We extend existing approaches considering not activity logs, but document versioning information. Thus, we derive information about activities from document logs. Additionally, we derive also informational and organizational aspects of the process. Hence, we create our models using extended workflow nets to represent not only behavioural but also these additional aspects. Altogether, incremental workflow mining, in our understanding, means providing the models as soon as we get the first log information and improving these models as soon as additional log information is available.

3   Solution

In this section, we present our main ideas. We start with the architecture of the system, where incremental workflow mining can be applied. Then, we describe our approach and show the example. The methods used for our approach are concluding this section.

System Architecture

The coarse architecture of our system for *incremental workflow mining* is presented on Fig. 3. It consists of a Document and Version Management System, Resource Management and Workflow Management System with its User Interface. The Resource Management System contains information about the user's interactions with documents. The Workflow Management System stores information about all the generated processes. We assume, that the processes are not defined manually, hence the information about the processes is not present in the system at the very beginning. The User Interface is used for representing the processes to the user in a comprehensive manner.

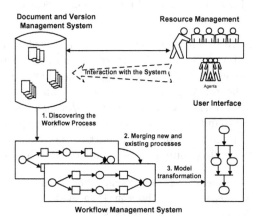

Fig. 3. Mining Architecture Schema

The users work with the Document and Version Management System committing the new versions of documents and entering the versioning log messages. The versioning log consists of *records*. Each log record contains information about the committed document, the user who committed it, the timestamp and a comment. The versioning log contains many logs related to different processes. The *execution log* is a part of the versioning log that consists of records related to the process that has to be discovered.

Following the incremental workflow mining approach, the processes are discovered and inserted to the Workflow Management System, where they are maintained. The processes are then transformed and presented to the user in an understandable format. The user, considering the presented process, continues working with documents. This cycle actually describes the work of the user and the roles of the systems involved in the *incremental workflow mining*.

Incremental Mining Approach

This section presents the basic idea of *incremental workflow mining*. Figure 4 shows the Mining Architecture Schema in detail. The Document and Version

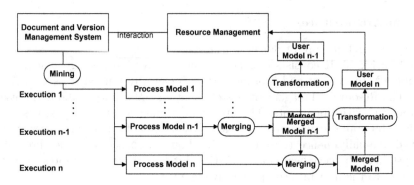

Fig. 4. Incremental Mining Approach Schema

Management and the Resource Management Systems are shown here. The Workflow Management System maintains the process models, which are derived during the steps of the approach. In rounded rectangles, the algorithms for deriving the process models are shown: *Mining*, *Merging* and *Transformation*. The *Process Models* are derived after the execution of the *Mining* algorithm, the *Merged Models* – after *Merging* and the *User Models* – after *Transformation*. The steps of the approach are enumerated in the left part of the schema.

The incremental workflow mining approach consists of the following steps:

```
Step 0. Let <Process Model>, <Merged Model> and
        <new Merged Model> be equal to null;
Step 1. Discover process model from
        versioning log ("Mining") -
        get <Process Model>;
Step 2. If <Merged Model> exists,
        then execute Merging algorithm ("Merging")
            and get <new Merged Model>,
        else let
            <Merged Model> be <Process Model>;
Step 3. If <new Merged Model> is not null
        then
            if <new Merged Model> is not equal
              to <Merged Model>
            then let <Merged Model> be
                <new Merged Model>
              and go to Step 1,
            else Stop:
        else go to Step 1.
```

It is possible that the versioning log contains either one or several execution logs. In case of several execution logs, incremental worklfow mining can be used immediately in batch mode.

The precondition(Step 0) is: there exist no generated models.

The first step is necessary for getting the first structure of the process. The *Mining* algorithm of the process model generation from an execution log has to be performed here. The main idea of this algorithm is represented in the example in Sect. 3. Since we get the input information from the Document and Version Management System, we can derive dependencies among activities from the accessed documents. Thus, for each record in the execution log, we have the context of activity: preconditions, output document and user. The preconditions are the documents already committed to the system. The output document is the document committed by the activity. The user is the agent who committed the document. From the timestamps of the commit, we can also get the information on the order of activities and, consequently, model the process.

The second step is the execution of the *Merging* algorithm, which refines the existing model by merging it with the process model, produced in the first step. This algorithm is the central point of the research in *incremental workflow mining*. It can be used for stepwise refinement of the existing process after getting a new process model by means of discovering new possible relations between versioned documents.

With the aid of the *Mining* and the *Merging* algorithms, the process is improved incrementally, thus, an initial ad-hoc process is becoming structured. This is the way, how ad-hoc or collaborative workflow can become structured [5].

The third step includes checking of the conditions of the loop of the approach and checking, whether an execution can be stopped. The execution has to be stopped as soon as the new merged model and the old merged model are equal. The implementation of this algorithm must contain additional guard conditions, which exclude the situation of stopping of the execution on early steps, because of the coincidence of execution logs.

As soon as any merged model is generated, the user has to be advised to work with the documents according to the discovered process. The idea is to present the existing process model in an appropriate comprehensive format to the user. This comprehensive format can be derived from the merged model using the *Transformation* algorithm.

The future research in the area must also deal with the incremental user support and the user behaviour. Thus, the work of the user should be supported the following way: during the first executions, the process model should be just shown to the user; later, the user should be advised about the further steps; at last, when the process model is stable, the user could be enforced to follow the model. From the point of view of the user behaviour, *incremental workflow mining* can be either interactive or non-interactive. In case of interactive incremental workflow mining, the process refinement is executed immediately after every user change in the execution log. In case of non-interactive incremental workflow mining, the process refinement is executed only after finishing the log. Non-interactive workflow mining can be used during the first executions, when the process is not clean and is supposed to be significantly changed by every execution; interactive workflow mining can be used for the ultimate improvement of the process.

Example

The following example presents the information that was taken from the CVS logs [18]. These logs are a simple version of the logs that could come from a software company changing the design and the code, testing the code and reviewing the design.

The log presented in Table 1 contains information about the documents, their versions (revisions), timestamps, authors committed the documents, and comments (CVS logging information).

Table 1. CVS log 1

Document	Revision	Date	Author	Comment
Design	1.1	01.01.04 14:30	Design Eng.	Modify
Code	1.1	01.01.04 14:30	Design Eng.	Modify
Test Results	1.1	10.01.04 18:45	QA Eng.	Test Unit
Design Review	1.1	15.01.04 10:00	System Eng.	Review Design

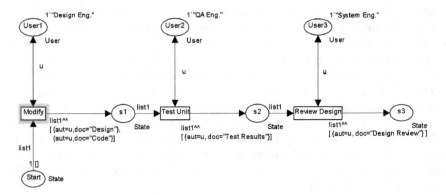

Fig. 5. Process Model generated from CVS Log 1

From the information presented in the log, the process model representing the sequence of activities, information about documents, produced by activities, and users, involved in executing them, can be generated. The current process model is specified using High-Level Petri Nets [19] as shown in Fig. 5. This model will be generated using the *Mining* algorithm.

As it was already described in this section, the *Mining* algorithm supports the generation of the process model using one execution. The current High-Level Petri Net model consists of the following nodes: transitions, places of type User, and places of type State. Transitions represent the derived activities; the names of the transitions are derived from the user comments in the CVS log 1, see Table 1. The places of type User represent the user information; for our example, it is the name of the user who executed the commit. The places of type State

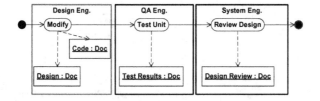

Fig. 6. User-Oriented Model generated from Process Model

Table 2. CVS log 2

Document	Revision	Date	Author	Comment
Design	1.1	01.02.04 14:30	Design Eng.	Modify Design
Code	1.1	05.02.04 12:15	Design Eng.	Modify Code
Design Review	1.1	11.02.04 11:00	System Eng.	Review Design
Test Results	1.1	15.02.04 19:30	Developer	Test Unit

represent the current state of the system. A state is a set of records of type *User × Document*; when the place is marked, this set contains the documents checked into the Document Versioning System and the users who executed the commit. For example, in Fig. 5 the transition "Modify" is derived from first two rows in Table 1, it contains two preset places: "User1" of type User with token "Design Eng." and "Start" of type State with token "[]" (empty list) and two postset places: "User1" and "s1" of type State. The arcs between transitions and places of type User go in both directions and contain the variable of type User as inscription. For example, there are two arcs from transition "Modify" to place "User1", both are inscripted with the variable "u". It means that "Design Eng." can execute the activity "Modify". The arcs between transitions and places of type State contain list variables and operations on them. For example, the arc from the place "Start" to the transition "Modify" contains the variable "list1" and the arc from "Modify" to "s1" contains the variable "list1", concatenation "∧∧" and the list "[$aut = u, doc = "Design", aut = u, doc = "Code"$]", which contains the information about two documents committed to the system and the user who did it. It means that after executing "Modify" the documents "Design" and "Code" were committed to the system by "Design Eng.". The order of the activities is generated according to the "Date" information of the log.

As soon as such a model is generated, it can be transformed to the user-oriented format using the *Transformation* algorithm; then it will be presented to the user for analysis. The corresponding model, represented as a UML Activity Diagram [20], is shown on Fig. 6.

To show the refinement of the existing model, we present the second CVS Log, see Table 2.

From this log, the process model can be derived, using the *Mining* algorithm, see Fig. 7.

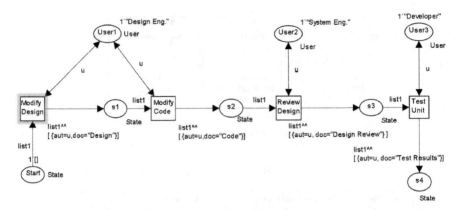

Fig. 7. Process Model generated from CVS Log 2

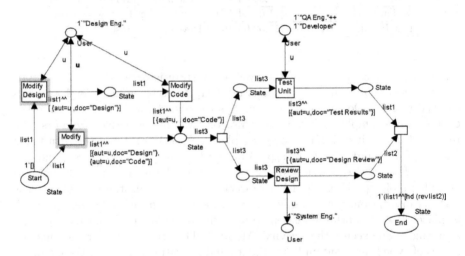

Fig. 8. Merged Process Model

The generated process presents additional details about the documents: in the first process, documents "Design" and "Code" were committed simultaneously, now we can discover the order; in the first process the document "Test Results" was committed by user "QA Eng.", now it is committed by "Developer"; in the first process "Test Results" was committed earlier then "Design Review", in the second log – in the reverse order.

Thus, now we have a second process model that contains additional information about the process. By means of the *Merging* algorithm, we can refine the first process using the second one. Merging of the processes gives the following information, see Fig. 8.

This model is transformed to the user-oriented format to be presented to the end user again[1], see Fig. 9.

---

[1] Here we use Activity Diagram syntax used in UML2.0.

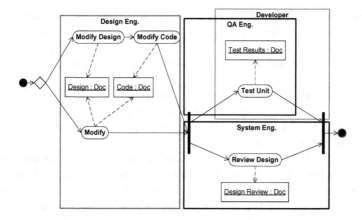

Fig. 9. User-Oriented Model generated from Merged Model

By means of the merging algorithm, we discovered the alternative: the Design Eng. executes either the "Modify" activity or "Modify Design" and "Modify Code" activities, and the concurrency: "Review Design" and "Test Unit" activities can be parallel, additionally "Test Unit" can be executed either by "QA Eng." or by "Developer".

Methodology

This section presents the methods of getting an appropriate input information and realization of the *incremental workflow mining algorithms.*

Methods of working with input data must deal with execution log information and representation of it. The main question in this context is: which kind of methods should be used to detect document dependencies, to discover, what documents belong to the same activity. This problem is tightly connected with the problem of deriving the exact preconditions of the activities, described already in this section. The existence of the predefined informational model and the policy of using the Document Versioning System in company is a prerequisite for solving these problems.

We assume that the execution log is structured in the following way: each record of the log refers to a document and document status, each record refers to a person and each record has its own timestamp. Transaction-based systems, like ERP, CRM and others, that either integrate or incorporate Document and Version Management, usually provide such information in a form, that could be converted to the desired one, according to the structure, defined above. Product Data Management (PDM) Systems [21], like Teamcenter by UGS, Windchill by PTC, SAP PDM and others, can also provide an appropriate input information. Software Configuration Management (SCM) Systems [21], like CVS, Visual SourceSafe by Microsoft, IBM Rational ClearCase and others, also contain the information, sufficient for input to the *incremental workflow mining algorithms.*

The timestamp in the log is used for extracting the order information. From the information about the user either user assignment or user availability or other useful resource information can be derived. The document status information is necessary for understanding the object flow, changes in the states of particular documents.

There are several types of methods, that have to be used for *incremental workflow mining*, such as methods of defining the process specification, ontology modeling of business process management concepts, model transformations and verification of defined models.

The process specification methods include such formalisms as workflow nets and high-level Petri Nets, which is suitable for the integration of control flow and object flow in one specification. Some subclasses of workflow nets could be defined for specifying the type of nets, closer related to the problem area.

For checking the soundness of the generated process and/or verification of some rational properties appropriate techniques of analysis of Petri Nets and verification of Petri Net systems should be used.

Ontology modeling has to define the relations between entities, used for describing the workflow process, and must incorporate different aspects of business process management, such as Informational, Organizational and Behavioural. Meta-modeling techniques, which could be put to the MOF/UML [22] framework for more precise definitions and possibility of future implementation, can be used here.

4   Future Work

The focus of this paper is on the motivation and some first ideas on incremental and interactive workflow mining. The examples show that the use of information on different aspects of the processes helps solving this problem. We are currently working on the details and on the prototype implementation of this approach.

In future, we have to deal with such problems as deriving the preconditions of the activities and inferring the names of the activities. Deriving the exact preconditions of the activities is an open problem, because this information is not available in the versioning log. By default, all the documents committed to the system before the execution of the activity can be a precondition. Thus, for improving the mining and getting real preconditions, we need the informational model - the model of document dependencies. This informational model must be given by the user as the input data for the *Mining* algorithm.

The other open problem is inferring the names of the activities, this information is also not available in the versioning log. The only details about the names can be taken from the user commit comments. Thus, for improving the mining and getting real names of the activities, we need the conventions on the commit comments. The comment must contain information about the real activity that was executed, e.g. add, modify, remove. This conventions should be also given as the input for the *Mining* algorithm.

If the informational model and the conventions were not given to the *Mining* algorithm, we can not be sure that the *Merging* algorithm works correctly, since the processes to be merged can differ significantly. Thus, using the Document Versioning System is not sufficient, the company must have a predefined policy. Having this document management policy is a prerequisite for successful *Mining* and *Merging*.

In this paper, we have used information from CVS for mining the processes. Other systems in the area of PDM and ERP basically provide the same information. Thus, the approach should be applicable to these areas too. In order to ease the applicability of our implementation to the other areas, it will work on a system-independent log format.

We are well aware of the fact that the mining algorithms need to be improved and we think that the improvements strongly depend on the application area. These improvements need more careful investigations, which can only be obtained by case studies. Since we are interested in software engineering processes and in particular in improving the CMM, our case studies will be in this area.

5   Conclusion

In this paper, we have presented ideas for algorithms supporting *interactive workflow mining* from different perspectives. These algorithms use data on the main aspects of business process management: Informational, Organizational and Behavioural. Since the required information about the activities of the software process is usually not available, we start with deriving this information from the logs of the Software Configuration Management system. The example of Sect. 3 illustrates the idea of the algorithm and the benefits of this approach:

- Our approach does not need information on the existing activities; rather, we can mine the information about activities from the versioning logs. We call this part of our approach "activity mining". Activity mining is not considered by classical approaches [23] since they work on logs of activities, which requires that the activities are defined already at this stage. Our approach works without explicitly defining activities.
- The use of the information from different aspects helps us to come up with process models very early without having seen many logs of many process instances. In contrast to classical approaches, which derive the dependencies among activities from the order in the logs, we derive the dependencies among the activities from the accessed documents. This allows us to immediately mine a model for an activity having its context. Therefore, a model of the process can be derived even after the first execution and we can have a model right from the beginning. Of course, these models are incomplete initially, but they can be interactively improved while the versioning logs are being produced. We call this "interactive workflow mining".
- Another mode of operation is to mine a process from the log once the execution has finished and to merge it with process models mined earlier. We call this "incremental workflow mining".

Altogether, this approach supports mining process models from ad-hoc executions without having any predefined information on them. This way, our approach supports increasing the repeatability of the processes, in terms of workflow terminology the ad-hoc processes become administrative.

In terms of the CMM, this means lifting the maturity level of some enterprise to defined.

References

1. Paulk, M.C., Curtis, B., Beth, M., Chrissis, Weber, C.V.: Capability Maturity Model for Software (SW-CMM). Technical Report CMU/SEI-93-TR-024, Carnegie Mellon University, Software Engineering Institute (1993)
2. SEI Carnegie Mellon: Capability Maturity Model Integration (CMMISM), Version 1.1. Technical Report CMU/SEI-2002-TR-012, Carnegie Mellon, Software Engineering Institute (2002)
3. SEI Carnegie Mellon: Process Maturity Profile. Software CMM 2004 Mid-Year Update. Technical report, Carnegie Mellon University, Software Engineering Institute. (2004)
4. Weijters, A., van der Aalst, W.: Workflow Mining: Discovering Workflow Models from Event-Based Data. In Dousson, C., Höppner, F., Quiniou, R., eds.: Proceedings of the ECAI Workshop on Knowledge Discovery and Spatial Data. (2002) 78–84
5. Leymann, F., Roller, D.: Production Workflow: Concepts and Techniques. Prentice-Hall PTR, Upper Saddle River, New Jersey, USA (1999)
6. van der Aalst, W., van Hee, K.: Workflow Management: Models, Methods, and System. Cooperative Information Systems. The MIT Press (2002)
7. Kindler, E.: Using the Petri Net Markup Language for Exchanging Business Processes? Potential and Limitations. In Nüttgens, M., Mendling, J., eds.: XML4BPM 2004, Proceedings of the 1st GI Workshop XML4BPM – XML Interchange Formats for Business Process Management at 7th GI Conference Modellierung 2004, Marburg Germany, March 2004, http://wi.wu-wien.ac.at/~mendling/XML4BPM/xml4bpm-2004-proceedings-pnml.pdf   (2004) 43–60
8. van der Aalst, W., Weijters, A.: Process mining: a research agenda. Comput. Ind. **53** (2004) 231–244
9. Cook, J.E., Wolf, A.L.: Discovering Models of Software Processes from Event-Based Data. ACM Trans. Softw. Eng. Methodol. **7** (1998) 215–249
10. Mannila, H., Rusakov, D.: Decomposing event sequences into independent components. In: V. Kumar, R. Grossman (Eds.), Proceedings of the First SIAM Conference on Data Mining, SIAM. (2001) 1–17
11. Agrawal, R., Gunopulos, D., Leymann, F.: Mining Process Models from Workflow Logs. In: Proceedings of the 6th International Conference on Extending Database Technology, Springer-Verlag (1998) 469–483
12. Herbst, J., Karagiannis, D.: An Inductive approach to the Acquisition and Adaptation of Workflow Models. citeseer.ist.psu.edu/herbst99inductive.html (1999)
13. Herbst, J., Karagiannis, D.: Integrating Machine Learning and Workflow Management to Support Acquisition and Adaptation of Workflow Models. In: Proceedings of the 9th International Workshop on Database and Expert Systems Applications, IEEE Computer Society (1998) 745
14. Weijters, A., van der Aalst, W.: Process mining: discovering workflow models from event-based data. In: Proceedings of the 13th Belgium-Netherlands Conference on Artificial Intelligence (BNAIC 2001). (2001) 283–290

15. Weijters, T., van der Aalst, W.: Rediscovering Workflow Models from Event-Based Data. In Hoste, V., Pauw, G., eds.: Proceedings of the 11th Dutch-Belgian Conference on Machine Learning (Benelearn 2001). (2001) 93–100
16. Schimm, G.: Process Miner - A Tool for Mining Process Schemes from Event-Based Data. In: Proceedings of the European Conference on Logics in Artificial Intelligence, Springer-Verlag (2002) 525–528
17. zur Muehlen, M., Rosemann, M.: Workflow-Based Process Monitoring and Controlling Technical and Organizational Issues. In: Proceedings of the 33rd Hawaii International Conference on System Sciences-Volume 6, IEEE Computer Society (2000)
18. Fogel, K.F.: Open Source Development with CVS. Coriolis Group Books (1999)
19. van der Aalst, W.: High level Petri nets Extending classical Petri nets with color, time and hierarchy. (http://tmitwww.tm.tue.nl/staff/wvdaalst/courses/pm/pm.html)
20. OMG: UML 2.0 Superstructure Specification. Version 2.0 ptc/03-08-02, Object Management Group (2003) Final Adopted Specification.
21. Dahlqvist, A.P., Asklund, U., Crnkovic, I., Hedin, A., Larsson, M., Ranby, J., Svensson, D.: Product Data Management and Software Configuration Management - Similarities and Differences. (URL: citeseer.ist.psu.edu/dahlqvist01product.html)
22. OMG: Meta Object Facility (MOF) specification. Technical report, Object Management Group (2002)
23. van der Aalst, W., van Dongena, B.F., Herbst, J., Marustera, L., Schimm, G., Weijters, A.J.M.M.: Workflow mining: A survey of issues and approaches. Data & Knowledge Engineering **47** (2003) 237–267
24. Murata, T.: Petri Nets: Properties, Analysis and Applications. In: Proceedings of the IEEE, 77(4). (1989) 541–580
25. Reisig, W., Rozenberg, G., eds. In: Lectures on Petri Nets I: Basic Models. Volume 1491 of Lecture Notes in Computer Science. Springer-Verlag, Berlin (1998)

A Framework for
Coping with Process Evolution

Brian A. Nejmeh[1,2] and William E. Riddle[3,4]

[1] Senior Partner
INSTEP Inc., Lancaster, Pennsylvania, USA
[2] Associate Professor of Information Systems and Entrepreneurship,
Messiah College, Grantham, Pennsylvania, USA
nejmeh@instep.com
[3] Senior Solution Architect
Solution Deployment Affiliates, Santa Fe, New Mexico, USA
[4] Senior Scientist,
Fraunhofer IESE, Kaiserslautern, Germany
riddle@WmERiddle.com

Abstract. To survive, companies must rationally, rapidly and incrementally evolve their processes in response to changes in customer desires, market pressures, personnel availability and capability, business goals, and available technology as well as many other business-context factors. A Process Evolution Dynamics Framework allows process change agents to address this critical need by rationally describing, understanding, learning from, planning and managing process evolution efforts in a manner that addresses rapid, unpredictable changes to their company's business context. The framework may be based on an experience-based categorization of process evolution-related activities highlighting their collaborative maturation of a company's process knowledge base. In addition to clarifying and facilitating a company's process evolution efforts, the framework suggests several topics which should be addressed by the process research and empirical-study communities.

1 Introduction

A company's business, engineering and operational processes are major determiners of the company's success. It is through these processes that the company identifies customer needs, develops and delivers quality products, applies leading edge tools and techniques, competes within its market segments, demonstrates conformance to regulatory and contractual constraints, manages its out-sourcing and sub-contracting arrangements, and keeps its workforce up-to-date professionally. Process deficiencies in any of these areas can lead to serious failures, including: reduced market-share, decreased profitability, increased time-to-market, insufficient workforce capability and productivity, and non-effective, inefficient business performance.

To prevent problems and their potentially disastrous results, companies look to standards to understand *why* their processes should have various properties, maturity frameworks to understand *what* activities should be included in their processes, and best practices to understand *how* the activities might best be carried out. Successfully

M. Li, B. Boehm, and L.J. Osterweil (Eds.): SPW 2005, LNCS 3840, pp. 302–316, 2005.

addressing all three of these concerns assures that a company's processes continuously match the company's needs and objectives.

Work-to-date on these *why*, *what* and *how* concerns has addressed several aspects of evolving a company's processes over time. Taken collectively, the results support the definition of *improvement game plans*: carefully defined, organized and managed sequences of process change activities. Standards – for example, ISO 9001 [1] and the Business Standards Institute's information integrity standard [2] – help identify goals and requirements for an improvement game plan. Maturity models – for example, the Carnegie Mellon® Software Engineering Institute (SEI^SM) Capability Maturity Model® (CMM®) [3] and Control Objectives for Information and related Technology (COBIT) [4] – identify and organize key practices and, as such, support the development of process designs and plans for process evolution via a series of staged exercises. Finally, best practice definitions – for example, as provided by the work on *agile methods* ([5], [6]) or as collected and promoted by the IEEE Computer Society [7] and the Project Management Institute [8] – support process improvement efforts by facilitating the specification of detailed, concrete activities and tasks within the processes.

As a result of a collective five decades helping companies – of many sizes and in many industry sectors – successfully evolve their processes, the authors have found that addressing the *why*, *what* and *how* concerns generally leads to "point solutions" which, while certainly very beneficial, are quickly over-taken by events. We have found it critical to additionally consider achieving major, long-term process evolution through narrowly focused, overlapping process change cycles addressing changes to business needs, constraints, requirements, and opportunities. We call this additional concern *process evolution dynamics*.

Our experiences lead us to conclude that properly addressing process evolution dynamics is the key process-related factor in assuring a company's success. Further, we have come to feel that: 1) the company's context (its customer requirements, marketplace positioning, workforce capabilities, profitability targets, etc.) is the major influence on the definition and sequencing of process change cycles, and 2) this context changes so rapidly, and often so radically, that the process evolution approach a company uses must be very flexible and adaptive. In sum: there is no "one size fits all" process evolution approach suitable for all the contexts that a company must cope with over time; and whatever approach is used to address a specific context must admit rapid adjustment to cope with changes to that context.

We have developed a Process Evolution Dynamics Framework to help companies effectively, efficiently and accurately manage the dynamics of their process evolution efforts. In this paper we focus on the framework itself, first discussing the problems it addresses (Section 2), then describing the framework itself (Section 3), and finally providing a case study illustrating its use to describe a process evolution effort (Section 4). At the end of the paper, and in the context of a summary of this paper's content, we identify several issues and topics that require empirical study and research (Section 5).

® Carnegie Mellon, Capability Maturity Model, CMM, and CMMI are registered in the U.S. Patent and Trademark Office by Carnegie Mellon University.
SM SEI is a service mark of Carnegie Mellon University.

2 Process Evolution Problems

Many companies have found that improvement game plans lead to significant, valuable results. In many cases, the improvement game plans are based on the CMM maturity model and move the company, step-by-step, from a primitive, ad hoc level of capability to a superior, optimizing level. The details of a variety of these efforts, and data demonstrating their cost-effectiveness and value, may be found in the SEI's Software Engineering Information Repository [http://seir.sei.cmu.edu]. Increasingly, improvement game plan-based efforts have changed from being a strict "march" from the ad hoc to the superior level to being more flexible and expansive by simultaneously addressing several levels [9], by interleaving a concern for other standards such as BS 7799 [2] and the People Capability Maturity Model [10] [11], and by skipping levels and shifting among maturity models [12].

Improvement game plans lead to significant process improvements, but the resulting processes are frequently "over-taken by events" by the time they are deployed throughout a company. Partially, this is because deployment – production and distribution of process documentation – and training can require a great deal of time. More importantly, it is because the company's business context can change quite rapidly and in totally unanticipated ways. Improvement game plan approaches tend to focus primarily upon project management and product engineering concerns. Some of the business-context influences that they fail to address are:

- real (as opposed to perceived) customer needs,
- positioning with respect to competition in the marketplace,
- profitability and operational objectives,
- out-sourcing and sub-contracting agreement negotiations,
- available technology opportunities, and
- workforce capabilities.

A failure to attend to these contextual influences diminishes, and sometimes totally erases, the positive effects of improvement game plans. First, improvement game plan-based efforts tend to focus on improvement rather than maintaining the *status quo* in the face of change. In industry sectors not subject to regulatory constraints or sectors or in which companies are not required to demonstrate specific levels of capability, maintaining the *status quo* is often much more of a driver than is improvement. Secondly, negative impacts frequently follow from a failure to consciously and directly address the business context and coordinate the many different, but interrelated, streams of process evolution activities that individually address different parts of the context. Visible symptoms of this lack of coordination include:

- redundant, duplicative, and inconsistent process descriptions; for example, process documentation and training materials that do not reflect the introduction of new engineering support technology,
- conflicting improvement plans; for example, training material update plans that are "out of synch" with the company's plans to demonstrate some desired level of process maturity,

- incomplete, inconsistent statements of requirements, needs, objectives, and constraints; for example, a process evolution activity specification that does not reflect the need to effectively compete in some new market segment,
- inappropriate resource allocation decisions; for example, a failure to fund and staff the development of workflow management support that would considerably reduce the cost of (re-)training the company's workforce, and
- deficient process documentation deployment; for example, the deployment of documentation which is out-of-date or fails to address all of a process performer's "What should I do now?" questions.

These symptoms stem from a failure to recognize two fundamental facts about process evolution. First, process evolution involves a variety of concurrent, inter-related, activity streams, each focused on some theme – process definition, process training, process appraisal, etc. – within some organizational unit – engineering, marketing/sales, finance, etc. Second, these streams are complimentary and mutually supportive.

As a result, process evolution efforts frequently fail to assure a company's long-term viability because the concurrent streams of activity are not coordinated, their results are inconsistent, and the streams do not effectively support each other. Exacerbating the situation is the fact that a noticeable lack of positive results frequently leads to a reduced resource allocation which, of course, only further diminishes the effect and value of the process evolution efforts.

To summarize:

- improvement game plans do provide valuable, cost-effective results,
- the impact of these results is often diminished because the business context changes before the results can be fully implemented,
- effective process evolution requires concentrated, broad-scope attention to the company's business context, and
- effective process evolution requires well-coordinated attention to several conceptually different, but highly inter-related, themes each of which is attempting to cope with changes to some part of the context.

3 Process Evolution Framework

We have developed a Process Evolution Dynamics Framework that allows a company's process change agents to describe, understand, learn from, plan and manage process evolution efforts. The basis for the framework is to recognize that each theme is addressed by a focused stream of activities and that there is extensive, complex inter-stream interaction. The framework's basic intent is to allow the activity streams, as well as the interactions among them, to be separately and concretely specified.

3.1 Framework Objectives

After actively participating in more than a dozen process evolution efforts, and reviewing reports and detailed records from more than a dozen others, we have found that: 1) most efforts – including the best planned ones – appear to be somewhat chaotic in nature, 2) there is always an order underlying the apparent chaos, and 3) this underlying order may be articulated in terms of interacting streams of activities belonging to one of twelve activity categories (described in the next Section)..

We have found that these activity categories are pertinent to both long-term efforts, lasting one or more years, and short-term ones, lasting only a few weeks or months. We have also found they are not only pertinent to process evolution efforts guided by well-defined plans but also to efforts that are relatively unplanned and unmanaged. Finally, we have found that the activity categories are pertinent to processes that govern a company's large-scale, engineering efforts – for example, its software development and maintenance processes – as well as to its more narrowly-focused, operational procedures – for example, its travel-reimbursement and report-production processes. We feel these activities form a "basis set" for process evolution – all process evolution efforts are comprised of a (perhaps complex) combination of activities, each belonging to one of the activity categories; no process evolution efforts involve activities which do not belong to one of the categories.

The purpose of the framework is to allow the "orderly chaos" underlying process evolution efforts to be clearly and succinctly articulated in terms of the twelve activity categories. One objective is to allow process change agents to discover and unambiguously describe complex, apparently chaotic, process evolution efforts. A second is to allow the change agents to transcend the details and gain a "higher level" understanding of "What happened?" A third objective is to allow the change agents to identify lessons learned and guidance that may positively affect the company's future process evolution efforts. The fourth and final objective is to allow the change agents to successfully plan and manage future process evolution efforts.

3.2 Process Evolution Dynamics Framework

The framework is depicted in Figure 1 using a "flower-petal" notation – first suggested by Kouichi Kishida [13] – to connote that the activities may be carried out in an arbitrary order but are sequenced according to how they use and produce process-related information. Twelve activity categories comprise the core of the Process Evolution Dynamics Framework. Each category has specific objectives which contribute to meeting the goals of four process evolution stages. Each also involves the accumulation and maturation of three categorically different kinds of process-related information. In the following, we first discuss the stages, then the three kinds of process-related information, and finally the activity categories themselves.

Process Evolution Stages. Several models have been developed to characterize improvement efforts. One is Shewhart's Plan-Do-Study-Act (PDSA) statistical quality-control model [14] underlying Deming's work on quality improvement [15]. Another is the QIP software engineering-oriented improvement model [16]. A third is the IDEAL software development process-improvement model [17]. The Process Evolution Dynamics Framework is based on an improvement model that mirrors She

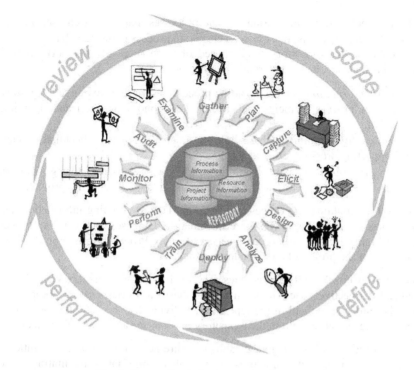

Fig. 1. Process Evolution Dynamics Framework

whart's model, simplifies the QIP and IDEAL models, and focuses on the activities occurring during process evolution. It has four stages:

scope. The goal during this stage is to establish a process evolution effort's context, requirements, progress-related metrics and plan.

define. During this stage, the goal is to develop descriptions of the processes that should be used and assure that they, and their descriptions, are complete, consistent and accurate.

perform. During this stage, the goal is to gather use-based qualitative and quantitative information about the quality of the processes and their descriptions.

review. The goal during this stage is to demonstrate process suitability and prepare for any future process evolution required to correct any failings that are discovered.

Process Evolution Repository. During a process evolution effort, the activities each use, modify and produce information relevant to some aspect of the processes being evolved or their performance. Over time, this information becomes a repository of all that is known about the company's processes and their effective, efficient, accurate performance. Also over time, the repository accumulates and organizes information about all of the versions and variants of the processes that have been used in actual projects[1]. The repository is, in essence, a corporate process knowledge base.

Conceptually, the repository is composed of three (logically distinct) databases, each holding a categorically different kind of information:

- a *Process Information* database holding process descriptions expressed, rigorously, in terms of process elements (activities, roles, conditions, etc.) and their inter-relationships,
- a *Resource Information* database holding assets (templates, checklists, policies, etc.) supporting process performance, and
- a *Project Information* database holding specific work products (designs, meeting minutes, white papers, etc.) produced during the course of a specific project.

The repository contains <u>one</u> Process Information database holding information about all of its process sets, <u>several</u> Resource Information databases each pertaining to collection of highly inter-related process sets, and <u>many</u> Project Information databases, one for each of the projects being conducted by the company.

Process Evolution Activity Categories. The twelve activity categories are depicted in Figure 1. Collectively, activities falling into these categories serve to complete and mature the information held in the repository. Individually, the activities use, modify and produce information held in the repository in order to satisfy specific objectives.

Gather. Activities in this category establish requirements for a process evolution effort – and the processes it will address – and collect information facilitating process performance. The objective is to find, filter and organize information that impacts the company's processes (e.g., regulatory constraints or budget/personnel-availability constraints) and their evolution (e.g., maturation frameworks), or can be used to support performance of the processes resulting from the process evolution effort (e.g., templates, checklist or best-practice specifications).

Plan. These activities develop plans for a process evolution effort and define the criteria used to measure progress and success. The objective is to define process requirements, measurable evolution objectives, and a manageable plan for the process evolution effort.

Capture. These activities gather and organize information about the company's should-be processes — the processes as they are currently specified. The objective is to establish a process architecture[2] and use it to organize and record the definition of the company's processes.

---

[1] By *project* we do not mean merely the projects a company uses to organize and track its work, the productivity of its workforce, its profitability, etc. A project may be formally commissioned and actively managed, for example, a project commissioned to develop a new version of a product. Alternatively, it may be neither formally commissioned – for example the "project" by which employees trade information about their experiences in carrying out their work – nor fully, actively managed – for example, the "project" by which a team collaboratively produces the company's Annual Financial Report.

[2] A process architecture specifies a set of process element types (for example, a `role` process element type) as well as formalisms for rigorously specifying process elements and relationships among them [18].

Elicit. These activities gather and organize information about the company's as-is processes, the processes actually being performed. The objective is to understand how process performers carry out the processes in practice, how the processes have been tailored and customized, and the workforce's individual and collective thoughts about possible changes.

Design. These activities specify the company's to-be processes — the processes the company wishes to use in the future. The objective is to define processes that conform to constraints, utilize the identified process performance resources, and reflect the workforces' experiences and expertise.

Analyze. These activities focus on the completeness, consistency and suitability of the processes and their descriptions. The objective is to analyze the processes and process descriptions to identify errors or anomalies (i.e., aspects of the processes or their descriptions that might be errors) and make appropriate change requests or suggestions.

Deploy. These activities disseminate descriptions of the processes throughout the company. The objective is to deliver new or revised process descriptions, help ongoing projects migrate to the processes as required and feasible, and gather information regarding the ease or difficulty of introducing the processes within the company.

Train. These activities provide on-the-job and course-based process education and training to new hires and the current work force. The objective is to establish the workforce's ability to accurately, effectively and efficiently carry out the processes.

Perform. These activities concern accurately, effectively and efficiently performing the processes during a project. Support for assuring process performance accuracy, effectiveness and efficiency may be provided by dedicated personnel ("process mentors") or electronically (i.e., via process enactment support). With respect to process evolution, the objective is to adapt the company's generic processes to a project's specific needs, gather qualitative process performance-related information, and reveal, through actual use, any problems with the processes and their documentation.

Monitor. These activities track process performance. With respect to process evolution, the objective is to obtain quantitative, longitudinal data about the performance of the process over many projects.

Audit. These activities involve reviewing the processes, and their performance, with respect to requirements levied by standards and maturity frameworks. The objective is to assess conformance to regulatory or contractual constraints.

Examine. These activities analyze and organize feedback from the other activities. The objective is to develop a prioritized list of potential process changes with an indication of their criticality, update current resources, and gather new resources resulting from use of the processes.

4 Example Framework Application

To illustrate how the Process Evolution Dynamics Framework may be used to describe the order underlying the (apparent) chaos of a process evolution effort, we provide a case study followed by a brief discussion of what it reveals about using the framework for describing process evolution efforts.

4.1 Case Study

A multi-national manufacturer has developed a set of processes governing the "birth-to-death" design, marketing, development, delivery and maintenance of their products' software components. Their products are subject to regulatory constraints levied by a Governmental organization. To date, they have been appraised at CMM Level II and wish to move to Level III. Prior to a Level III-oriented appraisal, they will be audited with respect to the regulatory constraints. Their processes are described in several Word documents, one per set of highly inter-related processes, for example, one document for their three different kinds of Peer Review processes and one for their Requirements Management processes. They are aware of many problems in their process documentation, ranging from simple inconsistencies (e.g., different role names in different documents) to process-logic errors (e.g., work products not produced before they are needed) to incompatibilities across their process sets (e.g., inconsistent definitions of the interfaces between processes in different sets). In addition, they are finding that manual maintenance of the documents is not only increasingly error prone but also starting to consume so much time that deployment of new versions can not be accomplished in a timely manner. Finally, they have received several requests for views better satisfying process performer needs (e.g., a table that reflects document production/usage by activities) and have recognized the need to provide views that support non-performance needs (e.g., views supporting workforce training, conformance audits and capability appraisals).

Evolution Effort Scope. The company's Software Engineering Process Group (SEPG) decides to focus on their software development processes and simultaneously prepare for their regulatory-constraint audit and Level III appraisal, correct the noted inconsistencies and errors, move from their Word-based documentation to Web-Guides[3], and include new process performance-related views as much as possible. They consciously decide to delay work on related processes, for example, process training and process documentation-deployment processes; before evolving these other processes, they plan to gain experience through performing them in the context of evolving the software development processes. Additionally, they consciously decide to delay producing audit- or appraisal-oriented views; again, they plan to use experience during the upcoming audit and appraisal to guide development of these views.

Evolution Effort Goals. The SEPG launches a process evolution effort having the following goals:

- G1: Update <u>all</u> of the company's software development processes in preparation for the upcoming audit and appraisal.

---

[3] By *Web-Guide* we mean process documentation web-sites developed using applications such as Dreamweaver [19], iNotion [20], Spearmint/PMC [21], and IRIS [22].

- G2: Correct errors and inconsistencies noted to date as well as problems and inconsistencies uncovered by several levels of review (by the SEPG itself, by personnel from various divisions invited to review the new processes, and by the workforce in general).
- G3: Convert the company's software process documentation to WebGuides to be deployed via the company's intra-net.

Evolution Effort Strategy. The SEPG decides to initially focus on just two of its software process sets – **Peer Review** and **Requirements Management**. By initially addressing more than one process set, the SEPG intends to develop a process architecture appropriate for all of its software development processes. By simultaneously addressing two process sets, it intends to define a reasonable approach to evolving a process set as well as an understanding of the inter-play among the evolution of different process sets.

After some, but perhaps not all, of the work on these two process sets has been completed, the SEPG plans to move on to its other software development process sets – Quality Assurance, Design and Implementation, Testing, etc. Because of time pressures, the SEPG plans to move on to addressing other process sets as soon as they feel that their approach to working on a process set is reasonably well-defined and stable. They are willing, in other words, to forego achieving a <u>perfect</u> process set evolution process in favor of achieving a <u>reasonable</u> process that may have to, itself, evolve over time.

Process Set Evolution Cycle. With respect to a process set, the SEPG plans to evolve its processes using a highly iterative steam of activities. This activity stream is described in the following and depicted, in terms of the framework's activity categories, in Figure 2.

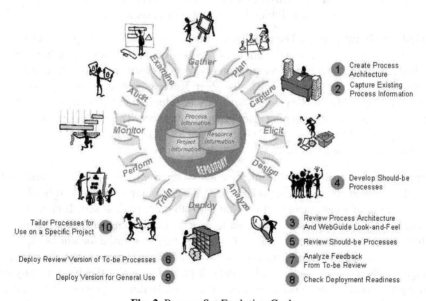

Fig. 2. Process Set Evolution Cycle

1. Define a process architecture pertinent to the process set's processes.
2. Capture the information in existing Word documentation.
3. Generate an example Web-Guide and review it to validate the process architecture and the Web-Guide look-and-feel.

    Iterate activities 1-through-3 as necessary.

4. Improve the process definitions and correct errors and inconsistencies noted to date.
5. Generate Web-Guides and have the SEPG use them to identify errors and inconsistencies in the processes and process descriptions.

    Iterate activities 4-through-5 as necessary.
    Iterate activities 1, 3-through-5 as necessary.

6. Deploy a test version of the Web-Guides for review by a select group of personnel with respect to the suitability of the processes in the process set.
7. Analyze the feedback from the review and identify issues that need to be addressed

    Iterate activities 4-through-7 as necessary.
    Iterate activities 1, 3-through-7 as necessary.

8. Assure that the processes, and their Web-Guides, are ready for deployment throughout the company.
9. Deploy Web-Guides throughout the company.
10. Tailor the processes to meet the needs of specific projects and the abilities and experiences of project personnel, noting not only the changes needed to tailor the processes but also any errors and inconsistencies in the processes or the Web-Guides.

    Iterate activities 4-through-10 as necessary.
    Iterate activities 1, 3-through-10 as necessary.

Cycle-to-cycle Influences. The SEPG recognizes that changes to the processes within one process set will influence the changes needed to the processes in another process set. It plans to use changes to **Requirements Management** processes to understand the changes that might be needed to the **Peer Review** processes, and *vice versa*. It plans to address this cross-cycle influence by developing and evolving, through experience, a process for managing inter-process interfaces. The SEPG recognizes that this introduces a "broader scope" activity stream that coordinates changes across multiple process set evolution cycles.

Completion. The SEPG plans to incrementally increase the scope of its attention to all of the software development processes. At the beginning of its work, it has little to no knowledge of when it can start to "move on" to other process sets. It plans to continuously reflect on the results achieved to date to decide whether or not the process architecture and Process Set Evolution Cycle are ready to be used for addressing additional process sets. It recognizes that work on additional process sets may lead to changes to the processes addressed to date. It plans to address this by gradually expanding the scope of the process-to-process interface definition process. It recognizes that this introduces yet another activity stream.

4.2 Case Study Discussion

The case study indicates that the evolution of a process set may be described as a stream of activities, each falling into one of the activity categories. Mapping the activities to the categories highlights the activities' objectives by indicating the information they may use and should produce. It also highlights the information flow constraints that order activity performance; while the activity stream is defined as if the activities are performed sequentially, they may, in actuality, proceed concurrently with the flow of information introducing any necessary ordering. Finally, it highlights the kinds of activities which have not been included thereby helping the SEPG understand potential failings in its Process Set Evolution Cycle.

The case study indicates that additional activity streams will be needed to handle the evolution of non software development-related process sets (e.g., the Interface Definition process set). The Process Set Evolution Cycle defined above could be used to evolve these other process sets. In all likelihood, however, these activity streams would be different, if only because they are carried out by other personnel and are conducted in other timeframes. These activity streams could be described and mapped to the Process Evolution Dynamics Framework's activity categories; because of length restrictions, these descriptions and mappings are not included in this paper.

As explained in the case study, the process evolution effort appears to be rather orderly. This, in part, demonstrates that the framework allows the "order underlying the chaos" to be described. Further demonstration comes from considering that:

- in every Process Evolution Cycle, ten activities are iteratively and concurrently performed with synchronization being effected by information flow,
- the company that is the subject of this case study has 14 software development-related process sets and many other process sets (for example, their Conformance Audit, Capability Appraisal, and Process Training process sets), and
- there will be a process governing the interactions among the Process Set Evolution Cycles for the software development-related process sets as well as other process sets to address the interactions between these cycles and cycles for other, non software development-related, processes.

In short, there will be hundreds of activities all proceeding concurrently but ordered by well-defined rules for information flow. The overall effort will, without a doubt, appear to be chaotic; but there is an underlying order and this can be exposed by using the Process Evolution Dynamics Framework.

5 Summary and Future Work

We have defined a Process Evolution Dynamics Framework we believe facilitates rational, rapid, incremental process evolution in response to changes to customer desires, marketplace structure, personnel availability and capability, business goals, and available technology as well as many other business-context factors. We believe that the framework fosters the business context-oriented co-evolution of a company's processes – by achieving major, long-term process evolution through narrowly focused, overlapping process change cycles – and that this has several key advantages:

- maintain management attention and support in times of resource restrictions,
- provide the value and pertinence demonstrations needed to gain personnel support,
- match the pace of current-day marketplace, business-need, workforce and technology changes, and
- gather the lessons-learned experience and process-performer insights needed to make valuable additional changes.

The framework is based on a categorization of process evolution-related activities that we have found, through experience, to be critical and fundamental. The framework identifies the activity categories and highlights their inter-dependencies in terms of their collective, collaborative maturation of a company's process knowledge base.

In this paper, we have rationalized and defined the framework and provided a case study illustrating its use to describe process evolution efforts. We have also alluded to additional work [23] in which we have found that the framework may also be used to help process change agents understand, learn from, plan and manage process evolution efforts. This additional work addresses several topics we feel warrant the attention of the process research and empirical study communities. These topics include:

- Empirical Studies: Develop empirical evidence that the framework reflects a broad spectrum of actual situations and leads to process evolution issue resolutions that are better than those achieved through improvement game plans.
- Process Evolution Understanding: Develop visualizations allowing process change agents to transcend the detailed descriptions such as depicted in Figure 2 and articulate lessons-learned, experience reports and guidance that may be considered for incorporation into the company's processes during future process evolution efforts.
- Process Evolution Planning: Define a process evolution planning process providing guidelines and scenarios based on various process evolution contextual parameters and drivers suggested by the framework.
- Process Evolution Process Evaluation: Use the framework to identify factors and measures useful in evaluating alternative process evolution approaches with respect to efficiency, effectiveness and value.
- Process Evolution Tool Suite Selection: Use the framework to identify factors and measures useful in comparatively evaluating commercial and research-prototype tools suites supporting process evolution.

Acknowledgements

This work has been influenced – directly and indirectly – through the authors' collaborations with many people in many organizations including: University of Michigan, Software Design & Analysis Inc., Fraunhofer Institute for Experimental Software Engineering, Software Engineering Institute, and TeraQuest Metrics Inc. People at these organizations who have had a major impact include: Dave Barstow, Fabio Bella, Marc Kellner, Beth Layman, Jürgen Münch, Alexis Ocampo, Don Oxley, Dick Phillips, John Sayler, Henry Schneider, Joyce Statz, Ian Thomas and Lyn Uzzle.

References

1. International Standards Organization (ISO), *Quality Management Systems: Requirements*, ISO 9001 (International Standards Organization, Geneva, Switzerland).
2. *Information Security Management – Specification for Information Security Management Systems*, BS 7799-2 (Business Standards Institution (BSI) Group, London, United Kingdom, 2002).
3. *Capability Maturity Model for Software, Version.1.1*, CMU/SEI-93-TR-024, ADA 263403 (Carnegie Mellon University, Software Engineering Institute, Pittsburgh, Pennsylvania, 1993).
4. *Control Objectives for Information and related Technology (COBIT) – Release 3.1* (Information Systems Audit and Control Association, Rolling Meadows, Illinois, 2004).
5. P. Abrahamsson, O. Salo, J. Ronkainen and J. Warsta, Agile Software Development Methods: Review and Analysis, VTT Publications 478 (VTT Technical Research Centre of Finland, Vuorimiehentie, Finland, 2002).
6. J. Highsmith and A. Cockburn, *Agile Software Development: The Business of Innovation*, IEEE Computer (September, 2001), pp. 120-122 (IEEE Computer Society Press, Los Alamitos, California).
7. *IEEE Software Engineering Standards Collection*, CD-ROM (IEEE Computer Society Press, Los Alamitos, California, 2003).
8. *A Guide to the Project Management Body of Knowledge (PMBOK® Guide)* (Project Management Institute (PMI), Newtown Square, Pennsylvania, 2000).
9. P. Ferguson, G. Leman, P. Perini, S. Renner and G. Seshagiri, *Software Process Improvement Works!*, CMU/SEI-99-TR-027, ESC-TR-99-026 (Carnegie Mellon University, Software Engineering Institute, Pittsburgh, Pennsylvania, 2002, November 1999).
10. B. Curtis, B. Hefley and S. Miller, *People Capability Maturity Model* (Addison-Wesley Publishing Co., Boston, Massachusetts, 2001).
11. V. Subramanyam, S. Deb, P. Krishnaswamy and R. Ghosh, *An Integrated Approach to Software Process Improvement at Wipro Technologies: veloci-Q*, CMU/SEI-2004-TR-006 (Carnegie Mellon University, Software Engineering Institute, Pittsburgh, Pennsylvania, 2004).
12. R. Nichols and C. Connaughton, *Software Process Improvement Journey: IBM Australia Application Management Services*, CMU/SEI-2005-TE-002 (Carnegie Mellon University, Software Engineering Institute, Pittsburgh, Pennsylvania, March 2005).
13. K. Kishida, *Informal Remarks during the Second International Software Process Workshop, Coto de Caza, California, March 1985*, Software Engineering Notes (August 1986), (ACM, New York, New York).
14. Walter A. Shewhart. *Economic Control of Quality of Manufactured Product* (Original Publication: 1931) (Re-issue Edition: American Society for Quality, Milwaukee, Wisconsin, December 1980).
15. E. Deming, *Out of the Crisis* (MIT Center for Advanced Engineering Study, Cambridge, Massachusetts, 1986).
16. V. Basili, G. Caldiera, and D. Rombach. The Experience Factory. *Encyclopedia of Software Engineering Vol. 1*, J. Marciniak (ed), pp. 469-476 (John Wiley & Sons Inc., Hoboken, New Jersey, 1994).
17. R. McFeeley, *IDEAL: A User's Guide for Software Process Improvement*, CMU/SEI-1996-HB-001 (Carnegie Mellon University, Software Engineering Institute, Pittsburgh, Pennsylvania, 1996).
18. W. Riddle. *Coping with Process Specification*. Proceedings 2003 Integrated Design and Process Technology Conference, IDPT-2003, Austin, Texas, December 2003 (Society for Design and Process Technology, Austin, Texas).
19. Dreamweaver. macromedia, San Francisco, California.

20. iNotion. I-Logix, Andover, Massachusetts.
21. Spearmint/PMC Tool Suites. Fraunhofer Institut Experimentelles Software Engineering, Kaiserslautern, Germany.
22. IRIS. Osellus, Toronto, Canada.
23. B. Nejmeh and W. Riddle. *Coping with Process Evolution*, Technical Report 2005-01 (Solution Deployment Affiliates, Santa Fe, New Mexico, in progress).

Software Process Management: Practices in China*

Qing Wang[1] and Mingshu Li[1,2]

[1] Lab for Internet Software Technologies,
Institute of Software, Chinese Academy of Sciences,
No 4, South Fourth Street, Zhong Guan Cun, P.O. Box 8718, Beijing 10 00 80, China
[2] State Key Lab of Computer Science,
Institute of Software at Chinese Academy of Sciences,
No 4, South Fourth Street, Zhong Guan Cun, P.O. Box 8718, Beijing 10 00 80, China
wq@itechs.iscas.ac.cn, lms@admin.iscas.ac.cn

Abstract. Software process management has been proven a useful means to help software organizations improve their development processes and produce high quality products. It focuses on providing process-related products and services to software developer. Chinese software industry is developing rapidly. Effective software process methods, technology and tools that help them produce quality products while reducing the costs are in desperate need. This paper discusses the current state of project management in Chinese software companies and presents a solution and practices meeting this need.

1 Introduction

Software engineering is an engineering discipline with goal of ensuring the software development and production under the cost control, schedule prediction and quality achievement [1].

Software engineering concerned with all aspects of software life cycle from the early stages of requirement analysis to system maintenance. Since the concept of software crises was first defined in 1970's, software engineering has been evolved and extended into a variety of directions and areas by researchers and practitioners, trying to eventually solve the problem. Though numerous achievements have been made, the expected objective is far away from coming true. From 1980s, the software process technology began to attract people's attention. It tries to use well defined processes to plan and control the development activities of software, the necessary visibility out of development team is provided and the shared vision of project in organization is established and maintained, to ensure the software relative products are delivered under budget, on schedule and satisfying the custom's need [2].

Software process technology adopts many successful process methods and technologies from manufacturing industry. It also follows the commonly principle of modern quality management concepts [3], such as customer focus, decision making

---

* Supported by the National Natural Science Foundation of China under grant Nos. 60473060, 60273026 as well as the Hi-Tech Research and Development Program (863 Program) of China under grant Nos. 2004AA112080, 2005AA113140.

M. Li, B. Boehm, and L.J. Osterweil (Eds.): SPW 2005, LNCS 3840, pp. 317–331, 2005.

based on actual project situation data and reasonable analysis, and continual process improvement.

The objective of software process management is institutionalizing the activities of software development with process method [4], performing these activities under plan, with clearly identified objectives and shared vision, and finally delivering custom satisfactory products. The essential problems that the software process management must solve are software estimate, project and process planning, project monitoring and control, performance evaluating [5], and continual process improvement.

Chinese Academy of Science (ISCAS) has been focusing its research on the area of software process methods and technology since late 1990's. According to practices, it's appeared that the elements that affect products quality are people, technique and management. The three dimension's elements should be integrated to provide service for software processes. And then lead to improve process and promote technique compliantly. Based on these ideas, ISCAS provide a solution for software process management. This solution abstract the primary problem of software quality management, software development technique and people services supporting, address to help software organization develop and manage their software projects more effectively. The solution around software lifecycle, support primary software development activities from requirement elicit, implementation to testing and delivery, as well as the quality management activities, such as process definition, project planning and tracking, quality review and audit, process data and asset assembling, measurement and analyzing. Some supporting activities, such as training, knowledge information service, agreement review and monitor are included too. A powerful framework was constructed to integrate these research methods and a toolkit called SoftPM was developed. SoftPM provide a integrative system to help software organizations develop and manage their projects under a well defined software process discipline.

2   Process Issues Within Chinese Software Industry

Nowadays, Software industry becomes the sunrising industry with the rapid development in China. According to the statistics of Chinese Software Industry Association (CSIA) [6], in 2003, the annual sale of information products in China is 1880 billion, ranked the third in the world. The sale of software products among them is 160 billion with an increase by 45.45% than 2002, among which 2.5% is from globe software products sale. By the end of 2003, there are more 8700 software companies and more than 620 thousands software practitioners in China. All data shows a dramatic increase.

Chinese government has enacted several supportive policies and established various funds to accelerate the development of software industry. To enhance the development and deployment of software industry, from 2001, the national software industry bases and software export bases was planed based on the excellent software parks which have been developed from 1995. By 2004, there are 11 national software industry bases, 6 national software export bases that have got assessed and approved. The 863 software incubators are sponsored by Chinese Ministry of Science and technology with the goal of promoting software industry through technical incubation. There are fifteen 863 software incubators have been approved by 2004. All this provides a very advantageous environment for the rapid development of software industry.

However, software industry in China is yet in the beginning stage. Most software companies have their management and technique in an ad hoc style. Many companies haven't established the formal and appropriate process management system. To address it, the advanced software process model must be introduced and applied compliant with the Chinese situation. There are more than 100 software organizations deployed CMM or CMMI by 2004, but not all of them get benefit from it in deed. Actually, the CMM/CMMI is a descriptive model in the sense that it describes essential attributes of a software process would normally be expected to be. It does not constrain how the software process is implemented by an organization. The CMM/CMMI is not prescriptive, and it does not tell an organization how to improve. In any context in which the CMM/CMMI is applied, a reasonable interpretation of the practices should be used. Software process improvement occurs within the context of the organization's strategic plans and business objectives, its organizational structure, the technologies in use, its social culture, and its management system [7]. CMM/CMMI must be appropriately interpreted when applied, solutions and tools supporting when applied will be more helpful. In fact, the lack of method and technology for supporting the application of CMM/CMMI and similar standards is the bottleneck of process improvement efforts in China.

As we said before, although some related standards and software process model, such as CMM, ISO 9001, provide the methodology guidance to establish and maintain the software process, they just solve the problem of what need to do. How to do it also needs the practices of application method and technology.

Moreover, process management is also costly. How to involve the related thing work together, provide the way to incorporate knowledge to perform better, leverage the resource and examine business trend? Some powerful and effective supporting tools are required. Actually, especially in China, many software companies can not apply ISO9000, CMM and CMMI effectively. The difficulties are: 1) software process is also a discipline, the theory concept and primary principle should be taught and spread, 2) the technical solution to develop software is also very important, the process improvement must be concurrent with the appropriate technology enhancement, otherwise they will fall in discomfiture resulted in disjoint of management and technique. The absolute and inherent essence is serious lack of the support tools and related practices. There is an urgent need of some effective tools and application practices that are compliant with Chinese nature.

In its initial phase, the software quality engineers in China are very insufficient. Most project managers and software quality assurance people only have a rough understanding about software process technology. The lower level of applications results in the ineffective use of the advanced methods, technologies and tools. The consulting and practices guidance must be required to help understand and use them.

3   A Solution for Software Process Management

Research on software process technology is across a broad spectrum. The primary genres are 1) addressed by the overall architecture, behavioral characteristics of processes and higher level capability to fit the business and mission goals of organization, (called *macroprocess*); 2) focused on precise, complete, detailed and unambiguous definition of software processes to help human-machine synergies inherent in software processes, (called *microprocess*). The trend of unifying the two ways is also emerged. Actually, the latter provides a rigor granularity and strength of the macro process management in the former. And the ideology of macro management promotes the definition to practice and effect.

Based on these, ISCAS presents a solution for software process management that integrates the management, technique and people which the key elements affect the process, from precise process modeling to macro process control. The framework obeys the concept of Total Quality Management (TQM), conforms the inherent of software process, explore a total solution for software process management.

Our Solution has three levels, as shown in Figure 1. The bottom level is research work, such as the process modeling methods, measurement model, requirements elicitation, knowledge management and so on. The middle level is the integrated framework with three platform, they are:

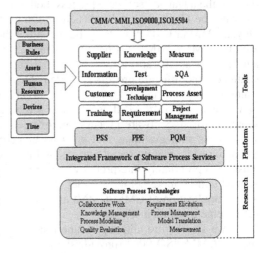

Fig. 1. The concept of solution

- Platform for Quality Management – PQM
- Platform for Product Engineering – PPE
- Platform for Service Supporting – PSS

The top level is tools which are integrated in the three platforms.

The solution provides a collaborative working environment for senior managers, project managers, developers, SQAs, customers, suppliers and so on.

The features of the solution are as follows:

- Serving for Lifecycle
- Depending on measurement
- Supporting continual process improvement
- Having an open integrated framework

3.1 Serving for Lifecycle

Our solution implemented and provided basic activities to establish and evolve the quality of software [8] that is around whole software lifecycle, as shown in Figure 2.

As the evolving of quality in the whole lifecycle, the different technique and process services are needed.

At the first, eliciting customer's requirement is important. The method and technique to support requirement development and management is expected. After requirement is confirmed, the internal quality is monitored and controlled under the appropriate technique solution and process management. Before delivering, measurement and evaluation are applied to verify and validate the external quality and quality in use of software products. In addition, some services such as training, customer, supplier and

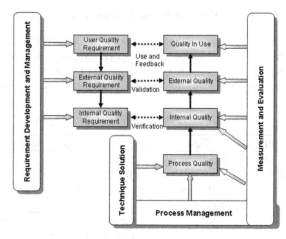

Fig. 2. Serving for lifecycle

general information are asked through the lifecycle. All above method and technique are included and supported by our solution.

3.2 Depending on Measurement

Measurement is one of the essential elements of software processes. Without measurement, it's hard to well understand software process and produce high quality product. When you can measure and describe the thing use numbers, you can understand what is actually going on.

Effective measurement can

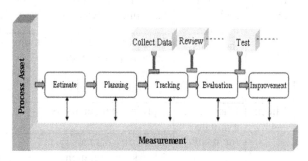

Fig. 3. Process management based on measurement

be used to help identifying, analyzing, and solving the problems arising during the development process, to evaluate and improve the capability maturity of processes, and to predict the quality of process products [9], [10].

In our solution, measurement is the basis of any kind of process management, not only for higher maturity level organizations, but for organizations at lower level. Actually in CMMI, measurement and analysis is a basic process area was categorized in maturity level 2. This solution presents a active measurement model for process control and improvement [11].

In our solution, Based on appropriate measurement, software organizations can establish their standard processes and process assets reasonably and consistently, guiding the development through various engineering stages such as estimate, planning, tracking, evaluate and improvement, as shown in Figure 3.

3.3 Supporting Continual Process Improvement

1930s, W. A. Shewhart presented the famous PDCA cycle for quality improvement. By the end of 1950s, some experts in quality management like W. Ewards Deming, Joseph Juran contributed the concept of TQC (Total Quality Control). TQC provides a framework for the improvement of process and system, based on PDCA. Nowadays,

Table 1. The activities categorize by PDCA and mapping to CMMI

PDCA	Task	Basic Activities	CMMI PA
Plan – P	Diagnose, estimate and planning	1.estimate and requirement management 2.define project processes 3.project development plan	PP, REQM, PPQA,MA
		9.define organization standard processes 10.quality assurance plan	OPF,OPD, OPP, MA PPQA,
		17.determine the objective of project quality 18.measurement plan 19.process performance baseline 20.indicator system for product evaluation	MA, OPP
Do— D	Perform and monitor the plans	4.task report, 5.project report 6.supplier service	PMC, SAM,CM
		11.quality report, 12.trainning service 26.customer service 27.test 28.requirement elicit	ISM, IPM OT,PI, TS, RD,IT, VER,VAL
Check —C	Check and evaluate the result	7.project data analysis	MA,PPQA QPM
		13.quality data analysis 14.risk management	PPQA,RS KM
		21.quantitatively process control 22. process status analysis 23.quality evaluation	QPM
Act— A	Analysis and improve the process assets	8.process improvement plan	DAR OID,OEI
		15.process documents management 16.process assets management	
		24.process evaluation and improvement	
		25.root causal analysis and resolution	CAR
Deploy the next cycle for continual improvement		8.process improvement plan 9.define organization standard process 19.process performance baseline 20.indicator system for product evaluation	CAR,OID, OPF,OPD, OPP

ISO9000, CMM/CMMI serials and ISO/IEC 15504, all are derived from the concept from these [12].

Our solution is based on TQM and compliant with ISO9000/CMM/CMMI. We categorize all the activities by PDCA cycle as shown in Table 1.

In table 1, each activity has a number, they are not ordered top down, but ordered by PDCA cycle from lower level improvement to higher level's.

When an organization sets up its process management system, each activity can be mapped to the reference process model compliant with PDCA, such as CMM, CMMI and ISO9000.

For example in our solution, if an organization establishes a quality system that refer to CMMI, he can select the related activities depend on level of CMMI and the mapping of CMMI and PDCA to generate the appropriate tools-support system, as illustrated in Figure 4.

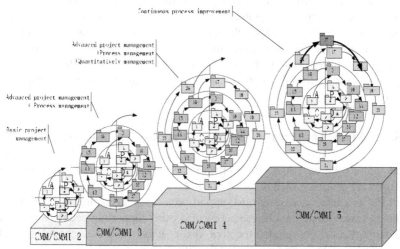

Notes: the numbers of activities refer to Table 1.

Fig. 4. The solution mapping to CMM/CMMI

3.4 Having an Open Integrated Framework

Our solution also provides an open infrastructure. It follows the three-tier architecture and based on J2EE, therefore it is platform-independent.

Customers can select different system software and configure the run time environment. The basic configurable system items it can be deployed on as listed in Table 2.

The solution supports software organizations establish their management system compliant different standards and models, such as ISO 9000, CMM, CMMI and so on.

Internationalization support allows the generation of Chinese, English, Japanese and other language version automatically with respective resource file.

Table 2. The system software environment for the solution

Class	Chinese Commerce Software	International Commerce Software	Open Source Software
OS	Redflag Linux. Co-Create linux, CS&S Linux	Windows XP, Windows NT. Solaris	Redhat Linux
DBMS	KingBase ES	SQL Server. Oracle. Sybase	Mysql, MaxDB. PostgreSQL
Application Servers	OnceAS, Apusic	WebSphere. WebLogic	Tomcat

Another important feature in our solution is that it can integrate other tools developed by the third parties. As figure 1 illustrate, the solution includes three platforms, each platform integrated some tools, and the third party's tools also can be integrated here. For example, the COCOMO tools can be integrated into PQM. These tools provide the basic activities for software process management. While adopting the solution, customer can select different tools and configure to appropriate support system compliant their capability level and/or continual improvement objective.

4   SoftPM: A Toolkit for Software Process Management

Based on our solution, ISCAS develop a toolkit to help software organization manage their software process which is called SoftPM.

SoftPM is a integrated system to support project managers, higher level managers, engineers, tester, quality assurance people and other supporting people work together, share the collected data and respective vision, understand the schedule, effort and quality of project and communicate effectively.

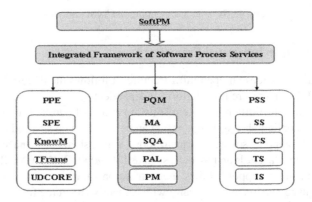

Fig. 5. The three levels of SoftPM

4.1 Platform for Quality Management – PQM

PQM is the most important platform in SoftPM. It covers most process activities list in table 1. PQM includes four tools to supports primary project and process management activities. The four tools can be combined according to increasing process improvement requirement. There are three product levels with the combination of four tools and compliant with the CMM/CMMI. Stage representation, i.e.:

- Basic project process management (compliant CMM/CMMI level 2)
- Defined process management (compliant CMM/CMMI level 3)
- Quantitatively process management

The four tools are:

- **Project Management – PM**

The goal of project management is to provide a shared vision to make the projects being developed under appropriate visibility and controllability, produce quality products while productivity is enhanced and cost is reduced.

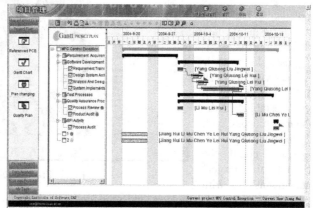

PM focuses on project planning (such as estimating the schedule, size and risk of project), project monitoring and control, improving

Fig. 6. Project plan made by Gantte

the efficiency of commitment and communication, collecting data for measurement, managing risks and analyzing project performance. PM uses Gantt view to establish and maintain the project plan and track the project development progress, as seen in Figure 6.

PM supports top-down task decompose and resource assign. The managers in each level just focus on what they need to do. He can allocate the sub-task to

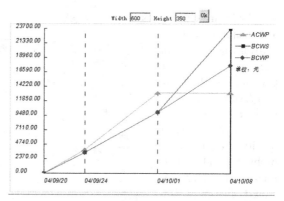

Fig. 7. Earn value of project cost

lower manager and assign the related responsibility and authority. The lower manager continual breaks down the task until the basic task unit, such as activities. The basic task units execute it and collect the related actual data. These data was assembled bottom-up to higher level manager and provide appropriate view.

For a given project, its process and development plan can be derived from standard process, imported from MS-Project or dynamically defined with the graphical component provided by PAL. PM also support multi-level project controls and facilitate large/outsourcing project management. Some necessary measure such as effort, schedule and earn value, is also applied in PM. Figure 7 presents the earn value measure for project cost.

- **Process Asset Library - PAL**

PAL defines, maintains the organizational standard processes and process asset, such as templates, historical data, assessment data and so on. PAL supports user define their processes visually even thought organization haven't established the standard process yet. All the activities of processes could be exported to Project Management with

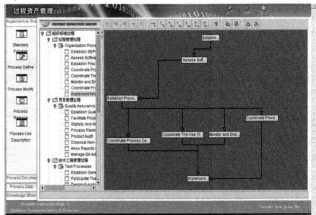

Fig. 8. Process definition

appropriate tailoring. Templates and guidelines are associated to each activity and make developers could perform their tasks easily.

Figure 8 illustrates the graphic interface of process definition.

- **Software Quality Assurance - SQA**

The major function of software quality assurance is to make quality planning (such as review/audit plan, test plan etc.), audit process and product, analyze quality data, issue problem and defect, track until them are closed. Figure 9 illustrates that SoftPM was applied to make quality plan and deliver quality report.

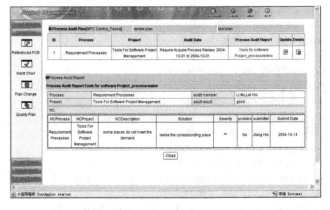

Fig. 9. Quality plan and assurance

- **Measurement and Analysis - MA**

Measurement and Analysis provides an open infrastructure to support organization to binding the measurement activities with the expect process quantitative management objectives. In MA a well–defined structure will be integrated into PM to enable data collection from project management activities easily. When an organization achieves high level maturity or capability, statistical process control (SPC) [13], [14] can be used to measure and control the performance of selected processes or sub-processes stability. Figure 10 illustrates how to select the sub-processes and projects under the quantitative management and then establish the quantitative objective.

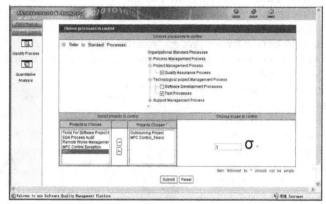

Fig. 10. Establish the quantitative objective

4.2 Platform for Product Engineering - PPE

The second platform in SoftPM is PPE. PPE is focused on solving the technical problems of product development, such as requirement eliciting, test, knowledge management to support the product development.

Currently, PPE includes four tools to support some engineering activities in software process. They are UDCORE (User-driven Domain-specific Component-based Requirements Elicitation), KnowM (Knowledge Management), TFrame(Test Framework) and SPE(Software Product Evaluation).

4.3 Platform for Service Supporting - PSS

The third platform in SoftPM is PSS, which is focused on provide customer service, supplier service, training service and general information service.

5   Application of SoftPM in China

From 2000, the variety versions of SoftPM were released in succession. They are SoftPM version1.0, SoftPM version 1.5, SoftPM version 2.0, SoftPM version 2.5 and SoftPM version 2.6. All of these versions have been applied in about 100 software relative companies. These companies provided many valuable feedback and practical experiments. Some of them use SoftPM many years. They contribute to and get benefit from each version upgrading.

5.1 Guidelines the Process Management and Improvement

In China, there are many software organizations applied SoftPM to establish and improve their software process management system. SoftPM helps them define the standard and project's processes, establish and maintain the process assets library, perform project management and quality assurance activities, collect the data for measurement, measure and evaluate the status of process performing and so on.

Use SoftPM, software organizations which are rated in CMMI ML2 can define their projects software process visually, estimate the size of software product, plan and track the project resource, schedule, work products and quality check list with Gantt graph, audit and review the processes and products quality, manage work products configuration, collect data and measure them for project management and software process improvement. The organizations which are rated in CMMI ML3 can define their organization standard processes and tailor to projects

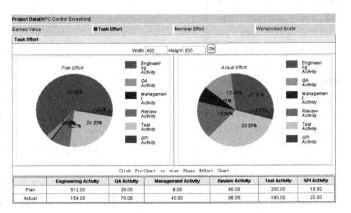

Fig. 11. Measurement for effort distribution

software process visually, elicit, implement and manage their customer requirement and deliver a customer satisfied products depend on our PPE and PQM platform, as well as execute the quality management activities the CMMI ML2's organizations executed. The organizations which are rated in and above CMMI ML4 can establish their process performance gradually and manage their processes and products quantitatively. Figure 11 is applied SoftPM to measure the efforts distribution for each software development activities.

SoftPM is not only applied to general process management, but also very useful to process improvement. Actually, quantitative management is the foundation of continual improvement. The key

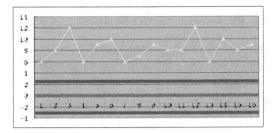

Fig. 12. The X-chart for schedule deviation

problem of quantitative process management is to establish the baseline of process performance. Process improvement is continually refined. The baseline is established and optimized gradually too. We usually apply SPC for process control. But the SPC applied must compliant the status of process. It's obvious that only the appropriate measurement will contribute to the organization. Unfortunately, many organizations collect many data but hardly use it correctly. In the case, the work for data collection is just a waste. Measurement should provide the useful information to help process control and improvement. We ever investigate many software companies in China, most of them don't know how to setup the effective measurement. For example, one of these companies wants to measure and control the schedule deviation. They used a normal baseline and use X-chart. They get the chart as figure 12.

As the figure 12 illustrates, almost all of the data exceeds the limit. They just know the schedule executed has some problem, but what is the reason remains unclearly. So they don't know how to correct and improve it.

After applied SoftPM, in this case, the process is not stable and the performance baseline hasn't been setup. Some other measurement algorithm such as deviation chart is suggested. Deviation chart uses $\mu \pm \sigma$ to measure the deviation of sample data. Figure 13 illustrates the schedule deviation of two teams. It can provide some valuable information to analyzing the causal of resulting in the deviation.

For figure 13(a), the average of schedule deviation is 0.71, which means the schedule executing conform the plan in the mass. But the standard deviation is 7.97, it means the capability of the team varies largely. The corrective action should be taken to improve the personal process capability and team process capability. For figure 13(b), the average of deviation is 10.58, it means the schedule is always delayed about 10.58%. But the standard deviation is 0.76, it means the capability of the team is stable, and the corrective action should be taken to improve the estimate and planning.

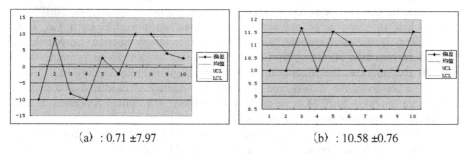

(a) : 0.71 ±7.97   (b) : 10.58 ±0.76

Fig. 13. The distribution measure for schedule deviation

Some companies, with the application of SoftPM, got the CMM assessment or CMMI appraise more effectively. Hangzhou Sunyard system engineering Co. Ltd applied SoftPM since 2002 to improve their software process. Sunyard got the assessment of CMM level in Aug. 2002 and CMM level 3 in Aug. 2003. Until 2004, the annual sale exceeds 25millions US dollars. As its report, the application of SoftPM increases the productivity effectively, the quality of products achieved the equivalent level of international high quality products, but the cost is reduced much more. The benefit result from applying SoftPM is more than 1 million US dollars.

Anyway, SoftPM provide a powerful support toolkit for software organizations to manage their process effectively. The toolkit covers CMM/CMMI Level 2-5. According to the feedback of customers, use SoftPM can save 35% effort of SEPG, SQA and project managers.

5.2 Wide Application

SoftPM has been used in many areas in China. The national software industry bases and 863 software incubators are important mechanisms to promote the software industry development with good environment for investment, new start-ups and incubating. SoftPM has been accepted and applied in 8 of 11 software bases, located across Beijing, Shanghai, Guangdong, Xian, Chengdu, Jiangshu, Zhuhai, Changsha, and all of the 863 software incubators. These bases and incubators attract and aggregate many software companies together, especially the small and middle companies. SoftPM was applied in more than 100 companies of them.

Some software bases and incubators applied SoftPM to establish the Common Technology Supporting System – CTSS to serve the local software companies and improve the process management capability and level. For example in Beijing, 863 software incubator takes the lead to apply SoftPM to establish the CTSS for Beijing software industry in 2003. There is hundreds of software companies have became the members of the CTSS. They access to the common process service through the SoftPM- customization system. Additionally, they can also apply SoftPM in enterprise level to support the internal process management and process asset safety. In Guangdong, the Software Park and incubator apply SoftPM to extend the resource and capability of service to the Zhujiang river Triangle area. The application of SoftPM improves the level of process and quality management of software companies within the park and incubator. The average benefit increased every year of companies within park and incubator is more than 200 million US dollars.

Besides the software companies in these software parks and incubators, SoftPM is also applied in many large software organizations, such as Chinasoft Co. Ltd, CS&S(China National Computer software and technology service Corporation), Beida Jade bird and NECAS. SoftPM helps software organizations promote their productivity, enhances the effect of process management and reduces the cost of management, cuts down the rework and improves the quality of products. The benefit result from applying SoftPM is more than 40 millions US dollars depended on the statistical data provided by partial software companies.

We investigated three software parks and incubators applied SoftPM from Guangdong, Henan and Xian. The statistical data is presented in Table 3:

Table 3. The data of benefit applied SoftPM in some software parks and incubator

National software parks /863 software incubators	Increase Benefit	Profit	Tax
Guangdong	200	36	5
Henan	25	6.2	3.6
Xian	62.5	——	7.8
Total	287.5	42.2	16.4
Notes:	Unit: Million US dollar		

There are another 13 national software parks and 863 software incubators. If we use the smallest data from Table 3 (25million) as base of calculation, the total benefits will be more than 600 million US dollars for all software parks and incubators which use SoftPM.

6 Conclusion

Software process technologies bring the new solutions for meeting the software crisis. Many achievement and practices have proven it is effective. Software process management is one of the primary research communities. It focuses on establishing the institutionalized process to address the ad hoc and sightless project development. In China, software industry has been developing rapidly. More and more new and small or medium size software companies are emerging. All of them are in lack of mature project management support and in desperate need of advanced and formal software management technology to help them promote their process capability and products quality.

This paper discussed a solution for software process management in China, and a toolkit SoftPM implemented to support the software organizations adopt the solution. It helps software organization take continual process improvement from immaturity to maturity. SoftPM was applied in many software organizations in China. It has been welcome. Moreover, our solution is also general for software process management. It's sure that SoftPM is suitable for the software organizations outside China too.

References

1. Lan Sommerville: Software Engineering 7th Edition, Addison Wesley Publishing Company (2004)
2. Evelyn Stiller, Cathie LeBlanc: Project-Based Software Engineering, Addison Wesley Publishing Company (2002)
3. International Standard: ISO 9001 Quality Management System – Requirements (2000)
4. Mary Beth Chrissis, Mike Konrad, Sandy Shrum: CMMI Guidelines for Process Integration and Product Improvement, Addison Wesley Publishing Company (2004)
5. Barry Boehm, Chris A., Winsor B. Sunita C. Bradford K. C., Ellis H., Ray M., Donald R., Bert S.: Software Cost Estimation with COCOMO II, Prentice-Hall, Inc (2000)
6. China Software Industry Association: Annual Report of China Software Industry (2004)
7. Mark C. Paulk, Bill Curtis, Mary Beth Chrissis, Charles V. Weber: Capability Maturity Model[SM] for Software, Version 1.1,Technical Report, CMU/SEI-93-TR-024, ESC-TR-93-177 (February 1993)
8. International Standard: ISO/IEC 9126-1 Software Engineering – Product Quality - Part1: Quality Model (2001)
9. Jim Lawler, Barbara Kitchenham: Measurement Modeling Technology, IEEE Software, Vol.20 No.3 (May/June 2003) 68-75
10. Stephen H. Kan: Metrics and Models in Software Quality Engineering 2nd Edition, Addison Wesley Publishing Company (2003)
11. Qing Wang, Mingshu Li, Xia Liu, An active measurement model for software process control and improvement. Journal of Software, Vol.16 No.3 (March 2005) 407-418
12. CMMI Product Team: Capability Maturity Model Integration, for SE/SW/IPPD/SS V1.1, Continuous Representation, CMU/SEI-2002-TR-011,ESC-TR-2002-011 (2002)
13. William A.Florac, Anita D. Carleton, Measuring software process-Statistical process control for software process improvement, Addison Wesley Publishing Company (1999)
14. Wang Qing, Li Mingshu, Measurement of software Requirement Based on SPC, Journal of Computer, Vol.26 No.10 (October 2003) 1312-1317

Process Elements: Components of Software Process Architectures

Jesal Bhuta[1], Barry Boehm[1], and Steven Meyers[2]

[1] Center for Software Engineering, University of Southern California,
Los Angeles, California, USA
{jesal, boehm}@cse.usc.edu
[2] Software Process Group,
1968 Adams Blvd, Los Angeles, California, USA
steve@softwarepg.com

Abstract. To reduce the complexity and time spent in building life cycle plans, project managers often reuse process assets from past projects. Such impromptu reuse is risky when the assets being reused were not created with strategies that make it reusable. In elaborating Osterweil's "Software Processes are Software Too" insight, Boehm et al have expressed the duality between software products and processes as: "If a given approach is good for software products, then its process counterpart is good for software processes." In this paper we discuss the duality between product and process reuse. We propose the development of process elements, "process counterparts to software components," which can be built with reusable strategies. These process elements can then be integrated with other process elements to develop software plans. We also present the results of an experiment that was conducted on several projects using our approach.

1 Introduction

Building project plans from scratch can be difficult and time consuming. In order to reduce the complexity and time spent, project managers often reuse process assets from past projects in developing the current one. However, impromptu reuse of process assets across different projects, similar to ad hoc product reuse, is risky and unadvisable, especially when the process was not created with strategies that make it reusable. Processes lacking the flexibility, quality, and maintainability for reuse are likely to be ineffective when applied across diverse projects. This is because they may not share common success criteria, their project context and objectives will differ, and other project-specific assumptions may not hold. For example, a traditional waterfall implementation for building a system using Commercial Off the Shelf (COTS) products is likely to fail [29]; since the waterfall process, amongst other things, does not account for frequent vendor upgrades to COTS packages [4]. Another problem project managers' face when planning software projects is estimating the effort and resource for individual activities. Cost estimation models such as COCOMO [9] and COCOTS [1] provide a project and phase level process estimate, but do not accurately estimate the per-task effort and resource allocation. In elaborating Osterweil's

M. Li, B. Boehm, and L.J. Osterweil (Eds.): SPW 2005, LNCS 3840, pp. 332–346, 2005.

"Software Processes are Software Too" insight [30], Boehm et al in [16] have expressed the duality between software products and software processes as: "If a given approach (disciplined programming, requirement definition and validation, reuse, risk management) is good for software products, then its process counterpart is good for software processes." In this paper we will discuss how this duality can be applied between product and process reuse and its effect on plan reuse.

As with to product reuse, it is not possible to reuse entire project plans across multiple projects given that project parameters such as available resources, project objectives, and domain are dissimilar in different projects. However, if discrete elements, much like software components, are built with reusable strategies it is possible to integrate them to create software development plans used across multiple projects. These elements, based on past experience, can provide information on the effort and resources required to implement them. Also, each element will provide value to the overall project by reducing risk, increasing the probability of success, and improving the projects visibility. In this paper we will define and describe "Process Elements", a component counterpart of process architectures. Additionally we show how one can build and use process elements within an organization.

The next section will provide background and related work; section 3 will define and discuss the process element. Section 4 provides an overview of developing and using process elements, within an organization. Section 5 describes an experiment and empirical results gathered during the experiment.

2 Related Work

There is a significant amount of literature that describes the building reusable product assets and reusing them across multiple projects [19, 21, 24, 25, 26, 33, 37]. Few researchers have however explored the possibility of developing the process counterpart of such product assets. Tailorable fault project processes have been developed around commercial tool suites such as the Rational Unified Process. Similar tailorable corporate software processes have been developed and used in response to such evaluation criteria as the Software CMM [31, 35]. Reusable process components have also been enabled by process programming research environments such as Little Jil [17]. Process researchers have also defined process patterns, which describe a proven, successful approach and/or series of actions for developing software [2, 3]. However, few have attempted to split the patterns into small discrete parts that serve a purpose in the project [32].

In [16], authors present an open architecture for software process asset reuse. In this paper we will extend their work so that it can be accommodated in multiple type of projects, and project domains.

3 Process Elements Definition and Description

In [20] authors describe a Process Element simply as "a component of a process". We expand the definition above to "a Process Element (PE) is a group of project activities, and/or other process elements related by logical dependencies, which when executed (or enacted) provides value to the project". Process Elements, like software components, have input and output interfaces, defined by pre-conditions and post-conditions. Within a process element, the project activities and sub-process elements are classified as variants and invariants. Additionally, PE's incorporate feedback from a knowledge base that has information on past project plans. Figure 1 shows the overall PE interactions. In the reminder of this section we will describe each of the interacting elements of a PE and provide an example.

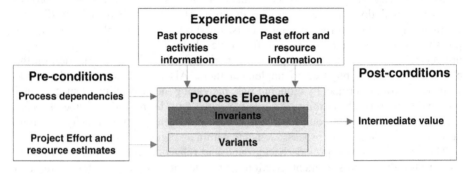

Fig. 1. Process Element Interactions

Pre-Conditions
The pre-conditions of a PE include its dependencies, i.e. artifacts and information that it will need for execution and the project effort, schedule and/or resource estimates. The dependencies of a PE usually include the results provided by predecessing PEs. The effort, schedule and resource estimates are used to determine the effort and resources of the activities and sub-process elements within the PE.

Post-Conditions
The post-conditions define the results obtained from executing a PE. These may be in the form of abstract models, information and analysis, or simply risk reduction. Results from one PE usually form the input or dependencies of another PE.

Process Element
As defined earlier the process element consists of a set of activities and/or sub process elements. Both activities and sub process elements are classified as variant or invariant. Unlike software components, which are usually treated as a black box, process elements will most likely undergo some sort of customization to meet the objectives of the project at hand. Variant activities are those that can be modified, and if required even removed from the process element, without significantly impacting the results produced by the PE. Invariant activities on the other hand, may be tweaked but cannot be extensively modified, since upon such modification the PE can no longer guarantee to produce the initially promised results.

Experience Base
Process elements should take into consideration the implications of past projects from both within and outside the organization. Incorporating past project schedule, effort,

and relationship information within the process elements will produce empirically proven project plans. Additionally, they should also include organizational and industry best practices. The past effort information for the process element can be used to determine the percent of overall project effort and resources required to implement the process element.

Process Element Example
In figure 2 we present the USC Spiral COTS-Based Application (CBA) Framework initially published in [15]. Each block in this framework indicates a process element. The arrows indicate the direction of data and control flow, and hence dependencies between the process elements. Figure 3 indicates the COTS Assessment Process Element, a sub process element of the framework.

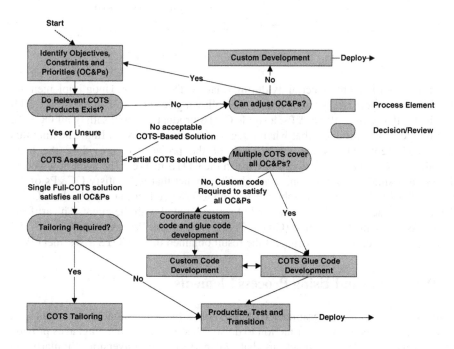

Fig. 2. USC CBA Spiral Framework

The COTS Assessment PE requires the Objectives, Constraints and Priorities (OC&Ps) of the project. This information as seen in the framework is provided by an earlier process element "Identify Objectives, Constraints and Priorities". The COTS Assessment element itself is composed of multiple variant and invariant PEs. Each of these in turn is composed of process elements or activities. Activities within a variant PE such as the "Market Trend Analysis" can be modified, or even removed by the project manager, if enough market information is already known. Alternately an invariant PE such as the "Detailed Assessment", although it can be tweaked, should not be modified or removed since this may significantly reduce the overall value provided by the COTS assessment PE; in that inadequate detailed assessment may

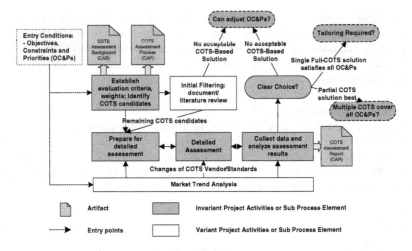

Fig. 3. COTS Assessment Process Element

result in higher risk and uncertainty during final COTS selection. Upon implementing this PE, the project will present one of the following results: no combination COTS candidates that satisfy all OC&Ps, a single COTS product that will satisfy all OC&Ps, or multiple COTS products that when integrated cover all OC&Ps. Implementing this process element reduces the overall risk of the project, by providing the team visibility into what exists or does not exist in the COTS market. The team now knows if there is a single, combination, or no COTS product that will satisfy OC&Ps of the project. Further if there is a combination or no COTS product that satisfy the OC&Ps the team can identify the ones that could be renegotiated with the client. The artifacts COTS Assessment Background (CAB), COTS Assessment Process (CAP) and COTS Assessment Report (CAR) document the result obtained in the COTS assessment PE.

4   Developing and Using Process Elements

In the present day, if a programmer wishes to convert a string variable into an integer, (s)he does not need to write a function to do so. Most programming languages provide libraries that already have functions that will perform the conversion. Similarly, an organization could provide a library of process elements to the project planners that they can use to rapidly build project plans.

A framework for the development and use of process elements is provided in figure 4. The figure consists of three distinct divisions. The topmost division indicates the infrastructure required by the organization, specifically for developing process elements. The bottom left portion indicates a project repository that stores information about projects developed in the organization. The bottom right portion indicates the planning activities within a single project. The developers of process elements use information from the Project Repository to identify the prominent process elements and patterns for the organization. They evaluate the best possible set of activities for a specific PE and store them along with any additional contextual information and

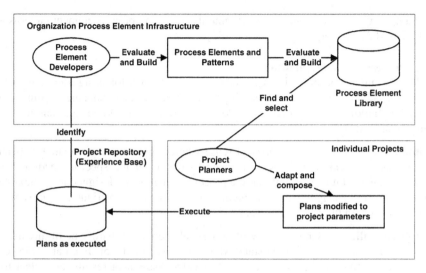

Fig. 4. Developing and Using Process Elements

examples in the process element library. The project planners find and select the PEs from the library for their projects. They adapt and compose the PEs to build a plan that will satisfy project parameters. When the project is completed the project plan as executed is stored back in to the project repository for evaluation to furnish new parts of the Process Element Library (or Experience Base as in Figure 1).

In this section we will focus on the specific activities of developing, and using process elements. Information regarding the development of a Project Repository and Experience Base can be found in [5].

4.1 Process Element Development

This section describes the development aspects of process elements including design of process elements, qualities the PEs should possess for them to be reusable, estimating the effort, and resource for each process element in a project and finally dealing with cross-cutting concerns in the project.

4.1.1 Process Element Design

There already exists a large amount of literature for designing reusable software components, such as the 3Cs (Concept, Content and Context) model in [37], the commonalities-and-variabilities (C&V) approach in [22], and the "rules of threes" in [6]. In the 3Cs model the concept of a software component is represented by an abstract set of specification, a family of implementations represents the content, and project parameters represent the context. Similarly, one can apply the 3Cs model to PEs where the concept is represented by the value provided by the element, its content is the set of activities, and effort, resource estimates, and its context is the project parameters. The (C&V) approach is similar to the process invariants-and-variants approach shown in Figure 3. Additionally, using the "rules of threes" process developers can identify patterns in which these process elements occur in the project.

An example where authors identified commonly occurring process element patterns in COTS-based Applications is provided in [32].

4.1.2 Process Element Qualities

In [24, 25] authors propose the Ada code reuse guidelines for design-for-reuse in 4 groups, i.e. adaptability, comphrensibility, independence, and robustness. Similar to these when building process elements, process developers should design them to have similar qualities:

Adaptability: Unlike software product reuse where components are treated as black box, process elements are likely to be modified to meet the specific needs of the project. To be used it is essential that the process elements are designed to be flexible, where a project manager can add, modify and remove the variant activities with minimal impact on the process element.

Comphrensibility: Having a library of process elements will hardly be of any use if the project managers do not understand what each task stands for. Even at the lowest level project activities such as "analyze the COTS assessment results and select the top 3 COTS products" would require some sort of explanation for managers new to COTS-Based Systems development. Every process element and project activity must accompany at a minimum some help information that defines:

- what the PE or activity does,
- value the PE provides,
- how can one execute it, and
- what resources are required to execute it.

Additionally, help can contain the context information about projects where the process element has been successfully executed, and the average absolute and/or percentage project effort required for implementing the PE.

Independence: Process elements should be independent, in that it should be possible to reuse a single element without adopting other unrelated ones.

Robustness: Activities within process elements should be correct, and fault-tolerant in being able to deal with discrepancies in their preconditions. An error in a process element or its interface can have far reaching consequences encompassing multiple projects.

4.1.3 Cost Estimation for Process Elements

Cost estimation for individual process elements over a long term requires organization-specific calibration. Such calibration can be done using data collected from past projects. Model-Based (System) Architecting and Software Engineering (MBASE) and Rational Unified Process (RUP) provide phase distribution percentages for effort and schedule in the four phases of inception, elaboration, construction, and transition [9, 27, 34]. Similarly, one could collect information for individual process elements, and identify their distribution in the overall project. The calibration however will require the consideration of the project domain and the project development method. Figure 5 [14] shows the percentage of total project effort spent in the major effort sources of COTS-Based Application (CBA) projects for three different types of CBA projects as well as non-CBA projects. As we can see in the figure, even within CBA projects there is a significant difference in distribution of effort amongst project activities in Assessment intensive CBA (ACBA), Tailoring intensive CBA (TCBA), and Glue-code intensive CBA (GCBA).

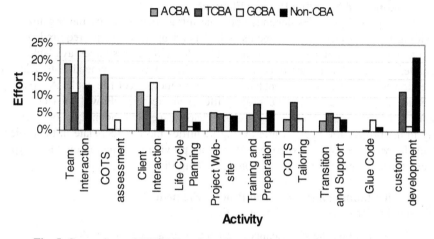

Fig. 5. Comparison of COTS-Based Application and Non-COTS Effort Sources

Effort estimation for individual process elements will also depend upon project constraints. In Schedule As Independent Variable (SAIV) projects [11], the effort and resources allocated per process element will be calculated based upon the available schedule. Similarly, for Cost as Independent Variable (CAIV) [18] projects' effort and schedule will be calculated based on available resources.

4.1.4 Cross Cutting Concerns Within Process Elements

In software applications non-functional requirements or aspects of the application, are usually realized in more than one software product component [23, 36]. Similarly, the various aspects of the project such as dependability, security, and quality are more often than not realized in multiple process elements. In such cases, the value provided by the string of process elements across the project is usually greater than the sum of the value provided by individual process elements. An example of such realization is shown in figure 7. The level of service aspect here encompasses multiple process elements, in different project phases. In the inception phase the project team needs to identify the level of service requirements, while in elaboration they are required to prototype and identify the desired and acceptable levels of service. The level of service aspect example here will also add project activities in the Architecting and Design PEs in inception as well as elaboration phases.

4.2 Using Process Elements

In order to reuse software components the developers are required to [19]

- find a component,
- select a component,

- understand the components selected, and if required
- adapt the components.

When reusing process elements the project planner will undergo a similar set of steps.

4.2.1 Finding and Selecting Process Elements

The finding process for PEs depends upon the infrastructure set by the organization providing them. Selection of elements will depend upon the value required by the project, the status of the project in the life cycle, and the resources available. For example, if the value required is defect reduction, it is recommended to add an inspection PE, if it has to be executed early during the project life cycle. Alternately to reduce defects late during the project life cycle, testing PE will provide better results than inspection. This is because software inspections identify more defects early in the project life cycle, while testing identifies more defects late in the project life cycle. More extensive Experience Bases can provide information on which types of defects are better found by inspection and testing PEs [10].

4.2.2 Understanding and Adapting Process Elements

Understanding process elements involves the:

- Understanding the significance of each project activity in the PE
- Understanding how each activity is related to others in the PE
- Understanding the variants and invariants of the PE, and exploring alternate variant activities when required
- Understanding the dependencies and results of the PE
- Understanding how to execute the PE.

An in-depth understanding of the PE will enable the project planner to allocate optimal resources to execute the process element. Additionally, it will provide the planner with the ability to modify the process element to suit the project parameters.

4.2.3 Process Elements Within the Spiral Framework

Figure 6 shows the anchor point milestone-elaborated Win Win spiral initially published in [15]. It returns to the original four segments of the spiral [7], and adds stakeholders' win-win elements in appropriate places. It also emphasizes concurrent product and process development, verification and validation; adds priorities to stakeholders' identification of objectives and constraints; and includes the Life Cycle Objective (LCO), Life Cycle Architecture (LCA), and Initial Operational Capability (IOC) anchor point milestones [8] also adopted by the Rational Unified Process. Figure 7 shows an instance of a hierarchical process plan for an assessment intensive COTS-based application. It describes process elements in the phases of inception and elaboration in details.

In the inception and elaboration phases, the plan implements the four original segments of the spiral model, "Identify OC&Ps", "Evaluate Alternatives with respect to OC&Ps", "Elaborate product and process definitions", and "Verify and Validate process definitions", in the process elements I4, I5, I6, I7, and E4, E5, E6 and E7 respectively. Additionally, it incorporates the anchor point milestones and related activities in I8 and E8.

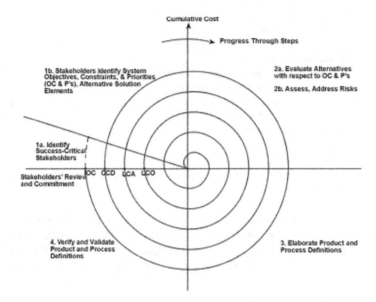

Fig. 6. Anchor Point Milestone-Elaborated Win Win Spiral Model

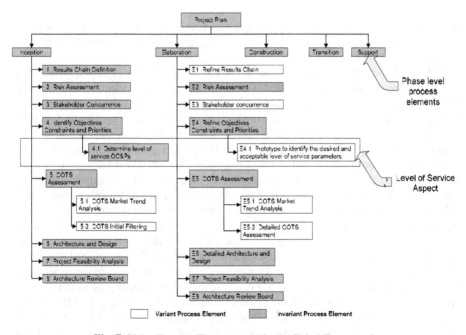

Fig. 7. Using Process Elements within the Spiral Framework

Task Name
⊟ **COTS Assessment Process Element - Detailed Assessment**
Collect detailed information on COTS packages that passed initial filtering
Create evaluation criteria for detailed assessment
Review available documentation on COTS packages
Evaluate products against the evaluation criteria
Select top N products for evaluation using prototypes (prototyping may be time consuming)
⊞ **COTS Tailoring Evaluation**
⊞ **COTS Integration Evaluation (when more than 1 COTS packages will be used)**
⊞ **Evaluation of COTS economic and strategic criteria**
Identify top n COTS combinations, based on technical evaluation, system OC&Ps, and COTS prototype results
Document the results in COTS Assessment Report
⊞ **Quality Management Review**
Detailed assessment milestone

Fig. 8. Breakup of the Detailed COTS/Technology Assessment Process Element in the MS Project Template form

The process elements in figure 7 can be further divided into sub PEs and activities. An example of the process element E5.2 – "Detailed COTS Assessment" in the MS-Project template is provided in figure 8. The PE "Quality Management Review" in the above example is a quality related crosscutting concern, which will span multiple PEs.

5 Experiment Using Process Elements

In the fall semester of 2004 we conducted an experiment using process elements in CSCI 577, a graduate level software engineering course. This section describes the experiment and the results derived.

CSCI 577 focuses on the development of a software system [12], requested by a real-world client. Over the last few years we have received requests to develop software systems for e-services, research (medicine and software), and business domains. Graduate students enrolled in the course form five or six person teams to design and implement a project requested by a real-world client, over a course of 2 semesters (24 weeks). During these 24 weeks the project goes from its inception and elaboration to construction and transition phases. The first semester involves the inception and the elaboration phases where the students negotiate mutually satisfactory (Win Win) OC&Ps with their clients and design a feasible solution that will satisfy them. During this process they undergo two Architecture Review Board (ARB) meetings where the instructors provide technical and business feedback to the teams [8]. The first ARB is the Life Cycle Objective (LCO) review where teams present at minimum, one feasible architecture that will satisfy the project OC&Ps. In the second ARB – the Life Cycle Architecture (LCA) review the teams select and present a single architecture and justify that it is feasible technically as well as from a business perspective. Based on the reviews and client feedback, a handful of the projects proceed to the next semester where they are built and deployed. In the second (spring) semester, the team members are re-distributed and undergo a Rebaselined

Life Cycle Architecture (RLCA) where the teams accommodate any additional or modified OC&Ps since the last review in their architecture and design. The team next moves on to the construction phase where they implement the system; first the top-priority core system requirements, which are presented at the Core Capability Drive-thru (CCD) and then the schedule-driven next-priority system requirements up to the Initial Operational Capability (IOC) phase. Finally, the project moves on to the transition phase, where the team transitions the system and any related information on the client site. Over the life cycle of the project the teams use the MBASE guidelines [13, 28] to guide them in the development and documentation of the success, process, product and property models.

The experiment was conducted during the inception and elaboration phases. We created a set of process elements for CBA and traditional (new code) projects, and made them available in two Microsoft Project template files on the course website. The elements were arranged in the pattern that was most commonly observed in the course. It was completely optional for students to use these templates. At the LCO stage, of the 17 teams in the class, 6 used a significant number of process elements critical to their project.

The percentage grade-scores for the "Milestones and Products" section in the life cycle plan of the project at the LCO stage are illustrated in figure 9. The scores were produced by the course graders without knowledge of which projects used the PEs, nor did the creators of the PEs have any involvement in the course grading. We selected the "Milestones and Products" section of the MBASE guidelines at the LCO stage since it provides the most information regarding the present and future plans of the project; and by LCO project teams have had sufficient exposure to the project planning concepts to plan ahead for the future phases. From the graph we see that projects, which used process elements to build their plans, obtained a higher score than projects that did not. The average percentage score of projects using process elements was 82% as opposed to the 57% for projects that did not. A 2-group t-test on

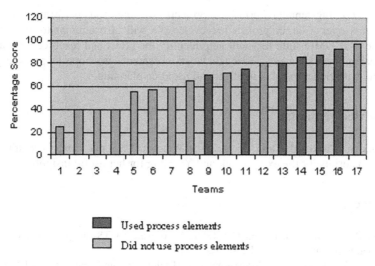

Fig. 9. Milestone and Products section scores at LCO

the team scores found the difference to be statistically significant. The two-tailed p value was 0.448, while the 95% confidence interval of this difference was from 0.552 to 40.404 %. The results of the test, although not conclusive are sufficient to warrant further research and experimentation. Of the projects that used process elements in the graph above, projects 16 and 15 used them without any modification; project 14 significantly modified one PE; projects 13 and 9 added one additional PE and customized one PE; and project 11 modified and used just 2 process elements critical to their project.

While this experiment is not entirely sufficient to demonstrate that composing process elements to build software development plans will be successful, the initial results look promising. In the forthcoming annual series of projects we plan to perform more extensive experiments, and measure the results over a larger project life cycle.

6   Conclusion and Future Direction

Software reuse principles can be applied to process elements as well as product components. Using process elements coupled with Win Win Spiral Model's Risk Driven approach and process patterns enabled project teams to develop better quality software life cycle plans. In this paper we have provided an initial set of principles for developing and composing process elements for CBA and traditional projects within the Win-Win Spiral framework. While additional experimentation is required to obtain more concrete conclusions, the initial results look extremely promising. Lessons learned from the initial experiment included:

- Providing concise and clear help files along with process elements, especially for process elements that are unfamiliar to the development teams
- Providing guidelines on the activities within process elements that can be modified and the ones that cannot.

In the coming annual series of projects we plan on performing extensive experiments over a larger project life cycle. We will also attempt to build models using the COCOMO suite that will help identify the effort and resource estimates for individual process elements. Through these increments we hope to provide project managers with richer insights in effort and resource planning.

Acknowledgements

We would like to thank Tami Perez, Jizhe Wang and Sophia Yang for helping us in creating materials for the experiment, and Ye Yang for her useful insights.

References

1. Abts C., Boehm B., Clark E.: COCOTS: A Software COTS-Based System (CBS) Cost Model. Proceedings, ESCOM 2001, (2001) 1-8
2. Ambler S., McGibbon B.: Process Patterns: Building Large-Scale Systems Using Object Technology. Cambridge University Press (1998)

3. Ambler S., McGibbon B.: More Process Patterns: Delivering Large-Scale Systems Using Object Technology. Cambridge University Press (1999)
4. Basili V., Boehm B.: COTS-Based Systems Top 10 List. IEEE Computer, May (2001) 91-93
5. Basili V., McGarry F.: The Experience Factory: How to Build and Run One. 19th International Conference on Software Engineering, Boston, Massachusetts, May (1997)
6. Biggerstaff T.: Design Recovery for Maintenance and Reuse. IEEE Computer July (1989) 36-49
7. Boehm B.: A Spiral Model of Software Development and Enhancement. IEEE Computer May (1988) 61-72
8. Boehm B.: Anchoring the Software Process. IEEE Software. July (1996) 73-82
9. Boehm B., Abts C., Brown A. W., Chulani S., Clark B., Horowitz E., Madachy R., Reifer D., Steece B.: Software Cost Estimation with COCOMO II Prentice Hall (2000)
10. Boehm B., Basili V., "Software Defect Reduction Top-10 List," IEEE Computer Jan (2001)
11. Boehm B., Brown A. W., Huang L., Port D.: The Schedule as Independent Variable (SAIV) Process for Acquisition of Software-Intensive Systems. USC CSE Technical Report Nov 2003
12. Boehm B., Egyed A., Port D., Shah A., Kwan J., Madachy R.: A stakeholder win-win approach to software engineering education. Annals of Software Engineering Volume 6 Issue 1-4 (1998) 295 - 321
13. Boehm B., Port D., Abi-Antoun M., Egyed A.: Guidelines for the Life Cycle Objectives (LCO) and the Life Cycle Architecture (LCA) deliverables for Model-Based Architecting and Software Engineering (MBASE). USC CSE Technical Report (1999)
14. Boehm B., Port D., Bhuta J., Yang Y.: Not All CBS Are Created Equally: COTS Intensive Project Types. Springer Verlag 2002, ICCBSS 2002, Feb (2003) 36-50
15. Boehm B., Port D., Yang Y., Bhuta J., Abts C.: Composable Process elements for Developing COTS-Based Applications. Proceedings of the ACM-IEEE Symposium on Empirical Software Engineering August (2003)
16. Boehm B., Wolf S.: An Open Architecture for Software Process Asset Reuse. Proceedings of the 10th International Software Process Workshop (1996)
17. Cass A., Lerner B., Sutton S., McCall E., Wise A., Osterweil L.: Little-JIL/Juliette: a process definition language and interpreter. Proceedings of the 22nd international conference on Software engineering (2000)
18. Cost as Independent Variable (CAIV). http://www.ar.navy.mil/aosfiles/tools/turbo/topics/u.cfm
19. Dusink L., Katwijk J.: Reuse Dimensions. Proceedings of the 1995 Symposium on Software reusability Volume 20 (1995) 137-149
20. Feiler P., Humphrey W.: Software Process Development and Enactment: Concepts and Definitions. Second International Conference on the Software Process (1993)
21. Gacek C., Boehm B.: Composing Components: How Does One Detect Potential Architectural Mismatches? Proceedings of the OMG-DARPA-MCC Workshop on Compositional Software Architectures January (1998)
22. Jacobson I., Griss M., Jonsson P.: Software Reuse. Addison Wesley (1998)
23. Kiczales G., Lamping J., Mendhekar A., Maeda C., Lopes C., Loingtier J., Irwin J.: Aspect-oriented programming. 11th European Conference Object-Oriented Programming, Volume 1241 of Lecture Notes in Computer Science, June (1997) 220-242
24. Kim H.: Ada Code Reuse Guidelines for Design-for-Reuse. Master's Thesis, Department of Computer Science, University of Durham, Durham, England, U.K., June (1996)

25. Kim H., Boldyreff C.: An approach to increasing software component reusability in Ada. Proceedings of 1996 Ada-Europe International Conference on Reliable Software Technologies (1996) 89-100
26. Kim H., Boldyreff C.: Software Reusability Issues in Code and Design. ACM SIGAda Ada Letters, Volume XVII, Issue 6 (1997) 91-97
27. Kruchten P.: The Rational Unified Process: An Introduction. Addision-Wesley (1999)
28. Model-Based Systems Architecting and Software Engineering (MBASE) Guidelines, URL: http://sunset.usc.edu/cse/pub/research/mbase/MBASE_Guidelines_v2.4.0.pdf
29. Morisio M., Seaman C., Parra A., Basili V., Kraft S., Condon S.: Investigating and Improving a COTS-Based Software Development Process. Proceedings of the 22nd International Conference of Software Engineering June (2000) 32-41
30. L. Osterweil: "Software Processes are Software Too," Proceedings of 9th International Conference of Software Engineering , ACM/IEEE, 1987
31. Paulk M.: Key practices of the capability maturity model Version 1.1. Research Access for Software Engineering Institute (1993)
32. Port D., Yang Y.: Empirical Analysis of COTS Activity. 3rd International Conference on COTS-Based Software Systems Feb (2004)
33. Rakic M., Medvidovic N.: Increasing the Confidence in Off-the-Shelf Components: A Software Connector-Based Approach. Proceedings of the 2001 Symposium on Software Reusability (2001) 11-18
34. Royce W.: Software Project Management A Unified Framework. Addision-Wesley (1998)
35. Software Engineering Institute: The Capability Maturity Model: Guidelines for Improving the Software Process. Addison-Wesley Professional (1995)
36. Tarr P., Ossher H., Harrison W., Sutton S.: N Degrees of Separation: Multi-Dimensional Separation of Concerns. Proceedings 21st International Conference on Software Engineering (1999) 107-119
37. Tracz W., Edwards J.: Implementation Working Group Report. Reuse In Practice Workshop, Software Engineering Institute

Process Programming to Support Medical Safety: A Case Study on Blood Transfusion

Lori A. Clarke[1], Yao Chen[1], George S. Avrunin[1], Bin Chen[1], Rachel Cobleigh[1], Kim Frederick[1], Elizabeth A. Henneman[2], and Leon J. Osterweil[1]

[1] Department of Computer Science, University of Massachusetts
Amherst, MA 01003, USA
{clarke, yaoc, avrunin, chenbin, rcobleig,
kfrederi, ljo}@cs.umass.edu
[2] School of Nursing, University of Massachusetts
Amherst, MA 01003, USA
henneman@nursing.umass.edu

Abstract. Medical errors are now recognized as a major cause of untimely deaths or other adverse medical outcomes. To reduce the number of medical errors, the Medical Safety Project at the University of Massachusetts is exploring using a process programming language to define medical processes, a requirements elicitation framework for specifying important medical properties, and finite-state verification tools to evaluate whether the process definitions adhere to these properties. In this paper, we describe our experiences to date. Although our findings are preliminary, we have found that defining and evaluating processes helps to detect weaknesses in these processes and leads to improved medical processes definitions.

1 Introduction

It has been estimated that there are approximately 98,000 deaths per year in the United States resulting from medical errors [7]. The Institute of Medicine (IOM) reported that many medical errors are caused by faulty processes and conditions that lead people to make mistakes or fail to prevent them [6]. Although the IOM advocates using more information technology in order to help improve medical care, it does not indicate what kinds of technology should be employed.

In the University of Massachusetts Medical Safety Project, software engineering researchers from the Department of Computer Science have been working with researchers and medical practitioners from the University of Massachusetts School of Nursing and from Baystate Medical Center to evaluate how selected technologies might help reduce medical errors. Although it is not possible to totally eliminate mistakes, it is our hypothesis that medical processes can be defined in such a way that mistakes are less likely to occur.

Medical processes tend to be complex, concurrent, and exception-prone. They tend to involve multiple practitioners with very different perspectives about the on-going process. Thus, we are interested in a process language that can capture this complexity yet still be understandable to a (trained) medical professional. Moreover, the proc-

M. Li, B. Boehm, and L.J. Osterweil (Eds.): SPW 2005, LNCS 3840, pp. 347–359, 2005.
© Springer-Verlag Berlin Heidelberg 2005

ess language should be precise enough to support static analysis techniques and to eventually drive simulations and executions.

To date we have experimented with using the Little-JIL process programming language [11], the Propel property elucidation system [10], and several finite-state verification systems, specifically LTSA [1, 9], SPIN [5], and FLAVERS [4]. In this paper we report on our experiences using these technologies to define and evaluate a in-patient blood transfusion process. In-patient blood transfusion plays a vital process in modern health systems. Although in-patient blood transfusion errors are rare, when they do occur, they can result in death and are among the most serious types of medical errors. Thus, we use in-patient blood transfusion as an example to demonstrate how our approach is effective at improving the safety of medical processes.

The rest of this paper is organized as follows. Section 2 presents a brief overview of the Little-JIL process programming language. Section 3 presents part of the in-patient blood transfusion process as specified using Little-JIL. Section 4 describes how properties are specified using Propel and the results of our analysis using finite state verification. The final section highlights our results and discusses future work.

2 Little-JIL Features

Little-JIL is a visual language for coordinating tasks that are to be executed by either computation or human agents. A process is defined in Little-JIL using hierarchically decomposed steps, where a step represents some specified task to be done by the assigned agent. Steps may also indicate any prerequisites, postrequisites, and exception handling behavior that should be associated with the step. Non-leaf steps, in addition to the above, also indicate the order for processing all substeps. The language has precise enough semantics that Little-JIL programs can be executed or can serve as the subject of careful static analysis.

To help the reader understand the blood transfusion process example, we first give an overview of the semantics and notation of Little-JIL. For a detailed description of Little- JIL, see the Little-JIL Language Report [11].

Steps. Steps are the basic elements of Little-JIL programs. As shown in Figure 1, each step has a name and a set of badges to represent the control flow, exceptions handled, prerequisites, and postrequisites. Each step need only be defined once, but can be referenced many times. References are represented by a step with the name of the referenced step, but with no badges. Although not shown in our examples here, steps also can indicate the resources required, including the agent responsible for step execution.

Step Execution. At run-time, a step can be in one of five states: posted, started, completed, terminated and retracted as shown in Figure 2. When a step is eligible to be started, it is moved into the posted state. It is started when the agent assigned to the step obtains the resources that it requires and begins to do the work. If the step is finished successfully, it is moved into the completed state and resources are released. If the agent fails to complete the work, the step is moved to the terminated state. A step is retracted if it is withdrawn from an agenda after having been posted but without being started by the agent. In the analysis phase, we often want to refer to a specific

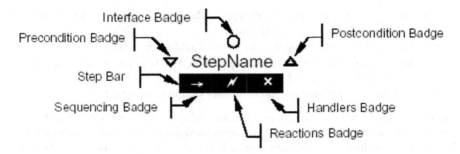

Fig. 1. Little-JIL step icon

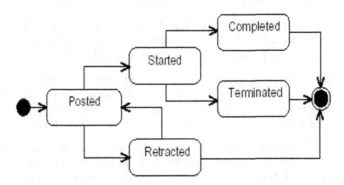

Fig. 2. States associated with Little-JIL step execution

state of a step. To do this, we append the state name to the name of the step. Thus, "Transfuse_ STARTED" refers to the step "Transfuse" when it is in the started state.

Step Sequencing. Every non-leaf step has a sequencing badge, which defines the order in which its substeps execute. A sequential step indicates that its substeps are to be executed from left to right and is only successfully completed after all of its substeps has successfully completed. A parallel step indicates that its substeps are to be executed asynchronously and that it cannot be successfully completed until all of its substeps successfully complete. A choice step allows the agent to dynamically select a substep to execute among its substeps. A choice step is considered completed only after one of its substeps have completed. A try step indicates that its substeps are executed from left to right until one of them has been completed. A try step is successfully completed only if one of its substeps successfully complete.

Exception Handling. A step in Little-JIL can throw exceptions when aspects of the step fail. For example, if a prerequisite is not satisfied, it may indicate that an exception is to be thrown. A thrown exception is handled by a matching exception handler associated with the parent step of the step that throws the exception or, if no such handler is found, the exception is rethrown by the parent step.

An exception handler has an associated control-flow badge that indicates how the step catching the exception executes after the handler finishes. There are four kinds of control badges:

- continue: the step catching the exception should continue as if the substep that throws the exception completed successfully;
- complete: the step catching the exception should be completed;
- rethrow: the step catching the exception should be terminated and the exception rethrown to the parent of this step;
- restart: the step with the exception handler should be restarted.

Requisites. Each step may have a prerequisite and a postrequisite. Requisites provide a way to check entry and exit conditions associated with a step. A prerequisite has to be completed before its associated step is initiated. A postrequisite has to be completed before its associated step is completed. When a requisite cannot successfully complete, the associated step is terminated and an exception is thrown.

Deadlines. Deadlines determine the time by which a step must be completed. Deadlines are used to define the maximum time allowed for a certain task. If a step continues to execute past its stated deadline, an exception is thrown.

Resources and Agents. The interface to a step specifies the resources used by the step, where agent is a special type of resource. For example, in a medical process, the agent might be a nurse, doctor, patient, or computer system. Each step must have an agent; if no agent is declared, the agent is inherited from the parent step.

Diagrams. To facilitating viewing, Little-JIL programs are decomposed into diagrams, where a diagram usually fits into a single window. Diagrams are usually used to decompose a Little-JIL program into conceptually meaningful subprocesses.

3 In-Patient Blood Transfusion Example

We have used Little-JIL to model a real-world in-patient blood transfusion process. This process model consists of 23 Little-JIL diagrams, comprised of about 112 steps. In this section, we present a few of the Little-JIL in-patient blood transfusion diagrams to give the reader an indication of what the model looks like.

An in-patient blood transfusion process cannot start unless there is a blood transfusion order from a physician. One order may require that several units of blood product be transfused to the patient. Once the required units have been transfused, the process completes. Figure 3 shows the top diagram of this process.[1]

In the root step, In-Patient Blood Transfusion Process has a prerequisite step Physician Prescribes Blood Transfusion. There is a cardinality "+" adjacent to the edge between the In-Patient Blood Transfusion Process step and Carry Out Physician Order for Transfusion step, which means that Carry Out Physician Order for Transfusion will be done at least once. Since In-Patient Blood Transfusion Process is a sequential step, instances of Carry Out Physician Order for Transfusion must be executed sequentially. Before Carry Out Physician Order for Transfusion starts, the agent

---

[1] In the actual In-Patient Blood Transfusion Process diagram (a modified version of which is shown in Fig. 3), the Single-Unit Transfusion Process step is replaced by an intermediate step called "Perform Transfusion". The Single-Unit Transfusion Process (Fig. 4) is really a substep of the Perform Transfusion step. This missing intermediate step is not shown because of space considerations.

(agent assignments are not shown) must check the form signed by the patient, indicating consent for the blood transfusion. If the consent form is not signed, a NoPatient-Consent exception will be thrown and then handled by the No Patient Consent exception handler associated with the In-Patient Blood Transfusion Process step.

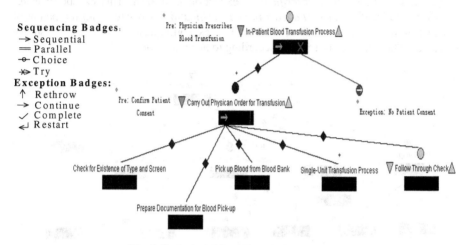

Fig. 3. In-Patient Blood Transfusion Process

Since this handler is a continue exception handler, as indicated by the right arrow, after completion of the handler, the process continues the sequential execution of the *In-Patient Blood Transfusion Process* step, meaning that the "next" instance of the *Carry Out Physician Order for Transfusion step* may start. If the consent form is signed, the agent can start to execute *Carry Out Physician Order for Transfusion*. The *Carry Out Physician Order for Transfusion* step has five substeps: *Check for Existence of Type and Screen, Prepare Documentation for Blood Pick-up, Pick up Blood from Blood Bank, Single-Unit Transfusion Process,* and *Follow Through Check*. The right arrow sequencing badge specifies that these substeps should be executed one by one, from left to right. Each one of these substeps is a reference to a step defined in another diagram, so none of these steps are elaborated in this diagram. There is a cardinality "+" adjacent to the edge between the *Carry Out Physician Order for Transfusion* step and *Single-Unit Transfusion Process* step, which means that *Single-Unit Transfusion Process* will be done once per unit of blood product.

Figure 4 shows the diagram that elaborates the *Single-Unit Transfusion Process* step. According to clinical research, the most common adverse outcomes during blood transfusions are caused by a failure to detect that an incorrect unit had been issued at the bedside [7]. To prevent such common errors, bedside checks are recommended. Thus, in our process definition, there are two bedside checks, *Verify Patient Identification* and *Product Verification*. *Verify Patient Identification* requires that the identity of the patient be established.

The *Product Verification* step definition, which is shown in Figure 5, requires a visual comparison of the information on the transfusion tag with the blood product bag. All identifying information on the blood product, the transfusion tag, and the patient identification armband must be verified. Thus there are four substeps to be executed: *Verify*

Product Tag Matched to Product Label, Check Product Expiration Date & Time, Verify Product Tag Matched to Patient Armband, and *Verify Product Type Matched to Patient Record.* Since these verification steps are independent of each other, they can be done in any order, as indicated by the parallel sequencing badge. If any of these substeps finds a discrepancy, a *FailedProductVerification* exception is thrown. This exception is rethrown to the handler Handle*Failed Product Verification* associated with the parent of *Product Verification,* step *Bedside Checks.* This exception handler, although not shown here, would handle this discrepancy according to hospital policy.

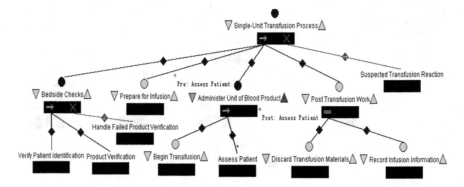

Fig. 4. Single-Unit Transfusion Process

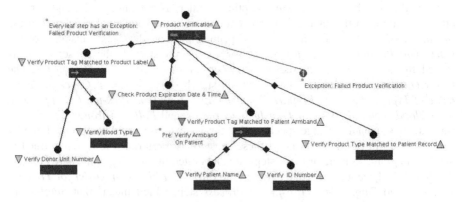

Fig. 5. Product Verification Process

4   Analyzing Processes

Although we have only shown a small part of the in-patient blood transfusion process, it is easy to see that it quickly becomes quite complex. The Little-JIL definition tersely describes complex control flow. This is both a strength and a weakness. It is a strength because medical professionals can understand the process definitions and help to describe them and develop improvements to them. Moreover, the process definition can easily be decomposed into subprocesses (e.g., diagrams) so that one's focus can be directed to relatively small, coherent aspects of the process. This terseness is a weakness, however, because it is easy for humans to overlook or misunderstand some of the complex flows through the system or among subprocesses. This is particularly true when exceptions or parallel execution can occur [2].

One way to help validate a process is to use analysis techniques to verify that important policies are not violated by the process definition. These policies can be represented as formal properties stated in terms of the states of the steps. We then apply finite-state verification techniques to determine if these properties will always hold on all possible traces through the process. For example, for the transfusion process, patient identification on the patient's armband must match the patient information on the tag affixed to the blood product before that unit of blood product is transfused. If this property does not hold for the process definition, the finite-state verification tool will provide a counterexample trace through the system showing where at least one such violation occurs. We can use this trace to identify and correct the error in the process and then try to reverify the revised process definition.

In this section we first describe some of the properties that need to be verified for the blood transfusion process and how we represented those properties and then describe what techniques we used to verify these properties.

4.1 Representing Properties

It is a surprisingly difficult task to determine the properties that should be verified. In the medical field, policies often exist that are a starting point for these properties. Below are some example policies often associated with the in-patient blood transfusion process:

- The patient's informed consent must be confirmed prior to carrying out a physician's order for a blood transfusion.
- The patient's identification must be verified immediately before obtaining each blood specimen.
- The patient's identification must be verified prior to administering each unit of blood product.
- Verifying that the patient's identification on the armband matches the patient's information on the tag affixed to the unit of blood product must precede administering that unit of blood product.
- The information for the unit of blood product must be verified by two healthcare professionals prior to administering the unit of blood product.
- The expiration date and time for the unit of blood product must be checked before starting to administer that unit of blood product.
- The patient's status must be assessed immediately before administering each unit of blood product.
- The patient's status must be assessed immediately after administering each unit of blood product.
- If a transfusion reaction is suspected, the transfusion must be stopped immediately.
- If a transfusion reaction is suspected, the physician and the blood bank must be notified.
- If a transfusion reaction is suspected, the the patient's information and the information for the unit of blood product must both be re-verified.

Such policies are often vague, however, and need to be translated into a precise instantiation based on the process that is actually being applied. For example, "confirm patient consent" must be represented in terms of the consent form that is actually used at the hospital where the process is being applied. Moreover, who is to do this confirmation and how is this confirmation documented?

Beyond that, finite-state verification requires a rigorous representation of each property. It is rare for English descriptions to describe accurately and unambiguously all the situations that need to be considered. The Propel system [10] is designed to help users consider all the situations associated with formulating a property. Propel provides a question tree that guides the user through the options that should be considered. Figure 6 shows an example of the question tree. After making some initial selections in this question tree, the user can continue to select options from the question tree or can choose instead to select options from a template of English phrases, called disciplined natural language (DNL), or from a finite-state automaton (FSA) template. Figure 7 shows the Propel GUI when formulating the DNL and FSA representation of the resulting property.

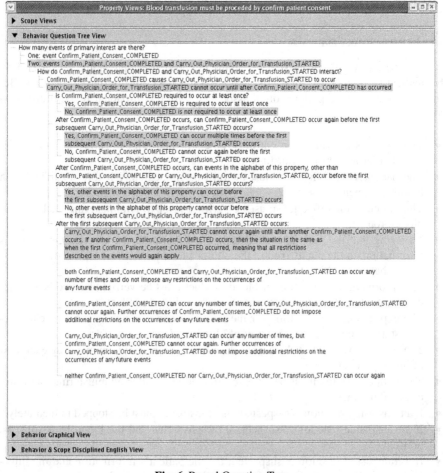

Fig. 6. Propel Question Tree

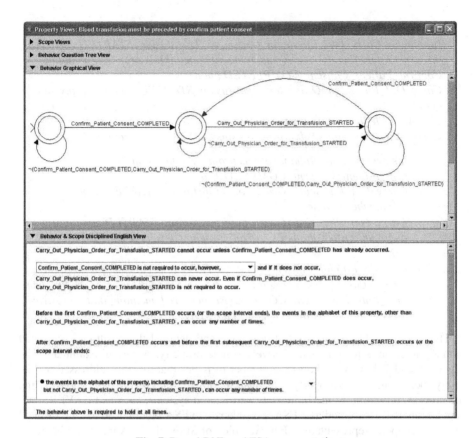

Fig. 7. Propel DNL and FSA representations

Thus, after using Propel, the first policy:

"The patient's informed consent must be confirmed prior to carrying out a physician's order for a blood transfusion."

would be represented by the following disciplined natural language:

Carry_Out_Physician_Order_for_Transfusion_STARTED cannot occur unless Confirm_Patient_Consent_COMPLETED has already occurred.

Confirm_Patient_Consent_COMPLETED is not required to occur, however, and if it does not occur,
Carry_Out_Physician_Order_for_Transfusion_STARTED can never occur. Even if Confirm_Patient_Consent_COMPLETED does occur,
Carry_Out_Physician_Order_for_Transfusion_STARTED is not required to occur.

Before the first Confirm_Patient_Consent_COMPLETED occurs (or the scope interval ends), the events in the alphabet of this property, other than Carry_Out_Physician_Order_for_Transfusion_STARTED, can occur any number of times.

After Confirm_Patient_Consent_COMPLETED occurs and before the first subsequent Carry_Out_Physician_Order_for_Transfusion_STARTED occurs (or the scope interval ends), the events in the alphabet of this property, including Confirm_Patient_Consent_COMPLETED but not Carry_Out_Physician_Order_for_Transfusion_STARTED, can occur any number of times.

After the first subsequent Carry_Out_Physician_Order_for_Transfusion_STARTED occurs:

- *the events in the alphabet of this property, other than Confirm_Patient_Consent_COMPLETED or Carry_Out_Physician_Order_for_Transfusion_STARTED, could occur any number of times;*
- *Carry_Out_Physician_Order_for_Transfusion_STARTED cannot occur again until after another Confirm_Patient_Consent_COMPLETED occurs;*
- *Confirm_Patient_Consent_COMPLETED can occur and if it does, then the situation should be regarded as exactly the same as when the first Confirm_Patient_Consent_COMPLETED occurred, meaning that all restrictions described on the events would again apply.*

The reader might be surprised at how long and detailed the resulting disciplined natural language is for this one relatively simple property. A careful examination of Figures 6 and 7, however, shows the number of issues that must be addressed in precisely specifying such a property. The resulting FSA would be the basis for verifying the process definition. Some finite-state verification systems, such as FLAVERS, accept a property represented as a FSA. For others, the FSA would need to be translated into their property representation. For example, for SPIN, the FSA must first be translated into linear time temporal logic.

4.2 Process Verification

There are several finite-state verification tools that could be used to determine if the process definition is consistent with a property. To date, we have investigated using three such tools: SPIN, FLAVERS, and LTSA. To facilitate using different tools, we first translate the Little-JIL process into an intermediate representation, called the Bandera Intermediate Representation (BIR). BIR was specifically designed to support finite-state verification and thus was a natural choice [3]. Once we have the BIR representation, we translate BIR to the internal form required for the particular verifier. Figure 8 depicts this two-state translation process.

A common problem with finite-state verification is that the size of the state space that must be explored grows too large. Direct translation of a process usually results in a model that is too large to be verified. Therefore, we use several optimizations and abstractions to reduce the size of the model generated. Some of these transformations have been previously reported [2, 8] and some are currently being investigated. All the transformations that are used must be shown to be conservative for the property and process definition. This means that a process will not be reported to be consistent with a property unless that is indeed the case for the unoptimized version as well.

False positives, violations that do not correspond to any real trace through the system, can be a problem but are less likely to occur for process descriptions than for detailed designs or source code.

All the verifiers that we have used have been able to find (the same) errors in the process and to prove interesting properties about the in-patient blood transfusion process. All of them have some limitations and their translation and optimization process is being improved to address these concerns. FLAVERS is currently best able to handle the larger problems, but requires more insight about the constraints that must be introduced to eliminate false positives.

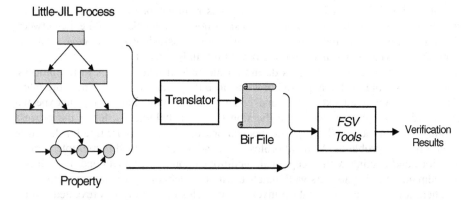

Fig. 8. The Little-JIL translation to BIR and then the BIR translation to the expected input for the selected Finite-State Verification (FSV) tool

5 Conclusions and Future Work

We have successfully used Little-JIL to specify a real-world, non-trivial in-patient blood transfusion process and verified that the process satisfies some important safety properties. We have also learned a considerable amount about the strengths and weaknesses in the technology that we are using.

The Little-JIL process language has been extremely useful in representing the in-patient blood transfusion process. Surprisingly, the medical professionals have become very adept at understanding the Little-JIL processes. It has turned out to be an excellent medium for describing the in-patient blood transfusion process and discussing alternative processes. The medical professionals have shied away from actually creating the process definitions. Instead they rely on the computer scientists to create the process definitions, although they are quick to point out problems or suggest improvement. As noted, there is also a tension between the expressiveness of the process language and the analyzability of the resulting processes. Humans like flexible processes, but such processes are much more difficult to analyze since they result in more choices and thus more cases to consider.

As might be expected, simply rigorously defining a process uncovers problems with that process. Often there were disagreements among the medical professionals about the process definitions. Sometimes this could be attributed to the different roles that medical professionals have (e.g., the nurse's view versus the doctor's view), but sometimes these disagreements revealed a real problem in the underlying process and an opportunity for a medical error to occur. In the future we are interested in exploring how best to decompose (and then compose) the process definitions according to the different roles.

Property specification also helped improve the process definitions. In considering a property, it often became clear that the process definition omitted important details. The medical policies that we had available before trying to define the process were useful, but the extra detail required to formulate a property resulted in a deeper understanding of the problem that eventually was reflected in the process definition. For example, thinking about how patient consent is required before an in-patient blood transfusion revealed that we needed to consider how long a delay could exist between the initial consent and the transfusion, how many transfusions could occur with one consent, and what would happen if the patient rescinds consent.

The verification of the process definition did indeed reveal errors in the process. Some were problems that appeared obvious once they were revealed. The more interesting errors involved exceptions and concurrent behavior that lead to unexpected event orderings. We found the verification useful in helping us debug the process definitions (and the translators). The medical process definitions are ripe for detecting event-ordering problems. Medical professionals are often involved in multiple parallel activities and dealing with exceptional conditions upon exceptional conditions. It is a problem domain that appears well matched with the technology we are applying.

There are many areas of future investigation. This case study has revealed limitations in the process language, the property specification approach, and the verification tools. For example, all three technologies need to be extended to have better support for timing constraints. The process language needs better support for visualizing the process. The property specification framework is still awkward to use, and the verification tools need much improved, process-specific optimization techniques. The Little-JIL to BIR translator currently does not support recursion. To handle recursion, we simply unroll the recursive step up to a given bound, but this might make the verification unsound.

The medical professionals are very interested in evaluating different kinds of medical processes, not just in-patient blood transfusion processes. In addition to improving safety, they are interested in improving efficiency with respect to turnaround and throughput. They would like to see how efficiency is affected by different symptom mixes (e.g. ankle sprains versus cardiac pain), different resources, different resource allocation strategies, and different processes. Such evaluations will depend on doing extensive simulations using real event histories. Finally, in the long term it would be desirable to actually execute carefully evaluated processes in the clinical setting. These processes could help medical professionals track and prioritize their numerous tasks.

Acknowledgments

We would like to thank Stephen Siegel, Jamieson Cobleigh, Sandy Wise, Ethan Katz-Bassett, and Barbara Staudt Lerner for their many helpful suggestions with this work.

This material is based upon work supported by the National Science Foundation under Award No. CCF-0427071, the U. S. Army Research Office under Award No. DAAD19-01-1-0564, and the U. S. Department of Defense/Army Research Office under Award No. DAAD19-03-1-0133.

Any opinions, findings, and conclusions or recommendations expressed in this publication are those of the author(s) and do not necessarily reflect the views of the National Science Foundation, the U. S. Army Research Office, or the U. S. Department of Defense/Army Research Office.

References

1. Cheung, S.C., Giannakopoulou, D., Kramer, J.: Verification of liveness properties using compositional reachability analysis. In: Sixth European Software Engineering Conference and Fifth ACM SIGSOFT Symposium on the Foundations of Software Engineering, Zurich, Switzerland (1997) 227-243
2. Cobleigh, J.M., Clarke, L.A., Osterweil, L.J.: Verifying properties of process definitions. In: ACM SIGSOFT International Symposium on Software Testing and Analysis, Portland, OR (2000) 96-101
3. Corbett, J.C., Dwyer, M.B., Hatcliff, J., Robby: Bandera: A source-level interface for model checking Java programs. In: 22nd International Conference on Software Engineering, Limerick, Ireland (2000) 762-765
4. Dwyer, M.B., Clarke, L.A., Cobleigh, J.M., Naumovich, G.: Flow analysis for verifying properties of concurrent software systems. ACM Transactions on Software Engineering and Methodology 14(3) (2004) 359-430
5. Holzmann, G.J.: The model checker SPIN. IEEE Transactions on Software Engineering 23(5) (1997) 279-294
6. Institute of Medicine: Crossing the Quality Chasm: A New Health System for the 21st Century. The National Academies Press, Washington DC (2001) 23-38
7. Kohn, L.T., Corrigan, J.M., Donaldson, M.S., (eds.): To Err is Human: Building a Safer Health System. National Academy Press, Washington DC (1999)
8. Lerner, B.S.: Verifying process models built using parameterized state machines. In: ACM SIGSOFT International Symposium on Software Testing and Analysis, Boston, MA (2004) 274-284
9. Magee, J., Kramer, J.: Concurrency: State Models & Java Programs. John Wiley & Sons (1999)
10. Smith, R.L., Avrunin, G.S., Clarke, L.A., Osterweil, L.J.: PROPEL: An approach supporting property elucidation. In: 24th International Conference on Software Engineering, Orlando, FL (2002) 11-21
11. Wise, A.: Little-JIL 1.0 language report. Technical report (UM-CS-1998-024), Department of Computer Science, University of Massachusetts, Amherst, MA (1998)

Translation of Nets Within Nets in Cross-Organizational Software Process Modeling*

Jidong Ge, Haiyang Hu, Ping Lu, Hao Hu, and Jian Lü

State Key Laboratory for Novel Software Technology,
Nanjing University, Institute of Computer Software,
Nanjing University, Nanjing 210093, China
gjd@ics.nju.edu.cn

Abstract. Software process technology is very important to improve the software quality. Some process models have been developed for process management during the software development process. Today's software corporations
become so large and geographically distributed that modeling cross-
organizational software process becomes an important topic. In this paper, we
use nets within nets to model cross-organizational software processes based on
mobile agent systems. For indirect analysis of the model of nets within nets, this
paper presents translation rules from nets within nets to flat nets, which pre-
serve the soundness property. For enhancing the flexibility of execution, we introduce weak synchronous concept into the model of nets within nets.

1 Introduction

Software process technology is very important to improve the software quality [6]. In
the modern idea of quality management, the three most important elements about
quality are processes, people and technology. It is a good idea to improve software
quality and productivity by improving software process management. In the past
decades, some process models have been developed for process management during
the software development process. Today's software corporations become so large
and geographically distributed that they must often operate across the organizational
boundaries, so modeling cross-organizational software process becomes an important
topic. In this paper, we use nets within nets [12] to model cross-organizational software processes and improve the flexibility and the scalability based on mobile agent
systems.

In this paper, we view the software process as a special workflow, and model
workflow process model by Petri nets or WF-nets [1], then by nets within nets [12]
for cross-organizational processes based on mobile agents.

The most important idea in the model of "nets within nets" is "Petri nets as token
objects" [12], that is, substituting Petri nets for token objects. In the Valk's paper, nets

* Supported by NSFC (60273034, 60233010, 60403014), 863 Program of China
(2004AA112090, 2002AA116010), 973 Program of China (2002CB312002), JSFC
(BK2002203, BK2002409).

M. Li, B. Boehm, and L.J. Osterweil (Eds.): SPW 2005, LNCS 3840, pp. 360–375, 2005.

within nets are also called object Petri nets, but they are different from the definition of Lakos' [9]. In this paper, we focus on the definition of Valk's. When token objects replaced by Petri nets, the Petri net model becomes a higher order Petri net model, which is the most important difference between the model of nets within nets and the traditional Petri net models. Here, the model of nets within nets can be called multi-dimensional Petri net model, and the traditional Petri net model including Pr/T nets, colored Petri nets and hierarchical Petri nets can be called flat Petri net model.

In the model of nets within nets, the tokens have their own autonomous behaviors, which is different from the traditional Petri net model. For example, in traditional place/transition Petri nets, tokens are indistinctive. In colored Petri nets or Pr/T nets, tokens have some data structures but not self-behaviors. The tokens' autonomous behaviors are analogous to the behaviors of software agents or mobile agents, so the model of nets within nets can be used for agent based process modeling [7].

Using mobile agent technology is a good approach to improve the flexibility and the scalability of process management. Mobile agents can represent roles of software process participants to get across the boundaries of software organizations, so this model provides a paradigm of cross-organizational processes, which is well suited for the large software corporations to manage their large processes in the global strategy.

The model of nets within nets enhances the capability of modeling mobility, which is the important advantage of this novel model, but the direct analysis for this model is difficult. In this paper, the authors provide a set of equivalent translation rules from multi-dimensional Petri nets to traditional flat Petri nets so that the model of nets within nets can be indirectly analyzed under the translated traditional flat Petri nets with many existing analysis approaches.

The paper is structured as follows. Section 2 presents the basic concepts and notations of Petri nets and WF-nets. In section 3 the model of nets within nets and *NN-*WF-nets and NN-sound are defined. Section 4 gives a set of translation rules from nets within nets to flat nets and some proofs for preserving soundness property. Section 5 introduces the concept of weak synchronous relation and related translation rules. The paper closes with a conclusion and an outlook to the further work.

2   Basic Notations of Petri Nets and WF-Net

With the idea of "Software Processes are Software too" [10], it means that developing software processes is very like developing software. The control structures of software processes are similar to the control structures of programming language. Because the control structures of Petri nets have the same equivalent expression as the programming language, Petri nets can be used to model software processes [3]. Aalst has listed three good reasons for using Petri nets for process modeling and analysis [1]: *formal semantics despite the graphical nature, state-based instead of event-based and abundance of analysis techniques.* In this paper, we view the software process as a special workflow, and model the workflow processes by Petri nets or WF-nets [1], then by nets within nets. In this section, we introduce the basic notions and notations used throughout this paper. We first define Petri nets.

Definition 1. Petri net
(1) A Petri net is a 3-tuple $PN = (P, T, F)$ where
  a) P is a finite set of places,
  b) T is a finite set of transitions, $P \cap T = \phi$
  c) $F \subseteq (P \times T) \cup (T \times P)$ is a set of arcs (flow relation)
(2) The preset of a node $x \in P \cup T$ is defined as $\bullet x = \{y \in P \cup T \mid (y, x) \in F\}$
    The postset of $x \in P \cup T$ is defined as $x \bullet = \{y \in P \cup T \mid (x, y) \in F\}$

Definition 2. WF-net [1]
A Petri net $PN = (P, T, F)$ is a WF-net (abbr. of Workflow net) iff:

  (1) PN has two special places: i and o. Place i is a source place: $\bullet i = \phi$. Place o is a sink place: $o \bullet = \phi$.
  (2) If we add a transition t^* to PN so that $\bullet t^* \{o\}$ and $t^* \bullet = \{i\}$, then the resulting Petri net is strongly connected.

In WF-net, the transitions represent the activities of software processes, while the tokens and the places represent the enable conditions of the process activities.

WF-net model based on traditional flat Petri nets has powerful expression, but in the traditional flat Petri nets, the tokens do not have the self-behaviors, so the flat Petri nets cannot model mobility directly. While, modeling mobility is important to build cross-organizational computing for large software enterprises. In this paper, we use the paradigm of nets within nets [12] to model mobility. In the model of nets within nets, the tokens in system net level have their own autonomous behaviors, which enhance the capability of modeling mobility. This paradigm can improve the flexibility and the scalability of the software processes.

3   Nets Within Nets and NN-WF-Net

The most important idea in the model of "nets within nets" is "Petri nets as token objects", that is, substituting Petri nets for token objects.

The model of nets within nets has the hierarchy concept similar to the traditional hierarchical Petri nets. But there are differences about the hierarchy concept between the model of nets within nets and the model of the traditional hierarchical Petri nets. The hierarchy concept comes from the substitution of the elements of Petri nets. In the model of nets within nets, the substitution is Petri nets for token objects of the system level nets. While in the model of traditional hierarchical Petri nets, the substitution is Petri nets for places or transitions of the super level nets. So, here to distinguish these two different hierarchy concepts, we call the hierarchy concept of the model of nets within nets as dimension, which is a higher-order paradigm of Petri nets, or called multi-dimensional Petri nets.

Here, we refer to Valk's definition about the model of nets within nets [12]. The simplest paradigm of the model of nets within nets is Unary Elementary Object System (abbr. Unary EOS or UEOS). The idea of "nets within nets" can be expressed in the formal definition of EOS.

Definition 3. EOS - Elementary Object System [12]
A Unary elementary object system is a 4-tuple $EOS = (SN, ON, \rho, OPS)$

(1) $SN = (P, T, W, M_0)$ is an elementary net system with $|M_0| = 1$, called system net of EOS.
(2) $ON = (B, E, F, m_0)$ is an elementary net system, called object net of EOS, and
(3) $\rho \subseteq T \times E$ is the interaction relation set between the transition sets of the two level nets. The interaction relation set ρ is used to describe synchronous relation between SN and ON.
(4) OPS (abbr. of Organizational Place Sets) is a partition of the place set in SN, which can be used to model mobility and define the organizational boundaries clearly.

Figure 1 is an example of the EOS. On the right side of this figure, SN is the system net, and on the left side of this figure, ON is the object net. Both of the SN and the ON have initial markings, in SN marked in p1, while in ON marked in b1. There is an interaction relation set between SN and ON, whose elements are labeled with <ix>. For example, i1:(t2, e2)∈ ρ, is an element of the interaction set. In the definition of EOS, we can observe that the EOS is a multi-dimensional Petri net, which is the essential difference from the traditional flat Petri net.

In Figure 1, $\rho = \{(t2, e2), (t7, e2), (t3, e3), (t4, e3), (t9, e4)\}$

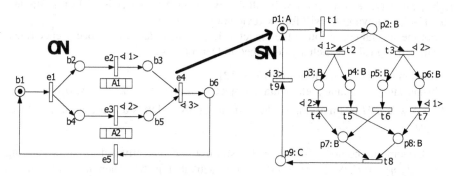

Fig. 1. A scenario of software processes modeled by EOS

In the system net of Figure 1, the places are labeled with logic places: A, B, C. In fact the places in SN are divided into some organizational place sets. For example, in the SN of Figure 1, there are three organizational place sets: A= {p1}, B= {p2, p3, p4, p5, p6, p7, p8}, C= {p9}. The organizational place sets represent the organizational boundaries. In the same organizational place set, the token objects will not run across the organizational boundaries when the transitions firing in SN. While across different organizational place sets, the token objects will run across the organizational boundaries when the transitions firing in SN. For example, when t1 firing, the token object in p1 will go from p1 in place set A to p2 in another place set B, across the organizational boundary between A and B. When t2 firing, the token object in p2 will go from p2 to p3 in the same place set B, not across the organizational boundary.

In Definition 3, the token objects in *SN* replaced by object nets can be viewed as software agents or mobile agents assigned with special tasks, which run in the system environment and can migrate from one place to another place. On the other hand, the system net can be viewed as system environment in which mobile agents run. Hence, object nets can be also called agent nets. Mobile agents are encapsulated computational entities. The process logic described by object nets can be encapsulated in mobile agents as their own behaviors. Mobile agents can represent some roles to run across the organizational boundaries. The model of nets within nets provides a kind of multi-dimensional process modeling. The object nets can be used to model micro-processes, while the system nets can be used to model macro-processes. So, this paradigm can be naturally used to model cross-organizational software processes, which is well suited for the large software organizations to manage their large processes in the global strategy.

Here is a scenario of software process modeling in Figure 1. The *ON* describes a process that a software testing organization A sends two testing reports: A1 and A2, which need the other software organization B to review. The transition e2 and e3 in *ON*, mean reviewing the testing report A1 and A2 separately. After t1 and e1 firing, the two testing reports and the token object come into place p2 in the organization B. The token object in p2 means that the organization B has a choice when reviewing these two testing reports. Because of the interaction relations (t2, e2) and (t3, e3), both reviewing A1 and reviewing A2 have opportunities to happen. If selecting the right path t3-t7, reviewing A1 will follow reviewing A2. Otherwise selecting the left path t2-t4, reviewing A2 will follow reviewing A1.

For the special definition of the model of UEOS, there are special occurrence rules, or called firing rules, which are described in Definition 4.

Definition 4. Occurrence Rules for *EOS* [12]

A bi-marking of a unary elementary object system $EOS = (SN, ON, \rho)$ is a pair (M, m) where M is a marking of the system net *SN* and m is a marking of the object net *ON*.

(1) System-autonomous firing: A transition $t \in T$ is activated in a bi-marking (M, m) of *EOS* if $\rho(t) = \phi$ and t is activated in M. Then the follower bi-marking (M', m') is defined by $M \xrightarrow{t} M'$ (w.r.t. *SN*) and $m = m'$, written as $(M, m) \xrightarrow{[t, \lambda]} (M', m')$ in the case.

(2) Object-autonomous firing: A transition $e \in E$ is activated in a bi-marking (M, m) of *EOS* if $\rho(e) = \phi$ and e is activated in m. Then the follower bi-marking (M', m') is defined by $m \xrightarrow{e} m'$ (w.r.t. *ON*) and $M = M'$, written as $(M, m) \xrightarrow{[\lambda, e]} (M', m')$ in this case.

(3) Synchronous firing: A pair $[t, e] \in T \times E$ is activated in a bi-marking (M, m) of *EOS* if $[t, e] \in \rho$ and t and e are activated in M and m, respectively. Then the follower bi-marking (M', m') is defined by $M \xrightarrow{t} M'$ (w.r.t. *SN*) and $m \xrightarrow{e} m'$ (w.r.t. *ON*), written as $(M, m) \xrightarrow{[t, e]} (M', m')$ in this case.

Here, the λ means empty occurrence sequence. The definition of notation of $\rho(t)$ and $\rho(e)$: $\rho(t) := \{e \in E \mid (t,e) \in \rho\}$ and $\rho(e) := \{t \in T \mid (t,e) \in \rho\}$.

According to Definition 4 of the occurrence rules, there is a following firing sequence in Figure 1 as an example: $[\lambda, \text{e1}], [\text{t1}, \lambda], [\text{t2, e2}], [\text{t4, e3}], [\text{t5}, \lambda], [\text{t8}, \lambda]$ $[\text{t9, e4}], [\lambda, \text{e5}]$.

In this definition for occurrence rules, the system-autonomous firing means the only actions of the system net, while the object-autonomous firing means the only actions of the object nets, which assigns the autonomous self-behaviors to the token objects. The synchronous firing means the synchronous actions between the system net and the object nets.

Based on the model of nets within nets, we can define the *NN-WF-net* [1] for cross-organizational process modeling. Here, we extend the workflow net in the paradigm of nets within nets.

Definition 5. *NN-WF-net* comparison to the *WF-net* in Definition 2
An *EOS* = (*SN*, *ON*, ρ) is a *NN-WF-net* iff:

(1) *SN* is a *WF-net*. *SN* has two special places: *is* and *os*. Place *is* is a source place: $\bullet is = \phi$. Place *os* is a sink place: $os \bullet = \phi$. If we add a transition t^* to *SN* so that $\bullet t^* = \{so\} t^* \bullet$ and $\bullet = \{is\}$, then the resulting *SN* is strongly connected.

(2) *ON* is a *WF-net*. *ON* has two special places: *io* and *oo*. Place *io* is a source place: $\bullet io = \phi$. Place *oo* is a sink place: $oo \bullet = \phi$. If we add a transition e^* to ON so that $\bullet e^* = \{oo\}$ and $e^* \bullet = \{io\}$, then the resulting *ON* is strongly connected.

Figure 2 is an example of *NN-WF-net*, the left is *ON*, while the right is *SN*, and both of them are WF-nets. Between *SN* and *ON*, there are interaction relations defined by the set ρ.

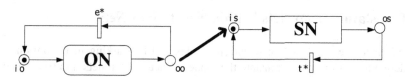

Fig. 2. *NN-WF-net for* cross-organizational process

Soundness is an important property in WF-net [1]. Comparing with the soundness of WF-net in Definition 6, we define the soundness of NN-WF-net in Definition 7.

Definition 6. Soundness of WF-net [1] (for flat nets)
A procedure modeled by a WF-net *PN* = (*P*, *T*, *F*) is sound if and only if:

(1) For every state *M* reachable from state *i*, there exists a firing sequence leading from state *M* to state *o*. Formally: $\forall M (i \xrightarrow{\ *\ } M) \Rightarrow (M \xrightarrow{\ *\ } o)$

---

[1] Note: *NN-WF-net* is the abbreviation of nets-within-nets workflow nets.

(2) State o is the only state reachable from state i with at least one token in place o. Formally: $\forall M \ (i \xrightarrow{\ *\ } M \wedge M \geq o) \Rightarrow (M = o)$ (Here, $M \geq o$ means more than place o have a token.)

(3) There are no dead transitions in (PN, i). Formally:

$$\forall t \in T \ \exists M, M', \ i \xrightarrow{\ *\ } M \xrightarrow{\ t\ } M'$$

The first two requirements can be described as proper termination while the last one states that there are no dead transitions (tasks) in the initial state i.

Definition 7. Soundness of NN-WF-net (for nets within nets), abbr. NN-soundness
Let EOS be a NN-WF-net, it is NN-sound iff.

(1) $\forall (M, m) ((is, io) \xrightarrow{\ *\ } (M, m)) \Rightarrow ((M, m) \xrightarrow{\ *\ } (os, oo))$, (is, io) is the initial state of NN-WF-net, while (os, oo) is the final state of NN-WF-net.

(2) $\forall t \in T$, if $\rho(t) = \phi$, then $\exists (M, m), (M', m') \ (is, io) \xrightarrow{\ *\ } (M, m) \xrightarrow{[t, \lambda]}$ (M', m') ; if $\rho(t) \neq \phi$, then $\forall e \in \rho(t)$ $\exists (M, m)$, $(M', m') \ (is, io) \xrightarrow{\ *\ } (M, m) \xrightarrow{[t, e]} (M', m')$.

(3) $\forall e \in E$, if $\rho(e) = \phi$, then $\exists (M, m), (M', m') \ (is, io) \xrightarrow{\ *\ } (M, m) \xrightarrow{[\lambda, e]}$ (M', m') ; if $\rho(e) \neq \phi$, then $\forall t \in \rho(e)$ $\exists (M, m)$, $(M', m') \ (is, io) \xrightarrow{\ *\ } (M, m) \xrightarrow{[t, e]} (M', m')$.

The model of nets within nets has powerful expression for process modeling [8], because it enhances the more capability of directly modeling mobility than traditional flat nets. But, as multi-dimensional Petri nets, the direct analysis is difficult. So, we try to design a translation approach to decrease the dimension of the model. The translation from nets within nets to flat nets builds an equivalent bridge so that the model of nets within nets can be indirectly analyzed with many existing analysis approaches, which reduces the difficulty of the analysis.

4   Translation from Nets Within Nets to Flat Nets

According to the definition of occurrence rules and bi-marking in Definition 4, we can define a set of rules to translate the model of nets within nets into traditional flat Petri net equivalently.

Rule 1. Translation from nets within nets to flat nets
Translation from *EOS* to Translated *EOS*, abbr. *TEOS* is defined by following. Given an *EOS* = (SN, ON, ρ) in Definition 3. Let Translated *EOS*, *TEOS* = (TS, TT, TF) is a flat net translated from *EOS*, iff: (a)-(c)

(a): $TS = P \cup B$
(b): $TT = T\bar{\rho} \cup E\bar{\rho} \cup \rho$
$T\rho := \{t \in T \mid \exists e \in E, (t, e) \in \rho\}$, $T\bar{\rho} := T \setminus T\rho$
$E\rho := \{e \in E \mid \exists t \in T, (t, e) \in \rho\}$, $E\bar{\rho} := E \setminus E\rho$
(c): Construction of *TF* by a set of translation rules: (1)-(3)

Rule (1): $\forall ti \in T_{\bar{p}}$,

$\left\{ \begin{array}{l} \forall px \in \bullet ti \ \text{in} \ SN, \text{then} \ (px, ti) \in TF \ \text{in} \ TEOS \\ \forall py \in ti \bullet \ \text{in} \ SN, \text{then} \ (ti, py) \in TF \ \text{in} \ TEOS \end{array} \right.$

Rule (2): $\forall ej \in E_{\bar{p}}$,

$\left\{ \begin{array}{l} \forall bx \in \bullet ej \ \text{in} \ ON, \text{then} \ (bx, ej) \in TF \ \text{in} \ TEOS \\ \forall by \in ej \bullet \ \text{in} \ ON, \text{then} \ (ej, by) \in TF \ \text{in} \ TEOS \end{array} \right.$

Rule (3): $\forall ik : (ti, ej) \in \rho$, then add a new transition $tiej$ to TT, ie. $tiej \in TT$

$\left\{ \begin{array}{l} \forall px \in \bullet ti \ \text{in} \ SN, \text{then} \ (px, tiej) \in TF \ \text{in} \ TEOS \\ \forall py \in ti \bullet \ \text{in} \ SN, \text{then} \ (tiej, py) \in TF \ \text{in} \ TEOS \\ \forall bx \in \bullet ej \ \text{in} \ ON, \text{then} \ (bx, tiej) \in TF \ \text{in} \ TEOS \\ \forall by \in ej \bullet \ \text{in} \ ON, \text{then} \ (tiej, by) \in TF \ \text{in} \ TEOS \end{array} \right.$

TS is the place set of *TEOS*, which combines the place set *P* of *SN* and the place set *B* of *ON*. *TT* is the transition set of *TEOS*, which combines the transition set *T* of *SN* and the transition set *E* of *ON*, but removing $T_{\bar{p}}$ and $E_{\bar{p}}$, then adding new transitions for every interaction relation of ρ,

TF is an arc set of *TEOS*. The following rules (1) (2) (3) are defined for the arcs of *TEOS*. These rules are defined according to the occurrence rules of Definition 4.

In fact, the rule (1) is according to System-autonomous firing of Definition 4, the rule (2) is according to Object-autonomous firing, and rule (3) is according to Synchronous firing.

The rule (1) and rule (2) mean remaining full places and partial transitions of both *SN* and *ON*, which is easily understood. Here we combine the structure of two-dimensional into a flat net, and remain the structure as originally where there is no synchronous interaction relation between *SN* and *ON*. But for the synchronous interaction set ρ, we define the rule (3). Given a pair of synchronous transitions *(ti, ej)*, which have a synchronous relation, rule (3) deletes *ti* and *ej*, then adds new transition *tiej* to *TT*, removing the preset of both *ti* and *ej* to be attached with the transition *tiej* as preset, removing the postset of both *ti* and *ej* to be attached with the transition *tiej* as postset respectively. Figure 3 shows a local scenario of the translation rule (3) in Rule 1.

According to the translation Rule 1, the EOS can be equivalently translated into a flat net. Figure 4 shows an example of the translation from Figure 1.

The translation from nets within nets to flat nets is a process to decrease the dimensions of the model of nets within nets, which will reduce the difficulty of analyzing the model of nets within nets, since there are many existing approaches for traditional flat nets.

This paper only presents a paradigm of translation from the two-dimensional nets into the flat nets, but under the idea of this translation approach, the *k*-dimensional *(k>2)* nets also can be translated into the flat nets step by step.

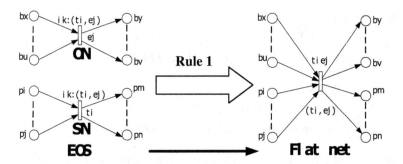

Fig. 3. Local scenario of the translation rule (3) in Rule 1

The paradigm of nets within nets divides the global process logic into object nets and system nets and combines the two level nets with the interaction relation set ρ. This approach is suited for describing the global processes and local processes separately. During modeling cross-organizational processes, we can use the paradigm of nets within nets, which can improve the flexibility and the scalability of software processes, also enhance the understandability of cross-organizational process models. However, during the analysis and the verification, the paradigm of nets within nets is very difficult to be analyzed directly. The translation rules can help us to analyze the model of nets within nets by analyzing the translated flat nets with many existing analysis methods.

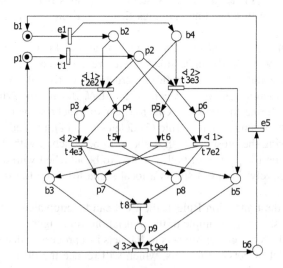

Fig. 4. A translation from Figure 1

For the indirect analysis of *NN-WF-net* (Definition 5), we define the Translated *NN-WF-net* according to Rule 1 in Definition 8.

Definition 8. Translated *NN-WF-net*, abbr. *TNN-WF-net* (see Figure 5)
A Translated *EOS*, *TEOS* = (*TS, TT, TF*) is a *TNN-WF-net* iff:

(1) *TEOS* is a flat net translated from an *EOS*.

(2) *TEOS* has two special transitions: *it**, *ot** and two special places: i, o. *it** $\bullet$ = {*is, io*}, $\bullet$ *it**={*i*}, $\bullet$ *ot**= {*os, oo*}, *ot** $\bullet$ ={*o*}, $\bullet$ *i* =ϕ , *o* $\bullet$ =ϕ .

(3) If we add a transition *tt* to TEOS so that $\bullet$ *tt* = {*o*} and *tt* $\bullet$ = {*i*}, then the resulting Petri net is strongly connected.

Figure 5 shows the Translated *NN-WF-net* for cross-organizational process modeling from Figure 2.

The *NN-WF-net* can be used for multi-dimensional process modeling. In the lower level, the geographically distributed organizations define their own processes as object nets, while the higher level organization defines the higher level processes as system nets and the interaction relations between two level nets. This provides a paradigm of combining the distributed modeling and the global modeling, which can improve the flexibility of process modeling and executing, and enhance the scalability of cross-organizational process management.

About the process detail, the distributed organizations themselves maybe know more clearly than the higher-level organization. It is a good idea to let distributed organizations define their own process models. Then the higher-level organization compose the lower level processes as object nets into the higher-level process as system nets.

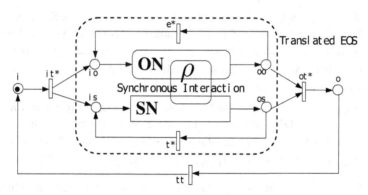

Fig. 5. Translated *NN-WF-net* from Figure 2

Soundness is an important property of workflow net. For the translation Rule 1, we try to prove that this translation preserves the soundness property, i.e. NN-WF-net is sound (see Definition 7) if and only if TNN-WF-net is sound (see Definition 6). To construct this proof, we need Definition 9 and Lemma 1.

Definition 9. Compatible Firing Sequence

Let EOS = (*SN, ON*, ρ) be an elementary object net and TEOS = (*TS, TT, TF*). For EOS, let σ_1 = $t_1t_2t_3...t_n$ be a firing sequence of EOS and σ_2 = $u_1u_2u_3...u_n$ be a firing sequence of TEOS. We call σ_1 and σ_2 are compatible iff:

(1) t_x = [λ , *e*] in EOS $\Leftrightarrow$ u_x = *e*, in which *e*$\in$ *E* in TEOS.

(2) t_x = [*t*, λ] in EOS $\Leftrightarrow$ u_x = *t*, in which *t*$\in$ *T* in TEOS.

(3) t_x = [*t, e*] in EOS $\Leftrightarrow$ u_x = *te*, in which *e*$\in$ *E* and *t*$\in$ *T* in TEOS.

According to Definition 9, a firing sequence σ, either in an EOS or in its translated net TEOS, will determine only one firing sequence σ', which is compatible to σ.

Lemma1. Let TEOS is translated from EOS by Rule1. EOS has initial bi-marking (M, m), TEOS = (TS, TT, TF) has initial marking S and $S = M+m$. σ_1 is a firing sequence of EOS and σ_2 is a firing sequence of TEOS. If σ_1 and σ_2 are compatible, then $(M,m)\xrightarrow{\sigma_1}(M',m') \Leftrightarrow S\xrightarrow{\sigma_2}S'$, in which $S'=M'+m'$.

Proof. The proof is organized in the following two parts:

(1) Suppose for EOS, $(M,m)\xrightarrow{\sigma_1}(M',m')$. We shall prove by induction on the length of σ_1. The case $|\sigma_1| = 0$, i.e. $\sigma_1 = \varepsilon$ is trivial, so let $|\sigma_1| = n$ and we have $(M,m)\xrightarrow{\sigma_1}(M',m'} \Rightarrow S\xrightarrow{\sigma_2}S'$ in which $S = M'+m'$. Now $\sigma'_1 = \sigma_1 t_{n+1}$ and $(M,m)\xrightarrow{\sigma_1}(M',m')\xrightarrow{t_{n+1}}(M'',m'')$.

   (a) If $t_{n+1} = [\lambda, e]$, then the marking m' would enable e in ON. According to Rule 1, the transition e is also enabled in TEOS at S', so there exists $S\xrightarrow{\sigma_2}S'\xrightarrow{u_{n+1}}S''$ in which $u_{n+1} = e$ and $m'\xrightarrow{e}m''$. It is easy to see that we have $S'' = M'+m'' = M''+m''$, so we have $(M,m)\xrightarrow{\sigma_1 t_{n+1}}(M'',m'')\Rightarrow S\xrightarrow{\sigma_2 u_{n+1}}S''$.

   (b) If $t_{n+1} = [t, \lambda]$, then the marking M' would enable t in SN. According to Rule 1, the transition t is also enabled in TEOS at S', so there exists $S\xrightarrow{\sigma_2}S'\xrightarrow{u_{n+1}}S''$ in which $u_{n+1} = t$ and $M'\xrightarrow{t}M''$, It is easy to see that we have then $S'' = M''+m' = M''+m''$, so we have $(M,m)\xrightarrow{\sigma_1 t_{n+1}}(M'',m'')\Rightarrow S\xrightarrow{\sigma_2 u_{n+1}}S''$.

   (c) If $t_{n+1} = [t, e]$, According to Rule 1, M' would enable t in SN and m' would enable e in ON, thus S' would enable te in TEOS. Similarly, we have $S\xrightarrow{\sigma_2}S'\xrightarrow{u_{n+1}}S''$ in which $u_{n+1} = te$, $M'\xrightarrow{t}M''$ and $m'\xrightarrow{e}m''$, then $S'' = M''+m''$, so $(M,m)\xrightarrow{\sigma_1 t_{n+1}}(M'',m'')\Rightarrow S\xrightarrow{\sigma_2 u_{n+1}}S''$

According to the proofs in (a) (b) and (c) we can conclude that $(M,m)\xrightarrow{\sigma_1}(M',m')\Rightarrow S\xrightarrow{\sigma_2}S'$ for any compatible firing sequence σ_1 and σ_2.

(2) Suppose for TEOS, $S\xrightarrow{\sigma_2}S'$. We can also prove it by induction on the length of σ_2. This can be proved analogously to (1). ⌐

Theorem 1. Let TNN-WF-net be translated from an NN-WF-net by Rule 1. NN-WF-net is NN-sound (see Definition 7) iff TNN-WF-net is sound (see Definition 6).

Proof. We organize the proof in the following two parts, part (1) proves the sufficient relation; part (2) proves the necessary relation.

(1) Suppose that TNN-WF-net is sound.
$[is+io]$ is the marking where only place is and io each has one token, while $[os+oo]$ is the marking where only place oo and os each has one token and other places in TNN-WF-net have no token (see Figure 5). σ_1 is a firing sequence of NN-WF-net and σ_2 is a firing sequence of TNN-WF-net.

(a) For the NN-WF-net, let $(is, io) \xrightarrow{\sigma 1} (M, m)$. According to Lemma 1, it is easy to see that in TNN-WF-net that there exists a firing sequence σ_2, and S is a marking of TNN-WF-net, $[i] \xrightarrow{it^*} [is+io] \xrightarrow{\sigma 2} S$, in which σ_1 and σ_2 are compatible and $S = M+m$. Since TNN-WF-net is sound, there exist a firing sequence σ'_2, $S \xrightarrow{\sigma' 2} [os+oo] \xrightarrow{ot^*} [o]$. According to Lemma 1, there will be a firing sequence σ'_1 which is compatible to σ'_2 and $(M, m) \xrightarrow{\sigma' 1} (os, oo)$.

(b) Let $t \in T$, if $\rho(t) = \phi$: Since TNN-WF-net is sound, there will also be a transition t in TNN-WF-net, and exist $[i] \xrightarrow{it^*} [is+io] \xrightarrow{\sigma 2} S \xrightarrow{t} S'$. According to Lemma 1, there will be a firing sequence σ_1 which is compatible to σ_2 such that $(is, io) \xrightarrow{\sigma 1} (M, m)$ and $S = M+m$. According to Definition 8, it is easy to see that $(M, m) \xrightarrow{[t, \lambda]} (M', m')$. If $\rho(t) \neq \phi$: $\forall e \in \rho(t)$, Since TNN-WF-net is sound, there will be a transition te in TNN-WF-net and exist $[i] \xrightarrow{it^*} [is+io] \xrightarrow{\sigma 2} S \xrightarrow{te} S'$. According to Lemma 1, there will be a firing sequence σ_1 which is compatible to σ_2 such that $(is, io) \xrightarrow{\sigma 1} (M, m)$ and $S = M+m$. According to Definition 8, we have $(M, m) \xrightarrow{[t, e]} (M', m')$.

(c) Let $e \in E$, if $\rho(e) = \phi$: Since TNN-WF-net is sound, there will also be a transition e in TNN-WF-net, and exist $[i] \xrightarrow{it^*} [is+io] \xrightarrow{\sigma 2} S \xrightarrow{e} S'$. According to Lemma 1, there will be a firing sequence σ_1 which is compatible to σ_2 such that $(is, io) \xrightarrow{\sigma 1} (M, m)$ and $S = M+m$. According to Definition 8, it is easy to see that $(M, m) \xrightarrow{[\lambda, e]} (M', m')$. If $\rho(e) \neq \phi$: $\forall t \in \rho(e)$, Since TNN-WF-net is sound, there will be a transition te in TNN-WF-net and exist $[i] \xrightarrow{it^*} [is+io] \xrightarrow{\sigma 2} S \xrightarrow{te} S'$. According to Lemma 1, there will be a firing sequence σ_1 which is compatible to σ_2 such that $(is, io) \xrightarrow{\sigma 1} (M, m)$ and $S = M+m$. According to Definition 8, we have $(M, m) \xrightarrow{[t, e]} (M', m')$.

According to the proofs in (a), (b) and (c), we can conclude that EOS is NN-sound.
(2) Necessary relation can be proved analogously as (1). ⌟

According to the Theorem 1, the translation Rule1 preserves the soundness property of the NN-WF-net. So, the NN-soundness property of NN-WF-net can be equivalently verified by checking the soundness property of its translated TNN-WF-net.

5 Weak Synchronization and Strong Synchronization

Because the synchronous relation restricts the enable conditions of the transition firing, for practical application, we define a new weak synchronous relation to relax the condition of firing, which can enhance liveness and flexibility of the model.

Definition 10. Weak Synchronization and Strong Synchronization

(1) For $(t, e) \in \rho$, a state (M, m), if t is activated in M, and e is not activated in m, then $(M, m) \xrightarrow{[t, \lambda]} (M', m)$.
(2) For $(t, e) \in \rho$, a state (M, m), if t is not activated in M, and e is activated in m, then $(M, m) \xrightarrow{[\lambda, e]} (M, m')$.

(3) For $(t, e) \in \rho$, a state (M, m), if t is activated in M, and e is activated in m, then
$(M, m) \xrightarrow{[t,e]} (M', m')$.

For the above three firing rules for the synchronous relation (t, e), if rules (1) (2) and (3) are all allowed, the synchronous relation is called weak synchronization. If only rule (3) is allowed, the synchronous relation is called strong synchronization, which is described in Definition 4.

According to Definition 10, the weak synchronous relation means that object nets can fire without *infinitely* waiting the synchronization of the system nets, and also means that system nets can fire without *infinitely* waiting the synchronization of the object nets. In practical application, weak synchronous relation can be fixed with a *duration value*. Within the duration, it must select strong synchronous firing as (3) in Definition 10, and when beyond the duration, it can select weak synchronous firing as (1) or (2) or (3) in Definition 10. The value of duration represents the degree of waiting synchronization. If the value of duration is *infinite* it means strong synchronization. If the value of duration is *zero*, it means no synchronization. When modeling, the weak synchronous relation can be marked with a capital character W (See Figure 6), so that it can be distinguished with the strong synchronous relation. For the weak synchronization, we define a translation from nets within nets to flat nets as Rule 2.

Rule 2. Translation with weak synchronous relation.
Translation from *EOS* with weak synchronous relation to Translated *EOS*, is defined by following. Given an $EOS = (SN, ON, \rho)$ in Definition 3. Let Translated *EOS*, $TEOS = (TS, TT, TF)$ is a flat net translated from *EOS*, iff: (a)-(c)

(a): $TS = P \cup B$
(b): $TT = T \cup E \cup \rho$
(c): Construction of TF by a set of translation rules: (1)-(3)

Rule (1): $\forall ti \in T$,
$\begin{cases} \forall px \in \bullet ti \text{ in } SN, \text{ then } (px, ti) \in TF \text{ in } TEOS \\ \forall py \in ti \bullet \text{ in } SN, \text{ then } (ti, py) \in TF \text{ in } TEOS \end{cases}$

Rule (2): $\forall ej \in E$,
$\begin{cases} \forall bx \in \bullet ej \text{ in } ON, \text{ then } (bx, ej) \in TF \text{ in } TEOS \\ \forall by \in ej \bullet \text{ in } ON, \text{ then } (ej, by) \in TF \text{ in } TEOS \end{cases}$

Rule (3): $\forall ikW : (ti, ej) \in \rho$, then add a new transition $tiej$ to TT, ie. $tiej \in TT$, and assign the duration of $tiej$ with the duration of (ti, ej)
$\begin{cases} \forall px \in \bullet ti \text{ in } SN, \text{ then } (px, tiej) \in TF \text{ in } TEOS \\ \forall py \in ti \bullet \text{ in } SN, \text{ then } (tiej, py) \in TF \text{ in } TEOS \\ \forall bx \in \bullet ej \text{ in } ON, \text{ then } (bx, tiej) \in TF \text{ in } TEOS \\ \forall by \in ej \bullet \text{ in } ON, \text{ then } (tiej, by) \in TF \text{ in } TEOS \end{cases}$

Compared with Rule 1, *TS* is the place set of *TEOS*, which combines the place set *P* of *SN* and the place set *B* of *ON*. *TT* is the transition set of *TEOS*, which combines the transition set *T* of *SN* and the transition set *E* of *ON*, and adding new transitions for the interaction relation set ρ,

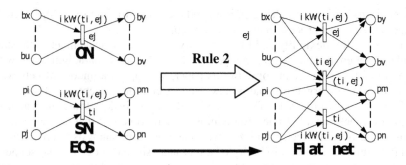

Fig. 6. Local scenario of the translation rule (3) with weak synchronous relation

TF is an arc set of *TEOS*. The following rules (1) (2) (3) are defined for the arcs of *TEOS*. These rules are defined according to the occurrence rules of Definition 4 and weak synchronous of Definition 10.

In Rule 2, the rule (1) is according to System-autonomous firing of Definition 4, the rule (2) is according to Object-autonomous firing, and rule (3) is according to Weak Synchronous firing.

The rule (1) and rule (2) in Rule 2 mean remaining the elements and the structures of both *SN* and *ON*. For weak synchronous relation, the rule (3) in Rule 2 is the same as the rule (3) in Rule 1.

According to the translation rules for weak synchronous relation, the EOS with weak synchronous relation can be equivalently translated into a flat net.

Figure 6 shows a local scenario of the translation rule (3) in Rule 2, a translation supporting weak synchronous relation.

Theorem 2. The translation Rule 2 also preserves the NN-soundness property of NN-WF-net.

The proof is similar to the Theorem1. Here is omitted due to the length limitation.

With the weak synchronous and duration concepts, the model of nets within nets can be better used to model cross-organizational process.

6 Related Work and Conclusions

Petri net model is a good formalism for software process modeling. W. Deiters and V. Gruhn et al. presented a FUNFOST net model used in MELMAC system [3]. Aalst presented the definition of workflow nets [1]. Verbeek has developed an inter-organizational workflow nets using XRL/Flower [14]. Both of them are based on traditional flat nets, which cannot model mobility directly and define the organizational boundaries clearly.

As a novel multi-dimensional Petri net model, Valk presented the definition of nets within nets [12]. The model of nets within nets enhances the capability of modeling mobility and is well suited for cross-organizational process modeling.

In the design perspective of workflow systems, T. Cai et al. at Dartmouth College developed a workflow system based on mobile agents, called DartFlow [2]. M. Divitini et al. also provided a system concept of inter-organizational workflow based on agent coordination [5]. Mobile agent is a good technique for improving the flexibility and the scalability of process management system.

To improve the flexibility and the scalability of process management in the cross-organizational environment, we combine the advantages of the paradigm of net within nets and mobile agent technology. In this paper, we apply the model of nets within nets to model cross-organizational process, and extend the concept of WF-nets in the paradigm of nets within nets. Then, we provide an equivalent translation approach from multi-dimensional Petri nets to traditional flat Petri nets so that the model of nets within nets can be indirectly analyzed with many existing analysis approaches. The translation rule reduces the difficulty of direct analysis and preserves the soundness property. For enhancing the flexibility of execution, we introduce weak synchronous relation into the model of nets within nets. This is the main work of this paper. Petri net model has firm mathematical foundation, so this translation will provide a base for verification and analysis of cross-organizational process model.

In this paper, we focus on the control process perspective of the software processes. For a complete software process support system, resource perspective, data perspective and organizational perspective are included. In our opinion, the control process perspective is the kernel of process model, and other perspectives can be added around the control process perspective. This is the future direction of our work.

Acknowledgements

We want to thank Professor R. Valk, Dr. M. Köhler and Dr. B. Farwer of TGI Group, Hamburg University and Dr. K. Misra of Department of Computer Science, Warwick University for their valuable suggestions.

References

1. W.M.P. van der Aalst: The Application of Petri Nets to Workflow Management. *Journal of Circuits, Systems, and Computers*, (1998) 21-66
2. T. Cai, P. A. Gloor and S. Nog: DARTFlow: A Workflow Management System on The Web Using Transportable Agents. Dartmouth College PCS-TR96-283
3. W. Deiters and V. Gruhn: The FUNSOFT Net Approach to Software Process Management. *International Journal on Software Engineering and Knowledge Engineering*, (1994) 229-256
4. J. Desel, J. Esparza: *Free choice Petri nets*. Cambridge University Press (1995)
5. M. Divitini, C. Hanachi, C. Sibertin-Blanc: Inter-Organizational Workflows for Enterprise Coordination. *Coordination of Internet Agents: Models, Technologies, and Applications*, Springer (2001) 369-398
6. W. S. Humphrey: *Managing the Software Process*. Addison-Wesley (1989)
7. M. Köhler, D. Moldt, and H. Rölke: Modelling mobility and mobile agents using nets within nets. Proc. of *Application and Theory of Petri Nets 2003*, Springer-Verlag, LNCS 2679 (2003) 121-140
8. M. Köhler and H. Rölke: Properties of Object Petri Nets. Proc. of *Application and Theory of Petri Nets 2004*, Springer-Verlag, LNCS 3099 (2004) 278–297
9. C. Lakos: From Coloured Petri nets to Object Petri nets. Proc. of *Application and Theory of Petri Nets 1995*, Springer-Verlag, LNCS 935 (1995) 278-297

10. L. J. Osterweil: Software Processes are Software too. Proc. of *ICSE* (1987) 2-13
11. W. Reisig: *An Introduction to Petri Nets*. Springer (1985)
12. R. Valk: Petri nets as token objects: An introduction to elementary object nets. Proc. of *Application and Theory of Petri Nets*, Springer-Verlag, LNCS 1420 (1998) 1-25
13. R. Valk: Concurrency in Communication Object Petri Nets. In G. Agha et al. editors, *Concurrent Object-Oriented Programming and Petri Nets*, Springer-Verlag, LNCS 2001 (2001) 164-195
14. H. M. W. (Eric) Verbeek, A. Hirnschall, and Wil M. P. van der Aalst: XRL/Flower: Supporting Inter-organizational Workflows Using XML/Petri-Net Technology. Proc. of *WES* 2002, Springer-Verlag, LNCS 2512 (2002) 93-108

M(in)BASE: An Upward-Tailorable Process Wrapper Framework for Identifying and Avoiding Model Clashes

David Klappholz[1] and Daniel Port[2]

[1] Stevens Institute of Technology, Department of Computer Science,
New Jersey, USA
d.klappholz@worldnet.att.net
[2] University of Hawaii at Manoa, Department of Information
Technology Management, 2404 Maile Way, E601k, Honolulu, Hawaii, 96822
dport@hawaii.edu

Abstract. MBASE (Model-Based [System] Architecting & Software Engineering) is a framework that can be wrapped around any software development process to deal with project failures caused by "model clashes." Existing MBASE guidelines have all been designed to cover large classes of projects, and are intended to be tailored down, based on risk considerations, to the project at hand. Experience has shown that tailoring down is quite hard to learn and apply; based upon this observation, we are developing M(in)BASE, a minimal version of MBASE intended to be tailored up. In this paper, we review the fundamentals of MBASE, discuss, in detail, the reasons for creating M(in)BASE, and describe M(in)BASE.

1 Introduction: MBASE

Even when a sophisticated software development process is used, projects often fail. A prime reason for this failure is unresolved, often undetected, differences among stakeholders' sets of assumptions – their "models" – of various aspects of the project. MBASE [1,2,3,4,5,9,10] is an approach to identifying "model clashes" so that their risks can be dealt with. Rather than being a development process, MBASE is a framework that can be wrapped around any type of development process, from light-weight Agile to heavier-weight Plan-driven.

A relatively heavy weight set of MBASE guidelines [10] has been used in USC's CS577 for a number of years, and a number of variants have been used in industry and government projects [6,7,8]. All have been designed to cover a wide variety of project types, i.e., to be more general than is required for any specific project, and to be tailorable down, based on risk conditions, to the project at hand. MBASE's adoption has been limited for various reasons, chief among them, we believe, that performing risk-based tailoring down – especially tailoring down for use with agile processes -- is fundamentally harder than performing risk-based tailoring up. In this paper we review MBASE and introduce M(in)BASE, a "minimal" version of MBASE intended to be tailored up, as required, to the project at hand.

Existing versions of MBASE start with the observation that in considering model clashes, it is useful to divide stakeholders' models into the following four categories:

M. Li, B. Boehm, and L.J. Osterweil (Eds.): SPW 2005, LNCS 3840, pp. 376 – 388, 2005.

-Success models: sets of assumptions that must be satisfied in order for the stakeholder to consider the product and project to be a success.

-Product models: sets of assumptions about the details of the product, e.g.: the product's operational concept; the product's scope; the product's environment, i.e., people and other hardware/software with which the product will/should interface; the product's requirements, the product's architecture / design; etc.

-Process models: sets of assumptions about the way the product will be developed and put into operation, i.e., about the way the project will be run/managed.

-Property models: sets of assumptions about such aspects of the product or process as cost, schedule, performance, and "ilities" such as reliability, portability, extensibility, maintainability, security, etc.; i.e., properties whose extents can be placed on either absolute or relative scales.

Numerous examples of all four types of assumptions/models may be found in [9].

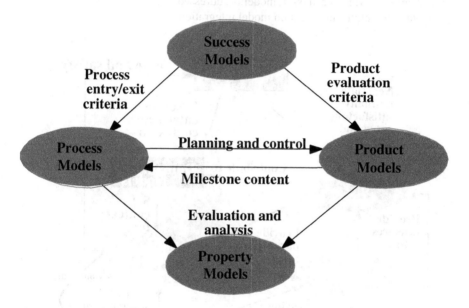

Fig. 1. MBASE Model Integration Framework

MBASE, as a process add-on framework, is defined in terms of five "invariants" [9]. That is, a project can be an MBASE-XP project, an MBASE-Waterfall project, an MBASE-Spiral project, etc. A project being run according development process X is an MBASE-X project if and only if it adheres to the following principles/invariants:

-(i) the model integration framework shown in Figure 1 has been added to X.

-(ii) the process integration framework shown in Figure 2 has been added to X

-(iii) developers use the Life Cycle Objectives (LCO), Life Cycle Architecture (LCA), and Initial Operational Capability (IOC) milestones/anchor points [13] as stakeholder commitment points for proceeding from stage to stage of the project.

-(iv) a stakeholder win-win relationship is defined and sustained, in a fashion compatible with X, for the purpose of dealing with model clashes, throughout the project's life-cycle. This means that periodically:

-success-critical stakeholders are identified-each stakeholder participates in the integration of models relevant to him/her

-models are modified, as required

-all critical stakeholders come to an agreement on the latest, updated models to be used to further pursue the project

-(v) model integration activities are risk-driven as are contents of all artifacts produced during model integration That is, each of the following is decided through an evaluation of its risk-reduction value:

-the number of times that stakeholders meet between anchor points

-the specific issues/models dealt with in developing project artifacts, other than LCO-, LCA-, and IOC-mandated issues/models (see below)

-the detail with which each issue/model is addressed

-the total amount of time spent on model integration

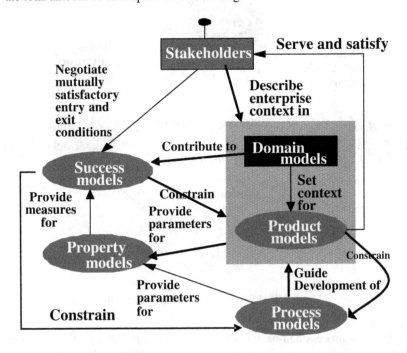

Fig. 2. MBASE Process Integration Framework

Detailed examples of the use of the integration frameworks may be found in [9]

Regardless of the process used in a development project and regardless of whether that process requires that models be discussed only verbally or written down to either loose or tight specifications, it is clear that the developers must create models in the following product- and process-related areas:

-Operational Concept: product's objectives and relation to organization objectives; product's scope; people and other software with which the product will interact; operational scenarios; perhaps, the direction in which the objectives are likely to evolve over time.

-Requirements: product's detailed functions, perhaps prioritized; details of product's interfaces; necessary quality attribute (reliability, availability, maintainability, etc.) levels

-Architecture/Design: logical and physical elements/components that will constitute the product, and their relationships.

-Development Plan: the development process to be used; schedules and milestones; individual developers' responsibilities.

-Business Case: project rationale, including costs, value-added and return on investment estimates; process rationale, requirements satisfaction; project risk assessment.

In all current versions of the MBASE guidelines, the models to be created are organized under artifacts named Operational Concept Definition (OCD), System and Software Requirements Definition (SSRD), System and Software Architecture Definition (SSAD), Life Cycle Plan (LCP), and Feasibility Rationale Description (FRD).

2 MBASE Guidelines

You The key to finding and eliminating model clashes is the use of the model integration and process integration frameworks; but doing so directly is far too much work for the average software developer, even for one who understands the theoretical underpinnings of the frameworks. The obvious solution to this problem is to provide the user with:

-A (maximal) set of specific models to develop within each of OCD, SSRD, SSAD, LCP, FRD, and CTS; that is, a set of models that cover all possible MBASE projects, with the typical MBASE proviso that the question of how elaborate each model should be for a specific project, or whether it need be developed at all, be based on the risk-based principle of "if it's risky not to do it, then do it; if it's risky to do it, then don't."

-For each pair of members of the (maximal) set of models to which a particular model or process integration applies, a detailed description of how the members of the pair must integrate.

Additionally, the user might be provided, for each specific model, with examples of situations in which risk considerations dictate that the model is necessary, and how elaborate it should be.

All of these are included in existing "MBASE guidelines," which may, therefore, be thought of as M(ax)Base Guidelines in the sense that they suggest that:

-one start with an assumption of maximal model construction
-one decide upon actual model construction through the use of a risk-based tailoring-down process.

Given that there really can be no set of models – and model-pair integrations – that cover all possible software development projects, the original MBASE (M(ax)BASE)

guidelines were designed, more or less, to cover all foreseeable CS577 projects and CS577 educational goals [14,15,16].

One problem with the M(ax)BASE approach is that, from 1998 to 2004, in order to correct perceived omissions and to accommodate previously unseen types of project, the M(ax)BASE guidelines grew from a relatively large 86 pages to an unacceptably large 355 pages. This growth occurred in spite of a conscious effort to minimize and reduce the size of the guidelines. The data points in figure 3 below shows the growth of the guidelines from 1998 to 2004 The exponential curve which has been fitted to the data points has an R2 value of 0.96. While there is no theoretical reason to believe that this is indeed a predictor of the growth of the M(ax)BASE guidelines, if it were, the size in 2007 would be 666 pages! We must note that there were always very good reasons for adding to the guidelines. Each year the MBASE development team has carefully:

-evaluated feedback from CS577, especially problem areas and size and quality of deliverables
   -reviewed:
   -current development trends
   -research goals
   -legacy, consistency, and support issues such as instructional materials and follow-on projects
   -industry affiliate requests
   -and many other issues.

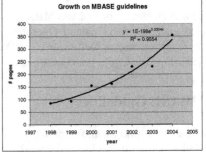

Fig. 3. Growth of MBASE Guidelines

The team has then proposed and hotly debated changes to the guidelines. Despite earnest effort, it seems that the fundamental approach to M(ax)BASE dictates that the guidelines will grow.

The complexity of the guidelines has grown to the point at which they are extremely difficult to follow, even with the addition of electronic templates [17], several "deliverables management" tools [18], and a very sophisticated and elegant "Electronic Process Guide" based on the Spearmint process description system [12,19] developed at the Fraunhofer Institute. This latter fully web-based guide, supplied as a presumed aid in using the MBASE guidelines, has over 1000 hyperlinked pages and remains relatively unused by both CS577 students and industry. With such an explosion of information it is not surprising that CS577 students do not read the entire guidelines. In fact they resort to using only the templates and then later, adapt archived artifacts from previous years' projects (often leaving in traces of the original project(s)!). Given the size of the guidelines and of support materials it has become very hard to keep everything aligned to the MBASE invariants. This latter issue erodes confidence in achieving MBASE's very objective – identifying and avoiding model clashes. To make matters worse, frustration has increased as the need has arisen to adapt to new project types (e.g. COTS-based), to new tools (e.g. Easy Win-Win and Rational Rose), and to new processes (e.g. XP and RUP). The very coherence and integrity of the guidelines has become problematic.

As it turns out, to students whose primary goal is a good grade, and for whom quality software is secondary, the maxim "if it's risky not to do, then do" is more visible than "if it's risky to do, then don't." As a consequence, the result of students' risk management has translated into an alarming increase in the size of artifacts produced, with an attendant lowering of quality (We suspect that an analog of this would hold in industry due to contractual and productivity pressures.)

Regardless of project type, CS577 student teams have tended to produce an instance of each type of model described in the guidelines, even when totally uncalled for. For example, students often produce UML class models for the (presumed) internals of COTS products that are to be integrated into software under development -- even though source code is unavailable, and only interfaces are of any importance.

The fact that it is, apparently, harder to learn what models not to build in a given situation than to simply build all possible models, often results in wasted effort, confusion and uncertainty for all stakeholders, including IV&V teams. LCO, LCA, and IOC reviews become less successful and less fruitful; and, worst of all, in direct opposition to MBASE's purpose, rather than decreasing, the incidence of model clashes often increases. Indeed, this seems to be a classic case of "if I had more time I would have written a shorter letter" syndrome.

Because of the large number of model-pair integrations, many between a model in one model group (OCD, SSRD, SSAD, LCP, and FRD), and a model in a different group (see examples below), even minor changes have caused major (cascading) breakage to the guidelines. Because of the overhead of corrections/updates and of the attendant required updating of lecture slides, evaluation rubrics, and TA training, CS577 instructional staff have often had no choice but to use out of date and inconsistent teaching materials.

On the industry side, MBASE has been adopted by companies like Rational, XEROX, TRW, Litton, FAA, and the Air Force CISR Center. However none of these organizations have truly adopted MBASE in its entirety. Rather, they have taken parts of MBASE and adapted them to their exiting process. For example, Rational has adopted the LCO, LCA, IOC lifecycle anchor points as part of RUP [11]. Although these appear to be examples of "tailoring down" the MBASE guidelines, they really aren't. Tailoring-down means reviewing each item and reducing, adapting, or removing the item if leaving it in poses a risk. Selectively picking bits of MBASE violates the fundamental purpose of the integration framework. Recall that it is this integration framework that is the primary means for identifying and avoiding model clashes, and so this presumed benefit is lost by selectively picking items and using them without regard to their original integrations.

3   M(in)BASE

The logical solution to consider for the problems created by M(ax)BASE is to create a M(in)BASE, i.e., a minimal set of models with model-creation risk management based upon the notion of:

-starting with a minimal version of each model
-adding detail when uncertain as to the adequacy of a model,
i.e., of tailoring up rather than tailoring down.

M(in)BASE is constructed by defining the minimal set of model types needed to embody the MBASE invariants, and adding to each relevant model pair a minimal amount of MBASE integration detail. Thus, for example, in M(in)BASE the OCD (Operational Concept Description) is specified as consisting of the following eight models:

1. Introduction
2. Initiatives and Expected Outcomes (Success Model)
3. Key Stakeholders & Win Conditions (Success Model)
4. System Boundaries and Environment (Property Model)
5. System Capabilities (Product Model)
6. Key Usage Scenario Prototype(s) (Product Model)
7. Operational Stakeholders & Win Conditions (Success Model)
8. Transition, Maintenance and Support Impacts (Property Model)

Each model category (OCD, SSRD, SSAD, LCP, FRD) is defined in terms of the milestone elements it should fulfill, e.g.:

Table 1. Models developed as part of the OCD will be used to contribute to satisfaction of the following milestone elements

OCD Success Criteria for LCO: Baseline operational concept, top-level feasibility considerations, architectural boundaries, and organization feasibility for at least one architecture	OCD Success Criteria for LCA: New system development project: Reasons why the system will be built Enhancement or modification project: Reasons why the system was built in the first place
• Initiatives and Expected Outcomes • Key Stakeholders • System Boundaries and Environment • System Capabilities	• Operational Stakeholders • Transition, Maintenance, and Support Scenarios

Each individual model has a relatively concise specification; for example:

- Initiatives and Expected Outcomes (Success Model)
This section lists outcomes beneficial to the sponsoring organization expected to result from the new system, major initiatives that will be required for the project to be successful, and any assumptions that will have to be satisfied to achieve the desired outcomes. This section is typically developed by starting with a list of desired

outcomes and working backwards, iteratively, to identify: additional outcomes necessary to the achievement of outcomes already known to be necessary; and initiatives whose satisfactory execution will be required to achieve the desired outcomes. One major initiative is always, of course, the development of the hardware/software constituting the new system. Other typical major initiatives are ones for dealing with transition, maintenance, and support.

- System Boundaries and Environment (Property Model)
This section describes the system to be produced in terms of what it does and what, if anything, it requires for its operation from other hardware systems, software systems, and humans. The system boundary distinguishes between:

-what the project team will be responsible for developing and delivering, on the one hand

-and, on the other hand, hardware systems, software systems, and humans with which the developers' system will interact, but over which the developers have no control and for which the developers have no responsibility.

Finally, each individual model comes with an indication of Stakeholder WinWin issues, Risk Issues, Risk Tolerance, and Model Integrations. Expanded M(in)BASE guidelines list all required individual model integrations. As an example, model integrations listed under Key Stakeholders & Win Conditions (Success Model) include:

• OCD 5 System Capabilities (Product Model): Each system capability must come from at least one key stakeholder win condition

• OCD 6 Key Usage Scenario Prototype(s) (Product Model): Each Key Usage Scenario should relate at least one key stakeholder win condition

• SSRD 2.1 Essential Success Requirements (Success Model): Each key stakeholders' (short term) win conditions must be satisfied by the essential success requirements

• SSAD 2 Logical Model (Product Model): For each logical model component, there must be relevant, essential or evolutionary, success requirements

• SSAD 3 Physical Model (Product Model): For each physical model component, there must be relevant, essential or evolutionary, success requirements

• LCP 2 Project Execution Plan (Process Model): The project execution plan must include steps to realize all key stakeholder win conditions

• FRD 2.1.2 Benefits: Value Added and Return on Investment (ROI) (Success Model): The benefits of achieving all key stakeholders' win conditions must be evaluated

• FRD 2.5 Stakeholder Concurrence (Success Model): All key stakeholders' win conditions must be accounted for by stakeholder concurrence

While M(ax)BASE guidelines specify that (analysis stage) use cases, a results chain, etc., must be included as models in the OCD, the basic M(in)BASE guidelines contain no such detail; expanded M(in)BASE guidelines, or a M(in)BASE textbook might include the following as possible Initiatives and Expected Outcomes models:

Table 2. M(in)BASE possible Initiatives and Expected Outcomes models

Model approach	Degree of formality
UML Use-case diagram where actors are initiatives, associations are contributions, uses are outcomes, notes are assumptions	Medium-high
The Results Chain is a useful notation for representing initiatives, contributions, assumptions, expected outcomes	Medium-high
The WinWin model explicitly relates stakeholder win-conditions, issues, options, and agreements which roughly translate into general initiatives, contributions and assumptions, specific initiatives, and expected outcomes	Medium
A simple two-column list of initiatives and related outcomes with notable assumptions	Low-medium
Stand-up meeting with paragraph summary of initiatives, outcomes and assumptions	Very low

For example, a "stand-up meeting with paragraph summary of initiatives, outcomes and assumptions," an extremely modest and low-cost model, is sufficient as a M(in)BASE Initiatives and Expected Outcomes model if the developers, perhaps using XP as their process model, deem there to be little/no/acceptable risk in not elaborating the model any further. Where the risk is significantly greater, a use-case model might be indicated.

Table 3 below provides a superficial comparison of M(in)BASE with M(ax)BASE based on their respective major sections, subsections, and numbers of pages:

Table 3. Comparison of M(in)BASE with M(ax)BASE major sections, subsections, and numbers of pages

Section	# pages		# Major sections		# sub-sections*	
	M(in)	M(ax)	M(in)	M(ax)	M(in)	M(ax)
OCD	7	41	8	6	8	23
SSRD	5	17	3	7	10	18
SSAD	3	128	6	5	6	20
LCP	2	30	3	5	3	15
FRD	5	18	2	5	7	12

*Note: If a major section has no subsections it is counted as one subsection

The above table is not exactly an apples-to-apples comparison as the M(ax)BASE guidelines provide details and elaborations specific to use in CS577, however it does underline logistical differences. That is, because tailorable-up M(in)BASE is far smaller and far less complex than M(ax)BASE, we believe it will be considerably more successful than tailorable-down M(ax)BASE because M(in)BASE should be far easier:

-to use -- subject to developers' having a solid background in risk assessment, and to the availability of material descriptive of standard modeling techniques and notations, from the lightest weight to the heaviest.

-to keep in line with the MBASE invariants

-to adapt to specific types of project, i.e., to perform generic tailoring up for classes of projects which by their nature, require heavier duty modeling.

-to be adopted by both academics teaching software development and industry developers.

4   The M(in)BASE Guidelines Project

The goals of the M(in)BASE work currently underway are to produce:

-a minimal set of model types that are general enough so that for (almost) all software development projects, regardless of the process to be used, a set of instances can be developed to cover the project's modeling needs.

-a list of specific model (type)-pair integrations required to identify, and help eliminate, all model clash types dealt with by the MBASE model and process integration frameworks.

-a compilation of actual risk issues encountered in software development projects, of a wide range of complexities, using a wide range of development processes.

-guidelines for the degree of elaboration required for each model type, or class of model types, based upon actual project risks.

-a compilation of examples of model instances, of various degrees of elaboration, together with the risk-based reasoning behind the degree of elaboration to which each was developed.

-instructional materials, including lecture slides and a textbook, to be used to teach both students and professional software developers to adapt M(in)BASE to their projects.

We have developed initial versions of the first two items on the list above, and are proceeding to develop the rest. Even though we are just at the start of the M(in)BASE project, the process of developing the model types and integrations, has served to elucidate at least two critical points regarding MBASE in general.

For one, it had previously been thought that all software development projects are sufficiently prone to model clashes as to justify the overhead of using MBASE, in one version or another. As it turns out, this is not true, because, in some cases, which we are beginning to learn how to characterize, model clashes are so unlikely as to counter-indicate MBASE's overhead; i.e., there are cases in which even the most minimal version of MBASE's has more overhead than justifies the small amount of risk reduction it provides. The following is an example of such a project:

-Consider a project whose goal is to develop software to convert data from the format required by one DBMS to the format required by a different DBMS; assume further that the company involved in this development effort is producing the data conversion software for public sale, rather than for use in migrating an application of its own from the first DBMS to the second one; suppose, finally, that the chosen developer has experience with both DBMS's and that the development is projected to be completed by one developer in two to three weeks, and is needed, to capture market sure, in a month at the latest. In this case the critical stakeholders' business needs are well-known up front as are technical software requirements; risks are well-understood and of very low magnitude; the project will pass through LCO, LCA, and IOC, but will probably reach LCO (identification of one feasible architecture) almost upon initiation, will probably reach LCA at or shortly after the same time as it reaches LCO, and will reach IOC a few short weeks later. In this case, the overhead of using MBASE is almost certainly higher than necessary, and would likely delay the production of the software or reduce its quality.

On the other hand, the following is a project for which MBASE's overhead is probably justified:

-Consider an e-services project to be done by a team of developers who have little experience working with one another, and have little exposure to the application domain; assume further that this is the first such project on which the customer, the owner of a medium-sized business, is embarking; assume, finally, that the best initial estimate of the size of the development team is five people. Even given its overhead, the use of MBASE is probably worthwhile because:

-the customer has likely thought very little about the details of the functionality required to satisfy both his/her needs and those of end users. The developers will, therefore, likely produce unusable software without going through a Win-Win process.

-risks relating to the customer's inexperience with software developers and software development, to the developers inexperience with the domain and with working together, and to the possibility that it is infeasible to produce software that will be usable and will satisfy the customer's business needs within time and budget constraints, make it most likely to either stop the project early or succeed in the development if all phases are risk-driven.

Starting to develop M(in)BASE has also led to a realization that not all projects are not MBASE prospects because not all projects need go through all three of LCO, LCA, and IOC. Examples of such MBASE non-candidates are (most) prototyping projects, which needn't go through IOC. Although some of MBASE's aspects might be applicable to such projects, all versions of MBASE, including the most minimal, come with the overhead of producing and integrating models that are not even used until IOC, resulting in clearly unnecessary overhead for projects that needn't go that far.

Finally, the M(in)BASE project has led us to the realization that some projects are, essentially, pre-architected and would suffer from considerable unnecessary overhead if MBASE were to be applied. An example of this type of project is one in which the use of specific middleware, along with, for example, specific server-end and client-end technology is mandated from the get-go, so that the overhead of the "architecting" in MBASE is not justified.

5 Future Research

On an informal level, it would be interesting, and far easier than with M(ax)BASE, to study the way users tailor M(in)BASE, especially with respect to their use of risk considerations.

On a more formal level, the basic question that must be answered is whether M(in)BASE will work better than M(ax)BASE; that is:

-will M(in)BASE prove to be easier to adapt to specific processes (e.g., to RUP, XP, Spiral) than is M(ax)BASE?
-does M(in)BASE deliver on the promised benefit of reducing risk due to model clashes?
-will more industry/government organizations adopt M(in)BASE than have adopted M(ax)BASE?
-will organizations that adopt M(in)BASE adopt the entire framework – required for dealing with model clashes?

On the issue of whether any version of MBASE delivers on the promised benefit of reducing risk due to model clashes, Al Said's USC PhD thesis [20] was a good start to the study of this question, but suffered from the fact that the very magnitude of M(ax)BASE made definitive conclusions extremely hard to achieve because relevant issues are obscured by the sheer magnitude of each studied project's documentation of its M(ax)BASE models. M(in)BASE's far smaller model documentation promises to be more amenable to the required analysis, and promises to enable us to include far more project instances in the study.

6 Summary

MBASE has proven to be valuable as a process wrapper framework for software engineering courses; many of its elements have been adopted in a variety of organizations. Logistical issues arising from the rapid growth and complexity of the guidelines have resulted in limited industry adoption and artifacts of questionable quality within the CS577 real-project software engineering course. Furthermore, we are finding it increasingly difficult to adapt the MBASE guidelines to new development tools and models (e.g. COTS, XP). The original purpose of MBASE, to identify and avoid model clashes, is difficult to assure within the current set of guidelines.

We believe the source of these problems to be the fundamental approach of "tailoring down" guidelines that attempt to address a broad range of project types and model choices. It is inherently difficult to apply the principle of "if it's risky to do it, then don't" to tailoring the complex MBASE guidelines.

The M(in)BASE project attempts to address the challenges of developing a stable, easily adopted and easily adapted version of MBASE by basing the approach on the principle "if it's risky not to do it, then do it" to guide in the "tailoring up" of a minimal set of MBASE models to a particular project.

References

1. Boehm, Port: Escaping the Software Tar Pit: Model Clashes and How to Avoid Them. ACM Software Engineering Notes (January 1999) 36-48,
   http://sunset.usc.edu/TechRpts/Papers/usccse98-517/usccse98-517.pdf
2. Boehm, Por: Conceptual Modeling Challenges for Model-Based Architecting and Software Engineering (MBASE). Proceedings, Conceptual Modeling (1997) 24-43,
   http://sunset.usc.edu/TechRpts/Papers/usccse98-513/usccse98-513.pdf

3. Boehm, Port, Egyed, and Abi-Antoun: The MBASE Life Cycle Architecture Milestone Package: No Architecture Is An Island. World International Conference in Software Architectures (1999) http://sunset.usc.edu/TechRpts/Papers/usccse98-510/usccse98-510.pdf
4. Boehm, Port. When Models Collide: Lesson From Software Systems Analysis. IT Professional, IEEE-CS (Janurary/February 1999) 49-56
5. Bohm, Port, Al-Said: Avoiding the Software Model-Clash Spiderweb. IEEE Computer, Vol.33, No.11 (2000) 120-122
6. Boehm, Port, Huang, and Brown: Using the Spiral Model and MBASE to Generate New Acquisition Process Models: SAIV, CAIV, and SCQAIV. Crosstalk (January 2002)
7. Boehm, Port. Balancing Discipline and Flexibility With the Spiral Model and MBASE. Crosstalk (December 2001)
8. Boehm, Basili, Port, and Jain: Achieving CMMI Level 5 Improvements with MBASE and the CeBASE Method. CrossTalk, Vol. 15, No. 5 (May 2002) 9-16
9. Klappholz, Port: Introduction to Model Based Architecting and Software Engineering (MBASE). Advances in Computers Edited by Marvin V. Zelkowitz, Elsevier Inc., Volume 62 (2004)
10. Boehm, B., Port, D., Abi-Antoun, M. and Egyed, A.: Guidelines for Model-Based Architecting and Software Engineering (MBASE), version 2.2, USC-CSE, (Feb.2001), http://sunset.usc.edu/Research/MBASE
11. Kruchten, P.: The Rational Unified Process. Addison-Wesley (1998)
12. MBASE Guidelines and MBASE Electronic Process Guide. USC-CSE. http://cse.usc.edu/research/MBASE/EPG
13. B. Boehm: Anchoring the Software Process. IEEE Software, Vol.13, No.4 (1996) 73-82
14. Port, Boehm: Using a Model Framework In Developing and Delivering a Family of Software Engineering Project Courses. 14th Conference on Software Engineering Education and Training (CSEE&T) (February 2001)
15. Boehm B., Egyed A., Kwan J., Port D., Shah A., and Madachy R.: Using the WinWin Spiral Model: A Case Study. (July 1999) (PDF)
16. B. Boehm, A. Egyed, J. Kwan, and R. Madachy: Developing Multimedia Applications with the WinWin Spiral Model. Proceedings, ESEC/ FSE 97, Springer Verlag (1997)
17. http://cse.usc.edu/classes/cs577a_2004/guidelines/MBASEtemplates/OCD_Templatev1a.doc
18. http://cse.usc.edu/classes/cs577a_2004/coursenotes/ep/Mdm.pdf
19. http://www.iese.fhg.de/Spearmint_EPG/
20. Al-Said M.: Ph.D. Thesis, University of Southern California, Department of Computer Science (2003)

Integrated Modeling of Business Value and Software Processes

Raymond Madachy[1,2]

[1] USC Center for Software Engineering,
Department of Computer Science, SAL 318,
University of Southern California, Los Angeles, CA 90089-0781
madachy@usc.edu
[2] Cost Xpert Group, 2990 Jamacha Rd., #250,
San Diego, CA 92019

Abstract. Business value attainment should be a key consideration when designing software processes. Ideally they are structured to meet organizational business goals, but it is usually difficult to integrate the process and business perspectives quantitatively. This research uses modeling and simulation to assess process tradeoffs for business case analysis. A model for commercial software enterprises relates the dynamics between product specifications, investment costs, schedule, software quality practices, market size, license retention, pricing and revenue generation. The system dynamics model allows one to experiment with different product strategies, software processes, marketing practices and pricing schemes while tracking financial measures over time. It can be used to determine the appropriate balance of process activities to meet goals. Examples are shown for varying scope, reliability, delivery of multiple releases, and determining the quality sweet spot for different time horizons. Results show that optimal policies depend on various stakeholder value functions, opposing market factors and business constraints. Future model improvements are also identified.

1 Introduction

Software-related decisions should not be extricated from business value concerns. Unfortunately, software engineering practice and research frequently lacks a value-oriented perspective. Value-Based Software Engineering (VBSE) seeks to integrate value considerations into current and emerging software engineering principles and practices [1].

This macroprocess research from [2] addresses the planning and control aspect of VBSE to manage the value delivered to stakeholders. Techniques to model cost, schedule and quality are integrated with business case analysis to allow tradeoff studies in a commercial software development context. Business value is accounted for in terms of return-on-investment (ROI) of different product and process strategies.

Many current practices are done in a value-neutral setting, such as standard earned-value techniques that track cost and schedule but not stakeholder or business value.

M. Li, B. Boehm, and L.J. Osterweil (Eds.): SPW 2005, LNCS 3840, pp. 389–402, 2005.
© Springer-Verlag Berlin Heidelberg 2005

The latter can be considered the "real" earned value. A value-oriented approach provides explicit guidance for making products useful to people by considering different people's utility functions or value propositions. The value propositions are used to determine relevant measures for given scenarios.

Two major aspects of stakeholder value are addressed here. One is the business value to the development organization stemming from software sales. Another is the value to the end-user stakeholder from varying feature sets and quality. Production functions relating different aspects of value to their costs were developed and are included in the integrated model.

It is a challenge to tradeoff different software attributes and particularly between different perspectives such as business and software development. Software process modeling and simulation can be used to reason about software value decisions. It can help find the right balance of activities that contribute to stakeholder value with other constraints such as cost, schedule or quality goals. A related approach to VBSE is the iDAVE static spreadsheet model used to estimate the ROI of investments in software dependability [3].

Some important elements of VBSE that this research includes are stakeholders' value proposition elicitation and reconciliation, business case analysis, and value-based monitoring and control. It is assumed in this modeling context that a benefits realization analysis has been performed to substantiate a new product initiative, though the model can clearly be used in this capacity. The stakeholder values of profit and ROI have also already been elicited. These steps have been performed in the field for companies in which this business case model has been applied.

2   Model Overview

The system dynamics model represents a business case for commercial software development. The user inputs and model factors can vary over the project duration as opposed to a static model. Inputs can be modified interactively by the user during the course of a run and the model responds to the midstream changes. It can be used dynamically before or during a project. Hence it is suitable for "flight simulation" training or actual project usage to reflect actuals to-date.

The sectors of the model and their major interfaces are shown in Fig. 1. The software process and product sector computes the staffing profile and quality over time based on the software size, reliability setting, and other inputs. The staffing rate becomes one of the investment flows in the finances sector, while the actual quality is a primary factor in market and sales. The resulting sales are used in the finance sector to compute various financial measures.

Fig. 2 shows a diagram of the software process and product sector. It dynamically calculates effort, schedule and defects. The staffing rate over time is calculated with a version of Dynamic COCOMO [4] using a variant of a Rayleigh curve calibrated to the COCOMO II cost model at the top level. The project effort is based on the number of function points and the reliability setting. There are also some parameters that determine the shape of the staffing curve.

There is a simple defect model to calculate defect levels used in the market and sales sector to modulate sales. Defect generation is modeled as a co-flow with the software development rate, and the defect removal rate accounts for their finding and fixing. See [2] for more background on these standard flow structures for effort and defects.

Fig. 3 shows the market and sales sector accounting for market share dynamics and software license sales. The perceived quality is a reputation factor that can reduce the number of sales if products have many defects (see the next section).

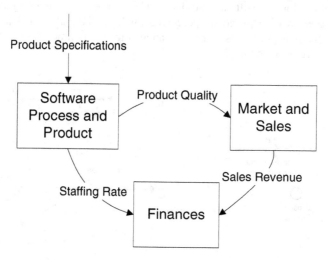

Fig. 1. Model sectors and major interfaces

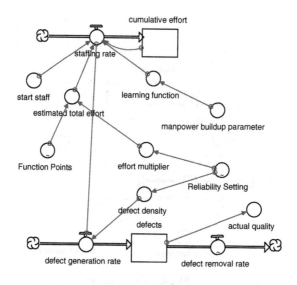

Fig. 2. Software process and product sector

The market and sales model presented herein is a simplification of a more exten-sive being used in industry that accounts for additional marketing initiatives and soft-ware license maintenance sales.

The finance sector is shown in Fig. 4. Investments include the labor costs for soft-ware development, maintenance and associated activities. Revenue is derived from the number of license sales. Sales are a function of the overall market size and market share percentage for the software product. The market share is computed using a potential market share adjusted by perceived quality. The additional market share derivable from a new product is attained at an average delay time. More details of the overall model are provided in [2].

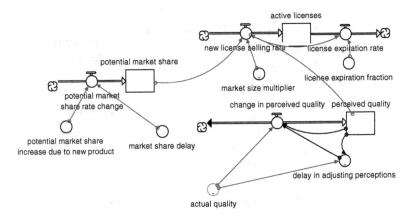

Fig. 3. Market and sales sector

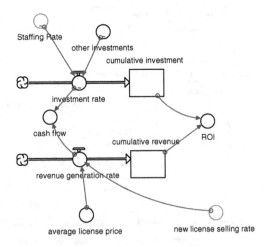

Fig. 4. Finance sector

2.1 Quality Modeling and Value Functions

For simplification, software reliability as defined in the COCOMO II model [4] is used as a proxy for all quality practices. It models the tradeoff between reliability and development cost. There are four different settings of reliability from low to very high that correspond to four development options. The tradeoff is increased cost and longer development time for increased quality. This simplification can be replaced with a more comprehensive quality model (see Conclusions and Future Work).

The resulting quality will modulate the actual sales relative to the highest potential. A lower quality product will be done quicker; it will be available on the market sooner but sales will suffer from poor quality.

Several rounds of a continuing Delphi poll of software marketing experts were conducted to help quantify the relative sales impact of different quality levels. Now the mapping between reliability and the relative impact to sales from the Delphi results is captured as a production function and used in the model with the latest refined numbers.

Collectively there are two value-based production functions in the model to describe value relationships (they are illustrated in the first applied example). A market share production function addresses the organizational business value of product features. The business value is quantified in terms of added potential market share attainable by the features. The relationship assumes that all features are implemented to the highest quality. Since the required reliability will impact how well the features actually work, the relationship between reliability costs and actual sales and is needed to vary the sales due to quality.

The value function for actual sale attainment is relevant to two classes of stakeholders. It describes the value of different reliability levels in terms of sales attainment, and is essentially a proxy for user value as well. It relates the percent of potential sales attained in the market against reliability costs. Illustrations of the production functions are shown in the next section.

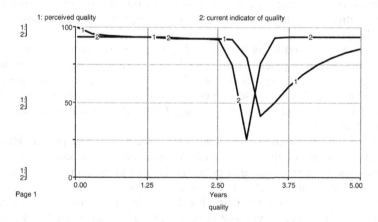

Fig. 5. Perceived quality trends with high and low quality product deliveries

The market and sales sector also has a provision to modulate sales based on the perceived quality reputation. A perception of poor quality due to many defects will reduce the number of sales. A bad quality reputation takes hold almost immediately with a buggy product (bad news travels fast), and takes a long time to recover from in the market perception even after defects are fixed. This phenomenon is represented with asymmetrical information smoothing as shown in Fig. 5 with a variable delay in adjusting perceptions.

3 Applied Examples

Three representative business decision scenarios are demonstrated next. The first one demonstrates the ability to dynamically assess combined strategies for scope and reliability. The second example looks at strategies of multiple releases of varying quality. Finally the model is used to determine a process sweet spot for reliability.

3.1 Example 1: Dynamically Changing Scope and Reliability

The model can be used to assess the effects of individual or combined strategies for overall scope and reliability. This example will show how it can be used to change product specifications midstream as a re-plan. Static cost models typically do not lend themselves to re-plans after the project starts, as all factors remain constant through time. This dynamic capability can be used in at least two ways by a decision-maker:

- assessing the impact of changed product specifications during the course of a project
- before the project starts, determining if and how late during the project specifications can be changed based on new considerations that might come up.

Three cases are simulated: 1) an unperturbed reference case, 2) a midstream descoping of the reference case and 3) a simultaneous descoping and lowered required reliability. Such descoping is a frequent strategy to meet time constraints by shedding features.

The market share production function in Fig. 6 relates the potential business value against the cost of development for different feature sets. The actual sales production function against reliability costs is shown in Fig. 7, and it is applied against the potential market capture. The four discrete points correspond to required reliability levels of low, nominal, high and very high. Settings for the three cases are shown in both production functions.

Fig. 8 shows a sample control panel interface to the model. The primary inputs for product specifications are the size in function points (also called scope) and required reliability. The number of function points is the size to implement given features. The size and associated cost varies as the number of features to incorporate.

The reliability settings on the control panel slider are the relative effort multipliers to achieve reliability levels from low to very high. These are input by user via the slider for "Reliability Setting". The attainable market share derived from the sales production function in Fig. 6 is input by user on the slider "Potential Market Share Increase".

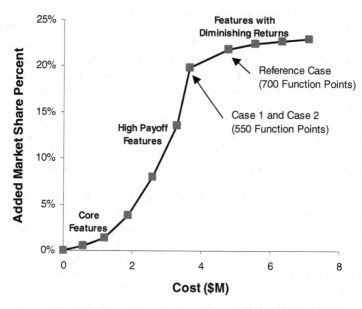

Fig. 6. Market share production function and feature sets

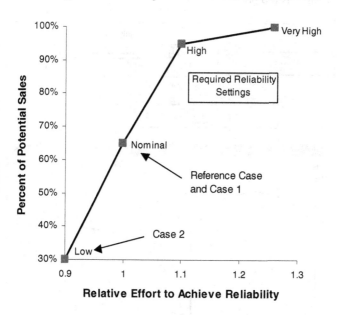

Fig. 7. Sales production function and reliability

Fig. 8 also shows the simulation results for the initial reference case. The default case of 700 function points is delivered with nominal reliability at 2.1 years with a potential 20% market share increase. This project is unperturbed during its course and the 5 year ROI of the project is 1.3.

Trend comparisons between the three cases can be visualized on Figures 8-10. Fig. 9 illustrates the initial case perturbed early to descope low-ROI features (see Fig. 6 for the points on the production function). The scope goes down to 550 function points and the staffing profile adjusts dynamically for it. The schedule is reduced by a few months. In this case the potential market share increase is lowered by only two percentage points to 18%. With lower development costs and earlier delivery the ROI increases substantially to 2.2.

A combined strategy is modeled in Fig. 10. The scope is decreased the same as before in Case 1 (Fig. 9) plus the reliability setting is lowered from nominal to low. Though overall development costs decrease due to lowered reliability, the market responds poorly. This case provides the worst return of the three options and market share is lost instead of gained.

There is an early hump in sales due to the initial hype of the brand new product, but the market soon discovers the poor quality and then sales suffer dramatically. These early buyers and others assume the previous quality of the product line and are anxious to use the new, "improved" product. Some may have pre-ordered and some are early adopters that always buy when new products come out. They are the ones that find out about the lowered quality and the word starts spreading fast.

A summary of the three cases is shown in Table 1. Case 1 is the best business plan to shed undesirable features with diminishing returns. Case 2 severely hurts the enterprise because quality is too poor.

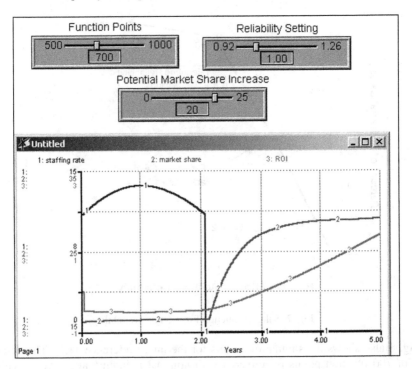

Fig. 8. Sample control panel and reference case (unperturbed)

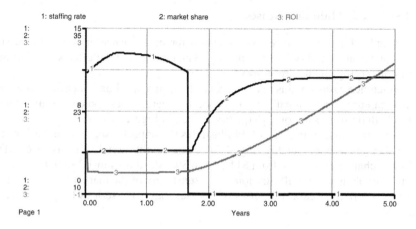

Fig. 9. Case 1 - Descoping of low ROI features at time = .5 Years

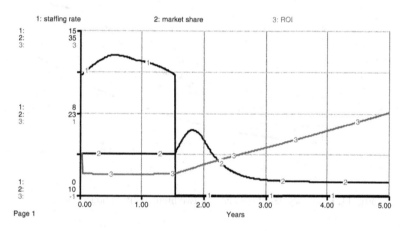

Fig. 10. Case 2 - Descoping of low ROI features and reliability lowering at time = .5 years

Table 1. Case summaries

Case	Delivered Size (Function Points)	Delivered Reliability Setting	Cost ($M)	Delivery Time (Years)	Final Market Share	ROI
Reference Case: Unperturbed	700	1.0	4.78	2.1	28%	1.3
Case 1: Descope	550	1.0	3.70	1.7	28%	2.2
Case 2: Descope and Lower Reliability	550	.92	3.30	1.5	12%	1.0

3.2 Example 2: Multiple Releases

This example shows a more realistic scenario for maintenance and operational support. Investments are allocated to ongoing maintenance and the effects of additional
releases of varying quality are shown.

The reference case contains two product rollouts at years 1 and 3, each with the potential to capture an additional 10% of the market share. These potentials are attained
because both deliveries are of high quality as seen in Figures 11-12.

A contrasting case in Figures 13-14 illustrates the impact if the second delivery has
poor quality yet is fixed quickly (Fig. 4 shows the quality trends for this case). This
results in a change of revenue from $11.5 M to $9.6M, ROI from 1.3 to 0.9.

This example is another illustration of the sensitivity of the market to varying quality. Only one poor release in a series of releases may have serious long term consequences.

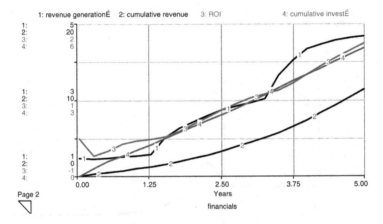

Fig. 11. Reference case financials for two high quality product deliveries

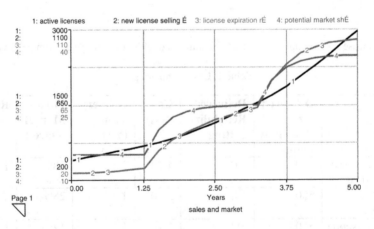

Fig. 12. Reference case sales and market for two high quality product deliveries

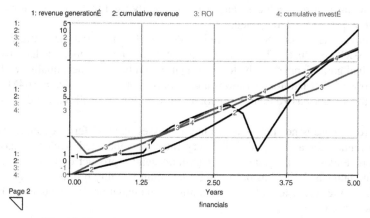

Fig. 13. Financials for high and low quality product deliveries

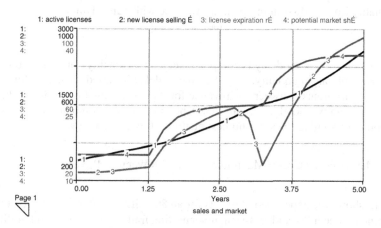

Fig. 14. Sales and market for high and low quality product deliveries

3.3 Example 3: Finding the Sweet Spot

This example derived from [2] shows how the value-based product model can support software business decision-making by using risk consequence to find the quality sweet spot with respect to ROI. The following analysis steps are performed to find the process sweet spot:

- vary reliability across runs
- assess risk consequences of opposing trends: market delays and bad quality losses
- sum market losses and development costs
- calculate resulting net revenue to find process optimum.

The risk consequences are calculated for the different options. Only point estimates are used for the sake of this example. A more comprehensive risk analysis would consider probability distributions to obtain a range of results. Probability is considered constant for each case and is not explicitly used in the calculations. Only the costs (or losses) are determined.

A set of runs is performed that simulate the development and market release of a new 80 KSLOC product. The product can potentially increase market share by 30%, but the actual gains depend on the level of quality. Only the highest quality will attain the full 30%. Other parameterizations are an initial total market size = $64M annual revenue, the vendor has 15% initial market share, and the overall market doubles in 5 years.

A reference case is needed to determine the losses due to inferior quality. The expected revenues for a sub-quality delivery must be subtracted from the maximum potential revenues (i.e. revenue for a maximum quality product delivered at a given time). The latter is defined as delivering a maximum quality product at a given time that achieves the full potential market capture. The equation for calculating the loss due to bad quality is

$$\text{Bad Quality Loss} = \text{Maximum Potential Revenue with Same Timing} - \text{Revenue.} \qquad (1)$$

The loss due to market delay is computed keeping the quality constant. To neutralize the effect of varying quality, only the time of delay is varied. The loss for a given option is the difference between the revenue for the highest quality product at the first market opportunity and the revenue corresponding to the completion time for the given option (assuming the same highest quality). It is calculated with

$$\text{Market Delay Cost} = \text{Maximum Potential Revenue} - \text{Revenue.} \qquad (2)$$

Fig. 15 shows the experimental results for an 80 KSLOC product, fully compressed development schedules and a 3-year revenue timeframe for different reliability options. The resultant sweet spot corresponds to reliability=high. The total cost consisting of delay losses, reliability losses and development cost is minimum at that setting for a 3-year time horizon. Details of the intermediate calculations for the loss components are provided in [2].

The sweet spot depends on the applicable time horizon, among other things. The horizon may vary due for several reasons such as another planned major upgrade or new release, other upcoming changes in the business model, or because investors mandate a specific timeframe to make their return.

The experiment was re-run for typical time horizons of 2, 3 and 5 years using a profit view (the cost view is transformed into a profit maximization view by accounting for revenues). The results are shown in Fig. 16.

The figure illustrates that the sweet spot moves from reliability equals low to high to very high. It is evident that the optimal reliability depends on the time window. A short-lived product (a prototype is an extreme example) does not need to be developed to as stringent reliability as one that will live in the field longer.

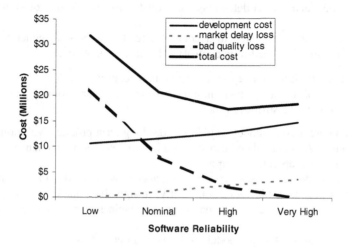

Fig. 15. Calculating reliability sweet spot (3-year timeframe)

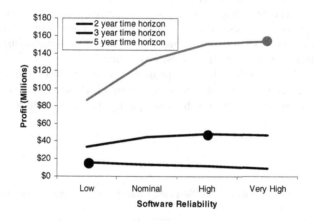

Fig. 16. Reliability sweet spot as a function of time horizon

4 Conclusions and Future Work

It is important to integrate value-based methods into the software engineering discipline to improve processes and maximize software utility. To achieve real earned value, business value attainment must be a key consideration when designing software products and processes. This work shows several ways how software business decision-making can improve with value information gained from simulation models that integrate business and technical perspectives.

The model demonstrates a stakeholder value chain whereby the value of software to end users ultimately translates into value for the software development organization. It also illustrates that commercial process sweet spots with respect to reliability are a balance between market delay losses and quality losses. Quality does impact the bottom line.

The model can be elaborated to account for feedback loops to generate revised product specifications (closed-loop control). This feedback includes:

- external feedback from user to incorporate new features
- internal feedback on product initiatives from an organizational planning and control entity to the software process.

A more comprehensive model would consider long term product evolution and periodic upgrades. Another related aspect to include is general maintenance by adding explicit activities for operational support.

The product defect model can be enhanced with a dynamic version of COQUALMO [5] to enable more constructive insight into quality practices. This would replace the current construct based on the single factor for required software reliability.

Other considerations for the model are in the market and sales sector. The impact of different pricing schemes and varying market assumptions on initial sales and maintenance can all be explored. Some of these provisions are already accounted for in a proprietary version of the model.

The model application examples were run with idealized inputs for sake of demonstration, but more sophisticated dynamic scenarios can be easily handled to model real situations. For example discrete descopings were shown, but in many instances scope will exhibit continuous or fluctuating growth over time.

More empirical data on the relationships in the model will also help identify areas of improvement. Assessment of overall dynamics includes more collection and analysis of field data on business value and quality measures from actual software product rollouts.

References

1. Boehm, B., Huang, L.: Value-Based Software Engineering: A Case Study. IEEE Software, Vol. 20, No. 2 (2003)
2. Madachy R.: Software Process Dynamics. IEEE Computer Society Press, Washington D.C. (2005)
3. Boehm, B., Huang, L., Jain, A., Madachy R.: Reasoning about the ROI of Software Dependability: the iDAVE Model. IEEE Software., Vol. 21, No. 3 (2004)
4. Boehm B., Abts C., Brown W., Chulani S., Clark B., Horowitz E., Madachy R., Reifer D., Steece B.: Software Cost Estimation with COCOMO II. Prentice-Hall (2000)
5. Chulani S., Boehm B.: Modeling software defect introduction and removal: COQUALMO (COnstructive QUALity MOdel). USC-CSE Technical Report 99-510, (1999)

Process Technology to Facilitate the Conduct of Science

Leon J. Osterweil[1], Alexander Wise[1], Lori A. Clarke[1], Aaron M. Ellison[2],
Julian L. Hadley[2], Emery Boose[2], and David R. Foster[2]

[1] University of Massachusetts, Department of Computer Science,
Computer Science Building, Amherst, MA 01003
{ljo, wise, clarke}@cs.umass.edu
[2] Harvard University, Harvard Forest, P.O. Box 68,
Petersham, Massachusetts 01366, USA
{aellison, jhadley, boose, drfoster}@fas.harvard.edu

Abstract. This paper introduces the concept of an analytic web, a synthesis of three complementary views of a scientific process that is intended to facilitate the conduct of science. These three views support the clear, complete, and precise process documentation needed to enable the effective coordination of the activities of geographically dispersed scientists. An analytic web also supports automation of various scientific activities, education of young scientists, and reproducibility of scientific results. Of particular significance, an analytic web is intended to forestall the generation of scientific data that are erroneous or suspect, by using process definitions to prevent incorrect combinations of scientific results. The paper also describes experiences with a tool, SciWalker, designed to evaluate the efficacy of this approach.

1 Introduction

1.1 A Vision and a Caution

The Internet has created the need for a new focus on the processes by which science is done. Worldwide scientific collaborations such as Globus [1], and specific projects such as GriPhyN [2] are beginning to use the Internet to create opportunities for scientists to make data available to worldwide communities, thereby enabling expedited collaborations among geographically distributed researchers. While this creates opportunities through the broader availability of more comprehensive scientific analyses, it also creates the need for stronger and more effective control of dataset distribution and utilization. We believe that an essential component of this control is definition of the processes by which datasets and other key artifacts of science are developed, evolved, and promulgated.

If the vision of broad collaboration among geographically dispersed scientists is to be achieved, the scientists must be sure that they have the same view and understanding of the collaborative activity in which they are engaged. This suggests the need for some medium that is effective in supporting clear, complete, and precise communication about the scientific processes in which all are participating to help assure that the collaboration will produce correct results. Another benefit of such a

M. Li, B. Boehm, and L.J. Osterweil (Eds.): SPW 2005, LNCS 3840, pp. 403–415, 2005.

medium is its value as the basis for the development of definitions of scientific processes that might be promulgated and published, thereby facilitating community consensus and aiding in the education of younger scientists.

Whereas clear, complete, and precise process definitions can facilitate successful coordination and community education, executable process definitions can do much more, potentially helping define the way in which computers and communications technologies can be harnessed to take off of the shoulders of scientists many of the (especially more mundane and straightforward) steps of such processes. One immediate benefit of this is the possibility that such executable definitions of scientific processes might speed the rate of scientific discovery, by supporting automation of tedious activities such as dataset management and communication. This capability also offers the possibility that these processes might be used by independent scientists to validate published scientific results, thereby facilitating the reproducibility of results, an activity that is at the very core of the conduct of modern science.

Such a process definition capability could address another key concern, namely that scientific datasets might be used in misleading and incorrect ways if the precise context in which they were created is not communicated to, and respected by, other scientists. Scientific results are derived through increasingly complex sequences of scientific processes, such as sampling, cleaning, transformation, data mining, statistical inference, and evaluation. Often different processes are performed by different scientists at different times and in different places. And, while the data resulting from these processes is readily available, the processes themselves generally are not. We are concerned about the resulting difficulty of independent reproduction of scientific results, as the need for reproducibility is a bedrock requirement of modern science, and the possibility that different scientific teams may misapply results due to differences in their understandings of how scientific datasets have been produced. The lack of clear understandings of the processes by which these datasets have been produced thus stands to create less agreement, rather than more, and a reduced basis for being able to have the kinds of careful and precise debates needed to arrive at understandings of why differences exist, and how to resolve them. Ultimately, we are concerned that lack of understanding of the processes used to create datasets will inevitably cause some scientists to combine results in ways that will lead to incorrect or misleading conclusions.

In order to avoid this situation, the processes used to generate published data and results, including the tools and algorithms employed by those processes, must be clearly, completely, and precisely defined, and then made readily available. The magnitude of this task should not be underestimated. Modifications to any of the tools, algorithms, or subprocesses used in a scientific process may be inadvertent, as when a software package is updated or the underlying operating system is modified. Lacking awareness of these modifications, subsequent scientific processing (e.g., that done in order to reproduce results) may proceed under the incorrect assumption that the original scientific process is being executed. But if changes to the process have been made, then the original scientific process may indeed not have been repeated, leading either to different results or to the false conclusion that confirmation of prior results has occurred (see [3] for a recent example of the impact of changing algorithms on EPA's particulate matter standards for air quality).

We believe that sounder and more efficient science can facilitated by the Internet, but only if the expedited access to data that it allows is tempered by use of process definitions capabilities of the sort that we describe in this paper.

1.2 A Strategy

To ensure that scientific datasets are adequately well documented to support effective collaboration, education, automation, and reproducibility, and, moreover, to guard against misuse of datasets, potentially resulting in confusion and faulty science, we propose that every dataset generated by a research project should have attached to it structured process metadata that formally describes the processes by which the data were derived, including the sequence of tools, techniques, and intermediate datasets used. The representation of such process metadata information is intuitively what we refer to as an *analytic web*. In the next section we provide a more formal definition of this notion.

In the meantime, however, we can be more specific in stating the goals in developing the concept of an analytic web to be to:

• Facilitate scientific community understanding by providing a medium for the clear, precise, and complete communication about scientific processes;
• Promote effective collaboration in scientific discovery by larger, and geographically more dispersed, communities;
• Support expedited scientific activity by effective incorporation of computer and communications technologies into scientific processes;
• Forestall the possibility that scientific datasets will be misunderstood and misused, thereby leading to faulty scientific results.

The remainder of this paper describes our approach to creating technologies for defining analytic webs, and our early work to evaluate this approach.

2 Formal Description of an Analytic Web

An analytic web is a formal representation of a scientific process, in the form of structured metadata that completely and accurately describes the process, and is sufficient to support execution of the process. Our research suggests that an effective way to represent an analytic web is by means of a coordinated collection of three specific types of graphs – a dataflow graph, a dataset derivation graph, and a process definition graph – all of which were originally developed for use in defining and controlling software development projects (e.g., [4]). In this paper we demonstrate the use of these three graphs by applying them to the formalization of different aspects of a specific ecological data processing process of considerable scientific interest and importance. We argue that the analytic web represented by these three graphs makes an important contribution to assuring the understanding, executability, and reproducibility of this process, and to science in general.

2.1 Dataflow Graphs

A dataflow graph (DFG) defines which types of datasets are acted upon by which types of processes (tools, activities) in order to produce other types of datasets. A DFG documents the relationships among datasets and process types, which are inherently generic. Examples include "rainfall data", "statistical package", or "interpolation via regression". A DFG is analogous to a recipe: "combine flour, eggs, seasonings, milk and water to make a batter". Like a cookbook, the clarity and comprehensibility of a DFG facilitates the reproduction of scientific processes.

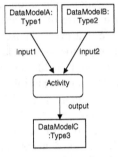

In the DFG shown in Fig. 1, the rectangular nodes represent the types of the datasets to be created and used, the rounded nodes represent the tools, techniques, and human activities that are to be performed, and the edges represent the flow of datasets into and out of these processes. Thus, this figure specifies that "DataModelA", an artifact of type "Type1", and "DataModelB", an artifact of type "Type2", are both required as inputs to an activity, called "Activity", which then produces "DataModelC", an artifact of type "Type3" as its output.

Fig. 1. Dataflow Graph

2.2 Dataset Derivation Graphs

In contrast, a dataset derivation graph (DDG) documents the instances of datasets produced by the actions of specific tools operating on other specific datasets. Dataset instances, which are uniquely specified, are the usual focus of attention in scientific processes. Examples include "rainfall data collected at the Harvard Forest on 1 June 2004 at hourly intervals", "SAS version 6.1", or "non-linear regression using nls2 [5]". Continuing the analogy of thinking of a DFG as a specification of a recipe, then the

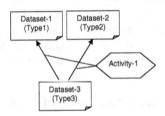

Fig. 2. Data Derivation Graph

DDG specifies the specific items resulting from following that recipe. This, the DDG might specify all of the final and intermediate products generated in baking a spiced chocolate prune cake for Jane's 60th birthday following the Joy of Cooking 10th edition, 1978. Reproducibility demands the documentation provided by the DDG, namely the specific datasets and tools that were actually used.

The example data derivation graph (DDG) shown in Fig. 2 keeps track of the specific datasets that have been used and derived by the actions of the tools specified in a corresponding DFG. In the DDG, a clipped box represents each actual dataset (instance) created by executing a process. Each node is connected by an edge to the dataset(s) from which it was derived. The edge is annotated with a specification of the specific tool instance (e.g., the exact version of a statistical routine or software utility), or sub-process instance (e.g., a representation of another analytic web) used for the derivation.

Thus Fig. 2 specifies that "Dataset-3", an artifact of type, "Type3", was created by the actions of a tool recorded as "Activity-1", using as inputs "Dataset-1", an artifact of type "Type1", and "Dataset-2", an artifact of type "Type2".

2.3 Process Definition Graphs

The augmentation of the information in a DFG with the information contained in a DDG does not provide sufficient documentation to always define the way in which datasets should be, and actually are, produced. The DFG defines the nominal way in which types of activities and tools are to be sequenced in order to produce specified types of datasets and other artifacts. The DDG does indeed record the exact dataset and tool instances that were actually used to produce various dataset results. But the DFG cannot be relied upon to incorporate sufficient checks and controls to assure that the actual instances chosen for participation in the DFG-defined process are consistent with each other, and suitable for use in the process of generating valid scientific results. The DFG only assures that such results are of the right type. Moreover, the DFG is effective for defining nominal processes, and is generally ineffective for defining how the process react when exceptional or unusual contingencies requiring non-nominal processing arise.

The detection and handling of such incompatibilities and non-nominal situations must be defined as part of any process if it is to be of genuine value to scientific investigation in the real world. Scientists generally are aware of such situations, and have appropriate remedies (although not always), but standard DFGs can make it hard or impossible to specify such contingencies and remedies clearly and completely. Therefore, our concept of an analytic web augments the information in a DFG with a more complete and articulate procedural description in the form of a process definition graph (PDG).

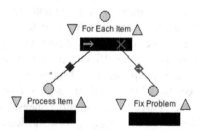

Fig. 3. Process Definition Graph in Little-JIL

A PDG defines the essential procedural details such as the order in which steps must be taken, but augments this with such additional features as preconditions for step execution, post-condition checks to determine whether or not processing has been successful, procedures to use when various exceptional conditions occur at various places in the process, conditions under which processing sequences are to be either iterated or terminated, and checking to assure that artifacts used are consistent with each other and with the activities employing them. In short, the PDG specifies the procedural flow of an analytic web, but also incorporates additional features to assure that dataset combinations are acceptable even when the process has to deal with exceptional conditions.

Figure 3 is a PDG specification, specified using the process definition language Little-JIL [6]. Space does not permit a full explanation of this language. Therefore, it must suffice to say that Fig. 3 specifies that the process "For Each Item" consists of repeated sequential executions of the "Process Item" activity, but that errors encountered in doing so are to be responded to by the execution of the "Fix Problem" activity, after which the next "Process Item" activity is to be initiated. More features of this language will be provided in the more comprehensive example presented in the next section.

3   An Example Analytic Web

We illustrate the need for, and the application of, an analytic web through an example drawn from the field of ecology. This example entails the processing and management of a type of data called eddy covariance data. The eddy covariance method is a commonly used technique for long-term measurement of the carbon exchange (e.g., the absorption of gases such as CO_2 into living organisms, such as plants) of whole ecosystems, and a useful tool in the study of global warming. Briefly, eddy covariance estimates CO_2 absorption by plant life such as forests from the covariance of CO_2 concentration and vertical wind velocity [7]. CO_2 measurements are taken continuously over an extended period by a structure, called a flux tower, located at a fixed location in the midst of a forest. Due to the variability in the accuracy of the data for a variety of reasons due to environmental conditions, researchers at Harvard Forest use a set of processes to identify unacceptable measurements and replace them with statistical estimates.

To identify and replace unacceptable measurements, first, they discard observed values of CO_2 flux if the wind direction is unsuitable for flux measurements. A particular wind direction may be unsuitable because local topography in a given direction from the flux tower creates unpredictable turbulence patterns, or because the forest of interest does not occur over a sufficient fetch in that direction. Second, the researchers examine the relationship between friction velocity, $u*$ (a measure of turbulence in meters per second, which equals the square root of vertical momentum flux), and CO_2 flux for several weeks of nighttime measurements. Flux is plotted against $u*$, and a threshold value of $u*$ ($u*_{threshold}$) is identified beyond which CO_2 flux does not increase significantly. Observed values of CO_2 flux are discarded if $u* < u*_{threshold}$. If data from all wind directions are suitable, the $u*_{threshold}$ criterion typically results in the discarding of <50% of the nighttime observations of CO_2 flux. On the other hand, if some wind directions are unsuitable, >75% of the nighttime observations may be rejected.

Finally, the researchers need to fill the gaps in the dataset that result from discarding observed values of CO2 flux by estimating the values that would have been observed if $u* \geq u*threshold$. To fill these gaps, they fit regression models of the reliable observations (CO_2 flux | $u* \geq u*$threshold) to the measured environmental variables. For nighttime observations, the predictor variables are soil and air temperatures and, occasionally, soil moisture [8].

3.1 Dataflow Graph Model

The data flow graph (DFG) for the process described above is illustrated in Fig. 4. The boxes, "Tower Data", "Environmental Data", "Selection Criteria", "Aggregated Data", "Excluded Data", "Rejected Data", "Selected Data", "Interpolated Data", and "Row-Filled Data" all represent types of data used in creating a usable dataset. As models are also fixed data types, the model type, "Interpolation Model", is also represented as a box. Processes are represented by ovals: "Create Aggregated Data", "Segregate Data", "Create Interpolation Model", "Apply Interpolation Model", "Merge Datasets", and "Revise Selection Criteria" are all types of actions that are applied to particular types of datasets. Diamonds indicate points in which the same dataset is used as input to more than one action or subprocess.

Of particular interest is the action, "Revise Selection Criteria", in which the criteria used to partition the data may be modified after examining the results of interpolating and merging the data. Intuitively, the DFG suggests that new criteria have been created, and that they are to be applied to previous datasets, generating new "Row-Filled Data". The DFG also suggests that this iteration might be continued indefinitely, causing the successive generation of new criteria and new output data. While this intuition is probably correct, we note that it also illustrates a key inadequacy of the DFG, alluded to earlier. The DFG is incapable of specifying precisely which criteria are to be applied to which datasets. Indeed, it is conceivable that scientists may wish to apply new criteria to some previous datasets, or to all previous datasets, or to no previous datasets. The DFG provides no guidance about this. As we shall see, the DDG is capable of recording what datasets actually are created, and the precise datasets and activities that had been used in doing this. But the DDG and DFG together are still incapable specifying what should have been done, and what perhaps would be scientifically unsound. The need for such specification is provided in an analytic web by the PDG, as shall be seen.

Presumably it is vital that there be a precisely defined relationship between each dataset and the model from which it was created. Relationships of this sort are quite familiar to software configuration management practitioners, who rely upon configuration management (CM) tools and technologies to assure needed consistency. Up until the popularization of remote access to data, researchers were better able to exercise informal configuration management processes in their own domains, generally being capable of assuring consistent application of models and tools to appropriate datasets, and thereby assuring that they could themselves reproduce the results of their scientific investigations. However, a number of forces are encouraging the sharing of data, models, and tools among scientists in disparate locations and research groups, including pervasive access to the Internet, and mandates from funding agencies such as US National Science Foundation. This sharply increases the likelihood that a scientific investigator might access datasets remotely, and then use incorrect or inappropriate tools or models to process these datasets. Indeed, as noted

above, the ability of other scientists to reproduce published results is central and
essential to the establishment of the validity of such results. Thus, Internet access to
datasets and models should ideally expedite and facilitate such reproduction, thereby
improving the quality and the rate of scientific progress. But, configuration
management mishaps clearly increase the risk that just the opposite might happen,
with inappropriate combinations of datasets and tools causing an inability to
reproduce scientific results, adding to uncertainty.

In our example, Harvard Forest researchers are continually getting new datasets
from their flux tower, and creating new models, often based upon analysis of the
outputs from previous models. In their work they have created sizeable bodies of
"Row Filled Data" datasets, predictive models, and datasets produced by those
models. Informal internal configuration management procedures tend to assure the
scientific integrity of their results. But, Harvard Forest datasets or models are
accessible by the operators of other flux towers, increasing the opportunities for
validation of scientific results through their reproduction. Moreover, Harvard Forest
researchers access datasets generated by other flux towers in an attempt to validate or
improve their own models. In both cases, it is vital that the remote accessor of such
data have the benefit of documentation or descriptions (such as definitions of the
processes by which the datasets were created) in order to assure configuration
mismatches do not cause the risk of creating invalid scientific analyses and datasets.

To illustrate the problem, Fig. 5 depicts the state of the execution of the process
whose DFG is shown in Fig. 4, at the beginning of the second iteration. As in Fig. 2,
boxes with clipped corners denote specific dataset instances. Each clipped box
represents the dataset derived by the application of the activity from which it
emanates to the dataset(s) input to that activity.

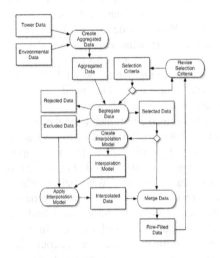

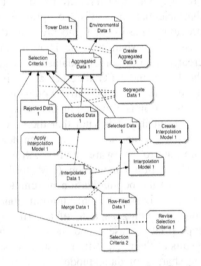

Fig. 4. Example Dataflow Graph   **Fig. 5.** Example Data Derivation Graph

Fig. 5 seems to provide a clear view of how certain datasets have been created, but
the continued execution of this process will lead to the creation of increasing numbers
of instances of datasets and models of the various types depicted. Thus, with iteration,

there will be a growing number of instances of "Tower Data", "Environmental Data" and "Interpolation Model".

But, a process definition graph (using for example, the Little-JIL shown in Fig. 6) enables the specification of the configuration management information needed to ensure that specific process executions are consistent with rules or properties derived from correct process executions. Again, without delving too deeply into the syntax and semantics of Little-JIL (see [6] for a complete description), there are two details of particular import in this diagram. First, a single instance of "Aggregated Data" is used to create an instance of "Row-Filled Data", but the '+' on "Create Row-Filled Data" permits multiple instances of "Row-Filled Data" to be created from that instance. This specification removes ambiguity left by the DFG (note that other specifications, resolving the ambiguity in other ways, can also be specified using a PDG. This specification is offered only as an example). Second, the "reference" to "Apply Selection Criteria" that appears as part of "Evaluate and Revise" ensures that when the selection criteria are revised, they are applied to the same instance of "Aggregated Data" as in the previous iteration, again clearing up ambiguity left by the DFG. Without the ability to add these clarifying specifications, there would seem to be little or no protection from the improper selection of datasets as inputs to process activities, with the consequent production of results that may be incorrect or of questionable validity.

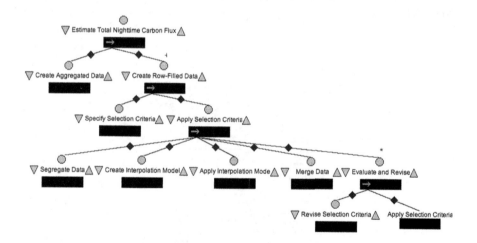

Fig. 6. Example Process Definition Graph

It seems important to note at this point that others (e.g., Estublier and his colleagues [9, 10]) have long ago noted that process definitions should be essential components of software configuration management systems. The work we describe here confirms that observation, and demonstrates that it extends beyond software configuration management, and also applies to scientific dataset configuration management.

4 Experimental Evaluation Through the SciWalker Tool

To gain some experience in assessing the value of the analytic web concept, we have developed a prototype tool, called SciWalker, as a vehicle for exploring the value of analytic webs. SciWalker supports the creation of two of the three analytic web graph representations (namely DFGs and DDGs). This capability is intended to demonstrate the value of the analytic web approach in supporting clear communication among scientific collaborators, as well as supporting education.

SciWalker also supports the execution of DFGs that it has been used to define, supports the ability to access datasets remotely across the Internet, and makes locally produced datasets available to others via the Internet. These capabilities are intended to demonstrate how analytic webs can speed the development of scientific results, and serve as facilitators for supporting reproduction of scientific results.

We performed some experiments using SciWalker to develop analytic webs that define the carbon flux process discussed in Section 3 of this paper. This experiment was designed to determine how readily such analytic webs could be defined and modified, how effective they were in communicating scientific processes to other scientists, and how easily they could be used to support remote access to datasets. A subsequent version of SciWalker will incorporate the third type of graph (the PDG), and will then be the basis for further experiments aimed at determining how effective an analytic web is in preventing inappropriate or incorrect combinations of datasets and models.

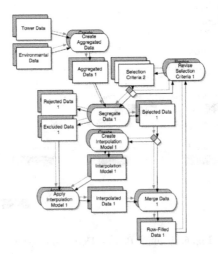

Fig. 7. Stacked DFG/DDG View

Rather than depicting DDGs independently, SciWalker depicts dataset instances as stacks piled atop the boxes (types) in the DFG representation (Fig. 7). Our early experience in using this depiction of instances has confirmed our expectation that this approach is indeed helpful to working scientists in clearly showing the specific dataset instances that have been created in successive (iterative) applications of an analytic web. The instances in SciWalker are all accompanied by specific metadata annotations, viewed through clickable menu items that provide exact and specific information about how they were generated. This approach to providing such key metadata has also proven to be useful and well received.

By using SciWalker to estimate nighttime carbon exchange from eddy covariance data, the Harvard Forest researchers were able to quickly determine the effect of varying $u^*_{threshold}$ on estimated nighttime carbon flux from a forest, without employing specific statistical tools that might be inaccessible to others who are interested in recreating or modifying their analysis. Simultaneously, the tool created a complete audit-trail of the process that is easily accessible via the Internet. With this audit-trail, data that were included or excluded can be easily retrieved and examined. Other researchers have examined effects of $u^*_{threshold}$ on estimates of carbon flux [11-13], but not through procedures that are easily accessible or repeatable. The researchers have indicated that SciWalker is a step forward both in ease and speed of data processing and analysis for them as individual researchers, and also a great leap forward in communicating their data analysis procedures to others.

While influences of $u^*_{threshold}$ on ecosystem carbon flux estimated from eddy covariance data have been examined in several papers, effects of other meteorological variables have been examined less frequently. Wind direction is of particular interest, because forest composition is rarely uniform around a flux tower. In general, one cannot relate carbon flux to a specific type of forest without limiting the range of wind directions that provide acceptable data for processing. As carbon exchange estimates and statistical models of carbon exchange for one forest cannot be applied to other forests unless the forest composition is similar in the two areas, it is often important for researchers to partition eddy covariance data by wind direction in order to confine measurements to a specific forest type. SciWalker seems to be a perfect tool for supporting this, by allowing for the specification of the range of wind direction for included *versus* excluded data. In the case of the Harvard Forest estimates of carbon exchange by a hemlock forest, they included data only if the winds were from the southwest (180-270° compass bearing) because of the relatively small size of the hemlock forest they were studying, and the position of the flux tower in the northeast corner of hemlock-dominated forest. Using SciWalker, they are now examining the effects of using other ranges of wind direction, thereby including other forest types within the eddy covariance footprint.

5   Discussion, Conclusions, and Future Directions

There is an important need to develop tools and techniques that will facilitate the production of high quality scientific results. Internet access can clearly help, by making important datasets more accessible to more scientists, thereby facilitating broader collaborations. But such capabilities must be balanced by additional capabilities for helping scientists to understand the ways in which the datasets they access have been developed. In this paper we demonstrate that the concept of an analytic web can be used as the basis for providing process metadata capable of providing scientists with the information that they need in order to assure that their use of remotely accessed datasets is safe and correct. An analytic web consists of three different graphs that together provide this capability, but also offer the promise of facilitation of education, effective application of computer support for scientific investigation, and catalysis of community debate about most effective scientific methods.

Our proposal to create analytic webs as syntheses of three specific types of graphs seems quite promising, based upon our initial work with the SciWalker prototype and its application to eddy flux data used to estimate whether forests are sources or sinks of CO_2. In its current implementation, SciWalker incorporates only two graphs, data flow graphs and data derivation graphs. Our preliminary use of this prototype has indicated that these two graphs can be used effectively to support process definition, computerization of some process steps, and reproducibility of results. In addition, our application of SciWalker already has led to new scientific insights and interesting new results.

Future versions of SciWalker will incorporate the PDGs necessary to support assessment of the correctness of the use of datasets, and process reliability. It is our goal that scientific analyses eventually be accompanied by process certification metadata derived from the (presumably successful) application of formal process analyzers to our process metadata. These certifications would then be usable by other scientists to guide them away from dangerous misuse of datasets or combinations of processes. The net result will be science that is not only more rapid and efficient, but also more reliable and reproducible.

Acknowledgments

This material is based upon work supported by the National Science Foundation under Award No. CCR-0205575. Any opinions, findings, and conclusions or recommendations expressed in this publication are those of the author(s) and do not necessarily reflect the views of the National Science Foundation.

We are also grateful to many colleagues who supported this work and contributed key ideas that have led to our analytic web concept and our SciWalker prototype tool. In particular, we wish to thank Ed Riseman, Al Hanson, David Jensen, Paul Kuzeja, Howard Schultz, Bert Rawert, George Avrunin, and Mohammed Raunak for their advice, support, encouragement, and many stimulating conversations.

References

1. *Globus consortium description.* http://www.globus.org/
2. *GryPhyN project description.* http://www.globus.org/about/news/GriPhyN.html
3. Dominici, F., A. McDermott, and T.J. Hastie, *Improved Semi-parametric Time Series Models of Air Pollution and Mortality.* Journal of the American Statistical Association, 2004(99): p. 938-948.
4. Ghezzi, C., M. Jazayeri, and D. Mandrioli, *Fundamentals of Software Engineering.* 2nd Edition ed. 2003, Upper Saddle River, NJ: Pearson Education, Inc.
5. Huet, S., et al., *Statistical Tools for Nonlinear Regression: A Practical Guide with S-Plus and R Examples.* 2nd Edition ed. 2004, New York, NY: Springer-Verlag, Inc.

6. Wise, A., *Little-JIL 1.0 Language Report*, in *Computer Science Technical Report*. 1998, University of Massachusetts: Amherst, MA.
7. Baldocchi, D.D., B.B. Hicks, and T.P. Myers, *Measuring Biosphere-Atmosphere Exchanges of Biologically Related Gases with Micrometeorological Methods*. Ecology, 1998(69): p. 1331-1340.
8. Savage, K.E. and E.A. Davidson, *Inter-annual Variation of Soil Respiration in Two New England Forests*. Global Biogeochemical Cycles, 2001(15): p. 227-350.
9. Belkhatir, N. and J. Estublier. *Software Management Constraints and Action Triggering in Adele Program Database*. in *1st European Software Engineering Conference*. 1987. Strasbourg, France.
10. Belkhatir, N., J. Estublier, and W.L. Melo. *Software Process Modeling in Adele: The ISPW-7 Example*. in *Proceedings of the 7th International Software Process Workshop*. 1991. San Francisco, CA: IEEE Computer Society Press.
11. Hollinger, D.Y., et al., *Spatial and Temporal Variability in Forest-Atmosphere CO2 Exchange*. Global Change Biology, 2004.
12. Barford, C.C., et al., *Factors Controlling Long- and Short-term Sequestration of Atomspherics CO2 is a Mid-latitude Forest*. Science, 2001(294): p. 1688-1691.
13. Saleska, S.R., et al., *Carbon in Amazon Forests: Unexpected Seasonal Fluxes and Disturbance-induced Losses*. Science, 2003(302): p. 1554-1557.

Process Definition Language Support for Rapid Simulation Prototyping

Mohammad S. Raunak and Leon J. Osterweil

Department of Computer Science,
University of Massachusetts,
Amherst, MA 01003, USA
{raunak, ljo}@cs.umass.edu

Abstract. This paper suggests how an appropriately designed and architected process definition language can be an effective aid to the rapid generation of simulations, which are, in turn, capable of providing important insights. The paper describes how the features of the Little-JIL process definition language helped in the rapid generation of simulations that shed important new light on the effectiveness of various collusion strategies in influencing the outcomes of various auction approaches. The paper describes how Little-JIL's approach to modular reuse and its separation of process concerns both turn out to be of particular value in supporting rapid prototyping. The simulation results obtained are themselves interesting, as the paper also suggests that the auction idiom is highly relevant to resource allocation in software development. Thus, the insights gained into the efficacy of various collusion approaches have particular relevance to software process research.

1 Introduction

There is currently considerable interest in using process definitions as the basis for important decisions about such matters as resource allocation, coordination of agents, and procedural issues. Because of the importance of such matters, technologies that are effective in supporting the precise, clear, and complete definition of processes seem to have broad and important applicability. Further, it seems particularly important to evaluate such process definitions carefully to be sure that they are correct and effective, which can then become the basis for their systematic, iterative improvement. We have long argued that software process development has a close parallel to application software development [14, 15]. This parallelism suggests that tools and techniques used in the latter should be expected to be applicable also to the evaluation of processes. From this analogy we know that there are two major types of approaches to evaluation, namely static and dynamic analysis. In earlier papers we have described our work in the static analysis of processes [7]. This work has shown that static analysis can be an effective approach to identifying defects in processes. This paper addresses a dynamic analysis approach, namely simulation.

Simulation seems to be a particularly useful approach to the evaluation of processes. Process simulations can support the quantitative determination of flow times

M. Li, B. Boehm, and L.J. Osterweil (Eds.): SPW 2005, LNCS 3840, pp. 416–432, 2005.

for executions of processes, the impacts of making certain resource allocation decisions, and the projected behavior of processes under various hypothesized loading conditions. Various authors have previously appreciated this, and have already begun to investigate technologies that support process simulation, and the effectiveness of these technologies [11]. While we agree with the value of this approach, our own work has increasingly demonstrated that it is often difficult to determine just which simulations best provide desired insights. Indeed, our work suggests that one set of simulation runs often raises as many questions as it answers, and inevitably leads to the desire and need for many subsequent sets of different simulation runs. Thus, because it is often the case that the analyst is unclear about the exact process that she/he wants to study, we have found that it is helpful to be able to rapidly create prototype simulations as a key support for the process of rapid exploration of the questions that arise as simulation runs suggest further sequences of elaborative simulations of processes. In grappling with the problem of how best to support the need for rapid process simulation generation, we have concluded that the appropriate process language architecture and execution tools are very important in this task.

We note that this observation itself mirrors similar observations that have been made by developers of simulations in application software domains. Simulations have been shown to be valuable in providing precise answers and insights when the questions and issues are narrowly drawn. Getting the questions appropriately narrowed down, however, can take considerable effort, often in the form of evaluation of sequences of preliminary simulations. Thus the value of being able to create simulations rapidly has been previously understood [19]. This points to the value of flexible simulation generation aids, such as the one that we will describe in this paper.

While our work seems to support the value of automated process simulation capabilities, it has also shown that simulation generators can lead to simulations that are largely interpreted, and consequently inconveniently slow. Our work has demonstrated that, while it is helpful to have rapid simulation generators to help identify the precise simulation that can provide results of great interest, once the simulation has been identified, it seems important to then code the simulation in a compilable language in order to assure that massive quantities of simulations needed for reliability of results, can be executed in acceptably short amounts of time.

All of the above has reinforced in our minds the desirability of an executable design language for processes. In our work we used our Little-JIL process definition language to specify simulation designs. Our Juliette interpreter was used to run these preliminary simulations, emphasizing the value of an executable design. After suitable preliminary simulations, we then moved on to the need to run massive amounts of simulations, at which time we used the Little-JIL designs as the basis for facilitated coding of the desired simulations in Java.

In this paper we describe our work, not only emphasizing the value of an executable process definition language, but also emphasizing how the particular separation of concerns in our language greatly facilitated the rapid generation of preliminary simulations, thereby expediting the definition of the massive simulations that eventually yielded the process analysis results that we sought.

2 Related Work

Simulation has long been used as a powerful tool for analyzing software performance in wide range of application areas. Simulation of software processes has also received a lot of attention over the last twenty years, during which time a wide variety of simulation approaches have been suggested and explored. Kellner et al. [11] provides a nice overall picture of the work in software process simulation, focusing primarily on the diversity of approaches to process simulation, addressing the different issues, and suitability of various approaches to dealing with them. In particular, [11] talks about eight different simulation approaches and language categories including state based process modeling, discrete event simulation and system dynamics. [6] shows how simulation can be of benefit in supporting software process improvement in the context of such approaches as the Capability Maturity Model (CMM). [18] provides some experience-based insights into the effectiveness of knowledge based simulation (KBS) and discrete event simulation (DES) of processes. [13] presents the need and usefulness of combining both discrete event and system dynamics approaches to simulation while simulating software processes.

Although researchers have not looked at issues related to rapid simulation prototyping for software processes, the need has been established in other system simulation domains. For example, [19] discusses the usefulness of rapid simulation and software prototyping for the architectural design of embedded multiprocessor systems.

There is ample literature studying auctions from the various perspectives of Economics, Management Science, Operations Research and Computer Science. Economists mainly look at the auction mechanism from the game theoretic perspective and try to identify optimum price determination that maximizes the utility of the seller and/or the bidder. They also try to reason about the behaviors of the bidders and their impact on the outcome of the auctions. Although most of these analyses are based on probabilistic models, a small but influential trend has been to study market mechanisms through laboratory experiments using discrete event simulation. The work described here is in that spirit.

Computer Scientists and Management Scientists have looked at different variations of auctioning mechanisms for multiple items [3, 17]. Their primary objective has been to devise auctions that are efficient in the determination of the optimal winner. Other researchers in computer science have looked into the capturing of auction processes with rigorous process language and statically analyzing the auctions to verify correctness and completeness [7].

Identifying vulnerabilities in auctions is a very important issue for better auction designs [12]. Some recent work attempts to identify collusive behavior of bidders by analyzing bidding patterns [1, 2]. These efforts, however, are few in number and limited in scope. Stochastic analyses usually fall short of providing a good picture of the outcome of an auction in a setting where there is the possibility of dynamic behaviors of bidders, and where the opportunity for collusion is present. Researchers have opted for empirical study based upon simulation of auction processes with actual human bidders [8, 9, 10].

3 Our Approach

The vehicle for our exploration of the value of a suitable executable process design language and architecture was our Little-JIL process definition language [21]. One of the key architectural features of Little-JIL is its separation of concerns [5]. In particular, the most noticeable feature of a Little-JIL process definition is its visual depiction of the agent coordination aspect of a process (to be described in more detail shortly). Equally important, however, are the definitions of agents and their behaviors, and artifacts and their flows. Neither of these process concerns is explicitly represented pictorially in Little-JIL. While this makes them less immediately noticeable, they are no less important. Of particular importance for this research is the fact that these concerns are separately defined, and separately modifiable.

To understand the importance of the separation of these concerns to the need for rapid prototype generation, we employed Little-JIL as a vehicle for the study of processes in the domain of auctions. An auction is a form of price negotiation that is usually a highly decentralized activity. Participants in auctions are essentially distributed agents coordinated to achieve a goal. There is a large literature addressing the enormous variety of different kinds of auctions. Indeed there are probably at least thousands of different kinds of auctions [12], all of which have somewhat different characteristics. The different kinds of auctions have been devised in a continuing attempt to find the most efficient ways to arrive at an accurate determination of the fair value of a commodity.

It is important to also note, however, that much of the diversity in types of auctions, and the continued lively investigation of auctions, is aimed at understanding the effects of various kinds of collusions among bidders. While there is a considerable amount known about how various different auction strategies may be vulnerable to, or resistant to, different forms of bidder collusions, much more needs to be known. We believe that simulations of various kinds of collusive activities operating in the context of different kinds of auctions have the potential to yield these important understandings.

Our research entailed the use of Little-JIL as a vehicle for supporting the rapid generation and execution of simulations of the different ways in which different auctions responded to bidder collusions. As will be seen, the Little-JIL architecture proved to be particularly useful in this work, as the pictorial coordination concern proved to be effective in defining the different auction processes clearly, precisely, and completely, while the agent definition concern, independently defined (in this case using Java), proved quite effective in defining different collusion strategies. Our Juliette process interpreter, drawing upon the combined coordination and agent definitions, supported the simulation of the different auctions.

It is worth noting here that the selection of auction processes for this research is far from irrelevant to software process concerns. We believe that the auction idiom, and indeed the auction vehicle itself, especially as elaborated using notions of agent collusion, are quite relevant to software development process concerns. We note, for example, that a significant aspect of the software development process involves the allocation of resources or agents to the various development tasks. The effective determination of the most effective allocation of agents (e.g. designers, programmers, testers) might well be modeled, and indeed carried out, as an auction, where the bidders are software engineers bidding for specific tasks. Communications among these agents should be expected, as is the case of collusive bidders in an auction process, although communication among software developers is generally useful in arriving at effective task assignment, in contrast to the situation in auctions. Thus, our focus on auctions is more than simply illustrative of our ideas about process language architecture, but also seems relevant to the development of superior software development agent allocation strategies.

3.1   The Little-JIL Process Language

Little-JIL is a process definition language [5, 21] that, along with its interpreter Juliette [4], supports specification, execution, and analysis of processes involving multiple agents. In this work, we used Little-JIL to capture and simulate auction processes and agent interactions. As noted above, the most immediately noticeable aspect of a Little-JIL process program is the visual depiction of the coordination specification of the process. This component of the Little-JIL process program looks initially somewhat like a task decomposition graph, in which processes are decomposed hierarchically into steps. The steps are connected to each other with edges that represent both control flow and artifact flow. Each step contains a specification of the type of agent needed in order to perform the task associated with that step. Thus, for example, in the context of an auction, the agents would be entities such as the auctioneer, the bidders, as well as, potentially, the manager setting up collusion amongst the bidders. The collection of steps assigned to an agent defines the interface that the agent must satisfy to participate in the process. It is important to note that the coordination specification includes a description of the external view and observable behavior of such agents. But a specification of how the agents themselves perform their tasks (their internal behaviors) is NOT a part of the coordination specification. The behaviors of agents are defined in a separate specification component of the Little-JIL language. More will be said about this shortly. But it is important to note that Little-JIL enforces this sharp separation of concerns, separating the internal specification of how agents carry out their work, from the specification of how they coordinate with each other in the context of carrying out the overall process. In particular, the definition of a particular specific auction is defined separately from the definition of how the bidders might collude with each other.

   The central construct of a Little-JIL process is a step. Steps are organized into a hierarchical tree-like structure. The leaves of the tree represent the smallest specified units of work, each of which is assigned to an agent that has characteristics consistent with those defined as part of the definition of the step. The tree structure defines how the work of these agents will be coordinated. In particular, the agent assigned responsibility for executing a parent node is responsible for coordinating the activities of the agents assigned to execute all of the parent's children.

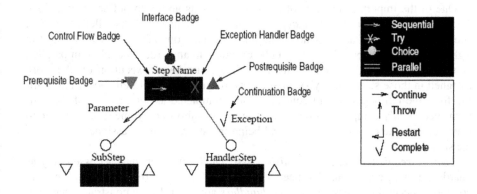

Fig. 1a. A Little-JIL step construct   **Fig. 1b.** Control flow and continuation badges

Figure 1a shows the graphical representation of a Little-JIL step with its different badges and possible connections to other steps. The interface badge is a circle on the top of the step name that connects a step to its parent. The interface badge represents the specification of any and all artifacts that are either required for, or generated by, the step's execution. Of greater importance for the work described in this paper, the interface badge also represents the specification of any and all resources needed in order to support the execution of the step. Chief among these resources is the single resource designated as the step's execution agent. Below the circle is the step name. A step may also include pre-requisite and/or post-requisite badges, which are representations of steps that need to be executed before and/or after (respectively) this step for the proper performance of the step's execution. Inside the central black box of the step structure, there are three more badges. On the left is the control flow badge, which specifies the order in which the child substeps of this step are to be executed. A child of a step is connected to the parent by an edge emanating from the parent and terminating at the child. Artifact flows between the parent and child are indicated by annotations on this edge.

On the right of the step bar is an X sign, which represents the exception handler capabilities of the step. Attached to this badge by exception edges are any and all handlers defined to deal with exceptions that may occur in any of the descendants of this step. Each handler is itself a step, and is annotated to indicate the type of exception that it handles. Here too, artifact flow between the parent and the exception handler step is represented by annotations on the edge connecting them. This edge also bears an annotation indicating the type of exception handled.

In the middle of the step bar goes a "lightning sign" (not shown in Fig. 1), which represents the message handling capabilities of the step. Attached to this badge by message handling edges are any and all handlers defined to deal with messages that may emanate from any step in the process definition. The message handling capability is quite similar to the exception handling capability, but, while exception handlers respond only to exceptions thrown from within their substep structure (a scoped capability), message handlers can respond to message thrown from anywhere (an unscoped capability). If there are no child steps, message handlers, or exception handlers, the corresponding badges are not depicted in the step bar.

One of the important features of the language is its ability to define control flow. There are four different non-leaf *step kinds*, namely "sequential", "parallel", "try" and "choice". Children of a "sequential" step are executed one after another from left to right. Children of a "parallel" step can be executed in any order, including in parallel, depending on when the agents actually pick up, and begin execution of, the work assigned in those steps. A "try" step attempts to execute its children one by one starting from the leftmost one and considers itself completed as soon as one of the children successfully completes. Finally a "choice" step allows only one of its children to execute, with the choice of which child being made by the agent assigned to execute the step.

The *pre-requisites* and *post requisites* associated with each step act essentially as guards, defining conditions that need to hold true for a step to begin execution or to complete successfully. *Exceptions* and *handlers* are control flow constructs that augment the step kinds. The exceptions and exception handlers work in a manner that is similar in principle to the way in which they work in well known contemporary application programming languages. Exceptions indicate an exceptional condition or error in the process execution flow, and handlers are used to recover from, or fix, the consequences of those situations. When an exception is thrown by a step, it is passed up the tree hierarchy until a matching handler is found. There is control flow semantics involved with handler steps to indicate how the program flow will continue once a raised exception has been handled by the defined handler. Figure 1b shows four different types of continuation semantics for handlers. With these semantics, a process definer can specify whether a step will continue execution, successfully complete, restart execution at the beginning, or rethrow the exception for a higher level parent step to handle.

As noted above, a complete Little-JIL process definition also contains definitions of *artifacts* and *resources* to complement this coordination definition. *Artifacts* are entities such as data items, files, or access mechanisms that are passed between parent and child steps. They provide information required for execution of a step and can be used to carry results of the step execution back to the parent. Again, as noted above, the artifact definition, indeed the specification of the type model used to support artifact definition, is a separate concern in Little-JIL, and is orthogonal to the coordination definition.

In an analogous way, the resource (and thus agent) definition is also separate from, and orthogonal to, the Little-JIL coordination definition. Specifically, how an agent carries out a particular task is independent of the coordination dictated by the process. Of course, however, the outcome of a process is influenced by the behaviors of the agents, which are, in turn, specified within the resource model. Consequently, the outcome of a process is similarly affected by the way in which specific resources are bound as agents to the various individual process steps at various points during process execution.

3.2 Auction Processes

We opted to investigate different auction processes and combinations of different bidder behaviors in a potentially collusive environment. In the course of our investigations of how these behaviors affected auction outcomes, we wound up modeling many different types of auctions, including open-cry or ascending bid (English) auctions, double auctions, first-price sealed-bid auctions and finally repeated sealedbid auctions. Space does not permit us to describe the all the details of these different types of auctions. The interested reader can find these details in [16]. But it is important to sketch out some of their salient properties as this helps us to explain how certain properties of Little-JIL were particularly useful in supporting the rapid creation of prototypes of auctions of these types.

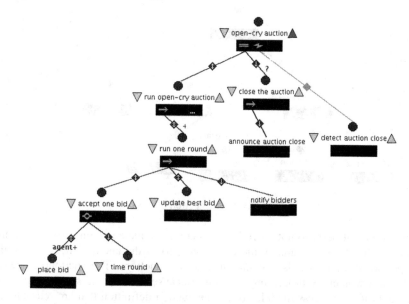

Fig. 2. An open-cry (Ascending bid/English) auction

In an ascending-bid (English) auction, the auction type that is most commonly depicted in movies and novels, the price is successively raised by the auctioneer until only one bidder remains, and that bidder wins the object paying the final price that was bid. A Little-JIL coordination definition of this type of auction is depicted in Figure 2.

A double auction differs from an English auction in that both buyers and sellers submit bids and offers in an auction round. The auctioneer opens this bidding, and then periodically closes the bidding, completing a round. At the end of a round, the auctioneer identifies matches between the bids of buyers and sellers, finalizing the sale of items so matched. Figure 3 shows a Little-JIL coordination definition that describes such a double auction process. As you can see "double auction" is a parallel activity between running the auction and checking to make sure that the auctioneer has not called a stop to the auction. The step "run double auction" has a pre-requisite step "check auction close" that identifies whether the next round should be placed or not.

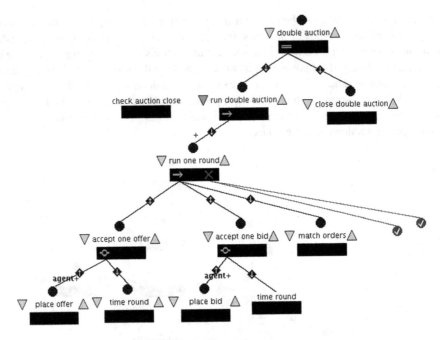

Fig. 3. A double auction process

The important point to note here is that there are some common activities in these auction processes. For example, the auctioneer closes the auction after a predefined time period. Placing of bids is common to all the auctions. The auctioneer needs to decide on a winner by processing the bids. Because of this, one should expect that there ought to be process modules from one auction definition that are reusable, and reused in other auction process definitions. Little-JIL encourages and supports such reuse, as can be seen by examining these process coordination definitions. For example, the "accept one bid" module of the double auction process is taken "as-is" from our ascending-bid/open-cry auction process.

Examples of more extensive successful reuse can be seen in additional auction process definitions. Our work continued with the definition of sealed-bid auctions. In a first-price sealed-bid auction, each bidder independently submits a single bid without knowing others' bids, and the object is sold to the bidder with the highest bid. The bidder pays his price (first price) to get the object. Auction of this type are currently very common and popular.

A repeated sealed bid auction is an important variant of this type of auction. It is a series of sealed bid auctions where auctioneer announces the results of the auction after every round, and then initiates a new auction for new batch of goods or services that are essentially identical to those just sold. Governments and large corporations carry out much of their procurement activities through exactly this kind of repeated sealed-bid auctions. Because of the enormous economic importance of such auctions, they have been the subject of much analysis, much of which has focused on their resistance, or vulnerability, to certain kinds of bidder collusion. The bidders, after receiving the announcement of the outcome of a round, can potentially attempt to collude or decide on their bids individually. In either case, the bidders place their bids and auctioneer collects the bids, processes them to identify the winner and announces the winner before initializing the new round.

For space constraint, we are not showing the Little-JIL coordination definition of a repeated sealed bid auction. However, it is important to note that this process reuses the entire definition of a single-round sealed bid auction, in a striking demonstration of reuse. The single round sealed bid auction, in turn, reuses some steps from the open cry auction definition.

There are other features of Little-JIL that foster reuse and rapid prototyping, but they require familiarity with other features of the language that we address now. Specifically, it is important to note that some edges are annotated with cardinality symbols, for example the *agent+* notation on the edge from the "accept one bid" step to the "place bid" step. This notation represents the *resource bounded cardinality* feature of Little-JIL process descriptions. The child step of an edge containing such a notation is instantiated once for each of the agents available as an active bidder at the time of instantiation of that step. Thus, for example, if we specify that the agent for a bidding step must be collusive, then one step will be created for every bidder whose agent behavior (as defined in the resource factor of the Little-JIL process definition) is defined to be collusive. A bidding step will be instantiated only for the collusive bidders and each of them will be given the task of bidding in that step. In contrast, if a step's agent specification specifies only bidders, then that step will be instantiated for all bidders, both collusive and non collusive. If an edge is annotated with '*?*', then that step will execute only if an agent satisfying the requested characteristics is available. Thus, the step may or may not execute at all. For example, in the repeated sealed-bid auction process there is a collusion step connected to its parent by an edge annotated with a "?" indicating that it will get executed only if there exists collusive bidders in that auction round.

One net effect of these properties of Little-JIL is that a given fixed auction process can be executed, and evaluated, against a variety of different bidder collusion scenarios very straightforwardly. Indeed, the auction coordination definition may not need to be changed at all in order to evaluate the resistance of a particular auction to a variety of collusive threats.

Conversely, it is correspondingly straightforward to evaluate the relative resistances of various auctions to a fixed collusive threat. Because the code for defining how agents will collude with each other is contained largely in the agent definition factor of Little-JIL, it is also highly reusable across the range of different auction processes. In our work, we have been able to plug in the agent code written to support one auction process, and use it to support a different one, with minimal or no changes to the agent code. Thus, Little-JIL's separation of concerns allows us to quickly change an overall auction process, by changing either the auction or the agent behavior, but then reusing the other part with little or no change. This has enabled us to create and evaluate a wide range of auction processes very rapidly.

3.3 Modeling Collusions

We have already noted that agent behaviors, such as collusions in an auction, are defined in Little-JIL as part of the agent definition factor of the language. Thus, our repeated sealed bid auction did not explicitly model the details of the collusive behavior. It is expected that these behaviors may best be defined in other languages, specifically those that are more strongly algorithmic or computational. On the other hand, there is no reason why agent behaviors cannot be defined as Little-JIL coordination, using the power and convenience of the Little-JIL coordination language itself. Thus, as an example, Figure 4 shows one possible definition of collusive behavior, which we have used in many of our simulations.

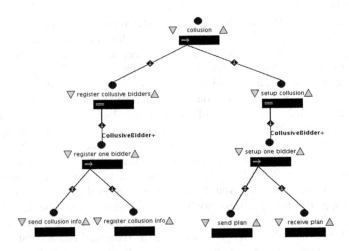

Fig. 4. A collusion process example

The collusion protocol presented here describes the scenario where each collusive bidder registers with a collusion manager. While registering, the bidders submit their valuation for the auctioned object to the collusion manager. The manager then sets up the collusion by sending a collusion plan back to the registered bidders. The plan includes what each of the bidders should bid in that round. It is important to note that we indeed used Little-JIL to define a number of collusions in our preliminary auction research, as the language's encouragement and support of reuse facilitated the rapid creation of prototype auctions that differed from each other only in modest perturbations of collusive behavior.

Thus, for example, the strategy used by the collusion manager to decide on the instructed bid, in the case of the collusion shown in Figure 4, be made independent of both the auction process and the overall collusion strategy itself. This allows us to quickly create a new prototype for a different type of collusion while running the same auction and using bidders who intend to collude in the same way.

4   Experiences and Challenges

4.1   Auction Results

After a few iterations aimed at identifying the simulation that seemed to be most promising for investigation, we zoomed into an intensive and detailed examination of the repeated sealed bid auction where bidders have the opportunity to collude. We ran several experiments using our process simulation vehicle. Our aim in the experiments was to see how the number of collusive bidders impacts the outcome of an auction. We were also interested in investigating the dynamics of multiple colluding rings operating in a repeated auction environment. We developed automated agents with bidding strategies based on game theoretic models. We allowed for changes of behavior amongst the bidders. A non-collusive bidder can become collusive and join a ring after a few rounds of auction based on the history information made available to the bidder. We modeled our bidders as risk neutral agents placing their bids according to a pareto-optimal bid producing a Nash equilibrium [20]. The bidders were made increasingly complex in later experiments. The bidding strategy was primarily modeled as a decision problem influenced by a lot of factors and parameters. If there are multiple colluding rings present, we allowed colluding bidders to switch rings under certain conditions. As noted earlier, we modeled the collusion with communication amongst the bidders through a center, the collusion manager. The center's role was to decide on the profit sharing mechanism of the colluding bidders and instruct participating bidders to bid according to the prescribed strategy. Here we present a very brief, but representative, summary of our experimental results to demonstrate the usefulness of such a simulation study. A more detailed discussion about the modeling of the bidding strategy and the results of different experiments we performed is to be presented in subsequent papers.

In this experiment, we used a fixed number of ten non-collusive bidders participating in the auction. However, after a fixed number of rounds, we updated bidder behavior and made a non-collusive bidder collusive. As the auction progressed through subsequent rounds, more and more bidders became collusive. Our object was to identify whether the collusive ring needs to achieve some kind of threshold size in a sealed-bid auction in order to consistently be successful in rigging the auction. We observed that with a specific auction model and bidder behaviors, the collusion starts to take over when around 70% of the bidders participate in the collusion. In another experiment, we have been investigating the conditions under which one dominant colluding ring drives other rings out of competition. The initial results have shown some interesting trends. We will present the details of our experiment setup and evaluations in subsequent papers.

4.2 Simulation Experience

The process definition and execution framework supported by Little-JIL and Juliette facilitated our efforts, and enabled us to execute hundreds of cycles of process definition, execution, evaluation, and evolution in a short space of time. The simulations we developed often provided intriguing results, causing us to feel the need for validation. Thus, one of our early activities entailed the generation of some large scale simulation outputs that could be verified against analytic results. The validation of these early simulation results encouraged us to go on to simulations that entailed complex, yet realistic, collusions that are not amenable to analytic verification. These simulations seem to add to the body of knowledge about the effectiveness of various collusions against particular auctions.

In order to obtain these results, we felt it was necessary to perform massive amounts of simulation runs of various configurations of colluding bidders, against the auction processes that we had decided to study. It was not initially obvious, however, which type of auction, and what type of collusion, was worth this evaluation through massive quantities of simulation runs. We felt that there was a need for the flexibility of rapid changes of process, collusion and bidder strategies necessary in order to identify the specific auctions, collusions, and bidder behaviors that were likely to be of most interest and value in auction research. The factoring of process coordination, agent assignments and actual agent behavior that we leveraged out of the Little-JIL/Juliette framework supported the separation of concerns in a process language framework that enabled the considerable amount of exploration of this sort that we found to be needed.

Once the specific simulations that needed to be evaluated through massive experimentation became clear as the result of a considerable period of this preliminary evaluation, the drawbacks of an interpreted language became apparent. The auctions that we wanted to simulate extensively entailed ten or more bidders, with the process itself consisting of more than eighty steps for every auction round. Dozens of auction rounds were necessary.

As Little-JIL is an interpreted language, executing processes with Juliette is naturally far slower than would be the execution of the same processes programmed in a compiled language. Moreover, Juliette was designed to support distributed process execution. This distributive support is accomplished through a lot of remote method invocations (rmi) which incurs large network communication time, which in turn makes the executed process slow. With real humans in the loop for placing the bids from distributed terminals, the simulator created with this infrastructure can be sufficient to produce realistic results. However, if one wants to focus on producing massive simulation results in a short period of time through automated agents, automated process execution falls short of providing that level of efficiency. In our experiments with ten bidders, each round of sealed-bid auction took about two to three minutes to finish depending on the number of bidders colluding. More colluding bidders result in an increased number of total steps for that auction round. In an experiment where the number of collusive bidders increases with time, the execution time for each auction also rose sharply. Toward the end of a thirty round experiment, each auction cycle took up to six minutes on average to finish. However, we did not intend to produce massive simulation with the distributed process execution framework of Little-JIL/Juliette. At this point, we used our process definition as the architecture of the intended simulation engine and rapidly coded out the simulator in a compiled language, Java. The beauty of this switching was the ability to reuse a lot of agent code. As agents were a separate concern in our process language and were written in Java in the Little-JIL/Juliette framework, it was easy to plug in the agent code in later simulations.

4.3 Process Language Experience

We have gathered some important insights regarding process programming in general and Little-JIL/Juliette framework, in particular, while implementing this simulation infrastructure. We have used Little-JIL as an executable design language to create a meta-model infrastructure to build simulators.

Little-JIL provided us with rich process notations to depict the architecture of the simulation hiding unnecessary details. We were able to capture the behaviors of a range of auction processes quite accurately, with relatively little effort being put into creation of the different processes. For example, Little-JIL's concurrency control features were particularly useful in defining the simultaneous placing and accepting of bids by the bidders and auctioneer respectively. Little-JIL also helps to describe certain steps succinctly. The agent bounded cardinality in *place bid* step succinctly, yet effectively, selects for instantiation steps executed only by agents available to carry out the work. Specifying different attributes of the agents allowed us to assure the selection of the agent appropriate to perform any particular task at any particular process execution instance.

We note (in passing, only to save space) that Little-JIL also incorporates some timing semantics. In our repeated sealed-bid auction process, we have used a deadline construct (a clock-face on a step interface) on the *place-bid* step. This indicates that the step has to be completed by the agent within a specified period of time. Otherwise it will be retracted and a *deadline expired* exception will be thrown. The inclusion of deadline semantics in the language supports the definition and evaluation of an even richer collection of auction processes.

Juliette, the Little-JIL interpreter, takes a little-JIL process and executes it in a way that is assured to be completely consistent with the Little-JIL semantics, through the use of finite state machine semantics that are used to define Little-JIL and also drive Juliette. Juliette, moreover, deals with a resource manager that is the repository of all resources (and, therefore agents) that are available for participation in the execution of the process. Thus, Juliette has the ability to acquire resources required to complete each step (agents etc) incrementally, and in real time, as the process execution proceeds. Juliette also manages the numerous data that flows from step to step throughout the process.

One shortcoming of the Little-JIL coordination language is the absence of semantics to support specification of artifact flow between sibling steps. As noted above, artifact flow in Little-JIL is defined to take place between parent and child. But this posed a continuous problem in our auction processes, as it complicated the representation of how bids flow from bidder to auctioneer, and how results flow from auctioneer to bidder. We have used the message passing semantics of using reactions and reaction handlers in Little-JIL to represent this type of lateral dataflow in our simulated processes. New versions of Little-JIL are due to incorporate features that would alleviate this shortcoming, and these features are clearly necessary to facilitate research of the type that we have been describing.

5 Concluding Remarks

Little-JIL, a rigorous process language, has been used to define a wide range of processes. Static analyzers have been applied successfully to reason about processes defined by this language. In this paper we have utilized the factored nature of the Little-JIL language, its separation of concerns, and its flexible execution environment, to develop a simulation framework to perform dynamic analysis of a specific type of distributed process, auctions and collusions in auctions. We demonstrated the utility of an executable process language in providing support for rapid simulation prototyping. We have also presented our case for the need of quick simulation development for identifying the right focus that needs further investigation. Our findings pointed out the issues important for process based simulation development. We investigated a number of simulations and finally zoomed into reasoning about auction outcomes in a repeated sealed-bid auction scenario with the presence of collusive bidders.

Although auctions have been extensively studied analytically in Economics and Operation Research areas, there are certain characteristics of auctions that are difficult to study analytically. Researchers have used laboratory experiments with small numbers of human bidders to study some such characteristics [8, 9, 10]. In our study, we utilized the theoretical findings of auction researchers to model automated bidders to run large numbers of auction simulations with varied parameters. We have found that in a repeated sealed-bid auction with risk neutral bidders, there seems to be a certain threshold governing a collusion's effectiveness in the auction. We also identified the effect of collusion when multiple rings of differing size are present in an auction. These insights should help us better understand the effectiveness of collusion in auctions and in turn, allow us to design better auction processes that are resistant to collusive behavior.

The demonstration of auction analysis through simulation indicates the clear potential for dynamic analysis of software processes. Auction processes are economic activities used widely for efficient resource allocation. This type of resource allocation and task assignment are, however, also common activities in software development processes. Like an auction environment with collusion, side communication amongst agents in a software process and bidding for work is not uncommon at all. However, the exact software process to study may require iterative prototyping of the process simulation. It is therefore our contention that there is a lot of merit in using flexible process language to produce executable simulation designs through rapid prototyping.

Acknowledgements

This research was partially supported by the Air Force Research Laboratory/IFTD and the Defense Advanced Research Projects Agency under Contract F30602-97-2-0032, by the U.S. Department of Defense/Army and the Defense Advance Research Projects Agency under Contract DAAH01-00-C-R231, and by the National Science Foundation under Award Nos. CCR-0204321 and CCR-0205575. The U.S. Government is authorized to reproduce and distribute reprints for Governmental purposes notwithstanding any copyright annotation thereon. The views and conclusions contained herein are those of the authors and should not be interpreted as necessarily representing the official policies or endorsements, either expressed or implied of the Defense Advanced Research Projects Agency, the Air Force Research Laboratory/IFTD, the U.S. Dept. of Defense, the U.S. Army, The National Science Foundation, or the U.S. Government.
Prof. Abhijit Deshmukh helped us a lot in guiding us towards the more interesting auction processes to study. His valuable input allowed us to model the collusions and

bidding strategies of the automated bidders. Conversations with Prof. George Avrunin were also very helpful in this regard. Sandy Wise and Aaron Cass have been very helpful in providing insights and advice about the Little-JIL language, and the Juliette interpreter. Ethan Katz-Bassett and Amr Elssamadisy helped us during the simulation modeling and implementations of the initial auction processes.

References

1. Aoyagi, M.: Bid rotation and collusion in repeated auctions. Journal of Economic Theory Vol. 112 (1) (2002) 79-105
2. Bajari, P., Summers G.: Detecting collusion in procurement auctions. Antitrust Law Journal Vol. 70 (2002) 143-170
3. Byde, A.: A comparison among bidding algorithms for multiple auctions. Technical Report, Trusted E-Services Laboratory, HP Laboratories Bristol (2001)
4. Cass, A.G., Lerner, B.S., McCall, E.K., Osterweil, L.J., Sutton Jr., S.M., Wise, A.: Logically central, physically distributed control in a process runtime environment. Technical Report No. UM-CS-1999-065, University of Massachusetts, Department of Computer Science, Amherst, MA (1999)
5. Cass, A.G., Lerner, B.S., McCall, E.K., Osterweil, L.J., Sutton Jr., S.M., Wise, A.: Little-JIL/Juliette: A process definition language and interpreter. In: Proceedings of the 22nd International Conference on Software Engineering, Limerick, Ireland (2000) 754-757
6. Christie, A.M.: Simulation in support of CMM-based process improvement. Journal of Systems and Software, Vol. 46(2). (1999)
7. Cobleigh, J.M., Clarke, L.A., Osterweil, L.J.: Verifying properties of process definitions. In: Proceedings of the International Symposium on Software Testing and Analysis (ISSTA2000), Portland, OR (2000) 96-101
8. Isaac, R.M., Plott, C.R.: The opportunity for conspiracy in restraint of trade: An experimental study. Journal of Economic Behavior and Organization Vol. 2 (1981)
9. Isaac, R.M, Valerie, R., Arlington W.W.: The effects of market organization on conspiracies in restraint of trade. Journal of Economic Behavior and Organization, Vol. 5. (1984) 191-222
10. Isaac, R.M., Walker, J.M.: Information and conspiracy in sealed bid auction. Journal of Economic Behavior and Organization, Vol. 6. (1985) 139-159
11. Kellner, M.I., Madachy, R.J., Raffo, D.M.: Software process modeling and simulation: Why, what, how. Journal of Systems and Software, Vol. 46(2) (1999)
12. Klemperer, P.: Auction theory: A guide to the literature. Journal of Economic Surveys, Vol. 13(3) (1999) 227-286
13. Lakey, P.B.: A hybrid software process simulation model for project management. In: Proceedings of the Software Process Simulation Modeling Workshop, Portland, OR (2003)
14. Osterweil, L.J.: Software processes are software too. In: Proceedings of the Ninth International Conference of Software Engineering, Monterey, CA (1987) 2-13
15. Osterweil, L.J.: Improving the quality of software quality determination processes. In: R. Boisvert, (ed.): The Quality of Numerical Software: Assessment and Enhancement. Chapman & Hall, London (1997)
16. Milgrom, P.R., Weber, R.J.: A theory of auctions and competitive bidding. Econometrica, Vol. 50(5). (1982) 1089-1122
17. Sandholm, T.: Algorithm for optimal winner determination in combinatorial auctions. In: Proceedings of the International Joint Conference on Artificial Intelligence (IJCAI), Stockholm, Sweden (1999) 542-547

18. Scacchi, W.: Experience with software process simulation and modeling. Journal of Systems and Software (1999)
19. Thuente, D.J.: Rapid simulation and software prototyping for the architectural design of embedded multiprocessor systems. In: Proceedings of the 19th annual conference on Computer Science, San Antonio, Texas (1999) 113–121
20. Vickrey, W.: Counterspeculation, auctions, and competitive sealed tenders. Journal of Finance, Vol. 16 (1961) 8-37
21. Wise A.: Little-JIL 1.0 language report. Technical Report No. UM-CS-1998-024, Department of Computer Science, University of Massachusetts, Amherst, MA (1998)

Evolving an Experience Base for Software Process Research

Zhihao Chen[1], Daniel Port[2], Yue Chen[1], and Barry Boehm[1]

[1] Center for Software Engineering, University of Southern California,
Los Angeles 90089 California, USA
{zhihaoch, yuec, boehm}@cse.usc.edu
[2] Information Technology Management, University Hawaii, Honolulu 96822 Hawaii, USA
dport@hawaii.edu

Abstract. Since 1996 the USC Center for Software Engineering has been accumulating a large amount of software process experience through many real-client project software engineering practices. Through the application of the Experience Factory approach, we have collected and evolved this experience into an experience base (eBASE) which has been leveraged successfully for empirically based software process research. Through eBASE we have realized tangible benefits in automating, organizational learning, and strategic advantages for software engineering research. We share our rationale for creating and evolving eBASE, give examples of how the eBASE has been used in recent process research, discuss current limitations and challenges with eBASE, and what we hope to do achieve in the future with it.

1 Introduction

Software processes are widely applied in development of software-intensive systems in the commercial, aerospace, and government sectors. They tell people that what to do, who should be doing what, when and how to build the software. While what people most concerns are: are they effective or not, are their guidelines efficient, can they reduce the risks, are there any best practices, do they fit the cultures ... Software processes need to be validated, and refined in the continuous practices. On the other hand, software process research relies on having a base of high quality empirical process-related data collected from the planning and execution of software development projects. It is a challenge to acquire and sanitize these data. In addition, such data tend to be poorly structured, evolve unpredictably, and grow rapidly making them difficult to effectively archive, manage, and subsequently access. Since 1996 the University of Southern California's Center for Software Engineering (CSE), and NSF center for empirical software engineering center (CeBASE) [16] since 2000 have been evolving a software process experience base (eBASE [1]) that are collecting graduate-level, real-client, real-project software engineering practices from the developments of e-service applications along with a full lifecycle of project artifacts such as Unified Modeling Language (UML) models, cost and effort estimates, and risk reports. These academic, governmental, and industrial software engineering activities in our center have generated more than 30 GB of project data since 1996.

M. Li, B. Boehm, and L.J. Osterweil (Eds.): SPW 2005, LNCS 3840, pp. 433–448, 2005.
© Springer-Verlag Berlin Heidelberg 2005

Without a doubt, eBASE has proven a boon to software process research. Empirical models are being accumulated, so as validated guidelines for selecting processes and technologies and the best practices. It can be used for software process research, project decision-making and project support. We use it to support planning of future projects. Software developers use the experience base to learn the processes, avoid recurring mistakes, and plan and control their projects from the previous similar projects. With the study of the data in the experience base, we try to understand the trends in e-services projects and their effort implications, and identify sources of effort reduction/increase. We also try to provide the guidelines for future software project development and management. With the validated and refined software processes, people can avoid the same mistakes, solve the recurring issues, and apply the similar models in future projects.

eBASE has been successfully served to inform our industry and government affiliates, including Motorola, Xerox, SAIC, NASA's Jet Propulsion Laboratory, etc. [2], of emerging process-related issues and to provide them with the validated and refined software process, and guidelines in software engineering practices. That interest extends from the science community to the government and industry communities, and that empirical research conducted in the software engineering empirical data can be of interest to all software-related communities, is a testament to the efficacy of eBASE [2]. Examples of some of the process research that has been enabled through eBASE are: empirical development activity and effort models, top-10 risks, Commercial Off-The-Shelf (COTS) activity effort models, UML model sizing and effort, WinWin attribute conflict resolution, COTS risks, COTS project types, and many others!

eBASE began with the modest objectives of providing project artifact examples and helping automate and streamline project development and management. It has evolved well beyond this into an invaluable organizational learning and strategic research tool not only for the CeBASE but also for all software organizations. We attribute this in part to our adoption of the Experience Factory (EF) approach [3,4,5,6] which we will be discussed in Section 2. Also in section 2 we describe our objectives and rationale for creating eBASE, the initiatives undertaken in its development and their subsequent benefits. In section 3 we describe how eBASE data is collected and organized and the experience management system (EMS) used to access eBASE data. Section 4 provides numerous examples of process research enabled though eBASE, followed by challenges of evolving an eBASE in Section 5 and some current work on addressing these challenges and conclusions in Section 6.

2   eBASE Objectives, Rationale, Results and the Experience Factory

The general objective of eBASE is to collect and enable access to a diversity of empirical data, process information, models, process knowledge and experience (hereafter collectively referred to as experience) arising from software development practice in a highly accessible format. It is available primarily to the CeBASE collaborators and secondarily to the general public. The content of the eBASE was initially based on experience stemming from previous and current work conducted by

CSE, for example COTS based and Defect reduction techniques. In the future we expect collaborators of CeBASE (students, researchers, educators, and practitioners) to collaborate in various groups and share experience within and outside those groups. The objective for eBASE is modest enough: provide software developers with the validated and refined software models, software processes, project knowledge, project experiments and develop guidelines. With eBASE, project data have captured, structured, packaged, and formalized. We have a set of methodologies governing how to structure the data. We have processes, procedures and role governing how to manage the data with the supporting tools.

eBASE has benefit beyond supporting *automation* and improving efficiency. The improved uniformity enabled us to use eBASE to collect project statistics (see Table 1) to aid in software process improvements such as reducing project risk, improve project productivity, review success, and client satisfaction. This enabled a kind of *organizational learning* feedback and control system where new techniques, tools, and methods were introduced and their effects could be measured in a tangible way. For example introduction of the first Model-Based (System) Architecting and Software Engineering (MBASE) guidelines [11] in 1997 reduced the final artifact page count from an average of 230 to 154.

The success of our primitive eBASE inspired the *strategic application* of process research. Previous experiences were used to identify key problem areas, and new techniques were developed to address these areas then used in the software processes. The re-sults were compared to previous measures to see if the expected benefits were realized. For example, we observed that from 1996-1998 a high percentage of project teams were failing their life cycle objectives (LCO) review [7] even though passing their life cycle architecture (LCA) review later.

Table 1. Project Statistics

Metric	USC 1996-97	USC 1997-98	USC 1998-99	USC 1999-00
Fall Semester: LCO/LCA Package				
Teams	15	16	20	22
Students	86	80	102	100
Applications	12	15	17	22
Teams failing LCO review	4	4	1	1
Teams failing LCA review	0	0	0	0
Pages, LCO Package	160	103	114	-
Pages, LCA Package	230	154	167	-
Client Eval (1-5, 5 Best)	4.46	4.67	4.74	4.48
Spring Semester: IOC Package				
Teams	6	5	6	8
Students	28	23	28	35
Applications	6	5	6	8
Teams failing IOC Acceptance review	0	0	0	1
Applications satisfying Clients	5	5	6	7
Application not overtaken by events	6	4	4	4
Applications continued	3	3	TBD	4
Applications used	1	3	TBD	5
Client Evaluation	-	4.15	4.3	4.75*

After study of the failing projects LCO artifacts we speculated that due to the fixed schedule, these teams were not able to discover and negotiate feasible architecture options quickly enough to present a viable LCO. To address this we introduced Simplifiers and Complicators [8] in 1998-1999 which resulted in a significant reduction in the number of LCO review failures.

The infrastructure of the eBase has evolved based on the ideas of the Experience Factory (EF) [3,4,5,6]. It is this approach that defines a framework for Experience Management (EM). The EF fosters organizational learning (as exemplified previously), which means that the organization manages and learns from its own experience. The EF approach teaches the organization to observe itself, collect data about itself, build models and draw conclusions based on the data, package the experience for further reuse, and most importantly to feed the experience back to the organization and for sharing it within and outside the organization. The basic framework for EF is illustrated in Figure 1.

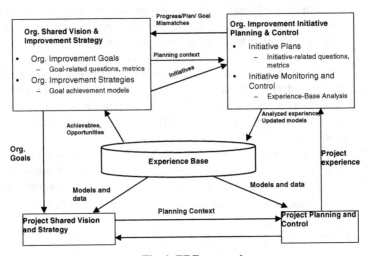

Fig. 1. EF Framework

The EF approach has been successfully applied to different organizational settings. It has been applied by individual organizations for utilizing their own experience and sharing experience within the organization, such as NASA GSFC. It has also been applied to groups of organizations for inter-organizational sharing of and learning from experience, such as the Software Engineering Center (SEC) consortium. The EF approach was designed for software organizations and takes into account the software discipline's experimental, evolutionary, and non-repetitive characteristics.

The EF helps organizations improve their experience management by implementing a framework for sharing experience within the organization as well as within the community. Through the EF we have evolved the eBASE beyond our original imitative of storing of projects on the web. These initiatives have each resulted in numerous direct and indirect long-term benefits to software development practices. These can be summarized within the following three areas that have been exemplified previously:

1. *Automating* - Centralizing access, Remote access, Reduced printing, Easier artifact review (grading)
2. *Organizational learning* - Feedback for course improvement, Uniform structure and formatting (especially models and file structure), MBASE refinement, Difficult areas, Historical record

3. *Strategic application* - Empirical data for process research projects, MBASE evolution, Recognition (affiliates, other research institutions, general public, funding orgs.), Attract new research and researchers, Attract new project clients.

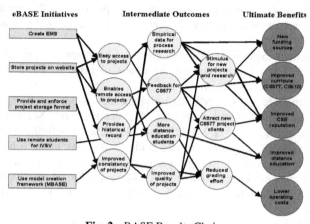

Figure 2 indicates a Results Chain [17] based on the above areas of benefit for eBase. It describes how the eBASE initiatives relate to intermediate benefits and ultimately to the longitudinal goals for the empirical research.

Figure 2 provides insight as to how the benefits of eBASE cascade and compound from relatively modest

Fig. 2. eBASE Results Chain

initiatives. Compounding benefits is a fundamental aspect of the highly iterative and integrated EF approach. These benefits have significant and measurable. For example, an indication of "stimulus for new research projects" is a count of the number of projects that directly utilize eBASE. While we have not kept precise records, roughly 26 of 48 current process research projects listed on the CSE utilize eBASE in some non-trivial way. Many of these projects have led to new eBASE initiatives (e.g. the Experience Management System) and these will are elaborated in subsequent sections.

3   The CSE Experience Management System (EMS)

The software projects produce a number of complex artifacts, all to be stored in eBASE. These include:

-   1) domain models; 2) requirements; 3) architecture models (often visual in nature such as UML class diagrams); 4) lifecycle plans (e.g. tasks, Work Breakdown Structure, schedules); 5) business case models; 6) construction and test plans; 7) review documents and meeting notes; 8) source code trees 9) effort reports; 10) project progress reports; 11) cost models, e.g. COCOMO II (COnstructive COst MOdel) [20] runs. 12) prototypes; 13) WinWin negotiations; 14) user manuals; 15) metrics; 16) project web pages.

There are multiple versions of these artifacts as they evolve through the lifecycle (e.g. LCO, LCA, Initial Operational Capability - IOC milestones [7]). In addition, there are no standards for how these artifacts are produced, stored, or formatted. There are MS Word, Rose, MS project, Visio, and HTML files. Requirements are sometimes specified in UML, others in plain text. Even the directory structure for the project websites vary wildly. To make matters worse, we also collect and archive course related artifacts such as project client feedback, individual student self-evaluations, grades, lecture notes, lecture slides, course readings, development guidelines, grading criteria, and so forth. More recently we are also collecting process research results such as simplifier and complicators, COTS process elements, effort analysis, risk tables, and an rapidly increasing number of others projects. With such a diversity of artifacts, it is clearly a challenge to effectively collect, archive, and access these artifacts for eBASE.

The Experience Management System (EMS) initiative is an attempt to provide structure and capabilities to reign in and control the chaos of eBASE. Figure 3 presents the context and activities for the EMS.

To provide a grounded structure for the EMS, its activities and system capabilities are formulated around the Model-Based [System] Architecting and Software Engineering (MBASE) framework [9,10,11]. MBASE provides detailed definitions of the anchor point milestone elements [7] and a process guide for deriving them. It has intermediate milestones to serve as commitment points and progress checkpoints with the set of anchor point milestones: Inception Readiness Review (IRR), Life Cycle Objectives (LCO), Life Cycle Architecture (LCA), Initial Operational Capability (IOC), and Product Release Review (PRR).

The software projects are (mostly) developed using MBASE framework [9,10,11]. For the EMS this provides a natural archival structure for project artifacts in terms of the MBASE deliverables and suggests good data ingest points based on the anchor point milestone reviews (e.g. LCO). As an example, we have EMS guidelines to structure the project artifacts in the inception and elaboration phases (LCO and LCA milestones) where we collect the projects:

- 1) operational concept description (OCD); 2) system and software requirements definition (SSRD); 3) system and software architecture description (SSAD); 4) life cycle plan (LCP); 5) feasibility rational description (FRD); 6) project UML models; 7) project prototype; 8) win-win negotiation report; 9) weekly progress reports; 10) risk assessments; 11) client meeting notes; 12) project quality reports; 13) effort data on the various development activities.;

Later in transition and maintenance phases (IOC), any new or updated project artifacts of inception are collected. These include:

- 1) iteration plan; 2) test plan; 3) test description and results; 4) peer review plan; 5) source code; 6) quality management plan; 7) release description; 8) transition readiness assessment; 9) iteration assessment; 10) report, transition plan; 11) user's manual; 12) acceptance test plan and description; 13) support plan, packaged tools and procedures; 14) regression test package, size report; 15) training materials; 16) close out re-port and estimation effort report.

After the collection of the data, we classify the projects into different catalogues based on project characteristics by using different criteria. Projects are classified by project domain, project type, and COTS type. Some project attributes like customer, developers, number of developers, project name, team and academic period are also added into the projects. The EMS has a search by project attribute capability which helps researchers and students locate relevant project data quickly. The EMS also provides full text search of all project artifacts regardless of format and file type.

Users of the EMS also give us additional project information such as project ratings, comments, and discussions. The system also collects a variety of usage statistics like page visits, page traffic, country of origin, referring host, file type, page URL, connection-from info, search keywords, OS, browsers, etc. We can easily find out what kinds of eBASE information users are looking at and their general profiles. Foe example, people from more than 60 countries have accessed our eBASE though the EMS.

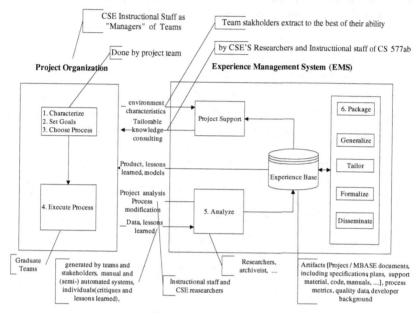

Fig. 3. The EMS System

4   Summaries Process Research Enabled from eBASE

Now that we have discussed the background of eBASE, we turn to the primary focus of this exposition. That is, once eBASE had been sufficiently established (e.g. structure and capability from the EMS) and populated with data, it enables an impressive variety of high-quality, empirically based process research. Rather than argue the validity of this statement, we believe it is self-evident by virtue of the numerous, non-trivial examples that we now present. Rather than detail each particular project, we shall provide a concise summary, references, an example, and a description of how the eBASE enabled the research.

Effort activities and distribution. The eBASE contains project effort reports for over 100 projects. In addition to coding effort, the reports provide a host of detailed process activity effort data such as review planning, COTS assessment, inspections, training and preparation, client communications, and so forth. There are a limitless number of valuable effort studies than can be made with this data. One such example is to validate the popular RUP activity level distribution by phase illustration [12]. This diagram suggests a breakdown in the amount of effort to invest for top-level activities such as management, requirements, coding, etc. Figure 4 was produced by aggregating the detailed activities into representatives of the top-level RUP activities and graphing these over the project lifecycle. We see that the software projects generally follow the suggested Rational Unified Process (RUP) activity level distributions. This is notable given that the software projects are generally small, short, fixed schedule projects. To the best of our knowledge, this is the first empirical validation of the RUP activity level distribution illustration.

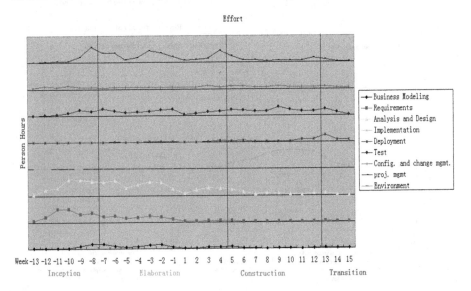

Fig. 4. The software project activity level distributions

UML sizing studies. Project size measurement has been an important application of eBASE as size is a reliable predictor of development effort, schedule, and cost [13]. There is considerable interest on utilizing UML model metrics such as number of use-cases and class diagram complexity for program sizing. The EMS has effectively helped researchers explore the relationship between UML models, code size, and effort by adapting tools such as Code Count for use on the project artifacts to get counts of attributes of use cases, sequence diagrams and class diagrams and correlate

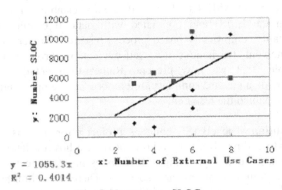

$y = 1055.3x$
$R^2 = 0.4014$

Fig. 5. Use-case vs. SLOC

them with effort from the effort reports and lines of code. Figure 5 is example of the correlation between external Use-cases and SLOC from the projects.

To date, our sizing research has demonstrated that some of the early UML metrics (i.e. number of high-level use cases and number of classes) are moderately well correlated with SLOC counts for the eService projects [14]. It indicates a potential for organizations to estimate project effort based on UML model statistics once UML usage definitions and counting rules are more standardized.

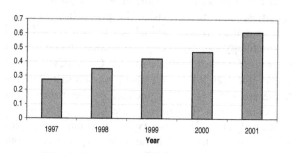

Fig. 6. Growth of COTS Intensive Projects

Growth in COTS projects. COTS has always posed a challenge for the projects. Despite numerous attempts at providing explicit COTS process guidance, projects that utilize a high-degree of COTS have difficulty adapting the MBASE guidelines (e.g. producing UML class diagrams for inaccessible COTS code) and a low success rate. This trouble seemed to get worse every year and we were not making much progress on a remedy. Our first question was to try to get a handle on how much of a problem this was and might be in the future. The eBASE revealed that the fraction of COTS based applications (CBA) projects undertaken per year was growing fast (see Figure 6). By 2001 over 60% of the projects made intensive use of COTS versus 28% in 1997. It was clear that there was a major shift in development practice and our course guidelines had not kept pace with this change! We also found that, indeed, industry had also been experiencing a rapid growth in CBA projects.

COTS project types. Since CBA's had become the majority, we had to confront our difficulties in providing effective guidance for CBA project develop-ment. An investigation into eBASE was con-ducted as to how effort was being expended wi-thin COTS projects. The idea behind this was to try to identify risky COTS development areas and provide more eff-ective means of add-ressing these risks (under the assumption "where there is effort, there is risk"). Remarkably, this investigation revealed that CBA's vary widely in how effort is expended between COTS assessment, tailoring, and

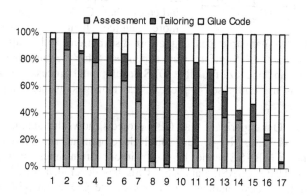

Fig. 7. COTS Effort Distribution in eBASE Projects

glue-code (see Figure 7). Further investigation into the eBASE reveled that these distributions result from three main strategies for developing CBA's: find and use COTS products without modification to cover all desired capabilities (assessment intensive), find and adapt COTS as needed (tailor intensive), find and integrate multiple COTS as components in a custom built application (glue-code intensive).

The decision as to which approach to use is driven primarily by the systems shared vision, economic constraints, and desired capabilities & priorities (DC&P's). We have observed these approaches will differ considerably in regards to the development focus, critical activities, and project risks. In particular, we have observed that, the particular way that the MBASE guidelines have to be adapted depends on the primary COTS use strategy employed (e.g. assessment intensive) and is proportional to the intensity of effort within each of the CBA development activities (assessment, tailoring, and glue-code). We have also observed that there are considerably different risks in these areas and strategic guidance on the management of these risks is critical to a successful project. Trying to "force-fit" a project of one type into a general process was extremely risky. We have experienced many examples of this, even within our process research. We found that the initial hypothesis for our Constitutive COTS Cost Model (COCOTS) [18], that CBA effort is proportional to glue code size, was false when 4 of the first 6 the CBA's turned out to be A- and T-type projects, with a good deal of effort and not much glue code. As a result, we had to come up with different estimators for the A and T effort.

Table 2. COTS Project Activity Sequences

No	Effort Sequences			
	Incp.	Elab.	Cons.	Tran.
1	A	AC	ATG	C
2	A	AT	A	A
3	A	(TG)A	G	G
4	A	A(TG)	A(TG)	G
5	AT	AT	T	T
6	A	T	TG	G
7	AT	T	T	T
8	AT	(AA)TG	(TGC)	G
9	A	AT	TG	G

COTS activity sequences. To address the COTS process risk issue raised above, a further investigation into the eBASE was made to analyze the weekly progress reports and the weekly risk reports to get the specific sequence in which COTS assessment (A), tailoring (T), glue-code (G), and custom code (C) effort was expended. Table 2 indicates that CBA's are even more unique than previously thought. Even projects with similar strategies and effort distributions had unique COTS "signatures" as to how COTS effort was expended. This demonstrated conclusively that there can be no "one size fits all" COTS development process. Each particular CBA project needs to "compose" a process that manages its particular COTS risks to its particular degree.

Compsable COTS processes. Our experience with CBA projects shows that standard software development process, e.g., risk-driven spiral development, risk-driven, WinWin spiral development, or MBASE cannot be used without, often-times severe, modification to the process. Using eBASE data USC-CSE has developed a set of project-motivated composable process elements, in terms of the COTS (A)(G)(T) activities, for developing CBA's as well an overall decision framework for applying the process elements. Figure 8 shown below illustrates this framework (each process element has a more detailed illustration not shown). It has been used as a basis for guiding students for whom the standard process guidelines don't apply to aid them in the successful planning and execution of their COTS-based projects. As has been the case with the results of other empirically-based research conducted using eBASE, data is collected from each new offering of the course and is used to improve both the (relatively new) process elements and the framework.

Simplifiers and Complicators and High Level Architectures. In his seminal work, "The Two Cultures", C.P. Snow found that science and technology policymaking was extremely difficult because it required the combined expertise of both scientists and politicians, whose two cultures had little understanding of each other's principles and practices.

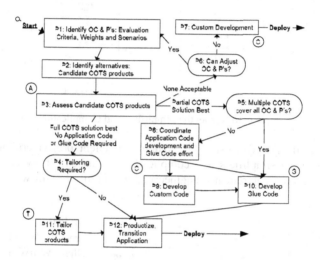

Fig. 8. CBA Effort Decision Framework

During the first three years of the center for software engineering, over 50 real-client requirements negotiations were conducted for digital library applications projects. Most projects involved professional librarians as clients and 5-6 person teams. It was found that their two-cultures problem is one of the most difficult challenges to overcome in determining a feasible and mutually satisfactory set of requirements for a software development project.

When the cause of the problem finally started to hit home, we started experimenting with expectations management and domain-specific lists of "Simplifiers and Complicators" and high-level architectures – derived through use of the eBASE by analyzing previous years' project documentation, including weekly effort and top-n risk reports -- as a way to address the two-cultures problem for software requirements within the overall digital library domain [8].

Figure 9 shows a small part of the table of developer-side Simplifiers, Complicators, and High-Level Architectures (Simple Block Diagrams). Client-side tables were also developed, and they are updated as the eBASE grows – by about 20

Type of Application	Simple Block Diagram	Example Project Nos.	Simplifiers	Complicators
Multimedia Archive		1, 2, 3, 4, 7, 12, 13, 14, 15, 16, 17, 18, 21, 24, 25, 26	• Use standard query languages • Use standard or COTS search engine • Uniform media formats	• Natural language processing • Automated cataloging or indexing • Digitizing large archives • Digitizing complex or fragile artifacts • Rapid access to large Archives • Access to heterogeneous media collections • Automated annotation, description, or meanings to digital assets • Integration of legacy systems
Selective Dissemination of Information		New library material notification	• Use of existing or standard information base • Well defined distribution points • COTS notification and event processing • WWW/internet based • Restricted interests vocabulary and filtering structures • Single information base	• Volatile or ill-defined interest or filtering criteria • Complex distribution • Multiple distribution formats • Heterogeneous information sources • Complex filter reasoning • Automated interest update

Fig. 9. Sample entries from the Simplifiers and Complicators Catalog

projects per academic year, using the student and client project critiques (specific questions regarding simplifiers and complicators are asked). They are taught as a critical part of the requirements engineering aspect of the software engineering education.

WinWin negotiation results. We plowed through the WinWin negotiation files within eBASE to determine which stakeholder types were most concerned with which quality attributes, and how frequently various attribute conflicts were raised as Issues and how they were resolved as Options. This served as the basis for the Quality Attribute Risk and Conflict Consultant (QARCC) [19] tool. A sample of this analysis is shown in Figure 10.

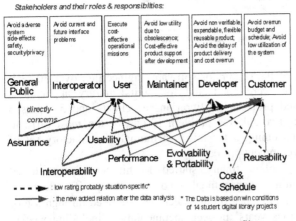

Fig. 10. Quality attribute and stakeholder conflicts

Risk Management. A critical aspect in the planning and execution of software development projects is the identification of risks and their management/mitigation.

The subject is covered in every general Software Engineering textbook such as and is taught in virtually every Software Engineering education. Nevertheless, understanding and identifying risks is difficult to teach and difficult to learn. Every few years Prof. Barry Boehm updates and disseminates a list of the top-10 software development risks based on industry surveys and software engineering practice data. The latest list is discussed in each project, and all developers are required to submit, on a weekly basis, top-n risk reporting forms of the form shown below to the eBASE. (The list shown is from Asian Film Database project.)

Table 3. Top-5 risk from Asian Film Database project

Risk Items	Weekly Ranking			Risk Resolution Progress
	Current	Previous	# Weeks	
COTS availability	1	1	5	Performed multilingual natural language processing COTS survey. Applied for academic discount.
Personnel shortfalls	2	4	4	Two members are not available for this week. Other team members will put extra effort this week.
Effective access for Asian Films	3	3	3	Performed an initial analysis on efficient storage management techniques. Will need to do look more into this matter in the following weeks.
Digitizing Indian Films	4	2	3	Due to its fast growing rate, there is a need for additional effort to digitize Indian films. Ask staff to assign a work study for this task.
Storage space	5	5	2	Plan for additional budget for more storage space to store. Discuss alternatives, tradeoffs with weekly customer reviews.

Without the top-10 lists as a guide, most Computer Science students and most beginning software developers would be at a loss to get started in identifying the top risks in their own projects; more advanced software developers would likely miss risks of novel types as they arise as a result of changing times. The published top-10 risk lists are developed, each year, through a process that involves analyzing top-n lists from the most recent offering of the latest projects in eBASE, sending a summary to CeBASE collaborators as suggestions, and reviewing their responses.

5   Challenges in Evolving the EMS

Our experience base is not only a knowledge base for software engineering research. Experience is explicit knowledge underlying processes, products, and technologies, which built up through individual learning from the experience of the people involved; knowledge is used in previously unknown contexts with some certainty and experience describes events in one specific context that can only be used carefully [5,6]. Here we define "Knowledge" describes the facts. "Experience" describes how to use those facts. People could have that kind of knowledge but they perhaps still cannot solve the problems as they maybe do not know how to apply them. They have to use the knowledge in different circumstance, and in different issues to learn what the right way to apply the knowledge is. When they find it, it can be called experience. To the organization, experience stands more value than knowledge.

While we have realized a great deal of benefit from our eBASE, we face many challenges moving forward. Some of these challenges include:

Everything keeps changing
Change is, of course, inevitable and unstoppable. However, consistency, stability, and controlled repeatability are the hallmarks of quality research. This is difficult to achieve within eBASE when so many uncontrollable variables are in play, some minor, others insurmountable. For example, the milestone review dates for each semester and each year vary between 1 to 3 weeks. The effort reporting categories quite naturally have evolved since 1996 as new development practices come into fashion (e.g. COTS, UML, and Extreme Programming - XP). New software tools and faster, cheaper hardware are utilized every year making baselines difficult to establish (e.g. some things that used to take a lot of time and effort no longer do). Before 2000, effort data was in HTML format, now it's stored in a DB table. The MBASE guidelines are updated and revised annually, sometimes making radical changes to the structure, format and process. New practices are introduced (simplifiers and complicators, RUP, XP, etc,). An unforeseen challenge is that our project client base is rapidly changing. Not only are the client project domains more diverse, our client base is also maturing. That is, some clients have become "veterans" who have a significant impact on the projects they are involved in and the operation of the course. More recently, the number of new projects has had a tremendous increase (from about 25 to over 50). The impact of this is significant on the challenge to uniformity. It is difficult to acquire enough quality, real-client projects, leaving us to create "proxy" projects or double-up some projects (i.e. run the same one with multiple teams).

Missing needed information
New information needs to be added into the experience base such as course schedules (they are in different places), guideline changes, new practices, team composition, size and attrition data, expanded grade information, research projects and results.

The structure is awkward
There is no standardized structure for the representation of the diverse experience data we generate and collect. In particular, there is increasingly use of diverse multi-media information such as video, audio, and dynamic HTML. In addition, there is a high-degree of dependencies between and within experience data, so adding new structure causes a lot of breakage and re-work. It is impossible to anticipate all possible evolutions. These problems tend to cause the data to be "blobbed" together is a weak, yet general format. This makes the data difficult to mine (i.e. correlate, operate, summarize, query, etc.).

There are limitations from current technologies
The evolution of EMS depends a lot in AI, database, and language technologies. The effective representation, archival, and mining of the kind of data we collect for eBASE is a highly active research area.

Most experience base researchers are consumers not contributors
They use the data and keep their results private. New incentives need to be introduced to encourage EMS users to contribute to eBASE. Researchers leverage the eBASE

data to find and publish valuable results. Data providers seldom get rewarded in this or any other meaningful way.

Other

There are a host of "annoying" difficulties such as problems with schema migration; variable numbers of fields per record; changing data definitions; the lack of good project metadata; and the lack of good front-end capabilities for eBASE exploration and data mining.

We are still working on how to provide more convenient ways for researchers and developers to use the experience base, and how to provide more valuable data to people. A long way still needs to go. Fortunately, we are making progresses.

6 Conclusion and Discussion

From a modest beginning, we have evolved and eventually realized great benefit from an eBASE of the software project experiences. These benefits go well beyond technology supported automation such as centralized access to project data. The EF approach has directed the evolution and use of eBASE to achieve benefits within organizational learning and strategically beneficial software process research. Every year it becomes more important and essential to the objectives and activities of software engineering education and practices. Software development experiences are a very valuable organizational resource and should be made easily accessible to all. In particular, process experience needs to be institutionalized as "corporate memory" where it can expand and evolve without critical dependence of any individual (this is particularly important in an academic environment where students are continuously entering and graduating).

But some of the most basic questions are unanswered:

- How do we create a truly useful Experience Base?
- How do we enable people to collaborate and share experience?
- What do different user groups (researchers, educators, practitioners) need in terms of tools processes and experience in order to do their work in a more efficient way?

We are still working on how to provide more convenient ways for researchers and developers to use the eBASE, and how to infuse it with more valuable data. Furthermore, if we want to apply EMS concept to the industry, we still need to determine an effective, general, powerful representation of experience.

References

1. http://ebase.usc.edu/index.html
2. http://sunset.usc.edu/affiliates/general/index.html
3. Basili , V., Caldiera, G., McGarry, F., Pajerski, R., Page., G., Waligora, S.: The software engineering laboratory: an operational software experience factory. International Conference on Software Engineering archive. Proceedings of the 14th international conference on Software engineering table of contents, Melbourne, Australia; ISBN:0-89791-504-6 (1992) 370 - 381

4. Basili, V. R., Caldiera, G., Rombach, D. H.: The Experience Factory. Encyclopaedia of Software Engineering -2 Volume Set (1994) 469-476

5. Althoff, K.-D., Decker, B., Hartkopf, S., Jedlitschka, A., Nick, M. & Rech, J.: Experience Management: The Fraunhofer IESE Experience Factory. In P. Perner (ed.), Proc. Industrial Data Mining Conference, Leipzig, 24.-25 (July 2001), Institut für Bildverarbeitung und angewandte Informatik

6. Rech, J., Decker, B. & Althoff, K.-D.: Using Knowledge Discovery Technology in Experience Management Systems. Proc. Workshop "Maschinelles Lernen (FGML01)", GI-Workshop-Woche "Lernen - Lehren - Wissen - Adaptivität (LLWA01)" (2001), Universität Dortmund

7. Boehm, B.: Anchoring the Software Process. IEEE Software (July 1996) 73-82.

8. Boehm, B., Abi-Antoun, M., Port, D., Kwan, L.: Requirements Engineering, Expectations Management, and the Two Cultures. International Conference on Requirements Engineering (June 1999). http://sunset.usc.edu/TechRpts/Papers/usccse98-518/usccse98-518.pdf

9. Boehm, B., Port, D.: Escaping the Software Tar Pit: Model Clashes and How to Avoid Them. ACM Software Engineering Notes (January 1999) 36-48

10. Boehm, B., Port, D.: When Models Collide: Lessons from Software Systems Analysis. IEEE IT Professional (January/February 1999) 49-56

11. Boehm, B., Port, D., Abi-Antoun, M., and Egyed, A.: Guidelines for the Life Cycle Objectives (LCO) and the Life Cycle Architecture (LCA) deliverables for Model-Based Architecting and Software Engineering (MBASE). USC Technical Report USC-CSE-98-519 (1998)

12. Kruchten, P.: The Rational Unified Process (2nd ed.). Addison-Wesley (2000)

13. R. Park: Software Size Measurement: A Framework for Counting Source Statements. CMU/SEI-92-TR-20 (1992), Software Engineering Institute, Pittsburgh, PA

14. Chen, Y. , Boehm, B., Madachy, R., Valerdi, R.: An Empirical Study of eServices Product UML Sizing Metrics. ACM-IEEE International Symposium on Empirical Software Engineering (August 2004)

15. Boehm, B., In, H.: Aids for Identifying Conflicts Among Quality Requirements. Proceedings, ICRE-96 and IEEE Software (March 1996)

16. Boehm, B., Basili, V., Port, D., and Jain, A.:Achieving CMMI Level 5 Improvements with MBASE and the CeBASE Method. CrossTalk, vol. 15, no. 5 (May 2002) 9-16

17. Thorp, J.: The Information Paradox: Realizing the Business Benefits of Information Technology. Mcgraw-Hill (February 1999)

18. http://sunset.usc.edu/research/COCOTS/

19. Boehm, B., In, H.: Cost vs. Quality Requirements: Conflict Analysis and Negotiation Aids. Software Quality Professional, Vol. 1, No. 2 (March 1999) 38-50

20. Boehm, B., Abts, C., etc: Software Cost Estimation With COCOMO II. Prentice-Hall, ISBN 0-13-026692-2 (2000)

Experiences in Discovering, Modeling, and Reenacting Open Source Software Development Processes

Chris Jensen and Walt Scacchi

Institute for Software Research, University of California, Irvine
Irvine, CA 92697-3425, USA
{cjensen, wscacchi}@ics.uci.edu

Abstract. Process discovery has been shown to be a challenging problem offering limited results. This paper describes a new approach to process discovery that examines the Internet information spaces of open source software development projects. In particular, we examine challenges, strengths, weaknesses and findings when seeking to discover, model, and re-enact processes associated with large, global OSSD projects like NetBeans.org. The longer-term goal of this approach is to determine the requirements and design of more fully integrated process discovery and modeling mechanisms that can be applied to Web-based, open source software development projects.

1 Introduction

The goal of our work is to develop new techniques for discovering, modeling, analyzing, and simulating software development processes based on information, artifacts, events, and contexts that can be observed through public information sources on the Web. Our problem domain examines processes in large, globally dispersed open source software development (OSSD) projects, such as those associated with the Apache Web server [16], Mozilla web browser [24], GNOME [9], and integrated development environments like NetBeans [18] and Eclipse [4]. The challenge we face is similar to what prospective developers or corporate sponsors who want to join a given OSSD project face in trying to understand how software development processes and activities are accomplished. As such, our efforts should yield practical results.

OSSD projects do not typically employ or provide explicit process models, prescriptions, or schemes other than what may be implicit in the use of certain OSSD tools for version control and source code compilation. In contrast, we seek to demonstrate the feasibility of automating the discovery of software process workflows via manual search and analysis methods in projects like NetBeans by analyzing the content, structure, update and usage patterns of their Web information spaces. These spaces include process enactment information such as informal task prescriptions, community and information structure and work roles, project and product development histories, electronic messages and communications patterns among project participants ([5], [26], [29]). Likewise, corresponding events that denote updates to these sources and other project repositories are also publicly accessible. Though such ethnographic discovery approaches net a wealth of

M. Li, B. Boehm, and L.J. Osterweil (Eds.): SPW 2005, LNCS 3840, pp. 449–462, 2005.

information with which to model, simulate, and analyze OSSD processes, they are limited by a lack of scalability when applied to the study of multiple OSSD development projects (cf. [13]). Subsequently, it suggests the need for a more automated approach to that can facilitate process discovery.

In our approach, we identify the kinds of OSSD artifacts (e.g. source code files, messages posted on public discussion forums, Web pages, etc.), artifact update events (e.g. version release announcements, Web page updates, message postings, etc.), and work contexts (e.g. roadmap for upcoming software releases, Web site architecture, communications systems used for email, forums, instant messaging, etc.) that can be detected, observed, or extracted across the Web. Though such an approach clearly cannot observe the entire range of software development processes underway in an OSSD project (nor do we seek to observe or collect data on private communications), it does draw attention to what can be publicly observed, modeled, or re-enacted at a distance. That is the focus of our effort.

Our approach relies on use of a process meta-model to provide a reference framework that associates these data with software processes and process models [15]. As such, we have been investigating what kinds of processing capabilities and tools can be applied to support the automated discovery and modeling of selected software processes (e.g., for daily software build and periodic release) that are common among many OSSD projects. The capabilities and tools include those for Internet-based event notification, Web-based text data mining and knowledge discovery, and previous results from process discovery studies. However, in this study, we focus on identifying the foundations for discovering, modeling, and re-enacting OSSD processes that can be found in a large, global OSSD project using a variety of techniques and tools.

2   Related Work

Event notification systems have been used in many contexts, including process discovery and analysis ([3], [30]). However, of the systems promising automated event notification, many require process performers to obtain, install, and use event monitoring applications on their own machines to detect when events occur. While yielding mildly fruitful results, this approach is undesirable for several reasons. This includes the need to install and integrate remote data collection mechanisms with local or project-specific software development tools, and it is unclear who would take on such effort within an existing OSSD project.

Prior work in process event notification has also been focused on information collected from command shell histories, applying inference techniques to construct process model fragments from event patterns (object and tool invocations) [8]. They advise that rather than seeking to discover the entire development process from enactment instances, to instead focus on creating partial process specifications that may overlap with one another. This also reflects variability in software process enactment instantiation across iterations. This imparts additional inconvenience on project developers, and relies on her/his willingness to use the particular tools that monitor and analyze command shell events (which can become intractable when a developer uses tools or repository services from remote networked systems). By doing so, the number of process performers for whom data is collected may be reduced well below the number of participants in the project due to privacy concerns and the hassles of becoming involved. While closed source software engineering organizations may mediate this challenge by leveraging company policies, OSSD projects lack the ability to enforce adoption of such event-capture technology.

Cook and Wolf [3] utilize algorithmic and statistical inference techniques to model processes where the goal was to create a single, monolithic finite state machine (FSM) representation of the process. However, it is not entirely clear that a single FSM is appropriate for modeling complex processes. Similarly, other FSM-related process representation schemes such as Petri-Net based FUNSOFT [6] offered a wide variety of activity and state-chart diagrams. It appears however that these representations may lack scalability when applied to a process situated within a global organizational context involving multiple tools, diverse artifact types, and multiple development roles across multiple networked sites of reasonable complexity, which is typical of large OSSD projects (cf. [9]).

Last, while process research has yielded many alternative views of software process models, none has proven decisive or clearly superior. Nonetheless, contemporary research in software process technology, such as Lil Jil [2], [21] and PML [19] argues for analytical, visual, navigational and enactable representations of software processes. Subsequently, we find it fruitful to convey our findings about software processes, and the contexts in which they occur, using a mix of both informal and formal representations of these kinds [28]. We employ this practice here.

3 Problem Domain

We are interested in discovering, modeling, simulating, and re-enacting software development processes in large, Web-based OSSD projects. Such projects are often globally distributed efforts sometimes involving tens, hundreds, or thousands of developers collaborating on products constituting thousands to millions of source lines of code without meeting face-to-face, and often without performing modern methods for software engineering ([26], [27]). Past approaches have shown process discovery to be difficult, yielding limited results. However, the discovery methods we use are not random probes in the dark, nor do they simply apply prior approaches. Instead, we capitalize on contextual aids offered by the domain. Some of these include:

- Web pages, including project status reports and task assignments, may be viewed and classified (informally) as object types.
- Asynchronous communications among project participants posted in threaded email discussion lists, which address process activities indicated by process identifier keywords (e.g., design, release, testing, etc.)
- Transcripts of synchronous communication via Internet chat (cf. [5]).
- Software problem/bug and issue reports, which reveal information on software bug reporting and maintenance/repair processes
- Testing scripts and results, which highlight project-based software testing practices

- Community newsletters, which highlight project milestone events (e.g., system releases, turnover of core developers in the projects)
- Web accessible software product source code directories and repositories, which carry timestamps and other identifiers indicating when source code objects were checked in/out, and versioning information.
- Software system builds (executable binaries) and distribution packages, which are constructed and released on a periodic basis (daily, candidate (alpha, beta), and final release (distribution version)
- OSS development tools in use in an OSSD project (e.g., concurrent version system (CVS), GNU compiler collection (gcc), bug reporting (bugzilla) (cf. [10])
- OSS development resources, including other software development artifacts and process fragment descriptions (e.g., How-To guides, lists of frequently asked questions (FAQs), etc.) [26]

Each OSSD project has locally established methods of interaction, communication, leadership, and control [14], whether explicit or implicit ([26], [27]). These collaboration modes yield a high amount of empirically observable process evidence, as well as a large degree of unrelated data. However, information spaces are also dynamic. New artifacts are added, while existing ones are updated, removed, renamed and relocated, else left to become outdated. Artifact or object contents change, and project Web sites get restructured. In order to capture the history of process evolution, these changes need to be made persistent and shared with new OSSD project members. While code repositories and project email discussion archives have achieved widespread use, it is less common for other artifacts, such as instant messaging and chat transcripts, to be archived in a publicly available venue. Nonetheless, when discovering a process in progress, changes can de detected through comparison of artifacts at different time slices during the development lifecycle. At times, the detail of the changes is beneficial, and at other times, simply knowing what has changed and when is all that is important to determining the order (or control flow sequence) of process events or activity. To be successful, tools for automated process discovery must be able to efficiently access, collect, and analyze the data including areas of the project Web space such as public email/mailing list message boards, Web page updates, notifications of software builds/releases, and software bug archives in terms of changes to the OSS information space [26], [27].

To prove the viability of our process discovery approach, we demonstrate it with a case study. For this task, we examine a selected process in the NetBeans project, which is developing an open source IDE using Java technology[1]. The "requirements and release" process was chosen for study because its activities have short duration, are frequently enacted, and have a propensity for available evidence that could be extracted using automated technologies. The process was discovered, modeled informally and formally, then prototyped for analysis and reenactment. The full results of our initial case study may be found elsewhere [22]. The discussion of our process discovery and modeling methods and results follows next.

---

[1] The NetBeans project was started in 1996, and SUN Microsystems began project sponsorship in 1998. At present, more than 60 companies are participating in the project through their developers. In 2004, the project passed the threshold of more than 100K developers contributing to the project.

4 Process Discovery and Modeling

Discovery of open source software processes relies on several data models. Firstly, we need to determine what aspects of the process we wish to discover, defined by our process meta-model. This meta-model is neither specific to our domain (OSSD processes), nor software processes. To capture OSSD software processes, we need a means of setting the problem domain within the terms of the meta-model. Such is the task of the reference model. Once this is done, we may begin looking for instances of processes within a corpus, in this case the OSSD project Web repository.

The meta-model we use is that of Mi and Scacchi [15]. It provides us with a vocabulary to describe the processes we examine. Our meta-model defines processes hierarchically: processes are composed of tasks (sets of related actions) and atomic actions. The hierarchy may be further divided (e.g. sub-processes, subtasks, and so forth) to achieve an arbitrary degree of decomposition. Each activity is defined in terms of process entities: agents that participate in the process activity, tools used by those agents in the performance of the activity, and resources that are the product of and are consumed by performance of the activity (see Figure 1). We find these to be a minimal set of entities necessary to describe a process. This meta-model is augmented with control-flow grammar in the process markup language (PML) [19] we use to formally represent software processes to show the order in which activities and instantiated.

Unlike Cook and Wolf's approach, we apply *a priori* knowledge of software development for discovering processes. Accordingly, we use a reference model [11] to help identify possible indicators (e.g., developer roles, probable tool types, input and output objects) that a given activity has occurred. We do this by creating a taxonomy of the process entities within the problem domain. Thus, we enumerate the types of tools (and resources, activities, and agents-roles) we expect to find referenced in the project corpus (e.g. "email client") as well as instances of those tools (e.g. "Mozilla Thunderbird"). This framework provides a mapping between the tool, resource, activity, and role names discovered in the community Web with a classification scheme of known tools, resources, activities, and roles used in open source communities. The instances are necessary for discovering process entities used within the corpus while types and genericity/hierarchy aid us in abstracting the instance data into a more general process model spanning multiple enactments.

Although we would like to achieve some degree of automation in discovering open source software development processes, it is unreasonable to assume that a complete solution is possible due to the heterogeneity of data available within and across project information corpora. Instead, we seek to automate as much as possible in order to ease the effort inherent to the task. To this end, our methodology incorporates general information gathering independent of document type, augmented by some analysis techniques specific to the type and structure of the data available. Thus we automate the tasks that are easy to automate and provide value to make the effort worthwhile. And, we do manually tasks for which automation is either too difficult or does not provide payoff to validate effort required.

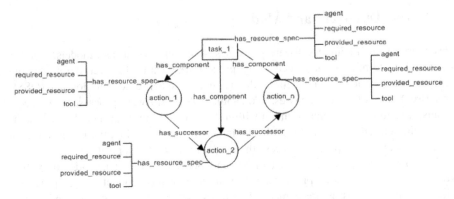

Fig. 1. Software process meta-model (cf. [15])

We use indexing at the core to do much of the legwork of general information gathering. We use this index to identify actions, tools, resources, and agents within artifacts in the corpus. These are correlated across artifacts according to usage and update information available. While we are able to tune the reference model to contain instance values of actions, resources, and tools (e.g. "submit defect report", "x-test-results", and "Issuezilla," respectively), identifying process agents by proper names a priori is not possible. Such identification requires document specific analysis techniques. These include parsers for extracting names, user handles, and email addresses from threaded mailing lists, chat logs, defect reports, and versioning repositories. Once extracted, they are looked up in the index and added to the action-tool-resource tuples already identified. Such document specific analysis may also be used to uncover heretofore-unknown instances of other process entities (i.e. actions, resources, and tools) in similar fashion and is essential to obtaining accurate timestamps in documents that aggregate multiple software artifacts (e.g. threaded mailing lists containing multiple messages within a single system file).

Document specific analysis provides rich results with a cost. There are many types of data and standards for document structure even for a single type of data and these vary highly across OSSD projects. As a result, a broad array of tools specifically tuned for each project corpus is required to obtain rich results. Such an array is painstaking to develop, although available off-the-shelf partial solutions ease this burden. Further, integrating large result sets from multiple data sources into a single process model of any degree of formality is a complex task in itself. Our reference model can suggest process entity tuples that are related and the temporal information we are able to extract provides a timeline of activities. However learning activity control flow and asserting an activity hierarchy remain somewhat an art as opposed to a science.

The discovery of processes within a specific OSSD project begins with a cursory examination of the project Web space in order to ascertain what types of information are available and where that information might be located within the project's Web site. Structure and content of the project Web space give us an idea of what happened in terms of process actions, agents, tools, and resources, whereas artifact usage and update patterns tell us when process activities happened as noted above.

To situate the process within its organizational context, we look for modes of contribution within the development process. The modes of contribution (development roles) can be used to construct an initial set of activity scenarios, which can be described as *use cases* for project or process participation.

Though best known as a tenet of UML, use cases can serve as a notation to model scenarios of activities performed by actors in some role that use one or more tools to manipulate artifacts associated with an enterprise process or activity within it ([7], [29]). The site map also shows a page dedicated to project governance hyperlinked three layers deep within the site. This page exposes the primary member types, their roles and responsibilities, which suggest additional use cases. Unlike those found through the modes of contribution, the project roles span the breadth of the process, though at a higher level of abstraction. Each use case can encode a process fragment. In collecting use cases, we can extract out concrete actions that can then be assembled into a process description to be modeled, simulated, and enacted.

When aggregated, these use cases can be coalesced into an informal model of a process and its context rendered as a *rich hypermedia*, an interactive semi-structured extension of Monk and Howard's [17] rich picture modeling construct. The rich hypermedia shown in Figure 2 identifies developer roles, tools, concerns, and artifacts of development and their interaction, which are hyperlinked (indicated as underlined phrases) to corresponding use cases and object/role descriptions (see Figure 3). Such an informal computational model can be useful for newcomers to the community looking to become involved in development and offers an overview of the process and its context in the project, while abstracting away the detail of its activities. The use cases also help identify the requirements for enacting or re-enacting the process as a basis for validating, adapting, or improving the process.

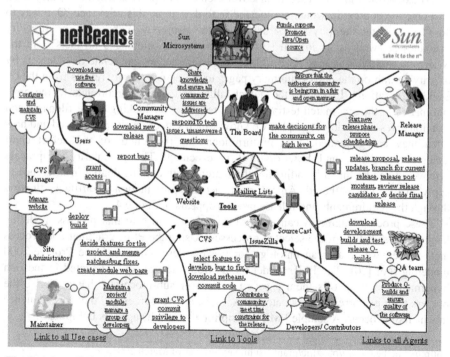

Fig. 2. A hyperlinked rich hypermedia of the NetBeans requirements and release process [22]

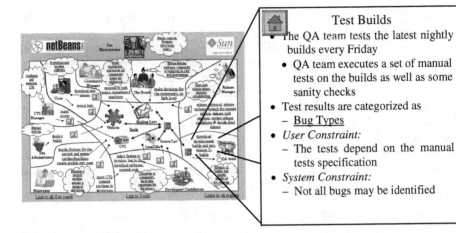

Fig. 3. A hyperlink selection within a rich hypermedia presentation that reveals a corresponding use case

A critical challenge in reconstructing process fragments from a process enactment instance is in knowing whether or not the evidence at hand is related, unrelated, or anomalous. Reliability of associations constructed in this fashion may be strengthened by the frequency of association and the relevance of artifacts carrying the association. If text extraction tools are used to discover elements of process fragments, they must also note the context in which are located in to determine this relevance. One way to do this is using the physical structure of the project's Web site (i.e. directory structure), as well as its logical structure (referencing/referenced artifacts). In the NetBeans quality-assurance (Q-Build) testing example, we can relate the "defects by priority" graph on the defect summary page[2] to the defect priority results from the Q-Build verification. Likewise, the defect tallies and locations correlate to the error summaries in the automated testing (XTest) results[3]. By looking at the filename and creation dates of the defect graphs, we know which sets of results are charted and how often they are generated. This in turn identifies the length of the defect chart generation process, and how often it is executed. The granularity of process discovered can be tuned by adjusting the search depth and the degree of inference to apply to the data gathered. An informal visual representation of artifacts flowing through the requirements and release process appears in Figure 4.

These process fragments can now be assembled into a formal process modeling language description of the selected processes. Using the PML grammar and process meta-model, we created an ontology for process description with the Protégé-2000 modeling tool [20]. The PML model builds from the use cases depicted in the rich hypermedia, then distills them a set of actions or sub-processes that comprise the process with its corresponding actor roles, tools, and resources and the flow sequence in which they occur. A sample PML description that results appears in Figure 5.

---

[2] http://qa.netbeans.org/bugzilla/graphs/summary.html as of March 2004.
[3] http://www.netbeans.org/download/xtest-results/index.html as of March 2004.

5 Process Reenactment for Deployment, Validation, and Improvement

Since their success relies heavily on broad, open-ended participation, OSSD projects often have informal descriptions of ways members can participate, as well as offer prescriptions for community building [26]. Although automatically recognizing and modeling process enactment guidelines or policies from such prescriptions may seem a holy grail of sorts for process discovery, there is no assurance that they accurately reflect the process as it is enacted. However, taken with the discovered process, such prescriptions begin to make it is possible to perform basic process validation and conformance analysis by reconciling developer roles, affected artifacts, and tools being used in modeled processes or process fragments (cf. [1], [23]).

As OSSD projects are open to contributions from afar, it also becomes possible to contribute explicit models of discovered processes back to the project under study so that project participants can openly review, independently validate, refine, adapt or otherwise improve their own software processes. Accordingly, we have contributed our process models and analyses of the NetBeans requirements and release process in the form of a public report hosted (and advertised) on the NetBeans.org Web site[4].

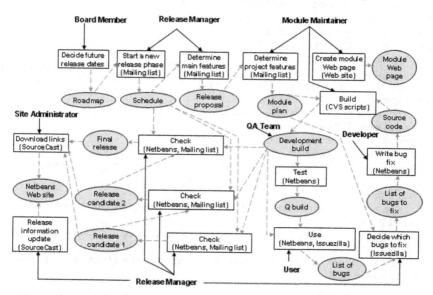

Fig. 4. NetBeans Requirements and Release process flow graph [22]

Process re-enactment allows us to recreate, simulate, or prototype process enactments by navigationally traversing a semantic hypertext (i.e., PML) representation of the process [19], [25]. These re-enactment prototypes are automatically derived from a compilation of their corresponding PML process model, and the instantiation of the complied result in a Web-based run-time (enactment)

---

[4] See http://www.netbeans.org/community/articles/index.html, as of May 2003.

environment [19]. One step in the process modeled for NetBeans appears in Figure 6, drawn from the excerpt shown in Figure 5. In exercising repeated simulated process enactment walkthroughs, we have been able to detect process fragments that may be unduly lengthy, which may serve as good candidates for downstream process engineering activities such as streamlining and process redesign [25]. Process re-enactment also allows us, as well as participants in the global NetBeans project, to better see the effects of duplicated work. As an example, we have four agent types that test code. Users may carry out beta testing from a black box perspective, whereas developers, contributors, and SUN Microsystems QA experts may perform more in-depth white-box testing and analysis, and, in the case of developers and contributors, not merely submit a report to the IssueZilla issue tracking system,[5] but may also take responsibility for resolving it.

```
sequence Test {
  action Execute automatic test scripts {
  requires { Test scripts, release binaries }
  provides { Test results }
  tool { Automated test suite (xtest, others) }
  agent { Sun Java Studio QA team }
  script { /* Executed off-site */ } }
action Execute manual test scripts {
  requires { Release binaries }
  provides { Test results }
  tool { NetBeans IDE }
  agent {users, developers, Sun Java Studio developers, QA team}
  script { /* Executed off-site */ } }
iteration Update Issuezilla {
  action Report issues to Issuezilla {
    requires { Test results }
    provides { Issuezilla entry }
    tool { Web browser }
    agent{users, developers, Sun Java Studio developers, QA
team}
    script {
        <br><a href="http://www.netbeans.org/issues/">Navigate to
Issuezilla </a>
        <br><a        href=http://www.netbeans.org/issues/query.cgi>
Query Issuezilla </a>
        <br><ahref=http://www.netbeans.org/issues/enter_bug.cgi>
Enter issue </a> } }
```

Fig. 5. A partial PML description of the testing sequence of the NetBeans release process

We are also able to detect where cycles or particular activities may be problematic for participants, and thus where process redesign may be of practical value [25]. Process re-enactment prototypes are a useful means to interactively analyze whether or how altering a process may lead to potential pitfalls that can be discovered before they lead to project failure. Over the course of constructing and executing the prototype we discovered some of the more concrete reasons that there are few

---

[5] See http://www.netbeans.org/kb/articles/issuezilla.html, as of March 2004.

volunteers for the release manager position. The role has an exceptional amount of tedious administrative tasks that are critical to the success of the project.

Between scheduling the release, coordinating module stabilization, and carrying out the build process, the release manager has a hand in almost every part of the requirements and release process. This is a good indication that downstream activities may also uncover a way to better distribute the tasks and lighten her/his load. The self-selective nature of OSSD project participation has many impacts on their development process. If any member wishes not to follow a given process, the process enforcement is contingent on the tolerance of her/his peers in the matter, which is rarely the case in corporate development processes. If the project proves intolerant of the alternative process, developers are free to simply not participate in the project's development efforts and perform an independent software release build.

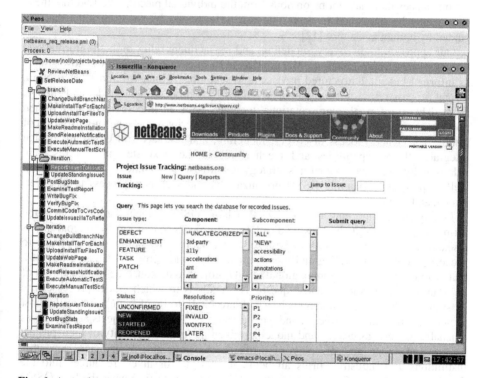

Fig. 6. An action step in a re-enactment of the NetBeans requirements and release process, specified in Figure 5

6   Conclusion

Our goal is to obtain process execution data and event streams by monitoring the Web information spaces of open source software development projects. By examining changes to the information space and artifacts within it, we can observe, derive, or otherwise discover process activities. In turn, we reconstitute process instances using PML, which provides us with a formal description of an enactable, low-fidelity model of the process in question that can be analyzed, simulated, redesigned, and refined for reuse and redistribution. But this progress still begs the question of how to more fully automate the discovery and modeling of processes found in large, global scale OSSD projects.

Our experience with process discovery in the NetBeans project, and its requirements and release process, and our case studies discovering, modeling, and reenacting processes used in the Mozilla and Apache HTTPD projects suggest that a bottom-up strategy for process discovery, together with a top-down process meta-model, can serve as a suitable framework for process discovery, modeling and re-enactment. As demonstrated in the testing example, action sequences are constructed much like a jigsaw puzzle. We compile pieces of evidence to find ways to fit them together in order to make claims about process enactment events, artifacts, or circumstances that may not be obvious from the individual pieces. We find that these pieces may be unearthed in ways that can be executed by software tools that are guided by human assistance [12].

Our approach to discovery, modeling, and reenactment relies on both informal and formal process representations. We constructed use cases, rich pictures, flow graphs as informal but semi-structured process representations which we transformed into a formal process representation language guided by a process meta-model and support tools. These informal representations together with a process meta-model then provide a scheme for constructing formal process descriptions. Thus demonstration of a more automated process discovery, modeling, and re-enactment environment that integrates these capabilities and mechanisms is the next step in this research. Additionally, we have applied this strategy towards socio-technical OSSD process as well as processes spanning OSSD organizations and seek new process to discover, model, and reenact.

Finally, it is important to recognize that large OSSD projects are diverse in the form and practice of their software development processes. Our long-term goal in this research is to determine how to best support a more fully automated approach to process discovery, modeling and re-enactment. Our study provides a case study of a real-world process in a complex global OSSD project to demonstrate the feasibility of such an approach. Subsequently, questions remain as to which OSSD processes are most amenable to such an approach, which are likely to be of high value to the host project or other similar projects, and whether all or some OSSD projects are more/less amenable to such discovery and modeling given the richness/paucity of their project information space and diversity of artifacts. As government agencies, academic institutions and industrial firms all begin to consider or invest resources into the development of large OSS systems, then they will seek to find what the best OSSD processes are, or what OSSD practices to follow. Thus discovery and explicit modeling of OSSD processes in forms that can be shared, reviewed, modified, re-enacted, and redistributed appears to be an important topic for further investigation, and this study represents a step in this direction.

Acknowledgements

The research described in this report is supported by grants from the National Science Foundation #0083075, #0205679, #0205724, and #0350754. No endorsement implied. Mark Ackerman at the University of Michigan Ann Arbor; Les Gasser at the University of Illinois, Urbana-Champaign; John Noll at Santa Clara University; and Margaret Elliott at the UCI Institute for Software Research are collaborators on the research described in this paper.

References

1. Atkinson, D.C. and Noll, J. 2003.. Automated Validation and Verification of Process Models, *Proc. 7ᵗʰ Intern. IASTED Conf. Software Engineering and Applications*, November.
2. Cass, A.G., Lerner, B., McCall, E., Osterweil, L. and Wise, A. 2000. Little JIL/Juliette: A process definition language and interpreter. *Proc. 22ⁿᵈ Intern. Conf. Software Engineering*, 754-757, Limerick, Ireland, June.
3. Cook, J. and Wolf, A.L. 1998. Discovering Models of Software Processes from Event-Based Data, *ACM Trans. Software Engineering and Methodology*, 7(3), 215-249.
4. Eclipse Web Site, 2005. http://www.eclipse.org
5. Elliott, M. and Scacchi, W., Free Software Development: Cooperation and Conflict in A Virtual Organizational Culture, in S. Koch (ed.), *Free/Open Source Software Development*, Idea Publishing, Hershey, PA, 2004.
6. Emmerich, W. and Gruhn, V., FUNSOFT Nets: a Petri-Net based Software Process Modeling Language, *Proc. 6th ACM/IEEE Int. Workshop on Software Specification and Design*, Como, Italy, IEEE Computer Society Press, 175-184, 1991.
7. Fowler, M. and Scott, K. 2000. *UML Distilled: A Brief Guide to the Standard Object Modeling Language*. Second Ed. Addison Wesley:
8. Garg, P.K. and Bhansali, S. 1992. Process programming by hindsight. *Proc. 14ᵗʰ Intern. Conf. Software Engineering*, 280-293.
9. German, D., 2003. The GNOME project: A case study of open source, global software development, *Software Process—Improvement and Practice*, 8(4), 201-215.
10. Halloran, T., and Scherlis, W. 2002. High Quality and Open Source Software Practices, *Proc. 2nd Workshop on Open Source Software Engineering*, Orlando, FL, May.
11. Jensen, C. and Scacchi, W. 2003.Applying a Reference Framework to Open Source Software Process Discovery, in *Proc. 1ˢᵗ Workshop on Open Source in an Industrial Context*, OOPSLA-OSIC03, Anaheim, CA October..
12. Jensen, C. and Scacchi, W. 2004. Data Mining for Software Process Discovery in Open Source Software Development Communities, submitted for publication.
13. Jensen, C. and Scacchi, W. 2005, Process Modeling across the Web Information Infrastructure, *Software Process—Improvement and Practice*, (to appear).
14. Jensen, C. and Scacchi, W. 2005b, Collaboration, Leadership, Control, and Conflict Negotiation in the NetBeans.org Open Source Software Development Community, *Proc. 38ᵗʰ Hawaii Intern. Conf. Systems Sciences*, Kona, HI.
15. Mi, P. and Scacchi, W. 1996. A Meta-Model for Formulating Knowledge-Based Models of Software Development, *Decision Support Systems*, 17(4), 313-330.
16. Mockus, A., Fielding, R., and Herbsleb, J., 2002.Two Case Studies in Open Source Software Development: Apache and Mozilla, *ACM Trans. Software Engineering and Methodology*, 11(3), 309-346.
17. Monk, A. and Howard, S. 1998. The Rich Picture: A Tool for Reasoning about Work Context. *Interactions,* 21-30, March-April.
18. NetBeans Web Site, 2005. http://www.netbeans.org

19. Noll, J. and Scacchi, W. 2001. Specifying Process Oriented Hypertext for Organizational Computing. *J. Network and Computer Applications* 24 39-61.
20. Noy, N.F., Sintek, M., Decker, S., Crubézy, M., Fergerson, R.W. and Musen, M.A. 2001. Creating Semantic Web Contents with Protégé-2000. *IEEE Intelligent Systems,* 16(2), 60-71.
21. Osterweil, L. 2003. Modeling Processes to Effectively Reason about their Properties, *Proc. ProSim'03 Workshop,* Portland, OR, May 2003.
22. Oza, M., Nistor, E., Hu, S. Jensen, C., and Scacchi, W. 2002. *A First Look at the Netbeans Requirements and Release Process,* http://www.ics.uci.edu/cjensen/papers/FirstLook NetBeans/
23. Podorozhny, R.M., Perry, D.E., and Osterweil, L. 2003, Artifact-based Functional Comparison of Software Processes, *Proc. ProSim'03 Workshop,* Portland, OR, May 2003.
24. Reis C.R. and Fortes, R.P.M. 2002. An Overview of the Software Engineering Process and Tools in the Mozilla Project, *Proc. Workshop on Open Source Software Development,* Newcastle, UK, February
25. Scacchi, W., 2000. Understanding Software Process Redesign using Modeling, Analysis, and Simulation, *Software Process—Improvement and Practice,* 5(2/3), 183-195.
26. Scacchi, W., 2002. Understanding the Requirements for Developing Open Source Software Systems, *IEE Proceedings—Software,* 149(1), 25-39.
27. Scacchi, W., 2004, Free/Open Source Software Development Practices in the Game Community, *IEEE Software,* 21(1), 59-67, Jan-Feb. 2004.
28. Scacchi, W., Jensen, C., Noll, J. and Elliott, M., 2005, Multi-Modal Modeling, Analysis, and Validation of Open Source Software Development Processes, *Proc. 1ˢᵗ Open Source Software Conference,* Genova, IT (to appear).
29. Viller, S., and Sommerville, I., 2000. Ethnographically Informed Analysis for Software Engineers, *Intern. J. Human-Computer Interaction,* 53, 169-196.
30. Wolf, A.L. and Rosenblum, D.S. 1993. A Study in Software Process Data Capture and Analysis. *Proc. Second Intern. Conf. on the Software Process,* 115-124.

Application of the V-Modell XT – Report from a Pilot Project

Marco Kuhrmann[1], Dirk Niebuhr[2], and Andreas Rausch[2]

[1] Technische Universität München, Software & Systems Engineering, Boltzmannstr. 3,
D-85748 Garching b. München, Germany
kuhrmann@in.tum.de
[2] Technische Universität Kaiserslautern, FB Informatik – AG Softwarearchitektur,
Gottlieb-Daimler-Straße D-67653 Kaiserslautern, Germany
{niebuhr, rausch}@informatik.uni-kl.de

Abstract. The new V-Modell XT has replaced the well-known V-Modell 97 as obligatory development process standard IT-projects of Germany's government and military service. During the development of the V-Modell XT a wide Beta-test phase was planned, enabling the project partners to make first experiences in practical use. Furthermore, the pilot projects enable all participants to come closer to the new standard and learn more about its strengths and weaknesses. After having a short look at the new concepts of the V-Modell XT, we present some experiences made during the pilot project "Development of the WiBe software" for the German Department of the Interior. We will present some experiences we made and provide some quantitative data of products created during the project.

1 Introduction

During the past years, IT-projects became more and more complex and extensive. Looking at the high degree of IT-systems penetration [1] of the every-day life, it becomes more important that IT-systems work accurately. A malfunction of a coffee-maker is quite annoying but tolerable, dysfunctions like the failed lift-off of the Ariane V-Rocket or miss-leaded Patriots during the 2nd Gulf War are certainly not acceptable. To avoid errors in such dimensions, a clearly-structured, well-defined modell for (software) development processes is required [4]. The Chaos Report [2] by "The Standish Group" e.g., lists criteria that can improve the chances of finishing IT-projects successfully. Modells like the new V-Modell XT [6] pay attention to these suggestions and support IT-projects from start to finish.

During the development of the new V-Modell XT in the WEIT-project, a wide beta test gathering phase was planned for collecting experiences in pilot projects using the V-Modell XT. In this paper, we want to present our results and experiences we made during the first phases of the WiBe-project, which is the first one developed according-ingly to the V-Modell XT in cooperation with BMI/KBSt (http://www.kbst.bund.de). Thereby, we point out what our main goals are and how to achieve them using the

M. Li, B. Boehm, and L.J. Osterweil (Eds.): SPW 2005, LNCS 3840, pp. 463–473, 2005.
© Springer-Verlag Berlin Heidelberg 2005

V-Modell XT. We also provide some quantitative data like the number of products created during the project or the number of products for certain milestones to show the efficiency of the V-Modell XT. We also want to outline some complications we encountered during the project.

2 The V-Modell XT – Overview

The new V-Modell XT is a unitised modell for (software) development processes [3, 5, 6], which can be customised for specific project requirements.

It doesn't focus on the question *how* something should be done anymore, but on the point *what* has to be available at a fixed deadline and in what *quality*. It clearly defines *"Who"* has to do something, *"What"* someone has to do, *"When"*, *"How"*, and *"Using what"* someone has to do it. The "Who"-dimension is defined by a *Role-Modell*, the "When"-dimension by an *Activity-Modell*, the "What"-dimension by a *Product-Modell* and the "Using what"-dimension contains references to tools, methods and other related standards. We will briefly discuss the basic concepts now.

Products

Products are the **ultimate centre** of the V-Modell XT – they are the central points of interest [6] and represent the project results. Products can be documents like the *Project Manual*, codes or the *System* itself. Provisional results are products as well, e.g. a document that still is in development.

Products can be classified into *initial*, *dependent* and *external* products. All products created in a particular project are logically grouped by content dependencies (*Product Groups*). A certain product can be divided into several *topics* so that simultaneous development and management of a product is supported as well. All products of a project are stored and managed in a *Product Repository/Library*.

To get a maximum quality of all products, the V-Modell XT defines a lot of measures for *Quality-assurance*. Regarding the products, there are, for example techniques based on a *Product-State-Modell* or a *Consistency-Modell* [6].

Activities

The relation between activities and products is quiet simple: *Each product is finished by one activity* [6].

As a sample, the *Project Manual* (product) is created by the activity *"create the Project Manual"*. Because of the tight coupling between products and activities, there are **no** activities defined in the V-Modell XT that work on other things than products.

Compared to other process models, the V-Modell XT doesn't know logical orders or orders in time. This for example means that there no input-products for an activity are defined. Every activity is focused on only one product.

Similar to products, activities can be logically grouped into *Activity Groups*. Thus a topic is created by a so called *Sub Activity* in this modell.

Roles

A role in the V-Modell XT is a concept, which clearly defines the responsibilities for certain products. Furthermore they describe the competences the people, who will assigned to a role, should have.

At first, a role is independent from a particular organisation structure. During the project's set-up, the V-Modell XT roles are assigned to participating persons while planning the project. One role should *always* be assigned to *one* person [3, 6]. Exactly one role is responsible for a product's creation but can be supported by other participating roles for a concurrent development. Compared to other process models, e.g. the V-Modell 97 or the RUP, where roles are more assigned to activities than to products, this is a novelty.

Process Module

A *process module* focuses on a concrete problem within the V-Modell XT [6]. Each process module is a self-contained unit which can be used, changed and extended independently from other process modules.

The process module is a component-like concept, which breaks off the monolithic architecture of the V-Modell 97. It contains all relevant *products*, *activities* and *roles*, necessary to solve the associated task [5]. Process modules have to be processed completely[1], meaning that all relevant products have to be created and all relevant activities have to be executed.

Project Types

The V-Modell XT defines three types of projects – one *development modell* for a client and one for an agent. Furthermore a *quality modell* for organisations is defined [5, 6] as well. A project type encapsulates what process modules have to be used in a particular project.

Strategies for Project Operation

Strategies for project operation (SPO) define in detail, in which order *decision points* (quality gates for products of a project stage, comparable with a milestone) have to be met within a project [6].

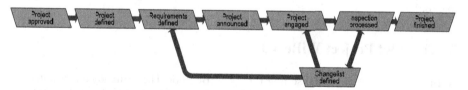

Fig. 1. SPO Placing of orders and realization of system development projects (client)

More than one strategy for project operation can exist for a project type. The SPO "Placing of orders and implementation of system development projects (client)" is mentioned as an example in Fig. 1. A SPO clearly defines the order of building certain products. Compared to other process modells, this is a novelty.

Tailoring

Tailoring is one of the most important concepts of the V-Modell XT. It enables a project manager to *trim* the V-Modell XT *to fit a specific project's characteristic* so that only the necessary products have to be created and no unnecessary activities are executed [5, 6].

---

[1] "Completely" refers to the result of the Tailoring and further adaptations.

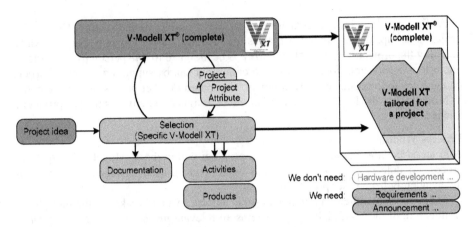

Fig. 2. Tailoring mechanism and subsetting

Let us give an example: Process modules for hardware development are not necessary for the development of a software system and are, thus, redundant.

At the beginning, a project can be characterized by several so called *project attributes*. Based on these attributes, necessary activities and products for the specific project are identified [6].

The resulting, project-specific V-Modell XT (left side of Fig. 2) in general consists of a subset (see right side of Fig. 2) of the available process modules of the complete model. Furthermore a SPO, a set of roles and the required products are fixed after the Tailoring. Thus only project relevant products will be filled out and only necessary activities will be executed within a project.

Compared to the V-Modell 97 an initial project-plan is exportable after the Tailoring, too!

3   The Pilot Project WiBe 4.0

At first, we present the initial setting for the WiBe pilot: There already exists software supporting the process of making economic decisions described in the WiBe 4.0 business concept [7]. This software is installed on about 900 computers and is used every time a project exceeds a fixed budget. The existing software shows weak points in dealing with modern requirements. Aspects we considered as difficult are:

- *Technical problems*: missing network and multi-user capabilities, incompatibilities with modern software like Windows XP
- *Functional problems*: the new version of the business concept economic decisions are based on is not supported by the old software system

Another goal is to become independent of a particular software provider. Due to the BMI/KBSt not owning the old software code, the new software should be available as source code as well. After deciding to develop new software for WiBe, the BMI/KBSt and the V-Modell XT team initiated this project as a pilot.

The following paragraphs report of this pilot project and will give some impressions of the practical application of the V-Modell XT. With developing the new WiBe 4.0 software, we wanted to address topics like the integration of the new business concept, network and multi-user capabilities as well as the redesign of the technical architecture and paying more attention to ergonomic questions. Furthermore, we wanted to order a software system which is completely owned by the client after finishing the project including all codes and documents.

3.1 Realising the Project Using the V-Modell XT

In this project we are in the role of the client. Our team consists of employees of the BMI/KBSt, the TU Kaiserslautern and the TU Munich. This project is tool-supported by in-Step V-Modell XT Edition made available by microTOOL GmbH Berlin (http://www.microtool.de).

Kick-Off and Project's Tailoring

The project's type is *system development project (client)*. During the Kick-Off, the first step was the Tailoring for gaining the required *process modules* and *products*.

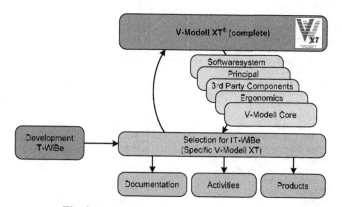

Fig. 3. Project-specific Tailoring for IT-WiBe

In Fig. 3 the Tailoring for WiBe is shown. The Tailoring result has to be documented in the Project Manual. All decisions for or against a particular project attribute should be documented there. The Tailoring provides a so called *application profile*, consisting of a project type, a set of process modules and a strategy for project operation[2]. For the current project WiBe the selected project modules are:

- "Project Management", "Quality Assurance", "Configuration Management", and "Problem and Change Management",
- "Requirements Specification"
- "Placing of Orders, Project Monitoring and Finishing (client)".

---

[2] As the project is of the type system development project (client), the strategy for project operation is already fixed, as at the moment only the SPO Placing of orders and realization of system development projects (client) is provided for this project type.

The elements listed in the first item are the obligatory ones of the V-Modell XT that are selected in every project per se (the so called V-Modell XT core [6]). The default-selection of the core elements ensures a minimum level of quality in each project.

Planning the Project
The V-Modell XT doesn't dictate a fine-grained process model. The type of the project and the strategy for project operation only define the *order of reaching* the project's decision points and what products have to be finished by then [6].

As we have mentioned before, an initial project-plan can be derived from the Tailoring. This initial plan only sketches the coarse time frame. The next step in our project was to plan the project in detail (assigning roles, activities, setting deadlines etc.)

Name	Zustand	Startdatum	Enddatum
IT-WiBe V4	in Bearbeitung	28.05.2004	30.09.2005
EP1 Projekt genehmigt	durchgeführt	28.05.2004	28.05.2004
EP2 Projekt definiert	durchgeführt	31.05.2004	04.01.2005
EP3 Anforderungen festgelegt	durchgeführt	13.07.2004	21.12.2004
Projekt planen (Anforderungen festgelegt)	durchgeführt	21.07.2004	21.07.2004
Anforderungen (Lastenheft) erstellen	durchgeführt	13.07.2004	21.12.2004
Projektstatusbericht (Anforderungen festgelegt) erstellen	durchgeführt	21.12.2004	21.12.2004
Prüfspezifikation Lastenheft erstellen	durchgeführt	21.12.2004	21.12.2004
Anforderungen (Lastenheft) prüfen	durchgeführt	21.12.2004	21.12.2004
PFE (Anforderungen festgelegt) herbeiführen	durchgeführt	21.12.2004	21.12.2004
Anforderungen festgelegt	bestätigt	10.09.2004	08.10.2004
EP4 Projekt ausgeschrieben	durchgeführt	08.07.2004	21.12.2004
EP5 Projekt beauftragt	in Bearbeitung	21.12.2004	18.03.2005
EP6 Abnahme Konzeption erfolgt	bereit	31.01.2005	22.03.2005
EP7 Änderungsplan Konzeption festgelegt	bereit	14.02.2005	08.04.2005
EP8 Abnahme Stufe 1 erfolgt	bereit	31.03.2005	12.04.2005
EP9 Änderungsplan Stufe 1 festgelegt	bereit	13.04.2005	14.04.2005
EP10 Endabnahme erfolgt	bereit	15.04.2005	31.05.2005
EP11 Projekt abgeschlossen	bereit	17.03.2005	30.09.2005
PM-Aktivitäten	in Bearbeitung	31.05.2004	28.07.2004
KM u. ÄM-Aktivitäten	bereit	08.07.2004	31.05.2005
Jour Fixe, CCB	geplant	17.06.2004	24.12.2004

Fig. 4. Planning the WiBe project using a supporting tool (German UI-version)

The supporting tool we chose delivers capabilities to assign dates to process modules and decision points as shown in Fig. 4.

An Example: Basically there is no statement *how* to create the Specification Sheet, but *when* it has to be finished and who is responsible for it. So at first the project manager should assign a responsible person who has a corresponding role and should define a deadline, when this specific document has to be built. Detailed planning a project means to plan a particular phase of the project. In our pilot we have planed only the current phase and the following one.

The project manager and the steering committee now can prepare, start or finish certain project's stages. As shown in Fig. 4, the project can be realised using an *activity-oriented approach* The activity "create Requirements (Specification Sheet)" for example can only change its state to *finished* if a corresponding Quality-assurance process (activity "test Requirements (Specification Sheet)") has been carried out with a successful result as well. This is only one possible view on the project. A product-oriented approach is possible as well, e.g. the decision point *project defined* can only be reached if the product Project Manual is in the state *finished*.

To give a short impression of our project, we will give a short overview of how we specified the requirements in the pilot project in the following section.

Requirements' Specification

The requirements specification is ***now*** one of the *core responsibilities of the client* in the V-Modell XT [4, 6]. It provides rules and templates showing, how to structure requirements. On the other hand it is flexible enough to give a wide range of project-specific customization.

According to the WiBe project we used this fact for a specific *Use Case-based* requirements engineering process which is shortly described in Table 1.

Table 1. Requirements engineering process in WiBe

Task	Description
Functional analysis of the business concept	– business concept in cooperation with the principal – core functionalities and other points of interest
Analysis of user interaction with the existing application	– user interaction – work flow and dialog/mask flow
Decomposition of the application's main tasks and Use Case assignment	– identifying and grouping of the tasks – building the application's core components – Use Case assignment for the components
Use Case and activity description	– Refinement of the Use Cases and their detailed description – Description of the activities

Thus we extracted the requirements for the system step by step. The Specification Sheet as well as the single topics were permanently reviewed in a concurrent running review process. The reviews were made internally by the project members as well as externally by participating industrial partners[3]. The Quality-assurance documents like test specifications or test protocols that have been created during these reviews are not a part of the particular product. They have to be managed separately in the product repository.

According to the V-Modell XT, the Specification Sheet does not only consist of functional and non-functional requirements. There is a lot of *context information* as

---

[3] Several industrial partners were involved in development of the V-Modell XT. As the WiBe project was set up as a pilot project, reviews for core products were carried out partly by those partners, which had been involved in the development of the correspondent part of the V-Modell XT.

well, which both gives the potential agent a feeling for the project's background and has to be taken into account as well. On the other hand, the client is forced to review the requirements with the focus: "Is the system realizable the way I want to?"

This information is structured by the predefined topic-structure of the Specification Sheet provided by the V-Modell XT product reference. An example for this context information is the topic "sketch of complete lifecycle and system architecture".

The Big Picture and the Project's Results

At this point, we want to give an overview about the results we obtained until the decision point "project announced" on the client's side and look a little bit forward as well.

Fig. 5 shows the first four decision points, together with their associated products. The topics every product consists of are not shown in detail here, but sketched. As you can see, the number of documents to be built up to this point is quite small (just 7 documents). Only the products *relevant* for the decision points listed in the Figure.

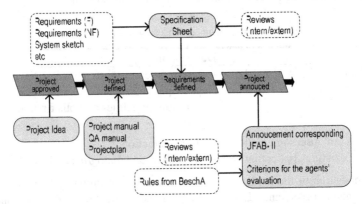

Fig. 5. The big picture: WiBe state until decision point: project announced

Not listed are *organisational documents* or documents for quality assurance: for almost every document shown here, at least two further documents exist – at least one *test specification* and a *test protocol*. Organisational documents are the ones that are related to the regular project meetings like an action item list or protocols.

These products are defined in the core process modules of the V-Modell XT and will occur in every V-Modell XT-based project.

Looking Forward

To put it all in a nutshell let us give you some quantitative data, now. Currently, the project has passed the next decision point *project engaged*.

Up to this point the project team has created about 220 documents at all. This number lists *all* documents, including action items, risks, meeting protocols and so on. Many of these documents are the project manager's all day work. The number of relevant documents is *much smaller*. At least 15-20 core documents like the Project Manual have to be created. Compared to the V-Modell 97, there is just one area, the client has to invest more resources: the requirements engineering phase. During this phase we created about 55 Use Case descriptions, which were unified in the Specification Sheet to one document.

In Fig. 6 we want to point out this statement again. As you can see, only eight documents, excluding project management ones, are needed to pass all three sketched process stages.

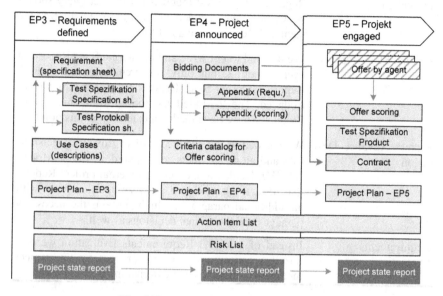

Fig. 6. Documents for some decision points

Customisation of the V-Modell XT

One of the most important features of the V-Modell XT is that every customer can build a specialised version which meets his requirements as good as possible.

This enormous flexibility was used in the WiBe project for customisation as well. In Table 2 we summarised some customisations. These customisations were discussed and decided within the project meetings and had of course to be documented in the project manual.

As an example for this, we will give you a few more details about the product *Project Advance Decision*. A Project Advance Decision is used for a well-defined break between particular project stages, so that the next one can be entered. According to the V-Modell XT, a Project Advance Decision usually is a stand-alone document, which contains the formal decision to pass a decision point. In our project, we decided, to not make a separate decision document for each Project Advance Decision, but to integrate the decision into the corresponding reports that have to be created in every stage.

We made this commitment to enable a more simplified reporting mechanism that corresponds to the project's volume and is less work for all participants.

The V-Modell XT is explicitly prepared for such customisations. As we learned during the project, sometimes there is no alternative to a customisation. In the WiBe project for example, the Bidding Documents have to meet the UFAB-III standard which differs structurally to the V-Modell XT's required documents. This requires hand-work because such situations are not tool-supported at the moment.

Table 2. Project specific customization of the V-Modell XT for WiBE

Product	Decision
Project Diary	Regarding to the V-Modell XT a Project Diary should be written. We decided not to do. We will provide technical Reports instead of this.
Internal State Reports	We decided to not write single Internal State Reports at every meeting, but only for preparation of external Reports. Internal State Reports are documents we introduced. The V-Modell XT doesn't know this type of Product. So we have made an extension at this point.
Project Advance Decision	We decided to not produce Project Advance Decisions as stand-alone products as required in the V-Modell XT. We decided to extend the external project Reports that have to be produced at every decision point with an additional paragraph, which contains the necessary passages and the formal decisions as well.
Requirements Evaluation	Instead of a formal Requirements Evaluation we preferred a continuously review process by the project members themselves and external industry reviewers.

A reached customisation decision and the corresponding documentation make thinks really easy. All made decisions have to be documented in the Project Manual and are *obligatory* for the whole project.

4 Summary

The WiBe project is the first pilot project in the V-Modell XT Beta-test phase. Many of the new concepts have been proven as very inventive and practicable, e.g.:

- *Communication* – project meetings and a well defined reporting make the whole process clear to everybody
- *Flexibility* – we were able to customise the V-Modell XT in order to meet our requirements, thus we could focus only on relevant tasks during project operation. Looking at certain tasks, we used the flexibility to meet the participants' personal interests as well as for integration of existing external standards, which define for example the way that bidding documents have to be created.

Lessons we've Learned

Some lessons we have learned are: The new V-Modell XT is quite simpler to use compared to the V-Modell 97.

Despite the strict activity policies, the product-centered viewpoint allows much more flexibility. Because of this new orientation, the Tailoring is much easier to understand and overview.

Remember: the V-Modell 97 contains about 180 activities and about 100 products. The project manager have to know all those things if he wants to tailor the model. This leads to a very complex Tailoring mechanism which was documented in a separate book and required specialists.

The newc V-Modell XT has a new grouping unit – the process modules. At the moment, the V-Modell XT provides about 20 modules. These modules are the base for the Tailoring process and much easier to handle and understand.

Because we are still working on other pilot projects as well, we can say that an average Product Repository after the Tailoring process consists of 30-40 document templates. As we have mentioned before, this number also includes templates for the project management products, thus an average V-Modell XT project consist of less as 20-25 core documents (products) that have to be created and maintained..

Conclusions

Nevertheless we have to say that the first contact with the V-Modell XT in the pilot project was sometimes a little strange because there are some learning efforts.

So some project phases at the beginning were not conform to the V-Modell XT and we had to invest a lot of work in correcting the mistakes made during this period. Furthermore, we had to realise, that the V-Modell XT doesn't cover all requirements related to flexible tool-support for unforeseen management rules and formal questions. As an example, we sketched the problems according to the Bidding Documents required by the UFAB-III compatible announcement. No tool supports such special structures, thus hand-work is necessary.

We assume that these problems will happen again in further projects. To avoid this upfront trainings are held or are currently in preparation. The trainings will address a wide range of customers from the ordinary employee to the top manager.

On the other hand, the V-Modell XT is still in development, thus there will be a well-defined further developing within the next few years.

References

1. Balzert, H.: Lehrbuch der Softwaretechnik Band 1/2, Spektrum Akademischer Verlag, 2. Edition, ISBN 3-8274-0480-0 (2000)
2. The Standisch Group: Chaos Reports, http://www.standishgroup.com/chaos_resources/index.php
3. Gnatz, M., Deubler, M., Meisinger, M., Rausch, A.: Towards an Integration of Process Modeling and Project Planning. In: ProSim 2004, The 5th International Workshop on Software Process Simulation and Modeling (May 2004)
4. Bergner, K., Broy, M., Moll, K.-R., Pizka, M., Rausch, A., Seifert, T.: Erfolgreiches Management von Softwareprojekten. In: Informatik Spektrum, Band 27, No.5 (2004) 419–432
5. Meisinger, M., Rausch, A., Deubler, M., Gnatz, M., Hammerschall, U., Küffer, I., Vogel, S.: Das V-Modell 200x – Ein modulares Vorgehensmodell. In: 11. Workshop der Fachgruppe "Akzeptanz von Vorgehensmodellen"(Gesellschaft für Informatik) (April 2004)
6. The V-Modell XT Portal: http://www.v-modell-xt.de
7. Röthig, P.: WiBe 4.0 – Empfehlung zur Durchführung von Wirtschaftlichkeitsbetrachtungen in der Bundesverwaltung, insbesondere beim Einsatz der IT. Schriftenreihe der KBSt, ISSN 0179-7263, Band 68 (August 2004)

A Road Map for Implementing eXtreme Programming

Kim Man Lui and Keith C.C. Chan

Department of Computing,
The Hong Kong Polytechnic University,
Hung Hom, Hong Kong
{cskmlui, cskcchan}@comp.polyu.edu.hk

Abstract. This paper proposes an implementation roadmap that shows how in-experienced software teams in industrial developing areas in China can adopt eXtreme Programming (XP) to produce software applications. Inexperienced teams unfamiliar with XP can face difficulties in adopting at once all twelve XP practices in a "big bang" implementation strategy. Intuitively, a step-by-step approach might seem more practical; however, XP practices are heavily inter-twined and mutually dependent, creating problems in terms of prioritizing and justifying one instructional sequence over another. We propose a way to techni-cally analyze the complex interrelationships between XP practices by identify-ing cluster patterns. These patterns can then be used to assist us in sequencing the introduction XP practices, helping both inexperienced teams and classroom learners in using XP. This work has value in both industrial and educational contexts.

Keywords: Managing Inexperienced Software Teams, Test-Driven Develop-ment, Visual Data Mining, XP in China.

1 Introduction

There has been in China in recent years a considerable and increasing demand for custom-made commercial software. This has seen a parallel increase in the number of software teams operating there, doing outsourcing or developing product in-house. Such teams are often small, inexperienced and lack practical knowledge of software development application methodologies. Our goal is to help these teams produce better software in such environments, with the view to developing a suitable paradigm for quickly improving their software development products and processes.

Conventional software models, like CMM, are heavyweight and, where teams are inexperienced, the straightforward adoption of such models is impractical as it is time-consuming both to train a team of inexperienced programmers and to have them implement the model. Such models are additionally unsuitable in that they emphasize process capability and process maturity, and fail to provide the support that inexperi-enced teams need in order to write better software and deliver business values. e<u>X</u>-treme <u>P</u>rogramming (XP) would appear to offer a more suitable approach because XP practices address programming management issues such as test case automation and

M. Li, B. Boehm, and L.J. Osterweil (Eds.): SPW 2005, LNCS 3840, pp. 474–481, 2005.
© Springer-Verlag Berlin Heidelberg 2005

coding standards. This kind of emphasis would assist in improving the overall performance of inexperienced teams and increase the ability of teams to run software projects on budget and on time.

An important part of an XP approach is its implementation. A big bang approach to roll-out is not likely to work for inexperienced teams. This paper proposes an alternative, explaining it in terms of an implementation road map and using a visual data mining (VDC) technique to reveal a pattern that shows how twelve eXtreme Programming practices support each other, thereby helping us to prioritize XP practices.

It is not within the broad scope of this paper to explore the IT decisions made by manufacturing companies in developing areas but as a matter of background we might proffer a number of tentative explanations as to why they might prefer to establish in-house IT development teams and/or seek services from small local software houses rather than using commercial off-the-shelf (COTS) software. One reason may be that company decision-makers believe that their operations are unique. Another reason may be the low cost of local programmers. A third reason may arise from the fact that in many companies in China the IT Department is under the Finance Division and there may be a misperception about the ease with which computer programs can be designed.

Section 2 provides some background about inexperienced software teams in China. Section 3 reviews two major representations of software models that influence approaches to XP adoption. Section 4 proposes an XP implementation road map based on patterns of XP practices revealed by visual data mining. Section 5 discusses the road map and its potential applications in industry and in the classroom. Section 6 describes the contributions of this work.

2 Inexperienced Software Teams

In well-developed cities in China, well-trained and experienced developers are readily available for software projects. However, as many new manufacturing plants are now being built in developing areas, numerous small local software teams, either in-house or external, software house, have been established to provide logistics, purchasing, and manufacturing solutions. These software teams have the following common features [1, 2].

i.   The team members are not well trained in Software Engineering and Software Project Management.
ii. The teams have a high proportion of inexperienced programmers
iii. Teams have a high turnover of good members as programmers seek opportunities in nearby well-developed cities.
iv. The educational background of team members is in an IT education system that focuses on individual skills such as practical tools and computer languages, neglecting team dynamics such as software project management.
v.   Team members rarely consider trying new ways to solve old problems
vi. Team members prefer step-by-step guidance when learning and applying new skills
vii. They are willing to accept comments about their mistakes; however, they might repeat the same kind of mistake after some time. This is a sign of immaturity and/or weak self-discipline.

Clearly, these are deficiencies that must be addressed. A systematic approach to these deficiencies will seek to educate teams and will create a work framework that improves efficiency and delivers business values. At the same time, however, we are aware of the costs and ROI (Return of Investment) involved in implementing any staff education scheme. Where staff turnover is high, the costs associated with staff training must of course be weighed in the balance along with other commercial considerations. In this respect, we believe that our approach does not run the risk of overinvestment and may even contribute to staff retention.

3   Implementing and Assessing a Software Model

A software development model can be implemented and/or assessed in a number of ways. Capability Maturity Model Integration (CMMI) for example has two representations: Staged and Continuous [3]. In staged models, a set of process areas are clearly prioritized for implementation in different stages. In continuous models, less specific guidance is provided as to the order of implementation. Rather, process areas are measured for assessment and from this is derived a capability profile. At a specific point in time, then, a capability profile can be used to guide process improvement.

eXtreme Programming similarly may be implemented and/or assessed in a staged style or a continuous style, as shown in Fig. 1. Nawrocki et al. [4] have defined an XP maturity model (XPMM) that distinguishes between different levels of advancement in XP practices. They prioritize twelve eXtreme Programming practices in terms of maturity. For example, different levels may represent an "On-site Customer" at different levels: at Level 2, the customer can be collaborating through the Internet; at Level 3, the customer pays frequent visits to the development team; at Level 4, the customer should be available on a daily basis. (Note that Level 1 is not compliant at all.)

Inexperienced software teams are not able to adopt XPMM because they need time to fully understand how each practice works individually and, most importantly, how

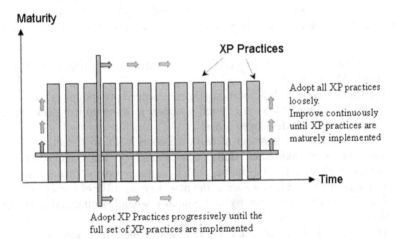

Fig. 1. Staged and continuous implementation

the practices support each other, which, as can be seen from Fig 2, can be rather complicated. Intuitively, one approach might be for inexperienced programmers to start with three or four XP practices and then to adapt more practices step-by-step. However, once again with reference to Fig 2, it is by no means a simple matter to determine which practice(s) should be introduced first, nor would it be any easier to explain the why and how of this ordering to inexperienced programmers.

4 Toward eXtreme Programming from Testing

Explaining Fig 2, Beck observed that XP practices require other XP practices to keep them in balance [5]. The strength of XP comes from the interactions of the parts. To manage inexperienced software team using eXtreme Programming, we thus need to find a way to demonstrate to such teams how the twelve XP practices interact.

It should be noted that it would be wrong to prioritize the practices only according to the number of their links. All of the practices are important and inherent to the XP approach [5], yet it is clear that, with eight links, testing may be a suitable starting point as it offers the greatest number of alternative next steps.

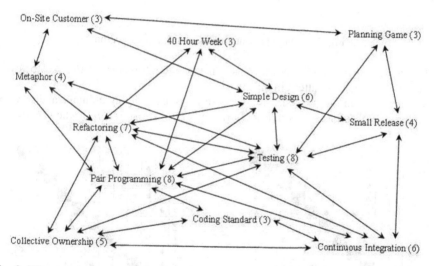

Fig. 2. XP practices support each other. A line between two practices indicates that they reinforce each other. [5]

Visual data mining lets human visualization participate in the decision making of an analytical process. It is a visual tool for revealing complicated data patterns. Applied to Fig 2, this technique may reveal a pattern in Fig. 2 which would be of assistance in designing a road map to XP implementation.

4.1 Exploring XP Practices Using Visual Data Mining

Let us revisit Fig 2. Some practices have many links with others, e.g. eight at Pair Programming, while some have three links, e.g. On-Site Customer. This kind of relationships is noticeable in a graph because only one vertex (i.e. one XP practice) is looked at in relation to the others. However, when we try to look at two or more vertices simultaneously, the picture may not be so coherent.

A graph with n vertices can be represented by an $n \times n$ matrix, where the entry at (i,j) is 1 if there is an edge from vertex i to vertex j; otherwise the entry is null. For example, in the graph shown in Fig 3, there is an edge ① between two vertices, Testing (T) and Metaphor (M). The graph can be presented in a matrix as shown on the right side in Fig 3. At (row T, column M) and at (row M, column T), ① is marked twice corresponding to the single edge ① of the graph. Thus, the matrix is asymmetric.

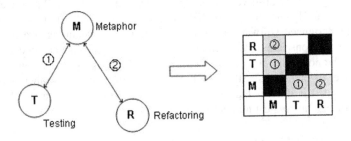

Fig. 3. Graph representation vs. matrix representation

In this way, Fig 1 can be re-drawn as a matrix, the left picture in Fig. 4. However, there is no meaningful pattern in this matrix.

The next step in our analysis involves a series of exchanging columns and rows of the matrix. We define a function $f(i,j)=(i+1,j)+(i-1,j)+(i,j+1)+(i,j-1)$ where $(i,j)=1$ if

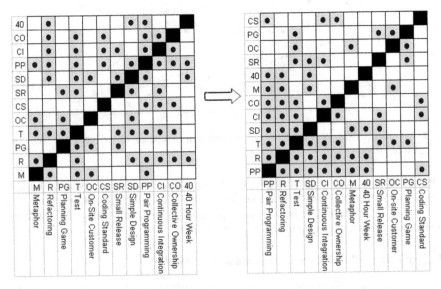

Fig. 4. Clustered patterns discovered by visual data mining

the square at row i and column j is marked; otherwise $(i,j)=0$. The total value of $f(i,j)$ over the matrix is $\sum_{j=1}^{12}\sum_{i=1}^{12} f(i,j)$. By exchanging any two rows and their corresponding columns, some points may move away from others, which decreases the total value of $f(i,j)$. Similarly, points may move closer to each other, which increases the total value. Thus, $f(i,j)$ over the matrix can be used as a heuristic function for breadth-first searching; that is, rows and their respective columns are exchanged to maximize the total value of $f(i,j)$ [6]. Fig. 4. (right hand side) shows a result after searching that reveals a cluster pattern.

4.2 From Testing to a Full XP Set

To draw a conclusion from that result (the right hand picture in Fig. 4), we need more information. As mentioned, one XP practice, Testing, stands out. Testing is the core of Test-Driven Development (TDD). As explained in [7], TDD is an iterative process implemented in five sequential:

i.   Use an XUnit tool and quickly add an automated unit test specifying a piece of functionality that we are going to write
ii. Run all unit tests including the one just added in Step (i) and see the new unit test fail as that part of the code has not yet been written.
iii. Quickly write the simple code to pass the new unit test
iv. Run all tests and see them all succeed
v.   Refactor the code

Note that (i), (ii) and (iv) are about Testing in XP; (iii) about Testing and Simple Design; and (v) about Refactoring. From this perspective, TDD is a subset of XP. Thus, Fig 5 should be able to show us this subset and indeed we can circle one single region where these three practices are represented. The XP practices form a cluster by themselves in Fig 5 because of their relationships depicted in Fig 2. It should be noted that Fig 5 is mathematically equivalent to Fig 2.

According to TDD and Fig 5, we can try to implement XP by adopting Test, Simple Design and Refactoring at Phase I. We then add one practice at phase II, two practices at phase III and the remaining practices at phase IV. In this way, we can draw four contour lines, shown in Fig 5. Note that Pair Programming, which involves partner rotation and Collective Ownership are closely connected. Both should be included in the same phase. Therefore, Phase II contains Continuous Integration and the practices at Phase I.

Fig 5 is produced from Fig 2 using a visual data mining technique and provides an easy reference for defining a road map to XP adoption for our own development environment. For managing inexperienced programmers, who may lack self-discipline, we should move Code Standard to Phase I. Thus, Table 1 illustrates a complete four phase road map that can be used to assist inexperienced teams adopt eXtreme Programming. Note that Table 1 is almost the same as Fig 5, except that Code Standard is adopted at Phase I.

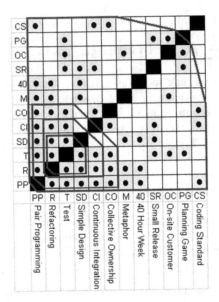

Fig. 5. An XP implementation map (note that Fig 5 is mathematically equivalent to Fig 2)

Table. 1. A four phase XP implementation road map

Stage	XP Practices
1	Testing, Simple Design, Refactoring and Coding Standard
2	Continuous Integration
3	Pair Programming and Collective Ownership
4	Metaphor, 40 Hour Week, Small Release, On-Site Customer, Planning Game

5   Inexperienced Teams at Work and Student Teams in Classroom

It is difficult for inexperienced teams to learn from the software experience of others because they teams cannot associate it with their own knowledge and experience. Such teams need step-by-step instructions and learn best when knowledge is well-structured. The purpose of our road map is to facilitate the learning of inexperienced teams by providing a clearer picture of the relationships among XP practices. So far, we have obtained considerable positive feedback when using our method with in-house software teams in China seeking to implement eXtreme Programming.

Our method has the advantage that it educates software teams so that they understand what they should adopt and why. But, out method has some limitations. It does not provide a timetable for the length of each implementation phase. Neither does it suggest how many phases a software team should go through in adopting the full set of eXtreme Programming practices.

Although the characteristics displayed by teams of university students in classrooms are in most respects the inverse of those of inexperienced work teams as described in Section 2, it is our belief that the clarity that our method offers can equally be applied in student instruction in XP practices. There are two kinds of difficult for students: appreciation and complexity.

In appreciation, some XP practices at Phase IV such as On-Site Customers and 40 Hour Week appear to be very simple, but students can fully appreciate them only when they run software projects in real world.

Complexity means the understanding of the reinforcement between XP practices. In our experience teaching eXtreme Programming, we have found that while students are usually able to explain the objectives of individual XP practices, they rarely have any insight into how its twelve practices reinforce each other. It is hoped that our proposed method will help students to gain this insight.

6 Contributions

Because making XP work is a matter of achieving synergy between the practices and visual data mining is an effective tool for displaying the complicated relationships among XP practices, the primary contribution of this work come from its use of visual data mining to clarify how the twelve XP practices support each other, thereby reducing the learning burden for students and practitioners. Compared with experience-based knowledge, our XP road map is easily explained to inexperienced programmers, and can be used to guide inexperienced software teams as they initially adapt parts of XP and thereafter continuously improve their XP implementation. In industry, organizations can use the proposed road map in their own roll-out of eXtreme Programming, adapting it to match their culture and environment. In education, this paper can serve as supplementary materials for XP learners and coaches.

References

1. Lui, K.M. and Chan, K.C.C., Managing Inexperienced Programmers by Managing Design-Coding, *Proceedings of European Software Process Improvement*, Denmark, pp. 2.9-2.19, (2000) On-line at http://www.iscn.at/select_newspaper/people/polytechnic.html
2. Lui, K.M. and Chan, K.C.C., Inexperienced Software Team and Global Software Team *Knowledge and Information Technology Management: Human and Social Perspectives,* Edited by Gunasekaran, A., Khalil, O., and Syed, M.R., Idea Group, Hershey, PA, (2003), pp. 305-323.
3. Ahern, D.M., Clouse, A. and Turner, R., *CMMI Distilled*, Addison-Wesley, (2001).
4. Nawrocki, J., Walter, B. and Wojciechowski, A., Towards Maturity Model for eXtreme Programming, *Proceedings of the 27th EUROMICRO Conference*, IEEE Computer Society, Los Alamitos, pp. 233-239, (2001).
5. Beck, K. *eXtreme Programming Explained: Embrace Change*, Addison-Wesley, (1999).
6. Ibrahim, M.E. and Lui, K.M., Use of Knowledge Discovery Techniques in Management Accounting, *International Review of Accounting*, Vol. 4, October, (1999), pp.22-38.
7. Beck, K. *Test-Driven Development by Example*, Addison-Wesley, (2003).

Automatically Analyzing Software Processes: Experience Report

Rodion M. Podorozhny, Dewayne E. Perry, and Leon J. Osterweil

Texas State University, San Marcos, The University of Texas at Austin,
The University of Massachusetts, Amherst

Abstract. Sound methods of analysis and comparison of software processes are crucial for such tasks as process understanding, process correctness verification, evolution management, process classification, process improvement, and choosing the appropriate process for a certain project. The purpose of our research is to lay the foundations for a systematic and rigorous comparison of processes by establishing fixed methods and conceptual frameworks that are able to assure that comparison efforts will yield predictable, reproducible results. The analysis framework presented here assumes that the comparison will be done relative to a fixed standard feature classification schema for the processes used, and with the use of a fixed formalism for modeling the processes. The aspect of the system described in this paper is focused on functional analysis of processes according to the predefined comparison topics, well formedness constraints, and instrumented agents. The paper describes our experience using our analysis system and its application to a logistics software process from the telecommunication domain.

1 Introduction

This work presents a novel approach for analyzing and comparing software processes that enables one to significantly increase the objectivity and repeatability of comparisons. To our knowledge, this is the first attempt at a partially automated analysis and comparison of software processes based on the artifacts they produce. While our work focuses on the application of our analysis system to software process analyses and comparisons, it is more general. It is also applicable in domains other than software process, such as data-based comparison of software applications for evaluation of continuous program optimization techniques ([9]).

It is our belief that certain tasks (e.g. software development) are very unlikely to be completely automated in the foreseeable future if ever. Thus there will be a need for software process systems with human involvement in their execution. We believe that the operation of such systems can be properly described and analyzed with the use of the concept of a software process as introduced in [11].

One of the hallmarks of a mature scientific or engineering discipline is its ability to support the analysis, comparison and evaluation of the artifacts with which it deals. Systematic analyses and comparisons rest upon classification.

M. Li, B. Boehm, and L.J. Osterweil (Eds.): SPW 2005, LNCS 3840, pp. 482–497, 2005.
© Springer-Verlag Berlin Heidelberg 2005

Thus we believe that the establishment of a discipline of process engineering requires the development of techniques and structures for supporting the classification, comparison, verification, evaluation, and improvement of processes. Systematic, rigorous and automatable analysis techniques can help achieve the goals of process engineering.

The analysis system discussed here assumes that the analyzed and compared processes are in the same problem domain and have a similar purpose, but might have certain differences in how they achieve their goals starting from the input of the same kind and providing output of the same kind. Our approach is based on the analysis and comparison of artifacts produced by the processes along the execution paths prompted by similar input (e.g. similar formal requirements for a software system fed to different software development processes). Thus our approach also makes an assumption that the intent of the analyzed processes is in response to the similar input is comparable and produces comparable artifacts.

In this paper we describe our experience analyzing and comparing two versions of a telecommunications logistics process, what results we get from the process analysis, how our system compares to other approaches, and lessons learned from the experience.

2   Logistics Process Example

As our example we used a telecommunications ordering process employed by Telcordia. The ordering process elaborates the activity of adding a service to a customer. This company uses a proprietary process specification language for rigorous specification of such logistics processes. Their logistics processes also use a predefined set of artifact formats. In addition to the format specification, there is a set of well-formedness conditions defined for the artifacts. One of the challenges the developers of these processes face is the task of change management. After a change is made to the process the developers have to make sure that the process still produces artifacts complying with the well-formedness conditions. If the new version of the process produces an undesirable result then the developers have to find out the cause. This is not always as trivial as it would seem even for relatively small processes as not a single developer understands the process in its entirety. There are also different possible interpretations of the process by developers. The suggested comparison approach alleviates some of these problems by providing a rigorous analysis of process artifacts and suggesting possible causes for the differences based on such an analysis.

The study assumed that two seemingly identical versions of the same process need to be compared to find out if the artifacts produced comply to a certain well-formedness condition, and to point out the reason for the differences if there are any. Such a set-up is likely to highlight the benefits of the artifact-based trace analysis technique that can be used to complement the static analysis of the process template specification such as by Jamieson Cobleigh et al. ([4]).

The representation of the motivating example process template is depicted in Fig. 1. We use the Little-JIL process language ([2]) to show software processes

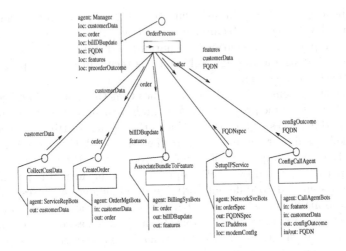

Fig. 1. Order process

in this paper. The visual representation of the Little-JIL is based on a functional decomposition. The steps are depicted as rectangles with a step's name above the rectangle.

The steps' interfaces include specification of an agent class (*agent:* prefix)[1], local parameters (*loc:* prefix), input parameters (*in:* prefix, and output parameters (*out:* prefix). The data flow is depicted along the decomposition links: the inscriptions near the arrow into a step contain input parameters and that near the arrow out of a step contain output parameters. A complete process specification also includes the resource model that specifies the agents available in the environment, the artifacts specification, and the agents' problem solver components specification that define the transformations from input artifact formats to output ones. The process program declares the agent classes for steps. The actual agents are bound to steps during process execution, therefore it is possible to run the same process template in different environments.

An example of a well-formedness condition for this telecommunications ordering process is the need to base voice communication service on a data communication service. If the ordering process does not establish that a customer ordering the voice communication also needs the data communication then the process creates malformed artifacts that result in billing the customer for the voice service that will not function. To avoid this scenario the executing software process (including the template and functionality of the agents responsible for performance of the steps) has to be shown to comply with the well-formedness condition. Any differences and their possible causes must be found, be they in the process template or agent functionality, and must be reported. Our comparison approach suggests a rigorous and automated way to provide these results.

---

[1] An agent is an entity responsible for execution of a step.

3   Steps in Analyzing and Comparing Processes

In this section we discuss the use of an analysis system to analyze and compare the example processes. Figures 2 and 3 illustrate the steps required by the analysis system illustrated in the Little-JIL.

The current implementation of the process focuses on an artifact-based analysis and comparison of two software processes. The software processes are assumed to have structured artifacts with predefined formats such that the processes specify transformations between the artifact formats.

The process of analysis and comparison shown in Fig. 2 is automated by a toolset. The steps for process execution and trace analysis are completely automated. The rest of the steps such as creation of the base framework, process modeling, comparison topics specification have to be executed by a user in a systematic way by following guidelines. The toolset assists the user in executing the non-automated steps. For instance, it provides the Artifact Meta-Format for artifact base framework specification and an agent framework for process specification. The non-automated steps are provided with guidelines for a systematic manual execution.

3.1   Artifact Ontology Specification

The analysis process starts with constructing an initial base framework (BF) for the artifact section (step **Construct initial BF**). The **base framework** denotes a problem domain specific framework for artifacts, software process decomposition units, and process features that can be derived on their basis. The base framework can be thought of as a classification schema or ontology that provides guidelines for grouping comparable activities, artifacts, or features of

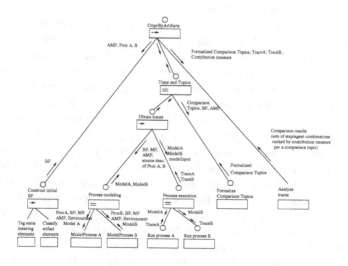

Fig. 2. Steps in analysis and comparison

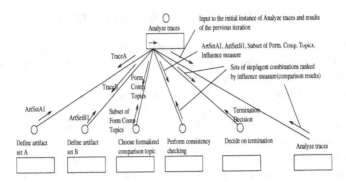

Fig. 3. Analyze traces

software processes from the same problem domain. Software processes are likely to be in the same problem domain if their purpose and functionality overlap.

The step is decomposed into the **Tag same meaning elements** and **Classify artifact elements** substeps to be executed sequentially. This step has a substantial subjective involvement of a human user. The BF can be constructed either from an existing ontology or it is generalized from the artifact formats of the analyzed processes. The goal is to identify the semantically overlapping portions of the artifact formats and tag the semantically similar elements of those formats. This is done in the **Tag same meaning elements** substep based on the source descriptions of the processes **Proc A** and **Proc B**. The output of this substep is a table of correspondence of artifact elements from the original process descriptions and their common naming. The correspondence is needed only between artifact elements in the overlapping portion of the semantics of artifacts. Such an overlapping is likely to exist in processes from the same problem domain and with the same purpose.

In the case of our analysis system we used a common artifact meta-format (**AMF**) and the artifact element naming conventions for tagging. Thus artifact elements are classified according to the AMF (step **Classify artifact elements**) and artifact elements with the same meaning are named the same in the process models and artifacts of the same class. The **Tag same meaning elements** substep precedes the **Classify artifact elements** since it is beneficial to reduce the number of elements to be classified. This reduction is the result of giving the same names to the elements with the same meaning, so the classification decision is made only once for both same named elements from different processes. In our example the BF corresponds to the formats of artifacts used by the telecommunications process. The process's authors at Telcordia have already specified the artifact formats rigorously. Since the two analyzed processes use the same artifact formats the task of identifying common ontology (BF) is simplified. The categories of the artifact elements map directly to the categories of the ontology. To obtain the BF specification in our example we wrote every artifact template from Telcordia's source process specification in the AMF. Thus we obtained BF specification for all categories in artifacts used by both analyzed versions of

```
<Node>
  <MetaComponentClass>
    <Attribute attrClass="java.lang.String"
        name="name"
        value="customerData"/>
    <Attribute attrClass="java.util.Hashtable"
        name="children"
        value="Customer1223027"/>
    <Attribute attrClass="java.lang.String"
            name="customerPhoneNumber"
        value="000-000-00-00"/>
    <Attribute attrClass="java.lang.String"
        name="defaultName"
        value="defaultValue"/>
    <Attribute attrClass="java.lang.String"
            name="customerStreetAddress"
        value=""/>
    <Attribute attrClass="java.lang.String"
            name="customerZipCode"
        value="11111"/>
  </MetaComponentClass>
</Node>

<Node>
  <MetaLinkClass>
    <Attribute attrClass="java.lang.String"
        name="name"
        value="association"/>
    <Attribute attrClass="java.util.Hashtable"
        name="children"
        value="Customer1223027RequestsServiceReq8745"/>
    <Attribute attrClass="java.lang.String"
        name="type"
        value="association"/>
  </MetaLinkClass>
</Node>
```

Fig. 4. Example of BF specification

the process: *customerData, order, billDBupdate, FQDN, FQDNSpec, features, modemConfig, IPaddress, preorderOutcome, configOutcome.* An example of BF specification is shown in Fig. 4. This figure shows specification of BF artifact categories *customerData* and *association*. The category specifications also indicate their properties. The actual artifacts used by pre-ordering processes would contain elements that map to these categories and that might be considered their instances. A user would specify the BF categories manually using the Artifact Meta Format to describe the artifact BF categories found in the original description of the analyzed or compared process.

3.2   Process Modeling

Once the artifact section of the BF is defined, the modeling of the processes in the same executable process modeling formalism can proceed. The input to this step includes the base framework (**BF**), process modeling formalism (**MF**), artifact meta-format (**AMF**), and the source description of the analyzed processes **Proc A** and **Proc B**. It is preferable to feed rigorous specifications of processes elaborated to the level of manipulation of the lowest level decomposition units of artifacts.

This step is further decomposed into modeling of the individual processes that can proceed in parallel. This step may require substantial human involvement but can be automated in the case if the source descriptions are rigorously defined by building a translator from the formalism used in the source descriptions to the common formalism used for analysis.

The expressiveness of the process formalisms can influence the analysis results if they do not allow modeling of the artifact elements or steps that manipulate them related to the comparison topics. The output of the modeling step consists of the process models in the common modeling formalism (**ModelA, ModelB**). In our implementation we use the Little-JIL as the common modeling formalism for process analysis and comparison. Thus the modeling involves representation of the functional decomposition of the process, specification of the process step interfaces, specification of the artifact formats in the AMF, specification and development of the agents to execute the steps, instrumentation of the agents per a step kind, specification and development of the step-specific GUIs, and the definition of the environment to be the same for both processes (the developed agents are included into the environment).

The original Little-JIL has been extended to generalize the agent and instrumentation specification for individual problem domains. The user must take care not to overspecify the agents beyond the elaboration of the lowest level activities from the source processes. If the source processes assume certain common low level activities then it is advisable to use the same implementation for the agents from both processes. The extended Little-JIL agent architecture allows for reuse of agents' problem solving components. The Little-JIL artifact specification and the agents must use the artifact formats specified in AMF and complying with the naming conventions for the artifact elements with overlapping semantics.

In our implementation of the analysis system the user would specify the process template in the Little-JIL using the visual editor. An example of a process template we created is shown in Fig. 1. We created two process templates for the analyzed processes.

The user would also specify the agents for the process template using Java and the domain specific agent framework. The framework allows specification of low level agent actions (operations) and then specifying the sets of actions that agents must execute in response to incoming events. In our case the vast majority of events processed by agents are generated by the Little-JIL interpreter. These events carry information about assignment of certain tasks to agents. A task corresponds to an instantiation of process steps. Any task assigned to an agent goes onto that agent's agenda list. The agent framework simplifies the specification of agents by providing a uniform way to specify actions and by providing a generalized way to instrument the process. Every time a certain agent executes an action the information about the action's result is written to the artifact trace. The user only has to specify an action without explicit specification of the instrumentation code.

The analysis system is limited by the level of elaboration of the source processes. If the source process does not describe the activities at the level of ma-

```
...
public synchronized void
    started(AgendaItemEvent evt) {
    AgendaItem item = evt.getAgendaItem();
    ...
  if (itemName.equals(ResetModemStepName)) {
    ...
    GetFQDN getFQDN = new GetFQDN();
    ArchGraph[] args = {modemConfig};
    ArchGraph fqdn = getFQDN.execute(args, agentStepID);
    item.complete();
    ...
  }
}
```

Fig. 5. Example of specification of NetworkSvcBots agent's problem solver

nipulation of artifact elements then this method is unlikely to be applicable. The generalized instrumentation components simplify the user's task in the process modeling stage. Nevertheless, the user must make subjective decisions regarding continuity of the artifact concerns. The user must decide on the kind of operation a given agent performs on a given artifact element when performing a certain step ($Operations = (Create, Derive, Retain, Modify)$). Thus every agent, when executing, would add an entry to the annotation lists of the output artifact elements explaining the operation it performed on that element and noting agent and step IDs and the timestamp. Also, the user must decide which output artifact elements are going to inherit the annotation lists from the input artifact elements. It is this decision that ensures the continuity of artifact concern traces. It is likely that specifics of a given problem domain might simplify this task. For instance, in logistics processes there is often a limited, predefined set of artifact formats with predefined and explicit relationships between elements from artifacts of different stages of a process.

Actions comprise the problem solving component of an agent. Part of the problem solver for the NetworkSvcBots agent is shown in Fig. 5 as an example. In this figure the *started* method is invoked in response to an event signifying the start of a certain task assigned to an agent. If the task's name is *ResetModemStepName* then the agent will perform the *GetFQDN* action among others. The example shows the generalization of action specification. An action is instantiated and then the action is executed when it is passed the input artifacts in a graph-based Artifact Meta-Format (implemented as ArchGraph). Having a set of domain specific actions it is fairly easy to create agents using this framework. The user would create or reuse a set of actions specific to the problem domain of analyzed processes so that to specify agents. Thus agents for the two versions of the pre-ordering process reused a number of actions.

First we wrote a set of actions in Java for the agents of the analyzed processes. The actions used the artifact categories specified in the AMF to represent manipulation of artifacts. For instance, the *getFQDN* action manipulates the artifact BF category *FQDN*. Then we wrote the automated agents that used the actions. Our analysis system also allows for specification of human-assisting and human-modeling agents by providing a framework for step-specific GUI specification.

For instance, the agents we specified for the analyzed process in Fig. 1 are *ServiceRepBots, OrderMgtBots, BillingSysBots, NetworkSvcBots, CallAgentBots.*

3.3   Process Execution

The next step of the analysis system, **Process execution**, requires execution of the so modeled and instrumented processes (**ModelA, ModelB**) on the same input (**modelInput**). The result of such an execution is a set of two traces of artifacts whose elements are annotated with a list of operations, agents, and steps that were performed on them. The annotation lists in an artifact would cover the trace until this artifact is produced. Thus product artifacts would contain the most comprehensive annotation lists. The annotations of artifact elements are partially ordered by timestamps by construction via the instrumentation code that is run during the process execution. Thus every artifact element relevant to the comparison topic[2] must have a history of all manipulations done to it in the annotation list. This step outputs the traces of artifacts with annotation lists (**TraceA, TraceB**). The traces follow the execution paths through the process models **ModelA, ModelB** that correspond to the same input **modelInput** and hence are considered comparable.

The user obtains the artifact traces automatically by starting the Little-JIL environment and running a process specification with the environment containing the domain specific agents. Since the artifact ontology and consequently the artifact formats used by the agents of the processes are the same then it is possible to conduct a meaningful analysis and comparison of the artifacts. In our example we ran the analyzed processes and obtained two traces of annotated artifacts specified in the AMF. Unlike the BF specification in Fig. 4 the artifacts contain the actual elements corresponding to the BF categories. An example of *customerData* artifact specification is shown in Fig. 6. It was produced automatically by running the process.

3.4   Comparison Topic Specification

The step for definition and formalization of comparison topics (**Formalize Comparison Topics** step) can be executed after the initial BF is constructed and in parallel with the **Process modeling** and **Process execution**. This is reflected by auxiliary decomposition steps **Trace and Topics** and **Obtain traces**. This step implies specification of comparison topics in terms of first order logic formulas operating on the artifact elements with common naming conventions. This step outputs **Formalized Comparison Topics** as a set of first order logic formulas. In the case of our example the comparison topic is whether both processes fulfill the requirement that a voice service must rely on an existing data service in the customer's service configuration. This requirement is reflected in a relationship from the voice service to the data service in the *billDPupdate* artifact.

---

[2] The one that needs to be checked in order to determine if an artifact complies with a certain comparison topic.

```
...
<Node>
  <MetaComponentInstance>
    <Attribute attrClass="graph.model.ComponentClass"
        name="class" value="customerData"/>
    <Attribute attrClass="java.lang.String"
        name="name" value="Customer1223027"/>
    <Attribute attrClass="java.lang.String"
        name="customerPhoneNumber"
        value="617-234-92-32"/>
    <Attribute attrClass="java.lang.String"
        name="customerName" value="Edward Jackson"/>
    <Attribute attrClass="java.lang.String"
        name="customerStreetAddress"
        value="962 Hill Dr."/>
    <Attribute attrClass="java.lang.String"
        name="customerZipCode" value="01403"/>
  </MetaComponentInstance>
</Node>

<Node>
  <MetaLinkInstance>
    <Attribute attrClass="java.lang.String"
      name="class" value="association"/>
    <Attribute attrClass=
        "graph.model.ComponentInstance"
      name="source" value="Customer1223027"/>
    <Attribute attrClass=
        "graph.model.ComponentInstance"
      name="dest" value="ServiceReq8745"/>
  </MetaLinkInstance>
</Node>
...
```

Fig. 6. customerData artifact in graph-based AMF

One version of the process checks for the data service and establishes the necessary relation. The other version omits this action and produces a malformed artifact which would lead to a failure of the service request set-up in a deployed telecommunications process. This comparison topic is formalized as a first order logic rule in the Xlinkit rule specification language ([3]). The formalized comparison topic is phrased as $\forall vs \in voiceservices \; \exists link \in associations$ s.t. $link.source = vs \wedge link.destination = ds, ds \in dataservices$. The Xlinkit rule specification we wrote for the comparison topic in our example is shown in Fig. 7.

3.5 Artifact Trace Analysis

Next, the analysis process calls for analysis of artifact traces **TraceA, TraceB** by way of consistency checking to the formalized comparison topics. This analysis is done in the **Analyze traces** step. The step's input consists of **Formalized Comparison Topics** and annotated artifact traces **TraceA, TraceB**.

The step's output forms the results of the artifact-based comparison - consistency links between formalized comparison topics and process artifact elements and sets of step/agent combinations ranked by the contribution measure per a comparison topic. One of the main outcomes of such an analysis is comparison of consistency links from the same comparison topic to artifact elements in different processes. The consistency links help highlight whether:

```
...
<consistencyrule id="wellform1">
  <header>
    <description>
      Voice service should be associated to data service
    </description>
  </header>
  <forall var="vs" in="$voiceservices">
      <exists var="1" in="$associations">
            <and>
                <equal op1="$vs/@name"
          op2="$1/@source"/>
            <exists var="ds" in="$dataservices">
              <equal op1="$ds/@name"
                op2="$1/@dest"/>
                  </exists>
          </and>
      </exists>
  </forall>
</consistencyrule>
</consistencyruleset>
```

Fig. 7. Comparison topic example

- both comparison processes comply with a certain comparison topic,
- both comparison processes violate a certain comparison topic,
- one process complies with a certain comparison topic while the other violates it.

The annotation lists help point out the steps and agents that are responsible for the analysis outcome. In addition, it is very likely that the sets of step/agent combinations from different traces (processes) corresponding to the same comparison topic are comparable. Such pairs of sets can give insights about the functional similarities or differences between processes and aid the user in making a more objective process comparison.

Choice of initial artifact sets. The set of product artifacts quite often is most useful to be used as the initial artifact set because they contain the most comprehensive annotation lists and they are likely to contain all the artifact elements that need to be checked for comparison topics. Another advantage to this choice of the initial set is high likelihood that the product artifacts are explicitly defined in the process source description. To reduce the amount of computation it is advisable to choose artifacts that are known to be relevant for the chosen comparison topics. Thus, the initial artifact sets **ArtSetA1** and **ArtSetB1** are defined by the steps **Define artifact set A** and **Define artifact set B**. At this point the user can use the developed toolset to specify the artifact sets to be analyzed from the lists of artifacts in the traces. The toolset visualizes the artifacts as graphs based on their Artifact Meta-Format specification. A general layout of the toolset's interface is shown in Fig. 8. In our example, using the toolset's interface, we chose the artifact trace produce by one analyzed processes as **ArtSetA1** and the artifact trace produced by the other analyzed process as **ArtSetB1**.

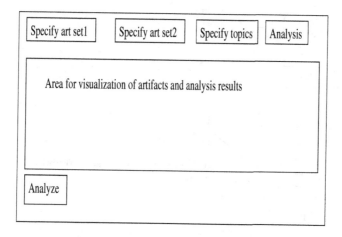

Fig. 8. Process analysis toolset GUI

Choice of comparison topics. Once the artifact sets are chosen, the user should choose the comparison topic to be used for consistency checking. This is done in the **Choose formalized comparison topic** step. The process analysis toolset also lets the user to choose the topics from a list of files with specification such as in Fig. 7.

Checking of artifacts' consistency to formalized comparison topics. Once the initial artifact sets for both processes and the formalized comparison topic are chosen, the comparison process runs a consistency checker that produces consistency links between the formalized comparison topics and artifact elements of the analyzed processes. The current implementation of the comparison process uses the Xlinkit consistency checker by Christian Nentwich et al. ([3], [10]). Next, the user analyzes the two sets of artifact elements that have consistency links to the same formalized comparison topics, but belong to different processes. By using the toolset, the user clicks the "Analyze" button and receives results as sets of consistency links between the specified comparison topics and artifact elements. The toolset also shows the steps and agents responsible for the consistencies or inconsistencies based on the information collected in the annotation lists of the traces. An example of analysis results is shown in Fig. 9. In the figure the *billDBupdate* artifact is shown as a graph. The rule *wellform1* corresponds to the comparison topic specified in Fig. 7. It stipulates that any voice service must be based on a data service. In this case the consistency link from the rule's representation points to the artifact element responsible for the complience (*Voice service*). The toolset also points out that the step **Associate Bundle to Feature** and agent **BillingSysBots** are responsible for the complience.

In our example, after we chose the artifact sets and chose the file with the comparison topic, we pressed the "Analyze" button and received results repre-

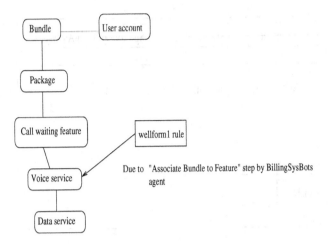

Fig. 9. Example of analysis results

sentation that indicated the consistency link between the *wellformed1* topic and *voice service* artifact element of the *billDBupdate* artifact for the first process. The toolset also showed it was due to the way agent *BillingSysBots* performed step *Associate Bundle to Feature*. There was no consistency link from the *wellformed1* topic to elements in the artifacts of the traces of the other process. Thus the two processes were functionally different due to actions the *BillingSysBots* agent performed in step *Associate Bundle to Feature*.

4   Selected Comparison with Other Process Analysis Approaches

In their earlier work on this topic, Xiping Song and Leon Osterweil proposed techniques and structures for a disciplined and rigorous software process comparison, and demonstrated their use by carrying out classifications and comparisons of processes drawn from the narrow and specialized domain of software design processes [12], [13]. These comparisons were guided by a formal comparison process, Comparison of Design Methods (CDM), and were performed according to a fixed base framework. The base framework can be thought of as a classification schema and provides guidelines for grouping comparable activities, artifacts, and features.

The need to compare modeled processes according to a fixed base framework was also recognized somewhat earlier by Sjaak Brinkkemper et al. ([8]). However, their comparison had no guidelines as explicit and formal as the CDM. The BF suggested in ([8]) has a flat structure as well. The content and construction method are different from the BF in our approach. The BF classes in ([8]) are constructed on the basis of the elements of the process and artifact decomposition units of the compared processes.

Analysis of in-place software processes and measurement of the correspondence of a particular process execution to its model have similar goals with process comparison in that they attempt to evaluate processes. Some fairly recent work in these directions has been done by Jonathan Cook and Alexander Wolf ([5], [6], [7]).

While the above mentioned work by Alexander Wolf, David Rosenblum, Jonathan Cook is a kind of retrospective analysis just as ours is, the kinds of properties investigated by them focused on real-time performance of process activities.

One of the more recent approaches in process comparison is by Abrahamsson et al. [1]. The authors present comparison of Agile processes. They use an ad-hoc comparison method for comparing processes by high level topics. The focus of their comparison is on organizational and activity sequencing issues rather than on the functional differences. This is primarily due to the fact that Agile software development processes (such as Extreme Programming) omit any description of the guidelines for artifact transformation by their activities. Instead they focus on organizational and activity sequencing issues.

5   Lessons Learned and Future Directions

The lessons learned from using our process analysis system to compare and analyze the two versions of the telecommunications logistics processes center around the artifact focus, the substantial amount of preparation, and the utility and advantages of the use of the system.

Artifact Focus. The focus on artifacts produced by processes is a very useful one. First, it represents the raison d'etre of processes: the production of processes and services on the basis of various input artifacts. Second, it avoids the tarpit of the widely varying and differing ways that one might accomplish the same tasks. The focus is on the results of the tasks and activities, which parts of the process affect them in which ways, and whether they have certain desired properties or not. And finally, while the ways in which artifacts may be produced vary widely, the artifacts themselves in the same domain are far more likely to be much less variable and far less the subject of disagreement.

Initially, Substantial Preparation. Process analysis and comparisons do not come for free. There is, at least initially, substantial preparation to set the stage for the analysis system. Currently very few processes are sufficiently specified – in fact, this posed a significant problem in our research: there were very few process descriptions in use that we could find that were defined in enough detail to perform our experiments with our analysis system. However, if we are to mature as an engineering discipline and move out the current craft stage, this will have to change.

While there is substantial initial preparation, it should be noted that this preparation serves in a variety of ways for subsequent analyses and comparisons or processes in the same domain. For example, once the processes have been formally specified, they may be used in a variety of comparisons and analyses. Once the base framework has been established for a given domain, it can basically serve for the analyses and comparisons of other related processes. The same is true for the ontology and well-formedness conditions. They are substantially applicable to other work in the same process domain.

Advantages. First, the most obvious advantage is the level of automation provided by the process analysis system. Once the initial preparation has been done, the rest of the analysis is done automatically depending on what input is provided to the system. This is a significant improvement in the state of the art for process comparisons and analyses.

Second, the various analyses and comparisons are repeatable. The points of variability are well defined and have been determined in the preparation. The only remaining point of variability is that where human responses are required in the execution of the processes and that input is controllable as part of the system execution.

And finally, as understanding of the processes grows, the various automated analyses and comparisons can be extended and evolved in various ways to provide deeper knowledge of the processes under consideration.

Limits. Because of the artifact focus, little has been done at this point to support various useful kinds of process performance analysis. For example, we currently do not support time and cost analyses for process - i.e. comparisons of race and lapse times of processes, nor the amount of effort involved in process execution.

References

1. P. Abrahamsson, J. Warsta, M. T. Siponen, and J. Ronkainen. New Directions on Agile Methods: A Comparative Analysis. In *Proceedings of the 25th International Conference on Software Engineering (ICSE 2003), Portland, USA*, pages 244–254, May 2003.
2. A. G. Cass, B. S. Lerner, E. K. McCall, L. J. Osterweil, S. M. Sutton, Jr., and A. Wise. Little-JIL/Juliette: A Process Definition Language and Interpreter. In *Proceedings of the 22nd International Conference on Software Engineering (ICSE 2000), Limerick, Ireland*, pages 754–757, June 2000.
3. C.Nentwich, L.Capra, W.Emmerich, and A.Finkelstein. xlinkit: a consistency checking and smart link generation service. In *ACM Transactions on Internet Technology, 2(2)*, pages 151–185, May 2002.
4. J. M. Cobleigh, L. A. Clarke, and L. J. Osterweil. Verifying Properties of Process Definitions. In *Proceedings of the ACM Sigsoft 2000 International Symposium on Software Testing and Analysis (ISSTA 2000)*, pages 96–101. Portland, OR, August 2000.
5. J. E. Cook, L. G. Votta, and A. L. Wolf. Cost-Effective Analysis of In-Place Software Processes. *IEEE Transactions on Software Engineering*, SE-24(8):650–663, August 1998.
6. J. E. Cook and A. L. Wolf. Discovering Models of Software Processes from Event-Based Data. *ACM Transactions on Software Engineering and Methodology*, 7(3):215–249, July 1998.

7. J. E. Cook and A. L. Wolf. Software Process Validation: Quantitatively Measuring the Correspondence of a Process to a Model. *ACM Transactions on Software Engineering and Methodology*, 8(2):147–176, April 1999.
8. S. B. Geert van den Goor, Shuguang Hong. A Comparison of Six Object-Oriented Analysis and Design Methods. Technical report, University of Twente, Enschede, the Netherlands, 1992.
9. T. Kistler and M. Franz. Continuous Program Optimization: Design and Evaluation. *IEEE Transactions on Computers*, 50(6):549–566, June 2001.
10. C. Nentwich, W. Emmerich, and A. Finkelstein. Static Consistency Checking for Distributed Specifications. In *Proceedings of Automated Software Engineering 2001, San Diego, USA*, 2001.
11. L. J. Osterweil. Software Processes are Software Too. In *Proceedings of the Ninth International Conference of Software Engineering*, pages 2–13, Monterey CA, March 1987.
12. X. Song and L. J. Osterweil. Engineering Software Design Processes to Guide Process Execution,. Technical Report TR–94–23, University of Massachusetts, Computer Science Department, Amherst, MA, February 1994. Appendix accepted and published in Preprints of the Eighth International Software Proces Workshop.
13. X. Song and L. J. Osterweil. Experience with an approach to comparing software design methodologies. *IEEE Transactions on Software Engineering*, 20(5):364–384, May 1994.

Status of SPI Activities in Japanese Software: A View from JASPIC

Kouichi Sugahara[1], Hideto Ogasawara[2], Teruyuki Aoyama[3],
and Tetsuya Higashi[4]

[1] FUJIFILM SOFTWARE CO. LTD., 1-2-2, Manpukuji, Asao-ku,
Kawasaki 215-0004, Japan
ksugahar@ffs.fujifilm.co.jp
[2] TOSHIBA CORPORATION, 1, Komukai-Toshiba-cho, Saiwai-ku, Kawasaki,
212-8582, Japan
hideto.ogasawara@toshiba.co.jp
[3] Fuji Xerox Co. Ltd., KSP/R&D Business Park Bldg. 3-2-1 Sakado,
Takatsu-ku, Kawasaki-shi, Kanagawa 213-8508, Japan
Teruyuki.Aoyama@fujixerox.co.jp
[4] TOSHIBA MEDICAL SYSTEMS CORPORATION,
Ultrasound Systems Division
1385, Shimoishigami, Otawara-Shi, Tochigi 324-8550, Japan
tetsuya.higashi@toshiba.co.jp

Abstract. For the effective promotion of software process improvement (SPI) activities in the word, it is very important to establish a community beyond various social/organizational barriers. Like the auto-mobiles industry, to share various knowledge/experiences is to evolve one's own industry. To promote SPI activities in Japan, we established Japan SPI Consortium (JASPIC) in October 2000. In this paper, we describe the status of SPI practice in Japan through our experience in various activities in JASPIC, analyze current issues from software engineering point of view, and make some proposals for future action.

1 Introduction

A number of software process evaluation frameworks, such as CMM, ISO/IEC 15504, etc., have been proposed and being used in many software organizations all over the world. Also, many companies have installed a functional unit called SEPG in their organization toward software process improvement. However, still there are number of companies who can not proceed step forward because of the shortage of human resources and/or the lack of sufficient technical/managerial knowledge necessary for SPI.

To overcome these difficulties, it is important for SEPG staff in various companies to have opportunity for exchanging information beyond the boundary of organizations. Japan SPI Consortium (JASPIC) was established as a social mechanism to promote this kind of mutual exchange among SEPG people in Japanese software industry.

M. Li, B. Boehm, and L.J. Osterweil (Eds.): SPW 2005, LNCS 3840, pp. 498–506, 2005.

2 Birth of JASPIC

The keyword "Process Improvement" became popular in Japanese software community since the translation of Watts Humphrey's book "Managing the Software Process" was published in 1991 [3]. Around that time, many software companies were trying very hard to get ISO9000s certification, but some engineers, people like SPIN (Special Interest Group on Process) members in SEA (Software Engineers Association) have already moved their concern to CMM.

SEA is a volunteer organization established in December 1985 to provide a "place for software engineers or researchers, who are working in different environments such as software houses, computer manufacturers, computing service bureaus, universities, and research laboratories, to exchange their technical experience or knowledge freely beyond the barriers of existing social organizations. It has been conducted various activities to promote software engineering practice. One of the major technical events in SEA is annual Software Symposium (SS). SEA-SPIN was kicked off at the BOF session in SS-1996. In 1998, some of SEA-SPIN members volunteered to make official Japanese translation of SW-CMM Technical Reports TR-24 & 25 responding a request from CMU/SEI. They published the result open to public via official web page of SEA.

Then SEI released CMMI. Soon, strong needs for Japanese translations of various technical documents were emerged from the industry. But the large volume of translation task seems to be far beyond the work of small volunteer group. So, a new non-profit organization JASPIC was established in October 2000 as a joint effort of several SPI-sensitive companies.

3 Activities in JASPIC

The fundamental operating policy of JASPIC is "grass-root" or "bottom-up". The major activity in early stage (2000 - 2001) was to support translation work of CMMI documents. After that work was finished, a number of special interested groups for discussion and information exchange have been organized as the major function of JASPIC and is active until now.

Now the number of member companies of JASPIC grew up to about 30, including almost all of major software-oriented organizations. About the half of them are embedded systems manufacturers and the other half are software houses doing enterprise systems development and maintenance.

The regular activities of JASPIC are: (1) Bi-monthly general meeting, (2) Annual general assembly meeting, (3) Special interest groups (SIG) and (4) Annual SEPG Japan Conference (since 2003).

3.1 Theme of Special Interest Groups in JASPIC

SIG in JASPIC is organized in bottom-up style based upon grass-root proposal from members. Now, the following 10 SIGs are active:

(1) Practical Know-How SIG
    Exchange information got from SPI activities in each company.
(2) IDEAL SIG
    Discuss effective promotion style for each phase in IDEAL model.
(3) Change Management SIG
    Study how to deal with process change.
(4) Development Environment/Tool SIG
    Study of various open-source tools and use of them in process support environment.
(5) Statistical Process Control SIG
    Study statistical analysis and quantitative management in CMM level 4.
(6) Cyber Coaching SIG
    How to establish effective mechanism for externalization of SPI knowledge
(7) PSP/TSP SIG
    Intensive study of PSP/TSP.
(8) Core Competent Team SIG
    Discuss how to introduce PSP/TSP into the company.
(9) People Process SIG
    Discuss education/training issues of SPI.
(10) Future SIG
    Discuss future vision for JASPIC and prepare long-range action plan.

These SIGs represent what kind of SPI-related issues are now considered important in Japanese software industry.

3.2 Presentation Topics in SEPG Japan

JASPIC conducted Annual SEPG Japan Conference twice (2003 and 2004) successfully. There were about 40 presentations in each year, and the number of participants was about 500 (fairly large comparing similar events in Japan).

Figure 1 shows the classification of presentation topics according to CMMI process areas. And, Figure 2 shows the ration of CMM or CMMI related topics in the presentations.

At the 1st Conference in 2003, the number of non-CMM presentations to discuss SPI in general was little more than those on CMM process areas. Maybe because of SPPG2003 was the first conference of this kind in Japan. At the 2nd conference in 2004, the number of CMM-related presentations became majority (about 2/3). This trend shows the growth of practical interest about CMM. In the case of all presentations, many presenters discussed about organizational (OPF, OPD, non-CMM, etc.) and/or training issues in SPI activities.

3.3 SPI Promotion Examples Based on the Activity Results of JASPIC

After establishment of JASPIC, the chance of information exchange about SPI has increased. Moreover, various work products from SIG activities are being developed. In this section, we show the SPI promotion examples based on the activity results of JASPIC.

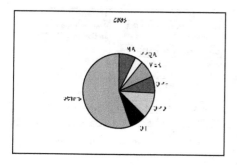
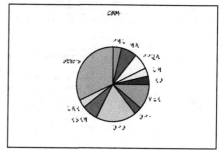

Fig. 1. Classification of Presentation Topics according to CMMI Process Areas

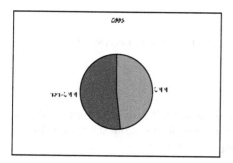
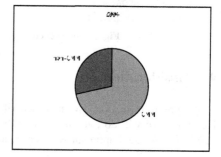

Fig. 2. Ration of CMM or CMMI Related Topics

3.3.1 Change of a Training Style

Conventionally, training such as development process or software engineering was performed in class room style in Japan. Training is very important to promote SPI activities. However, training of class room style is not necessarily effective and efficient.

In SEPG Japan, training is popular topic. In some presentations, there was a proposal that it was better to change a training style into workshop from classroom for effective training implementation. Many participants were received the stimulus from these presentations. After SEPG Japan, some practical results were reported at Bimonthly general meeting.

3.3.2 Application of SPC SIG's Products to Measurement Process

TOSHIBA is one of the JASPIC members, has been promoted SPI activities since 2000 [1].

SEPG leader training course is one of activity to accelerate SPI in TOSHIBA. The time schedule of this course is shown in Figure 3. The purpose of this course, which involves lectures and homework, is to provide the trainees with a detailed understanding of each phase of IDEAL, a basic understanding of CMM, and knowledge of techniques for promoting SPI. IDEAL consists of 5 phases, namely Initiating, Diagnosing, Establishing, Acting, and Learning.

Statistical Process Control SIG developed some materials for establishing measurement process. These materials are being used into metrics module and SW-CMM Level4 and Level5 module in this training course.

	1st term	2nd term	3rd term	4th term
1st day	Course introduction (1H)	Assessment method (3H)	How to introduce the PM technique (2H)	Presentations by participants (1.5D)
	SEPG overview (3H)		Six sigma method (1H)	
	IDEAL (1D) I, D phases	Process definition (4H)	Presentation methods (4H)	
2nd day		How to harmonize ISO9001 (3H)	CMMI overview (3.5H)	
	SW-CMM Level2, Level3 (2D)	Report of homework (1H)	Report of homework (1H)	Case study (0.5D)
		IDEAL (3H) E,A phases	IDEAL (3.5H) A, L phases	
3rd day		Metrics (5H)		H: Hour, D: Day
		SW-CMM Levels 4,5 (2H)		
4th day				
	How to practice SQA (3H)			

Fig. 3. Time schedule of the SEPG leader training course

4 Consideration

In the previous section, we have described about the SPI activities around JASPIC. Hereafter, we will do overall consideration and analysis about the status of SPI practice in Japan based upon software engineering point of view.

4.1 History of Software Engineering in Japan

In this section, we summarize the history of software engineering in Japan especially about quality management aspects of the technology [1] [2].

4.1.1 Before 1980s

In this period, the major concern in software industry was quality assurance of large application systems like banking, railroad seat reservation systems, etc. The major players were mainframe computer manufactures. They have applied their know-how accumulated in quality management in hardware manufacturing into software development. The result was very much successful and known as world famous "software factory system".

Also, in this period, QC circle approach, which was well known in hardware manufacturing area, was introduced into software field. It was rather easy to incorporate various support tools in software development environments because each manufacturer was using their own operating systems as the basis of environment. Many creative engineers invented their own software quality tools or management style and practiced in their projects.

4.1.2 1980s

In this period, IT industry's major concern was the "expansion of a scale", because of high-speed growth of Japanese economy. Many large application systems like 3rd generation banking systems were developed, and a large number of engineers from software houses were involved into these projects under Japanese style project subcontracting mechanism.

In this situation, it was necessary for system integrators (main-framers) to train subcontractors about their system for project management and quality control. For this purpose, there ware intensive effort of systematizing quality control and assurance methods. The representative examples were "SWQC" of NEC, "Ayumi System" of Fujitsu, etc. NEC's approach was an example of software design improvement system all over the organization different from traditional hardware manufacturing field. Fujitsu's system was a mechanism for transferring main-framer's software quality management approach into software houses in subcontracting scheme.

This period can be summarized as the glorious age of Japanese style software quality management. Generally speaking, technology change was rather slow; OJT (On the Job Training) of quality management was successful in many organizations.

4.1.3 1990s

From late 1980s, a rapid trend toward open systems has started. Also, globalization of world economy brought Japanese software vendors into fierce international competition in the international marketplace. Big and long-range projects have disappeared. Many open system development project were small in size and development cycle was very short. Also, style of software business was sifted from product-oriented one to service-oriented. Traditional quality management style succeeded in the domestic market became rather out of date in this new situation and resulted lot of confusion in project management and also in training.

At the same time, International standard ISO9001 has come out. Many companies started to get ISO certification for competition in the international marketplace. Also, other new framework like CMM, Six Sigma, etc. has come in. Many software companies who did not have strong technical identity rushed into certification racing. As a result, SPI activities in field projects were slowed down.

4.1.4 2000s

Still the general trend in the industry is looking for the new ideas imported from overseas. But other voices for the needs of re-evaluating the strength of Japanese style quality management became louder and louder. Some people are indicating needs to establish new role of Japan in the international software engineering community.

4.2 SPI in Embedded Software Development

One of the uniqueness of Japanese IT industry is the strength in the embedded system product manufacturing. In the past, importance of software components in these products was rather small comparing with hardware parts. Embedded software components were developed in rather ad hoc style.

But the size and function of embedded products has been increased rapidly. For example, in the case of high-function mobile telephone, the size of embedded software is several million steps. Nowadays, software development project teams consist of several hundreds engineers, and have a number of management layers.

One reason why many embedded system manufacturers joined JASPIC is that they were not accustomed to this kind of large-scale software development and wants to transfer quality/project management know-how from other members, especially from software houses working in other industrial sectors. Current issues in embedded software development are:

- How to coordinate hardware development unit with software development unit
- How to deal with rapid growth of software size and shortening of project cycle
- How to manage large scale development project

From now on, embedded software will become more and more important along with the penetration of a variety of products into the various aspects of society like automobiles, home electric appliances, mobile terminals, etc. Japan has been leading international market in some of these fields. In the future, it will be a unique role of Japan to make contribution to the world by combining its high quality hardware manufacturing process with new style of software quality/project management method.

4.3 Weakness of University Education

From industrial viewpoint, current university education of software engineering is insufficient, especially in terms of quality/project management. It is because of the large gap between academia and industry. Organization like SEA or JASPIC has been tried to narrow this gap, but still far way from completing its purpose. One other difficult social issue is the barrier of human resource exchange between two communities.

4.4 Status of SPI in Japan

The scheme of current scheme for SPI: The third party provides a process framework and development team execute that process, looks like effective at a first glance. But the failure of ISO9001 indicates that if developers did not have the ownership the process will not be used actually.

Following table shows the status of SPI activity in Japan based upon historical summary of software engineering and or experience in JASPIC. Table 1 shows the historical trends of SPI in Japan.

Table 1. Historical trends of SPI in Japan

Item	1980s	1990s	2000s
Process Owner	Developer	Special Staff	SEPG (or Developer)
Method of process Construction	Documentation based upon Experience	Given Model	Documentation based upon Model
Training	OJT	Classroom	Classroom and Workshop
Important Point	- Quality & Productivity - Personal Training	- Accordance with Model	- QCD - Skill development

In the period from late 1990s to early 2000s, many companies just tried hard to get certification of ISO9001 or to achieve CMM levels. But, presentations in SEPG Japan indicate that this kind of miss understanding of models is gradually disappearing.

After entering 2000s, QCD requirement for software projects became tighter and tighter. Also, globalization of development was accelerated in terms of outsourcing to

India or China. Under this situation, many software companies became more sensitive about balance of QCD in their development process, and sharpening their core skills for global competition.

4.5 SPI in Future

JASPIC member companies have been very eager to construct a knowledge-sharing community beyond the organizational barrier. They all know that it is necessary to rely on community power for solving various problems in SPI.

Usually, most of requirements and functions (user interfaces) of software system to be developed are given by customer. Software developers can only show their creativity in the process of implementing these requirements and functions as a real system. Fig 4 is the conceptual diagram of software development process.

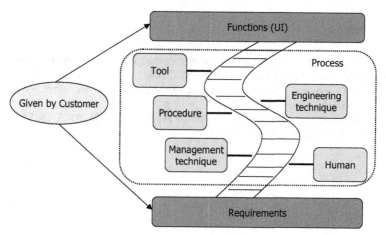

Fig. 4. Conceptual Diagram of Software Development Process

Recently, many companies are sensitive about information disclosure. Of course, we must be careful about information given from customers. But mutual exchange of process-related in-house information through mechanism is important and very useful for the development of software industry.

In JASPIC, member companies are sharing common issues in software process and jointly trying to solve problems. Rapid growth of the number of membership companies indicates that this open-process concept is accepted in Japanese software industry.

21century is the age of software. We should continue software process improvement activity to encourage software developers. For that purpose, it is needed to promote information exchange beyond various social/organizational barriers. JAPSIC is a test case to implement such a mechanism.

5 Summary

We have described short history of activity of JASPIC, and made an analytical consideration about the status of SPI in Japan. Unique character of Software Process

Improvement in Japan is that it is a collection of bottom-up cooperation among software engineers beyond the organizational barriers in which they are working. JASPIC is considered as a mechanism to promote this kind of mutual knowledge exchange. We hope to enlarge this movement into international domain in future.

Acknowledgements

The sustained cooperation with Mr. Kouichi Kishida, SRA-KTL Inc., Mr. Yukihiko Akasaka, NTT Data Corp., Mr. Takamasa Nara, Hitachi System & Services, Ltd., and Mr. Kouji Kondo, Sony Corp. has significantly influenced many views and details of this paper. Many fruitful discussions and debates with them are very much acknowledged and appreciated.

References

1. Hideto Ogasawara et al, "Evolution of Software Process Improvement Activities in a Large-Scale Organization", Proceedings, CONQUEST (2004) 213-220
2. Michael A. Cusumano, "Factory Concepts and Practices in Software Development", IEEE Computer, January-March (1991) 3-32
3. Watts S. Humphrey. "Managing the Software Process", SEI SEROES IN SOFTWARE ENGINEERING, Addison-Wesley (1989)

A Survey of CMM/CMMI Implementation in China

Zhanchun Wu [1,2], David Christensen[3],
Mingshu Li[1,4], and Qing Wang[1]

[1] Laboratory for Internet Software Technologies, Institute of Software,
The Chinese Academy of Sciences, Beijing 100080, China
[2] Graduate School of Chinese Academy of Sciences, Beijing 100039, China
{wzchun, wq}@itechs.iscas.ac.cn, mingshu@admin.iscas.ac.cn
http://www.cnsqa.com
[3] One Market Ltd. Co, P.O. Box 58004, Whitby, Wellington, New Zealand
david_c@onemarket.co.nz
http://www.spiregister.com
[4] Key Laboratory for Computer Science, The Chinese Academy of Sciences,
Beijing 100080, China

Abstract. Since 1999, the Chinese software industry has been using CMM/CMMI to improve software process. By November, 2004, more that 180 appraisals have been conducted. But the number of CMM/CMMI users is fairly low compared to the whole Chinese software industry. In addition, the growth rate of appraisal numbers has fallen during 2004. Limited research has been done to find out the obstacles for the wide-usage of CMM/CMMI in China. In this research, by investigating most of the organizations who have been appraised, reasons, success factors and benefits of CMM/CMMI implementation are identified, problems which negatively impact the CMM/CMMI usage are analyzed. Recommendations are made to the Chinese software industry and government to solve those problems, which could help those who want to or are using CMM/CMMI.

1 Introduction

In 1993, the Software Engineering Institute (SEI) released the Capability Maturity Model (CMM)[1] V1.1 with five staged maturity levels as a means to both appraise maturity level and guide process improvement effort for software organizations [1]. This model has since been widely accepted around the world, especially in India where the CMM helped many software companies to grow [2]. By August 2004, 3360 appraisals had been conducted for 2561 organizations worldwide, and more than half of the appraisals have been conducted outside the United States [3]. In 2004, the Capability Maturity Model Integration (CMMI) which integrated CMM for many disciplines replaces the CMM. The two CMMI representations (staged and continuous representation) provide more flexibility for process improvement [4].

---

[1] CMM, CMMI, Capability Maturity Model, Capability Maturity Model Integration are trademark of Carnegie Mellon University.

M. Li, B. Boehm, and L.J. Osterweil (Eds.): SPW 2005, LNCS 3840, pp. 507–520, 2005.

Before 1999, except for the multi-national company like Motorola, CMM was a strange term to the Chinese software industry. The breakthrough appeared in July, 1999, when Advanced System Development Co. was rated as CMM level 2. By November, 2004, 184 appraisals based on CMM/CMMI have been conducted for 134 software organizations [5].

By using CMM/CMMI, software organizations get some benefits such as more disciplined management, improved project controllability and product quality[6]. These positive results suggest that more Chinese software organizations should use CMM/CMMI.

But now, the number of companies which use CMM/CMMI is fairly low compared to the whole Chinese software industry, say, less than 2% (134 out of 8900 software organizations), and the growth rate of appraisal numbers went down in 2004. Furthermore, higher maturity organizations are rarely seen, only 19 by now. Compared to well-developed software nations like the United States and India, Chinese software enterprises are rather immature. There is very little research on finding obstacles which prevent CMM/CMMI being widely used in China.

To present an overall picture of CMM/CMMI implementation in China, this paper researched background information of most organizations who have been appraised (122 out of 134). The information includes organization size, product type, and geographic location.

Further, Survey forms were sent to software companies and process improvement consultants. By analyzing the data, this paper tries to answer such questions as: who is using CMM/CMMI, and why? What are the benefits? What are the problems? Meanwhile, recommendations are made to the problems. Hopefully, these recommendations will help existing and potential CMM/CMMI users.

2   Current Status in China

In recent years, the Chinese software industry developed rapidly, especially after the State Council issued No.18 Policies in 2000 [7] which spurred the growth of the Chinese software industry. Since then, nearly 2000 software companies have been established each year. By 2004, there are 8900 software organizations around China.

But the Chinese software enterprises are still rather weak in terms of profitability and size. In 2002, the global software market was $662.5 billion, but only 2% was taken by the Chinese enterprises while American took 40%. In addition, only 1/3 of the software companies claimed profitability.

Roughly 6000 Chinese companies have less than 50 employees, only 240 have more than 200 people, 25 have more than 1000 employees. On the other hand, our neighbor India, who has a very successful software industry, has almost 400 thousands software engineers, and more than 1000 Indian software companies have greater than 300 employees.

For maturity levels, the majority of the 134 CMM/CMMI–appraised Chinese software organizations are CMM2 while 19 of them are CMM/CMMI4 or above. In India where successful implementation of CMM/CMMI and other quality systems plays an important role in the software society [8], 300 companies have been appraised at different maturity levels, and 48 are CMM5 in early in 2003.

By following the CMM/CMMI-rated organizations list provided by a major CMM/CMMI consultancy company in China, we examined each organization's website, if any, to find background information such as size, product type, related news, local government policies etc. This information provides us with an overall image of CMM/CMMI implementation in China.

2.1 Maturity Profile and Growth Rate

From 1999 to November, 2004, there were 184 CMM/CMMI appraisals for 134 software organizations in China. Among the CMM appraisals, 100 are CMM2, 46 are CMM3, 8 are CMM4 and 9 are CMM5. There are 8 CMMI2, 11 CMMI3, 2 CMMI5 appraisals too. As shown in Table 1. From 2001-2003, the number of appraisals rose rapidly. By November, 2004, the growth rate of appraisal numbers began to fall, as shown in Figure 1.

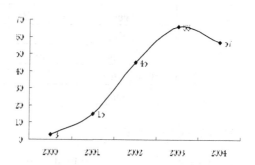

Fig. 1. Number of appraisals 2000-2004

Table 1. CMM/CMMI maturity profile in China

	CMM	CMMI
Level2	100	8
Level3	46	11
Level4	8	0
Level5	9	2

2.2 Geographic Distribution

60% of the CMM/CMMI appraised organizations are concentrated in Beijing, Shanghai, and Guangdong where the software industry is developed better than in other areas. See Table 2.

There are special cases. In some provinces, local government provides strong support to CMM/CMMI implementation for local software enterprises. This support includes rewarding each "successful" appraisal within a designated time, organizing and coordinating training, consulting and appraisal activities for local software companies. In most cases, a "successful" appraisal is an appraisal that results in a specified Maturity Level for the company

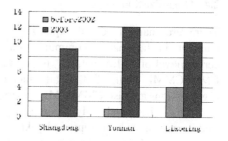

Fig. 2. Rapid growth in some special areas

being appraised. This strong support makes the number of appraisals rise quickly within the area. For example, before 2002 only two companies reached CMM2 in Yunnan province [9], but in 2003 there are 10 companies rated as CMM2. Similar support is provided by Shandong and Liaoning capital city's government [10], [11]. See Figure 2.

Table 2. Number of the appraisals in different geographic areas.

Area	Quantity	Area	Quantity
Beijing	54	Liaoning	10
Shanghai	13	Shandong	9
Guangdong	13	Zhejiang	4
Yunnan	13	Jiangsu	3

2.3 Organization Size

The term SIZE here refers to total number of employees in an independent entity as opposed to the number of software developers (for instance, the total number of employees in a whole company or a whole indecent R&D center). The reason we use total employee number is that CMM/CMMI is a systematic approach. In addition to the development team, the quality department, HR department etc. are also involved in process improvement effort.

Figure 3 shows different organization size. From the figure we can see, only 12% of organizations have less than 50 people, 74% have over 100 people and 58% have more than 200 employees.

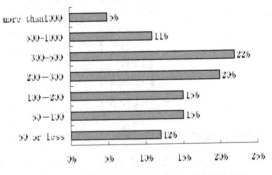

Fig. 3. Organization size

2.4 Organization Type

There are many types of organization using CMM/CMMI. Because biding for contracts in the finance, communication, or e-government areas typically requires a certain level of CMM maturity, more organizations developing such applications use CMM/CMMI, taking 2/3 of all, than other organization types. Outsourcing type organizations are also CMM/CMMI users, taking 10%.

On the other hand, only 5 companies developing general application software or middle ware have been appraised, taking only 4%. See Figure 4.

From the above information, we can see that there are quite few CMM/CMMI users in China (less than 2% of all software organizations), and only 57 appraisals were conducted in 2004. The appraisal growth rate is lower than 2003.

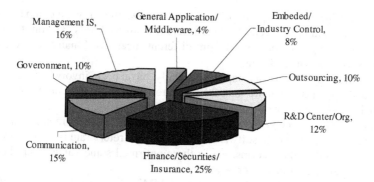

Fig. 4. Organization types

The majority of the appraised organizations are at the lower levels of maturity, and there are few higher maturity companies for the time being. Compared to the Indian software industry, this result is not very satisfactory.

In China, CMM/CMMI appraisals are conducted mainly in the areas where the software industry is well-developed or CMM/CMMI is strongly supported by local government. And most CMM/CMMI users have more than 100 people, majoring in finance, communication, and government application areas and outsourcing.

3 CMM/CMMI Implementation Survey

3.1 Survey Method

After obtaining background information of those organizations who have been appraised as discussed in the previous section, we designed survey forms consisting of multiple choice and open-ended type questions which cover the 5 topics listed below for both software organizations and SPI consultants. The objective of this survey is to provide a deeper understanding of CMM/CMMI implementations in China.

1. Drivers for using CMM/CMMI
2. Success factors to CMM/CMMI implementation
3. Benefits
4. Problems
5. Continuous improvement

The reasons we use SPI consultants as information source are, 1) consultants are independent to any software organizations, and could provide authentic and objective feedback. 2) consultants are process improvement professionals, and could provide a more comprehensive pictures about CMM/CMMI implementation. 3) consultants have deep understanding of the software companies that they work with, and could be the representative of the software organization. We finally chose 5 consultants who represent 50 companies.

To ensure the reliability and authenticity while remaining representational, we carefully selected software companies to issue survey forms. The selection criteria are

1) there is at least one third-party personnel that knows the software company, so that returned data could be verified. 2) from different maturity levels. 3) from typical size and application type companies. 4) from different locations. Finally, we selected 30 companies to issue survey forms.

Meanwhile, authors of this paper personally have been involved in consulting, training and appraisal for more than 20 software companies, and could further verify authenticity and reliability of the returned survey data.

By now, we have received return survey forms from 23 software companies and 4 consultants who represent 38 software companies. The return rate is about 80%.

Once we received these forms, we further confirmed some vague data via e-mail, phone calls and face-to-face interviews.

The returned survey forms are from 14 CMM2, 7 CMM(I) 3 and 2 CMM4 or above companies. The size of these companies is from fewer than 50 to more than 1000 people. Besides consultants, different roles filled in the survey forms including senior managers, quality managers, project managers, SQA, and developers. So the information is not biased.

3.2 Survey Results

Major Drivers of CMM/CMMI Usage
In the survey form, we listed a set of possible reasons for using CMM/CMMI, and left a blank row for companies to list any other reason they felt to be important. By sorting the selection frequency (similar sorting method are used throughout this research), the top three drivers listed in table 3.

Table 3. Major drivers

Rank	Drivers	Frequency
1	Self need	83%
2	Customer required	79%
3	Government reward	34%

From consultants survey form, we find the similar result. But for the small-medium size enterprise (SMEs), all consultants believe that government supporting policy is the top1 driver.

Success Factors
We define success as whether the CMM/CMMI can help software organizations meet their business needs and solve their problems. According to our survey data, 39% claim CMM/CMMI is "Very helpful", while 57% think "Somewhat helpful" and 4% say "Not at all". Since 4% represents only one company in the survey, we eliminated this data because further investigation is needed to find out if the answer is true.

After summarizing the returned survey forms, three major success factors are listed below.

1) Senior management not only clearly defines process improvement goals and provides resources, but also is personally involved in and monitors the process improvement activities.

2)   SEPG members should have both management and technical experience, and higher capability to coordinate and communicate.

3)   Developers welcome software process improvement, as long as the process can help their work.

SPI Benefits

From our survey data, the top 3 major benefits are "More disciplined management", "Project controllability improvement" and "Quality improvement". Table 4 shows the ranking sorted by selection frequency.

Table 4. Major benefits for all

Rank	Benefit	Frequency
1	More disciplined management	91%
2	Project controllability improvement	78%
3	Quality improvement	43%

Since the majority of Chinese software organizations have below 200 employees, we can not expect CMM/CMMI to be widely used without their active involvement. Therefore, in addition to overall results, we draw separate pictures for SMEs, both for benefits and problems discussed in the next session.

By prioritizing benefits selection frequency of the SMEs, we see the results in Table 5 that "More disciplined management" becomes the overwhelmingly No.1 benefit which is somewhat intangible. Yet the SMEs also improved project controllability and product quality, the effectiveness, compared to the larger organizations, is not that notable.

Table 5. Benefits for the SMEs

Rank	Benefit	Frequency
1	More disciplined management	95%
2	Project controllability improvement	58%
3	Quality improvement	33%

SPI Problems

Table 6 shows the problems according to all of the survey data. Again, we list the problems especially for the SMEs as show in Table 7.

Table 6. Major Problems for all

Rank	Problem	Frequency
1	Over-complex and dogmatic process	65%
2	High cost	52%
3	Other	<5%

Although cost is a universal problem, it is more severe for SMEs. To understand deeply why cost influences SMEs more than the larger ones, we compare three companies' SPI investment and revenue. Company A has more than 500 employees, company B has about 150 employees, and company C has 60. See Table 8. From the table, the large company investment-revenue ratio is 0.7% which is much lower than 5-13% for the SMEs. For large companies with decent revenue, 0.7% of their yearly revenue is not a heavy burden, but for the small and medium size company , 5-13% is unbearable.

Table 7. Problems for the SMEs

Rank	Problem	Frequency
1	High cost	92%
2	Over-complex and dogmatic process	85%
3	Other	<5%

Table 8. Cost comparison among large , medium and small companies

	Company A	Company B	Company C
Effort (man-year)	15	13	10
Capital /year (kRMB)	1100	800	500
Revenue (kRMB)	200,000	22000	6000
Investment/revenue ratio	0.7%	5%	13%

The second major problem is "Over-complex and dogmatic process". When interviewing SPI consultants, we find that since CMM/CMMI tells just "what to do ", SPI consultants often provide advices on "how to do it" at a strategic level while leaving intensive, time-consuming tactical SPI effort to the clients, such as deeper understanding of CMM/CMMI, carefully defining processes which match both their own environment and CMM/CMMI requirements. Unfortunately many software organizations simply take the advices of how to define a set of CMM/CMMI-compliant processes and forget process usability which is hard to improve in a short period of time. After all, there is normally an appraisal deadline set by outsiders, in most cases, the government rewarding time-constraint. This makes many organizations' processes look CMM/CMMI compliant, but is very complicated and dogmatic to use.

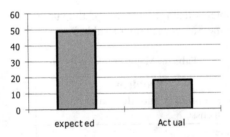

Fig. 5. CMM3 appraisals: expected vs. actual

1/3 of the software organizations complain about lack of automated supporting tools. And this makes the above two problems even worse. For example, each KPA requires measurement and analysis. Manual data processing brings extra management overhead. In addition, it is error-prone and not timely, and consequently does not help process improvement very much, if not making procedures more complex.

It is interesting to note that, there is no evidence to support the CMM critics "ignorant of the dynamics of innovation" [12], [13]. From all survey forms returned, none selects the choice "CMM goes against innovation".

Continuous Process Improvement Issues

According to the SEI [3], after another 19 months improvement, a CMM2 organization could reach CMM3. In China, before 2002, there 49 CMM2 organizations, but in 2004 there are only 18 of 49 rated CMM3. See Figure 5.

Thus we investigated the continuous process improvement issues. From returned survey forms, 27% of organizations would like to "improve to higher maturity levels when sitting on lower levels", while others give a negative answer. The reasons for NOT moving to higher maturity levels are shown in Figure 6.

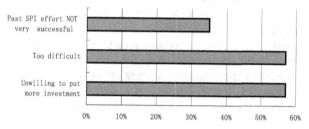

Fig. 6. Reasons for NOT moving to higher maturity levels

4   Analysis and Recommendations

According to the survey results, high cost, over-complex and dogmatic process are the two major problems for CMM/CMMI-based process improvement, especially for the SMEs. Consequently, complex and dogmatic process limited the effectiveness of process improvement. These problems prevent CMM/CMMI being widely used.

4.1   Impact Analysis

There are two contributors to the cost, or investment. First, labor-effort. To satisfy KPA goals, management overhead should be put in. For instance, SQA, SEPG and SCM altogether take 10-20% of development effort. Secondly, fixed fees. Appraisal fees which cost 300-800kRMB in China. Plus, other fees such as extra training and hardware/software facilities required. For any software organization, the SPI labor effort is both inevitable and bearable. But when we add the fixed fees of which appraisal fee take most part, things changed. For larger companies with decent revenue, roughly 0.7% investment-revenue ratio is acceptable, while 5-13% is relatively high for SMEs. See in Table 8.

Furthermore, the somewhat intangible benefit of "more disciplined management" received by SMEs make them more cautious when investing on process improvement activities. In fact, the government reward (about 500kRMB in some areas) plays a major role for SMEs appraisals [9], [10], [11].

CMM/CMMI is not born to be complex and dogmatic [14]. As mentioned before, time-constraints mean that some software organizations do not have time to skillfully use CMM/CMMI and define processes to improve their usability. These complicated and dogmatic processes, when executed, because some troubles which reduce the effectiveness anticipated, especially for SMEs. A typical scenario is like this: for a small team (3-5 people) in a small company, requirement changes could be done in hours. But by following the ill-defined CMM/CMMI-compliant process, they have to propose formal application forms, update requirement status table, run a formal meeting to evaluate change impact, get official approval from all stakeholders, etc. The procedures could take days, or even weeks while doing the same thing.

These two problems cause negative impacts on CMM/CMMI implementation, and become major obstacles to CMM/CMMI large-scale usage in China. First, due to the recent reduction or suspension of government support [15], SMEs are unable to bear the cost by themselves to use CMM/CMMI, and on the other hand there are a limited number of large software companies (240 in China). So it is natural to see the growth rate of appraisal numbers fell down in 2004.

Second, the complex and dogmatic process, though it could be reinforced by senior management, reduces SPI effectiveness. And this, in turn can not help companies. The "NOT very successful" process improvement effort not only prohibits companies moving to higher maturity levels, but also sets bad examples for other software organizations to improve their process based on CMM/CMMI.

4.2 Recommendations

It is has been proved that once the process improvement does not satisfy an organization's needs, the SPI effort could not be rated as successful, or helpful [16], [17]. Meanwhile, we also believe that process improvement should solve software organizations' business problems. In other words, SPI should meet an organization's needs and solve business problems. Based on this philosophy, we present the following recommendations which focus on business needs and problems to both government and software organizations.

a) Problem-measurement Approach
In order for the CMM/CMMI to be successfully used, a company must accurately define the problems that it wants the CMM/CMMI to solve. Meanwhile, specific measurements should be defined which can be taken within the company so that a company can understand the impact, positive or negative, that their improvements are actually making, and hence ensure that the implementation of their procedures, techniques and processes is actually benefiting their business and their customers. The more business problems are solved, the more benefits are received. And this makes the high cost more worthwhile.

b) Partial Improvement At a Time
Based on continuous process improvement concepts, CMMI continuous representation provides more flexibility for organizations to improve their processes. For instance, if the major weakness of a company is to control their projects, Project

Planning and Project Monitoring and Control should be the first two PAs to be introduced for projects. Once they are proved to be successful, other PAs could be introduced as needed until they reach a maturity level. And then move to a higher level.

This method could reduce the process complexity and cost because the implementation scope is limited.

Furthermore, we are happy to see now that, from the interviews with consultants, more companies are rationally think about the SPI effectiveness. The "Partial improvement at a time" method is more helpful to those who want to receive more benefits rather than a rushed appraisal certificate.

c) Supporting Tools

Obviously, automatic tools could improve management efficiency and reduce management overhead. Meanwhile, automatic tools could reflect the SPI effort effectiveness such as improved quality over time, in a timely manner. Such on-time support is also necessary for recommendation (a).

d) Government Policy Adjustment

Without government support, it's hard to imagine how to initiate nation-wide CMM/CMMI-based process improvement. But the government policy should be move away from rewarding CMM/CMMI appraisals based on achieving a specified Maturity Level. Rather than rewarding Maturity Level ratings, policy should reward actual measured business improvements as outlined in (a) above.

5 Conclusions

In China, those who are implementing CMM/CMMI are relatively large organizations driven by their own needs and customer requirements. SMEs using CMM/CMMI are mainly due to the government encouragement policies.

Though benefits like "more disciplined management", improved "project controllability " and product quality have been seen, problems such as high cost and over-complex process reduce process improvement effectiveness, and became the major obstacles which limited the CMM/CMMI usage in China . We have already seen that the number of CMM/CMMI users is not very large (134 out of 8900, less than 2%), and appraisal growth rate fell in 2004. The majority of appraised organizations are at lower maturity levels, while few software organizations reach CMM4 and above.

Without solving these problems properly, large number of CMM/CMMI users and higher maturity organizations can not be expected. Thus we put some recommendations to both government and software organizations which hopefully can help to alleviate the negative impact of these obstacles, and consequently make CMM/CMMI more widely used in China.

We suggest that, CMM/CMMI-based process improvement should be treated as a means to meets enterprises' business needs and problems. Particularly, the recommendations are for a problem-measurement approach, partial improvement and government policy adjustment. Proper supporting tools are also highly recommended.

Further research is necessary to solve those problems associated with effective CMM/CMMI implementation methods, alternative process improvement practices and partial improvement methodologies.

Acknowledgement

This research is supported by the National Natural Science Foundation of China under grant Nos. 60473060, 60273026 and the Hi-Tech Research and Development Program of China (863 Program) under grant Nos. 2004AA112080, 2005AA113140.

Thanks to the SPI experts from Beijing SPIN and Soft Tech, an American-based consultancy company. They have provided valuable data and information to this research.

Colleagues Feng Yuan, Meng Huang, Juan Li, Xinpei Zhao and Fengdi Shu spent lots of time to review this paper. Professor Xiaoyong Huai and Yongji Wang gave many constructive suggestions. Their works are highly appreciated.

References

1. Mark C.Paulk et. al.: Key Practices of Capability Maturity Model^{SM} Version1.1, Technical Report CMU/SEI-93-TR-24/25 (1993)
2. SEI: Process Maturity Profile of the Software Community, Aug (2004)
3. Qingyong Ji: Suggest from Indian software industry, http://tech.sina.com.cn/it/2004-12-21/1606480894.shtml
4. CMMI Product Team: Capability Maturity Model® Integration (CMMI^{SM}), Version 1.1, December (2001)
5. Marketing department: Quarterly Marketing Report, Soft Tech, December (2004)
6. Xiaoyu Sun: Neusoft CMM experience, http://www.csdn.net/news/newstopic/9/9678.shtml
7. The States Council: No. 18, Some policies to encourage software and integratedcircuits industry (2000)
8. Shanghai Foreign Trade Committee: Status of Chinese software industry, http://www.shec.gov.cn:8001/shec/jsp/cyfz/cyfz_cyfzdt.jsp
9. Wu Xi: Kuming software, http://chengdu.ccw.com.cn/market/200303/0317_06.asp
10. Qingdao city government: Regulations on promoting software industry in Qingdao (2002)
11. Fei Xie, Yingchun Qiu: Shenyang Government Policies on Supporting CMM, http://media.ccidnet.com/media/ciw/1196/g0201.htm
12. Reidar Conradi: Improving Software Improvement, IEEE Software, July/August (2002) 92-99
13. James Bach: The immaturity of CMM, American Programmer, September (1994)
14. James D. Herbsleb, Dennis Goldenson: A Systematic Survey of CMM Experience and Results, ICSE, Berlin, Germany (1996) 323-330
15. Xioang: Beijing policies, http://www.china.org.cn/chinese/kuaixun/230696.htm
16. Michael Diaz, et. al.: How Software Process Improvement Helped Motorola, IEEE Software, September/October (1997) 75-81
17. Pablo Straub, et. al.: Incremental, collaborative Software Process Improvement in a Tiny Software Group, Proceedings of the XXII International Conference of the Chilean Computer Science Society (2002) 187-194

Appendix: List of Software Organizations Above CMM/CMMI3 November, 2004

CMM 3 List

1. Neusoft Group
2. TopSoft Group
3. Software Department, Lenovo Group Co., Ltd.
4. UFsoft Co., Ltd
5. Beijing NEC IC deseign Co.Ltd
6. Institute of Software, Chinese Academy of Sciences (ISCAS)
7. Chinasoft Network Technology Co., Ltd.
8. Wonders Information Co., Ltd.
9. Kingdee International Software Group Co., Ltd.
10. But'one Information Corporation
11. Powerise Software Park Co. Ltd.
12. Shanghai Baosight Software Co., Ltd.
13. Modern Hi-Tech Development Co., Ltd
14. Langchao Common Software Co., Ltd.
15. China Software SolutionsCenter
16. Suntek Technology Co., Ltd
17. Chengdu R&D Center of ZTE
18. PFU Shanghai Co., Ltd.
19. Platinum China Co., Ltd.
20. CVIC Software Engineering Co., Ltd.
21. HangZhou Sunyard System Engineering Co.,Ltd.
22. Shenzhen YLINK Computing System Co., Ltd.
23. Guangzhou Sinobest Information Technology Ltd.
24. BearPoint Global Development Center,Shanghai
25. Hangzhou Handsome Electronics Co., Ltd.
26. PeCan Co Ltd.
27. Yutong Sunshine Information Technology Corporation Ltd.
28. Beijing Founder Electronics Co., Ltd.
29. Peking University Founder R&D Center
30. Shanghai Newtouch Software Company, Ltd.
31. Chinasoft Co., Ltd.
32. SureKAM Corporation
33. Shanghai Boke Informaiton Co. Ltd.
34. Gever Tech
35. Natian Group
36. Beijing PANSKY Science and Technology Group
37. Foresee Technology Co. Ltd
38. Guangzhou Huawei Software Co. Ltd.
39. 615 Institute of Avichina Industry and Technology Company Ltd.
40. iSoftStone Technologies Ltd
41. NEWGRAND Software Co., Ltd
42. Information Department of ICBC Beijing Branch

43.Guangdong Sunrise Electronics
44.Shanghai Xinguo IT Ltd.
45.Wuhan KMSoft IT Ltd
46.DHC

CMM4 List

1. Huawei Indian R&D Center
2. Huawei Beijing R&D Center
3. Bamboonetworks Guangzhou
4. Huawei Nanjing R&D Center
5. Software Department, Lenovo Group Co., Ltd.
6. Shanghai Baosight Software Co., Ltd.
7. Kingdee International Software Group Co., Ltd.
8. Chengdu R&D Center of ZTE

CMM5 List

1. Motorola Asia-pacific Telecommunication Solution R&D Center
2. Global Software Group-China Software Center (Motorola)
3. Neusoft Group
4. Motorola Chengdu Software Center
5. Dalian Haihui Sci-Tech Co., Ltd
6. Huawei Indian R&D Center
7. Hunan Changsha Newsky Technology Group Co., Ltd
8. DHC
9. China Software Solutions Center (HP)

CMMI3 List

1. Bright Oceans Corporation
2. Golden China Telecom Services Co.,Ltd
3. Shenzhen Financial Electronic Settlement Certer
4. Oceansoft information system Co., Ltd
5. Top Founder Information Systems
6. Shanghai Primeton Informations technology Co.Ltd
7. Fujian Fujitsu Communications Software Co., Ltd
8. Shanghai Xinguo IT Ltd.
9. American International Assurance IT Co., Ltd.
10.Sony Shanghai Technology Center
11.CHINA PUTIAN Institute of Technology

CMMI5 List

1. Hunan Changsha Newsky Technology Group Co., Ltd
2. Bamboonetworks Guangzhou

Author Index

Lecture Notes in Computer Science

For information about Vols. 1–3750

please contact your bookseller or Springer